THE
GODS

ALAIN / THE GODS

Translated by Richard Pevear

A NEW DIRECTIONS BOOK

For Inna and Robert
in translation –

– Richard
10/16/84

© Éditions Gallimard 1934
Copyright © 1973, 1974 by Richard Pevear

Grateful acknowledgment is made to the editors and publishers of *Antaeus* and *The Hudson Review*, where some of the material in this book first appeared.

Manufactured in the United States of America
First published clothbound and as New Directions Paperbook 382 in 1974
Published simultaneously in Canada by McClelland & Stewart, Ltd.

Library of Congress Cataloging in Publication Data

Chartier, Émile, 1868–1951.
  The gods.

  (A New Directions Book)
  Translation of Les dieux.
  CONTENTS: Aladdin.—Pan.—Jupiter. [etc.]
   1. Religion—Philosophy. 2. Truth. 3. Gods
I. Title.
BL51.C513   200′.1   74-8291
ISBN 0–8112–0547–9
ISBN 0–8112–0548–7 (pbk.)

New Directions Books are published for James Laughlin
by New Directions Publishing Corporation,
333 Sixth Avenue, New York 10014

CONTENTS

FOREWORD

"Ulysses, wrapped up and sleeping under the leaves, like a shepherd's fire, is Ulysses none the less." This one sentence from *The Gods* is a paradigm of the constructive principles of Alain's thought and a model of his prose. The image of Ulysses, fire under leaves, the powerful nature of the man hidden behind a tattered appearance, is a condensed figuration of two widely separated moments in the *Odyssey*. But in context it is more than an allusion, it is a primary, active image. Alain is talking about the Homeric idea of gods wandering the world in human disguises, of which Ulysses, since he is not a god, is a metaphor: just as Ulysses is hidden under a beggar's rags, so it might be a god; the reserved fire of his nature is godlike, an image of the god-in-disguise. But the sentence contains something else, the mention of the shepherd's fire, which is the most memorable thing about it. The counterpart of that brief image, in Homer, is a long simile that describes the way a man who must spend the night in the open, not by a hearth, will conserve his fire for morning by burying a fresh stick in the embers. That is why Alain says, with such odd precision, a *shepherd's fire*. In neither case is the image merely a "vehicle." The construction of the Homeric simile is dialectical, it is more of a disruption than an illustration, it argues with the main line of the narrative and corrects or adjusts our view of it. The texture of the simile, the question of its structure, is the basic question of *The Gods*.

In his essay "The Storyteller," Walter Benjamin observed that "an orientation toward practical interests is characteristic of many born storytellers." *The Gods* is a book of images and image-readings. But for Alain the realm of images is wider than we would expect: the gesture of an old farmer resting during a walk over his fields, the shape of a loaf of bread, the layout of an iris garden, the cobwebs in stable windows, the angular

1

intersections of city streets, the furrow drawn by a plow, the paths that cows make across a meadow, the balance, the yard-stick, the coin are all readable images. The figures of the gods are familiar to us, their world is the perpetual world of statues, pictures, myths. But the lore that Alain has gathered belongs to another perpetual world, one that has no "status" in the categories of thought or in the partial records of history, and which might be called the world of labor. The meeting, opposition, and interpenetration of these two worlds is the source of the old art of storytelling, and is therefore both the source and the subject of Alain's thinking in *The Gods*.

"Counsel woven into the fabric of real life is wisdom," says Benjamin, using an appropriate metaphor. The resident craftsman, the weaver, is one prototype of the storyteller. War stories are not invented at the front; storytelling naturally accompanies the peacetime arts. Stories are, besides, literally woven out of hundreds of intersections known as words. And the fabric of our existence is such that people who are constantly at war, whose peacetime life is also a kind of war, will lose the art of storytelling and will find themselves speaking a language of migratory ciphers. "The art of storytelling is reaching its end," Benjamin writes, "because the epic side of truth, wisdom, is dying out." And further, "The earliest symptom of a process whose end is the decline of storytelling is the rise of the novel at the beginning of modern times. . . . What differentiates the novel from all other forms of prose literature— the fairy tale, the legend, even the novella—is that it neither comes from oral tradition nor goes into it." It is a curious fact, in this connection, that Alain once thought of becoming a novelist. He did not follow that inclination, perhaps because he was already too much of a philosopher, that is, a lover of wisdom. What was natural to him was not the novelist's long form, the construction of a definitive "world," but the brief, provisional images of the storyteller, the opposing of the world of myths and the world of labor, the storyteller's freedom to bring diverse materials together, to create anachronisms. The novelist is an observer of life, but in the end his observations are wholly transformed into fiction and take on the consistency of fiction. His images are not constructed on the dialectical principle of the Homeric simile or the storyteller's story. Dreams, myths, and the history of historicism have the consistency of fiction, as does the reasoning of the systematic philosopher. But thought implies the interruption of reasoning. That is the function of Alain's method, and of his humor, which is a quality of the free spirit. The storyteller is an older figure than the novelist, and even older than the epic poet; yet the remarkable thing is not that he is older but that he persists alongside them, which means that he stands in a place that is not visible to history. From there he is able to interrupt and ask questions.

That, roughly speaking, has been the place of popular culture, by which I mean the inner life of working people and its poetic objects, in relation to the ruling powers of historical civilization. And that explains why certain political convictions are inseparable from Alain's study of religious images, why in one aspect *The Gods* is a critique of power and of political idolatry. It may also explain his rather humorous references to Marx. Alain's socialism was not based on the "laws" of history, it was, as he would have said, physiological. His dialectic is more pervasive and detailed than Marx's because it takes place in individuals, not only between classes, and because it is recurrent rather than successive. But Marx is furthest from Alain in his methods, which he adopted from historicism and systematic philosophy, and with which he fashioned an obligatory, inevitable truth, a truth based on the notion of power.

The attitude of the teller and of the listener to the story is in each case a free one. The teller does not disappear into the story and the listener is not absorbed by it; the one is always a man speaking, the other a man listening, and the story is something offered and considered between them. Its truth can only be tested experimentally. Thought offered and considered in the same way is counsel, the most humble face philosophy can show us, the most familiar, the most reminiscent. The naïveté of the story as an instrument of thought is its best recommendation. It is that kind of naïveté, I think,

3

that Bertolt Brecht had in mind when he said, "The naïve is an aesthetic category, the most concrete of all. . . . The opposite of a naïve approach is naturalism." Naturalism in the theater is like empiricism in philosophy; they are both born of a distrust of representations, and that distrust leads them to attempt an absolute representation, which is the highest degree of illusion. "Let them see that you are not conjuring, but working," Brecht advised his actors. The naïve method is the most concrete because it lets the teller be seen in the act of telling, the actor in the act of acting, the thinker in the act of thinking, and thus reaffirms the living world. Paradoxically, the naïve image in its provisional nature is a more complex form of utterance than the most difficult proposition. Its complexity is dramatic, not semantic. The script only comes to life when it is performed, and each time it is performed under new circumstances. There is no definitive performance of a play, no definitive telling of a story, no idea that puts an end to thought.

The material of *The Gods* comes from daily life and common tradition, but also from the works of philosophers, novelists, poets, physicists, historians. If Alain tells many stories, he also recounts many ideas. His discovery of the recountability of ideas marks the extent of his break with the philosophy of his own youth, what he always called "the philosophy of the schools," which was a mixture of mathematics, psychology, and historical criticism. It would be a great misunderstanding of *The Gods* to consider it a historical study of religion. It would also be a misunderstanding to consider *The Gods* an attempt to reconstitute past beliefs, a work of cultural anthropology, in the manner of Kerényi. Though Kerényi seems close to Alain when he writes, in *Prometheus*, "Our assumption that *human existence* was the chief determinant of these mythical figures . . . distinguishes our mode of observing and interpreting ancient mythology from all previous attempts characterized by astral or 'naturist' theories," he is still a scholar; his work is the careful excavation of a site that is no longer there. Whereas Alain says, "In some way I am reading two texts one on top

4

of the other. . . . The past leads me back to the present, and always presupposes the present in my thought." The world that appears in Kerényi's words is "spiritually" reconstructed in the scholar's mind's eye. The world that appears in Alain's words is physically construed. The trees, flowers, birds, animals, seas, springs, winds and tides, sun and moon in *The Gods* have their own natural being and presence; they must be sensed physically in order to be understood metaphorically as the substance of the gods. The provisional nature of images is answered by the continuity of the material world through time. That is the configuration of Alain's thought, the ground of storytelling and of the realism of poetry. He does not locate truth on one side or the other. Instead he takes us into the workshop, he demonstrates the cross-grained, intricate, dialectical process of image-making itself.

Alain's prose is extremely concise. That is the only difficult thing about it. He has a way of depicting and interpreting an image in the same breath, and his thought moves by quick associations that are not always marked in the writing. His style is abrupt, elliptical, and gnomic. I have tried to keep its rhythm and character in English.

Alain worked by improvisation. He once described his handwriting as a kind of carving: ". . . my pen is always trying to go through the paper . . . ; my writing is like wood sculpture, and I have to make shift with the cut of the chisel; how can I revise it?" (*propos* of 14 April 1923). He believed, as he says in the same place, that an artist "can only invent as he works and as he perceives what he is working on." But he also wrote, in the *Système des Beaux-Arts* (1917): "When a man gives himself up to inspiration, I mean to his own nature, I see nothing but the resistance of the material that could save him from hollow improvisation and the instability of the spirit." Alain's material sense was very strong. And, for example, the art of psychological shading was foreign to him. He was not a modeler. He dispensed with certain ramifications of sensibility as he dispensed with much of the rhetoric of

5

French prose. Style, for him, was a question of heightening the resistance of language. And for the same reason he preferred to work within strict formal limits.

The basic model for all of Alain's writings was the brief essay he called the *propos*. The word means a conversation, a talk. These miniature essays make up a large part of his work; between 1903 and 1936 he wrote over five thousand of them, an average of one every two and a half days. They were first published, weekly and then daily, in a radical newspaper, the *Dépêche de Rouen*, and later as monthly collections in his own journal, *Libres Propos*. The nature of the *propos* grew out of the unusual working conditions Alain set himself: to fill two pages, at one sitting, with no revisions. In fact, he would not erase a sentence once it was put down; he would make his thought follow his words. In a note written in 1908, he compared the *propos* to the *stretto* in a fugue, the abbreviated repetition of the subjects, which come together "as if they were passing through a ring. The material crowds in, and it has to line up, and pass through, and be quick. That is my acrobatic stunt, as well as I can describe it; I have succeeded perhaps one time in six, which is a lot. . . ." In the same note he says, "It is not the desire for fame that makes me write, but rather a lively political passion, which will not let me consider without horror the present state of letters, emptied of all richness and force. One would like to have talent and not sell it to the highest bidder. I am trying to find out what my talent is, and what sort of virtue I claim to have." Each of these statements is clear in itself, but they have to be taken together. Pure play (art plus acrobatics) is one term in Alain's writing; ethical conscience and a passionate involvement in the world are the other. There is no simple way to read him.

A number of Alain's later books are collections of *propos*. And the form turns up again in the short chapters of *The Gods*. The beautifully integrated structure of the book, which is at once temporal, hierarchical, and circular, does not preclude the fact that it was produced in a single, sustained act of improvisation. Alain first touched on the subject of *The*

Gods in a note written in 1911: "If religion is only human, and if its form is man's form, it follows that everything in religion is true." Twenty-two years later the book was written out, in the month of September, while he was staying at the village of Le Pouldu on the coast of Brittany.

RICHARD PEVEAR

NOTES AND AN ACKNOWLEDGMENT

The French word *esprit* means *spirit*, and also *intelligence* and *wit*. Alain uses it in all three ways, occasionally in all three ways at once. *Spirit* and *esprit* share the same root metaphor, and have essentially the same range of meanings, and in this translation I have used *spirit* for *esprit* most of the time, but *intelligence* or *wit* when it is clear that Alain intends one of those meanings only. There are two chapters entitled "Spirit" in *The Gods*, one at the end of Book III, the other at the start of Book IV. In the former, the word *esprit* is used in the sense of *wit*, as the context will make clear. But Alain means to say that wit is a quality of the spirit, and rather than obscure that idea by using *wit* throughout, or in the title, I have used *spirit* when possible and *wit* when necessary.

Quotations from Alain's notes and letters in the Foreword and in the Biographical Note are taken, unless otherwise attributed, from the introductory chronology by Maurice Savin in *Propos*, Bibliothèque de la Pléiade, ed. Maurice Savin. Paris: Gallimard, 1956.

I would like to express my gratitude to M. Albert Laffay, of Paris, a friend of Alain's, a distinguished critic and teacher of English, who corrected the first version of this translation with great care and great enthusiasm.

R.P.

INTRODUCTION

A man who takes philosophy in the right way, that is, for his own salvation, once described to me his experience of a vision, which, he said, had shown him the possible truth in what he had always thought of as a long series of errors. One day he was riding on a train, letting his eyes wander over a hilly landscape, when he saw a monster with a huge head, powerful wings, and several pairs of legs, climbing up one of the hills towards a village; a terrifying sight. It was only a fly on the window. This short moment of error and belief delighted him. The truth, he said, deceives us about ourselves; error is far more instructive. To his mind all the visions in history could be explained by this simple example, and by the luck of having surprised consciousness in its most primitive state. That was a hasty conclusion. On the contrary, I plan to move very slowly into this formidable subject. But since the method I intend to follow is rarely used, it will not be wrong of me to anticipate somewhat and present to the reader, at first in abstract form, the guiding idea of the present study.

Our knowledge of things often comes to us through a pane of glass; and the fly is not really necessary. With the slightest movement, the irregularities of the glass roll across our view like waves, rippling and twisting the images; from which I draw this first warning: that we always see through something like a pane of glass, and the glass is in motion. But setting aside this important idea, which reveals the truth of so many well-known distortions, for example the stick that seems broken in a glass of water, what I want to look for here is the imagination; by here I mean in the pane of glass that distorts one thing and another as I move; and I find that the imagination is precisely that movement. I understand then that I not only see all things as if through another pane of glass, which is myself, but that, moreover, the various movements I make, be it intentionally,

9

if I act, or emotionally, if I am afraid, or simply through the continual transports of respiration and circulation which sustain life, never cease to distort what I see, what I hear, what I taste, what I smell, what I touch. I might think that this time I have got hold of error properly speaking; and at bottom it is because of the uncontrollable impulses within him that a madman no longer knows where he is, or what he sees, or what he is doing. It is clear that we are all a bit mad in this sense, and that wisdom consists in eliminating as much as one can that portion of oneself in what one knows. That this can be achieved, the various sciences show; but it cannot be achieved without difficulty, which makes us understand that order we are forced to follow from the abstract to the concrete, selecting, out of the mass of our continual astonishment, first numbers and distances, then types of motion, then the effects of shock and encounter, then the intimate combinations which are called chemical; which leads us, by an arduous path, to some understanding of the movements of life and brings us finally face to face with our own passions; demonstrating that the cause of our errors was at first eliminated only provisionally, and that the disturbances of the knowing subject must finally take their place among positive truths. We know enough about this process to affirm that everything would be true, even a madman's extravagances, if we could know everything.

Spinoza says that there is nothing positive in error, which means that in God man's imagination is entirely true. I doubt my own ability to form, in the style of this abstruse master, an intuition of that wisdom of the prophets and soothsayers that should be one with the meditation of the sage. Nevertheless this great idea cannot be avoided, even if, to my mind, it is wise to delay its arrival; which means that we promise a doctrine according to which all religions are true, and at the same time we put it off for as long as we can. If I could think of the gods in god and as god, all gods would be true; but it is the human condition to question one god after another, one appearance after another, or better, one apparition after another, always pursuing the truth of the imagination, which is not the same as the truth of appearance. I perceive the stick in water as broken, but I certainly do not try to straighten it; on the contrary, I measure the distortion, I draw knowledge from it about the properties of water and light. The rainbow is likewise a vision only for someone who does not understand, here as in other cases, the refraction of colors. These illusions are not denied but confirmed.

The difficulty is entirely different for those of our visions that result wholly from the tumultuous impulses of the human body and the passions that result from them, such as fear or hope. For there are distortions which can always be explained physically. A tired eye sees its own fatigue in the form of flying spots; the sick ear mixes its own buzzing with all external sounds; simply by stopping my ears with my fingers I can create a silence which is not true, and yet is true. There is nothing imaginary about these things. As I have realized in studying the arts, the imagination always withdraws and conceals itself. It is not true that the moon appears larger at the horizon than at the zenith. Apply your measure here as you have with the broken stick, and you will find something new, though familiar, something all too rarely considered, which is that the appearance of the moon is the same in both cases. You think it looks larger, but that is not what you see. This example, gone over many times, has given me great insight into our most surprising errors. It seems to me that I am following Spinoza to the letter here, because this time the error really is nothing. But physics will also have to go, since it can only tell me: "Your error is not where you think it is." Of course, I might examine my own judgment; and I am far from despising that kind of research, though it is very difficult and evidently without object. But once again I will have missed the imagination. For it is clear that if I do not see that the moon appears larger at the horizon than at the zenith, at least I think I see it, and with all my heart. Is it the surprise, astonishment, perhaps terror, of finding this pale face among the roofs and chimneys? I am persuaded that it is. Forgive me for this long development of such ordinary examples. The meaning of the moon on the horizon, which seems to look larger, but does not look larger, is something that I have been unable to make anyone else understand.

People shake their heads, or even become angry with me, perhaps because of the prospect of great changes in great questions. Now I have all the leisure I need, and I am counting on a host of other, more accessible arguments, to bring more than one reader back to this difficult point.

The imagination is entirely within the human body and consists only in the impulses of the human body. Holding fast to this principle, at least as a tool, I came to consider another vision which is no longer a vision, but is far more disturbing than the rising moon. Dizziness invades us and almost throws us over the edge, when we see a cliffside drop away beneath us. But it does not drop away; that is not true. Colors and shadows still have the same appearance; yet we feel ourselves falling, we try to hold back, we are afraid; which is what gives the abyss its frightening appearance. Yet this appearance does not appear in itself; we think it appears. The truth is that one must pay long attention to perceptions of this sort in order to arrive at some correspondence between such muscular preparations and vivid emotions and what we take to be the physical aspect of things. The stereoscope offers another good example of this experience, but only on reflection can it teach us anything; for each of us thinks at first that he is looking at a relief, whereas we are looking at a certain manifestation in the colored images, in no way like a relief, which touches us with a slight alarm, and by the separation and withdrawal of our body, makes us feel the distance to be crossed or the menacing third dimension of the pictured objects. I conclude, too quickly of course, that the moon on the horizon would not seem so large to us were it not for a slight impulse of fear and surprise which, if we measure it with ultimate precision, in no way changes the image of the world that results from the interplay of light and the structure of the eye.

The same thing happens when we see the head of a grazing cow or a man's face in the foliage of a tree, or when we recognize a profile in the cracks in a wall. We do not change the least thing in what we see. The change remains purely imaginary, meaning that it is entirely in an attitude of the body and in a kind of mimicry which disposes us within ourselves as we would be in the face of such an object. But to complete the reader's enlightenment, if he happens to be interested in these problems which may smell too much of school, I advise him to meditate for a while on the cube in which all the angles are visible, or on the drawing of a stair that is in all the textbooks, which one can see from above or below at will, without changing the lines in any way; from which it will be understood that the change we experience then is not in what we are looking at but rather in a certain way of using the object we are thinking about, a way which is prepared for in our bodies. And following this method of analysis, which is so far removed from our real dramas, we find ourselves nevertheless enlightened about the nature of the gods. For, it is important to notice, we understand that the appearance of the world, even under the strongest emotions, is always the same and always true. From this realization, and without self-indulgence, we form that notion of the invisible which is essential to our subject, and to which I shall return more than once. We seek our own emotion in the same irreproachable image from which the physicist takes his measurements; we call that image to account for the outsize interest it holds for us, and the image cannot respond. Out of its silence we form the hidden and lurking presence, the mysterious other side of reality which makes us believe that everything is full of souls, or, as Thales said, that everything is full of gods. What Thales may have meant by that, if he really said it, is a question that I will take out of the hands of the historian and pose for each of us, and first of all for myself; for these illusions I have spoken of remain as powerful, in their way, as the spectacle of the world remains pure and faithful in appearance, as it always does. The primitive man thinks crudely but aims well, and this contrast between technical perfection and confusion of thinking must lead us to avoid from the start the idea that the world itself is deceptive—following Descartes, of course, who took the right path, but keeping a tight hold on the assertive eloquence of our passions. Certainly we have more than one reason to consider the object-world as we would a society of men, after our own image and the image of our companions. Religion springs from a thousand sources, and those sources

13

will always sing. I will try to explain in more than one way that the past is not far behind us and that our childhood begins again with each moment. But the best test is always the most ordinary experience, which repeats to us, as many times as we like, that we are deceived by ourselves and not by the world. The gods refuse to appear; and from this miracle which never takes place religion develops into temples, statues, and sacrifices. But I must also put forward another idea, of which I will not develop all the intricacies. The miracles of religion, which do not appear, are all recounted in stories. On the subject of language, there is still much to be said. When we speak, in gestures or signs, we fashion a real object in the world; the gesture is seen, the words and the song are heard. The arts are simply a kind of writing, which, in one way or another, fixes words or gestures, and gives body to the invisible. These new objects, poems or temples, are made of the same material as the world. And no doubt it should be said that the ambiguity of the world, which is not of the world, is even less easy to suppose in works of art, where movement and form have on the contrary something regulated and finite about them which turns us away from idolatry. A Greek temple has no within; it announces that its marble is only marble; and poetry itself, and music above all, show by other means the same grain and the same homogeneous crystal. Pure object, entirely external; which never ceases to purify our passions, but which also never ceases to awaken them; as if, in this particular case, we were under an injunction to come back to ourselves. And the legend, through the one fact that it is invariable, again submits our wild thoughts to the rule of the object, that is, to a form of experience. But, on the other hand, through the repetition of a measured and almost felt emotion, the invisible redoubles its presence. And because the experience is perfectly complete, we lose all our means of investigation, or else we exercise them on the side, like people who make a pious inventory of the sculptures at Chartres, and discover the lamb, the lion, and the eagle, which leaves belief in its primitive state. So that a new temple for a new god always drives out some woodland deity, but always establishes a second degree of idolatry.

Each of us thinks he is capable of questioning a verbal account of events. In reality we are in a very poor position for questioning such accounts. The object itself is lacking; and thus experience, which samples, walks around, double-checks, and measures, is not directly possible; but that means it is impossibile. The criticism of stories is a form of scholasticism, entirely founded on the ruinous notions of the possible and the impossible. In this kind of research, one cannot avoid the ridiculous idea of Renan, who claims that it is impossible for a severed leg to grow back, when everyone knows that the leg of a crayfish will grow back. And Hume was right to mock the king of Siam who believed that ice was impossible because he had never seen it. The antipodes were also considered impossible. And for my own part, I will always come back to these rather pointed remarks, with the purpose of recalling what everyone says but few really use for the governing of their thought: that it is the experience of the object, and only the experience of the object, that decides. From which it will be understood that emotion, which is the root of belief, can find nothing in a story to disbelieve. A miracle recounted can no longer be established; that is, it can no longer be denied. Here the strict method of understanding leads to a surprising result, and to a strictness of criticism which we are not quite prepared for. For it is a waste of time to deny a story; and it is something more; it is a loss of judgment through negligence; and it is certainly the loss of an occasion for self-instruction. There is a story in Herodotus about a group of sailors who claimed to have seen the sun from the other side, that is, from the north; a detail that might have seemed highly doubtful, but which, on the contrary, became proof to better instructed men. And yet this is a minor argument, for there would have been more to say about such a story, and even with verifying details it could still have been a lie. No, what is bad about not believing a story because we judge it absurd, is that we thereby uncover an immense area of weakness in ourselves, and a defenseless credulity, since we are forced to believe whatever seems normal and self-explanatory to us. That is not how I conceive of the free spirit. And I would prefer, like Montaigne, to believe everything I hear, down to the smallest details, but always with reservation, and with an equal distrust, or, if you will, an equal confidence in the unbelievable and in the believable; which is to leave the problem open. This succinct exposition, which deserves a great deal of thought, enlightens my great subject in many ways. For on the one hand we know that men believe what they are told more readily than what they see. But on the other hand, I gather that it is healthier to believe everything, which is to learn how to believe, and never to be closed up in what one believes. If our aim is to learn about human nature, we must leave what men say, absurd or not, in its naïve state, for it is worth a hundred times more than a plausible arrangement from which we can draw only commonplace conclusions. Of which you can be sure I will give more than one example.

But as yet we have considered language only from the outside. Language is a natural thing, like the liver and the kidneys. Nothing will make me believe that language, either spoken or mimetic, does not reveal in its own way the truth of the human structure and of the human situation. All the same, as it is not wrong to balance belief with that part of the intelligence that is always skeptical, I will first examine a bit more closely the language of gesture and all of the natural inscriptions that embody it, and then the language of the modulated voice. A man who lies down in the grass writes his form in it, as a dog or a hare does; and since man thinks and tosses around in his thoughts, I may say that man writes his thoughts in his bed of grass. In fact, it is not easy to read this writing; that is why all of the plastic arts are enigmatic. Man himself is an enigma in motion; his questions never stay asked; whereas the mold, the footprint, and by natural extension, the statue itself, like the vaults, the arches, the temples with which man records his own passing, remain immobile and fix a moment of man's life, upon which one might meditate endlessly; and this, properly seen, is my main object in the present study; for the great inscriptions are really Gods. But what must be noted above all is that there is no reason to suppose that these written characters ever tell anything but the truth about man, and therefore the truth of history. Not that man is always divine in his gestures and works;

certainly we can find bad acting in them, like the part of the fool. But at the same time, these works, or imprints, are not all objects of an equal piety. Powerful works, those in which one senses something worth the trouble of divining, are also centers of prayer, of miracles, of pilgrimages; which is to say that the faithful man, standing before these human images, finds himself brought back to his true condition and reconciled with himself by a better attitude. That is why these works are preserved. Moreover, they are imitated, and other artists learn to speak this great language as it should be spoken, that is, to fashion human truth in their own ways. They are inspired, as it is so well put, by beautiful works; and the masterpiece gives birth to new masterpieces that do not resemble it at all. Envy produces flat copies, but admiration leads a man to do his own work. From which it can be understood that, apart from errors of taste, which give themselves away, the history of art equals a succession of enveloped truths; and it is primarily because of this that humanity amounts to something.

There is more obscurity surrounding the subject of language that is spoken or sung. We know that this human bird song, though it never ceases to express the most intimate passions and feelings, is in itself unstable and always more or less secret, because of a natural complicity of affections, projects, and activities; and that is why languages are as distinct as nations; but what is more, experience shows that the national language itself is also broken down by local or professional accents and abbreviations; so that we must go to the roots to recover man. We know that institutions have always opposed this alteration, this perpetual erosion of languages. But above all the great works, poems, speeches, histories, memoirs, treatises, bring those who can read them back to a way of writing, and therefore of speaking, which calls for a ceremonial attention. Thus the Ionian dialect survives because of Homer; thus Montaigne, Sévigné, Voltaire, Montesquieu, and many others, have preserved beautiful language, and continually save us from our own speech impediments and first of all from our childish babbling, which we impose so naturally on those around us. That the power of these works depends upon a more explicit, or, if

17

you will, a less enigmatic truth, is evident in Pascal as in Montesquieu, in Stendhal as in Balzac. Therefore, ways of speaking which are preserved are found to be marked with truth, and already capable of sustaining argument and description with their syntax and vocabulary. But beauty is no less important; you feel it in prose, though it is not easy to account for this other truth, implicit, and as inexpressible as plastic truth, which results from the resonance and inflection of words. On the other hand, the gestures of the throat and of the whole body, in as much as they express human equilibrium and the harmony between men and things, belong almost entirely to poetry, which never ceases to rejuvenate thoughts that have become too well known by an always new way of attuning them to the visceral attitude. The beautiful, once again, is a faithful sign of the true, and anticipates the true. Let us add that poetry, even before writing and reading, contributes to the fixing of language, and corrects local accents and abbreviations with the rules of rhythm and rhyme, which the reciter is naturally inclined to respect and even proclaim. For these reasons, spoken language itself becomes a tool of thought which is far more precise than one might think. We know that the most rigorous logic is no more than an inventory of the connections which relate one manner of speaking to another. It is less well known that the vocabulary contains treasures of thought, and a sort of impossibility of describing badly, for anyone who is familiar with the great works. Auguste Comte has given more than one example of this, and I will point out, as items to orient and regulate research, only the familiar words: heart, people, bad, necessity, taste, grace, to repent, parliament, constitution; but I could cite all words consecrated by usage, and in each of them I would find a lesson in things and an article of humanity. Such detail is not necessary. It is enough if we recall that works of language, and principally those which have been the object of a cult, contain in all likelihood something more than what they seem to say, and that they are as enigmatic, and as worthy of being interpreted, as the statues of the gods. By now a method will have become clear; a method which I would call pious, which assumes that all religions are true. Thus I disagree with Pascal, who liked to say that the only successful religion is the religion that goes against nature and against proofs. But I find something in Pascal that I suspect is true of many others who call themselves believers, which is that he does not succeed in believing. I suppose that he was too much of a geometer, or to put it another way, that he was too little of a pagan to be a Christian.

BOOK I

ALADDIN

Chapter one

ONCE UPON A TIME

"Men are forever pursuing the gods," the shade of Socrates tells me, "as if they once had powerful servants and then lost them. They search everywhere. And they spend more energy praying to the invisible powers than it would cost them to get what they want for themselves." What we must realize is that the invisible powers do nothing. A palace is not built overnight, a field is not worked without oxen; and it takes many man-hours to redirect a river or drain a marsh. But the nurse-maids go on with their stories about how it is different in some far-off country, or was different long ago; as if such an absurd existence were desirable; as if man could ever have lived under the power of enchanters and fairies. But, says Socrates, since there is no country where goods come without labor, and since experience always confirms this rule, I asked myself long ago where such fictions could have come from. Then one day the oldest nurse told me, after a thousand other stories, the story of the condition in which all men used to live, and where their absurd ideas about favor, fortune, and prayer came from, ideas from which they have never since been able to liberate themselves. The old nurse told how once upon a time men lived among the giants, who were like themselves but far more powerful, and these giants always had a supply of bread, fruit, milk, and all that was necessary to sustain life, which they must have acquired in ways that cost them little, for they would always give away their goods to whoever knew how to please them. And the giants would also carry them wherever they wanted to go, provided they were asked in the proper way. So it came about that men never thought of working, nor of walking, nor of building wagons or ships; instead they became natural orators, and spent all of their time watching the giants,

23

figuring out what would please them or displease them, smiling at them or imploring them with tears in their eyes, or else simply pronouncing the necessary words, which had to be memorized exactly, though they had no understanding of the changes of humor that would come over the giants, their brusque refusals, or their sudden willingness. Now, if some man, in those days, had tried to get something for himself by his own industry, they would have laughed him to scorn; for the results of his labor would have been puny beside the immense provisions the giants had amassed; and besides with one false step the giants could easily have crushed those little beginnings of labor out of existence. That is why all human wisdom came down to knowing how to speak and how to persuade; and, rather than move things around with great effort, men chose to learn what words it would take to get one of the giants to do the moving. In short, their main business, or rather their only business, was to please, and above all not to displease, their incomprehensible masters, who seemed nevertheless to be charged with nourishing them and housing them and transporting them, and who eventually carried out their duties, provided they were prayed to. This kind of existence, in which men never knew whether they were the masters or the slaves, lasted for a long time, so that the habit of asking, of hoping, of counting on those stronger than themselves left indelible traces in human nature. That is why, nowadays, though there is no longer any trace of these giants, men search everywhere for them and always hope to see them again, and frequently call for them, and we do not know whether they miss, or long for, or fear that state of dependence under which, once upon a time, they had to manage, and which they may even have loved. For how should we not love the ones we count on for everything? And how should we not love the ones from whom we have everything to fear, as long as they do not do all the harm they might do? On the other hand, how should we not fear a little, even a great deal, those who serve us only because it pleases them? That is why, as if they were still waiting for the return of the giants, men do not forget to pray and make offerings, though no giant has ever shown himself, and they give thanks for any piece of luck, for instance if their hook catches a fish or their arrow strikes a deer in the right spot. The shade of Socrates added a number of other details that he said he had learned from the oldest of the nurses; intent, it seemed to me, upon giving an air of seriousness and truth to this unbelievable story. I imagine that he considered it even more unbelievable that men should exhibit such strange habits if there were no real experience behind them.

An idea is a fiction; and long experience has taught us that men can only perceive by means of an idea; the bare fact, above all if it is ordinary, seems used up in advance, and in any case it ends with itself. Who, for example, has sufficiently weighed this phrase of Descartes: "For we were children before we were men"? It is well known; it is too well known; whereas a fiction has need of us and is nothing without us. That is why I decided to go through with the fiction of the giants, although the reader will have seen by the third line where I was leading him. This ingenuous art of delaying judgment I have learned from the fabulists and from Plato. Whether I imitate them well or badly is of no importance; what is important is that the idea be formed and not simply presented. In what is not yet complete, connections are all-important; the mind looks for them and maintains them. Not to mention that my fable is like all fables and like everything imaginary: there is nothing imaginary about it. It is precisely the first condition of each of us to be carried around and waited on. Therefore our first experience, which is certainly true, nevertheless deceives us about everything; and therefore we come to mature experience with the ideas of a child, which are utterly false. This has been overlooked by many people though they are well aware of what it is to be a child. I will give ample attention to this series of corrected but preserved errors, and once again I will find a nucleus of truth in them. But the reader must learn to be surprised by what is not at all surprising, and to discover what he knows too well to be able to think about. Therefore all the old ruses are gathered here, and openly avowed. That is the theme not only of these reflections but of those to follow. For this half-involuntary delay is almost everything in the acts of religion. Men are afraid to complete their thoughts.

It is something to have discovered ambiguous and deceptive

perceptions; it is something also to show that the error in them is really nothing. But it is still not enough. What is necessary first of all is to recognize as the ground of the canvas the actual past of every man and the nearness of antiquity; and against that ground, errors that are fully consistent and always verified; a moving and always deceptive experience; even a sort of solemn initiation into error. Needless to say the truth of emotions is not thereby altered. On the contrary, the idea that external causes have no power except through the malevolence of some human agent is certainly of a nature to strengthen our courage with indignation; thus thought always finds itself king in the midst of things, recognizing no other evil than that which can come to repentance. That is a summary of childhood's judgment of life, which is doubtless only the yesterday of all our thoughts. And because error is the form of the discovery that corrects it, the false idea being preserved even as it is superceded, forgetfulness is the law of childhood; I mean that in childhood there is no remembrance, though memory is faithful and faultless. We push our childhood before us, and that is our real future. In this sense we can say that a mind that could know the object-world without any error would know nothing at all. But imperious need, imperious love, and imperious growth have first drawn good and evil according to man's measure. And the habit of obtaining by force of demand and expectation develops into courage and industry. There is a child in every inventor, no doubt more so than one might think. Such then is ambition, in him who was first a tyrant by necessity, and a tyrant of a tyrant. And such is the childhood of the spirit. So that the realization of Descartes has greater scope than he thought, though I am sure he always kept it before him.

I have already said that observation is no help to us in making this inventory of a past which is never far behind and which presses upon us so energetically. This story, like every story, is dialectical; it has nothing to do with physical change; no doubt it results from a continual reformation of judgment in the face of a passionately questioned insufficiency. The why of the child is often misunderstood. It means, "Why am I a child?" and also, "Why am I no longer a child?" The accelerated step from one awakening to the other must always be reconstructed in the face of the future, and in the movement of growth; and I believe that memory gives us only a feeble idea of it. We must therefore invent the dialectic of childhood, otherwise known as the stages of forgetting, of that forgetting which is the substance of dreams, and in a certain way the part of thought in all our endeavors, as Plato saw it. The creations of childhood must serve us here, which are games, songs, and stories, but always essentially stories. We must therefore find an order in these things. But as all of our sequences, outside of mathematics, and perhaps even in mathematics, are empirical, we need only try out one order for a better order to appear. And above all let the reader not ask for proofs; it is up to him to find them, and proofs only help to explain an order after the fact. I do not think that there is any other first term than that irrevocable past, that past which we were driven out of with no hope of return, and which we only wish to regret. I was nourished by rivers of milk; but that could not last. They drove me out of that paradise because I wanted to be driven out; and I work out this punishment, which is my own richness. Suddenly the richest and most constant fictions rise up before us; and even the subtleties of theology are already explained by the condition of beloved childhood, regretted and refused. Who would not wish never to die? Yes, but who would wish never to die, when the condition of life is that something is constantly dying? But we must divide up this mass of sentiment, and die away from the happy moment of beginning.

Chapter two

COCKAIGNE

Rivers of milk, mountains of chocolate, and things like that. The idea is that you live without working; nature gives all. We often look far off for what is right in front of us. And the life of Cockaigne is right in front of us: it is the life of a child. There is nothing imaginary about it. The child really finds all of his nourishment ready for him. Not that he gets it when he wants it or as he wants it; but certainly he has no idea that the very nature of things places an obstacle between desire and accomplishment; for this obstacle, if he suspects it, is a slight thing beside the wishes of his mother, his father, or the cook. And since he almost always succeeds, and in the end always succeeds, in seducing these capricious masters, by the strange use of signs, there remains as the ground of the canvas, and as a summary of physical laws, an inexhaustible abundance and a universe made entirely for man. At the beach, where I happen to be writing this, it is easy to see that the savage forces of the Ocean, the rocks and sand, are taken merely as conditions in the game. Even fishing is no more than a game. The nature of these obstacles is that they make the game possible, since it does not matter in the least whether they are overcome or not. The warning against going into the deep water comes long before the menace of the Ocean itself. Thus the obstacle is concealed, or by-passed. Certainly the necessity of food, shelter, and sleep speaks for a deeper necessity, the necessity of a world that guarantees nothing. But it can also be said that childhood knows no other obstacle than emotion, which at that age is almost entirely respect and love. And that is the experience which first instructs us. We all know that this experience, which proves false at every step, was true once and is more and more true as we move back toward the rivers of milk; for there was a time when this metaphor was not a metaphor; and there was also a time when human substance entirely enveloped the child and bathed him in the warmth of human blood. But there is no going back. One simply dreams that things are still that way somewhere. This paradise is always lost, and we pretend to regret it. We will never know enough about the element of pretense in fictions. Here children's games can instruct us. But we must make some divisions.

What I think should be noticed here, as with the age of gold, as with the earthly paradise, is a first state of innocence and ignorance, which we have left by our own fault; which is also very true; for the child chooses to be a man, and never stops making that choice. You might even say that he anticipates his destiny, by always despising the easy and seeking out the difficult, curious, in the midst of so many frivolous reproaches, about the real crime and the real punishment. There is something tragic in the child who deliberately misbehaves, and does not yet know what misbehavior is. He questions; he confuses words and signs; he digs up passions the way he digs water out of the sand. There is a presentiment of necessity here, which is as yet no more than fatality. But the original sin is everywhere, original in the sense that it is willed long before it is known; at the same time, what is already sensed, as if at the tips of one's fingers, is true necessity; and though it is first measured by the strength and does not reveal itself beyond the reach of his small hands, the child is never wholly unaware of it. For he drops his toy and cannot pick it up; he wavers on his feet and struggles to keep his balance. He hammers, but without breaking, he bumps into things, he hurts himself; he chews his rattle with his gums. The resistant world, in its small dimensions, is not yet formidable. But it may irritate him that, although it is not formidable, it never gives way. Labor begins at this point, but its bonds with need never show. The great obstacle is the word No, and the only sin is disobedience. A great and faultless myth grows out of this condition; a great myth which, remarkably enough, says only that it is no longer true. We will be less surprised, after these observations, by beliefs which have no real object, or whose only object is the absence of an object; and also by those strange experiences which were, and are no more, like an old man's recollections.

Man was condemned to labor. Very true. And very true also that he looked forward to it. But there is always treachery in this acceptance. Labor will never make the whole of the Universe exist. The margin of the real is extended as far as man, by great effort, extends it. But, beyond his pains, there is always the greater spectacle; and idealism remains true for the regions that human action cannot reach. Here there is more than one idea to be disentangled, as we already sense. But first, in the spirit of this chapter, we will have to keep with the idea of goods obtained without labor. The child's existence is never really without labor; it is only the necessity of labor that does not appear to him. He grows, he builds his muscles, and that is his labor; he studies, and he calls that labor; but the child does not earn his living; or if he does he is no longer a child. School, which is a time capsule, is a good representation of the place where labor goes unpaid; and from that a noble idea develops, as noble as are all the ideas of childhood, though experience will not leave much trace of it, which is that there is no honor in serf labor, and that merit is a finer thing than conquest. At first, knowledge is held above power; and the idea of working only for the sake of learning is the essential utopia; it is simply an extended childhood; and what we call curiosity, which promises more than it pays, is the result of muscular labor which does not grapple with the object-world but merely explores it. The pleasure of hiking, which is always deceptive, is a pure vestige of this kind of labor. There is a surprising discontinuity between the fatigue of the hiker and the meal he finds waiting for him. This discontinuity is everywhere in the perceptions of early childhood, as we shall see. In reality, the relationship between labor and food is the closest of all relationships; he who labors not, eats not; but it is also the most hidden relationship in the course of a child's life. Rousseau offered a cake to the winner of the race; but that has nothing to do with making the cake, or with growing wheat. The bond between muscular exertion and the things that restore energy is not always understood by grown men, for the simple reason that as children they first learn not to understand it. Sweets are put away in a box, or in the pantry. The problem is to open the box, or to open the door, neither of which is a form of production. No child will ever believe that he was refused something because there was nothing to give him; he always thinks that they did not want him to have it. This idea comes before all others, and it always will. With it we first try to understand poverty and wealth, and this abstract form gives us no real grasp of society and exchange. It is interesting to notice that a child's exchanges are ruled only by desire, with no notion of value. The appearance of desirable but previously hidden and invisible things, is an example of how the fantastic is never invented; it is the result of real experience.

The idea of a comestible universe is perhaps the most remarkable example, and the most natural, of an idea that is false but constantly verified. And men are always too willing to believe that the problem of distribution is first and foremost; thus they sometimes glimpse as in a dream that there would be enough goods for everyone if it were not for the greed of a few. Which is to believe that the totality of consumable goods is locked away somewhere; when the truth is that if labor should stop, human existence would immediately become impossible. The life of arctic peoples, who survive on raw seal fat and the blood of the moose, represents our difficult situation better than stories from warm lands where fruit hangs waiting for the knife. Besides, the extreme fertility of nature is itself a danger, not to mention the multiplication of the human species. But this pressing necessity, as near and as inexorable as gravity, cannot touch the child or he will perish. That is why his experience tells him that the world is good and well-meaning and that misery, like poverty, is always somebody's fault. The fruits of the earth are for everyone, they say. But are there any fruits of the earth? Gardens are deceptive. There are only the fruits of labor.

Chapter three

APPARITIONS

A child is first carried or wheeled around. He is handled like an object. He is told to look at one thing and another; he is dragged through labors and conversations which he neither wants nor foresees. Often I see him looking back with regret. These foreign movements carry him at first far beyond his own impulses; the world is thrown to him piece-meal. He rarely pursues or explores anything fully. Because of the time of day, or other reasons that he cannot understand, he is torn away from his experiments and made a spectator against his will. A woman who opens the window to watch a parade is not learning anything new; but what of the child in her arms? There is nothing real in his visions. Anything at all can follow anything else. Things appear and disappear according to some foreign will. The ease of travel in fairy tales is true experience in the beginning. Maybe not always easy. But the problem is always to overcome some particular obstinacy. Once consent is obtained, things go by themselves. This fantastic world is not invented, it is the real world, seen at first through the medium of the human world. Not only is everything ready-made, like the garden; even discovery follows the movements of the nurse. And again, when the child begins to explore on his own, he is faced with obstacles which are utterly invincible, and which are suddenly overcome with no difficulty at all; just as a cat waits for the door to open, and profits from his chance. For a long time a door is a magic obstacle. And familiar toys are often taken from a drawer that the child cannot reach. The sequence of things is broken up by dark hiding-places. And there are other eclipses, the sudden, short naps a child takes anywhere. The time changes, the place changes. Hiding things and then showing them is even a game. Maine de Biran said that vision is idealist, and that is always true for the reaches of the sky. But our earliest existence, because of the whims of those who carry us, shatters the great image of nature.

The human beings who surround us and serve us are far more consistent. Our mothers first enveloped us, and human substance is never far away. So that the portion of the universe that later on will be most mobile and least known, is what we first discover and recognize. The dialectical opposite, independent but familiar, is the child's mother, his father, his brother; it is the nurse, the maid, the cook, the gardener. Everything depends on them, material goods and visions of the world, and each of them has his province and his powers; but each of them also has his refusals. From which we see that the world of enchanters and witches is not at first imaginary. The apparitions of things are subordinate to the apparitions of people. And the functions of this strange physics are conjurations in a true sense. The main business of Faust is to call the devil by his name. This method does not surprise us as much as we might wish. More likely we recall that things used to be that way in the old days, when we would call a name and a powerful figure would come and open the door or the gate. But when I say that we recall it, I am saying too much; for to recall is to represent things to oneself, knowing that they no longer are and will never be again; whereas the magic that was natural to us, and always is to some degree, of obtaining things by means of signs, remains in the warp of our most positive notions; it is present to us as the other side of a house is present to us without our having to think that we saw it on a certain day, under certain circumstances; and it is more memory than recollection. In the same way fictions are familiar and present to us, though not perceived, as the other side of life, and the obverse of concrete reality.

What then is the real? As opposed to the incoherent spectacle of the world, the real is what is expected, what is obtained and discovered by our own movement. It is what is sensed as being within our own power and always responsive to our action. The child-physicist, as soon as he is left alone, beats on the table with his rattle or his fist. He is stubbornly repetitious. Thus he creates little fragments of a Universe, always measured to his strength and projects; like those paths that he explores from one end to the other. Nothing appears, once he holds the means of discovery. But dinner time comes; the toy is put back in its drawer; the child is carried off again into his dreams, which are realities for us, but not all of them; only the hunter-turned-cook knows the whole route from a bird on the wing to a succulent roast. Contrary to what we would think, it is the child who eats as one ought to eat, and it is the little man who makes noise with his fork.

Chapter four

PRAYER

Asking is the means. Knowing how to ask is the first knowledge. And language, to be exact, is the most ancient method of action. It begins with the cry, which is at first the only power the child has, a power which moves from afar and without contact. The school of the will is persuasion. To recognize, to smile, to name, are often the conditions for obtaining something which otherwise would only be held out and then refused. We must do what it takes. Politeness is a tool and a means long before the bow and arrow. And the power of names remains mixed in with our physical powers. We speak to things. But even if we consider language from every side, we will not arrive at a real understanding of how it is our first attempt to know or to change the world around us. And the unavoidable condition of naming before knowing should explain all the detours of knowledge. We talk, we tell stories, to ourselves and others. Our thinking life is first a speech, which carries over even into sleep. But what is to be noted above all is the advance that speech has over thought; which would hardly be believable did we not know that a child naturally speaks before he knows what he is saying. Analyze the dialogue between a mother and her child, and you will see that the child returns her words as if he were playing with a ball, and is surprised that he can hear his own voice as well as hers; this kind of echo is the first meaning of language and it always will be. It is a human resonance which later develops into music; but in another way, the music of words develops into magic, through the necessity of praying continually to the familiar spirits, the masters of toys, the masters of food, the sovereign lords of the doors, windows, and stairs. This method of obtaining, which is at first the only one, and for a long time the principal one, accounts for a function of words that is almost always forgotten in deference to the idea that we form our knowledge first and then express it. For, if the notion of an object always results from the efforts by which it is reached, and grasped, and mastered, then it is clear, if only because of the weakness of the child, that language is the first means of conquest, and therefore the first form of knowledge. People's names, polite phrases, imitative cries, the names of things, are at first directly bound up with our needs, our fears, our affections, our desires, and are all, in fact, "Open Sesames." Incantation, which, by means of exactness, repetition, and insistence, conjures up what it names, is the first physics. And this attitude of waiting and expectation is what preserves the power of expression in words. The movement of poetry, and even of the simplest story, is on the verge of giving body to what it names, almost gives body to it, and the attitude of the listener, even better if he is also the storyteller, is an attentiveness like the attentiveness of early childhood. Scheherazade piles tale upon tale, and so delays her execution; this story made up of stories only redoubles the listener's curiosity for the miraculous outcome, but he is always deceived by further promises. At the moment when we expect finally to see, more phantoms are announced; we must go on, renounce the end, be forever expectant. Orpheus bringing Eurydice back, is the essential text of the imagination. For it is true that emotions like fear, anxiety, surprise, create a kind of presence in our bodies, one that is even sensitive to touch, which is, as we see, the most deceptive of the senses; and it is also true that our senses are quickened by our own blood and disposition so as to produce the beginnings of phantoms—a humming in the ears, spots of color, butterflies in the stomach, pricklings, salivation, nausea, and other effects of heightened expectation; but these disturbing forms, if we should pay attention to them, would present us with nothing more than the structure of our own body, though in a state of flux. However, the inner murmuring of the body is effaced by speech, which is an object really produced and really perceived. Conjuration by means of words calls up all the spirits of our flesh and blood, but immediately disperses them by solemn ritual incantation, which opens a door of silence upon the outcome. These effects are powerful in the theater, and tell us why violent actions are kept off stage; for waiting is fulfilled by waiting.

The reality of the imagination is always in some impulse of the body; it cannot be otherwise. But in the end the art of naming and speaking upstages everything else, and the game of evocation is turned wholly toward the future, which is immediately past. All the devices of the old stories are designed to occupy us only with what takes place, and the double meaning of this phrase is quite remarkable. What takes place in a story is always what is about to take place. Our creation is annunciation; anticipation is the law of poetry, which means creation. This magic is prepared for by experience. We will be less surprised by rainmakers, who give names to the rain and imitate it with sounds and gestures, in hopes of making it appear, if we note that there was a time when naming was the only way, or the principal way, of making the enchanters appear, and through them, the desired object. Which is expressed summarily when we say that we first perceive all things through the medium of the human world. But I see that this idea is still hidden in the clouds of abstract evidence and cannot find its content without a fairly strict analysis of the real conditions under which we invent the gods. That men and above all children see man and man's will and man's capriciousness everywhere, is only roughly true; and if we look closer, it is not true at all. The child, like the man, sees no more than the world as it shows itself, and the world shows itself as it must, which means as it is. But speech, be it in story, poem, or prayer, fashions another world of objects, animals, men, and all else that can be given a name; a world which never appears. It is no easier for magic to evoke a man than a forest. The magic bond is not from an imaginary man to the things he brings or takes away; it is from the word to the invisible thing and the invisible man; and that presence which we seek behind real presence results from an imperious, let us say even an imperial, method of action which comes first for all of us. I must say, anticipating a great deal, that it is no less mythological to wish to change a man by means of words than it is, by the same means, to change dry rocks into a spring

37

of water. The real world of men is what it is, deaf and blind as the rocks, responsive only to diligence, to pulleys and levers, that is to say, to tools, efforts, labor; but this condition is not discovered at first, or it is more known than believed. What we believe are the old stories. No doubt we understand well enough by now why an apparition is always the story of an apparition, and no one can do better, in that case, than retell the story in the same terms; this constancy is important, and the child insists on it; for it is the whole object. We are surprised at the prodigious effect of prayers; I think that no one has ever believed more in prayers than in stories, but that is already a great deal. What is more, fairy tales are the stories of prayers answered; speech confirms itself. That is the virtue of speech.

Now we can turn to the famous story of *Aladdin* or *The Magic Lamp*. In it I see the world of childhood as it appears in our earliest experience. Riches, like food and diamonds, exist somewhere in dark, closed places. It is only a question of calling the servant who holds the key to these things. And the right way to call him is, with perfect naïveté, to imitate one of those gestures that servants make without realizing their importance, such as polishing a lamp. We must notice that real labor is thus reduced to the level of a sign; but it is raised up to that level according to the child's physics; for the child obtains everything by means of signs. In this case, as in all stories, one sign is laid over another; for the story itself is only a series of signs, and the narrator simply polishes all sorts of lamps, forgetting one as he reaches for the next. Not to mention that the little gods of our flesh and blood, the renewers of emotion, are first awakened in this reverie by the brightness of the lamp, which gleams here and there on the underground jewels. Thus the spirits of the earth take their place in the procession that leads to the higher gods. And the theologian who refuses to polish the lamp is wrong to think himself reasonable; he is not reasonable enough.

Chapter five

LABOR

A child is an idealist as long as he knows nothing of labor; and the same is true of any man who lives like a child. That, briefly, is the idea. It is well hidden. How many jobs there are in which polishing the lamp is simply a form of prayer! In a forgotten novel, *Balaoo*, the story of a monkey who was taught to speak and dress like a man, I have come across a very enlightening passage. I take stories at their word. Balaoo, the civilized monkey, used to go to the zoo of the Jardin des Plantes at night to pick up his brother Gabriel, and, after dressing him properly, would take him around to the cabarets. But Gabriel had the unfortunate habit of throwing himself on anything he wanted, like a lady's hat decorated with artificial fruit. After the commotion and their escape, Balaoo taught Gabriel the following lesson: "When humans want to eat something, they don't just take it; they have to show their intentions by putting down some money." A child might have the same idea about money; and it remains unchanged in many grown men. The Duc de Villeroy, when he was about to go out gambling, asked his footman, "Have they put gold in my pockets?" The words of an overgrown child, but no more unreasonable than the idea of the self-styled physicist who said that there is enough energy in a copper penny to turn a thousand machines. He was too naïve to remember that the energy in a penny, being in repose, would have to be separated into particles before it could do any work, just as a spring has to be coiled up, and that one would obtain as a result no more than the equivalent, at best, of the energy spent in working against the forces of cohesion in the penny. The noble duke also did not consider that the power of purchasing with gold rests on all of the work done in mills and factories from morning to evening, on

39

great exertions and great fatigue. And, for reasons contained in childhood itself, the child cannot understand that the treasures of Aladdin are the fruits of labor. That is why all of these characters live and think in enchanted ways with regard to that portion of the world that is no more for them than a spectacle. We know that Bishop Berkeley was persuaded that the world is only imagery within us, the imagery of our thoughts. For him the world was a bishop's supper. And the child-man Berkeley went as far as Newfoundland to preach, and came back, still persuaded that our perceptions have no substance. He let himself be carried by the ship, while others hoisted the sails. The passenger's job is no doubt the stupidest in the world; which is why there are travels and travels. We come back to the child who, by condition, is at first only a passenger, with no ability to steer himself and no need to. His proper labor, as I have said, is to grow, like the famous lilies which neither toil nor spin but rise up naked in the fields. The child, however, is given clothing, shelter, and food; and lives in a fairy tale. That is the idea that we must gather at its root.

Maine de Biran, the subprefect, touched the world by thoughtfully testing the resistance of his desk; and his *Memoirs* concerning touch, sight, and the other senses, have endured almost alone among the many philosophical tracts of his loquacious century. But the reason for believing what we hear is already behind us. The subprefect was a most positive thinker. He observed that we know as the real world only what we have revealed by an effort of will. For example, to explore a faint odor by purposefully sniffing it, is to make the odor dependent upon us, and at the same time to know that it is not dependent upon us. Our sense of touch immediately clarifies this first thought. For to receive a shock is only to feel ourselves; therefore we know only our own feeling. But it is entirely otherwise if we explore the surface of a solid object, for example the desk of a subprefect. For, moving by our own will, brushing the object with our fingers or leaning our full weight against it, we get a more or less moving impression, and one that can be repeated, and we discover all of these sensible events by an effort and a rule of motion that depend only upon us. In this process the world withdraws from us and begins to take on its own existence. In short, what makes existence is not appearance, it is appearance at the command and under the condition of labor. And what makes the world known as a reality are the bonds between labor and its effects, those laws, in other words, of which the mere spectator can have no certainty. That is why Maine de Biran says that vision is idealist. There is no labor possible in exploring something with our eyes. I turn my head; new colors come into sight, even the whole of the sky, with no difficulty; but we also know very well that vision alone gives us no knowledge of anything. The philosopher wished only to insist upon the fact that an active sense of touch, on the contrary, gives us the experience of reality that comes from effort. That is still only half the idea; effort is not labor; and the labor of the subprefect was almost all magic. But he was on the right path.

Leaving aside the valuable things he said about the blind geometer, the only profound man, and about the lighthearted geometer of the visible world, I would like to move one step beyond his idea, to compare blind labor, which feels the weight of the world on its tools, with the easy contemplation of a colorful spectacle that changes instant by instant with the slightest movement. Travel, it is true, is a form of labor, though we often give up and go by car. But considering even the most favorable case of an explorer or a mountain climber, in which felt labor accompanies the changes of spectacle, we will observe that there is no proportion between the labor and the change; there is still something miraculous here, an appearance reminiscent of the old stories. On the other hand, blind labor, working from one end of the field to the other, never ceases to pay out a stable change, where the laborer is established to continue it. Here there is no suspicion of idealism, because what is felt in the exchange between shoulders, arms, plow, and the resisting earth, is the antagonistic term, strongly bound in all of its parts by a nonarbitrary law. It is no small business to change the appearance of fallow land into the appearance of plowed land and it is labor that gives consistency to this series of visions, as the most profound physics has finally understood.

Therefore when the peasant takes a rest and looks around, it is not at the treasures of Aladdin, or any other kind of treasure, it is at his own labor, which he feels at the same time as he sees it. He has conquered his vision; he is master of it. This world is no longer a game. And two notions appear at the same time, which are correlatives, the notion of creative will and the notion of necessity. Of creative will, because action does not cease where knowing begins; of necessity, because it is only through labor that one is assured of the fidelity of the world, which could also be called the inertia of the world, which wipes out all promises and is worth more than promises; for on condition that one obeys and delves oneself, as a picking and shoveling creature, into the tissue of things, one learns finally what it means to will, which is also to will what one does not will. But I admit that if the peasant should happen to dig up a pot of gold, he would begin to dream, I mean to dream his own life; he would become a magician.

From which I have learned the full meaning of the word "visions." For popular language never weighs its words, it suddenly throws out the most profound idea, since it means by visions, or things that are merely seen, spectacles that are absolutely deceptive; deceptive, even if we should be certain of their sequence and recurrence; no doubt that is what the eclipses were to an Egyptian; and that is what they are to the mathematical astronomer, because thirty zeros cost him nothing; and it took a kind of blind attention and refusal of spectacle to introduce the idea of labor into events that are as far away from our hands as the movements of the heavenly bodies, the birth and decay of suns. But there is always a danger in the work of the clever student, who is never more than an intelligent visionary. For, as Maine de Biran says, the geometer who can see is satisfied with the spectacle he has made for himself with pencil and paper. He moves from evidence to evidence, from intuition to intuition; he lets the truth enter all at once. Whereas the blind geometer, who is the true geometer, starts with nothing; all that he thinks, he makes; he constructs and reconstructs his thought. A triangle for him is no longer a secret which looks back at us, so boldly that the clever student could not help drawing the eye of God within it. No, the triangle is a path that has been followed and remembered, according to the rules of physical movement; from which the proof is born, always as a form of self-awareness, and of understanding, as language so energetically expresses it. Yet this labor of the hands and of memory, which is also a pledge to oneself, is still only an imitation of true labor; and the difference between the two geometers is of no importance, as long as the geometer only gives birth to geometry; for geometry is always a question of possible worlds. On the other hand, if one wishes to push geometry toward concrete things, by means of mechanics and physics, it is the hands that will find the object; the idealist eye will never find it. However, this is not the place to explain so difficult an idea. I wanted to pay homage to Maine de Biran, because he has made me understand that visionaries are lighthearted men, alienated men, dreamers of the world, who never stop waiting for a miracle, that is, for treasure without work. These same visionaries seek proof of the existence of the world, without finding any proof; and I can well believe it; they do not know what existence is. Theirs is always the bishop's supper.

The child's situation is the same, though more natural. And I am trying to explain how childhood experience, though it is, and always is, an experience of the world, is the beginning of all error. The child knows nothing of labor. Games are a form of effort without lasting results; games are written in the sand, like hopscotch. They are erased and played again. We never find in them the sequence that exists in labor, where the result immediately becomes a means. This difference, which shows clearly in games that are wholly fictional, like parades, songs, dances, ceremonies, is even more striking in games that imitate various kinds of work; for nothing gets done; everything is merely spoken or mimed; games do not grapple with the world; the child is fed and housed by other means. He who does not grapple with the world, is ignorant of the world. He who does not know how to carry the law of labor down to concrete things, and bind them together according to the blind man's mechanics, cannot know what it costs to turn fallow land into a field of wheat. Everything is possible; anything can happen. And this, added to the broken perceptions and magic journeys of our earliest years, explains fairly well how everything is a miracle. Fairy tales express the surprises of a traveler who was transported while he slept; but on a deeper level fairy tales express a real life in which everything is obtained by prayer, in which nothing is gained by labor. The world nevertheless is as it is, and appears as it appears. But the mind, that god of gods, first plays in it like Ariel, and deceives itself without inventing anything. Over the past few days, while I have been writing, the ripe fields have turned into piles of wheat and piles of straw; and I knew nothing about it; I only saw that the decor had changed, through the agency of the earth-spirits who appear at the end of a field and arrange such things. My bread is brought to me in the same way. Where does bread come from? And who takes care of it? Even if I were concerned with it myself, even if I represented to myself the successive spectacle of plowing, sowing, growth, harvest, milling, and baking, it would give me only a better connected dream, I would not really know that I am nourished by men's pains. We are children and visionaries for a good part of the things we use, for almost all of them. The visionary geometer is fed on perfect triangles as he is fed on his little matinal bread, another miracle.

Chapter six

BOURGEOISIE

The bourgeois is a city-dweller; and the word says just what it means. It opposes commerce to labor, and first of all to the essential labor, which is in the fields. The natural opposition between bourgeois and peasant was extended to include workers in wood, and from them to coal miners and miners in general; and the definition of bourgeois is in no way changed by that; on the contrary, it is confirmed. The bourgeois is he who lives by persuasion. The merchant in his shop, the professor, the priest, the lawyer, the politician do nothing else. You will never see them changing the face of the earth or transporting things. What offers them resistance is not the object-world, it is man; and from that situation astonishing preconceptions are forever being reborn, which are at bottom only an ongoing childhood. The bourgeois matures through the art of making his nurses walk. This art is quite profound in a king, but it is never more than a more skillful childhood and a better magic wand. It amuses me to watch the official at a cornerstone ceremony; what a mason he is! He actually makes stones move simply by speaking. But this strange occupation never teaches him anything about stones. Why should fairy tales surprise us? There are many men for whom palaces are built on command. But a certain sum of money has to be placed at the foundation, as a sort of sign. This magic is real; and to pay is not to learn. But to cook a meal for the harvesters and carry it out to them, is also a form of payment, and one does learn from it. We have all seen the way a child will follow the cook around and make a game of carrying the salt shaker or saucepan. Such is the bourgeois, always tangent to the real. And we were all bourgeois once, even the sons of workers. And every worker becomes bourgeois again when he markets his skills, because that is a form of persuasion. I am not speaking of negotiators or union officials, for they are bourgeois anyway, and more so than ever when they pretend not to be. The mixture of fictions and realities which is the result of this double situation contains the secret of all our quarrels. All wars are wars of religion, though everyone denies it. We do not know how or why it is that we naturally deceive ourselves. We should see by this time that our errors are only memories of childhood. The spectacle of the world and the life of society might explain equally well all the pitfalls of the imagination and all the degrees of religion that stand behind the least of our thoughts. But childhood is more open; and through childhood we understand that we all got off to a bad start and that it could not be otherwise. It is only in this sense that the secret of the gods lies in fairy tales; and this first richness has been amply developed in the bourgeois situation. But here I must add, what will appear later in its proper place, that the bourgeois situation, and before that the child's, also leads to precious ideas, without which the adhering proletarian thought, which deceives itself least, would never have become conscious of itself. Animals are never deceived; they have no altars, no statues, no false gods; that is why they sleep and will go on sleeping.

Everything is religion in the bourgeois life; because requesting and persuading have no assignable rules; everything depends on the opinion of the one to be persuaded; and there is obvious risk in neglecting an artifice of form simply because one does not see the purpose of it. He who would be polite is never polite enough. That is why all conventions are tools for the task of persuasion. On the other hand, the proletarian dislikes politeness; he gets nothing by politeness, nothing from the earth, nothing from iron, nothing from lead. The bourgeois problem is the distribution of goods, the proletarian and peasant problem is their production. And we all do our share of bargaining. In a way, the beggar is the pure bourgeois, for he gets nothing except by means of an art of requesting, by making appealing signs; his rags talk. And, for the same reason, a worker who has been laid off is immediately condemned to be bourgeois. Here I am simply developing Marx's idea, according to which a man's knowledge, his emotions, and his religion all result from the way he earns his living. But this thought itself has great need of being applied; otherwise it is only a vision like any other. The proletarian, as long as he lives and thinks in terms of real labor, labor against the object-world, is naturally irreligious. But there is also no such thing as a pure proletarian. And again it must be said that the risk of the pure proletarian is to be deceived by politeness, by signs, by credit, by persuasion, in a word by religion itself. Because he thinks that there is no truth in these things. And yet, as I have already suggested, it must be that everything is true in the end; nonbeing is nothing and does nothing.

Every contract is an arrangement of signs that conceals an organization of labor. The first part is bourgeois, the second is proletarian. A legal process takes place in the signs and attempts to harmonize them; but it sometimes happens that the court is brought to the scene of the action, which puts a restraint on imagination, or, better, on incantation. All the same the surplus of human labors is enough so that the childish custom of acting through signs and only with signs suffices for many of us, and for a long time. From which comes a dialectic that is typically bourgeois, and which we must call idealist. This kind of thought, considered in its perfection, consists in working with the conceptions of the mind alone, which in fact are merely arguments. The threat to argument is contradiction, and the health of argument is conciliation. Utopias, as we see with Jaurès the professor, consist first of all in an arrangement of arguments. Is it true or is it not true that a social arrangement by explicit contract, extended to all, is contrary to the development of the individual and his strengths? I do not see, says the philosopher, that I am forced to deny the one if I affirm the other, and I prove it by affirming both. This is rhetoric in its pure state; and it plays no small part in those struggles that develop over poorly structured arguments. I find it a cause for wonder that so many men should be judged incapable of altering the course of events, even of events within their reach, simply because words are poorly organized. It is to die for grammar. On the other hand, Pangloss consoles himself for everything with new arguments; and this heroic grammarian is not as far as we might think from the illustrious Leibniz, the most skillful of conciliators. All the same we must account for irritation or conciliation by some more or less durable humor. Leibniz was happy; and our bilious determinist is not happy enough. A child stops crying if you sing to him, or if you turn him over or put him in his bath. One suspects that the apparent connection of arguments by Yes, No, and Distinguo, stands for another linking which takes place in the breast, the lungs, the whole body. In the same way, the true reason for the baby's bottle is not that it is called for with tears and cries. But childishness is always strong, and shows itself even in the highest seriousness, when the object-world does not answer for itself but is entirely assumed. Kant dared to say, what is immediately obvious, that an arrangement of words, however perfect, in no way speaks for an arrangement of things; which does away in advance and for good with the argument of arguments, which attempts to produce a concrete reality by assembling, in one argument, every conceivable perfection.

The people sense well enough how empty these arguments are; they are the babbling of overgrown children whom the people must feed and carry around in their arms. But the people suspect something else, which is that this pretentious game is the deeply serious translation of a state of affairs that goes beyond humors to the sources of humors, which are food supplies, houses, heat, light, and other goods. For words must lead to things, that is the basis of ontology. Whence a few obstinate thinkers have formed the idea of a dialectic which they rightly call materialist, according to which all theological systems translate a certain way of living and precisely a certain kind of work. We know that there is a god for each trade. But the bond between labor and belief is much stricter than the believers think. And because the philosopher innocently expresses, in his words, that he lives by words, there is need for a philosophy of philosophy. We have not fully perceived how the lower carries along the higher. It is nevertheless true that materialism is the sole support of the spirit. It is this that the doctrine of religions must make evident, following rustic paths. The god Limit rules over the cities, but his true face, which is faceless, appears at the edge of the field.

Chapter seven

FEAR

Magic works. In the life of childhood words really make things appear; first the servant, then his services, the keys to the doors, the garden, the toy, the bottle. In adult life many miracles take place because of words. Authority, favor, reputation, disapproval, contempt, excommunication either encourage or disrupt activity, and therefore health. Almost all wars are fought with words. War, bankruptcy, misery, prison, are no less real than riches or a throne. Thus the imagination triumphs and perishes in its opposite. Yet we know that the most terrible gods never appear. The invisible guides us. The sort of trance that comes over us in a deserted wood is nourished by silence, and thrives on what should appease it. We must now grasp, if we can, the reality of the imaginary, which is nothing. For this underside of vision, this enigma of vision, is the whole vision. When I hear what I think is a thief outside the door, I listen to his breath at the keyhole, and his breath is my own. The most formidable thief is the one I do not hear.

Every emotion is a presence. We are too quick to say that the sense of touch is never deceptive; that can only be said of the voluntary sense of touch. The touch of emotion is the false witness. What is emotion? Briefly, it is a preparation of the human body, an incipient way of acting which, in anticipation of its object, is on the point of doing what it would do if the object were there. But the essence of emotion is precisely in the watchfulness, or better, in the state of alarm of all our bodily functions, after the first shock. And the shock often comes from a little fall, perhaps only the drop of a hand, of someone who is sleeping in an uncomfortable position and thus wakes himself up, the way a man who falls asleep reading

49

his paper is awakened by the very surrender that comes with sleep. And, because the initial shock is promptly communicated to all of the senses by the nervous system, the alarm grows, and we are suddenly ready for anything, without knowing what. The felt increase of an anxiety which we do not know the reason for, is fear itself. The proverb says that joy is frightening; no doubt we are frightened by any impulse that comes over us against our will. And, because we are afraid of fear, it can be said that fear is the purest emotion.

Later on this naïveté is dressed up; manly strength turns fear into anger. But it is quite certain that a child is frightened of fear. He feels it coming at a certain time of day, in a certain place. That is the principle of what we call imagining, and the object-world plays almost no part in it; it is because we perceive nothing that we are left alone with our fear. That is why we can say that the only fear is fear of the gods. Fear of oneself, always, as we feel it in the fear of heights, or, at the opposite extreme, in the most intense conflicts. But let us first be sure of innocent childhood.

I once happened to observe a child's fear. The effects were obvious, the causes were beyond comprehension, and no doubt one would not have believed them. But I have learned how to believe. The child admitted that she was afraid of the swaying shadow of the plane tree by the road, projected against the wall by a streetlight. I said, "But you know it is only the shadow of a tree?" She said yes. I could see that that was not what frightened her. And yet she was afraid; and because of this perfectly simple image, she had a nightly encounter with fear. The only thing to do was move her to another room. We must not be too quick to say that the child imagined some human form waiting in ambush behind things. It was much less than that, in fact it was absolutely nothing. Stories of spirits and evil demons are no doubt the beginnings of a cure for the fear that has no object; the art of David begins there.

It is well known that we find it hard to be afraid for a given reason. Strange as it may seem, if we do not begin by being afraid, we will form no more than an insubstantial idea of fear. In the same way, we cannot hate unless we begin by being sad, and we cannot love unless we begin by being happy. This shows that there is an order in our affections, which always moves from the lower to the higher, and which we cannot reverse. As we do not fall in love at will, and according to our knowledge of perfections, so we do not come to be afraid simply with the idea that we ought to be afraid. It may even be that true fear is always distinct from the reasons we give for it, to the point that there may be only one way to incorporate fear into alarm, and that is by overcoming fear; which means that courage is already present in the condition of alarm. This view of the passions, once recalled, is of great importance for our subject. A little girl, finding herself alone for a moment, wanders across a hunting trail and comes face to face with a wolf, without being frightened; on the other hand, fear, lacking the wolf, invents a monster that defies description, and which is really nothing. I heard a story about a naturalist in Siam who saw a huge cat leap suddenly through a clearing; it was a tiger; and no doubt on reflection, telling the story over to himself or to someone else, he was afraid. That is often what happens in moments of danger, especially if the exchange of signs has not led to panic fear. And on the contrary a religious song can dispel fear, in the presence of the most terrible and evident danger, as we are told happened aboard the *Titanic*. I don't know how far heroic strength can go; but to man fear is always of more consequence than danger. One can sing marching to battle or martyrdom; what takes place in the moment of pain does not change the event, for the attack moves quickly. And, if I guess right, the very onslaught of the catastrophes that destroy us is the object neither of alarm nor of fear, nor even of remembrance, except perhaps for the witnesses.

Here we see once again, and closer-to, why stories are always deceptive. But the analysis of causes allows us to take one more step toward the gods. For it is clear that nothing is more effective than a story for awakening fear. I have said that it is of little importance that the objects described are not present; I understand now that it is of great importance that they not be. No doubt it is enough if our perceptions are so confused as to make us think we see, or to make us fear to see, as happens in the old evening story-sessions in the country, when the candle barely illuminates the recesses of the barn; only the narrator can be clearly seen, and the listeners are so strongly affected by what he says that they would believe anything. The evening storytelling in the *Country Doctor* is a good description of this kind of theater, which is far more moving than the stage monsters of the opera. But, passing over the heroic tale, which goes side by side with popular history, we will learn more about the power of stories from reading the *Courageous Hunchback*, which refers to the same setting, and which, starting out from realistic conditions, and at first allaying fear with courage, arrives at the limits of terror in the moment of peace following the real danger, when the head and limbs of the murdered man drop down the chimney into the fireplace. I don't want to tell the whole story here, though that is the only way to tell it. For contrast, I would have to tell the story of the *Cranes of Ibycus*, in which the sequence of events is perfectly natural and never fails to seem so; and the vengeful god is entirely in the spirit of the wrongdoer. But it will not be bad if the reader seeks out these great examples for himself, knowing that he will find the sequence of the gods there, in order, it being understood that religion makes no separations, and that gods and devils go together, if we may put it so, the way belly, breast, and head always go together.

Let us turn back to the solitude of the woods, and of silent nights, when fear is tasted in its purity and without the mediation of art. A man cannot see from behind, nor can he defend himself from behind. Even in front of him, in full daylight, a man sees only one side of a tree. Wild animals, if they are there, appear only for an instant. Often what seems like a deer or a wolf is only a stump with a couple of leaves hanging on it. But approach and examination are not as reassuring as we think. That the apparition that seized our hearts turns out to be only the trunk of a tree, is an ambiguous proof, since the Evil Genius of Descartes, who lives in all of our thoughts, may decide to undeceive us. I hope to bring to light, in the proper place, this great debate between intelligence and the always insufficient world. Right now we are concerned with childhood, in which experience is naïvely sought out and never proves anything. It has often been said that primitives are impervious to experience; but that separates them too far from us. The human debate is this: we seek the truth, and we will find it only within ourselves, through a purification of the thoughts that depend on us. That is what exorcism means; but it is necessary that man first believe sufficiently in his own intelligence. Exorcism, and the peace that it brings, at first hands us over to other powers which are also invisible, also hidden behind the trees. We will find, in the lyric movement of the *Phèdre*, another exorcism which comes close to revealing the gods of the earth, centaurs and satyrs, but in procession and by a kind of playing that is almost all voluntary. The fairy tales of childhood are also magic flute games which give a decent clothing to fear. Childhood is reassured by all of these rules, like the wand, the lamp, the magic carpet, Sesame, which make up a sort of coherent second world, a world, besides, that is attuned to domestic life, from which the child inevitably takes his first idea of law. Nature, always an unexplored domain, is far more frightening than stories, because nature offers no sufficient ritual. A simple stick, which is the ax and fasces of childhood, must be more reassuring than a weapon. And the weapon itself, the manly armament, serves only to increase superstition, because, as we see with the bow, it depends first of all upon the human body, and a man cannot shoot straight if he is shaking. What gives confidence is also what kills the enemy from afar. That is why we should say, and have said in effect, that it is the curse that kills and not the arrow. I prefer to think that the most formidable marksman is not the least superstitious of men, but on the contrary that he is more superstitious than the rest. One would be less superstitious if one always missed.

Chapter eight

GAMES

To better understand the emptiness of imaginary spaces, and the present absence we have been talking about, it is necessary to consider the poetry of acting, first of all in the child, who is an actor—and the word is full of meaning—in almost all of his games. I do not mean games of dexterity, like playing with a ball or a top, which are on the way to real physics, since they have almost no effect on things but only on the body. Other games, like rounds, made up of song, dance, ceremony, fashion a real object, twice real, because first we recognize the actor as one of our friends, and then, through the decisive experience of playing a character ourselves, we bring about a state of belief in others and in ourselves as well, and thus create a real and deceptive god. This mixture, which is natural in professional actors, was shaken up by Diderot, himself an actor, and always delighted with the uncertainty he leaves us in. There is for all that no real uncertainty about the development of emotion in the actor; for it always moves from the sign to the spectator, and returns to the actor via the audience-players, who also know their part. The actor makes believe, and believes himself, in his conceit, because others believe him. This development, this state of infatuation, this reliance on the simple sign, are everywhere in the actor's least gestures. The seriousness and self-assurance of the child, in the plays that belong to that age, come from the same source. I believe I have said that the theater of childhood, with its chorus and ensemble style, never invokes the invisible but rather makes everything visible, through the confusion of spectator and actor, something of which is preserved in the chorus of ancient tragedy.

It is entirely otherwise with games that imitate actions,

games of hunting, of war, games of cars and airplanes. Here the imagination never ceases to create, and what it creates is nothing. Movement never ceases to efface what has never appeared. The imagination in this case is quite frankly what it always is, the feeling of an impulse in itself. It is enough if this impulse is regulated by some accessory object. For example, a paper hat brings about a military attitude. A stick takes the place of a horse. The lion-tamer's whip suggests the lion. Sounds always add to the impression, because they return to the ear as objects. Moreover, for men themselves, the drum adds to the noise of marching feet, already eloquent in itself. As for the gesture, which is now our object, it is easy to understand that it works more energetically than any other language, for it is seen by the other actors and is in itself strongly, sometimes violently, felt. All the same I see no visionary illusion in this kind of game. A round object that disposes our hands the way they would be on a steering wheel takes the place of the whole automobile, but does not evoke it; neither do chairs arranged in a certain way take on the appearance of a car or a horse. The acting alone is enough. These games refuse the object-world, as they would also refuse such imitative toys as model cars, puppets, costumes, perhaps because these appearances interfere with the freedom of belief. The void of the imagination is what is sought out and loved. Once again, the imaginary is nothing but the perception and sensation of impulses in the human body; this realization is of great importance for our subject; for we now see that the gods have no need to appear. But there is something more to be learned from the games of acting. In the same way as a child learns to handle words before he can handle things, he also learns to handle himself and get used to himself before he attacks the objects of labor. That is literally what it means to see the world through the medium of the human form; which is not at all to say that things take on human form, for they never do; but rather that things, once we come to them, contradict the human form and give substance, if we can say that, to the emotion that reads a hidden life into them. Anthropomorphism is translated quite indirectly by allegorical statues.

Their likeness is external. Fairy tales tell us clearly that a sword is enchanted, that a spring is enchanted; which is not to say that we see, or even think we see, a human form in these things. No, the sword is never anything but a sword, the spring is only the sound and reflection of water. The occult, the soul of religions, never appears; it is awesome in the extreme. So much the better can we understand that when children play they do not have visions.

Self-deception is a fine word; it is something quite different from being deceived. Self-deception is active. The Stoics used to say that our passions are errors; no doubt they thought of error as more tumultuous, madder, more headlong than we think of it. "No one has condemned me to play the tragic hero," said Marcus Aurelius. The man of passion is an actor; he always begins playing a bit above his natural tone; he forces the role, and he is caught in it; he is caught in it because he thinks he has mastered it. Plato compared this strange form of self-government to tyranny, in which fits of anger are so promptly translated into action that the tyrant can only maintain control by ordering a worse evil for tomorrow, through a mixture of madness and logic. The theater develops the power of signs in itself, which makes up all dramas. When Montaigne reminds us that children are often frightened by a face which they themselves have scribbled on a piece of paper, he traces the exact curve of belief. The sorcerer's apprentice was too successful; but we must understand this old fable; he started out to frighten himself, and in the end he was scared to death. These dramas are absolutely internal, and for that reason, as Hegel liked to say, absolutely external; for the likeness answers back, and the world does also; two monologues fall into unison; and the brambles only catch at the one who runs away. The child plays at fighting, and gets some real bruises. He plays at falling in the sand; but gravity is not playing with him, and he finds in the sand a very serious rock. This kind of proof, though it is a form of experience, comes in by an unfortunate door. War is the essential drama. It is often proved, and very stupidly proved, that we did have enemies after all, because we have them now. A child is no more naïve than a man.

I imagine that games of hiding, of big-game hunting, of imitating animal calls, often end badly; but the child never talks about it; he sees the frontier, he does not cross over into the country of fear. I notice that there are conventions in this kind of game, as there are in the theater. There is more simplicity in the young child who is clapping his hands, claps too hard, hurts himself, becomes angry, and claps even harder. That is the course of crimes. But we must keep to the world of signs if we want to understand religions; for the response of the likeness and of the world easily leads to a kind of madness, which kills both gods and devils, the unseen powers. I remember a game that ended badly, but only because of fear. Our maid covered herself with a wolf-skin rug and chased after us, howling and moaning; in the end we were all screaming with terror, and a higher power had to intervene; and yet we loved the game. I also remember a child, more of a philosopher, who would sit and stroke a wolf-skin rug, saying "afraid" to himself in a very calm voice. He knew what to do with a wolf skin. It was a very short prayer, which many of us develop like this: "I am afraid of you; do not make me afraid." We stroke many kinds of wolf skins, knowing that we could believe if we wanted to, and even more than we would want to. But who knows? A famous mathematician said of one of his enemies, an atheist, who had just died, "He's burning now!" This way of playing with hell-fire might easily turn on the actor; and it always proves that he is a bit too fond of his baser passions. It could be that the flames of hell are the kind of flames they use in the opera, which sometimes set fire to the house.

Chapter nine

NEW MIRACLES

Lucretius is justly celebrated, and always read, because of the particular human miracle which, in the very act of driving out the gods, raises poetry to the sublime. Here nature finds her essential grandeur, inhuman and catastrophic, not in the spirit or soul that looks back at us from within things, but in the intrusion and continual assault of outside things, which reduces happening to a whirling of the cosmos. And the conquest of this blind order increases man's stature, and the stature of the universe, each according to its measure, the human concentrating into courage, the universe expanding in extent. Here the mind of the physicist is fully revealed, which demonstrates precisely that research into the most hidden secrets of nature is important above all for our own mechanics, and that the first and principal victory, which is best achieved in the simplest notions, is to pursue and drive out the spirits of the trees and springs. Lucretius, seeing straight here, though he always surprises us, goes as far as to say that the hypotheses we make to explain the rising and setting of the stars, the phases of the moon, the eclipses of the sun, are all good, provided that we leave the gods out of them. The essential work of physics, essential for justice itself, is once again to purify our knowledge of the world of its quantum of imagination, which means to move out of childhood. And what is the intellectual means, or if you will the mother hypothesis, which saves our suppositions from their own boldness? It is pure mechanism, or more precisely the atom, the eternal idea of external change. For the atom is nothing but a speck of matter, large or small, which is simply struck or pushed by other atoms, the atom having no other property in itself than that of being struck or pushed, which is what makes light, fire, ocean, land, vegetation, and man himself in so far as he is a thing; for man is a thing, and the mind is only strengthened by this strictly materialist view. I must go on to purify Lucretius himself and set him on the right road, the double road along which Descartes fearlessly walked. There is no trace of magic in Descartes; but, since we were children before we were men, Lucretius should be read before Descartes, and Homer before Lucretius, and the stories of Mother Goose before them all.

If error were not natural, we would have to despair of the human intellect; such is the reign of the false gods, under whom we live in deception. But spirits are natural, they are even established by controlled experience in the life of early childhood; and childhood always returns. We have memories of a god who served, who forbade, who threatened, and who is so aptly called god the father. But also, for other reasons, which are now fairly clear, we imagine a sort of servant behind or within things, who is never seen but who gives us what the things give us. And we must pay great attention here, for even the most attentive experience will prove to us unconditionally that concrete things, like pitch pine, rubber, zinc, or coal, serve us perfectly under conditions that are always the same, which shows only that the hidden spirit is not a capricious servant. People say that electricity is the genie in the lamp. I have only to flick a switch to have light, heat, even cold; and its apparent caprices can always be explained by the fact that I did something wrong. But what electricity is in itself, we have no idea. Yet there is no question, once we study it properly. The answer is copious, precise, and entirely other than what our marveling curiosity expected. For men watch dials, machines turn, other men make the machines, still others tunnel into the earth to extract iron and coal from it. It is a question of recognizing all of this labor in the presence of obedient light, in the motor that turns with the pressing of a button, in the tramcar that seems to move by itself. The truth is that we never fully succeed in understanding that there is no occult power in these things, that everything in them follows a closed system of operations, under the law

59

of equivalence, and that even the leaks in the system can be explained by a change in surrounding things.

The law of work is not revealed in its purity here, because it is drawn into the circuit of substances that seem to work by themselves, like coal, oil, or water power; and it is obvious that god's lightning costs man nothing; but lightning also does not work for man, and neither does a waterfall; neither does coal; only man works for man. We will learn this better from the simplest machines, in which matter remains inert and yields us only resistance or weight. For no one will claim that the weight that runs a clock gives us back anything other than a man's salary, that is, exactly, though with less effort and more duration, the labor it cost us to wind it up. No one will claim that a lever works by itself; it merely transforms man's labor. The same is true for the pulley, and for the block and tackle, though we will think that there is some magical multiplication of force in the block and tackle unless we have taken one apart and put it back together and tried it out several times. Here we have the alphabet of physics. But it has taken a long time for the true exorcism to be found. The notion of work and the evaluation of work are barely a century old; and many children are still unaware of them, because we do not lead them in that direction. We still teach them that each thing carries within itself properties that we can rely on. For example, zinc and an acetic solution together have the property of activating electromotive force. If a child asks why, he is usually told that no one knows why, that it simply happens. It would be better to compare the zinc to a clock's weight which has been wound up with great effort, or to a spring that has been coiled by hand, and the zinc sulphate to a weight on the ground or an uncoiled spring. It would be understood then that the zinc has no hidden power, that what is given and consumed is human labor. Or again, it seems that certain deposits, like coal and oil, are sources of energy which need only to be transported. But it is not enough to transport them, their energy must be bridled and harnessed, by generators, pistons, and wheels; more of man's work. And their very presence in the ground should be explained by some external labor, such as solar heat and the pressure of the earth, for the explanation divests coal of that occult power of heating and moving which is a sort of imaginary god. Thus the physicist often arrives at a clear reading of the universe in the least of things, in the flux and whirl of atoms, as Lucretius foresaw. But I am not dealing with physics now.

If with this understanding we attempt to educate children by means of physical and chemical experiments, we should not be surprised if we only confirm their familiar errors. For, under the appearance of zinc, sulphuric acid, glass, and things of that kind, you are introducing into the experiment, making active in the experiment, labors that go unseen, in mines, railways, factories. Workers, laboring men, are part of the process. But who thinks of them? The thread is broken; the capsule is sealed. I am not at all sure that the semi-educated physicist himself does not find these things miraculous; it is certain that children do, because the whole of their childhood has prepared them to see what is hidden come forth, as if from a secret drawer, by the inner virtue of the thing itself and the magician's art. And curiosity, so often celebrated, is simply the attitude of waiting for the miracle to take place. The sequence of real causes is hidden, and real causes mean work done. This error occurs in the judgments which I have called bourgeois, which result from a lingering childhood. Having received without paying in real labor, the kind of labor that moves things and feels their weight, we forget, we keep on forgetting, the real situation of man in the face of a universe that gives nothing for nothing. And our forgetfulness leads to the greatest injustice, ingenuous as childhood, and itself the consequence of childhood. If some of us have more with less work, it is only favor or luck, and the art of prayer, as the child believes. And, because the child cannot believe otherwise, education is both important and difficult. Every real lesson is a lesson in incredulity. The misfortune is that the bourgeois mind, because of greater leisure, is alone in knowing the artifice of mathematics, which is the beginning of all research, and besides is not well educated in it, because its manly labor consists in giving orders, or in praying and negotiating; whereas the proletarian, so well taught by his tools not to believe in good or evil spirits, dwells in the pure and simple negation of these things, without developing it into a representation of the world in terms of work. Therefore the proletarian too often thinks that his turn will come to cheat work, and that the discovery of occult riches will bring about a time when machines will run by themselves. I will add here, marginally, because the development would be endless, that the peasant's fetishism is of yet another sort; for after plowing and sowing his fields, he leaves unseen chemical forces to do their work. What peasant knows that plants are depots of atmospheric carbon? He thinks that the whole tree was waiting in the seed and in the ground. Yet another miracle. There is land that nourishes men easily. But I have learned better; I have learned that there is as yet no perceivable limit to the number of men that ordinary land can nourish, provided they work on it from morning to night, watering, fertilizing, weeding, thinning, transplanting. When labor thinks, and thought labors, the miracle will take refuge in man; it will be called courage.

THE TRUTH OF FAIRY TALES

Courage is the king of fairy tales and the god of childhood. It is a fine thing to see that in the enchanted forest weapons are of no use; all you need is a magic wand or a magic word, and not to be afraid. This is naked courage. The conqueror may strike with a sword, but it is a magic sword. Ulysses never touches Circe; it is enough if he threatens her. The lesson in these things is pure gold. For it is true that nature has no consideration for us; it is true that she understands none of our signs. It is true that we cannot intimidate her, or make her pity us. But this truth is among those that we always learn soon enough; it is among the truths that age us; it is no more than the diabolical fatality of nature, the objection to everything. This idea is like the hardening of our bones. Hard stones, hard man, it makes a hardheaded wisdom, a limit, a wall, a house; it makes a man cold, and soon he is no longer capable of forming the idea; he has become it. Men who are right, and do nothing.

I have often thought that childhood is the age of ideas; I mean the age in which man portrays himself alone and sees nothing else, as the knight, brandishing a stick instead of a sword, sees only the curve of his own courage. The windmills of Don Quixote are an excellent image of the enemy seen through the eyes of victory. We are well aware that victory will not end up the way it started out. And it has been said often enough that he who thinks his enemy is weak, cowardly, and poorly armed, is a fool; it is like choosing to believe that a river can be forded. The river answers; the enemy answers. This has all been said too many times. No one has a high enough regard for the idea of childhood, that courage suffices for anything. It is not true, of course, but it is profoundly true that all resources and measures are useless without courage.

And we are only too familiar with the capacity for making reasonable plans, and stopping there; this capacity is a measure of age. Courage runs out before strength, and this fatal advance is in imagination, because the imagination needs another kind of strength than the strength that relies on tools. Man dies over his tools, and that is called labor. Happy childhood is not deformed by the world in the precious time of growth; and neither are the child's ideas. It is right that everything should be easy in childhood, even self-awareness. The ideal as a whole comes from childhood, and is worn out with age.

It is profoundly true that the evil of childhood is fear without an object; therefore the ideal of childhood is courage without an object, that is, with no other means or obstacles than the self. To conquer fear, then, is to conquer all. And therefore magic in childhood is a power that opens up everything, and not only suppliant magic but the magic that commands with signs, which is to make signs as they should be made, abstract and pure. That is our first intention, and our first tentative drawing. Our life is at first a simple outline, a thin line that begins where it ends. The circle is a child; its law is entirely human. And how many men betray the circle! The straight line is the image of virtue; the descending curve is the image of vice, as the Pythagoreans, those sublime children, used to say. The fact is that these unsubstantial signs give us the key to things; but first they give us the key to ourselves. As we must venture upon heroic geometry before experience, so we must venture upon the heroic life before experience, and pledge ourselves to it provisionally. We are too quick to say that there is no such thing as courage; it was in the beginning, like God. It is what binds us. To what? To all that is human, to justice, friendship, fidelity, which are all rooted in courage. He is fortunate who finds only courage in them, for courage is their birth and their rebirth. And, truly, if we believe that the world itself is just, justice will get lost in a surfeit of proofs; but if we know that justice is only what we will, what we will against all experience, then we will seek reason in courage, and not the reverse, courage in reason. I will anticipate myself and say that piety, which is gathered and living here, must go without recompense; but the road to that realization is long. Homer was farsighted when he showed us the gods stirring up the flames of discord. How many gods stand between us and the true god!

I can at least glimpse, along this great road, the essential dialectic of childhood, which always goes from the abstract to the concrete, from the word to the thing, from gesture to act. Courage stops with the noble drawing of a sword, which is only a thin stick. To grasp the thing is to name it, which is to see things in the round that lack all dimension. It is to carry gesture through to the end, overlooking every obstacle; it is to see straight. That is how a judge reaches a decision, if he is any good; and we use the straight line to build a wall that is not at all straight. The metaphor that is about to die is perfectly alive; and that is also what we call thinking.

Comte had the idea, and it is worth a great deal, that the miraculous has never dared to touch the soul. The gods did not think to console Achilles by killing friendship. Nor have they ever changed a man's character, except by dreams and other external effects. Mephistopheles did not change Faust, and could not, except by offering him more and more. And, in our fairy tales, Prince Charming can be fixed to the floor like a nail, but he cannot be made indifferent to love. Even when the external spirits turn him into a bluebird, he returns to sing at his lady's window. He does what he can, but he knows what he wants. Of course, you may say that fairy tales are ignorant of love; no, they know sworn love, they know nothing of love foresworn; foresworn by the oblique power of nature. This love is not yet a great love; it will be, in defeat, if the whole of childhood does not perish with it. We must be thankful for the fact that everything is easy at the start. To say "Let there be light" is the essence of childhood; and Mephistopheles is right: the "Old Man" is the creator faced with the disaster of irreversible acts. The world is no doubt a chaos of irreversible acts. Faust become a child again is the image of the hero in anger.

These metaphors are my guides. Perhaps my way of taking metaphors has become clear; I take them very seriously. Coming closer to my subject now, I say that there is a truth in fairy tales, for there are truths and truths. There is a truth in things, which we cannot know without courage; but there is a truth in courage, which belongs to man alone, that is, to the man who thinks, loves, ventures. And, for example, the love potion in Yseult is a mixed truth; it does not belong to pure story, and I suspect the hand of some overly wise commentator, who has confused external with internal miracles. For what is forced love? It is love that is already dead. And the portion of love that is no more than a sickness, is no longer love at all, lacking the grace of the other, which is born and reborn out of nothing. It is necessary, then, to love despite the potion, if there is to be a potion. We may say that the potion is only an image; even so it is too strong. The magic sword is better; for no doubt it is more difficult to have confidence in a magic sword than in a real sword. But faith is that much better armed, armed only with itself. This is what fairy tales teach us, with their clear separation of good and evil characters; Cinderella is perfectly good, and her sisters are pure envy. Of course, that is not how things are; but a child begins by judging that way; that is how he learns to desire and fear. He will come back, and inscribe the truth and the variety of characters within the simple circles he has already traced out, as he will come by means of fairy tales to a vision of the world.

Having seen it, having conquered it, having changed it, he will no longer take labor for true wealth, if only he is mindful of himself. For if man wants to fly through the air, he will fly through the air, and once it is done, it will be nothing to him. Fairy tales see truly. Distances are crossed, time runs on. The great soul does its work and does not talk about it. For the difficult world is always the human world, with its enchanters and sorcerers, old men or young-men-old, who must be prayed to and persuaded, and whom fifty horses, even in a machine, cannot draw out of their shell. The fact is that nothing is gained by force. The tyrant is sick of flatterers, he longs for a friend. And thus through the mist of fairy tales, the end appears at the beginning. Power is dethroned, endlessly. In short, fairy tales are fetishist but not idolatrous. We must return to this condition of childhood, by a just mixture of diligence, false prayer, and true prayer, which is prayer to oneself.

66

BOOK II

PAN

Chapter one

ETERNAL HISTORY

Pan is not dead. And the god All will always be recognized by his goat's feet. The image says that man is half animal, which is true. There was a time, according to the historian of religions, when man lived in intimacy with nature, was one with her, and felt within himself, in his bones and blood, her slightest changes; animals still live that way, and plants especially, sensing the right time to flower. Man once lived like a plant; he grew up into the world, and that was his activity; he felt with the world, and that was his thought. But, like Molière's doctor, we have changed all that. People laugh at him for saying the heart is on the right side; but the hypothesis of a man who is no longer part of the world is no less ridiculous. Man is a thinking animal, who is no more divorced from his belly than he is from his heart or his head. And we should also be as little surprised by the wisdom of antiquity as we are by the ancient gods. We carry all of this with us, as we carry our childhood with us. Certainly a child does not think like a man or act like a man; but that is also a reason for thinking that there is no modern way of being a child. The truth is that childhood is eternal in any case, because it is preserved and repeated. And the feeling for nature is eternal also, as immutable poetry testifies. It is my experience that Homer and Plato are not far removed from us, and that experience would be perfectly common if people were not taught to reject Homer and Plato.

At the same time each of us also has the experience that nothing is repeated. Here on the coast of Brittany, everything is the way it was in Caesar's time; but I see that the rocks are ceaselessly worn away, and I know where sand comes from. The dunes are built up before my eyes, yet the cows come to pasture there, kicking and showing their horns to the dogs, as in the time of the *Odyssey*. In some way I am reading two texts one on top of the other. It is true that this particular dune is the product of other dunes, which were the products of other dunes, and so on; the present sends me back to the past; but it is also true that dunes have always been built up by the wind, and that the grain of sand seeks the lowest level as it always has done. The past leads me back to the present, and always presupposes the present in my thought; for I start out from the present, and it is the present that I learn from. There is a history of religions because events are irrevocable; but, on the other hand, events were irrevocable before as they are now. And it is always by identity that we judge difference, by the same that we judge the other, and by the other the same. These problems of Logic are not what interests me now. I simply want to explain that if we call the science of change Dynamics, and the science of the immobile Statics, I propose to attempt a Statics of religion, which is not at all the same as a history.

History is as miraculous as a fairy tale. In it the mind recognizes itself. Man was first astonished by everything, and worshiped all-powerful nature, the sun, fire, the harvests, animals; and during the same time, he attempted to act the way plants grow, which is by magic. I will call this mother religion the religion of nature, and for me the god Pan is the perfect embodiment of its naïve pantheism, in which the god All turns into a swarm of gods. Next, in the West, which is what concerns me, came the Olympian religion, in which the human form alone was worshiped, and the world was governed like a kingdom. I will call this religion of conquerors the religion of politics. I will also call it the religion of the cities, as opposed to the first, which is obviously agrarian. And as for the third, which has become no less popular on this promontory of Europe, under the name of Christianity, I can hardly be mistaken about it, in the light of the new values it has taught us, and I will call it the religion of the Spirit. And I see no other. These are, in fact, the stages of man's history.

What is more, I would say that these are the levels of man's body. We must simplify a great deal, for with too many details everything gets confused. Man is belly, which means desire and fear; man is heart, which means anger and courage; man is head, which means prudence and control. In proposing that he was always that way, I am not suggesting anything unbelievable; in proposing that he is still that way, I run no risk of being mistaken. Nor when I say our least thoughts arise out of desire and fear, through anger and courage, toward a kind of wisdom, every moment. This brief outline is enough to make it understood that the three religions, of desire, of courage, and of the spirit, are one now as they always were. To attempt to describe their various combinations, in eminent men or in the masses, to analyze progress, setbacks, real gains in that light, is the task of the historian. I will resolve the endless argument between the Dynamic and the Static for my own part, with the observation that we must first locate our problem in a brief, anecdotal story, and then boldly construct our theorems, in order to come back to a more geographical history, and to a more geological geography, as has already been done for inanimate things. This new kind of geology, then, will explain religions by the structure of man, in so far as it can be done, and should teach us on the one hand to hold them living together, and on the other hand to depict, in their purity, the highest values we know.

In the process I will be careful to preserve religion as such, grounding myself always in what has been said and told and preached. A soldier in the artillery once asked me what I thought of religion; he was pious, and he saw that I was not. I answered him off the top of my head, but the answer still seems to hold. I said, "Religion is a fairy tale which, like all fairy tales, is full of meaning. And no one ever asks if fairy tales are true." I have not finished mining that first vein. You see why I began with fairy tales, and why I propose to move on from story to story, always staying close to their metaphors; which is the way to discover our common philosophy instead of falling into the philosophy of the schools, which is without beauty.

Chapter two

THE SACRED WOOD

The peacefulness of the fields is always deceptive. The passions of envy and greed grow through the winter, while labor sleeps; not to mention real fears, of invaders and robbers, not to mention wolves and other wild animals. The appearance of peace comes from the openness of cultivated fields, where at the most we see only one or two men; these distances are silently at war. But I will set aside real dangers and, if I may put it so, real mysteries. With them, the imagination picks up a scent; actions are followed through. The peasant is brave, quick, resilient, as we see in times of war, where, amid a crowd of men, and in the face of real danger, the rustic gods have no place. On the other hand, the density of the woods has always been sacred. This darkness at midday and in midsummer is again imaginary; the forms of things are distinct enough, but they are constantly eclipsed as a man walks, by the very act of walking. Everything opens out and closes in again; each moment is a separate world; and the trees follow after us, hide each other, and reappear; the columns of temples copy these effects, even to the interlacing of the upper branches, but they bear man's signature; whereas the nature of the woods is profoundly alien to man. In that monotonous variety he is quickly lost. He is only happy there with other men, in the loud company of woodcutters and hunters, or in woodland festivities, which are a form of exorcism. Otherwise we only cross through the woods; we hurry through them, and that is the shape of our knowledge. When a man stops, his flight is only suspended. He questions his way, and his eyes focus beyond what he can see. Gardeners know how to handle questions and answers; but gardens are urban and political. Gardeners keep the trees pruned and the view open, which gives us a kind of second wind when we emerge from the woods. A wood is nothing like a garden; a little wood is bigger in its way than the most extensive garden; we always emerge from a garden, we emerge at every step; in the woods we are always going further in.

No one lives in the woods. Animals only go there to hide, and stay on the edges unless they are pursued. Man cannot live there; he uses the woods for lumber and firewood. Life in the woods is a fiction; the man of the woods is a fugitive; it does not occur to us that forests are as uninhabitable as the desert sands. We never fully realize that nature, with its vegetal invasion, is uninhabitable. Land-clearing is man's natural struggle; and the forests repel him. That is why the presence of a living creature, deer or hunter, is always a surprise. And again, through these screens of leaves and tree trunks, whatever moves is an apparition. We stand faced with surfaces that do not say a word, asking ourselves if this is a dream. Experience is all remembrance; at the moment it is only a story. Reality defies us with its ordinariness. Attention cannot make its examination. Examination is the whole of our science. The horror of the woods is therefore physiological. And the sacred wood of the muses is only a garden. The sacred is much closer to us than respect or even fear. The sacred has no object, or has one no longer. The sacred is the contrast between what we expect and what we see. What is truly ominous is the tree that is only a tree, the forest that is only a forest. It is rightly said that before the gods in human form came gods without form, compounded of absence. The vegetal world is never human; vegetal form denies man. We are sometimes fooled by it, mistaking some figure in the leaves, a dark eye that is only a glimpse of a tree trunk, or a gnarled branch that looks like a face or an arm; but this kind of apparition vanishes without any change, at a glance, more quickly than a deer, and more strangely, for we assure ourselves that there is nothing there and there was nothing there; we realize a hundred times over that nothing was there. This way of reassuring ourselves is frightening, and confirms something else, something absolutely other, absolutely formless. We do not know what, it is something that is always hidden, not behind a tree but within it; not within, because

73

all there is within a tree is fiber and sap; the inside of a tree is known in the same way as the outside, no more, no less; we need only gouge, cut, or split the wood. The same surface mocks us. The great or small fear is our own; it is like our shadow projected over things; and of course there is a mythology of shadows, but one that is only serious, I think, for the cult of politics; they have taken over from agrarian life a god who for a long time has not even frightened children. The shadow of our fear is of a transparent and shapeless density; touch it and it is lost. Like seeing a relief in what is actually flat. That is how we look at these specters, in the silence of the woods and even in the peacefulness of the fields. They are nothing that is not perfectly familiar, and we know it. But the more we know it the more we doubt it. The impatience of man when he does not want to live in fear drives him to act against the knot of wood or piece of stone that refuses a face, in order to complete the god. That is the great exorcism. Something dies in a statue; it is the woodland god, whose substance is absence and silence.

A woman who was far from foolish, and who could be brave when she needed to be, told me once that she did not dare look out at night at the darkness beyond the windows. "I'm afraid," she said, "of seeing something frightening." This impulse, which is perfectly natural, confirms all of the gods. For if we avoid the sacred spring or the enchanted grove, if we run away instead of looking closer, if we prostrate ourselves, then we can only offer hearsay evidence. All the same I think I understand that this refusal of a closer inspection is more calming than troubling, above all if one stands perfectly still, turned inward with bowed head; for it is always our own perceptions that lead us to imagine things, and it is our own movement that animates them. Prayer, whose naïve and mute image we have just grasped, is therefore also an exorcism, and more forceful than one might think. Sleep would be inexplicable if immobility did not extinguish thought. And mechanical prayer, following a rigid model, chastens the garrulous story we carry on within us. Furthermore, all of our most vivid passions exclude the trance without object. Misers believe in nothing; they are occupied with other fears and other expectations; but avarice also presupposes a political condition that is in some way urban. One religion blots out another. And yet, of the movement of prayer, which is in a way a rejection, there remains in each of us a great prudence with regard to what can be believed or even seen. At the level of agrarian religion, there is nothing that cannot be believed, and one god establishes the next. It is one type of tolerance to believe provisionally and without looking for evidence. A god is almost always the imminence of a god, or simply the possibility of a god. We hasten to believe, I would say, for fear of seeing. We never walk along the path of a god; we turn aside, and that is perhaps the perfection of belief, for it brings us peace of mind. Here we come upon the reason for our acceptance of stories, and in that sense belief is what we hand over on the spot, the way we hand over our money to robbers, very gladly. That is the moment of the invisible, and its favorite locale.

So it is that benevolent night conceals the visible and the invisible at once. In Homer's words, sleep comes alike to gods and mortals. And, unless I am mistaken, in the beautiful night expedition in the *Iliad*, the warriors meet up with none of the gods. The dangers of the night are too real perhaps; and what is hidden by night is of the same species as what is revealed by day. Imagination presupposes perception. No one likes to be alone at night. Instead night draws men together, and makes a sort of township. Not that men sleep as soon as the light dies, like hens. But it is no less true for all of us that the sun, the awakener, takes with it when it sets the garment of light that clothes all of our thoughts and imaginings. In my nursery school there was a dark room where troublesome children were put; you would think that the child would cry even louder, but in fact he would fall asleep almost instantly. The first and most useful thing to do with a wild horse is to cover his head with a sack, if you can. Thus, after the weariness of the day, and with friends nearby, man waits and hopes for sleep; it falls softly on his eyes; he does not have to wait long. Insomnia is utterly malicious, even diabolical, but it is a mark of agrarian religion that the opposition between devil and god has not yet been formulated. If you think of your rivals and of the business of empire, you will not sleep; but if you think of labor, you will sleep. The gods are outside. The sacred wood draws back into itself; it is beyond the door, and the door is closed. Which makes me think that all night-magic is out of doors. The witches hold their sabbath far away on the mountain; we have to go out to it. Stories alone can make these visions live; the storytelling itself is reassuring, and we only play at being afraid. From which we learn the value of the hearth and of our fellow men.

Then sleep comes, and dreams, which are helped on by the faint light and the first noises of morning. Man is not really afraid of dreams, and when he is, no doubt his own thoughts are what frighten him. The recurrence and importance of dreams belong to another religion, that of the immortals in human form. There is none of the mystery of things in dreams, I mean that we do not feel the lining of the extraordinary behind the ordinary in them; for if we take them at all seriously, they awaken us like danger. Apart from messages from the dead or from distant travelers, there is no symbolic or allegorical significance in the dream-world; it is the real that is allegorical, as all poems prove. Furthermore, dreams are almost all story, invented in the telling and in the light of day. The age of dreams, as far as we can say, is the age of fairy tales. In dreams we are children by consent; otherwise awakening would be inexplicable. We let ourselves be amused. There is no agrarian god in dreams because our attention is neither alerted nor deceived by them. It is in the nature of dreams that we cannot turn the object over or examine it; dreams do not arouse our curiosity, nor do they surprise us. It is theological to be deceived by dreams; and those who would see the stuff of the gods in them are asking too much. It is more likely that the gods are the stuff of dreams; and I would like to pause here for a moment, at this level of simplicity at which the gods are nothing that can be described. Like the water in a spring, so shadowy in its depths, so clear in the hand, the sacred wood is the image of nature, obscure in its transparency. There is nothing else there.

Chapter three

THE SEASONS

Order is above. When man lifts up his eyes, it is another, more virile form of prayer. Order is above, in the stars, in the phases of the moon, in the balancings of the sun. Order is here, in the sprouting grain, in the ripening wheat, in the messenger flowers; and in the yellow leaves. Nothing is deceptive. And therefore what we expect is precisely what happens. The brightening sky announces the sun, and no one asks for anything else. The sun is enough, the day is enough. The flower is made of the same stuff as the stalk. Spring is good; when will it come? It is here in the anemones. And the time for sowing comes after the plowing and harrowing. The sun is not a magician who gives and withholds; to pray is to work. Plato cites an old proverb: "Who would dare call the sun a liar?" To believe the sun, is to prepare the soil in winter and split firewood in August. An alert religion, that walks at the side of labor. Here is the celebration of the Annunciation, which is the essence of celebration. At this point I want to describe the religion that has no god, that celebrates the fidelity of nature, or the reconciliation of nature and man, and recognition in the old sense, which also means gratitude. I recognize the nightingale and the cuckoo. I recognize the swallow and the quail. I recognize the signs. I anticipate the event, embody it, name it; there is nothing behind it.

I enjoy describing our celebration of the sun, and I like to imagine what a primitive man would think of it. What do I mean? We draw the shape of the sun in the ground with the leaves of the iris; we carry around the image of bread; we plant roses. The primitive man will look for something more; and we will also. Celebrations must be brought down to what they really are. They are greater and more beautiful that way, just as a poem in which everything is real is the most beautiful of poems. We plant roses with no purpose in mind, simply because roses scatter their petals on the wind. We must not think that primitive peoples who celebrate the Spring are celebrating anything other than their own joy. As flowers open, men sing, and that is all there is to say. Do not look for gods; this faith celebrates itself.

The celebration of Easter is the same everywhere, provided that it follows winter. I wonder if people who are overly favored by nature really celebrate the sun; it is a reasonable cult, but not for them. It is more likely that, living too easily in their daily existence, yet prey to unforeseeable catastrophes, they are reduced to a violent fetishism. You cannot wish to be a peasant. Our chain of celebrations advances with the sun. Easter celebrates resurrection, in the light of clear evidence; Christmas celebrates birth, under the star of the annunciation; from far off, in the cold and snow. The Fête-Dieu is a day of thanksgiving; it celebrates happiness, which is the most beautiful kind of thanks. The wine festival is more tumultuous; the flight of the sun can already be felt; we crush the last juice from our joy; but in vain, for human feeling must follow the sun and the yellowing leaves into the mists of November, where the commemoration of the dead takes its proper place. Homer sought the dead in the Cimmerian mists. But I suppose that the commemoration of the dead was first celebrated in attitude; it was an exchange of signs and a sudden aging; and it still is. The celebrations of the spirit cannot live by the spirit alone. The backdrop of the world and the decor of the seasons are necessary. Those who celebrate Christmas in summer and Easter in autumn, as they do in Capetown or Australia, foster irreligion; in such decreed celebrations the body is out of tune with the spirit. The whole of Christianity must rest upon the whole of paganism. But the savants are city-dwellers and work by lamplight; and even if they should look for some vestiges of solar myth in the higher gods, they will see no more than a recollection of the old cult in the new. Memory cannot do very much; but the power of the sun is always the same. And the darkening of the year will always send us into retirement, curled up against the cold, as is only prudent. Christmas lacks strength and calls up the image of a child-god. But, not for any god, but because of the signs of false spring, people rejoice too early and devour their provisions, which is carnival, a celebration marked by contorted madness, a celebration with no future, promptly followed by penitence; for the cold weather returns, and with the cold, the fear of shortage, Lent, which lasts up to the explosion of Easter, though there is still a touch of winter in the idea of death and resurrection. These great movements are the movements of our joys and cares, and myths are first no more than the gestures with which we withdraw from the world or open out to it. Shellfish and starfish celebrate the tides. The sun waxes and ebbs like the tide; we open and close our shells; that is the ground of our ceremonies, which is embroidered upon by a variety of political beliefs. And to protect ourselves from history, we must not forget that childhood is political before it is pastoral, and that the gods in human form once again are the first to stand around each cradle. It is no less necessary to appreciate this separation of nature and man, which occurs in every man through his first labors, though the city and Caesar never cease to weave new garlands, garlands of iron, for our garlands of flowers, and thus revive the helmeted gods of the golden age. We will notice that peasant religion arrives at reason through its feeling for the great cycles which are the rhythm of our life; but that reason of State, which is strong in children, twists reason into the folds of another necessity, equally primordial, represented by the policeman at the corner of our country roads.

The gods are composite, as we are; I would even say that they are a composite of various animals, as we are. We still find the lamb, the ox, and the eagle, mixed in with branches and flowers, in the ornaments of our cathedrals as in the metaphors of Bossuet. Perhaps we sense that religion without images would no longer be a religion. Pushing further ahead, and staying close to our solar existence, we must ask ourselves if thought without images is still thought. The answer is physiological, and cannot be otherwise.

Das Was bedenke, mehr bedenke Wie. But physiology extends beyond the living body, as Darwin saw. Our environment shapes us, the sun shapes us, our prey shapes us, our companions shape us. As an organism reveals all of these things in its form, so religion, whichever it be, reveals in its thousandfold form all of its circumstances, and the form of man. And its real heartwood, if it has any, is enveloped in layer upon layer of bark, as it should be. Metaphor reverently covers what cannot go naked and live. Thus philosophy, in its imprudence, never ceases to lose the very spirit it seeks, while religion never ceases to lose it by saving it. We must live between the two.

If we thought in terms of the seasons and of peasant celebrations, we would think truly; if we thought of the country before the city, we would think justly, for the city cannot feed itself. Neither can the spirit feed itself. A temple gives us more to think about than a book, and temples are more at home in the fields and woods than standing above crowded buildings and torrents of men. The true pilgrim's route is empty of men but covered with footprints. At this point, on our pilgrimage, I will not let the human form stand between us and religion. There are thousands of reasons for believing in man, and thousands of reasons for not believing in him. There are only reasons for believing in Spring; it is life itself. "Be reverent before the dawning day," says the little uncle of Jean-Christophe. It is to awaken, it is to believe again. Life, in Darwin's eyes, implies the judgment that the world is good. To pray is therefore first of all to adapt, or, better, to recognize our aptness. Which is confirmed by Stendhal, the after-dinner melancholic, when he says that life is made up of mornings, otherwise called joyful beginnings. The songs of evening have the color of sadness; prayer at that hour is entirely spiritual; the world does not sustain it; it is itself disappearing. On the other hand, the song of morning rebounds off the given world and the spirit leaps out of itself. Without the noise of the street vendors nothing would get done and nothing would be thought. The city is full of lost mornings, and the gods are sad there.

Chapter four

ANIMALS

Everything I have just said, plants know better than we do. They flower even under the snow. Trees are wiser, they wait. Models of hope and prudence, as their leafy crowns show. For some, the sign is fecundity, even excess; for others of us, it is the meager flower, which stands less for strength than for knowledge, less for wealth than for faith. Both signs are important; the former awakens passions, the latter the spirit, which I want to consider first, in the calm features of the anemone and the violet. Also in the graceful birds, thrush, cuckoo, oriole, nightingale, which for us are a part of spring. The duck, the crane, the swallow write their signs in the sky. Our hens lay eggs while it is still cold, and the first nests are built before we think of nests. The joyful economy of plants and animals is divine to us; that is, a divination. And the idea of reading the future in the flights of birds is as old as man. Besides that, the daily prudence of animals, which can be seen in their labors and in their smallest acts, leads to the idea of another wisdom that is far simpler than ours, and which consequently throws light on the hidden side of ours. This is how animals appear from a distance.

But animal life is not a spectacle; animals hunt for their food, and are food for other animals. Their blood is like our blood. These violent analogies darken nature. They seize us more strongly in domesticated and trained animals, for these are almost our own likeness, and the differences are therefore more striking. It is urban, as it is also childish, to believe in the friendship of animals. Not everything is idyllic in this familiarity, for we eat cattle. If cattle trust us, they are quite mistaken. Which gives us reason not to be so trusting of cattle, even without considering the thrust of their horns. We also observe among trainers, who make a profession of loving animals, and who no doubt do love them after a fashion, a ready brutality; and thus we can say, with Aeschylus, that force governs and violence is never far off; and the results of force, with animals, are impulses of fear which in truth are highly improper. And thus familiarity itself comes between men and animals as a sort of veil that obscures their vision of each other. The tyrant never ceases to harden himself. How shall we analyze this strange human development, which explains, by analogy to the training of animals, a terrible part of politics? The peasant plays with his anger, and so does the gentleman. A man thrown to the ground five times in a row is in a state to treat his horse as he would never treat a man, for he would kill the man; I am forgetting about the human slave, who in effect shares the privileges of cattle. We foresee that the peasant religion will not always be good humored.

Domestic animals are therefore like a mirror of our faithlessness. We are afraid of them because they should be afraid of us. We serve, and believe, and obey them, and we kill them and eat them. This admixture is the sort that irritates our thoughts; and I see that thought is not yet free of it. Here certainly we find an idea of sin and hypocrisy. No doubt it takes a high degree of sympathy to be a trainer; and all trainers work by imitation as much as they can, like the English girl who leads a flock of turkeys dressed in a black cape and a red cap. This kind of propriety has turned clothes made of fur and feathers into ornaments; and the imitation of animal language comes even more naturally. Not long ago, a man might have been called the Bull, the Wolf, the Parrot. And because the trainer's skill, like other agrarian skills, is kept in a family, we can understand the use of animal totems, at least as a form of language, and the prohibition, according to caste, against eating the flesh of certain animals. But these are only fragments of agrarian custom. In fact, animals were once gods everywhere; the God-man alone could abolish that cult, when politics came to govern agriculture, and better still when slaves came to judge politics. The separation of man and animal is a great accomplishment of religion, and is still going on, but not without hesitation and regression, we might almost say not without regret. The man-wolf of the sculptors, and the siren of our metaphors, still witness to it, and so, more subtly, does the chimera, in the meaning that that word has taken on. This immense idea cannot be exhausted; it will be enough for us to touch upon it by degrees, and with precaution. These native beliefs, by their very nature, are accepted and rejected continually, like our friendship for cats.

For agrarian labor, there is no sharp distinction between the wild and the domestic. The same animal that stands beside the hearth or in the courtyard or the stable, shows up in the woods like an apparition, and tasks us to divine its invisible presence. It is this animal that gives body to our earliest fear. It is a god in its familiarity, and in its estrangement. Primitive hunters naïvely render their prey favorable, through civilities which simply translate a natural discretion. This kind of war has its rituals, like the other kind of war. Ajax slaughtering the herds, is a meaningful punishment. It is said that religion is the sense of the incomprehensible; and that is generally true; but real religion never works in general, and never thinks in general. Man avoids contradictions, as he avoids trees and rocks, by circling around them, always studious of the obstacle and imitating the obstacle as closely as possible. This gesture of the potter, the sculptor, the priest, is the form of rituals and cults. In it man is occupied with himself, and each of his movements is composed. That is the meaning of peasant immobility, which is a refusal to think. And it is not easy to understand the cult of the cow, or altars dedicated to the monkey and the elephant. In these ways the human body guards against thought. That one cannot improvise with animals or give way to one's first impulse before them, is the common experience of the herdsman, even more perhaps than of the horse trainer. Nature imposes immutable forms upon us. That is how sculptors are able to discover immutable form, and true style, which cannot easily be transferred to statues in human form. In short our thought circles around animal form, and will not enter into it. The cult stops, then, with external form, and its secret comes from prohibition, a natural development, since action regulates thought.

More profoundly, we are not permitted to think that animals

have intelligence, for that thought has no issue. The order of things would immediately be threatened if we dared to believe that the little calf loves its mother, or that it is afraid of death, or simply that it sees us. An animal's eye is not an eye. A slave's eye is also not an eye, and the tyrant does not like to look into it; although in this case, which is entirely political, we can imagine the slave's hatred, fear, or hope; whereas faced with animals we reject all such feelings, designing and completing, on the contrary, an impenetrable, impermeable form. Piety arms us against importunate thoughts; and once again agrarian prayer is a monster of inattention. It is from working with animals that man learns not to think. He turns away; and there is fanaticism in that movement. Animals cannot be our friends, or even our enemies; don't talk about it, talk about something else, or talk without thinking. Man with his finger to his lips, is the image of the silence he imposes upon nature, the image of rights refused. This hardness, this shrug of the shoulders, this return to work, this cessation of thought is in every gesture of religion. Ritual is an impenetrable refusal; the Sphinx, in one way or another, prefigures the ancient gods.

Chapter five

THE GREAT MYSTERIES

Violence is everywhere under the peacefulness of the fields. Thunder, lightning, storm and flood are excesses. Man circumscribes this intemperance; he learns not to fear it; he learns to fear it in himself; occasionally he plays with it, and it is a savage game. We must understand that religion could not have avoided this side of things without becoming shameful and secretive again. We must now deal with the dark pit that underlies all passions, and punishes them all. The spirit burns there as if at the stake. But sacrifice is a precaution against self-immolation. Ritual, the trembling bough. I descend into hell; may the stone gods protect me, for the spirit is helpless.

The spirit is lost through pride; and pride is neither principally nor at first a contemplative emotion; it is an irritated energy, an uncontrollable impulse, an anger that feeds on itself, more self-sufficient than dependent, and in a certain way a domination by excess. It is the tyrant's passion, and we are all tyrants. I take pride in its fleshly substance, and it is the first manifestation of the spirit. The common feeling is that spirits are not all good. Here, then, the spirit seeks out extreme affliction, and is consoled by a frenzy that is its own work. But we must move carefully at the beginning.

There is intemperance in nature, in the terrific force of storms, in the immensity of the sands, in glaciers and snow-capped peaks, in the exuberance of vegetal and animal life, in the excesses of the human masses in agitation. In all of these circumstances, man feels himself weak and pitiful; but he rebounds with the whole of his spirit; he tests his powers of daring and defiance; he finds them unlimited. Fear is conquered. Death is conquered. That is the feeling of the sublime, and there is sublimity in every excess. Drunkenness cannot be mediocre in a thinking being. That is the kind of madness that leads us to the contemplation of terrifying and inhuman things. We want the mountain peak to be even more savage, the waves to rise even higher, solitude to be even more terrible. Try me, universe, try me! This impulse drives us to great risks, to the scaling of mountains, to flight, to war, to all kinds of exploration. This form of courage is of lower origin than we would think. For pride is not wholly of the spirit; the hero feels in himself the force of a storm and an uncontrollable monster; and, as Plato saw, he holds anger ready to support the audacity of his mind. Not only does man judge himself king, he produces out of himself a force of nature that is no less marvelous than the forces surrounding him; and the growth of this reserved anger always promises more; so that he feels himself invincible and immortal, like nature itself.

The dance of the bacchantes is a crude example, but all the more remarkable in its unleashing of sensuality; the spirit plays for its own loss; and I would put this demoniacal dance in my hell, if I were to describe one, far sooner than the punishment of Tantalus, which makes a mockery of man. The wild dance of the dervishes is well above desires; it is actually a defiance of sorrow. Suicide appears in this same light, as well when its violence takes harmless forms, like the mania of the alpinists. The soldier's delirium is of the same order, and no more or less honorable, which is not a little. We must do justice here to certain cruel men, and, who knows, perhaps to the whole race of cruel men. For some of them do not spare themselves, they receive as many blows as they give; and they all test their strength against pity, which is, at its lowest and strongest level, a great humiliation; for we feel faint at the sight of blood. The victory over pity is formidable. It is a kind of fecundity. Which leads us to an understanding, even almost to an experience of the hells of ancient Mexico, where captives were slaughtered by the thousands; that was their way of celebrating. It is a prodigality of nature that attempts to equal the sun and the volcano. And it is the revenge of weakness, but also of strength. Far above the animals, who kill in order to eat, and flee unceremoniously. But in relation to my real subject, these premeditated and formalized human sacrifices are only a remnant, a ritual; and the god in them is external. At the level I want to come to next, the god is internal, and, if we look closely, is already the spirit.

Fecundity is an excess; spring is excessive. Its advent never goes by without drunkenness, and the essence of drunkenness is to be drunk on oneself, that is, on impulse and audacity, excess upon excess. Wine is a means of awakening these sleeping forces; and there is generosity in the drinker. Wines are called generous, but the spirit does not like to receive without giving. The pleasure of drinking is small beside the pure pleasure of securing even more pleasure, I would almost say of conquering even more pleasure. In the old language of the corporations, the hardiest drinker was called Sublime; these ways of speaking are intimations. Here again is a ritual. Here again is Bacchus. But to call him Bacchus is to hold him at arm's length. The god of the great mysteries is never named, he cannot be named. Ceres, mother of the harvests, is only a figure.

I do not believe that man has been able to give distance or a name to the powerful god of animals and men. Eros and Aphrodite are civilities. Indian art expresses something stronger in its heaping up and intertwining of animals; also in its multiplication of legs and arms. The god of fecundity is the organ itself, and the higher religions have conquered it with difficulty. By a reversal of reflection there appears among us a sort of mania, even in archeology, for discovering this symbol everywhere, which is so easily confused with the tree, the column, the obelisk. And the confusion is within us, since it is evident that all of our strength lies in all of our victories. No doubt the sublime in man attempts to conquer modesty as well as pity, and succeeds only by an intoxication that it is very hard to confess to; and so we brave everything. The witches' sabbath, more familiar to us than the mysteries of Eleusis, is a sort of deliverance, through the representation of the devil in the form of a goat. We pretend that the devil and his witches are of a separate, accursed world. Which, as each of us is aware, is to separate ourselves politically from the excessive part of our nature, and to renounce good as well as evil. But nothing is accursed, and the genius of Plato knew how to unite heaven and earth again, which puts us all back into question. We sometimes forget that Socrates conversed with Alcibiades; which is a way of speaking to oneself.

These frenzies are agrarian. The city gives us no idea of them. Maenads and witches return to the fields and mountains, as if to enter into closer combat with enormous nature. And it is there that these violent impulses, which expend, conserve, and increase, find another remedy than madness and death. For man continually wins his living from nature at the cost of labor and fatigue. There war and sensuality perish, after brief upheavals. The virgin carries flowers to the altar of Venus, and she blushes; this impulse of the blood says enough. The hay grows, and the cow waits, with her nose on the bar. The hens flutter; the fox watches. Thus fecundity calms its own waves; especially in our temperate lands, where spring is only an affair, and avarice, in her woolen dress, gives the orders. The god Limit is the strongest.

Chapter six

RITUAL

Man holds himself back. He does not eat the way
animals eat; if he did he would want to be worse than they
are. Nor does he kill the way animals kill. The sacrifice of an
ox to Jupiter or Neptune seems absurd at first; Jupiter lives
on ambrosia; and besides, after they burn the skin and fat of
the animal, men eat the meat themselves. Sacrifice is less an
offering than a way of killing; what is sacrificed, as it should
be, is the intoxication of killing, the bath of blood and entrails,
and other horrors that kill the killer. On second thought, then,
we must admire, as a reasonable practice, this prelude to dinner,
and this frankness in bringing butchery and cooking into the
light and making them ceremonious. And it is only a device,
though not entirely, to imagine that the god of politics is the
witness and ordainer of these things. It is to bring civility before its extreme opposite; and civility, in this difficult situation,
is always highly ornate. That is why the horns of the fatted
calf are gilded, why the bands are knotted, why it is the priest
or the chief who strikes the blow; and it is a bad omen if
the blow does not kill cleanly. Force is caught in this trap, and
is almost civilized. Next to which our hypocrisy makes us bar-
barians; we do not want to see the killing; all of our civility
goes into the eating. However it amounts to the same thing;
it is no more decent to grab your knife as if you were about
to kill a stewed beef or a roasted chicken a second time. The
carving of meats was a high office in the palace, not long ago; it
was graceful, like the movements of a dancer.

The village dance is a love ritual. I admire its seriousness and
the economy of its movements; you may say that madness
and seduction are only waiting for their chance; and it is true
that they are waiting. Peasants never have much faith in civili-

zation; they get what they can out of it, which is better than believing in it. The bows, the steps forward and back, and above all the slow farandole in which each dancer is held by all of the others, are the very negation of the bacchanalia. But are we not told also that the bacchantes killed Orpheus? These myths have a rich and clear meaning, once we are willing to accept, as a working hypothesis, that man is the sole ordainer of dances and cults. Man has never ceased to struggle against himself. The plumb line and the compass circle are triumphs of real philosophy; and before them the dance. Not to mention music, which, in the dance at least, is at first simply a way of marking the step, which is a precaution against violence, for a man who stamps his feet is already getting excited. Song regulates our cries, which would otherwise turn into fury, as happens in arguments.

Dramatic spectacles are also a form of ritual. And abstract philosophers are often surprised that people enjoy awakening pity, fear, and even horror in themselves, by their own effort. We enjoy experiencing these emotions because we enjoy overcoming them, even more so in a crowd, in the press of men, where emotions blow up like a storm. But the crowd is also immobile, silent, in full view of itself; what is more, in an access of precaution, the ancients interposed between the bound Prometheus and the seated spectators a second crowd, dancing in rhythm, who taught the larger crowd the right way to contemplate the afflictions of men and the wrath of the gods. Theater is religious. Or else it is the utterly irreligious comedian who delivers men, through the spectacle of their own very serious stupidity. For laughter disarms the furies, even the most voluptuous of them; and the most ancient experience has always found laughter to be healthful. It is a way of overcoming the gods where they are, in the breast and the belly; a way of liberating the thinking animal. Wit can do no more; but perhaps that is enough.

Poetry, prose, beautiful language are forms of ritual. We are sometimes surprised that we gain so little from novelties, for instance from the often expressive inventions of argot. We need only note that improvisation too easily takes the form of an affront, by forgetting to be human. And on the other hand prayer liberates, because it makes us feel safe, as we feel safe in gardens; one does not tire of serenity, because it is so quickly lost. Ritual gestures are never sudden or unforeseen; the sudden and the unforeseen are the most part of incivility. And as we must speak to a horse before touching him, so even more obviously must we speak to man, who is by far the most skittish of animals. There is an orational quality in all important works, even in the novels of Voltaire. Study the gestures of prayer; there is nothing violent in them. We interpret them from a distance, for example the gesture of raised arms, and they always express a sublime confidence.

Rituals, whichever they be, are always of use to labor, and have another, more hidden use, against passions; thus they preserve being and structure and overall health. There is as little left to chance in them as there is in the thatched cottages of the peasants. Horace promised the blood of a goat to his spring. At first the mind dreams wildly at the thought of water being so profaned, but that road leads nowhere. It is necessary first of all to quiet our misanthropy; then the purpose becomes clear, which is that a serum of blood is one way of filtering water. I have had pointed out to me as an example of absurd superstition the peasants' practice of not removing the spider webs from the small windows of their stables; the explanation is in front of your eyes, in the bodies of flies hanging from them. Let chance serve you; but always be ready to welcome it. Not long ago I noticed a ritual that was moving in appearance, and even more beautiful in its truth. I was watching an old man who could no longer do more than walk over his fields, and I saw him stop for a moment, motionless, on one knee. I thought he was praying. But when I pointed him out to a local woman, she said: "That's how people rest around here." Several times since then I have noticed the same posture, so appropriate for spring and autumn, appropriate also for old age, appropriate for thought. I do not mean to say that the old man was not praying; quite the contrary.

Chapter seven

ORACLES

Nature never ceases to prophesy. Trees, flowers, birds, insects, all advise us. The city-dweller watches the drift of the clouds or of smoke; and I know of an old woman who forecasts rain by watching her canaries; they sometimes spill water out of their dishes, and when they do it always rains. But this simple example can only mislead the imagination, for the signs turn out to be magical by coincidence. The canaries seem to speak in gestures; but in fact the little apparatus that keeps their water dishes at a constant level is a highly sensitive barometer, and the water overflows when the air pressure decreases. Thus one can tell the truth, and still be wrong. And we must note once again that experience, which is never deceptive, always deceives us. Descartes found that it could never be trusted, though in the end we may have to trust it. But Descartes is himself a difficult conquest. He too is an oracle, and people will go to his house as they once went to the oak at Dodona. In any case, oracles are worth as much as you are, and that is what the inscription over the doorway at Delphi says: "Know thyself."

There is no question that the city mind administered the oracles along with everything else. The sacred birds were mere functionaries, which is why Cicero was allowed to laugh at them. Agrarian religion, in every age, comes to die in the city; this movement is as eternal as the movement of the sea. I am not writing history; the order I am describing is to religion what roots are to the tree. If the city can only live on what it takes from the country, it is also true that country life is fugitive and cannot be caught without the city and its police. Therefore there has always been a theology of oracles. But the soul of oracles still wanders in the fields; it is there that its life is renewed. It is there that the flight of birds marks the change of seasons, the approach of a storm, or the presence of a snake or a cat. It is there that the call of a hen to her chicks makes us look for a hawk overhead. It is in the woods that the call of a jay from tree to tree lets us follow the movements of an invisible hunter. It is there that a rabbit leaping across our path makes us stop, hesitate, change our plans, or go back for a different rifle; for it means that the hunt is on, and that a more dangerous animal will follow. The true peasant lives by oracles; he interprets and arranges the signs; he bends his action after them. His interpretations are canny, and the will finds its way through them. Doubt remains; and where there is doubt, we can take our chances. The city-dweller, on the other hand, takes signs as absolute, because he has lost the thread that connects them to the world of things. But he only believes in signs because he despairs of making up his own mind; he tosses a coin, and the image of Caesar decides for him, as is only proper.

The flight of birds decides absolutely in the end, just as Caesar's decree decides which day will be Friday and which will be Sunday. But the spirit of oracles is more flexible, and of the same grain as the physical world. It remains true for what is far off, dangerous, or uncertain, that it is wiser to act with restraint. We realize that the adult example throws very little light on the superstitions of childhood, in which everything is either permitted or forbidden. Not to mention that fear works in favor of oracles, even in the hardest heads; for the mere thought of defying an oracle will send the arrow wide of its mark; not necessarily because it is contrary, but simply because it is thought of. It has been predicted that a certain peasant will die from falling on a pitchfork, in the exact place where his father died. If this thought occurs to him in that place, when he is a little off balance, he will end up on the pitchfork. And because stories relate these miraculous things according to another law, we always believe in signs more than we mean to, and even more than we think. We do not like oracles that come as a surprise to us; we prefer to seek out advice. We go to the temple only if we want to; there we hide all our fear, if we can; and it shows an admirable simplicity, and in fact a kind of wisdom, to say that no one can enter. The young man leaves his offering on the doorsill and goes away; he asks for nothing; this gesture is charming, because it is the gesture of happiness.

Let us go back to the life of the primitive hunters, the herdsmen, the migrants, the nomads. Not only does a bird, a flock of birds, the movement of an animal have meaning; even the stomach of a freshly killed animal is worth inspecting; from it one can learn what grains and fruits are edible in a new territory; one can find out if there is pasture land or a spring nearby. Besides, as we know, it is a good idea to be cautious and attentive when cleaning game; the meat will turn bitter if the bile duct is ruptured. This method of observation, and of respect, is naturally bound up with sacrifice. But I sense a more primitive emotion in it, an emotion born of deep sympathy. For wounds, especially the wounds of war, are also prophetic; and the resemblance of bloody entrails to that part of ourselves that foreshadows fear or courage, makes the reading of entrails tragic in itself. Perhaps it makes us feel our own presentiments, our own terrible foretaste of courage or flight, more vividly. Man is a terrifying oracle for himself, because the first signs are greatly intensified by the fear or hope they give us. Ajax knows already from the movement of his body that he will be brave and victorious. He says, "I feel that a god is urging me on." But the god has a name, and that takes us a step too far.

More naïvely, that is, in earlier times, man drew prophecies from the human body. Not only by human sacrifice, but also through ritual tortures inflicted on prisoners, from which came the use of torture under the Inquisition, or inquest, which was urban, even legal, and took place only yesterday. Did they hope, in these cases, to draw from the very quiverings of the flesh, secrets that the lips refused to utter, and perhaps could not utter? That means that they were counting on the involuntary; for what is less voluntary than the signs of suffering? This passionate curiosity is something other than the natural desire to carry out a threat. The spirit of vengeance is not the whole of it, and torture has more than one meaning.

The involuntary is what we see in simpletons, idiots, epileptics. These impulses have been called unconscious, a confusion of terms that has had serious consequences; but this scholasticism will pass. In truth, there is no consciousness that is not voluntary, and no thought that is not voluntary. And the oracular impulses of the uncontrolled body belong wholly to nature, like trees and springs, geese and rabbits. We have always felt that simpletons say more than they know; and in effect they say everything, out of their naïve bond with nature. They flutter like leaves on a tree, and make a noise of words, and invent gestures that we can almost understand. Hence the great interest in such accidental revelations, which, besides, are always bound, through the human body, to the preservation of the species, which is why some of these predictions are accurate. This condition is nothing like the child's; children are far more guarded and far more political. There is nothing political about the Pythia, though she is surrounded by politics. The Pythia is simply a body wholly possessed by nature, or perhaps given over to nature through some pharmaceutical process; though she also has her theatrical side, as do all madmen and convulsives. I think of the whirling dervishes, whom I have already described; this wild play-acting, which ends in demented fury, throws a great deal of light on all passions. The Pythia, then, is a madwoman who plays the madwoman, and she is studied much as birds or entrails are studied; for there is a sympathy at play in these things which disposes us to belief. As for the prophecy itself, which is always enigmatic, and perhaps ambiguous for dramatic effect, the man who labors or governs makes what he can of it, as he does with all beliefs, with a deviousness that we will never really understand. Tiberius punished his astrologer, and the astrologer understood the game very well. The impulse to punish the bringer of bad news is hateful in the tyrant, who has too free a hand; but it is a natural reaction in every man, and a sort of defense against despair, which is in that case the real messenger. In short, man gets out of prophecies as he gets out of any other difficulty. Superstition often conceals intention, and is always related to it. That is why the ambitious man is incomprehensible, and the flatterer is despised.

95

Chapter eight

THE MAGICIAN

Magicians are political; there is nothing Pythian about them, and nothing religious. The magician believes only in himself, and the theatrical part of the extravaganza is what saves this particular spirit from being its own tragedian. Magicians can be bought; the Pythia cannot be bought. And we also notice that confidence goes to the Pythia, whereas the magician is dogged by distrust. He is not loved; his glance is wary; there is a shrewd observer behind his eyes, as there is behind the eyes of the actor. And yet his looks promise more than is there, for this thinker, who is always overestimated, counts only on effects; no one is less concerned with real causes. That is what makes the magician credulous, though he is incredulous to the point of cynicism from another angle. What deceives the magician is the passion for control; for men often join together for causes that go unnamed, and which they need not even be aware of; yet the magician is suspicious of this double comedy, which is a diabolical irony. Such is Faust, and such is the poet, for they are both too successful.

I have pushed this complex portrait too far ahead; it speaks for another stage of man and a religion that is more urban than agrarian. I must admit that in this highly civilized world, which abounds in magicians, but very cautious ones, it amuses me to finish this portrait by telling the whole truth, though it is not at all pleasant for the magician. Nevertheless, we must go back and seek out the unfinished magician of the fields. Flocks of sheep make a fine procession, following after the man in the heavy shepherd's coat. He is their god. He comforts them, he heals them; he alone knows how to lead them to the slaughter-house; without his providence, they would die too soon. There is rarely a shepherd who does not pass for a magician. And I believe that the first rustic magicians were animal trainers, men whose patient efforts go unseen, and who suddenly reveal the most astonishing effects. All animals can be trained; but, as Lucretius saw, we cannot always include trained animals in our work. Snake charmers and lion tamers have no place in industry. The witches in our fairy tales appear surrounded by animals, almost always by dangerous animals. That is what leads me to think that the magician's art is always exercised principally upon animal nature, and perhaps also upon vegetal nature, and that it involves patience, an accumulation of techniques, and an excellent memory, and no real science whatsoever. Which does not keep us from saying that astronomy owes a great deal to the astrologers and chemistry to the alchemists. For these rainmakers came to their art by observing, measuring, keeping track of the weather and the growing seasons, and above all by preserving notable facts in their secret archives, which is what led them to the use of numbers, figures, and formulas, among other devices. And yet there remains a profound stupidity in all of these magic texts, and a credulity that far exceeds common opinion, whose suspicions are more than justified.

The highest religion, always bound up with the ancient gods as the soul is with the body, burned a number of magicians and witches at the stake. This impulse of vengeance comes from more distant, or rather from more humble sources. Common judgment always held the fairly profound idea that magicians act only for evil; such is the destiny of those whose abilities exceed their knowledge. Perhaps we should say that people resort to magicians above all because they fear them. Magicians are excluded from friendship, and they know it. It is their particular job to play only upon the basest part of man; and it is their consolation to despise him. No doubt they would never have chosen this sad occupation for themselves; more likely they were exiled and condemned to it, by an involuntary power. But we must also consider the effect of that childhood injustice which looks for magicians everywhere, and which divides the world into good and evil, thus confirming the one and the other. There is no family that has not made use of

97

some inoffensive dwarf, hunchback, or bogeyman in order to get the child to eat his supper or go to bed. This does man great harm, for he finally accepts his role of scarecrow; and that is a sort of diabolical friendship. It is like making people afraid of a dog by telling them that he is bad; even for a dog, this does not contribute to making him good, for the signs of warning and prohibition are repeated and imitated a thousand times as if in a game of mirrors; and eyes that realize they are frightening, are truly frightening. Such is the sinister gleam of the evil eye, which is universally feared, though people do not always admit it. It is easy to imagine that it makes the crops dry up, that it makes the cows die, that it is even fatal for children. But think of the repercussions within the person who knows or suspects that people think he has such power. The magician is always more of a magician than he wants to be. Spells and incantations are explained fairly well by this vicious circle, which the magicians often have not drawn so deeply themselves. They are hated, they are prayed to, they are paid, they are cursed, they are burned at the stake, and all of this comes of itself. All the evil of the imagination comes of itself. We see that it is necessary to separate out the thousand sources of religious passions. It would be absurd to think that the Church invented magicians. She found them, expelled and damned them, as she did all of the lower gods. People are sometimes indignant at the idea of hell, as if it were an invention of the priests; but hell comes of itself. I will attempt to pursue this idea; of course it will escape me, in its breadth and in its depth. Yet we must try. The magician despairs the moment we begin to hope.

Chapter nine

MEASURE

The sun's legacy, divided among the furrows of the field, is counted out in workdays, or better still in man-hours. An evil magician might increase the blight on the wheat; but he can never plow a three-day field in one hour, and without oxen. There remains a margin of black magic in all forms of affliction, in storms, drought, wolves, weasels and moles; but reason opens out over cultivated fields; the necessary seeds grow by reason of the furrows, and the beets grow by reason of the rows. Two plowed fields can easily be compared, either in terms of work, or in terms of their product. These relationships are before our eyes and under our hands. The two dimensions are figured by the cultivation itself, which lays out alignments and equal spacings. The number of shocks, the number of sacks, the number of plants, the number of man-hours, all of this is imposed by the task itself; and to know that one number depends on another, is to know number as it should be known. The crops grow from almost nothing, as we do. The pleasure of these evaluations is inexhaustible. The art of the surveyor, who was born a peasant, is continually judged in sales and divisions of land. And no one is less of a magician.

The measurement of work has remained hidden from physics for a long time; that is surprising, and it give us a first idea of the effect of urban magic, in which everything seems to depend on conventions. Work, says the professor, is measured by multiplying a force times the displacement of its point of application in the line of action. Six oxen plowing a furrow would embody the idea; no one can think that two oxen do as much work as six, or that a furrow of two times the length does not correspond to two times the work for the same number of oxen. Such measurements of work enable us to evaluate heavy and light soils, and, by comparison of their products, to determine their fertility. Peasant good sense, so justly celebrated, is not the result of chance. Perhaps because the relationship between geometry and arithmetic is here continually implied and continually recalled. A farm can be evaluated in acres, in workdays, in oxen, in horses, in men; all of these measures are interrelated and can only vary together. A herd of cows, a set of harnesses, a full table, are therefore embodiments of reason. Perhaps we have not given enough consideration to favor and luck, the two rulers of the city. We might say then that reason is born in the fields and dies in the city. If there are other laws in the city, and honest occupations as well, we will learn nothing about them from the banker or the prince.

Man has been defined as the tool-making animal. That is true, but it is not precise. Tools are evidence of thought and of a calculation of strength. The ancient scepter is a stick, and the same stick is itself a rule and a law. The earliest plow was simply a drawn stick; the furrow is the track of the stick, and neater work than a man could do by himself. Law, which is straightness of conduct, is inscribed by the plow. All tools are sticks; the yard measure is a stick. The lever is a stick; and the wheel, the soul of all machines, already appears in the turning of the simple tool. I will not go on with this analysis of tools; it is difficult, and would interrupt my subject. What is clear is that animals, even the most ingenious of them, have never thought of delegating their strength to things, or of making use of a resisting object, which is an obstacle and becomes a means. There is something political in tools, as there is in the scepter, and a piety of man toward man. Tools and weapons are an honored inheritance. And no doubt it was by an attachment to ancient form, and by the duplication of venerated models, that tools and weapons came to regulate action, as we see with the scythe. So there is superstition even in tools. But this kind of religion, which finds the whole of its development beside the hearth and in the cities, and which it would be better to study separately, is directly opposed to rustic religion, because the tool is an uncapricious servant, which can be tried out, tested, and examined in every possible way. The balance is a stick which regulates our thoughts; it is justice become an object, inflexible, and strictly good. Our thoughts, on the contrary, may rob us of courage by that deceptive instability which is, if we may put it so, their law. The agrarian divinities are a series of dissolving thoughts, thoughts that cannot be formed. And, on the contrary, tools and their imprint are lasting thoughts. The idea of placing one's confidence in every stable form is the religious idea itself; thus the notion of paganism as an irreligious religion is inseparable from religion itself, and the struggle of the gods of the city and the god of the spirit against the gods of the earth has never ended and will never end. The object that recalls us and that we come back to, the statue or the crucifix, is directly opposed to these apparitions which never occur more than once, and which can only be made into stories. There have always been and there always will be false gods, and the temple, so firmly drawn, measured, balanced, the temple, which is so resistant, is the limit at which they come to die; there is no mystery here, though we always think there is. One prays better in the midst of nature, says Rousseau; I would say rather that one prays too much. The old proverb is better which says, to labor is to pray; for what is prayer but the search for exorcism? The relation between impiety and piety is intimate to piety, as the temptations of the saints naïvely express; and whereas the thinker's temptation is pleasure, the saint's temptation is belief. Proteus is the best name for this enemy of the spirit, inasmuch as these almost violent metamorphoses, from tree to lion, to clear water, are an exact representation of the follies of the imagination, which are instantly lost. There is then something to think about in the geometric figure inscribed on Faust's threshold, which the devil cannot cross over. And the circle traced by a stick is magic, but only in its limitation and exclusion of magic.

LAND AND SEA

We have reason to think that the first cities were maritime settlements. For provisions constantly flow into them. The harvests of the sea grow by themselves and are replenished from day to day. This leads to unbounded expectations. The miraculous fish is the prototype of those miracles that are not miracles at all. On the other hand, the importance of tools, fish hooks, boat hooks, nets, boats, oars, sails, must have brought about a workman's mentality, and purely urban, for the furrow of a boat's wake immediately disappears. The opposition between violent nature and human shelter is more clearly marked in this kind of life. In the act of conquest, danger is always sudden. And I think, in the light of what fairy tales tell us, that miraculous events are more common in distant lands than on the seas. Water is monotonous; its force is regulated, as the coastline shows, and its obvious fluidity takes away all the mystery of change. Faced with the rise and fall of this balanced liquid, we realize that the part explains the whole. Here nature constantly reveals her inner workings. That is why the sea is more dangerous than terrifying.

The ship is a center and a school of politics, and the old comparison of the chief of state to the pilot of a ship should be examined afresh; for it is true that the politics on board ship hardly resembles the politics of cities, but it is also true that navigation suggests the rules of politics as politics would be under reason alone. On the sea, dangers are evident and of sudden effect; actions are easily judged, and there is no time for deliberation. Power is freely acknowledged on the sea; the best man gives the orders; and because those who carry them out join together under the chief, there is no favoritism, no abuse, no tyranny. Revolt would be so easy that there is no place for it; the situation is demanding enough in itself. It is impossible that this active existence, always twisting with the waves, and rescued each time, should not enlighten the spirit in a very particular way. One would assume, in the light of these conditions, which are all interrelated, that the seafaring mind is more cynical and less clouded than the land-bound mind, and, in short, that there is scarcely a sea divinity that has not descended from the woods and streams. When Ulysses is struggling in the sea, he trusts only to himself; it is in the estuary that he makes his prayer to the river. This summary view is not enough; we would have to trace back the ancestry of the Nereids and Tritons, and of the sirens, to find out if these divinities are not as much children of dry land as the *Flying Dutchman* is. But I do not want to get involved in such discussions; they represent a way of thinking about the gods that dulls the spirit. It will suffice if we observe that the most reasonable civilizations have always been maritime, and that in any case the labors of the seafaring life, the industry of the shipbuilders, trade, long voyages, and forced hospitality, as we see in the *Odyssey*, not to mention the actual government by the most able rather than the most ambitious man, have contributed much toward liberating men from the most primitive and least controlled part of their spirit. We must note, on the other hand, that the separation of men and women is far more marked in the seafaring life, where man is formed by labors that take him far from home, and under circumstances in which urban law is entirely forgotten. I have noticed a great contrast between the insouciance of a group of men playing ball, and the seriousness of women, who drive their men back to work, sometimes with the help of a stick. The peasant woman shares in almost the same tasks as the man, in the same prudence, the same worries, the same celebrations, the same prayers. Marriage and family life are more restricting for a man than the life of the sea, and naturally make him more pious and obedient, but also less enlightened.

Chapter eleven

POETRY

The agrarian gods are faceless. They are no more than the thing itself, which is divine by what surrounds it. A spring of water is mysterious because it is set in the mountains, among trees. Trees and the wind awaken each other. Thus the most familiar things always carry a strange significance, and an inexplicable resonance. The modern city-dweller retains something of this emotion which has no other object than the presence of the whole in each part; and the mythological apparatus of fauns, sylvans, naiads and dryads is reduced to the level of metaphor. The poet looks for nothing other than the cover of the woods, the tree, the spring; and the more he perceives these things as they are, the more he feels them as they are not in appearance; and the divine takes refuge entirely within real form, as the change in poetry and even in painting at our extremity of civilization reveals in a thousand ways. The miraculous in agrarian life, once it is represented by means of human form, is as cold, and for the same reasons, as Christian miracles are in epic poetry. What this idea bears out is that the woodland gods are imported from the city, that they are offspring of the gods of the hearth. Paganism is often bound up with the Olympian religion, which nevertheless is not agrarian but political. And these secondary gods are no more than inoffensive little deities, a very poor embodiment of sovereign nature and the real powers to which the peasant sacrifices flowers, grain, a lamb or an ox. That is why the poet of our day is in a better position than his Homeric ancestor to rediscover in its purity something of the sensibility of the peasant, who offers the blood of a lamb to the spring itself, a garland of flowers to the tree itself, his Easter without god to the vernal equinox itself. This god Pan, revealed in his precious form, which is all forms, from simple grass to the druidic oak, must not be taken for a new god, the product of enlightenment and reason. Pantheism has always been denounced by the religion of the spirit as a capital error, and I intend to explain little by little, in the course of these pages, that it is in effect a capital error, from which even the subtlest theologians do not always escape, for the reason that they have not traced out the progression of the gods and the war of the gods according to the order of structure, which is the truth of history. We will perhaps understand, in the light of the most frightening mysteries of agrarian religion, that pantheism was already a heresy, and a formidable one, in the time of Olympian Jupiter. It was a reawakening of the Titans, who were buried once and for all under their mountains; it was a resuscitation of the savage world against the spirit of the cities, the real source of the peacefulness of the fields.

It is essential to religion that the religion of nature be subordinated, though it is always preserved. That is why the famous proof of God by the beauty of nature is a scandal in the eyes of the spirit. Because first of all it is false. It is not true that everything is good and divine in nature, just as it is not true that the labors of the fields are easy and pleasant. This is a city-dweller's illusion. The peasant worships the snake after a fashion, but that does not keep him from killing snakes. And it is quite necessary to eat the flesh of cattle. Nature is severe and without tenderness, outside of man; within man she is even worse, and Jansenism is right. The offering to Venus is not in itself less tragic than the sacrifice of Iphigenia; and the word tragic, which comes from goat, seems to me to express rather forcefully even the very odor of our dramas. That is why seductive and intoxicating pantheism must continually be fended off and reduced to its proper level. It nourishes all that is above it, as the belly nourishes heart and head, but it is no more than the belly, whereas man is more than the belly.

That is why it takes all the techniques of rhythm and the whole grace of song to revive, within just proportions, this mother religion through which we have our being and against which we set our being, as the ambiguity of the animal glance occasionally reminds us. I wonder at the excessiveness of Descartes, who was no poet, and who stood inflexibly opposed to the very idea of the animal soul. This cool-headed soldier had to open up a difficult path. The poet can and will come back to his brother the tree and his sister the snake; but these two great images brought together in the biblical poem always rear their double menace, and here we can sense what is positive and worthy of understanding in a great myth. The time will come, no doubt, and may already have come, when we will stop asking these oracles if that is how things really were and what was actually said; instead, content that things should be presented and spoken that way in our fables, we will apply ourselves to understanding them. The metaphors of our poets have the same double meaning, which at once evokes and overcomes the inferior powers. No one asks if the snake in Valéry is really the same one as in the Bible, for it is precisely the same one as in the Bible. Yet no one really thinks that the devil took on that shape; the fact is that he has it. And the more we think of the snake as he is, the better and more boldly will we think of man as he is, and of the prudence necessary for the least of human existence, if it is not to fall back into animal dreams.

These moving and humiliating truths are made clear in the legend of the tempting serpent; but, because they no longer touch us with the force of real nature, the story passes by as if we did not realize that it has to do with us. Yet if we consider the real serpent, who speaks to us only of himself and of his own sufficiency, we will understand that the legend has to do with us, and that the spirit is a small bet on a very large table. That is how metaphor, moving side by side with our thoughts, cautiously awakens the true obstacle, which the abstract thinker too easily forgets. For Yes, No and the contradiction *in terminis*, are a kind of obstacle which also has its importance, but only for grammar; and logic only serves to support the poet's image and to surround it as with a cordon of police, which, along with rhythm and music, helps us to overcome the presence of the image, let us say even to withstand it, which is, once again, to conquer savage nature. Philosophy leads us further into wisdom, but it does not lead the whole man. And in the world of wise men, only Plato that I know of has understood this fact. Therefore read Gyges or Er once again, in order to put this first mass of reflection into place.

BOOK III
JUPITER

Chapter one

THE HEARTH

Ulysses, on Calypso's beach, thinks of the smoke above his roof in Ithaca, and wants to die. The house is a sacred place; and notice that this word means at the same time the worst and the best; because happiness is appeased horror; thus peace has two faces, as a wall has two faces. Outside, the house takes its form from the enemy, rain or wind; inside, it is a man's shell, the hollow imprint of his life; nothing is more eloquent than an empty seat; it is the first statue. In the midst of these presences and absences, the hearth-fire is king; it gives heat and light. The art of handling fire, which animals know nothing of, depends largely upon tools, largely upon human hands, largely upon prudence. We remember the girl in Dickens who reads all sorts of stories in the glowing embers. Proust, more subtly, listens through the door to a fire that stirs like an animal. It is a building that never ceases to crumble, the best image of transformation and the play of force. Kant cites the ancient philosopher's problem: "How much does smoke weigh?" Some have meditated on flying sparks; others on dead ashes; everyone on the warmth of flames, a warmth so obviously like the warmth of living bodies. The hearth is a center of metaphorical thoughts; and all of the shadows lead back to man; they are all dear to him. Here is the provision of another poetry, which is like the reverse image of external nature; dogs and cats belong to it only by sufferance; man is the god of animals. It is thus that day is mirrored in divine night, and that is why Christmas is the Easter of thought. However, the child God, worshiped by his mother, his father, the ox and the ass, signifies yet another birth, and a higher level of religion.

The spirit is lost once again in fire, and lost in the shadows. The athlete takes the best seat; it is his divine right. The old people vanish into the background, shades already, with nothing left but a dormant wisdom. This is how the doorway of dreams is made, with no architectural fantasy. Statues encircle the room, just stepping out from the walls. And in this inturned reflection upon order the exchange and composition of the various powers is carried out. "You will see my father," says Nausicaa, "he is seated by a column; but run first to my mother, who is at the hearth." However, this power of intercession presupposes an urban peace. At the peasant hearth, the shadows are more crowded; labors are closer and more urgent; long experience is more highly valued. Our oldest and most natural thoughts are simply a conversation between son and father. And whenever there is a question of source, culture, or limit, the older man says, "I remember what my father told me." I would say that commemoration is not only a matter of piety. The dead come to bear witness to what they alone know. When a man is dead, we are left only with the remembrance of what he said; we would like him to speak again; we apply to this evocation all the force of our spirit and the most fervent attention. Our tender affections would be satisfied with less. That is why the best men are not assured by affection alone of the brightest immortality; rather it is those who have a genius for action and the strongest memory. Caesar appears.

We will meet Caesar again. Piety was first filial, as language reminds us. The reason is that in agrarian existence, it is enough to have lived a long time to know a great deal; and labor on the earth is such that improvisation is less esteemed than ancient example, for success takes long years. The oldest member of the family is therefore king in intelligence. He is consulted in death. But, better still, he is consulted as greater than he was, for we are in a position to choose; he is consulted as strong, courageous, prudent, and in no way hesitant or doting, as he was known at the end of his life. He is not consulted with the thought that he is dead, or worse than dead. Besides the fact that such images would corrupt affection, it is also natural that the most urgent thoughts of the living efface the death of the dead; and this first piety was always full of precautions. It is the reason for the funeral pyre and the tomb; from which comes the widely held belief that the dead, if improperly buried, will come back in reproach, useless then in their mutilated form, useless and even malicious. This results in a kind of consolation that is quite forceful in any event; for, in the form of ghosts, the dead could not be consulted, and we would not even know how to love them. That is why the immortals are immortally young, immortal in their prime, and made beautiful by piety itself. But peasant art is limited to carving roots or modeling figurines in terra cotta; and these forms standing around the hearth suffice to evoke distant faces and thoughts that are always young. No doubt the proverb is like a statue in words, assured of memory by measure and rhyme; under this form the ancestor came back to life. And it was piety again to carry with one, like Aeneas, a host of faceless and perhaps nameless ancestors; for we certainly feel that the dead to be honored are legion, and we know from experience the value of humble virtues that will be forgotten. Such then were the lares and penates in all times and all countries. These little gods have nothing to do with nature; in fact they are a victory over nature, which kills as it nourishes, and which forgets everything, even itself, in its new beginnings. It is important to mark some gradations here, from the god of the outside and the daylight, who is always somewhat mad and often malicious, to the god of the house and of evening, who never fails to be wise and helpful. However we have still to separate ourselves from the former, for time must pass before the son reawakens into the glory of the father. The hearth is not isolated. The city surrounds it; the temple dominates it; and the gods of common power do not always have time to be good. *Ave, Caesar, morituri.* . . .

Chapter two

The Hero

It may be that there are no agrarian heroes. It is true that Hercules is a peasant; he kills dangerous animals, and an occasional cattle thief. But he also never quite makes it as a god. And the sea-adventurers are not perfect heroes either. The hero has almost no share in the belly; he is not concerned with plunder, and he is not essentially a protector. Perhaps he is not a legislator either, nor even a king; for these functions demand prudence, and an inclination to greed, from which the hero is very far removed. The hero is generous, and of a pure anger; by which I mean that he has as little intelligence as he has desire. But I am already exaggerating these characteristics, the way legends do. Perhaps there are only heroes of a moment. And yet this human moment is often poorly understood; it is overlooked because we forget, in our structure, the breast, and the impetuous heart, which, as the poet says, is awakened by its own beating. Man is almost always described in terms of need and prudence; that is, in terms of belly and head. We forget the part that spends itself freely, which is the heart, king of muscles, and symbol of the muscular system, which is utterly explosive. A muscle pulls like a horse; it is provoked by resistance, it is annoyed by obstacles; it is dying to win. This impulse has no purpose; it is its own purpose. The muscle pardons what does not resist; to what resists, it is cruel; cruel with a sort of cruelty against itself; brutal in its own strength. We know that when a frog's leg is cut off, the leg muscle will exhaust itself trying to jump if we merely touch it. We can reconstruct the hero by isolating the part that spends itself in action. The ensemble is a man, that is, a being that feels and thinks, and also a cringing belly, but which is subordinated by a structure that denotes an excess of energy and a sudden self-surrender. Pride is the essential passion of a being so constructed; but we must not judge pride in terms of the precautions of honor, which often contain a sort of greed, or a prudence with regard to anger. There is in true pride a sudden impulse, a perfect animal reflex, as when a horse, harnessed in its strength, suddenly pulls against its collar. When the harness of the muscles is aware of itself, evaluates itself, knows and judges itself, this sudden impulse is a sign of death or victory. It does not experiment, it throws itself into action. There is this moment of heroism in the blow of a fist, in the blow of an ax, in the stroke of an oar; but in these cases it is measured, because the unfeeling obstacle turns effort into labor.

The object that belongs to the hero and shapes the hero, is the enemy; that is to say, the equal, the much-praised equal, the rival in other words, and a rival whom he judges worthy of himself. Therefore there can be no complete hero without a solemn war, without some provocation, without the long anticipation of another hero, subject of fame and legend. Man loves rescue operations, hunting, and all kinds of risk, because there is a portion of the hero in him which never entirely sleeps. But for the full hero to emerge, he needs the hunt for man, the most dangerous of all; he needs a kind of agitation that belongs to the city and the assembly, the fear and hope of the weak, an insulting threat, a set time, a fixed place, a title put in question, a ceremony, a publicity, even a preparation, which is like an exercise between fear and courage; all, in fact, that we read about in the *Jerusalem* and in other heroic stories. And whoever looks closely at these violent stories will recognize in them our own wars, especially in their beginnings. This moment is human and it always will be.

We see perhaps how the hero differs from a horse that pulls until it is exhausted, though the resemblance between Achilles and his horse is also something to think about; for, by separating will from structure, and from the obstacle, we lose the whole of man; we even lose the poet. Every genius grows out of earth and blood, as language makes clear by using the same word for the invisible gods of the woods, and for the man who despises these gods to the point of giving them no thought, sufficient in himself, and rivaling the gods of Olympus in destruction or creation. It is therefore necessary to consider the human obstacle, in which man sees his own highest image. And the human obstacle is by nature strong in pride, and still stronger in defiance, stronger in the signs of force that are conceded to him, the supposed equal, mastering his own fear, and restraining himself only by a prodigious equilibrium, always a threat to himself; for the trembling of anger is a kind of omen. Thus the mad resolve of a horse, that would kill itself trying to pull down a mountain, becomes madder still in man with the first shuddering of fear, which he feels in himself, and senses in his opponent, and which advises him to spend himself first, in order to surprise the enemy, and to double the weight of his blow with assurance. This gathering and drawing in before the start, so noticeable in every difficult act, never coils the spring so tightly as it does in the hero, when he faces the human obstacle, declared, recognized, resolved. Not that death itself is taken as the end of action; it never is; the thought of death is excluded from this moment, along with the thought of defeat, for the thought would be death and defeat beforehand. But indignation tells him in advance that he must give all, and without hope, if he wants to fight with all of his strength. Saint-Simon, who was a just man out of simplicity and as if in spite of himself, always uses a particular epithet when he refers to the famous Condé. He calls him: *Monsieur le Prince le héros*. It is clear that he did not find the company of such a man very pleasant. But the repetition of this one phrase makes me feel all the more strongly his lightning judgment, his impulsiveness, the terror that he drove before him, his absolute pride, with no doubt of victory, all things which, though without great effect in those political times, were not without glory. And the example of this almost entirely bad character teaches me still more than does the character of Achilles, who is also neither gentle nor good. It is important to realize that the god of cities is not an amiable god, and is never admired without being feared; and not only because we admire what we fear; the people are more subtle than that;

they live in expectation of some reckless impulse which, for no reason at all, will suddenly shake the earth. The Jupiter of Homer, the conqueror of the Titans, without giving it a thought, takes good fortune from one barrel and misfortune from another, and out of that mixture makes each man's destiny. The poet touches here upon a kind of contempt that is well beneath contempt. When we say that we must pardon the hero for his lack of the little virtues, we have not said enough. Such then is this human fire, as inhuman as any other, which burns within the hearth of hearths.

Chapter three

Legend

This kind of storytelling is open and public. The hero's praises are sung, on a customary day, at the foot of his purified statue. Commemoration, in which architect, poet and rhapsode invest their own genius, even their own immortality, carries still further the pious labor of embellishment which is so natural to filial piety. And the listeners are all guardians of the legend, as the word itself says, for legend means what must be spoken. There is something supernatural in the hero, in his innate and total defiance, and in his heaping of excess upon excess, which is the law at least of his own will. This surviving spirit flies off by itself where no man can follow. The sky is the dwelling-place of the gods, because gravity is our nearest and most unrelenting enemy. But this place in the sky has other privileges. It is there perhaps that we seek our memories; for they are born first of all from nearby objects, and perception always nourishes them; but at the same time perception obliterates them; so that our attention, pursuing them, is turned naturally toward the clouds or the pure light. This brief moment of reverie, after we raise our eyes, is inexpressible, because what we are about to grasp is always disappearing into the mist or the sun; only speech remains to people those solitudes. And that is the natural apotheosis. The flames and smoke of the sacrifice also direct our glance. And the resemblance between this free warmth and the warmth of the living body leads us to imagine that life also flies off with the smoke from the fire. These concordant metaphors always govern the movement of our thoughts, once we refuse the object at hand in order to search for one that is better, more beautiful, more beloved. But, in truth, what gives consistency to the mystery of the invisible, is the real mystery of thought, the final object of all religions. For it is true that what is absent to our senses is still present in a certain way, if we think of it. This effect of the imagination, so intense in the experience of fear, is inseparable from all emotion as such, for emotion literally takes us by the body, it invades us. We are touched, we are seized, as these violent metaphors put it. We look for the object; we do not find it; we throw our words into the void; our words, because the gesture is more felt than seen, and speech has the privilege of returning to our ears as an object. That is why incantation is the eternal method for bringing back what are so aptly called spirits. I would like to add, in anticipation, that the spirit searches for itself as legitimately in the external world as within; however, the exact critique of this notion of notions would be out of place here.

We are talking about remembrance, and the pleasure of telling and listening to stories. They say that primitive peoples can only think in assembly. But primitive peoples are a fiction, like the age of gold. It is true for all of us, and it will always be true, that the assembly is the place for remembrance; for, once the object itself is gone, we need some testimony and some agreement in order to sustain reverie; every biography or chronology is based on the questioning of witnesses, and witnesses of witnesses. We know also that, if the assembly is large, there will be an order established, the priorities of age, for age is the witness of the past, and finally a reciter or reader. All eloquence presupposes rules that are basically acoustical, the purpose of which is not only to avoid ambiguity, but also to prepare, almost to measure in advance, the space of what will be said. Poetry is the natural form of this eloquence which must express only what everyone expects and recognizes. The poem does not only serve glory, it is glory itself.

At this point, it is necessary to explain the choice that is always made, in legends, between what is important and what is not important. I have already observed that, in the child's tales, mere labor against the object-world is simplified, if not eliminated, because all useful labors are performed without the child's help and away from his view. A journey is therefore a minor thing, covered in a few words, for the child is carried and he sleeps on the way. We find similar abbreviations in every legend and even in every history. The movement of childhood reappears in them; but it would not be able to survive childhood if it were not confirmed by better and more mature thoughts. The fact is that the labors of troop movement, transportation, digging, cutting trails, navigation, repairs, the arranging and setting up of camp, are in themselves monotonous and simple; they are done and forgotten. These long periods of preparation are abbreviated in all stories. A legion marches on foot from Pont-Euxin to Armorica, and it seems only natural to us. Even today the movements of war are almost all slow, but they flash by in the telling. The memorable drama begins only when the slow and heavy things are in place. And who thinks about transporting them once they are in place? Bonaparte, or Hannibal, crossed the Alps and fell on the enemy. The interest waits at the end of all those miles, for us as well as for the generals. Orlando mounts the flying horse; this means that the journey into battle is of no interest; one way or another it will get done, and no one will think any more about it. Children's stories are more frank than we are in this respect; our historians always forget how much work it takes. The real reason for this apparent ingratitude is the same in the one case as in the other; it is that the transportation of men and material is not really difficult, no more so than paving a road. The test of courage is what is important; that is the goal of the story; material means will always be disparaged; and deservedly so, since no preparations suffice without the power of daring. Against what? Against fear itself. All battles take place in our thoughts. All legends live in the clouds.

Chapter four

THE CITY

Tombs amaze us with their massive stones. From these stones so naturally arranged the race of divine men will be born. Long remembrance, long forgetting. Jupiter is father and king; these traits are clear enough. But death and apotheosis must necessarily be forgotten. Jupiter has always reigned in the sky; which is to say that human power has always been worshiped and has always been superhuman. But it takes the heaping up of stones and the heaping up of men, otherwise no one would ever have thought of subordinating lightning, clouds, and storms to man's power. Nature beats against the walls of the city; inside it is almost forgotten. Commemoration heaps up the stones and crushes celebration. In the time of Julius Caesar and of the foreshortened year of the usurers, Easter was no longer celebrated in the spring; it was a human Easter. It took the forder of rivers to reform things.

How the city crowds in around the temple, around the court, around the marketplace; how the sellers of religious objects, the sellers of legal robes, the sellers of eloquence open their shops close to the great gates of commerce, law, and ceremony, these things are well known; but the result is astonishing. What is significant about these stone beehives? That here external nature dies into flower gardens. Here the raging storm is scarcely heard. Here the faun and nymph are merely ornaments, and the spring bubbles through lead pipes. Man's hammer is everywhere. Help comes from men, danger comes from men, the storm comes from men; and we know only too well what the darkness may conceal. Two processions, one the miserable poor, the other the royal guard which is relieved at noon. An order that knows nothing of the seasons; a disorder that is a threat in any season. An armed wisdom, which never argues and cannot be argued with. A reason of State which salvages one day after another; the perfect labor of a moment, which must always be repeated. The blockade of force is sudden, and complete in its own being. Vertical thinking. People are happy enough, as children are, to be told what is forbidden and what is allowed; the reason why, the wall never says. There is no question about the path to be followed; a man goes through channels, like water. That is how credulity is turned into certainty. One gives the law, another the way, another the god. A new direction is a bold idea in the country; in the city it is impossible. The street is a brutalized country path. We never ask if we should respect a particular house or boundary. We turn where we have to turn. This angular power, which does not rule out new projects, but which bends them unceremoniously, defines the urban god as he appears at all times. This slow concealment of the hero, this costume of stone, fixes the statue to its base, which is as eloquent as the statue itself. And the nature of the city limits is not that they should not be crossed, but that they cannot be crossed.

It is worth noting that urban thought is self-assured, angular, frivolous, and subtle in the street-space that is left to it, serious and preoccupied within its limits. In the fields all thought is somewhat forbidden, somewhat permitted, like the paths that cows make. In the city, everything is permitted to thought, but it comes up against the impossible, which needs no explanations. "The Chinese wall!" said Painlevé of a rather clumsy arguer; we use the same tone when we warn someone: "You'll get run over!" It is not even a threat. When what seems to be a street is actually a dead end, it helps to know it; but you will know it eventually. These regulations of thought explain scholasticism, which is urban. But as the notary and the judge also rule over the fields, so the theology of the streets and sidewalks never ceases to civilize agrarian religion. It is thus that the hero stops disappearing beyond the sky. Everything is fixed in the image of the palace. The immortal has his guards, his porters, his ministers, his cup-bearers; they are his brothers and cousins, as the whole city knows. The hero governs, and there is only one way to govern. The gods have not stopped leaping about in the world; but they also sit in council. We find in the *Iliad* this mixture of decrees and wild exploits, and either way the warrior finds himself carried off, tripped up, stopped cold. Here the death of the gods is prepared, by Fate. Fate is like a wall; no one likes to run into the wall; that is why we follow along it.

We would not conceive of a race of gods simply by looking at the stones of the city; for the stones are self-sufficient. City-dwellers are assured and incredulous; there is almost no movement in their fantasy. But each day the peasants come to town bringing their mad gods along with their baskets of fruit. Something of the invisible Pan, god of a thousand shapes, always reappears in the political Olympus, just as the city architect, in return, plants at the bottom of a garden a stone Satyr playing on his triangular flute. This mixture belongs to all religions because it belongs to man. In it we will always find the child's fear and the child's hope, then the peasant's fear, less easily reassured, and then urban regulations, the offspring of another kind of fear, and of another kind of security. The child would never be what he is without protection, nor would the peasant be what he is without protection. The urban by itself is impossible; that is the meaning of morning deliveries, fruit baskets, milk bottles, the market; the country comes to the city as nourishment. But, on the other hand, the pure country life is a fiction that will always deceive us; for man seems to live in peace in the country, with his bread, his wine, his cheese. In fact the country would be plundered very quickly without the protection of the city. What is more, passions would set fire to the farms and villages; for man everywhere is suspicious and thinks dark thoughts; that is one of the fruits of intelligence. It is left to the city-dweller to enjoy the peace of the country, and to believe in it. The fact is that the cows make way for us; but it is not hard to imagine and to be afraid of the thrust of their horns. That is why it is unjust to love open nature, so still in the evening air, if one does not love established order as well. Besides, we would not know how to love open nature if we did not have recourse to a higher god; we would fear more than the cow's horns, we would fear the animal mind. It is necessary then that the agrarian gods be reduced to the level of ornaments. The faun makes us laugh; he would not make us laugh if we were to laugh at Jupiter. Thus the priest's strategy always wins.

Chapter five

THE ATHLETE

The Olympian religion could as well be called Olympic. Its god is the perfect man. That valor is everything in man, and that he has no reason to envy volcanoes, boa constrictors, wolves, is an essential idea; it is even the essential idea. It is therefore shortsighted to reject the gods in human form, and to return, thinking it an advance, to the worship of force and brute nature. And man strays again, or rather he is still on the way, when he chooses to worship the brutal side of man; for that side is nothing more than blind nature, nature that is stronger than we are. Socrates paid great attention to the fact that we can be conquered by ourselves, and that we can conquer ourselves. What does this mean? That is what Socrates asked Socrates. In any case it is only philosophy, and always a question. The questioner within us will also have his day. Ignorant of both answer and question, the athlete responded at Olympia; the sculptor responded; the poet responded, creating a race of gods, or immortal athletes. This first, memorable purification of man has more meaning than is commonly admitted. It was the natural impulse of the saints to put down as idolatrous the cult of the snake, the bacchic frenzy and the pure discus-thrower. The subtlety of the confessor had found out the hidden path from the last of these cults to the first. Man became king; it was a great step. But it is not easy to rule. The athlete and the sculptor have written down, in ineffaceable characters, that man must first rule over himself.

This is what the beauty of the athlete, the model of man, expresses. And Greek philosophy, so justly praised, has simply read its four famous virtues in the body of the strong man. To conquer oneself, and to govern oneself, that is the secret of moderation, courage, wisdom, and even justice. But to do as we like is a vain attempt, if we do not know first how to guide our hands. The lute player knows what he wants to do, but he may not know how to do it. And experience shows that it is always the whole body that weighs on the fingers, that cramps them, that makes them rebel. The constricted and rigid attitude betrays our inward fear of ourselves; and it is foolish to envy the virtue of a horse when we have not yet found our own force as men. With the discovery of the essential being of man, and of the essential strength of man, the grimace of the evil-doer is effaced from history, at least as a model; that grimace which is so surprisingly like the gnarls of a tree or the twisted features of an enraged animal. To be so ugly as to be frightening, is a technique of war, of which something remains in war-masks and helmets. A monstrous animal covers the head of Michelangelo's *Thinker*, but it is only an ornament; the monster has been demoted; there is no longer any question of thinking in terms of monsters. I mean that in the order of values, the athletic face wins out over the intemperate mask. However, because human problems are always the same, there is still a method, if we can call it that, in making oneself terrible to behold and in roaring instead of speaking. A warning to those who, going too quickly from the hundred-headed animal to the would-be pure spirit, take one step too many. This order is the true dialectic, as Hegel taught it, for in it everything has its place: mineral nature, vegetal nature, human nature, belly, breast, head, and finally the spirit. It is always true that the sequence of religions teaches us more about this order than do the essays of the philosophers. And yet this statement itself is the fruit of philosophy, not religion.

The level of religion we have now reached is entirely embodied in the athlete's immobile and enigmatic face; such are the gods. And the secret of this face is that it is wholly informed by the equilibrium of the body, which pulses with vital awareness and assurance; expressed by the belt, the auxiliary of audacity, if nothing else; but in perfection by the girding of the muscles, already an armor against fear, and by the great play of the legs, which reaches almost to the arms. Thus free and real self-knowledge is articulated, exported from the subaltern forehead, as if in unleashed streams, down to the least filaments of muscle. The face is stripped of dissembling and imitation. As the warrior has wiped off his monstrous war paint, which rules by opinion, so he wipes away all wrinkles, which come from expression instead of action, and are always the sign, even among our intemperate gymnasts, of a studied ability that goes against the art of being. However superhuman this image of man may be, it is no small accomplishment to have drawn it, and to have drawn it so close to man, with such human likeness, such earthly happiness. For once, then, man finds himself happy in his limits, and powerful in himself. What is lacking to him, he refuses, he holds himself apart from it. He refuses a hundred arms, as he refuses the complicity of tree, flood, and fire. These things are no more than indifferent means to him, like the eagle at Jupiter's side; means that are of no account. Man reigns.

No other life. Human life is enough. All that it needs is to last forever. All that athletic perfection needs is to remain forever at the point of maturity. God is a deathless man. And what else does the chief immortal do, in the minds of the commemorants, but appear always in his flourishing strength, himself his own conquest, satisfied with being, and absolutely reconciled with himself? Such are the Immortals. And this is no hollow idea. The athletic hero fills it out and gives it motion. Immortal, because in vitality and strength, the other idea, of fatigue, old age, and death, finds itself absolutely excluded. The only death present here is not an inward death, the death of the self. It is a foreign death, willed, and sought out; death at a fixed moment; death defied in single combat; death that can be conquered, and that the hero knows how to conquer. It is to die out of strength, not out of weakness. It is to die of an excess of life. The warrior cannot think of this sudden death as his own; he thinks of it as his opponent's; in himself and for himself he does not believe in it; let it fall upon his thoughts like a shadow, he marches over it, he crushes it under foot. Such is the morning of courage.

Chapter six

THE GODS OF HOMER

The gods are moments of man. This is not an abstract thought, it is written into the battles of the *Iliad* and the wanderings of Ulysses. Besides, once the gods have taken human form, how shall we recognize them if not by a grace of movement, a force, a glance, a word of advice, all the eminent signs of man? Or else in sudden impulses of hope, audacity, fear? Man looks about him or behind him for his friend, his ally, his enemy, whom such feelings or impulses ordinarily announce. Whether or not he finds them hardly matters, for man himself appears and disappears. The heat of battle, which drives everyone toward where the dust is thickest, carries men and the gods along pell-mell. These noonday visions are perfectly real. While theology, which is only a philosophy that lacks distance, can attempt to dissolve the new god into ancient nature and Jupiter into the immensity of the sky, poetry, adhering more closely to the actual movements of man, never ceases to vanquish the pantheistic monster, and to portray man simply as man, so naturally superhuman. For the miraculous is common experience in war, be it that the wounded enemy is lost in a mist; that courage and fear pass overhead like meteors; that the sword-strokes carry by a kind of guiding foresight; that one slip of the sword or bow announces others, which is only too true; that a friend protects us without our noticing it, or that a man is mysteriously separated from his friend as if by a curse. When the warrior flies off in pursuit of a phantom, it is only a loss of control, and perfectly natural; but the same event, the very same, is supernatural, as we have seen it with our own eyes. And the death of Patroclus, disarmed by Mars, stripped of his strength as of his armor, is precisely the death of an exhausted man. Man does not know himself. Though he knows that bread, meat, wine give him his dose of courage, never infinite, he does not really believe it. It is in the nature of courage, as of all passions, to look for other causes. Ajax says that a god urges him on; which means that he feels his hands and feet moving by themselves. And if, on the other hand, Jupiter today gives victory to the Trojans, it means that the Achaians' knees will not sustain them any longer. These metaphors are all true; their lines are firmly drawn; the scene is supernaturally what it would be physiologically. The Jupiter of Phidias is no more than a man; and it can even be said that he is greater than man only because he is perfectly human. Thus the battles in the *Iliad* are simply battles. Of course Achilles also fights with the Scamander, and that is more theological than religious; still it is true that the river fights back like a river in flash flood, which is something real. But the pure battle, the battle that is sought out and celebrated, is a human event, utterly human; all of its surprises and mysteries bear man's imprint. We must grasp this moment of human strength when, the monsters of nature being defeated and despised, the hero is the sole enemy worthy of man.

On the other hand, through the amassing of men, and the meditation of courage faced with itself, nature is returned to its own condition and is simply nature, as the Homeric similes express, revealing in a flash, and even in the thick of battle, this other truth which is no longer deformed by passions. Men are winnowed like wheat; but this chaff is simply chaff in the wind. Snow is ordinary snow in the image, and falls according to the law of things. The lion is simply a lion who leaps over the fence; his claws are simply claws. And the woodcutter on the mountain is simply a man who chops down trees, and is hungry. The shield of Achilles, in the most striking contrast to the fury of the man who carries it, shows us images of nature as it is, of labors, of marriages, of all that passes and returns and is repeated; here war itself is only plundering, another kind of harvest, as if the divine blacksmith had wished to inscribe on his work the truth that there are no gods. And that is just what the shield signifies, with its strength so precisely defined in layers of oxhide and sheet brass. Labor is everything and does everything. This is an eternal text, and the true mirror of man. But Achilles does not take the time to read it, nor does he give anyone else time to read it.

When the dust has settled, and the dead are burned, the idea that the hero is a god takes a strange turn. The human form seems closed in upon this great secret. The gods are everywhere. An unknown young man who gives directions, might be Mercury. A wise friend is Mentor, or Minerva. And, as Ulysses is hidden under a beggar's rags, it could just as easily be a god who shoulders his sack and begs from door to door. This prodigious warning, which is only wisdom, is the most beautiful fruit of heroic madness. For the hero always comes back to ordinary life; he eats, drinks, and sleeps. He is my human brother. And Ulysses, wrapped up and sleeping under the leaves, like a shepherd's fire, is Ulysses none the less. We must extend a credit of honor and hospitality to every shape of man; and the idea that any stranger may be a god in disguise, is among those that the future will not diminish. The Christian can say no better. Or rather, he ought to say better. Where there is only a man, there is god. Homer already makes this understood when he attributes human passions to the gods, and the petty stratagems of politics as well; to the point that sometimes, as in the case of the broken truce, the gods seem worse than man. In fact, the hero is also worse than man. And by that very fact, the god of Olympus is unmistakably human. This model is made for us, and within our range. Charity wins through, since even the gods have need of being loved and pardoned. The great idea of gods wandering the earth announces a new age, and thoughts less ruled by pride. The form of the athletic hero is already deposed; man recognizes himself by other, less brilliant signs, by signs that have to be interpreted and seen through. That is why I think that Chateaubriand went beyond the pagan sublime and even the Christian sublime, in what is perhaps the most beautiful passage in the *Martyrs*. To the Christian who has just given his coat to a beggar, the pagan, in his profound wisdom, says: "No doubt you took him for a god." "No," replies the Christian, "I took him for a man."

Chapter seven

CAESAR

Caesar is always preoccupied, even on campaign. He has made heroes in his own image; and, without considering courage, Caesar is well aware that a half dozen poltroons could easily cut him down. Caesar sleeps; he is confident; but in fact he is only confident halfway. He bargains with this force that is not himself, and that is never entirely in his hands. He makes believe. This device of the gods is their great weakness. To make believe is to stand apart from belief. And so he does not pay back the love he is given. His most valuable friends having descended to the level of means, he has no friends. All glory arises from equality and lives by equality; the suffrage of honor comes from the honor of suffrage. The peers always worry the king. He would prefer less liberal praises; would be less esteemed, perhaps even despised. From this point of view, the king is never just; he finds it necessary to underrate merit and to be fed on formal offerings; which is vanity, but turned toward very serious ends. This mixture occurs in every king. Majesty corrupts glory by a dissimulation that is part of the job. They think, but I know. It is thus that every king dismisses glory. And the face of the ingenuous hero is soon hidden behind an impenetrable secrecy; like the head of Medusa, petrified and petrifying. Besides, Caesar lives on the dead, and on the most beautiful of the dead. This turns friendship to ice. Even Agamemnon is no longer the mirror of Achilles; or he is a clouded mirror that does not return homage. Hence the detachment, the mysteriousness, the impenetrability of kings, which they pass on to the gods. This inhuman scrutiny makes certain only that it will not be scrutinized. Thus it awakens in those who are closest and most faithful a fear of offending which is a fear of being offended; a fear of examining which is a fear of doubting. This feeling makes for bold subjects, because all they have left is the consolation of obedience, in which they rival each other. But it also creates the desert that surrounds the principal tent. At bottom, power does not want to be loved the way men want to love it. The religion of power is therefore profoundly false and profoundly sad. Theologians cannot look at it without terror, for what they see is a series of evident but impossible propositions. "Whatever you offer to God, God offers to himself." We would like to believe that there is some metaphysical complexity here; but it is merely a device of intelligence to disguise the old lie with philosophy. No matter who the general is, we never offer him what he wants. And devotion, which is dishonored if it is not free, is offensive if it is not forced. Here all the dramas of military politics are gathered together, which history dresses up with incidents. Revolt is contained within obedience; it is in the weapon itself. It is imperative that the executant die. And because man, at this level of cult, has no other gods than his ancient kings, we understand the way Jupiter looks down on miserable mortals. It is not that he wants it that way, it is that men want it that way. Achilles destroys himself, and it is the enemy who will pay for it; the master waits. It is likely that the fury of men at war comes wholly from this expressionless god, who is worshiped as such.

Tiberius is worse than Caesar, and the court is worse than the camp, whose image it retains. The administration, which ranks and numbers men and things, allows intelligence to rise above strength, to rule by calculation. And the administrative official is even forbidden to commit suicide because of his valuable memory. The accountant thus stands higher than the fighting man, because he stands under him. The heroic world is turned upside down, and the most vile flatterer wins out over the honest soldier, or the so-called honest soldier, since every subaltern carries lies in his cartridge belt. Thus power is dishonored by an utter disregard for means. The royal guard is brutally efficient; and the Intelligence Service, as it is so accurately and terribly called in the British Empire, is false by the very nature of its work. We sense, in this life of empire, willfully blind as it is, that intelligence cannot join with power without maintaining a formidable silence toward others and within itself. The lying astrologer and the buffoon disguised by sincerity are the two friends of Tiberius, and Tiberius wants it known. Thus a mockery of order is established, but nobody laughs. It cannot be made into a god. But the sheer force of the Prince, eternally portrayed by Machiavelli, and always the same over the centuries, raises us little by little toward the Jewish contradiction, Job's dungheap and the sacrifice of Isaac, violent images of the play of arbitrary power.

In the Olympian compromise, the capriciousness of Jupiter is good natured, always moderated, according to agrarian commemoration, by the affections of his family and the quarreling of Juno. But destiny shows itself occasionally, as that necessity to be king which stands higher than the king himself. Likewise the father, in a real family, is often as hard and pitiless as the object-world; for he is the minister of the object-world; and if the harvest is meager, he must count out the rations. Ration is reason, and reason is not tender. But in the case of Jupiter, because of the mixture of the power of war with the power of industry, destiny is closer to the king, and stands in the shadow of his throne. It is there that he retrieves it, after he has let the immortal heroes have their play, after he has played himself, in human fashion, the game of feasting and loving. Destiny tugs at his sleeve, and reminds him that he is not on his throne to amuse himself. On the contrary, he is the slave of his own power. This blind force that he senses behind him, is force itself, whose law, though absolutely external, is the inner law of every king. The most ancient model of the law is an arbitrary decree, made by no one, but uttered, *fatum*, like a command. There is a god behind the highest god, as there is a king behind the king. This more than terrifying idea is nonetheless familiar, and always will be, as long as man gains power through Caesar and Caesar through man. For, by the rules of obedience, reason of State cannot be reason, and the word of the master cannot be retracted. The spirit fulfills the word, and it is therefore not by chance, but because of man's own structure, that the dialectic reigns over the humiliated spirit. The hero did not want this to happen.

Chapter eight

MERCURY

We always have to eat. All of the heroes and all of the kings in the world are supported and maintained in their dignity by work, by trade, by the double circulation of goods and money, by bankers, loan sharks, and misers. Tiberius is held by this rule as well as Caesar, and very firmly. To plunder is not to produce; it is, on the contrary, to reduce production to what is strictly necessary for the producer, and it is first of all to scare away provisions, which can be hidden more quickly and more effectively than men. Troops on the move are wise to pay their way; and war is always careful to keep its suppliers and furnishers out of the war. Thus another law is revealed, a law of strict integrity; for there is almost no exchange in which the establishment gives and receives at the same time, and the promissory note is what transports goods from one place to another. That is why the warrior stands watch over the market.

We all know that a price cannot be imposed. From this point of view every market is free. The refusal to buy, like the refusal to sell, is not only a way of stalling under pressure; these things must be openly translated, in terms of underbidding and overpricing. For the just price, endorsed by Caesar, is the price of the public market, and, without the just price, there will be no credit and no cash. The face of Caesar on the coin has more than one meaning. By it Caesar guarantees good faith; he resigns his own will to this metal that passes from hand to hand. The royal signature guarantees weights, but the scales are not far away. A precise poetry has invented the golden scales in which Jupiter weighs human destinies; weapons are placed on the pans, and heroes, and the gods. The symbol of the scales, the impartial judge, says more than Caesar would like; and yet it speaks for Caesar. It distributes among us a heavenly justice, which does not reign in heaven.

These contradictions would not exist among the gods if they were not first lodged in the least of our thoughts. At court everything depends on distributive justice, which creates merit and immediately corrupts it. Good and bad rewards are suddenly handed out, as if by chance, for power will have no rules, and it is too much like submitting to the flatterer to give him what he wants. Favor is everywhere along the avenues of the court, and is always inexplicable. This idea was carried over into the most sublime theology, and is the reason for the Jansenist's despair; for to trust in absolute power, or even in oneself, is clearly to usurp its prerogatives. Commerce falls under this strange law, and even brings it into play in leisure hours; for the principal power is reflected in lesser majesties, and vanity puts on airs at the counter; hence the misfortunes of Birotteau. But the other justice, commutative justice, is all the more clearly affirmed in this case. The opinion of the marketplace differs from the opinion of renown, and honor itself disappears before the balance of accounts, which never ceases to play in our thoughts.

There is an injustice burning at the heart of royal justice. There is an injustice concealed within the justice of the marketplace, since a promise rigorously kept is itself a trap. The two-way dealing of buyer and seller works only because of a two-way deception; for each of them always pretends that he has no need of the other. The buyer pretends to be poor, and the seller pretends to be rich; for the one disguises his low bidding, and the other disguises his high prices; as can be seen in the endless bargaining of the peasants, in contrast to the solemn and religious conclusion of the deal. There is the same strict integrity in Balzac's Gobseck. And this blend of guile and good faith is the reason why the blank face is the face that inspires confidence. But spendthrifts cannot understand this double virtue, which cheats them twice. It is a commonplace to say that commerce is theft; Gobseck himself laughs at the idea, for a good ploy is always a good ploy. Jupiter pays no attention to these things, he sends Mercury. This god, who is always plunging down from the sky, makes the connection between the governing spirit and the spirit of the laws. He is the god of things as they are. He is, properly seen, the enemy of catastrophes; he comes to save the lower order. Horace invited him to his modest celebrations: "Don't forget Mercury." His is also the name given to the shiny metal that slips through our fingers. And the wings on the god's feet are not the wings of victory, but rather the tireless motors of supply and demand. He is the busy spirit. He is the god who thinks of everything. Mythology has also thought of him.

You have all met him. He is the one whose thin black mantle floats over the funeral procession; it is he who dresses the heir in mourning, for a day. It is he who leads the shades away with his black wand; it is he who appeases them. The same god who will run to the marketplace tomorrow, the one who will ring the opening of the stock exchange; the god of closing and the final bid; the god who posts under his own name the just prices which are never just. Such is the ambiguous spirit who designs the strategy for a justice which Jupiter will finally underwrite. "Men," says the god of gods, "blame us for their misfortunes, when their misfortunes come from their own stupidity; nevertheless I will send Mercury down to advise them, though it will do no good." These beautiful images put our thoughts in place and rule over them first and always. For the spirit knows at all times that its well-aimed barbs cannot harm Jupiter, or Mercury, who are both only messengers. Power does not change, and the marketplace does not change. And the gods are made in man's image. For the attributes, divisions, and gradations of Olympus represent the invincible regulations under which man must accommodate himself and be resigned. And man's wariness of man is found even in hell. For Minos, Aeacus, and Rhadamanthus, the final arbiters, are former kings, but they have not been raised to the rank of gods. We ask justice of the gods, who never grant it; we do not ask justice of man, because we know that he will grant it. Plato accepted these popular images; he merely studied them, and was very careful not to alter them. Which means, you will notice, that he separates belief from knowledge, whereas an unenlightened criticism leads us from one belief to another. The famous allegory of the cave says all of this and more; for it is true that the shadows are deceptive, but it is also true that they are reflections of the truth, as the shadow of a tree projected against a wall brings together the truth of the tree, the truth of the wall, and the truth of the moon. Once you know that the gods are blameless, you will know everything.

Chapter nine

AESOP

The slave is a kind of animal. Somehow he must be forgotten; and what he thinks is of interest to no one. Otherwise everything would have to be changed. The gods of power and of order do not look down that far. If they did they would find their own negation, their precise negation. For, by an effect which the tyrant is always dimly aware of and which he avoids by means of his ministers of all degrees, divine power expires at the point at which consent is no longer an issue. No one tries to make a slave believe anything, except that what he believes does not matter. Force, become this explicit, negates itself. Animals are governed like slaves in agrarian existence, not without a kind of religion; but good sense warns us that the slave cannot be made a god; for we can invent a kind of animal thought; but the idea that a slave might be able to think, must be absolutely denied. This denial stands as an absence and a void in ancient thought, and also in all thought of empire; for slavery has its part at every level of such thought, but it is shameful and hidden. The slave is a naked man.

The greatest human fact is that the slave does think; and the Fable is his witness. This kind of thinking alone, because of the terrible pressure exerted on it from above, completely accepts its condition. We smile at the way the Fable makes animals talk and think, through a bold use of metaphor, which purposely cannot be believed, and so cannot offend. For animals do not talk, and men are not animals. Everything being false, the truth can show itself. There is more than one reason for fictions, as we have already explained. But this essential form of fiction is well explained by the fact that, under the rule of power, which never relaxes, no truth can be told. No doubt the law of the comic actor is that he must make himself unbelievable; and the most ancient comedies had to be absolutely unbelievable. Not that the king himself, if he hears the fable, does not have the right to see himself in it; but that is his prerogative; the fabulist, very ingeniously, maintains his theater of animals, and avoids instructing others. Even the moral is reassuring, because it applies to man, but with everything changed. It is no more than a comparison, whereas the truth of the fable is in the terrible image; there is no need to soften or transpose anything. The very fiction of talking animals expresses the play of force as it would be but for hypocrisy, and therefore simply as it is, for hypocrisy is a cover, but it changes nothing. And this itself is the slave's discovery, which only the slave could make. However little the rest of us may profit from the existing order, we still do not expose it.

Here, then, is the contrary of epic poetry, and the negation of all greatness, which is perfect atheism. No one is surprised that the lion is the strongest and takes all shares for himself; we see the play of his claws and everything is said. Each living thing does exactly what it can; the fable of the Fox and the Cat carries the idea to its limit. The cat climbs a tree, which the fox cannot do. All of the resources of wisdom go into measuring the length of a paw; the idea that the paw may not be able to do what it needs to do, is never presented. The system which is called historical materialism does not go that far, even in Hobbes, for whom the gods and fidelity are finally more useful than naked force. This idea itself, celebrated since under the name of Pragmatism, is a useful lie, but only if we bring it into play without believing in it. It is absolutely false to say that it is in the watchman's best interest to get himself killed for his master's sake. It is absolutely false to say that the intoxication of power leads men to die for Sparta or Rome. There is something else, as Socrates would say. There is what the spirit owes to itself, and an inward dishonor in using certain means. Here the true religion appears, the religion that is always denied. There is perhaps not a single person who believes in Plato. Why? It is not virtue that is frightening so much as the insurmountable notion of the free spirit. It has been necessary to invent a new supreme master for the free spirit, more pre-established truths and insoluble contradictions, in short, our irritating theology. It is nevertheless evident, in materialism itself, that its system would not exist if the spirit were not free; for materialism presupposes a method and an order which things as they are do not dictate, and which they even contradict. And materialism is forced to deny the revolt of the spirit, which is nevertheless its soul. The system of Lucretius denies Lucretius, and denies itself. Such is the inconvenience of being human. It is this that the fable conceals by piling up its brief dramas, in which the very idea of human likeness is constantly denied. Man looks and does not see himself. It is the very contrary of anthropomorphism. And, as anthropomorphism is everywhere, so the fable is everywhere. In the first, the spirit appears to itself and terrifies itself. In the second, the spirit rigorously crosses itself out, with strong and perfectly unmysterious lines. Even the moral is not of the spirit, inasmuch as it applies to man the simple law of animal life; we intend to judge, but we do not judge. We might go as far as to say that the spirit tests its freedom without wishing to engage it; which is to dismiss reflection. This device has opened the way for consistent materialism. We must admit that fables retain a friendship for the weak and a sense of mutual aid; but here again the idea of human likeness is avoided. The familiar title—crow, gazelle, tortoise, rat—is in itself destructive. There remain *The Two Pigeons* and *The Two Friends*, two oases of thought. Each soul saves itself as best it can, and there is no absolute slave. But the least amount of power excludes friendship. This severe and desertlike view shows well enough that power is not a god; and it shows more; it shows that power was never a god. It is a great moment, and eternal in each of us, when we deny justice absolutely. But, like every other idea, this idea gets lost in the image; thus absence is truer than presence. And the spirit stands behind man, always behind him, casting shadows and shadows of shadows, never anything more. Hegel drew great and forceful ideas from the opposition between master and slave. And it is true, as he said, that the slave forms out of necessity the rarest virtues and the most exact notions, whereas the master, by his very situation, loses virtue and loses the spirit. This, according to Hegel, is the mainspring of history, which, because dethronement is inevitable, is a continual revolution. But there will always be more to say; for, in the least of our thoughts, some master is always overthrown and stripped of his power. There is no man who does not doubt what he is certain of; that is the very notion of certainty. But that is also philosophy. The difficulty, in the present study, and especially in what will follow, is to see how, from fable to fable, the very notion of the spirit is formed without fault, by the gestures of man, which cast the most beautiful shadows.

Chapter ten

Spirit

The spirit loves mockery. Common speech, which never deceives us, throws this lively warning in our faces. Around and within power the spirit floats and plays. It is always self-sufficient. Laughter unties the knot; we are content enough not to be hanged on the spot. For we would be hanged in our own very serious devices; and gravity will always be the best symbol of force, just as anguish is the most common effect of government service. The spirit liberates us for a moment; it is better than prophecy. The spirit is friend and savior, now and always. Voltaire lived a long time. Find a better way if you can. I have to breathe while I'm waiting. I have to stay limber. We realize, of course, that laughter is the effect of seriousness. A physiological reaction, a release of tension; and something more. Animals know the brusque movement that brings a change of humor; a mere nothing can turn their heads. It is man's nature to cultivate and extend this sense of freedom. To be free in oneself, to be free of oneself, is the first object of reflection, and this object is laughter. The spirit adopts it, tries it out, becomes sure of it. Sometimes a serious prospect is enough to make us laugh. Which explains why extreme logic is ridiculous. We need merely arrange things in words, as the spirit would shape them without the shock of experience. Catastrophe, when it only touches ideas, makes us laugh; like a man whose chair suddenly collapses in the middle of a serious argument. But this kind of laughter is a bit too involuntary. It is better if the spirit senses its own strength in an inner catastrophe. The unforeseen, in its particular form, and because of its particular form, is the real prize. What we call wit always approaches a pure construction of the mind. Like the famous twin in Mark Twain, who describes how his twin brother was drowned in the bathtub: "Only I'm not sure whether it was him or me." The threat of seriousness is very clear here. It always is more or less. Kant cites the example of a man struck down by misfortune: "His wig turned white overnight." And there is the saying that Chamfort made up for the dark-minded Champcenetz: "He is building dungeons in Spain." That is why the spirit has great potential.

What potential? Basically this: that the power to demolish ideas confirms the power to create them. There is something ridiculous about an infinite number that is exactly twice an infinite number: as Cantor said of infinite pairs of boots, there are certainly twice as many boots as there are pairs. But laughter is also quite necessary in these attempts at pure equilibrium, and Plato knew it. He knew enough to laugh even on the verge of the most serious discovery. Thus, in the *Republic*, when justice has been flushed out by the definitions of the three other virtues, but no one has noticed it, Socrates, master of the hunt, cries: "Halloo! Halloo!" This device is rarely understood, perhaps for lack of seriousness. A device against infatuation, which always lies in wait for man; a device of the self against the self: Do not mistake conceit for wisdom. Never has a more expressive mimesis given us so strong a sense of how the spirit must remain master, and catch itself on the verge of its own impetuosity. This is what Plato always does, avoiding the eternal error that worships the creations of the mind as if they were gods. There stands fanaticism, drunk with its own proofs; and wit is directly opposed to fanaticism. That is why, among the heroes of the spirit, we must always include Voltaire, even though he refuses the honor, and precisely because he refuses it. The spirit is nothing, says the spirit. With each flash of wit, a system dies; a system completed and demolished in a single movement. A breath is all it takes; you would have tried using your muscles. This combat in the sky, this combat which we must call preliminary, and which must always be so, is revealed here, where it belongs, in the moment when the captivating gods risk death. Polyeucte smashed the ancient gods; that is his way of believing; he is afraid that he may not be strong enough; and it is this fear, in every action, that makes us swing wide.

We have misjudged the skeptic; we will always misjudge him. Montaigne is often misunderstood, in his very serious undertaking in which he knows that seriousness would lose everything. One enormous chapter, which is pure exercise, weighs down all of the others; and that is absurd, because it ought, on the contrary, to air them out. For Montaigne himself there is no doubt; or rather all doubt should be taken as a tool to carve out the truth, to mount it in gold, as he does in all of his judgments, on eloquence, courage, fear, obedience, custom, law, war, and peace, which are firm in their refusal to be trapped. In this underground labor, the tunnel never caves in on the miner. "What is more serious than an ass?" And the famous discourse of the theological goose (for, says the goose, isn't it obvious that this universe was created for geese?) is one of those irrefutable transformations that reveal our own mechanical thinking. The absurd saves reason, by throwing it out of the circle of its own productions, and by its explosive surprise. We must cite once more the most beautiful and disturbing story in Montaigne, about the son who has become head of the family and drags his father around by the hair; the father says nothing, until they reach a certain corner of the house, when he cries out: "Stop, my son! for I only dragged my father this far." We do not easily recover from a shock like that; it gives us a gigantic view of what the iron law would be, if reason were nothing but reason. After which we must cite, again from Montaigne, the fable, or whatever you would call it, of the wooden bowl, a more discreet story but one that partakes of the same wild gaiety. A child is making a little wooden bowl like the one his grandfather takes his soup in. His father asks him who he is making it for, and the boy replies: "It is for you." No order can stand against this way of describing. But I want to end on a lighter note. "Sweet sister grass," says Voltaire, "look! A frightful monster is coming who will eat us both in one gulp! Men call this monster a sheep." Systems and professors fall down in confusion. *Candide* is a profound book because it demolishes everything. The famous banquet of the kings takes its greatness from its dismissal of all greatness. Pangloss reasons well; he is irrefutable, and we laugh at him. And Senator Pococurante has such fine taste that he no longer likes anything. "I will describe the landscape," says Guillot the dreamer in *Liluli*. "But you're not looking at it!" says Polichinelle. "I see. . . , I see. . . ." "With your eyes on the ground?" "I see further, I see higher, I see the summit, the light." O Poetry! The gods depart; and with them depart the Furies.

BOOK IV

CHRISTOPHORUS

Chapter one

SPIRIT

The religion of the spirit has issued from a thousand sources. Never as a step by step construction; that would be philosophy; and not without risk, as we have already seen. But rather by means of new, moving, triumphant metaphors, which are, if we look closely, as old as the spirit itself. The gods always go together. And as the whole of paganism carried the spirit within it, so the spirit, loosed in lightning flashes, burns into the tree it strikes; and the marks of this lightning have brought more than one ancient sanctuary, spring, or altar back into veneration. Sacrifice and power, Jupiter and Pan are always with us. But from now on power is subordinate, like the eagle at Jupiter's side; nothing stands with it. Far from power, at the crossroads, we see a man executed on a wooden cross. I do not think that this fabric of images can be unraveled, or even that we should make the attempt, unless we first have some idea of the difficulties and contradictions that the notion of the spirit brings with it, often to the despair of those who have tried to form it. Let us take the spirit seriously, then, for a sort of review of its immediate data, if we can speak that way of what is neither given nor created, in a word, of the eternally absent.

The first and supreme paradox is that the spirit does not exist. We have strict methods for getting hold of what exists. The nets we use are ideas, and they are thrown out into experience, which, according to common sense, alone decides, provided that we question it properly. Once everything is prepared and the traps are set, using ideas and instruments copied from ideas, the watchful eye will be able to say if the star disappears behind the moon, and when; if the comet is moving, and how much, and in relation to what; if the tide, marked on a movable scale, rises higher today than it did yesterday. There is no arguing with this method. Yet these means have never located the spirit anywhere, either outside of man or within him, either in the living man or in the departure of the dead, either in the mouths of oracles or in the sanctuaries of healing. What they find are only wounds and scars, moving objects and moved objects, the transformations of an invariable energy, a sleight-of-hand trick. The miracles of true faith and the miracles of half-faith, and the juggler's game, have all been overturned and spread out on the table. And it has been proved a hundred times over that without food the hero will be unable to lift a finger. The spirit does nothing, and the spirit is nothing.

I think. Granted that this power changes nothing in the spectacle of the world, the power as such is immense. Knowledge is not a fact, since knowledge gathers facts. Perception does not exist in a place or in a body, since perception represents places and bodies to us. A place itself is nothing but a relationship; a thing is neither near or far. Time is nothing; for what is past is nothing once it is past, and what remains is absolutely and always present. Even the consciousness of these relationships, which are nothing, runs into every conceivable difficulty; for merely conceiving of them, we give them the same kind of nonbeing that is common to all of our ideas; and the very power of deceiving ourselves with the nothingness of forms is nevertheless something. I come back to myself, and then it seems to me that my self goes the way of all phantoms; I find nothing but my own voice:

> Amère, sombre et sonore citerne
> Sonnant dans l'âme un creux toujours future.*

In the soul? What is this within if not a without? We are thrown back again into things as they are, as they are under relationships which are not.

* Bitter, dark, echoing cistern, sounding
  An always future hollow in the soul.
                                        —Valéry, La Cimetière marin.

The spirit leaps ahead all the same, and never ceases to move through the full expanse of existing things, high, low, to the limits and beyond, through the small and the great, subdividing as easily as it multiplies; of which property numbers are the sacred symbol; for it is no more difficult to subdivide the smallest number than it is to go beyond the largest, to add to it, or to take it, whichever it may be, as a unit. Whatever the limits are, we find the spirit on the other side as well as on this side. To say that the spirit cannot occupy one body, since it knows other bodies, is not enough. The spirit is neither within nor without; it is the all in all. Beyond the known, it conceives of region after region; it is the whole of the possible; and where it may deny itself, it still is; it is present at its own death. However far being is extended, the spirit is greater; which is not to say only that it exceeds the limits; the very idea of a limit to the spirit is absurd, for the limit, once conceived, has two sides; the spirit exceeds everything in advance. When we say that it does not exist, we mean that it is more than existence. This simple description goes beyond all the hyperboles of theology.

The highest paradox, finally, is that the spirit is one and indivisible. If the unity between here and there were broken, there would be no more here and there. The universe is one, but in advance, because two separate universes are actually one, since we can think of them as two. Because the universe can do nothing about it, it is not the universe that is one. Spinoza, perhaps the only man to have conceived of the spirit, astonishes his disciples with the observation that extension is indivisible; and in effect, extension cannot lapse between two extensions; and this again is an image of unity. But he alone also has conceived of unity as we all think of it. For just as two spaces are always portions of a single space, so two spirits are actually one; the all in all is identical with itself; for if it contains many, it contains them in itself. The one need not gather its forces, for it can only gather them into itself, which is always presupposed. All possible forms of mysticism come together here; accept it as you will. It must be realized that there can be no explanations or proofs of this unity. No explanations, because the separation and reassembling of parts occur within the unity of the spirit, which therefore can never itself be assembled or broken down. No proofs, because all proof, even the skeptic's, presupposes the universal spirit. Those who glimpsed these things, without disentangling them from apparitions and powers, shaped out of metaphors the sublime, violent, and fanatical religion of the spirit, which at the same time fulfills and destroys them all, and which threatens, with each of its prayers, to destroy itself. This passionate nihilism is hardly gentle. The Furies pursue rare and atrocious crimes. According to the religion of the spirit, the crime of crimes is error. Lamartine tells of meeting a powerful Mohammedan chieftain, who was, he says, a polished and nobly hospitable man. Yet if anyone had doubted the absolute unity of God in his presence, merely in conversation, that person would have paid instantly with his life for this slight deviation of spirit. The fires of our modern inquisition shed their troubled light everywhere.

Chapter two

THE PEOPLE OF THE SPIRIT

Hegel gave this name to the Jewish people, and it is not an overstatement. The Bible is a terrifying book; but it is *the Book*. In the beginning there is nothing, and the spirit creates the way the mind thinks. Light first, and the rest as if by a subdivision of light. The sublime stands in this first act, as Longinus has said. Man cannot repeat it. Man is reduced to almost nothing; and his thoughts are reduced to almost nothing, except when that very condition is what he celebrates and sings. The spirit is straitened, if we can say that, in its metaphysical dimensions. Everything is decreed. Everything is foretold. Of course, ceremonies and sacrifices are carried out as they always were; but the entire cult is marked by unworthiness and inadequacy. Idolatry knows that it is false. The psalm alone finds grace, by its ritual killing of thought. The false gods are sacrificed; metaphors are sacrificed; what remains is the emptiness of the desert and a formidable, all-pervasive absence. In the face of which the only virtue is obedience, and all errors are equal. The only crime is to forget that man is nothing in the eyes of the Eternal. This view explains a kind of forgiveness and a kind of strictness which man cannot understand, but which nevertheless ring true, because every value is of the spirit. Since the finite spirit is inadequate, it must humble itself before the true greatness that is the measure of its own inadequacy. Reproached by his piety, man realizes, of course, that it is a great crime to be ignorant of the true god; but he realizes much more; he realizes that it is an even greater crime to belong to the people of God, for it is beyond his ability. We see what it means for a people to have to drag the Bible behind them. And along with the Bible, such contempt for mankind, and such contempt for themselves,

149

the pride of being nothing, and the essential irony of Job, who knows that he did not deserve punishment, but that his punishment is just. This spirit, which is always in the wrong, is in a sense indifferent to all wrongs, and devoid of hope, so much so that labor, pleasure, and suffering serve equally for passing the time. The Jew labors in the same way as he laments his fate; and this kind of purposeless attention often turns out to be more effective than the ambitious desire to rule.

All religions exist together, because all of man's parts exist together. "The heavens resound with the glory of God." Thus nature is degraded, as an arbitrary and incomprehensible creation; but at the same time nature is exalted, because everything is divine in the sense that everything is a symbol of God; which means that all things are raised to the level of metaphors, as a clothing of external and reflected beauty. This is a religion of gestures, entirely magical, but with no trace of magic. When the warrior-king raises his arms, his soldiers are victorious; if he lowers them, his soldiers are defeated. He gets tired; but two younger men hold up his arms, and the victory is won. This is an example of what Montaigne meant by "stories that do not say a word." This gesture imitates creation. It is the idolaters who turn gestures into acts. Madness in action, greatness in signification. Here is the role of materialism, carefully preserved by the very excessiveness of piety. Thinking could not exist without meaning; but that is not saying enough. A man's innermost thought is too miserably far from God ever to deserve expression; instead he must express God's thought, as the stars do; very poorly, of course, because man is small; but at least in harmony with this great theater; and therefore with an emphasis on humility, and naturally with a sort of dance to nature's rhythms, not to the movements of thought. Which would seem to be agrarian, but is really a sort of despair of expressing inexpressible greatness and inexpressible unity. It is a tragic poetry that is entirely external, itself sacrificed in vain images. A well-known theatrical aptitude, characteristic of metaphysical vanity. Ecclesiastes is the last word for the actor. Imitation in itself is simply a form of prayer; frenzy, despair, damnation are humbled in their own images, and the sin of feeling is punished with convulsions. Which is why convulsions are noble. Each image is therefore intended to express its opposite; and that is the soul of metaphor, because metaphor immediately denies itself, whereas the simile is developed at length. We must not confuse the biblical feeling for nature with purely agrarian feeling, nor the prophet Isaiah with the Delphic oracle. The imagination, in its pantheistic stage, seeks another nature behind nature, and the great secret in the convulsion itself; whereas the imagination of Israel knows itself to be cursed and impure in the eyes of the Eternal. Thus nature is handed over to God, under the reign of the pure Spirit.

Religion of the second degree, which is political, has never passed into metaphors. And it seems to me that the attribute of power, delegated to the pure spirit in a moment of abandon, must be taken as the shameful part of the religion of the spirit. I would pursue this essential error in the very efforts that the highest religion has never ceased to make to be free of it. Here the doctrine of grace and the image of the one whom Claudel called the scandalous victim, shine like beacons. In the Old Testament there is no grace. The spirit is an absolute tyrant. That is its way of existing. The spirit in its decrees is worse than the object-world; in the object-world there is always thing against thing and tyrant against tyrant; but with the spirit alone there is no recourse and no succor. Theology remains perfectly coherent, as long as the Perfect alone inspires it. For God cannot change. The fleshly tyrant is obstinate, and that pleases the courtiers, the royal guard, and all of us, as an image of our own sweet passions. The pure spirit is not obstinate, it simply *is*. It exists in the world only in the form of decrees. Thus everything is declared good in advance. Doubt is a sin, but is overcome in prayer. "Not for us the glory, not for us, but in Thy name." Thy will be done, thy bitter will. . . .

This vision of the spirit has not killed the spirit. The first school of intelligence is necessity, not when it is suffered, but when it is conceived as inevitable, as it would be in the infinite mind of God. We know besides that such necessity, rightly called absolute, is beyond our control, by common consent. But our mental sequences and well-ordered arrangements are, like numbers, a sort of image of God thinking. A biblical turn of mind will note the irony in our basic agreements with ourselves; at the same time, this exercise of agreeing without believing is a kind of intelligence that it is permissible to follow, provided that it is held in disdain. And the biblical mind, instructed in this game anyway by its own transactions, which are also orders from God, maintains a surprising advance over other, more rustic ways of thinking, which are still involved in being just and in usurping God's powers. The intellect is Jewish, and makes use of its theatrical gifts in abstract ways, playing upon the appearances of reason, to the great amazement of the peasants when they come to town for the fair. If there is a trace of criticism in these words, it must disappear in the presence of Spinoza, the most rigorous and steadfast of master-thinkers, and the model of the free man, even though he re-ties the threads of the Eternal. Having done justice to the philosopher, and perhaps to all philosophers, we must come back to religion, that story which does not say a word.

Chapter three

METAPHOR

Metaphor is essential to the religion of the spirit, because all degrees of religion exist at once, and the dignity of the spirit can only be preserved if it maintains images at the level of appearance. This is the meaning of poetic figures, and it is in effect a prophetic meaning, for poetic figures never cease to foretell another order and a new arrival. But, taken more humanly, metaphors also have the power to move the whole man, and to lead even the human body onto the ways of truth. If we have some understanding of this union of soul and body, we will be less surprised to see that poetry was always the first form of thought, and that it still is. A passion for clear reasoning leads to the forgetting of real conditions. But dance and music, by subordinating the dangerous art of speech, will always recall man to himself. *La Jeune Parque* is still the best introduction to psychology. But I will use cruder and more forceful examples; for it is well known that *La Jeune Parque* forces nothing.

In the Bible there is a story of how the trees set out to look for a king. They offered the kingship to each of the useful trees, the apple, the plum, the olive. And each of them gave the same reply: "Why should I be king of the trees?" At last they came to the thornbush, who replied: "Be king of the trees? Of course! But watch out!" We see immediately that this story is totally unbelievable, and that that is exactly why it delights us, for we expect something else; in fact, though it is only a fable, out of it, as out of the clouds, comes the flashing spirit of the Bible. But struck by this lightning, we are stupefied for a moment. For we are left holding a savage truth in our hands, a truth as piercing as the thorns on the thornbush. And, by refusing it at first, we will come to understand it fully. This the intellect alone would not dare to do; the intellect is in no hurry to reach such conclusions, and when it does finally reach them, it is exhausted with proofs, and comforted besides by the welcome suspicion that it may have overlooked something. The intellect is less strict than the spirit. The spirit, which is the final judge, does not exhaust us with arguments, it simply forces us to look. Why should a wise man want to rule? Not only does he have no need to, he also would not know how; or to put it a better way, it is not wisdom that would lead him to rule or teach him how. On the contrary, it is always the evil side of man that seeks power and that knows how to use it. This thought, once it is uttered, pierces through all tyrants and reaches God. But wait, the story was about trees, and it can hardly be true. It is thus that the truth of truth leaves its innocent trail and enables us to follow through an insupportable thought. This is active doubt; this is the beautiful beginning of the spirit; for it needs to be reassured about the truth itself. This Cartesian device is deeply hidden. We see how metaphor gives air and space for thought.

The Fox and the Crow, the celebrated fable, is no more open to exegesis. We do not ask if animals once talked like men. We do not ask if a crow can hold a cheese in its beak. These are not childish mistakes. We look for something else. And what do we find? An utterly mechanical description of passions, a description that overtakes them from below. Sterne writes that one evening out of boredom he paid three outlandish and reckless compliments to an ugly woman, a general, and a poet, just to see what would happen. That evening, he says, I made three friends that I will never be able to get rid of. We laugh at this story, but we do not believe it. Thought will never really understand the effects of flattery. If we had our eyes on the crow's beak, looking at these three well-dressed vanities, we would have seen the cheese fall. The fox perceives a beak that has to be opened; he talks about singing, he asks for a song; the beak opens, and the cheese falls according to the law of gravity; the crow thinks a moment later, a moment too late. Here passions are portrayed as Descartes would have had them portrayed; the mechanical animal is in effect one of the keys to man; and success in all kinds of negotiation is always due to causes that are simpler than we would think, expensive cars, comfortable chairs, proprieties, and open hands. A man holding a cup of tea cannot make a fist; he must think of other things. This idea is violent, I admit, and hardly believable. Animal cynicism, which is entirely dependent upon form and movement, is more instructive for us than proofs, the better if we are not on the defensive, because the story makes no claim to be true. We must notice that abstract thought is never accepted unless it is in tune with the passions, or else indifferent to all passions; and Leibniz says that a geometer who found geometry insulting to his vanity would easily reject all proofs. He had seen it happen.

These examples, which I have chosen for their simplicity, bring us very close to the great subject of revelation, and even push us into it. For we have a great many true ideas that we do not believe; they do not take us by the body, they do not touch us. But come an occasion, an object, a situation, something that we see before us and that we would not think of denying, and we may find ourselves transfixed by a familiar idea that was quite inoffensive before. These feints, which are not always welcome, find entry to us at a sensitive and unguarded point. It is thus that an event, an example, an image, sustain argument, and, by giving it color, resonance, solidity, finally make us certain with our whole being of what we would accept, reject, or ignore with our intellect alone. It is thus that a very real fear brings us face to face with the god of the woods and valleys, a confused but powerful idea, to which we must accommodate ourselves as we can; for our actions go on ahead of us. This is no longer simply to have an idea, it is to find ourselves in the process of forming it, and under the obligation to overcome it. It is thus that the imagination engages us, by the shock of surprise, of beauty, of sublimity; and the idea that everything must be preserved, even the thornbush, is religion exactly. Outside of these tragic problems, which will not wait, which take us by the throat, it must be admitted that we think easily and lightly, about anything at all. Every religion is revealed.

Chapter four

THE FIG TREE

The modern error, which occupies something like four thousand volumes, is the attempt to find out if religion actually was revealed, and where and when, and by what evidence we know it. It seems, according to an inverted piety, which is in fact impiety, that the revealed idea will be true only insofar as it can be established that the precise circumstances under which it was revealed were real, and exactly as they have been reported. This proof cannot be produced, because every proof of existence is a proof of experience, and there can be no experience of the past. But there is more to be said. No one asks if the trees really went in search of a king; no one asks if the fox really spoke to the crow. It is a question of a fresh understanding of the idea that lives in the story. If we learn from the story, then it is true in the way that stories can be true. Whether or not I know that Homer existed, it does not alter the beauties of the *Iliad*, or what knowledge of the gods and of himself a man can draw from the poem. Jesus denounced the Pharisee; I recognize myself in that image; I judge myself; this manner of speaking is driven into me, it pierces me like an arrow. I hope to escape by first examining the problem of whether or not Jesus really said that, telling myself that if Jesus never lived, what he said might well be false. This is a delaying tactic. It is a diversion whose purpose may be to make religion inoffensive, I mean for those who practice it. Our beliefs are rarely based on evidence; the mind is simply bemused by this kind of criticism. But the whited sepulcher is something real, and so is Pharisaism; what matters is not whether these things are true but how they are true. And if Jesus taught that one cannot have royal power, through armies and money, and at the same time save one's soul, what needs to be examined is not whether Jesus said this on such and such a day, but whether what he said is true. It is very true that we must believe, that we must start from belief, and hold to it, and always return to it; it is very true also that we must think about what we believe; that is what thought is. Comte often meditated on a particular sentence from the *Imitation:* "Intelligence must follow faith, never precede it, and never break with it." This maxim, which the reader is already prepared to accept, instead of being scared off by it, will become clearer if we examine the well-known parable of the barren fig tree.

Jesus hungered, and he came upon a fig tree in the way; but there were no figs on it; it was not the season for figs. Thereupon he cursed the tree, and it withered and died. This is unacceptable; and our exegete immediately tries to find out what witless copyist or misformed letters might be responsible for the remark that it was not the season for figs. But repeated experience has taught me never to change a text before I have tried seriously to understand it. For this difficulty disturbs me, and from what disturbs me I have often drawn great and important ideas, which my slack and abstract thought might otherwise have overlooked. And this, I claim, is a pious attitude, pious in the true sense; not because I promise to accept the absurd, but because I attempt to overcome the appearance of absurdity, which I obviously cannot do if I correct it first. My method proved sound in this case. For I told myself that, if it was not the season for figs, then it is also not a question of the fig tree, but of myself and my human brothers. I immediately started looking for human fig trees, and I did not have to look far. Not long ago a man said, speaking of the war, that that was not the season for figs, that is, for justice and truth, but that the season had now come. And others say, more simply, that the office is closed, that the unfortunate person will have to come back tomorrow; or, better still, that there are no funds available. To all of this there is no reply, for it is external necessity that commands, or, if we look closely, the order of power, the order of Caesar, which always invokes and always will invoke necessity against justice.

Not right now, I haven't got time, circumstances are stronger than you and I. Let us wait for the season for figs, that is, for sunlight and water. These people excuse themselves as the innocent fig tree might have done. And in a flash the curse comes over me. Is it not always because of circumstances that we put off repaying a debt? And it is by circumstances that the unfortunate Jean Valjean tries to prove to himself that he need not go to Arras to give himself up and save Champmathieu. But, says the Lord, are you fig trees, who receive everything from outside, and produce only under the right conditions? Or are you men, who know yourselves and even will yourselves to be free to distribute the reserves of your being as your own spirit dictates? Who renounces this privilege? Pilate, the great prefect, renounces it; his spirit washes its hands like the fig tree. Would he renounce it absolutely, expressly? I don't know. But I call him Lord who violently reminds us that the principal crime, perhaps the only crime, is to renounce in oneself the condition of being human. This Lord is demanding; Jean Valjean listens to him, and follows him, without asking if this Lord who is right was born before or after some other man, or if he was born at all. For it is easy to say that we could all live like administrative fig trees, always acting by the calendar and according to the edict of things, or of Caesar, and that this kind of life might even be pleasant, were it not for Jesus. What Jesus has said cannot be taken back; what has once been revealed cannot be withdrawn.

Turning this idea over and over in my mind, I realize that Jupiter is now replaced by another power, which is not only powerless, which not only refuses power, but which holds all power in judgment; that while it preserves power, rendering the pittance unto Caesar, it judges power and refuses it the highest value. And the fact is that political, or military, power is not really superior in value to the power of nature; for, *de facto*, power is power; and Rousseau was right, a robber's pistols are also a power. Should we respect them? This idea, from the *Social Contract*, is absolutely revolutionary, but it surprises us without enlightening us. It is not certain that Rousseau himself did not grant too much to external necessity;

for this necessity will never make it right to lie publicly or consciously, or to kill the innocent, or to refuse to pay for work done. If this becomes a subject of dispute, we will no longer see anything. I prefer the fig tree, in its solitude, far from Caesar and from this necessity that is handled like a weapon, and which forces me, and my thought, continually onto the field of battle. I am quite certain that the order of conscience, in Jean Valjean, did not force him like that; for, far from telling him not to think for himself, alone and without advice, it enjoined him to do so; enjoined him without forcing him, like the priest in *L'Otage* who tells the unfortunate Sygne: "It is for you, for you alone, to know your obligation. God himself does not ask this sacrifice of you; he simply waits. And if you decide that you are not obliged to do it, I will absolve you in the name of God." Thus the Christian revolution presents us with the pure idea of Free thought, which is often unaware of its origins, and which, furthermore, has yet to be measured in its fullness. But I admit once again that, all religions being together, Christianity has never entirely cleansed itself of power. That it has wanted to and still wants to, is obscure according to theology, but clear and almost blinding in its images. Consider for a long time the cross at the crossroads. That is what I call prayer. And, to finish with this subject, I will say that it is very important that a religion be idolatrous. Expressed in pure ideas, it is no longer religion, and it is not much of anything.

Chapter five

THE DEVIL

The Satyr is always ready to leap out from behind
a tree. It is possible, at any moment, that a tree stump, shaped
like a deer, is watching us. All things flee, appear, and hide as
we move. Noises bounce; echoes answer us. Like a bridge
spanning a river, the rainbow hovers over the flat earth. The
arched entrance to the city, the gateway of armies, is more
massive; we can touch it. We can pass through it; the push of
air under the arch sets us moving. Power is beautiful, the
athlete is beautiful, Caesar is beautiful. It is beautiful to die
for Caesar. False glory seduces us, but true glory is even more
seductive. Deceived at first by vanity, we save ourselves through
real power, which means instant death for anyone who resists.
We are lost in reality, which lies in wait for us as we come out
of our dreams. And if a man takes stock of things as they are,
how can we reproach him? Life comes first. I am a man of
the possible. It is not easy to govern; it is not easy to be
governed. To earn a living is not easy, and, as Proudhon said,
"A man of high position has one real thought—his salary."
Here is a scoundrel who ought to be despised, but he is one
of the prince's favorites; my last request, so obviously just,
depends on him. Cashiers and brokers must also be respected.
I walk on hot coals. We must tolerate evil to do a small amount
of good. Everything pulls at my sleeve. Ah! The devil! The
devil!

This interjection is as eloquent to the ear as the most perfect music. Ah! The devil! I almost forgot things as they are,
I almost forgot the way the world goes. Ah! The devil! I almost forgot that I need Caesar, that I need everyone. Ah! The
devil! My schedule is full of important things that are not
important at all, and that cannot be put off. The devil, as the

word says, is oblique power; a hare leaping across your path, or better still, a prince leaping across your path. The devil is an ambush; he is necessity as it reappears to the spirit. Mephistopheles is very smart; he thinks of everything; what a great politician he would make! There is an admirable development in *Faust*; the ideas in it ripen like fruit. Draw the line of descent from the little spaniel to the financier; it is always the same devil. He is fantastic in the beginning; but the older he gets, the more he resembles the incontestable. We must give way to the spaniel in human form. "That's how it is." Three times, before the cock crows . . .

This devil of a thousand shapes is born of the highest religion; he follows it like a shadow. For what can be done with the vegetal and animal gods who hold us by the belly? And what can be done with the crowned gods who hold us by the breast? They are all both real and deceptive. They are appearances, but true appearances. The worst is the one that proves truest, for a man really can become a king. The devil carries Jesus away to the mountain top and shows him all the powers of the valley, the woods, the fields, the cities, that are there for the taking. It is still to be a goat, but a goat with a golden hat and belt. All of this is temptation, and vice never goes unrewarded. Oh, unhappy mankind! as Plato already said. They will make the wrong choice. Everything deceives them. Who would not want to be powerful in order to help his friends? This voice which alerts us to our proper being and to the slavery we are about to throw ourselves into, has rarely been heeded. The devil, that goat, is more convincing, with his disguises, his sudden appearances, his prodigies; with the facility he procures for us to move like lightning, to take, to transform, to bestow, to rule. The child learns, before all else, that there is nothing that cannot be had for the right argument. And, on the contrary, the way of justice and labor is long. The devil! The devil!

In this diabolical mixture of falsehood and truth, of truth that is never true and falsehood that is never quite false, I recognize a perfect idea, in which all of the lower gods, the gods of nature, the gods of politics, are brought together. That they exist is obvious; they are nothing but existence; they are existence itself, in which we are trapped again and again. But existence is not a god. What could be stronger than a glacier? It heaps up mountains of rocks; it carves valleys; it melts into torrents and rivers; it floods fields and cities. Blind force; overwhelming. Caesar is blind also; he uproots, he razes, he shifts direction, according to oblique chance. Victories and defeats simply sketch out the angles of the world. An empire is like a river; the sand is stronger than the river; the wind is stronger than the sand. That is why Jesus said: "My kingdom is not of this world." The devil says clearly, without speaking, that his kingdom is of this world. But what a conjunction of legends, arts, and even words! What a leveling of all gods into this one word, devil! That he is damned for all time, is full of meaning. For the universe exists for all time, and is without value for all time. The spirit is deceived if it does not first believe in itself, and only in itself.

Descartes did not scorn to raise the devil to the height of his *Meditations*; he calls him the Evil Genius, and recognizes in him the power to deceive with evidence, and even with the truth. This is a rigorous denial of the external god; and from it follows, and must always follow, the moment of hyperbolic doubt. For we must make no mistake about it, Descartes rose from doubt of the uncertain to doubt of the certain. This doubt remains. It is hereafter attached to everything that appears, for things never appear in their truth; and it is the spirit armed with itself and with things that do not exist, called ideas, it is the spirit that will unravel the wonders of the rainbow, of snow, of the lodestone, and of the sun that is only illuminating to our eyes and only warm to our skin. This famous revolution took place in philosophy. But by analogy it enlightens the Christian revolution and its striking images. For it is true that the cult of the spirit is what gives value, and what puts the lower order in its place. But it is also true that the lower order will not stay in place for a single moment, and that it is unrelenting in its efforts to reduce everything else to its animal law. It is very exact to say that everything is a temptation, that every appearance is false because of the devil and true because of the spirit. Error is nothing, but it appears nonetheless. That is the essential being of the devil, and his damnation.

The consequences will be surprising. For it is the essence of the religion of the spirit to refuse miracles. That it does not deny them entirely, shows once again that all religions exist together in man, and that, as I must repeat, religions are less the stages of man's history than the stages of his growth. The surprising thing is that the religion of the spirit, though it is entangled with agrarian sorcery, and soiled by urban power, nevertheless has for its vocation the denial of all miracles, through its great image of the devil, who can always create the appearance of a miracle. We cannot do even limited justice to Christianity, unless we think of the troubled religions it has surpassed and condemned, reducing the oracles forever to the level at which they now stand, and provisionally denying the ancient world, in which everything was miraculous. Which is to say, and we cannot omit saying it, that the spirit is the judge of miracles; and, essentially, that the spirit can borrow nothing from miracles that does not strengthen it in itself, and that does not give it a firm resolve against the prestige of the marvelous. Even theology must finally admit that the true miracles are exceptions only for our dark and troubled minds, and that, on the contrary, they would conform to the law of the spirit if we knew all. It is thus that the eternal Descartes wrestles with the Evil Genius. Descartes is always threatened by error, and even, if we may put it so, certain of error; but he curses it in advance, and flies to his other life, where the spirit is certain of itself. We are also guided toward this other life, in the midst of the world's confusion, by the great images of the devil, and of the cross that dispels all apparitions. For the just man on the cross tells us enough, I think, and more than enough about necessity and power; and once we attach supreme value to this signum of humiliation, the devil will drop back down on all fours.

Chapter six

THE SAINT

We must say good-by to Greek beauty, which is only the delight in being strong. Nature and the city have both been reduced to their proper levels, and we have seen new temples arise and a new hero, commemorated according to a new kind of glory. Here, as Hegel has shown, the arts are more telling than arguments. For the new temple is closed in upon itself, even in the midst of the city; and the new athlete is also closed in upon himself, withdrawn. The sculpture of the human form can only refuse itself and deny itself, foretelling a disdain for the external, and, indirectly, the beauty of inwardness. Painting is more adaptable; and Hegel had good reason to call it essentially a Christian art. Not that it cannot be profane; but even then it brings equality to external things, granting at will the same diffuse beauty to all that shines in the light. But, above all, painting has the ability to grasp and master the fugitive inner life, through the expression of the face and especially of the eyes, in which we have learned to read the worth of a soul, and the value of infinite subjectivity. I have borrowed this phrase from Hegel, because I am unable to improve on it. The spirit housed within the body and yet greater than all worlds, the spirit which is only my "self" and yet is everything, appears more clearly in music and in poetry, which are the supreme arts of the spirit. This great succession of harmonious signs confirms for us the idea that the religion of the spirit is better preserved from impurity by its images than by arguments. We cannot erase what we value above all else; our highest pleasures, even when the devil lurks in them, keep us from entirely forgetting our nobler parts.

With this sort of propriety, we are still far from saintliness. Man is never proud of being an animal, either in his pleasures or in his anger. There have always been wise men who have held back from these two forms of excess, having recognized the connection between them, and that power, which is systematically cruel, leads naturally to orgiastic madness. Socrates said all that needs to be said about this subject. The emperor Marcus Aurelius and the slave Epictetus have pushed to the limit the concern with not dishonoring the governing part of man. They have a precise idea of human greatness, which they distinguish from clothing, wealth, and power. They seek it out and honor it under all appearances, which gives them a certain presentiment of equality and even of fraternity. Nevertheless they are pagans. Pascal sees the stigma of pride in them. They call themselves and know themselves to be sons of the world. Searching, as Christopher did later, for the most powerful of masters, they stop at the extensive greatness of the world, and they submit to it. "All that your seasons bring is fruit for me, O Nature!" We know that, in this roundabout way, they were able to accommodate Jupiter and the other Olympians, who were, according to their arguments, simply poetic names for the great forces of the world. And it was precisely by means of power that they drove their thought toward universal reason. "Nothing is more powerful than the world; nothing is greater, nothing is more beautiful; therefore the world is rational." It was not so much that they renounced power, since what they worshipped was the supreme power. They saw man as little; and this recognition led them to a kind of self-contempt, and perhaps to a ready contempt of others. As sons of the world, they were sons of pride. Perhaps, in attempting to understand the Christian images, we will come to realize that power dishonors even God. In the light of this idea we understand the Hebrew prophet, who spoke in the name of a terrible god, but a god outside the dimensions of the world, which are nothing in the eyes of the spirit. This double idea, of a great and beautiful spectacle, and of an absolute spirit, whose commandments surpass us, occurs again, as we know, in Christian theology. But there it rings false. It is never a first principle. It is a misjudgment of the sublime; for the sublime is not in power contemplated, it is in the reflection of the contemplation of power back upon the present and intimate spirit. And in any case, the idea of a governing order and of a governing spirit breaks down the notion of the spirit. For it means that everything is already said and done. Salvation comes from God and merit is nothing.

Here we recognize all the subtleties of grace, and the new order of charity, which throws down the old world and takes it up reborn; the center of meditation for a consciousness that relies only upon itself and yet only upon God. This paradox is given in the human situation. For the spirit in any one of us, however weak he feels, still has the ability to count beyond the highest number and to pass beyond all limits; but, more important, the capacity for error, which is inseparable from the capacity for thought, implies freedom, as Descartes realized, and as each of us feels. And freedom is positively supernatural, in that no representation of a mechanical object can give any idea of it. These notions throw the philosopher into labors that are exhausting, and that must always be repeated. It has been said often enough that consciousness put to the test, faced with an unambiguous task, or even in the search for what is best, quickly concludes that the principal error, perhaps the only error, is to pronounce man incapable of will. In these problems, which are themselves problems of will, the power of the spirit finds that it is threatened, within itself, by external power. It is always a question of choosing between the eternal Caesar and free consciousness. And, since Caesar's exact weight is not the issue, in this extremity of inward debate, there can be no recourse to measurement and remeasurement. The intellect is powerless. We must choose out of generosity, as Descartes would say, or out of charity, in the words of the apostle. But it takes a great deal of reflection to see no difference between them. The saint takes this step, through a precise sense of himself, and with good fortune.

When I say that religion is human and not inhuman, I am not committing myself to explain it fully. I say only that we must look at it attentively, and that, the more we look at it, the more we understand that the reflective man had to arrive at these subtleties, which are surprising at first, but all of which illuminate man in himself. Descartes certainly thought that out of his own freedom he worshiped a free God. This condition can be developed, provided that we do not let ourselves be taken in by the mirage of infinite comprehension. If the spirit is free, and if God is spirit, then what is offered to us is a grace and an aid that is nothing other than freedom itself. And to say that grace must be deserved and that one cannot deserve it without grace, is to say in the richest way and with what is doubtless the most beautiful of words, that we declare ourselves free, and that, because of the given nature of the problem, that declaration guarantees nothing; it is inexhaustible only if we believe it; and this very faith, which is the supreme and only faith, is free. Nature provides nothing; nature does not fall in with freedom once freedom is posited, any more than the courage of the evening serves for the next morning. This condition, in a sense abandoned and helpless, is nevertheless all help and the only help. You must save yourself, that is the divine inspiration. That is why Pascal, following Descartes more closely than he thought, affirms an order that is higher than spirits, who are themselves infinitely higher than things, and calls it the order of will or of charity. Love, that happy confidence, does not stop at the supreme spirit; it leaps beyond and discovers its own conception. The saint waits for us in that third heaven.

Chapter seven

THE TRINITY

I will help you; but it is you who will help yourself. For the free can only love the free. It is thus that power is withdrawn, and the ancient god, who is only frightening in his absence, is suddenly eclipsed. It would be impious to believe in him, and Jesus himself refused the help of the angels. Christian theology has naïvely preserved God the Father, the god of the Jews, the god of armies; but it considers that the Jews have been condemned for worshiping him alone. This sort of deposition reveals the full greatness of soul that belongs to the saints. For they do not deny power absolutely, but they leave it in the clouds, they do not invite it to their secret councils. That is how they interpret the alien power of the father, who belongs wholly to nature, and who must eventually be denied, though he always remains surrounded with respect. External law must give place to inner law; that is the future of the beloved son. This metaphor says very clearly what it means. The saint contemplates man in his humiliated perfection; he joins God and man in a single image; he considers that man and God are profoundly united in the free man; he sees this free man hung on a cross; he concludes, like Plato, who foreshadowed this great spectacle in his *Republic,* that such extreme affliction proves at least that virtue is not a means to power. A lesson for kings. But how comprehend that this Just Man is at once, and very certainly, entirely man and entirely God, as Hegel put it?

The theological subtleties which abound on this point are essentially academic; yet incarnation and redemption are forceful expressions of certain very touching human movements. But we must judge, in the light of our own real falls and our own real salvations, this conspiracy within the pure spirit, this voluntary sacrifice of the being who has come down from on high.

These pictures are drawn from nature, and presuppose reservations of will and of grace which can only be understood in terms of mechanism, or, if you prefer, in terms of logic, which is the same thing. It is once again an attempt to incorporate the miraculous into nature, which will never accept it. The idea that God, because of the enormity of man's crime, could only redeem him by sacrificing his own son, is nothing but calculation and pettifoggery; it brings no light to our real problems. In that case we are only matter, a manipulated herd. But what do we mean to say and what thought do we embody in the figure of the god-man? We must go back to the lost moments of transition and to the real ascension that shapes all of our thoughts. Anthropomorphism is in no sense a primitive error; and the Greek Olympus is really the first salvation of our ancient shudderings. Jupiter is a man, but does not become a god, except in relation to the snake, the cow, the wolf, the monkey, the elephant. Jupiter is not god enough; he is also not entirely a man; for he does not transcend himself and never judges his condition. He is easygoing, as Caesar will always be if he remains unchallenged. And it is because he is not enough of a man that he is not worthy of being a god. Jehovah, on the other hand, is no longer a man in any sense, and his way of being incomprehensible is not man's way, but rather the way of the "indescribable" that hides in the woods or in the clouds. He is a pure spirit which can no longer become flesh; he is cut off from man, and returns to man in the form of external wonders. From these vacillations we had to move closer to the true man. Religion, then, takes on flesh, the way logic takes on flesh, except that the spirit retains something of its sublime unruliness, which is at least an attempt at real infinity. And it is no small thing to have recognized and commemorated the spiritual model of man, crowned with thorns, who not only judges better than we do and loves better than we do, but who also suffers better than we do. This is the second moment of the spirit, which by a double movement raises us from the athlete to the saint, and leads us from the pure spirit to the spirit in brotherhood.

The wonder is that this dialectic, which is first of all poetry and human gesture, has thrown us as food for reflection the third term, spirit, which removes all ambiguity from the problem of our salvation. After the Passover of the spirit comes Pentecost with its tongues of flame, when the spirit is incorporated once again into our elements, and confided to each one of us. Which completes this great mythology by instructing us so that we will neither forget nor turn away from a future of trials, heresies, and persecutions. For, according to the spirit, nothing is thought or decided once and for all; on the contrary, everything must be recreated from the beginning and from before the beginning, under the law of freedom and love, but with the formidable responsibility of doubting precisely out of faith. We exist in this movement; it is hard for us to judge it. The cross-bearers cling to what they know, which means that they no longer know anything. Those who have thrown down the cross forget the condition of extreme affliction, and would have the spirit rule by Caesar's methods. This two-sided mistake comes from a false estimation of the spirit, which does not exist, which can do nothing, and which is utterly lost when it is made into an intellectual image; which finally can only live in continual incredulity. I have tried to point out this quality of believing nothing as it appears in the saint. For, with regard to ancient religion, the saint is that great spirit who does not permit himself to be taken in by what men believe, who refuses wealth and promises, blasphemes against Pan and Caesar, and who is separated from family, honor, power, and from his own inner wealth, for he has taken the measure of pride and even doubts his own salvation. This is what he calls charity, and it is very well named; for charity always goes directly against imposed beliefs; and self-love, here re-established at its center, goes against all that men believe so easily and so gladly about themselves. Our saints are poor and live in garrets, like all Saints, and they are devoted, without thinking themselves worthy, to a spark of the spirit that does nothing and promises nothing. But, as for the duty of saving it, though they have no hope, these doubters are never doubtful. That is why I have placed the whole of this book under the image of Christophorus, or Christopher, whose name means the Christ-bearer.

Chapter eight

CONFESSION

Under this heading, which has given rise to thoughtless polemics, I want to bring together some notions concerning admission, judgment, and penance, in order to throw more light on that invisible and secret other world in which everything is decided according to the free spirit and absolute friendship. This will give us a better idea of the road that has been won through the thickets of temporal superstition. For agrarian cults, punishment is pure constraint, and there can be no admission of guilt, because the error is purely external in nature. I do not always know what is forbidden, like sleeping under a particular tree or eating a certain kind of fruit or meat; I know my error by the punishment; that is, so to speak, how I learn. Under Caesar's regime, punishment is public and political; it must be recognized, even by the criminal. It is quite correct to speak of reason of State, and not merely of force of State. That is why they demand an admission of guilt, going by the theory that the punishment would be pointless if the guilty man did not realize what he had done, or what he intended to do. One of the tyrant's claims is that he is right, which means that there is no perfect tyrant. What is carried out in political punishment is precisely the will of the guilty man, as Hegel says; for instance, to be robbed if he is a thief, or to be killed if he is a killer, or to be terrified if he is a terrorist. The punishment is mental, just as politics is mental. But because of this need for justice, the admission must be forced. Naïvely forced by means of torture, or forced by operations on the mind. The abuse of force is less moving with the second method than it is with the first; it is no less of an outrage. At times it would seem preferable for a man to be struck down openly by force, as happens in war. Something of

171

this mentality remains in the efficiency of the police, who do not bother about intentions but simply clear the streets.

The opposite idea, the idea of free judgment, judgment of the self by the self, is worth preserving. And it is preserved, in the religion of the spirit. The practice of confession shows very clearly that the consideration of true values arrives as if by itself, and despite an inevitable admixture of formalities, at a very beautiful freedom and a very beautiful kind of friendship.

I do not believe that a man can know himself very well as long as he only confesses to himself. Not that we are always self-indulgent; there are also examples of magnified sins and excessive repentance. Often the idea of a moral failing, seen in anticipation, or even in retrospect, turns into a proud despair. Proud because the power of doing wrong, which is power itself, is nursed by a fund of anger that is similar to the great external forces. Remorse, which is far more active and enterprising than is commonly supposed, declares war, takes risks, and defies affliction. This point of profound misanthropy is remarkable in that it is always a fall. For the cult of power, according to an inexorable judgment, always moves toward the test of power in combat. "How can we do God's will," says Coûfontaine in *L'Otage*, "when our only way of knowing it is by contradicting it?" Here we get a brief glimpse of the tyrant's soul, which Plato alone has revealed; but the famous pages of the *Republic* are still very obscure to me; I can barely understand them. I think also of the pronouncements of Vautrin, in which we feel an excessiveness that is only too true, pronouncements we are unable to refute; for the words of a king are ridiculous if they are only words, and pointless if force stands behind them. Which shows, if we have gone through the levels of cult in their order, that political religion is only a stage, that it endures only because a higher religion negates it, and that we fall back, if we do not transcend it, to the religion of the wolf and the snake. This is the devil's logic; and theology has not neglected to say that it is primarily the inner logic of the devil, who is eternally damned by himself. These well-drawn myths refuse facile commentaries. That is why the Christian supernatural is ridiculous in epic poetry. For, insofar as splendid paganism has been not merely replaced but surpassed, the whole drama from then on takes place in the conscience, with regard to which external causes are only means, and are all held in contempt. The inadequacy of what we must call Christian paganism shows clearly in the *Jerusalem*, and even more clearly in the *Martyrs*. But the Gospels reject supernatural aid; which is all that needs to be said.

It remains true that the conscience that feels itself falling has need of an arbiter to deliver it, to make it rebound into faith and hope; so that despite its openness to ridicule, absolution is the proper end of confession; without absolution man would be lost through his own goodness. There are few confessors who do not know how to discern in any sin a rebelliousness of the spirit which turns the sin into a kind of god. It is very true that only faith can save us; and it is very true that proud sinfulness is precisely the opposite of charity. There is a perfect example of salvation in the encounter between Jean Valjean and the bishop. This legend, which, like all legends, comes from the people, is an adequate text for the servants of the spirit, who are always threatened by a gigantic despair. Success can only be gratuitous, as we are all aware.

Now, if we search for an arbiter, it may not be easy for us to find one among our friends, for the reason that we are afraid, not only of burdening our friends, but also of infecting them with the great hesitation, which comes with every evening and every morning. The unknown arbiter, who works in secret, who will even forget what we tell him, is sometimes better. What is most noteworthy in confession is that the admission is freely given and the advice is asked for. The arbiter waits and judges according to what he hears. "It is you yourself who will say it." The famous words of Socrates reappear in this conversation which, with the help of the other person, is nevertheless always a conversation with oneself. For, says the Jansenist confessor, if there is a sin of pride in preaching well, it is you who recognize it, and it is for you to say it. Anyone can see how this practice can be abused, but I am talking about its proper use, in order to bring some light to the difficult life of the spirit, which is always full of risk. The casuists have done more than people say. I will give an example from *Port-Royal*. The abbey of anchorites was threatened by an armed mob, the villagers took refuge in the abbey buildings, and the penitents, some of whom had been professional soldiers, took up their helmets and muskets again. But while they kept watch, they sent to ask M. de Sacy if they were permitted to use bullets; and M. de Sacy said no, they must be content with making noise. It was forbidden to do more. But this expedient was itself a lie, and the famous director had his scruples. He put first things first. He knew very well that the savage joy of conquest and the intoxication of blood might lead to boundless evil, under the beautiful appearance of courage; it was this spiritual evil that he feared, not the death of a few pillagers, who belonged to the other world, that is, to this world. It is an injustice to men, and, far worse, to oneself, to disavow the religion of the spirit, and, instead of protecting it from alien admixtures, to throw it into the common ditch. We throw ourselves into the ditch at the same time. The errors of religion are far less dangerous for religion than for those who criticize it without looking at its principles. And the devil appears once again at this point; for in his oblique way he passes out the arms of war, to be used against others, when what we seek are the arms of peace, for ourselves.

Chapter nine

THE VIRGIN

I do not intend to argue my way into any further clarification of the highest religion, which is always eluding itself. Instead I will try to show, by other examples, that poetry goes on ahead, and illuminates our thoughts today, as it always has. We are all vaguely aware that woman is not the slave of man, and that force, here more obviously than anywhere else, decides nothing. This has led the most outspoken of us to portray the rights of women in an abstract and shocking form; for, once again, behind any political system, however perfect we suppose it to be, stands force itself, which annihilates without looking. The law of contracts is beautiful in spirit, but it too is simply a way of equalizing the struggle, which leaves the weak with no recourse. These painstaking arrangements have turned out to be slower and less effective than the naïve imagery which the Christian revolution had to produce as an ethical model. For theology did not invent the cult of the mother; in fact, theology has always resisted it, while wordless contemplation has developed the initial myth along human lines. For in the continuous generation of the son who will replace the father, we know, from our own childhood experience, that the mother will always intercede at the side of governing power, until she has created out of her own grace almost the whole of paternal love, perhaps the whole of it. Because of this exchange of messages, which tempers external necessity, the Holy Family was a favorite subject for painters, and a source of happy meditation for the viewer, who was suddenly relieved of the image of Caesar and the bacchantes. For then nature supported the almost insupportable fiction of the god-man with the representation of a mother who constantly watches over her most beautiful hopes in the person of a child who is too small to bear them.

But this double weakness also represents the human order as it is for beautiful moments, under the protection of the eternal carpenter.

It is part of the order that the carpenter thinks of trees, of the ax, of the plumb line, of the square, of the outside world, and of its pitiless forces; thus he acquires an air of severity and authority that is not his by nature. The urgency and the order of labors speak through him; no one argues and no one will ever argue with the kind of power that belongs to wind, cold, and rain. There would be no temporal power of any sort if security did not depend on a blind world that destroys as it produces. Such then is man, always a bit too serious and preoccupied, in the presence of the free exchange of natural feelings. His thoughtful glance is turned toward the outside and the distance. The mother's thought is turned inward; and is still turned inward when she bends down over the new life she has formed, and which she always carries; still turned inward when she walks through the inside of the house, the human shell that is her domain. Plato's saying, "preserve the inner things," takes on a metaphorical meaning that is more literal than what he meant. For the within is the image of man, and is cast in human form, but this form itself signifies an inward law of formation, as sensible to a woman as the grip of an ax-handle is to a man. And I read in a man's face the sad task of destruction, while in a woman's face, by a sort of absence from the world, the happy task of creation and preservation. These two powers cannot be rivals; on the contrary, it is part of the order that each of them loves and completes the other. The child listens to this double language, and grows up in the double cult of things as they are and of man as he should be. These ideas are never hidden; each of us gives his own value to this double protection; each of us distinguishes the two powers, spiritual and temporal, down to their very roots. And yet, because of the ambiguity of laws which attempt to combine what cannot be combined, I can portray the two powers better by studying this family portrait with my eyes than by following, in conversation or in books, the abstract and fleeting thoughts that have been proposed on this great subject. External necessity never ceases to break up the human form. The external world is the invader, and thought stands on the ramparts.

We must give in, then; we must betray. But dangerous love betrays even more subtly, by an assault of pure animality, which is a kind of simplicity that is as much worshiped as feared. The whole of civilization bears upon this point of extreme union and imminent disunion. In the crypt of Chartres, beside a deep well, the guide tells us that in ancient times a sort of Virgin mother was worshiped in the same place. This idea has always been formed, destroyed, and recreated. Like every idea, it depends on us. Blessed be the face that reminds us of it, because once in a while it happens. This is what the mute image of Gretchen says in *Faust*. We can think of nothing better; we can think of nothing other; for I defy you to conceive of love only in terms of the divinities of the fields and woods, of the cow, the monkey, the Satyr; I am not talking about love in others, I am talking about the love that we feel, the love that we love. There is a great adventurousness in love, perilous and beautiful, but that leads to very serious consequences. That is why Faust trembles at the very mention of the *Mothers*, buried in the depths of nature; for there is a kind of profanation in finding them still there. And though it may be an iron law that we degrade what we love, I doubt if there is a man alive who surrenders himself entirely to this demoniac passion, so naturally bound up with ancient worship. He who saves himself a little, is raised up higher than he meant to be. And yet thought never comes cheaply. Even in physics there is a need for severity and purity, and for a separation of shadow and light, with that strong craftsman's hand that Michelangelo drew. I do not suggest entering a monastery; that is to turn away from life. But I see that a tolerable life implies moments of monasticism, each time we refuse a certain degree of injustice, of power, or of pleasure; these moments are our thoughts. He is fortunate who rejoices in his thoughts. What I know very well, is that diabolical thoughts will not remain thoughts for long. Of which Goethe's Mephistopheles is a chilling example. And it is not by a fortuitous metaphor that we even think of mechanics in terms of pure, or virgin, ideas. Without this glance toward the other world, we would be unable to see the world under our feet. Such are the ties of human substance. Plato wrote, with a smile, that the god in the *Timaeus*, having created this world of perfect proportions, rounded it off, closed it in on all sides, and has never set hand to it again. An admirable way of saying that man will only find man, wherever he looks, and that that is enough for his thousand lives of an instant.

Chapter ten

NOËL

Everything recurs; and justice is as weak today as it was yesterday. As weak, and as strong. The first impulse of a thought is young, alone in the poorest surroundings, the child of labor, and enlightened by labor, watched over by love and patience, watched over, wordlessly, by the ox and the ass, attended by the rich, who come bearing incense, humble because it knows that it has no use. The universe redoubles the splendor of its stars, which means nothing; it is bitter cold; dawn comes only for thought. Noël! Noël! The child is born! If only the doctors of the law will let him live.

Christmas has distinct resonances. It has all resonances. All myths come to take part in it. Each thing has its precise place in this assembly. Consider the ox and the ass, the Magi, the attentive parents. We must develop this rich image, and take it into our thought, but without ceasing to follow its irreproachable outlines. Christmas is first of all the celebration of spring, but the human celebration of spring. Flowers open to the sun; but men open like flowers through a scrupulous memory that has kept track of the days and nights. Easter is a celebration of nature; the first of January is a political celebration, which already braves the cold. Christmas is more attentive, more daring, closer to astronomy, which locates around the twenty-first of December that hesitation of the sun which it calls the solstice. Thus the pagan Christmas goes beyond the spirit of the fields and woods. The spirit takes up its lantern and sings the News:

> Awake, O beautiful sleeper,
> Awake, for it is day.

179

It is day for the spirit, in the longest night of nature. The wooden shoes, the night procession, the joyous consent, all of this taken together is the dawn of the spirit. The carols are man's bird song. Without waiting for nature, he renews his alliance with nature. Thus the song of Noël foretells another alliance. But let us go back to the image, because it says everything.

Christmas represents the human order, and what there is of truth in the political order, the family in its three-way power, of industry, love, and promise. The family embodies human continuity, the real object of political religion. Here the human form holds empire over the other gods. As the eagle, on Olympus, is no more than Jupiter's messenger, so here, by a more precise drawing, by a gesture that is closer to the human situation, the ox and the ass are mute and subordinate powers. With this view of agrarian labors, which will always come first, Caesar himself is reminded of his birth, Caesar, whose likeness is stamped on the peasant's small change. But the heavy kilogram, the measure of armies, is also in man's service, and, to describe the image exactly, is in the service of the spirit of hope. From which we conclude that political idolatry foretells something better than the rule of the strong. Then the three kings arrive, kings of armies and of wealth, who have come to worship the carpenter's son. This dethronement occurs in every speech from the throne. A sensitive ear will discern it; but the naïve image is more expressive.

A new religion rises up from this altar, the manger. And once again, if we question this spectacle that does not say a word, we will find the master-word. The spirit strays into self-worship through the prestige of well-ordered ideas; and more than one intellectual Caesar will be a tyrant of force, if he forgets the infant spirit which cannot be subjected to force, to whom all must be given and forgiven. Bishop Bienvenu does not ask Jean Valjean for proof; he grants him every virtue, and swears by him, and sings Noël into this human night. With even more certainty the mother sings Noël into the child's night, and will always sing, that he is the spirit, that he can speak, that he knows and recognizes, long before he speaks, knows, or recog-

180

nizes anything. For, as fairy tales say, an old witch beside the cradle can wither the flowers of the spirit to come. "You will be stupid, you will be envious, you will be a thief." These predictions are borne out by means of a persuasion in which the new-born spirit condemns itself. And through this fiction, which is not always a fiction, charity is fully revealed, charity which is more than love because it does not expect perfection. Man often obscures charity simply by making himself worthy of love; and it is out of self-love that the wisest avoid loving themselves. Yet, in the presence of the child, there is no doubt. We must love the spirit without expecting anything from it. There is certainly a charity of the spirit toward itself; it is thought. But look at the image; look at the mother.

And look at the child. This weakness is God. This weakness that has need of all of us is God. This being who would cease to exist without our care, is God. Such is the spirit, in relation to which even truth is an idol. Because truth is dishonored by power; Caesar enlists it, and pays it well. The child pays nothing; he asks for more and more. It is the severe rule of the spirit that the spirit pays nothing, and that no man can serve two masters. But how shall we say strongly enough that there is a truth of truth, which experience can never negate? The less proof a mother has, the more intent she is upon loving, helping, and serving. This human truth, which she carries in her arms, may be nothing that exists in the world. Nevertheless she is right, and she will be right even when every child has proved her wrong. A good word here for doctors who care for the mentally retarded and who wait, like prophets, for the least flicker of attention; they never lose hope; and they are right. There is, then, a truth of truth which defies fortuitous circumstances. And I would demonstrate, following Descartes, that there is no truth, however well verified and useful it may be, that does not rest upon an unverified truth, a truth that is useless, and that has no power whatsoever. But practical truth is an ungrateful child, and is punished a hundred times over by its own rewards. These ideas will perhaps become clear, and the spirit will know how to strip itself of power, of every kind of power; that is the highest kingdom. It was foreshadowed on

Calvary, in so eloquent and violent a fashion, that I will add no commentary to it.

End of the Fourth and Last Book

BIOGRAPHICAL NOTE

Alain was the pen name of Émile Auguste Chartier, who was born at Mortagne-au-Perche, Normandy, in 1868. His father was a veterinarian, greatly respected in the region for his knowledge of horses. His grandfather was a farmer. At eighteen Alain was said to resemble his mother closely; later he said of himself, "Alain is really a Norman, the exact image of one of the Norman types, with his tall, erect frame, regular features, and blue eyes." He attended the local school at Mortagne and the lycée at Alençon, and then spent three years (1886–89) at the Lycée de Vanves, where he studied philosophy under Jules Lagneau. In 1889 he went on to the École Normale Supérieure, from which he graduated in 1892 with a degree (*agrégé*) in philosophy. After teaching for a year in Pontivy, he moved to a new post at Lorient, where he spent the next seven years.

The years in Lorient were a period of political activity as well as intellectual activity for Alain. He joined in the socialist movement, took part in electoral campaigns, and ran for office himself; he also collaborated in the founding of a radical newspaper and of a free night university for workers. He produced a considerable amount of journalism, but also a series of dialogues on philosophical subjects, published under the name of Criton. (Six of these dialogues appeared over the next few years in the *Revue de Métaphysique et de Morale*; originally there were to be seven, but by then he had abandoned that mode and its way of thinking in favor of the *propos*. Later he said of them, "They are my Aristotle, and everyone knows I'm a Platonist.")

In 1900 Alain took a teaching post in Rouen, where he continued to support the cause of the Left with newspaper work and public speeches. In January 1903 he moved to Paris to teach, first at the Lycée Condorcet, then at the Lycée Michelet, and finally at the Lycée Henri IV. There he started another university for workers, originally located in Montmartre, later on the Place d'Italie. That summer the first of his *propos* appeared in the *Dépêche de Rouen*, under the name of Alain, beginning a collaboration that would last for the next eleven years and result in a five-volume collection of *propos*, published between 1908 and 1928 and reprinted after Alain's death under the title *Propos d'un Normand*.

Alain was deeply opposed to the policy of war. In the years just prior to 1914 the *propos* spoke more and more strongly against the events he saw coming. He said, in a letter, "I cannot leave this military question alone . . . I no longer think about astronomy." On July 31, 1914, two days before war was declared, he wrote: "After this the people, whether they win or lose, will be poor in

183

true noble blood; poor in protective, enterprising, generous spirits; rich in prudent, calculating, niggardly spirits. Rich in evasive and clever spirits; rich in impoverished natures. Rich in tyrants and rich in slaves. The blood-letting will take the best blood . . . Injustice will deliver its funeral orations; lessons in the beautiful dead, but for whom? I'm afraid we will see a great crop of hypocrisy, of pompous speeches and trivial speakers . . . I wish the shades of the heroes could come back, to admire the honorable peace they paid for with their lives."

However, by the seventh of August Alain had enlisted as a private in the heavy artillery. He was forty-six. "I am still physically strong; and I am stronger morally; I will add that to the pile." During the war, he continued to write. In 1915 a pamphlet entitled *Twenty-one Propos for the Use of Non-Combatants* was published, without approval of the censors. That was the only work he published. But the forced silence of this period enabled him to think through some longer problems, which resulted in several manuscripts, including the *Système des Beaux-Arts,* "written in the midst of the military uproar, and in which can be found, along with the means of expression proper to an experienced writer, a sort of solitude or forgetfulness of the reader that is hardly reminiscent of the *Propos d'un Normand.*"

In 1917 Alain was demobilized following an accident and went back to his classes at the Lycée Henri IV, where he remained until his retirement in 1933. Teaching was always an important part of Alain's life; he called it his *métier.* And he formed lasting friendships with many of his students, among them Jean Prévost and Simone Weil. But he disliked professors as a type, and often satirized them, the *docteurs* and *Sorbonnagres* of the *propos,* bureaucrats of the university system, "who give themselves titles and an air of majesty simply because they know a few languages and can recite tables of contents," and whose "pretended discussions consist in an exchange of compliments." And when he was offered the chair in philosophy at the Sorbonne, he declined it.

Alain bought a small house in 1917, in the village of Vésinet, near Paris, and from then on divided his time between there and Le Pouldu, in Brittany, where he spent the summers. He was uncomfortable during the years between the wars, and the *propos* show it. But it was also during those years that his thought reached its most integral expression, in books like *Onze chapitres sur Platon* (1928), *Entretiens au Bord de la Mer* (1931), and *The Gods* (1934). In 1951, the year of his death, he was awarded the first Grand Prix National de Littérature.

SELECTED BIBLIOGRAPHY

(The following is not a complete list. The information given is for the first edition of each book.)

A note on the journal *Libres Propos:*

After the war, Alain was not able to renew the relationship he had had with the *Dépêche de Rouen* from 1903 to 1914. However, in 1921 Michel Alexandre, a former student, founded *Libres Propos* for the purpose of printing Alain's *propos* in periodical collections. Over the years the journal expanded as other writers joined in the particular struggles Alain had undertaken, so that along with the *propos* Alain wrote for each issue it printed essays, articles, reviews, commentaries on events, satires, polemics, open letters and manifestoes. For example, Simone Weil wrote a number of articles for *Libres Propos* in the early thirties, and her essay *Oppression and Liberty*, which Alain considered "of the highest order," was originally to appear there; unfortunately the journal ceased publication before the chance came, and the essay was not published until 1955. The monumental edition of *Propos* published by Gallimard in 1956 was drawn largely from the pages of *Libres Propos*, as were several of the collections listed below.

Cent un Propos d'Alain ("One Hundred and One Propos of Alain"). Series of five volumes. Rouen and Paris: J. Lecerf, Wolf, 1908, 1909, 1911, 1914, 1928. Republished as *Propos d'un Normand*. Paris: Gallimard, 1952–60.

Quatre-vingt un chapitres sur l'esprit et les passions ("Eighty-one Chapters on the Spirit and the Passions"). Paris: Emancipatrice, 1917. New, enlarged edition, retitled *Éléments de Philosophie* ("Elements of Philosophy"). Paris: Gallimard, 1941.

Système des Beaux-Arts ("System of the Fine Arts"). Paris: Éditions de la N. R. F., 1920.

Mars, ou la guerre jugée ("Mars, A Judgment of War"). Paris: N. R. F., 1921.

Souvenirs concernant Jules Lagneau ("Recollections of Jules Lagneau"). Paris: N. R. F., 1925.

Éléments d'une Doctrine Radicale ("Elements of a Radical Doctrine"). Paris: N. R. F., 1925.

Le Citoyen contre les Pouvoirs ("The Citizen against the Authorities"). Paris: Kra, 1926. Introduction by Jean Prévost.

Sentiments, passions, et signes ("Emotions, Passions, and Signs"). Paris: Marcelle Lesage, 1926.

Les idées et les âges ("Ideas and Ages"). Paris: N. R. F., 1927.
Onze chapitres sur Platon ("Eleven Chapters on Plato"). Paris: Hartmann, 1928.
Entretiens au Bord de la Mer ("Conversations by the Sea"). Paris: N. R. F., 1931.
Idées ("Ideas"). Paris: Hartmann, 1932. (Contains previously published studies of Plato and Descartes, and a study of Hegel.)
Propos de Littérature ("Propos on Literature"). Paris: Hartmann, 1933.
Les Dieux ("The Gods"). Paris: N. R. F., 1934.
Propos de Politique ("Propos on Politics"). Paris: Rieder, 1934.
En lisant Balzac ("Reading Balzac"). Paris: Éditions des Laboratoires Martinet, 1935. New, enlarged edition, retitled *Avec Balzac* ("With Balzac"). Paris: N. R. F., 1937.
Stendhal. Paris: Rieder, 1935.
Les Saisons de l'Esprit ("Seasons of the Spirit"). Paris: N. R. F., 1937.
Minerve, ou de la sagesse ("Minerva, or On Wisdom"). Paris: Hartmann, 1939.
Suite à Mars ("The Mars Suite"). Paris: N. R. F., 1939. (Two volumes, separately titled *Convulsions de la Force* ["Upheavals of Force"], and *Échec à la Force* ["Forced Checked"].)
Les Vigiles de l'Esprit ("Vigils of the Spirit"). Paris: N. R. F., 1942.
Préliminaires à la Mythologie ("Preliminaries to Mythology"). Paris: Hartmann, 1942.
Les aventures du coeur ("Affairs of the Heart"). Paris: Hartmann, 1945.
Lettres à Sergio Solmi sur la philosophie de Kant ("Letters to Sergio Solmi on the Philosophy of Kant"). Paris: Hartmann, 1946.

Collected editions:

Propos. Ed. Maurice Savin. Paris: Gallimard (Bibliothèque de la Pléiade), 1956. (Collection of more than six hundred *propos*, arranged chronologically.)
Les arts et les dieux ("The Arts and the Gods"). Ed. Georges Bénézé. Paris: Gallimard (Bibliothèque de la Pléiade), 1958. (Contains twelve books, including *Les Dieux.*)
Les passions et la sagesse ("Passions and Wisdom"). Ed. Georges Bénézé. Paris: Gallimard (Bibliothèque de la Pléiade), 1960. (Contains twelve books, including *Onze chapitres sur Platon* and *Entretiens au Bord de la Mer.*)
Morceaux choisis ("Selections"). Eds. Maurice Savin and Albert Laffay. Paris: Gallimard, 1960.

Praise for
THE BABYLON CODE

"[This] book reveals the truth about the ancient teachings, religious legends, pagan doctrines, and false religious myths that have plagued Christianity and the Western world for centuries. THE BABYLON CODE is true to the prophetic Scriptures, especially those that have to do with the end times; carefully researched and well written, it is an enjoyable read. I recommend it to anyone concerned about today's worldwide chaos and the soon-to-come end of days that the Bible teaches us about."

—Dr. Tim LaHaye, minister, author, and
Christian educator

"Prophetic events are rapidly converging as we approach the wrap-up of history. At the same time, God has revealed pieces of the end-times puzzle to many different people. THE BABYLON CODE by Troy Anderson and Paul McGuire features amazing research from many experts that allows us to put the puzzle together."

—Sid Roth, host, *It's Supernatural!*

"Paul McGuire and Troy Anderson have written a powerful and compelling book, THE BABYLON CODE, which unravels the mystery code of ancient Babylon in the light of the prophetic Scriptures. The authors reveal, from the accounts of Babylon in Genesis and also in the Book of Revelation, prophetic signs that shed light on current events today and point to the nearness of the Lord's return to earth."

—Dr. Robert Jeffress, senior pastor, First Baptist
Church in Dallas, author of *Countdown to the Apocalypse*

"I am so glad that Paul McGuire and Troy Anderson decided to do this book. Without a doubt, there are powerful forces and secret societies that are working tirelessly to influence the direction of our society from behind the scenes. I believe that you will be shocked by what you learn in this book."

—Michael Snyder, publisher of The Economic
Collapse blog

"As the world hurtles toward cataclysmic end-times events, prescient clarity of cascading global affairs is desperately needed for all who will listen. Enter journalist Troy Anderson and prophecy expert Paul McGuire, who carefully uncover a prophetic mystery that began at the Tower of Babel and will culminate with the Battle of Armageddon."

—Dr. Thomas R. Horn, bestselling author

"As I look at Israel and other world events taking place around us, it is clear we are in the last days. Paul McGuire and Troy Anderson have given us an excellent resource to understand the times in which we live. I highly recommend you read this book."

—Jonathan Bernis, president and CEO,
Jewish Voice Ministries International

"Paul McGuire and Troy Anderson have done a masterful job in compiling and then synthesizing the work of more than one hundred Bible prophecy scholars. Their assessment points to the conclusion that we are, indeed, approaching the time of Christ's return. I especially appreciate their urgent call to all Christians to make good use of whatever time remains to bring the Good News of Jesus Christ...to people in every walk of life and every ethnic group around the world."

—Hugh Ross, founder and president, Reasons to Believe

"As you read this investigative book, you will be excused in thinking that you are reading the headlines of today's newspapers. Paul McGuire and Troy Anderson's summary of how the world began with a vision of globalization and will end with the same vision will encourage those who are anticipating the return of Christ. By the same token, it is an invitation for those who are living only for this life to come and place their whole faith in Christ alone."

—Michael Youssef, author of *Jesus, Jihad and Peace*

"As we move more and more into globalism, this book is a great outline and a road map as to how that happened. It began with Nimrod and will end with Antichrist. Through it all, we're to occupy until Jesus comes, and that message comes through clearly in this book."

—Jan Markell, founder, Olive Tree Ministries

"If you are wondering what on earth is going on in our world today, you must read this book. The research analyzed within is unparalleled and will give you the facts and insight you need to grasp a deeper understanding about the unbelievable changes taking place in the world today.

"THE BABYLON CODE will provide you with the information and clarity essential to be a Christian of vision equipped to think and live in accordance with a biblical worldview...This book will draw you to your own search of the Scriptures and will develop the assurance in your heart that the Bible is the infallible, inspired, inerrant Word of the Living God."

—Doc Beshore, president, World Bible Society, and host, Bible Institute of the Air radio program

THE
BABYLON
CODE

Solving the Bible's Greatest
End-Times Mystery

PAUL McGUIRE *and*
TROY ANDERSON

NEW YORK   BOSTON   NASHVILLE

Cover design by Jody Waldrup
Cover photography of Orion nebula by NASA/Corbis Images; photograph of sunrise over Australia by NASA/Getty
Cover copyright © 2015 by Hachette Book Group, Inc.

FaithWords
Hachette Book Group
1290 Avenue of the Americas, New York, NY 10104
faithwords.com
twitter.com/faithwords

Originally published in hardcover and ebook by FaithWords in October 2015.
First Trade Paperback Edition: October 2016

FaithWords is a division of Hachette Book Group, Inc. The FaithWords name and logo are trademarks of Hachette Book Group, Inc.

The publisher is not responsible for websites (or their content) that are not owned by the publisher.

The Hachette Speakers Bureau provides a wide range of authors for speaking events. To find out more, go to www.hachettespeakersbureau.com or call (866) 376-6591.

Please see page 379 for an extension of this copyright page.

Paul McGuire, PhD, and Troy Anderson are represented by Alive Communications, Inc., 7680 Goddard Street, Colorado Springs, CO 80920, www.alivecommunications.com.

Library of Congress Cataloging-in-Publication Data

McGuire, Paul, 1953–
   The Babylon code : solving the Bible's greatest end times mystery / Paul McGuire and Troy Anderson. — First Edition.
      pages cm
   Includes bibliographical references.
      ISBN 978-1-4555-8943-2 (hardcover) — ISBN 978-1-4789-6013-3 (audio download) — ISBN 978-1-4555-8942-5 (ebook) 1. Bible—Prophecies—Babylon (Extinct city) 2. Babylon (Extinct city)—In the Bible. 3. Bible—Prophecies—United States. 4. End of the world. 5. Bible—Prophecies. I. Title.
   BS649.B3M34 2015
   220.1'5—dc23
                                                                                    2015025987

ISBNs: 978-1-4555-8945-6 (trade pbk.), 978-1-4555-8942-5 (ebook)

Printed in the United States of America

LSC-C

10 9 8 7 6 5 4 3 2

We dedicate The Babylon Code *to the Hebrew prophets and the Ancient of Days who inspired them to write about a prophetic mystery in the Bible, code-named Babylon.*

From the Tower of Babel incident in Genesis to the famed accounts in the prophetic books of Isaiah, Jeremiah, Ezekiel, and Daniel, and ultimately to the apostle John's enigmatic description of "Mystery, Babylon" and "Babylon the Great" in Revelation, Babylon plays a central—though seldom recognized—role throughout the Bible.

The biblical writers told the tale of a powerful empire—one steeped in sorcery and the "magic of money manipulation"—that would reemerge in the last days as a global government, economic system, and religion under the control of the Antichrist and False Prophet.

Employing a variety of literary devices involving phrases, numbers, and riddles, these brave prophets and their investigative scribes laid out in exacting detail the stunning course of events that would transpire as mankind neared the end of history as we know it.

Many paid with their very lives to reveal this great biblical mystery, one that Daniel wrote would be "sealed until the time of the end" when only the "wise would understand."

Contents

THE
BABYLON
CODE

Introduction

The Great Biblical Mystery

Alas, alas, that great city Babylon, that mighty city! For in one hour your judgment has come.

—APOSTLE JOHN, REVELATION 18:10 NKJV

There is nothing more deceptive than an obvious fact.

—SHERLOCK HOLMES, *THE BOSCOMBE VALLEY MYSTERY*

The world-renowned evangelist Billy Graham, in an exclusive interview, said, "The Bible indicates that as the time for Christ's return approaches, evil and social chaos may well intensify. Are we living in those days?"[1]

It's the great question of our time. Are we now living in the last days of planet Earth?

If so, how will the apocalyptic events foreseen by the ancient prophets unfold? Are powerful forces now at work to create a global government, economic system, and religion as predicted in the Bible?

Unlocking a great biblical mystery that has puzzled scholars for nearly two thousand years, *The Babylon Code* unearths answers to these momentous questions.

In this book, we'll explore a prophetic enigma that begins in Genesis at the Tower of Babel and ends in Revelation with the Battle of Armageddon. The prediction involves "Mystery, Babylon"—the Bible's greatest end-times riddle—and reveals how an elite group of wealthy globalists and their interlocking network of transnational corporations, international banks, government agencies, think tanks, foundations, and secret societies are working to create a global government, cashless society, and universal religion as predicted in Scripture.

The world is at a final turning point. An unparalleled convergence and acceleration in end-times signs is now occurring. These harbingers are geopolitical, economic, scientific, technological, cultural, and moral. To ordinary men and women, these forces are overwhelming, as if a giant tsunami is about to drown everything they've ever known or dreamed of.

It's at this moment that every one of us is confronted with a choice. Either we can allow ourselves to be overcome by fear, leading to panic, or we can seek to understand the nature of the forces behind these events so we can survive.

In an out-of-control, upside-down world, *The Babylon Code* asks two urgent questions: Is it possible that God embedded a code in the Bible that could be cracked only in the end times? What if by decoding this prophetic cryptogram we could unlock the secret to both our salvation and our survival?

In these pages, we'll reveal the results of a five-year journalistic investigation that uncovered astonishing evidence that not only has the countdown to Armageddon begun, but the elite are involved in an international political and economic takeover—what one former U.S. official calls a "global financial coup d'état."[2] As we investigate this prophetic mystery sweeping across time, we'll unearth evidence that connects a secretive, international power structure with ties to ancient Babylon—the occult-enmeshed civilization where the "magic of money manipulation" originated—to what today's globalists call the "New World Order."[3]

Featuring scores of exclusive interviews with prominent world leaders and highly respected experts in geopolitics, economics, science, and theology, *The Babylon Code* is the first book by a mainstream, award-winning investigative journalist and a prophecy expert to explore the nexus between current events, secret societies, and end-times biblical predictions.

We'll also tell the intriguing backstory—a fateful tale of poetry, music, and a mysterious death involving Ludwig van Beethoven, "Ode to Joy" poet Friedrich von Schiller, and the Bavarian Illuminati—that brought us together to write *The Babylon Code*.

Follow us on our journey as we piece together this apocalyptic puzzle—uncovering what could be the biggest story and political scandal in modern history. Along the way, we'll unearth answers to the questions many have about the troubling events now transpiring in the world.

Recent polls and statements by world leaders demonstrate extraordinary public interest in this topic:

• A Barna Group survey found that four in ten Americans—and 77 percent of evangelical Christians—believe the "world is now living in the biblical end times." A similar poll commissioned by *New York Times* bestselling author Joel Rosenberg confirmed these results, finding that 41 percent of Americans believe that "events such as the rebirth of the State of Israel, wars, revolutions, instability in the Middle East, widespread national disasters, and the serious threat of a global economic depression are evidence that we are living in what the Bible calls the last days."[4]

• Israeli prime minister Benjamin Netanyahu recently told the United Nations General Assembly that "Biblical prophecies are being realized." Meanwhile, Pope Francis said the world has entered the "last times" and is at the beginning of a "piecemeal" Third World War.[5]

• A McLaughlin & Associates poll found that 80 percent of Americans fear a "Second Holocaust" in Israel—and 68 percent fear a "nuclear holocaust" in the United States—if the world does not take decisive action to stop Iran from building nuclear weapons. A recent Fox News poll found that 84 percent of Americans fear ISIS will soon launch terrorist attacks inside the United States.[6]

• Meanwhile, 28 percent of American voters believe a secretive power elite with a globalist agenda are working to create an authoritarian world government. Nearly 40 percent of Republican voters agree. A poll by Public Policy Polling—ranked by the *Wall Street Journal* as one of the nation's top polling firms—found that 19 percent of voters believe secret societies such as Yale University's Skull and Bones produce America's political and financial leaders to serve the wealthy elite. Further, the poll found that 17 percent of voters think a group of world bankers are slowly eliminating paper currency to create a cashless society and global economic system.[7]

The World Is at a Final Turning Point

These stunning poll results come amid an explosion of interest in the end times. In recent years, a seemingly nonstop series of crises has prompted many to ask whether the conclusion of the human epoch is quickly approaching. These concerns have intensified since the September 11, 2001, terrorist attacks—an event that shocked the world and that some saw as the biggest wake-up call in the nation's history. Since then, disaster after disaster has battered the planet—the Indian Ocean tsunami, Hurricane Katrina, the Haiti earthquake, the global economic meltdown, and the Fukushima Daiichi nuclear disaster. Recently, people worldwide have been intrigued by the convergence of a rare set of four blood moons and the biblical Shemitah, along with Sir Isaac Newton's end-times prediction known as "Newton's Riddle" regarding 2015–2016—asking whether these are portents of the beginning of the end. A number of prophecy scholars in recent years have uncovered biblical mysteries and riddles they say point toward the possible fulfillment of end-times prophecies between 2015 and 2028.

Nations are drowning in unparalleled levels of debt. Fears of a cataclysmic economic collapse and hyperinflation are rising. Tensions between Russia and America are growing, ISIS is warning the West of "Armageddon," and North Korea has threatened a nuclear strike on the United States. Some experts believe Iran may already have nuclear weapons—further raising the specter of the unthinkable. Meanwhile, the World Economic Forum says the world is experiencing record-breaking natural disasters and extreme weather, not to mention worsening global drought and famine.[8] Scientists are sounding the alarm about the dangers of mega-earthquakes and tsunamis, the Yellowstone supervolcano, solar storms, and massive tornadoes the likes of which the world has never seen before.

A report by the Intergovernmental Panel on Climate Change urged the world to prepare for more intense drought, famine, floods, freak weather, and heat waves—emphasizing that the "world's food supply is at considerable risk." Due to the dramatic and unprecedented planetary climate change, the globe is on the verge of massive food and water shortages. This is expected to lead to battles over food and water over the next five to ten years.[9]

A Brookings Institution report put it bluntly: The world is in an "unprecedented state of crisis."[10]

Is this the end of civilization?

Noam Chomsky, a political theorist and a professor of linguistics emeritus at the Massachusetts Institute of Technology who is considered "one of the world's most controversial thinkers," pondered that question in his recent article "The End of History?: The Short, Strange Era of Human Civilization Would Appear to Be Drawing to a Close." "It is not pleasant to contemplate the thoughts that must be passing through the mind of the Owl of Minerva as the dusk falls and she undertakes the task of interpreting the era of human civilization, which may now be approaching its inglorious end," Chomsky wrote.[11]

The question of whether civilization will indeed approach its "inglorious end" is now in our hands, Chomsky said in an exclusive interview. "Since 1945 we have lived in the shadow of possible nuclear war, and it was understood a long time ago that a nuclear war would have horrendous consequences, from which the power that initiated it would not escape," Chomsky says. "The threat has too often come ominously close, in part through foolhardy and irresponsible actions, in part through accidents that have been barely averted. Those dangers persist, but at least in this case we know in principle how to mitigate them. That is not so obvious from the twin threat of environmental catastrophe, towards which we are marching resolutely... For the first time in human history we have to decide whether we will bring human civilization to an inglorious end or will try seriously to carry the experiment forward."[12]

Chomsky's concerns are echoed in a recent study by professors and researchers at the University of Maryland and the University of Minnesota who found that civilization could be headed for an "irreversible collapse" because of unsustainable resource exploitation and increasingly unequal wealth distribution between the rich and the poor.[13]

A recent Oxfam report titled "Working for the Few" found wealthy elites have "co-opted political power to rig the rules of the economic game, undermining democracy"—creating a world where the eighty-five richest people own nearly half the world's wealth. The report found that 1 percent of the world's population control 46 percent, or $110 trillion, of its wealth. The richest 10 percent possess 86 percent of the globe's wealth. Noting growing public awareness of this "power-grab," the report found that increasing inequality is helping the rich undermine democratic processes and drive government policies that promote their interests at the expense of everyone else's.[14]

Meanwhile, a growing number of scientists, philosophers, and "tech billionaires" at Oxford, Cambridge, MIT, and the University of California, Berkeley, believe the world needs to start thinking seriously about the threat of human extinction. Curiously, they warn that one of the risks that threatens human civilization is a "world dictatorship" or a "global totalitarian state." These prestigious universities recently created several institutes to help humanity prepare for the Apocalypse, including Oxford's Future of Humanity Institute, Cambridge's Centre for the Study of Existential Risk, MIT's Future of Life Institute, and UC Berkeley's Machine Intelligence Research Institute. The physicists, philosophers, biologists, economists, computer scientists, and mathematicians at these institutes are "students of the apocalypse," *New Statesman* assistant editor Sophie McBain wrote in her story "Apocalypse Soon: The Scientists Preparing for the End Times." "Predictions of the end of history are as old as history itself, but the 21st century poses new threats," McBain wrote. "The development of nuclear weapons marked the first time that we had the technology to end all human life. Since then, advances in synthetic biology and nanotechnology have increased the potential for human beings to do catastrophic harm by accident or through deliberate, criminal intent."[15]

The Convergence

While secular experts warn of societal collapse and the end of civilization brought about by overexploitation of natural resources, the technological "singularity," and an "unimaginable level of income inequality," faith leaders say the roots of the world's problems are spiritual in nature and coincide with an unparalleled acceleration and convergence in signs of the last days.[16]

In an exclusive interview, Billy Graham—the famed evangelist who has preached to more people (2.2 billion) than any Protestant in history and has been on Gallup's list of the world's most admired men fifty-eight times since 1955, more than any other individual on earth—says he believes the world is approaching the "end of the age." "We're coming toward the end of the age, not the end of the world or the earth but the end of the age—the period that God has set aside for this particular time," Graham says. "There's a great deal to say in the Bible about the signs we're to watch for, and when these signs all converge at one place we can be sure that we're close to the end of the age. And those signs in my judgment are converging now for the first time since Jesus made those predictions."[17]

Graham's remarks follow a letter he released in the summer of 2012 comparing America to ancient Nineveh—the lone superpower of its time. When the prophet Jonah finally traveled to Nineveh and proclaimed God's warning, the people repented and escaped judgment. He believes the same thing can happen in America.[18]

The open letter to "America and its deceived people" was followed by Graham's *My Hope America* broadcast during the week of November 7, 2013—his ninety-fifth birthday. During what was described as the largest event in the six-decade history of the Billy Graham Evangelistic Association, Graham called on people worldwide to turn back to God. In his most recent book, *The Reason & My Hope: Salvation*, Graham warned that society "can't go on much longer in the sea of immorality without judgment coming."[19]

Greg Laurie, pastor at the fifteen-thousand-member Harvest Christian Fellowship in Riverside, California, and president of Harvest Crusades, says Graham is a "prophetic voice, and to me it's like Isaiah or Jeremiah standing up and telling our nation what we need to do. We would be wise to heed his warning and his admonitions and turn back to God because I believe God's prophet is speaking to us."[20]

Rabbi Jonathan Cahn, author of the *New York Times* bestselling books *The Harbinger* and *The Mystery of the Shemitah* and a descendant of Aaron, the brother of the biblical prophet Moses, says Graham's message has grown "more and more prophetic" in recent years.[21]

"Before God brings a nation into judgment, he sends warning," says Cahn, whose book *The Harbinger* is based on a real-life prophetic mystery he discovered in the Bible that unveils the September 11, 2001, terrorist attacks, the "War on Terror," and the 2008 global economic meltdown. "Before he brought judgment and destruction on ancient Israel, he warned them. *The Harbinger* is the revealing of how the same nine harbingers of judgment which appeared in the last days of ancient Israel are now reappearing on American soil."[22]

Philip Ryken, president of Wheaton College and the author of *Kingdom, Come: Looking Forward to Jesus' Return*, agrees that today's end-times signs—rampant immorality, growing religious apostasy, and the worsening persecution and slaughter of Christians worldwide—fit in with the biblical prophecies about the terrible times of the last days. At the same time, though, Ryken notes that the gospel is being preached throughout the world, including the last of the unreached people groups. "The fact that the gospel has now been proclaimed to more people in more places than at any time in the history of the world encourages us that the Great Commission is being fulfilled and reminds us that we are closer than ever to the fulfillment of the promise of Jesus that the gospel will be preached to the whole world and then the end will come."[23]

Joel Rosenberg—a former adviser to Netanyahu and the *New York Times* bestselling author of *Implosion: Can America Recover from Its Economic & Spiritual Challenges in Time?*—says he was taken aback by the Israeli prime minister's remarks before the United Nations.[24] Netanyahu's comments referred to a prediction in the Bible about the rebirth of the nation of Israel in the end times. Bible scholars consider the 1948 establishment of the State of Israel as the prophetic supersign that the world has entered the "end of the end times."[25]

"There are very few world leaders who believe Bible prophecies are coming true in our lifetime, much less are willing to say that publicly," Rosenberg says. "I'm trying to draw a little bit more attention to [Netanyahu's comment], its significance, and a question raised by it: If the prophecies related to the rebirth of the State of Israel have come true in our lifetime, when will other major Bible prophecies come true as well?"[26]

Is the World in the Run-Up to the Second Coming?

In addition to the rebirth of Israel, the Bible predicts a series of events in the run-up to the Second Coming—an explosion in knowledge, the development of "mark of the Beast" technologies, and ultimately the creation of a global government, cashless society, and false religious system.

Consider these recent stories:

- "Russian General Seeks Nuclear First-Strike Option Against US" (Sean Piccoli, *Newsmax*, September 4, 2014).
- "Gorbachev Issues New Warning of Nuclear War Over Ukraine" (*Newsmax*, January 10, 2015).
- "Pope Francis Warns the Global Economy Is Near Collapse" (Alexander C. Kaufman, *Huffington Post*, June 13, 2014).
- "ISIS, in Magazine, Warns of 'Armageddon' Against US, West" (Drew MacKenzie, *Newsmax*, September 16, 2014).
- "North Korea EMP Attack Could Destroy U.S.—Now" (Peter Vincent Pry, *Washington Times*, December 19, 2012).
- "Is There a Microchip Implant in Your Future?" (John Brandon, FoxNews.com, August 30, 2014).
- "Is the 'Mark of the Beast' the Future of Money?" (Catholic Online, April 2, 2014).
- "Pentagon Preparing for Mass Civil Breakdown" (Nafeez Ahmed, *Guardian*, June 12, 2014).

- "Henry Kissinger on the Assembly of a New World Order" (Henry Kissinger, *Wall Street Journal*, August 29, 2014).
- "Billy Graham Sounds Alarm for 2nd Coming" (Troy Anderson, WND.com, October 20, 2013).

As these headlines reveal, prominent world and faith leaders and military officials are openly talking about the possibility of a nuclear conflagration, a devastating electromagnetic pulse attack on the United States, a worldwide economic collapse, and the end of the world. Even more remarkably, experts in science, economics, and geopolitics across the political spectrum agree that the planet is facing a confluence of unparalleled dangers.

Polls show that there is widespread anxiety about the future. On one hand, many believe climate change poses an existential threat to humanity. On the other, leaders of many faiths say events in recent decades suggest ancient prophecies are coming true. Throughout the world, people sense something epochal is occurring.[27] The most optimistic—futurists, transhumanists, New Agers, and the "technorati"—believe humanity is on the cusp of a technology-driven quantum leap forward, a "climax in human cultural evolution" that will usher in a "techno-utopian" New Age era. Others, such as Tesla Motors and SpaceX founder Elon Musk, have warned that superintelligent computers might exterminate humanity following the "singularity"—a term coined by Google director of engineering Ray Kurzweil to describe the point in time when he expects computers to become more intelligent than humans. Kurzweil predicted this will occur by 2029.[28]

Others are alarmed by the deepening chaos and immorality in the world. A Barna Group poll found that 81 percent of Americans believe morality is in a free fall.[29]

Many believe the world is on the verge of an economic and societal collapse that will ultimately lead to what the Bible calls the Tribulation—a seven-year period of unparalleled mayhem that culminates in the Battle of Armageddon. It is commonly believed that this period will begin when the Antichrist—a charismatic but satanically inspired political leader—signs a peace treaty with Israel. During the first half of the Tribulation, the world will experience a time of peace and prosperity. But in the latter half, the Antichrist will consolidate his power and institute a global government, economic system, and religion with the help of the False Prophet. During this time, he will declare himself to be God, require universal worship, and demand that people take the notorious "mark of the Beast." Without it, people won't be able to earn a living or even buy the necessities of life. By the time of the final battle, prophecy experts believe anywhere from one-half to two-thirds or more of the world's population will have perished via war, disease, starvation, cataclysmic natural disasters, and the Antichrist's unparalleled bloody reign of terror.

Many today are unaware that we are now approaching the final battle for our world and that everything we see happening is connected with that conflict. Against this apocalyptic backdrop, the key question is: What powerful forces could bring about the unprecedented, end-times events predicted in the Bible—especially a global government and cashless society?

To understand what is happening today, we need to go back in time to Genesis. The Bible is embedded with a prophetic code that predicts what is happening now. This biblical riddle revolves around Babylon and the coming of a world-state, world economic system, and world religion.

The Origin of "Mystery, Babylon"—the First Secret Society

Thousands of years ago, a massive cataclysm destroyed everyone except a man named Noah, his family, and countless animals protected in a giant wooden ark. The biblical account of this famous story is corroborated by the fact that civilizations around the world have passed down knowledge of a great flood that wiped out the known ancient world.

When this massive deluge subsided, mankind sought to rebuild civilization and developed a secret occult plan the apostle John described in Revelation 17:5 (KJV) as "Mystery, Babylon." It's a prophetic riddle that has mystified Bible scholars ever since Jesus' beloved disciple penned those enigmatic words nearly two millennia ago. "Mystery, Babylon" was a secret system of knowledge that an ancient ruler named Nimrod tapped into when he built the Tower of Babel and ancient Babylon. Under Nimrod's rule, ancient man believed that the human race could survive and prosper by creating a worldwide government, economy, and religion.

Babylon was ruled by a secret society known as "Mystery, Babylon." Under this system, mankind believed that it could accomplish anything and become gods. According to Genesis, God looked down from heaven and saw into the hearts of men and their sinful desire to become gods. God judged ancient Babylon by confusing their language and scattering the tribes of humanity throughout the earth.

Despite this judgment, the dark, occult teachings of "Mystery, Babylon" were passed on from generation to generation through secret societies that arose in Egypt, Rome, China, South America, and even North America. One of the common themes of "Mystery, Babylon" was that it produced a secret society of god-kings who ruled the world's most powerful empires through political, economical, and spiritual systems.

In ancient Egypt, the pharaoh was a god-king. In ancient Rome, the caesars were worshipped as gods, and giant temples were built to consolidate their religious-political power. The great mystery hidden in the Incan and Mayan temples offers archaeological proof of the god-king system that began in Babylon. Through a succession of secret societies, "Mystery, Babylon" took root in Europe and eventually migrated to the United States.

In the early 1600s, a secret occult plan for America was conceived by English lawyer, statesman, and philosopher Sir Francis Bacon, head of one of the world's most powerful secret societies—the Rosicrucian Order. Bacon, who played a leading role in creating the British colonies, wanted America to become the head of a utopian new world—the New Atlantis, also the title of one of his books. Later, the Rosicrucian Order merged with the Bavarian Illuminati, an Enlightenment-era secret society founded by University of Ingolstadt law professor Adam Weishaupt in 1776, the year of America's birth. Although the Bavarian government officially banned these groups a decade later, many believe these secret societies infiltrated the world's most powerful banking families, the political realm, and European royalty. The evidence uncovered in our five-year investigation—which included more than one hundred interviews and the review of hundreds of books and tens of thousands of pages of government documents, academic papers, and news articles—reveals that these power brokers are actively working behind the scenes now to rebuild the ancient Babylonian system and bring about what globalists today call the New World Order.

Global Domination and a Cashless Society

In journalism, investigative reporters are often told to "follow the money" to uncover the real truth behind a story. Likewise, money and the "love of money" is a prominent theme throughout the Bible. In fact, it is such an important topic that it is the main subject of nearly half of Jesus' parables. In the New Testament, one in every seven verses deals with money. And while the Bible contains about five hundred verses regarding prayer, it contains more than two thousand verses about money.[30]

So it's no surprise that money and rampant materialism play an important role in the rise of "Mystery, Babylon" in the end times. As the world's governments amass unprecedented levels of debt, many are asking how it will all end. Many believe the global recession and the international debt crisis are just the beginning of events that will lead to the global economic system foretold by the prophets.

Today, for the first time in history since Genesis 11 and the Tower of Babel, the potential of a global government and cashless society is within mankind's reach. All the necessary components are in place for creating a socialistic world government—the surveillance state, political bodies such as the United Nations, electronic banking, and microchip implants. Not surprisingly, the headline of a recent FoxNews.com story asked, "Is there a microchip implant in your future?" "You can inject one under your skin and no one will ever notice," the author wrote. "Using short-range radio frequency identification (RFID) signals, it can transmit your identity as you pass through a security checkpoint or walk into a football stadium. It can help you buy groceries at Wal-Mart." During confirmation hearings for U.S. Supreme Court chief justice John Roberts, Vice President Joe Biden told him that a microscopic tag could be "implanted in a person's body to track his every movement." "There is actual discussion about that," Biden told Roberts. "You will rule on that, mark my words, before your tenure is over." While seldom mentioned in the mainstream media, the push for "global governance" has advanced significantly in recent years. At an upcoming UN summit, the nations of the world are scheduled to approve a sweeping set of sustainable development goals costing trillions of dollars, including unspecified "reforms of the mechanisms of global governance." The authors of the UN report containing these reforms note that the next fifteen years will be some of the "most transformative in human history."[31]

Meanwhile, biometrics, digital currencies, and similar technologies are moving the world ever closer to a cashless society. In a CNBC.com article—"Cashless Society: A Huge Threat to Our Freedom"—Signature

Bank chairman Scott A. Shay warned of the dangers of the "sprint to a cashless economy." Shay went on to say, "This will happen in such a way as to permit governments to exercise incredibly powerful control over all human behavior. While this may sound like a paranoid doomsday scenario to some, as a real-world financial professional, I believe that this scenario is not only eminently possible, but most of the technology is already available—albeit not yet fully marshaled—to frighteningly make it reality."[32]

Increasingly, these and similar articles are showing up in the mainstream media or in reports by think tanks and nonprofit organizations. Recently, Hudson Institute senior fellow John Fonte—author of *Sovereignty or Submission: Will Americans Rule Themselves or Be Ruled by Others?*—wrote that the world is at the beginning of an epic international political and ideological conflict between the forces of global governance and the democratic nation-state, especially the United States and Israel.[33]

"The concept of 'global governance' is in the air," Fonte wrote. "For many of the world's elites—who gather at places like Geneva, Davos, The Hague, UN headquarters in Manhattan, and wherever the G20 meets—global governance is the 'big idea.' Leading thinkers argue that today's global issues are too complex for the 'obsolete' nation-state system... We are told that 'sovereignty' must be redefined as something that is 'shared' or 'pooled.'" Fonte noted that there is nothing hidden or conspiratorial about the global governance movement or its goals. "The globalists' objectives are found, not in dusty memoranda or 'secret' Bilderberg or Trilateral Commission conferences, but on the websites of the United Nations, the European Union, the American Bar Association, Yale Law School, and the Ford Foundation."[34]

In a recent article in the prestigious *Financial Times*, "And Now for a World Government," Gideon Rachman went even further, saying that he believes the "formation of some sort of world government is plausible. A 'world government' would involve much more than co-operation between nations. It would be an entity with state-like characteristics, backed by a body of laws. The European Union has already set up a continental government for 27 countries, which could be a model. The E.U. has a supreme court, a currency, thousands of pages of laws, a large civil service and the ability to deploy military force."[35]

John W. Whitehead, a constitutional law attorney, president of the Rutherford Institute, and the author of *A Government of Wolves: The Emerging American Police State*, says the superwealthy now "run the show" and are cleverly orchestrating the creation of a global government without the knowledge of the vast majority of the world's population. This emerging "global state" will maintain "the semblance of the fictional nation-state, but operate like a global society"—at least initially. "Let's say there is a global secret government now," Whitehead says. "You wouldn't want it to look like a global government. You'd want different countries. People want to be American or Russian or French. They want to have nations...I think if you want a global society, you would keep the semblance of the nations and there would be something to keep people in check."[36]

During the transition to this new global system, the elite are using a multipronged strategy to ensure its success and avoid a worldwide uprising. This strategy involves corporate-controlled media that keep people entertained and distracted and usually report only information already vetted by the government, intimidation, and even arrests of those who object to what is happening, and the development of an aggressive surveillance state.

Whitehead calls this the "global electronic concentration camp"—a brave new world in which governments are partnering with corporations like Google to monitor people's e-mails, text messages, and telephone calls, and to track their movements with literally millions of cameras. "What's emerging, obviously, is a corporate state in America, but probably it will be stretching around the world with drones and satellites—a corporate global society. Look at China. China is a corporate state—a corporate tyranny."[37]

The New World Order

Since at least the early twentieth century, globalists have openly called for the creation of a New World Order. This began with President Woodrow Wilson in 1917, was picked up by Vice President Nelson Rockefeller in the late 1960s, and was championed repeatedly by President George H. W. Bush in the late 1980s and early 1990s. It has since been repeated by British prime minister Tony Blair, Soviet leader Mikhail Gorbachev, banker and philanthropist David Rockefeller, and Vice President Biden. "The affirmative task we have now is—is to actually create a new world order," Biden told the Export-Import Bank Annual Conference in 2013. In the wake of the global economic crisis, Pope Benedict called for the creation of a "global public authority." Even Adolf Hitler called for its creation: "National socialism will use its own revolution for the establishing of 'a new world order.'"[38]

"The New World Order, of course, is not exactly a new idea," says Jim Marrs, a former *Fort Worth Star-Telegram* investigative reporter and the *New York Times* bestselling author of *Rule by Secrecy* and *Crossfire: The Plot That Killed Kennedy*, the source for Hollywood director Oliver Stone's film *JFK*. "You can go all the way back through history and find people who talked about instituting a new order in the world. It's gotten to have the connotation that this means the push for a one-world government. I would even go so far as to say that the wealthy elite, this one percent, realize that they need to control everything if they are going to maintain their power and monopolies. So, yes, they are pushing for one-world socialism."[39]

The move toward global socialism—as detailed in the *Newsweek* cover story "We Are All Socialists Now: The Perils and Promise of the New Era of Big Government"—has its modern roots in books and articles written by the Fabian socialists of Great Britain. This includes playwright and London School of Economics cofounder George Bernard Shaw; H. G. Wells, a purported British intelligence operative and author of *The New World Order* and *The Open Conspiracy: Blue Prints for a World Revolution*; and Aldous Huxley, author of *Brave New World* and brother of Dr. Julian Huxley, an internationalist, president of the British Eugenics Society, and the first director of UNESCO—a specialized UN agency that promotes "global citizenship education." The Fabian socialists have had a far greater impact on the modern world than many would suspect. Jerry Bowyer, a chief economist at BenchMark Financial Network, wrote in a *Forbes* article that President Barack Obama is a Fabian socialist. "Fabians believed in gradual naturalization of the economy through manipulation of the democratic process," Bowyer wrote. "Breaking away from the violent revolutionary socialists of their day, they thought that the only real way to effect 'fundamental change' and 'social justice' was through a mass movement of the working classes presided over by intellectual and cultural elites."[40]

The rise of the New World Order aligns with prophecies in Daniel and Revelation regarding an end-times global government, economy, and religion that will hold the entire world in its grip. Many prophecy scholars believe some type of international crisis will serve as the catalyst facilitating the rise of the predicted global dictator who will oversee this Orwellian geopolitical-military, economic, and religious system.

"The Antichrist will initially be a man of peace and he will be a man with global and economic solutions," Greg Laurie says. "He will be able to get the Israelis and the Arab nations to sign some kind of peace agreement. He will come as a false messiah. So any talk I hear of a one-world currency and a one-world government is certainly a cause for concern if it means a move toward the end-times scenario spoken of in Revelation."[41]

Mark Hitchcock, a pastor, lawyer, prophecy scholar, and adjunct professor at Dallas Theological Seminary, says globalization is setting the stage for the fulfillment of end-times predictions. "The Bible tells us in Revelation 13 that there is going to be a one-world economy, a one-world religion, and there is going to be a one-world government in the end, and so to me the globalism that we see today points toward that," Hitchcock says. "How much longer will it take for the stage to be set? No one knows."[42]

The move toward a cashless society, the exponential growth of the surveillance state, and the development of mark of the Beast technologies are the necessary components for the total societal control the Bible predicts the Antichrist and the False Prophet will wield.

A recent Entrepreneur.com article noted that "implantable chips are already in use and growing." "It's only a matter of time before those [chips] migrate under our skin into our bodies," according to Peter Eckersley, the lead technologist at the Electronic Frontier Foundation.[43]

During the Tribulation, the Antichrist will require everyone—under penalty of death—to "receive a mark on their right hands or on their foreheads, so that they could not buy or sell unless they had the mark," according to Revelation 13:16–17 (NIV). Mark Hitchcock believes a cashless society is coming. "I think we are seeing the beginning of it already. When we look at our world today, we see things moving in that direction, and in some cases, rapidly. To me, the convergence of all these things is staggering."[44]

Is the Illuminati (If It Even Exists) Really Bent on World Conquest?

Amid this convergence in end-times signs, the central question is what forces could bring about the return of "Mystery, Babylon" and "Babylon the Great"—the final geopolitical, economic, and spiritual system described in Revelation 17–18. In recent years, a number of prophetic scholars have drawn parallels between the New World Order and the revived Roman Empire that the biblical prophet Daniel predicted would arise in the last days.[45]

These experts and esoteric researchers claim that the Illuminati—the pop culture moniker for the elite and their interlocking networks of transnational corporations, international banks, government agencies, think tanks, foundations, and secret societies—are behind the push to create a global government, economy, and New Age religious system "not seen since the Tower of Babel."[46]

While this power structure is known popularly as the Illuminati, former MI6 intelligence agent John Coleman calls its inner core "the Committee of 300." In his book with a subtitle of the same name, Coleman described this cabal as a highly organized secret society with "tentacles reaching into every level of government of the world, backed and run by men of the highest education and intelligence, with vast resources at their disposal."[47]

The late Georgetown University history professor Carroll Quigley, a noted expert on secret societies whom President Bill Clinton (one of Quigley's students) cited as an important influence, wrote about this hidden power structure in his classic 1966 book, *Tragedy & Hope: A History of the World in Our Time*: "The powers of financial capitalism had another far-reaching aim, nothing less than to create a world system of financial control in private hands able to dominate the political system of each country and the economy of the world as a whole. This system was to be controlled in a feudalist fashion by the central banks of the world acting in concert, by secret agreements arrived at in frequent private meetings and conferences."[48]

Fascinatingly, a 2011 study by the Swiss Federal Institute of Technology found that a very small core group of banks and giant corporations dominate the global economic system. The researchers found this core group—described as an "economic super-entity"—consists of just 147 very tightly knit companies, mostly banks.[49]

This power structure has many facets, front groups, and interlocking power centers, including the Bilderberg Group, Council on Foreign Relations, Royal Institute of International Affairs, World Trade Organization, World Bank, International Monetary Fund, Federal Reserve, CIA, MI6, Round Table, Trilateral Commission, Club of Rome, Bohemian Grove, Yale University's Skull and Bones, and UN, experts say.

The late Antony C. Sutton, a British and American economist and historian and a senior fellow at the Hoover Institution at Stanford University, wrote in *America's Secret Establishment: An Introduction to the Order of Skull & Bones* that the infamous Yale University society is a "multigenerational foreign-based secret society with fingers in all kinds of pies and roots going back to 'Illuminati' influences in 1830's Germany."[50]

Historians agree that the Bavarian Illuminati was an actual secret society. The big question is whether it survived the Bavarian government's 1786 ban on secret societies, still exists today in some form, or helped inspire and fund the creation of other secret societies and clandestine organizations.[51]

In his book *Rapture (Under Attack)*, Tim LaHaye, coauthor of the Left Behind series of end-times thrillers that has sold more than eighty million copies, wrote that he spent more than four decades studying the "satanically-inspired, centuries-old conspiracy to use government, education, and media to destroy every vestige of Christianity within our society and establish a New World Order. Having read at least fifty books on the Illuminati, I am convinced that it exists and can be blamed for many of man's inhumane actions against his fellow man during the past two hundred years...For twenty years my wife and I have worked tirelessly to halt the effects of this conspiracy on the church, our government, media, and the public schools...An enormous amount of evidence proves that the secularization of our once Judeo-Christian society has not been an accident but is the result of the devilishly clever scheming carried on by this secret order."[52]

One of the primary books about the Bavarian Illuminati was written by John Robison in 1798. Robison, a professor of natural philosophy at the University of Edinburgh, a contributor to *Encyclopaedia Britannica*, secretary to the Royal Society of Edinburgh, and a former Freemason, wrote in *Proofs of a Conspiracy: Against All the Religions and Governments of Europe, Carried on in the Secret Meetings of Free Masons, Illuminati, and Reading Societies*, that the Bavarian government had discovered documents in the possession of Illuminati members that contained plans for overthrowing the governments of Europe and "rooting out" Christianity. Although the Bavarian government had outlawed secret societies, Robison wrote that it was revived afterward under another name all over Germany: "It was again detected, and seemingly broken up, but it had by this time taken so deep root that it still subsists without being detected, and has spread into all the countries of Europe. It took its first rise among the Free Masons, but is totally different from Free Masonry."[53]

But Trevor W. McKeown, curator of the library and archives at the nine-thousand-member Grand Lodge of British Columbia and Yukon, says the Bavarian Illuminati existed for only eight years in the late 1700s and the historical records indicate it didn't have "any real effect on the beliefs, ceremonies or rituals of Freemasonry." The Bavarian Illuminati advocated the "extremely radical and revolutionary" ideas of separation of church and state, limits on the power of the state, and emancipation of the people. "So as far as Western civilization is concerned, the

Illuminati won, and each and every one of us is the recipients of those values," McKeown says.[54]

Muralist and radio host Robert Hieronimus, a co-Mason and author of *Founding Fathers, Secret Societies: Free Masons, Illuminati, Rosicrucians, and the Decoding of the Great Seal*, also rejects claims that the Illuminati infiltrated Freemasonry and "since then the Masons have served as the cover organization for men of power to control the rest of humanity." "I am not about to deny the existence of covert groups of powerful men who meet for shadowy purposes of mind control of the masses," Hieronimus—a Great Seal expert whose research has been used by the White House and the U.S. State Department and a highly acclaimed artist whose works include the famous "Woodstock Bus" and the prophetic *Apocalypse* mural at Johns Hopkins University—wrote in his book *The United Symbolism of America*. "However, I am wholeheartedly of the belief that this is not being done through the auspices of the modern Freemasons."[55]

Likewise, Jim Marrs agrees that the vast majority of Freemasons are not "sinister conspirators." "That's not the case at all," Marrs said on the History Channel special "Secret Societies. "But what Masonic historians and authors have made very, very plain is that within Freemasonry there's a small inner core, an inner circle if you will, of people who have some knowledge of the true agenda, and then you have the huge outer circle that basically doesn't even know the inner circle exists."[56]

Public fascination with the Illuminati, Freemasonry, and other secret societies has grown dramatically in recent years, especially since the release of blockbuster books and films like Dan Brown's *The Da Vinci Code* and *Angels & Demons*; and *National Treasure* starring Nicolas Cage. Secret societies and their symbols—pyramids, obelisks, temples, altars, and the all-seeing eye—are now pop culture phenomena that appear regularly in films, TV shows, music videos, music award shows, and Olympic Games ceremonies, and even on supermarket stands with publications like *Time* magazine's *Secret Societies: Decoding the Myths and Facts of History's Most Mysterious Organizations* and Devra Newberger Speregen and Debra Mostow Zakarin's *Secret Societies: The Truth Revealed*.

Illuminati is a buzzword among youth and is part of hip-hop culture. Musical artists such as Jay-Z, Lady Gaga, and others often flash the "pyramid signal" in their music videos and during concerts. "Jay-Z has an understanding of the magnetic power of some of these symbols—the Pentagram, the eye in the pyramid, the obelisk—and he uses them as an artist," Mitch Horowitz, editor in chief of Tarcher/Penguin and author of *Occult America: White House Séances, Ouija Circles, Masons, and the Secret Mystic History of Our Nation*, said on a recent *HuffPost Live* segment. "These things have deep historical roots, but they were popularized in the modern world by Freemasonry. The Illuminati as an organization existed kind of at the fringe margins of Freemasonry and they were very much attached to these symbols because they believed they communicated something about a universal search for meaning. There were many of the Founding Fathers, including [George] Washington, Thomas Jefferson, John Hancock, who also found these symbols appealing and they imbued our currency and the design of our capital with some of these symbols." On the *HuffPost Live* segment titled "Why Are People Obsessed with the Illuminati?," host Marc Lamont Hill spoke to Horowitz, as well as a columnist from the *Washington Post* and an editor at *Reason* magazine, about the Illuminati. Hill, a journalist, author, television personality, and associate professor at Teachers College, Columbia University, said people worldwide—and "not just people in tinfoil hats in their basements, but everyday people who go to work, who watch TV, who vote in elections, your friends, my friends"—believe "that the world is run by these people."[57]

Hill stated, "I begin from the premise that a small group of people run the world. That is empirically true when it comes to wealth, right—that one or two or three percent of the world controls like sixty-five to seventy percent of the wealth. It's no secret to anyone that decisions about how the world functions, who gets elected, and who is going to run are not really made in ballot boxes, but are made in private rooms. It's not a question of whether or not there is rule by the few. The question is: What is the nature of that organization? What is the nature of how power is organized? It could be the Illuminati. It could be the Bilderbergs. It could be people with wealth and money. It could be something else. That's what we want to unpack. So no one is disputing the idea that small groups of people run the world. The question is: What is the nature of that arrangement of power?"[58]

Our research into this question uncovered extensive proof that this "invisible government" or "secret government"—as President Theodore Roosevelt and journalist Bill Moyers have described it—is indeed the world's predominant power structure.[59]

Many of the Founding Fathers, U.S. presidents, prominent world leaders, and others, including George Washington, Thomas Jefferson, Yale University president Timothy Dwight, Harvard University president Joseph Willard, Abraham Lincoln, Theodore Roosevelt, Woodrow Wilson, Winston Churchill, and John F. Kennedy, warned of the dangers of the wealthy elite, their secret societies, and interconnected political and financial networks. They spoke of the "money power," the "invisible government," and "a small group of dominant men" with inordinate power and influence.[60]

Are the Illuminati still in existence? Is it—as some researchers have claimed—made up of thirteen wealthy and powerful families who trace their bloodlines back to the royalty of Europe, Rome, Egypt, and even ancient Babylon? If so, what exactly is it, what kind of power does it wield, and are its members really intent on controlling the world and its wealth? Or is the "Illuminati" simply the pop culture term for the real power structure in today's world, the plutocracy—the elitists who exercise power over the planet's governments by virtue of their extreme wealth?

A recent *Rolling Stone* article titled "Everything Is Rigged: The Biggest Price-Fixing Scandal Ever" offered intriguing insight into this question: "Conspiracy theorists of the world, believers in the hidden hands of the Rothschilds and the Masons and the Illuminati, we skeptics owe you an apology. You were right. The players may be a little different, but your basic premise is correct: The world is a rigged game. We found this out in recent months, when a series of related corruption stories spilled out of the financial sector, suggesting the world's largest banks may be fixing the prices of, well, just about everything."[61]

In his book *The Trillion-Dollar Conspiracy*, Jim Marrs wrote, "The global financiers—the global plutocrats of Wall Street, London, and Switzerland—have manipulated Western history for at least the past century." Now, Americans are living under the "tyranny of a New World Order"—a world run by elites connected to the Bilderberg Group, Council on Foreign Relations, Trilateral Commission, and similar organizations.[62]

Many of these people trace their lineage to the royals of Europe, Charlemagne, the Roman caesars, the pharaohs of Egypt, and even Nimrod. "The Rothschild banking dynasty, for example, they believe themselves to be the descendants of Nimrod, who was the ancient god-king of Sumer," Marrs says. "So there is a strange aspect to the whole thing, and yet when you actually begin to study it there is quite compelling evidence that this ruling elite—this 1 percent, this New World Order bunch, this Illuminati, whatever you want to call them—is actually just one and the same of the bloodlines that have come down through antiquity."[63]

The Reason for Our Hope

Regardless of the names people use to describe this clandestine power structure, our investigation uncovered significant evidence connecting the world's most infamous secret society, the Bible's greatest prophetic riddle, and what Billy Graham calls the "end of the age." Based on the extensive evidence laid out in *The Babylon Code*, we believe secret societies with roots in the mystery religions of the Tower of Babel and ancient Babylon are engaged in activities that are setting the stage for the fulfillment of end-times biblical prophecies.

However, this doesn't mean it's a fait accompli. God gave us free will, and we believe there is still hope. Throughout the Bible there are examples of people and nations turning back to God and escaping destruction.

We believe that there is a personal living God of the universe who ultimately controls the destiny of the world and that he embedded a code in the Bible that has largely remained an enigma for nearly two millennia. We also believe that God gave each man and woman the power to decipher this code by reading God's Word. Jesus Christ said, "You will know the truth, and the truth will set you free" (John 8:32 ESV).

When we understand this code the truth opens up to us. We discover that there is a force at work not only in the world but in our personal lives that is far greater than the chaos. Ultimately, that force for good is embodied in Jesus. Even in the middle of the pandemonium there is a real reason for hope, and that hope is Jesus.

At a certain point in human history, at a time known only to God, Jesus will return to this earth at his second coming. At that time, he will destroy the counterfeit New World Order, and "Mystery, Babylon" will fall. At the Second Coming, God will usher in a brand-new world, a new heaven, a new earth, and the New Jerusalem. Jesus will conquer death, and all those who put their faith in him will be given new bodies and live forever. Jesus said these words: "Behold, I make all things new" (Rev. 21:5 KJV). When we trust in that reality we have an unshakable hope.

In fact, Revelation is the Bible's greatest book of hope. It reveals God's final chapter in the story of humanity's salvation that began in Genesis. In the end, God is victorious. That's the great hope of our faith, and that's why "God's prophet" is sounding the alarm regarding the Second Coming.

Part I

A STORY OF APOCALYPTIC PROPORTIONS

Chapter One

"Mystery, Babylon"—the Bible's Greatest Prophetic Riddle

Upon her forehead was a name written, MYSTERY, BABYLON THE GREAT, THE MOTHER OF HARLOTS AND ABOMI-NATIONS OF THE EARTH.

—APOSTLE JOHN (REVELATION 17:5 KJV)

An enigmatic code in the Bible predicts what is happening now—a global political and financial coup d'état that is setting the stage for the end times.

The prophetic mystery foretelling this international takeover by the world's elite begins in Genesis at the Tower of Babel and ends in Revelation with the Battle of Armageddon. It revolves around "Mystery, Babylon"—the Bible's greatest end-times riddle—and reveals how an interlocking network of transnational corporations, international banks, government agencies, think tanks, nonprofits, foundations, and secret societies are working to create a global government and cashless society as predicted in the Bible.

Amid heightened instability in the world, discussions about "global governance" are intensifying, and many believe the world is just one crisis away from the creation of what globalists describe as the "New

International Order" or "Global Union."[1] Geopolitical experts say the world is now undergoing the most radical and revolutionary transformation in all of history—moving from independent nation-states to a global government.

Curiously, a prophetic code that began in Genesis and culminates in Revelation foretells the rise of what globalists today call the New World Order. This biblical mystery originates in ancient Babylon with the story of the Tower of Babel and Nimrod, ruler of the first world government. It reappears in Revelation—the New Testament's most enigmatic book—with the rise of "Mystery, Babylon."

But "Mystery, Babylon" is not as mysterious and secret as it may seem if you know how to decipher it. In *The Babylon Code*, you'll learn how to break the ancient secret code and come to see that all the visible clues regarding its existence and agenda are right before our eyes.

The Key to Unlocking the Babylon Code

The key to unlocking this biblical cryptogram is Babylon, the second-most-mentioned city in the Bible other than Jerusalem.

In a way, the biblical metanarrative—and all of human history—is really the story of the battle between the two archetypal cities, the earthly Babylon and the heavenly Jerusalem. The Bible pictures Jerusalem as the righteous city and faithful bride of Christ, but Babylon is revealed as the materialistic megalopolis of rebellion and sin.[2]

"Babylon is a cipher for the world system that is opposed to God," says Darrell Bock, the senior research professor of New Testament studies at Dallas Theological Seminary. "It's not a false Christianity, which is the way some people interpret it. It's not the Roman Catholic Church, which is how Protestants interpreted it during the Reformation. It is everything that is anti-God. And the reason it's called Babylon is because Babylon represented what the global empire at the time of Daniel was when a lot of the imagery for the end times was initially discussed in-depth in the Bible. Revelation picks up all that imagery and reuses it."[3]

Babylon, a highly sophisticated and influential ancient empire, embodies a significant biblical theme. Throughout the Bible, Babylon is a place of exile for the people of God and a place of spiritual power in opposition to God, Philip Ryken says.[4]

Though little-known and rarely discussed outside circles of Bible scholars and eschatologists, Babylon plays a pivotal role in the end-times prophetic scenario. "At no time in human history could we envision the book of Revelation being viable and believable until now," says Jeff Kinley, pastor of VintageNxt and the author of *As It Was in the Days of Noah*. "At no time in human history could the world be reunited under a common currency and under a common leader. Countries are economically teetering on the edge of collapse. When one country collapses, they are all tied to one rope. The time is really ripe for the resurgence of Babylon with a one-world government, and I see that as being very possible."[5]

The legendary Babylon—one of the greatest empires in world history—is mentioned more than three hundred times in the Bible. At its height, the city of Babylon—the most magnificent and famous city in the ancient world—had achieved a high level of civilization, with sophisticated knowledge of economics, astronomy, mathematics, medicine, chemistry, botany, and other sciences that ultimately benefited the entire world.[6]

The Bible—describing Babylon as the "glory of kingdoms" and the "golden city"—actually tells the story of three different Babylons from Genesis to Revelation. The first one is Nimrod's Babylon, an archetype of the Antichrist's end-times empire. Nimrod, the first world ruler, is best known for building a great city and the fabled Tower of Babel. The second Babylon is the empire of King Nebuchadnezzar II. While mostly remembered for destroying the First Temple and taking the Jews into captivity, the ruler of the Neo-Babylonian kingdom is also famed for

living like a wild beast during seven years of insanity in a foreshadow
of the "madness of the Antichrist." Last, Babylon reappears in the end
times as "Mystery, Babylon"—an apostate worldwide religious system—
and "Babylon the Great"—a corrupt worldwide geopolitical and economic system.[7]

The Revealer of Mysteries

The term "Mystery, Babylon" in Revelation 17:5 (KJV) has puzzled theologians ever since the apostle John penned those cryptic words on Pat-
mos nearly two millennia ago. In a heavenly vision, Jesus revealed the
end of days to his beloved disciple through a phantasmagoria of images,
numbers, phrases, and riddles—the Four Horsemen of the Apocalypse,
the mark of the Beast, the seventh seal, the number 666, the Antichrist, the False Prophet, the great whore of Babylon, and the Battle of
Armageddon.

"The Bible describes [John's] vision as 'Mystery Babylon,'" Greg
Laurie wrote in *Revelation: The Next Dimension*:

> Most of us love a really good mystery—a whodunit that keeps us
> turning pages or glued to our seat in front of the TV...In this
> passage, "Mystery Babylon" is introduced, pictured as a prostitute,
> dressed in red, and riding on a beast. A scarlet harlot...In many
> ways Babylon is what we might call a code word in the Bible, rep-
> resenting something more than its name...When we use the word
> *Hollywood*, we aren't necessarily talking about the actual city of
> Hollywood. We're speaking about the movie industry as a whole.
> It's the same thing when we say "Wall Street." There really is an
> actual Wall Street in New York City, but for the most part we're
> speaking of commerce or the stock market. It's the same thing with
> the term *Babylon*.[8]

The Bible often speaks of such mysteries—describing God as the "revealer of mysteries." In Jeremiah 33:3, the prophet wrote, "Call to me and I will answer you, and will tell you great and hidden things that you have not known" (NRSV). "The Bible contains many layers of meaning and application," says Steve Cioccolanti, founder of Australia-based Discover Ministries. "Jewish rabbis are trained to interpret the Bible on at least four levels: *pashat* (simple, literal meaning); *remez* (hinted, implied meaning); *drash* (searched out, metaphorical meaning); and *sod* (secret, mystical meaning). We always start with the pashat or most simple level of interpretation unless the text itself suggests a metaphor or hidden meaning is being used."[9]

The word *Mystery* in "Mystery, Babylon" comes from the Greek word *Mysterion*—a hidden spiritual truth—and hearkens back to biblical phrases referring to various biblical mysteries. Most Bible scholars say that Babylon is best understood figuratively or symbolically. Some note the apostle Peter referred to the Roman Empire as "Babylon," which the Bible says will rise again in the last days. Extrabiblical works, including the Sibylline Oracles, *Apocalypse of Baruch*, and Esdras, also use *Babylon* as a code word for "Rome." "Down through church history most Bible interpreters have thought that Babylon was some kind of code word for some other entity, like the Roman Empire, Roman Catholicism, apostate Christianity, or even the United States or Great Britain," according to Thomas Ice, executive director of the Pre-Trib Research Center.[10]

The word *Mystery* in Revelation 17:5 is also a reference to the ancient mystery religions of Babylon, Egypt, Greece, and Rome.

"It used to be called Gnosis, and it is secret knowledge that only the initiated can know," says S. Douglas Woodward, a former partner at Ernst & Young, an executive at Oracle and Microsoft, and a prophecy expert. "[The apostle] John uses the term to suggest it's not an obvious truth. It seems to be somewhat hidden and so it takes some searching—it takes some degree of initiation, if you will—to understand. Like most mysteries in the book of Revelation, the mysteries are basically broken; the code is broken—as my mama would say—'If you know your Old Testament.'"[11]

A Strange and Storied Tale

In fact, the Old Testament is almost as much the story of the Hebrews as it is of the Babylonians. The Old Testament is filled with references to Babylon, its advanced culture, mystical beliefs, formidable military power, and early system of banking.

This great civilization, once home to the world's largest city—Babylon—has a strange and storied history. Located in the cradle of the human race, Babylonia is in the geographic heart of the world's major landmasses. Most historians believe that inhabitants of the Mesopotamian region appeared around 6000 to 9000 BC. The earliest known records—hundreds of thousands of Sumerian cuneiform tablets—are from the middle of the fourth millennium BC.[12]

While no date is given, the biblical history of Babylon begins in Genesis 11:1–9 with the tale of Nimrod and the Tower of Babel.

Hugh Ross—an astrophysicist, president of the science-faith think tank Reasons to Believe, and author of *Navigating Genesis: A Scientist's Journey Through Genesis 1–11*—believes the evidence suggests that the Flood took place twenty thousand to fifty thousand years ago. Until recent times, the traditional date of Noah's flood was based on a seventeenth-century chronology of the history of the world by Church of Ireland archbishop James Ussher, who calculated that the Deluge occurred in 2349 BC. While the dates vary, ancient cultures throughout the world share common flood stories, the most famous of which is the Epic of Gilgamesh. "There are more than 300 Flood stories in multiple civilizations globally across the world," Jeff Kinley says. "Obviously, they didn't have Facebook or Twitter and couldn't tell each other about this story. So this was something that was common to all civilizations and I think that's evidence that something did happen."[13]

At the time of the Tower of Babel incident—perhaps forty thousand to eleven thousand years ago, according to Ross—the world's inhabitants spoke one language and lived together in the land of Shinar, ignoring God's instructions to Noah to "be fruitful and multiply, and fill the earth" (Gen. 1:28 NRSV). The biblical story tells how Nimrod, in a hubristic act of defiance, built a city and a gigantic tower to reach "to the heavens" (Gen. 11:4 NIV). Just as Adam and Eve were tempted by the serpent's promise of divinity in the Garden of Eden, those building the tower and this fortified city were likewise making a divine power grab.

"They basically shook their collective fists in God's face and said, 'We're not going to do what you told us to do and move around the earth and multiply. We are going to gather in this one place,'" Mark Hitchcock says. "So, God confounds their languages—scattering people throughout the earth. I think that's the genesis of the nations of the world and the languages of the world."[14]

Hungarian legends describe this tyrant as "Nimród the Giant"—a descendant of one of the "most wicked" sons of Noah. While the idea is controversial, some prophetic experts believe he was a Nephilim—the biblical term that refers to the offspring of a woman and a fallen angel as described in Genesis 6:1–4; Numbers 13:30–33; and Jude 4–8. Other Bible scholars say a "half-angel, half-human being would be an impossible anomaly." "The only apparent solution to all the problems posed by these verses is demon possession of both parents and progeny, not demonic marriage or procreation," wrote Dr. Henry Morris, founder of the Institute for Creation Research, in *The Henry Morris Study Bible*.[15]

The construction of the Tower of Babel was the first organized rebellion against God following the Deluge. Nimrod had unified the world in political and religious unity. The Tower of Babel—an inspiration for the European Parliament's building in Strasbourg, France—was the birthplace of the mystery religions of antiquity, experts say.

Curiously, European Union buildings, murals, paintings, statues, and stamps feature a wealth of imagery and symbolism from ancient Babylon. "They used the Tower of Babel as inspiration," says Kevin Farrington, a representative of a London-based publisher of Bible prophecy reports. "What we see in Europe is a reimagining of Babel in a modern-day form."[16]

In Europe, the European Parliament building is known as "The Tower of Eurobabel." An EU poster features artist Pieter Brueghel's painting of the Tower of Babel with the slogan "Europe: Many Tongues, One Voice." A statue of the goddess Europa riding a bull—an image reminiscent of the whore of Babylon riding the beast—stands just outside the EU headquarters building in Brussels, Belgium. The same image is featured on a colossal painting on the dome of the building, on a mural at the rival Parliament building in Strasbourg, and on a 1979 EU stamp. Meanwhile, the anthem of the EU—based on Schiller's poem "Ode to Joy," which Beethoven set to music in the final movement of the Ninth Symphony—concerns "the entering of a shrine of a pagan goddess and the uniting of all men in brotherhood, by the power of magic." Beatles cofounder John Lennon sang of Schiller's "brotherhood of man" in his signature song "Imagine"—the unofficial anthem for many of a utopian world of "peace and harmony." The song was played at the closing ceremony of the 2012 London Olympics, which featured occult symbolism and Elgar's "Nimrod" song. In an interview, Lennon described "Imagine" as "anti-religious, anti-nationalistic, anti-conventional, anti-capitalistic... but because it is sugar-coated, it is accepted."[17]

The dream of Schiller, Lennon, and many others dates back to the ancient world and the "Mysteries—the secret teachings of the ancients." As described in Genesis, the ancient Tower of Babel was a center of occult worship to unite the world in rebellion against God. "We could call the Tower of Babel the first 'United Nations building,'" Hitchcock wrote in *The End of Money*. This all played into Satan's grand strategy. He's been working furiously ever since to bring this diabolical plan to fruition.[18]

To thwart their designs, God confused their languages, and people eventually spread around the world. The account in Genesis, along with other biblical stories about the authoritarian nature of empires—makes it clear that a world government is a recipe for oppression and evil to "run out of control," Hugh Ross says.[19]

God's intervention marked the end of the first world government, but it was just the beginning of the occult-based belief systems created at the Tower of Babel. Nimrod built the tower to unite the world in the worship of fallen angels, or the "sky gods." The tower was the focal point of ancient Babylon's religion and the fountainhead of all the mystery religions—the "secret cults"—that passed their esoteric knowledge down through other occult societies over the centuries. The central thread running through these mystery religions is the idea that man can become a god.[20]

So God judged them. He saw it as an Antichrist system because they wanted to create a new global order in rebellion against him.

The Tower of Babel, the Zodiac, and the Messiah

The Babylonians, accomplished stargazers whose discoveries later contributed to the development of astronomy, also used the Tower of Babel as an observatory. They designed a planisphere—or star chart—as part of the tower, according to Ray Bentley, pastor of the five-thousand-member Maranatha Chapel in San Diego, California.[21]

But their astrology-based religion perverted God's original purpose for the heavens. In his book *The Holy Land Key*, Bentley pointed out that the book of Job refers to the "Mazzaroth"—the twelve signs of the

Zodiac. God created the constellations to communicate a biblical message of redemption to people before the Bible was written. The Zodiac was meant to point people to Christ. God gave the stars "for signs and for seasons" (Gen. 1:14 NRSV), and this truth was visible in the "heavens where people would notice it and could read it."[22]

The planisphere pictured the signs of the twelve known constellations. The tower was an attempt to preserve and hand down to future generations the original revelation from God written in the heavens. But the Tower of Babel reinterpreted this message, removing God from his position as Creator and placing humanity at the center of the universe.

Nimrod twisted the meaning of the stars, shifting the focus from the Creator to the creation. He told his subjects that the stars predicted their destinies. "In the modern horoscope, the stars tell you whether to buy a house, take a job, or marry someone," Bentley says. "It's all about making us god. Nimrod was the first human to self-worship. He declared his own glory. He was called a 'mighty hunter before the Lord.' He wanted to be lifted up in worship. So there are stories about Nimrod dying and being resurrected. Where did they get that idea? They got it from the Mazzaroth, which was later fulfilled in Jesus."[23]

Nimrod and the "Great Harlot" Semiramis

These stories—based on extrabiblical traditions, legends, and mythology; *The Two Babylons* by Presbyterian Free Church of Scotland theologian Alexander Hislop; and *The Prophecy Knowledge Handbook* by Dallas Theological Seminary president John F. Walvoord—have their roots in the tale of Nimrod and the woman thought to be his wife, the beautiful prostitute Semiramis.[24] While the story of Nimrod and the Tower of Babel is in the Bible, Semiramis isn't mentioned directly, and there is considerable mystery, controversy, and intrigue surrounding this enigmatic figure. Further complicating matters, the *Encyclopaedia*

Britannica contains an entry about the Assyrian queen Sammu-ramat, or Semiramis in Greek, who became a "legendary heroine" and "built Babylon" in the ninth century BC.[25]

In his book *The Babylon Connection?*, minister Ralph Woodrow explores the controversy, noting that the Bible contains no mention of Nimrod being married to Semiramis and that Sammu-ramat lived during an entirely different time period. "Some scholars have identified Nimrod with Sargon the Great, who lived about 2600 BC; others with Gilgamesh, the heroic figure of about 2200 BC; others with the Egyptian monarch Amenophis III of about 1411; and still others with king Tukulti-Ninurta I about 1246 BC," Woodrow wrote. "History about Semiramis is so confused, some have supposed there were two women by this name, and that one may have lived earlier."[26]

The conflicting accounts could be due to the sheer amount of time that has transpired since the Tower of Babel incident, which scholars believe occurred anywhere from four thousand to forty thousand years ago. Nevertheless, some experts point to verses in the Bible that seem to lend credence to the legends surrounding Semiramis. For example, the prophet Ezekiel mentions the name of her purported son, Tammuz, in Ezekiel 8:14. During the Preach the Word Prophecy Conference 2011 at Harvest Christian Fellowship, Tim LaHaye, coauthor of the Left Behind series, cited this verse in Ezekiel, saying, "And the women were weeping for Tammuz, the mother of Nimrod, the father of paganism and all idolatry."[27]

Also, John. F. Walvoord, a highly respected Bible scholar who served as the president of the Dallas Theological Seminary from 1952 to 1986, described Semiramis in *The Prophecy Knowledge Handbook* in this way: "The wife of Nimrod, who was the founder of Babylon, headed up the mystery religion which characterized Babylon. She was given the name Semiramis, and according to the adherents' belief, she had a son conceived miraculously whose name was Tammuz," Walvoord wrote. "He was portrayed as a savior who fulfills the promise of deliverance given to Eve. This was, of course, a satanic description which permeates pagan religions."[28]

According to extrabiblical sources and legends, Nimrod married the prostitute Semiramis, who in some accounts was actually Nimrod's mother. Wanting to conceal the nature of his marriage, Nimrod told his subjects that Semiramis was a goddess. Then, after catching her in the act of adultery, Nimrod got into a fight with Semiramis—the "Queen of Babylon"—and she killed him.

Pregnant at the time from her illicit affair, Semiramis concocted an alibi regarding the astrological prediction atop the Tower of Babel about the prophecy in Genesis 3:15 pertaining to humanity's future Savior— Jesus. Semiramis told her people that Nimrod was this savior and had given his life on their behalf. Claiming to be a virgin, Semiramis said Nimrod had visited her in a "flash of light"—supernaturally impregnating her in a type of counterfeit of the virgin birth of Christ. She said the baby in her womb was the reincarnated Nimrod.

Later, according to legends, she gave birth to Tammuz, who was worshipped as a deity. Meanwhile, Semiramis told her subjects that Nimrod had become the sun god. In Egypt, according to experts, Nimrod became known as the sun god Ra—associated today with the Eye of Ra or Eye of Horus—believed to be the inspiration for the all-seeing eye above the pyramid on the back of the dollar bill.

The dollar and the Great Seal are full of symbols from the secret societies of ancient Babylon and Egypt, including the pyramid, which is essentially an occult hierarchical organizational flowchart. Toward the top are the "illumined ones," who possess the secret knowledge of "Mystery, Babylon." The bottom of the pyramid consists of the masses born to serve the god-kings. This organizational system was implemented in Egypt where the pharaoh was considered the god-king. Likewise, the Roman Empire was a pyramid society with the emperor at the top.

Throughout the ages, the source of knowledge from secret societies such as the mystery cults of ancient Egypt, Greece, and Rome has flowed directly from the "mystery religions" of ancient Babylon.[29]

Over time, the story of Nimrod is believed to have evolved in different cultures to become the story of Ra, Osiris, Apollo, Zeus, and other deities. Semiramis became a goddess and this initiated the mother-goddess religions with the young child Tammuz, a theme repeated in countless religions. "Throughout Scripture references are found concerning Babylonian worship such as Ezekiel's protest of weeping for Tammuz (Ezek. 8:14)," Walvoord wrote. "Jeremiah objects to the heathen practice of offering cakes to Semiramis as the queen of heaven (Jer. 7:18). An offshoot of this was the worship of Baal which was one of the pagan religions of Canaan, and Baal is often identified as the same person as Tammuz."[30]

These tales about Nimrod, Semiramis, and Tammuz all have their roots in Babylon—the birthplace of the money changers, mystery religions, and pagan worship of the Virgin and Child.

"The ancient Babylonians worshipped these deities," says Carroll M. Helm, a retired associate professor of education at Belmont Abbey College in Belmont, North Carolina, and the author of *God's Mysteries and Paradoxes*. "They deified Nimrod and Semiramis, who called herself the 'Queen of Heaven.' It talks about her as the great whore in Revelation. She embodies this role because she called for blood sacrifices, human sacrifices. She instituted the shrine prostitutes that we read about in the Bible."[31]

From Babylon, this occult-based belief system spread throughout the world. In Egypt, the mother and child became known as Isis and Horus; in ancient Rome, Fortuna and Jupiter; and in Greece, Ceres/Irene and Plutus.

"In fact the New Age folks, especially the feminist groups, believe in this ancient mystery religion," Helm says. "They actually worship the mother goddess—the Semiramis of ancient Babylon. The New Age movement is a reemergence of ancient…religions. Of course, we have all kinds of offshoots of that with the occult and with witchcraft being really popular today."[32]

The Return of the God-Kings and Symbols of Babylon

Another central tenet of the mystery religions is the predicted coming of the "god-kings"—a reference to the ten "benevolent kings" that Greek philosopher Plato claimed ruled the world during the time of the legendary city-state of Atlantis. Revelation 17:12 refers to ten kings—under the helm of the Antichrist—who will rule the world during the last half of the Tribulation. Currently, the UN divides the world into ten regions. Prophecy scholars say the ten kings of Revelation may preside over these global regions one day. The most recognized one is the EU, which globalists view as the "model for a projected Global Union," but others are in various states of formation.[33]

Today, the belief in the god-kings that was passed down from culture to culture, beginning in Babylon and then Egypt, Greece, Rome, and Europe, is reflected in the architecture, monuments, and artwork in Washington, DC; Rome, Italy; and the EU.

The primary architecture involves the dome, which represents Semiramis's womb, and the tower—the phallic symbol of Nimrod. This started in Egypt with the pyramids and obelisk monuments. It's also seen in Washington, DC; New York City; Rome; Paris; and many other cities with domelike structures and obelisks. It's been repeated many different ways throughout history.

The Archenemy of God's People

After God confused their languages at the Tower of Babel, Babylon didn't rise to prominence again until about 2100 BC and then later during the reign of Hammurabi from 1792 to 1750 BC. Hammurabi is known for organizing Babylon's laws into a written system known as the Code of Hammurabi. After his death, the empire declined for many centuries until the time of Nebuchadnezzar, who reigned from 1124 to 1103 BC.[34]

But the greatest period of Babylonian supremacy occurred during the reign of Nebuchadnezzar II from 605 to 562 BC. At the time, Babylon, a significant commercial and trade center in the ancient world, was the dominant imperial power in the Near East. King Nebuchadnezzar's exploits—the destruction of the First Temple in 587–586 BC and the captivity of the Jews—are chronicled in the Bible. During the zenith of Babylon's glory, Nebuchadnezzar built the Hanging Gardens of Babylon, one of the Seven Wonders of the Ancient World. The towering walls of Babylon were considered impregnable and were so vast that five chariots could race abreast around the top of the metropolis.

A sizable portion of the books of the prophets—Isaiah, Jeremiah, Daniel, and others—are devoted to Babylon as both an instrument and a target of God's judgment. Isaiah viewed the destruction of Jerusalem in prophetic terms, and Jeremiah warned people not to "play the harlot" with Babylonian gods—predicting Jerusalem would suffer the fate of a rejected prostitute. They also preached judgment against Babylon as the "climax of judgment on the nations, since Babylon is the 'archenemy of God's people.'"[35]

Following Nebuchadnezzar's reign, the Persians, under Cyrus the Great, captured Babylonia in 539 BC from Nebuchadnezzar's last successor. As predicted by Jeremiah, the city's famous walls were torn down. Eventually, the empire passed in 331 BC to Alexander the Great, who planned to make Babylon the capital of his empire, but he died in Nebuchadnezzar's palace. After Alexander's death, Babylon was eventually abandoned—bringing to an end one of the greatest empires in history.

Daniel's Prediction of the End-Times Babylon

Prior to Babylon's exit from the world stage, the prophet Daniel—while exiled in Babylon—revealed God's prophetic plan for the future and the reemergence of Babylon in the end times. In one of the Bible's most famous passages, Daniel interpreted Nebuchadnezzar's dream about a giant statue of gold, silver, bronze, iron, and clay. He said it represented the empires that would rule over Israel, including Babylon, Medo-Persia, Greece, Rome, and a future empire under the control of the "little horn"—the Antichrist (Dan. 7:8 kjv).

"The book of Daniel is an account of rulers attempting to restore the one-world government of the days before the Flood and of Nimrod's generation," Hugh Ross says. "And so you have this story of four different world empires and how God acted to stop each of those empires from ruling the world."[36]

The interpretation of Nebuchadnezzar's dream relates to another key passage—Daniel 9:24–27. This involves a supernatural coding system known as the "seventy weeks" prophecy. Daniel knew Jeremiah had predicted that the Jews' captivity would last seventy years. So Daniel prayed for the restoration of Jerusalem. The angel Gabriel visited him, telling him that 69 "weeks of years," or 483 years, would transpire from the time the decree was issued to rebuild the Temple until the day Jesus rode into Jerusalem. The prophecy was fulfilled to the day. But Israel rejected and crucified Jesus, resulting in the suspension of the "seventieth" week. The world is now living in this interim period—the "church age." God's prophetic clock will resume after the Antichrist ratifies a seven-year peace treaty with Israel—triggering the Tribulation period, the final week of years.[37]

It's during these seven years of tribulation—a period of unparalleled plague, pestilence, famine, death, and destruction—that Babylon will reappear as the embodiment of the evil forces aligned against God. In

Matthew 24:21–22, Jesus said there would be great tribulation during this time, "unequaled from the beginning of the world until now—and never to be equaled again. If those days had not been cut short, no one would survive" (NIV).

During the Tribulation, the Antichrist and the False Prophet will rise to power, controlling the global religious system—"Mystery, Babylon"—and the worldwide geopolitical and economic system known as "Babylon the Great."[38]

Revelation, written at a time when the pagan political powers had partnered with a false religion and the followers of Jesus were under intense persecution, provides a great deal of detail about these two Babylonian systems.

The secrets contained in what we've dubbed the Babylon code are so important that one out of every ten verses in Revelation is about Babylon and two entire chapters, Revelation 17 and 18, are devoted to Babylon and its destruction before the Battle of Armageddon and the Second Coming. Revelation contains 404 verses, and 44 of the verses are about Babylon.[39]

"The topic that is more talked about than anything else in the book of Revelation is Babylon," Mark Hitchcock says. "It would probably shock most people to know that."[40]

The Bible's Greatest Riddle

Over the centuries, there has been a great deal of speculation among eschatologists about the identity of the final Babylon. Preterists, who view the events in Revelation as having already occurred, equate Babylon with Jerusalem, which was destroyed by the Romans in AD 70. Idealists view Babylon as one of many symbols in Revelation about the ongoing battle between good and evil. Futurists, who believe Revelation describes events leading up to Christ's return, have linked it to apostate Christendom, the Roman Catholic Church, the United States as a whole, Europe, Rome, Jerusalem, and even the rebuilt city of Babylon, a project now under way in Iraq. Prior to his death, former Iraqi dictator Saddam Hussein commissioned the rebuilding of the ancient city. The U.S. State Department has contributed millions of dollars to the "Future of Babylon Project." It is designed to attract "scores of 'cultural tourists' from all over the world to see the glories of Mesopotamia's most famous city."[41]

"Some think it's just some transtemporal city—it's just going to be whatever great city is dominating events in the end times," Hitchcock says. "Others take it to be Rome because of the reference to the seven mountains or the seven hills there. My view is that Babylon is the literal Babylon over in what is modern-day Iraq. It is right in the middle of about two-thirds of the world's proven oil reserves."[42]

While Iraq is usually assumed to be Babylon by some prophecy teachers, Cioccolanti notes that the ancient territory of Babylon could just as well refer to the Arabian Peninsula and nations such as Saudi Arabia, Qatar, and Yemen. "John gives us descriptions of 'Babylon' which are congruent with the Arabian Peninsula," Cioccolanti says. "In Revelation 17:6, John wrote: 'I saw the woman [Babylon], drunk with the blood of the saints and with the blood of the martyrs of Jesus.' Both Al Qaeda and ISIS are drunk on beheading Christians and minorities, women, and children. Who funds them? The money and weapons appear to trace back to the axis of Saudi Arabia–Qatar–Kuwait. These countries, which situate where ancient Babylon once was, are the state sponsors of Sunni terrorist groups." In Revelation 18, the apostle John notes that Babylon "sits on many waters," a description that doesn't fit Iraq but does fit Saudi Arabia—a country with thousands of kilometers of coastland that is flanked by both the Persian Gulf and the Red Sea. Saudi Arabia has the largest seaport network in the Middle East with eight major ports and three minor ones. "She trades by sea the oil that every nation drinks," Cioccolanti says. "Second, Babylon is a region that lives in luxury." In Revelation 18:3, the apostle John notes that the "merchants of the earth have become rich through the abundance of her luxury" (NKJV). "The oil-backed opulence that exists in the Middle East cannot be compared to any other nation's conspicuous consumption," Ciocco-lanti says. "From diamond-studded Mercedes to the world's first under-water hotel, the Arabian Peninsula has mind-blowing extravagance. It boasts 25 percent of the world's cranes, the world's tallest tower, largest shopping malls, largest indoor ski facility...you get the picture. When John was shown this Babylon of the future, he 'marveled with great amazement' [Rev. 17:6]. All of us do, even when we are accustomed to Western wealth and technology. Saudi Arabia, in all the above ways, would qualify as the most straightforward candidate for Babylon."[43]

In recent times, a growing number of experts have expressed alarm at the rise of "apocalyptic Islam" in the Middle East with ISIS slaughter-ing, beheading, and crucifying thousands of people, mostly Christians. For the first time in history, two nation-states in the Middle East are driven not by political ideology or religious theology but by "apoca-lyptic, genocidal end-times eschatology." "The Islamic Republic of Iran today is ruled by an apocalyptic, genocidal death cult," Joel Rosenberg wrote. He continued:

So is the Islamic State, also known as ISIS or ISIL. The former are Shia. The latter are Sunni. Both believe the end of days has come. Both believe their messiah—known as the "Mahdi"—is coming at any moment. Both are trying to hasten the coming of the Mahdi. Yet each has entirely different strategies to hasten his arrival or appearance on earth. ISIS wants to build a caliphate. Iran wants to build "the Bomb." ISIS is committing genocide now. Iran is preparing to commit genocide later. In the near term, ISIS is more dangerous. Why? Because ISIS is on a jihadist rampage right now. Robbing. Killing. Destroying. Enslaving. Raping. Torturing. Beheading. Because ISIS is a satanic movement. This is not mere terrorism. This is genocide. These are demon-possessed people making blood sacrifices to their god, and if they are not stopped they will murder millions and bring down one mid-eastern regime after another. As Americans, we dare not turn a blind eye to this threat. If we don't defeat the jihadists over there, they are coming here. Longer term, Iran is the most dangerous, especially if the President [Obama] approves the disastrous nuclear deal that is emerging. Why? Because the apocalyptic leaders of Iran are biding their time to build a nuclear arsenal capable of killing tens of millions of people in a matter of minutes.[44]

While Hitchcock, Rosenberg, and others debate what role the ancient Babylonia region will play in end-times events, prophecy teachers such as Hal Lindsey—author of *The Late Great Planet Earth*, the bestselling nonfiction book of the 1970s—Tim LaHaye, and Grant R. Jeffrey have taught for decades that Europe would play a central role in the last days with the emergence of the revived Roman Empire.

In *One Nation, Under Attack*, Jeffrey reiterated this position, warning that international financiers and powerful socialist forces are working to destroy the United States and pave the way for the rise of the Antichrist and a global government. These conspirators are working together with many willing accomplices in powerful positions in the United States and Europe. Jeffrey argued that "globalist multibillionaires" had bankrolled liberal-progressive political candidates—pulling the "strings of highly placed puppets in government."[45]

"In a very short time, the United States will be pushed to the sidelines of world events," Jeffrey wrote. "All of this is taking place just ahead of the emergence of the prophesied Antichrist. Satan's representative on earth will consolidate his power and establish his dictatorship, first over the revived Roman Empire and soon after that, over the entire world. And the American Empire, which rose to power with the blessing of God, will be so weak that it won't play a notable role in the culminating events of the 'last days.'"[46]

While many prophecy scholars still share this view, a number are now taking a closer look at America in the prophetic end-times scenario. One of the most prominent proponents of this view is the late Times Square Church pastor David Wilkerson, author of the bestselling book *The Cross and the Switchblade.* After the September 11, 2001, terrorist attacks, Wilkerson told his congregation that he believed America was the end-times Babylon depicted in Revelation 17–18 that is destroyed in one hour near the end of the Tribulation. "Everything will change in one hour or one day to bring down the Babylonian system of greed," Wilkerson told *Charisma* magazine in 2008.[47]

Wilkerson and others who hold this view note that Revelation 17 refers to the "great prostitute, who sits by many waters" (v. 1 NIV) that is destroyed in one hour. The apostle John wrote that the "woman you saw is the great city that rules over the kings of the earth" and sits "enthroned as queen" (17:18; 18:7 NIV). In these chapters, John wrote that the "Mother of Prostitutes and of the Abominations of the Earth" would be destroyed by fire, while the "kings of the earth who committed adultery with her and shared her luxury" and the merchants who grew "rich from her excessive luxuries" would "weep and mourn over her because no one buys their cargoes anymore" (17:5; 18:3, 9, 11 NIV).

Likewise, Woodward believes that America—the globe's remaining superpower with the world's largest military and economy—is the end-times Babylon described in Revelation 17–18. The Babylon of Revelation 18 is an economic giant that dominates global finance and is a supreme military power. Both descriptions fit America, which has the largest economy in the world, more than one thousand military bases worldwide, and the planet's largest navy, including more than eighty nuclear-powered submarines—half of which are equipped with nuclear missiles.[48]

"We take a very contrarian view," Woodward says. "We believe that America is at the center of what is happening in the world. We do not believe that Europe will be the powerbase of the Antichrist. We believe that America will be the powerbase of the Antichrist. We don't speculate on any particular American leader, but we believe there will be an American leader soon who heads up this empire and that leader will likely be the Antichrist. So, as succinctly as possible, America is at the heart of what happens in the end times and unfortunately it's on the wrong side."[49]

However, we believe "Mystery, Babylon" and "Babylon the Great" will have multiple geographic centers. We base this argument on the fact that Revelation refers to three components of the end-times Babylon—spiritual, economic, and geopolitical-military. It's a global government, economic system, and false religion. While no one can say with certainty where these will be headquartered, we believe the most likely power centers will be in the United States (Washington, DC, America's political capital; and New York City, the financial capital); Europe; and the Middle East, perhaps the rebuilt city of Babylon. The end-times Babylonian system will likely involve a global network of nations, including a transatlantic partnership between the United States and Europe's financial center—the "City of London," or the "Square Mile."

Regardless of how and where it arises, Revelation makes it clear that this end-times geopolitical, economic, and religious system will revolve around money and the mark of the Beast. According to the apostle John, those who refuse to take this mark on their right hand or forehead will face beheading. However, John warned that anyone who "worships the beast and its image and receives its mark on their forehead or on their hand" will be "tormented with burning sulfur in the presence of the holy angels and of the Lamb" (Rev. 14:9–10 NIV).

Further, Revelation and other biblical books offer clues as to the identity of those who will help facilitate the rise to power of the Antichrist and the False Prophet over this final Babylonian system. As noted earlier, Revelation 18 points out that the "kings of the earth who committed adultery" with Babylon "shared her luxury" and became rich. We believe these "kings" are today's elite.

In *Our Occulted History*, Jim Marrs touches on the connection between ancient Babylon, "the magic of money manipulation," and today's monetary system. He points out the existence since antiquity of an "international money power" that employs a variety of means to enrich itself, including "fraud, deception, assassination, and war," in order to "usurp the money-and credit-creating power of the various states it has sought to dominate."[50]

In ancient Babylon, the priests controlled the supply of money, checks were circulated, and "promises to pay" in silver were used to make loans. Such practices gave rise to an "international class of bullion brokers," or bankers.[51]

Over the centuries, the monetary systems of Babylon spread to other cultures. In fact, it was this very partnership between the money changers and the religious leaders of the Temple in Jerusalem that ignited Jesus' only violent outburst during his earthly ministry. The apostle Matthew gave this account: "Jesus went into the temple of God and drove out all those who bought and sold in the temple, and overturned the tables of the money changers and the seats of those who sold doves. And He said to them, 'It is written, "My house shall be called a house of prayer," but you have made it a "den of thieves"'" (21:12–13 NKJV).

Was Jesus' visceral reaction to the money changers in the Temple more than just righteous indignation at the misuse of God's house? Does the incident also offer another piece of the prophetic puzzle regarding the identity of those behind the rise of Babylon in the last days?

It certainly does for Marrs, who believes the same political, economic, and religious beliefs prevalent in ancient Babylon, the location of the world's first secret society, have been resurrected among today's secret societies and wealthy elite.

"They are concerned with global manipulation," Marrs says. "I would refer to them as elitists. They feel like that because of their bloodlines, because of their wealth, because of their power, that they should be in charge of the world. And I'm sure some of them even feel like they would be quite beneficial and benevolent, but still for myself, being a student of history and a huge supporter of freedom and liberty, I don't want anyone in charge of myself except myself.[52]

"I think we need to be aware of these people and I think we need to resist their attempt to just take over and control the entire world. They are pretty close now because they control the banking systems, they control the basic resources of the world, and as a result they pretty well control the political process."[53]

Chapter Two

The World's Most Infamous Secret Society

They that will be rich fall into temptation and a snare, and into many foolish and hurtful lusts, which drown men in destruction and perdition. For the love of money is the root of all evil.

—APOSTLE PAUL (1 TIMOTHY 6:9–10 KJV)

The world is full of obvious things which nobody by any chance ever observes.

—SHERLOCK HOLMES, *THE HOUND OF THE BASKERVILLES*

Many believe it has nearly unlimited wealth, power, and reach. It's known by many names: the "shadow government," "the invisible government," or what Masonic historian Manly P. Hall calls the "Order of the Illumined."[1]

Secret society experts say this mysterious group consists of wealthy families, transnational corporations, international banks, government agencies, think tanks, foundations, nonprofits, and secret societies. They claim it has many facets, front groups, and interlocking organizations, including the Bilderberg Group, Council on Foreign Relations, Royal Institute for International Affairs, Trilateral Commission, United

Nations, CIA, MI6, National Security Agency, Federal Reserve, World Bank, International Monetary Fund, World Trade Organization, Bank for International Settlements, Bohemian Grove, and Yale University's Skull and Bones.

In today's pop culture, the elite, cloak-and-dagger network purportedly controlling these organizations is known as the Illuminati—the rich and powerful secret society that gained international exposure in blockbuster movies such as Dan Brown's *Angels and Demons* starring Tom Hanks and *Lara Croft: Tomb Raider* featuring Angelina Jolie. This "shadow government" of wealthy elitists in international banking, politics, media, and industry is believed to be behind efforts to create a global government, monetary system, and universal religion. Not surprisingly, these elitists trace their roots to the Knights Templar, the "medieval equivalent of today's multinational corporations," and the "pioneers of international banking," according to the *Time* magazine special publication *Secret Societies*.[2] Today, this clandestine group is widely considered the world's most infamous secret society, though it's known by a variety of names.

"There is in truth a hidden hand that's working behind the scenes, behind all these apparently unconnected organizations, and they are advancing quietly, unseen an agenda for a world government, world central bank, world currency and world army and a micro-chipped population," conspiracy researcher and English writer David Icke said on the History Channel special "Secret Societies." "And it's not done openly because if we knew that was the agenda we'd scream very loudly."[3]

At a time when wealth and power are increasingly concentrated, many are asking who really runs the world, how much of the planet's wealth the elite control, and what influence they wield over politics and the news media.

A study by Princeton University professor Martin Gilens—detailed in the "Rich People Rule!" story in the *Washington Post*—shed some light on this question, concluding that the economic elites have substantial influence over the political process and average citizens have little or none. "We expected to find that interest groups and economic elites might have more influence than ordinary citizens, but what surprised us was that average Americans appear to have no influence really whatsoever over the policies the government adopts," says Gilens, a political scientist.[4]

Money, or rather political contributions made to politicians, is the key to understanding the influence of the elites. "The candidates that people can choose among when they go to the polls are candidates who . . . have already been sort of vetted by the money system," Gilens says. "And these are all people who have the support of the elites or they wouldn't be on the ballots to begin with. And so the choices that Americans have when they go to the polls are constrained by the role of money and the power of the economic elites."[5]

Given the influence of big money on politics, people are also intrigued by the nexus between the ruling elite and their secret societies such as Skull and Bones, Bohemian Grove, Freemasonry, and the most mysterious of all, the Illuminati.

"The structure by which the world is controlled by a few people, literally a handful at the very top, is like Russian dolls—one doll inside another, inside another, inside another," Icke said. "I call this web in which they all fit the Illuminati—the illuminated ones, illuminated into knowledge that the rest of us don't get—and that Illuminati has been manipulating for centuries to bring about what is now appearing before our eyes. Among some of the most famous people in the world today, you'll find that their rituals are an absolute mirror of the ones that were carried out in Babylon, in Egypt and the ancient world in general. It's an unbroken span of manipulation from the far ancient world to the present day."[6]

While some may be skeptical about the existence of the Illuminati today, historians agree it was an actual, Enlightenment-era secret society whose membership rolls included some of the most distinguished and influential men of the late eighteenth and early nineteenth centuries.

"The philosophy of the [historical Bavarian Illuminati] has carried forward through today's various secret societies—the Bilderbergers, the Council on Foreign Relations, the Royal Institute of International Affairs, and the Trilateral Commission—and these at their very inner core style themselves as globalists," Jim Marrs says. "The Illuminati as a distinct organization probably does not exist anymore—although it can be used as a catch-all term for the New World Order folks or the one percent or the one-world order guys."[7]

We, too, empathize with anyone who is skeptical about secret societies and conspiracy theories in general, as that was the case for both of us initially. There are so many outlandish, unproven, and nonfactual claims in print, film, television, and books and on the Internet that would initially discourage any sane person from taking the subject seriously. But when we began to dig deeper and separate disinformation from the truth, we found substantive proof regarding certain conspiracy theories and secret societies.

In addition, we discovered that the goal of many of these secret societies is ultimately to bring about a world state and cashless society. To our amazement, these goals are openly stated in dozens of reports on the websites of their organizations and were confirmed in interviews.

One of the most powerful organizations in this network today is the Bilderberg Group, a highly secretive organization that has generated media attention and controversy in recent years as some of the most powerful individuals in the world—Bill Clinton, Paul Wolfowitz, Henry Kissinger, David Rockefeller, Zbigniew Brzezinski, Tony Blair, and others—have met at luxurious hotels to decide "the future of humanity." In *The True Story of the Bilderberg Group*, award-winning investigative journalist and bestselling author Daniel Estulin claims that the Bilderberg Group—an organization that sponsors annual three-day conferences attended by bankers, economists, politicians, and government officials—has become a "shadow world government."[8]

"At the center of the global financial system is the financial oligarchy that is represented to a certain extent by the Bilderberg Group," Estulin says. "Members of this organization come and go, but the system itself has not changed in the decades since it was first created in 1954. You can even go further back in time to its roots in all the secret organizations. It is a self-perpetuating system, a virtual spiderweb of interlocking financial, political, economic, and industry interests. Now, what's important to understand is that organizations such as the Bilderberg Group, the Trilateral Commission, the Council on Foreign Relations, and Bohemian Grove are not the seats of power; they're the conduits of power."[9]

It's through these organizations that the "real controllers meet to decide the policies that they then take back to the other secret societies," Jim Marrs says.[10]

Half of Americans Believe a "Secret Cabal" Runs the World

Astonishingly, a recent survey by the University of Chicago found that 51 percent of Americans believe that "much of what happens in the world today is decided by a small and secretive group of individuals"—a so-called secret cabal.[11]

"In the popular media and scholarly community, it is quite common to disparage conspiracy theories as an expression of either paranoid cranks (e.g., the 1997 film *Conspiracy Theory*) or a particular type of right-wing politics," wrote University of Chicago Department of Political Science professor J. Eric Oliver and his student Thomas J. Wood in the study mentioned above. "Nationally representative survey data provides a much more complex picture of conspiracism's place in mass opinion. While the active propagators of conspiracy theories may be limited to fringe groups or the paranoid, the willingness to agree with conspiracy theories...is quite commonplace in the American public. Not only does half the American population express agreement with at least one of only seven conspiracy theories offered, large portions of the population exhibit a strong inclination towards a conspiracist predisposition."[12]

Jesse Walker, a senior editor at *Reason* magazine and the author of *The United States of Paranoia: A Conspiracy Theory*, says many people think of conspiracy theories as a phenomenon of those on the fringes—the far left and far right. "I argue, no, people believe in them in the center as well as the extremes, in the Establishment as well as among dissidents, and it's sort of at the core of the American experience," Walker says.[13]

The Bavarian Illuminati: A Historical Secret Society

This "secret cabal" is known in pop culture as the Illuminati, an enigmatic organization that is believed to be a continuation of secret societies stretching back to ancient Babylon—the site of mankind's first effort to create a world government and false religion in revolt against God.

The leaders of this rebellion have been operating in the shadows for thousands of years and have passed down the secrets of the Babylonian mystery religions—along with their wealth, power, and hidden plans—through a series of secret societies and bloodlines. The apostle John referred to this secret system of occult societies as "Mystery, Babylon."

Have you ever wondered why there is an unfinished pyramid on the back of the U.S. dollar bill with an all-seeing eye on it and the Latin phrase "Novus Ordo Seclorum," or "A New Order of the Ages," at the bottom? The symbols of these secret societies—pyramids, obelisks, domes, and the all-seeing eye—are prevalent in Washington, DC; Europe; Egypt; and throughout the world and originated among the ancient secret societies. It's the great mystery of the world concealed in plain sight.

Sumerian cuneiform tablets speak of secret societies. In Egypt, the pharaohs belonged to secret societies, such as the Mystery Schools of Egypt. Throughout recorded history, hundreds of secret societies have existed, including ones in ancient Babylon, Egypt, Greece, and the Roman Empire. In the Greek and Roman cultures, these aristocratic secret societies were known as the "secular mystery clubs" and played important roles in politics, religion, and history, as they still do today.[14]

In his landmark bestseller *The Secret Teachings of All Ages*, Manly P. Hall—described by the *Scottish Rite Journal* as "Masonry's Greatest Philosopher" and by Mitch Horowitz as an esoteric "scholar of mythic proportions"—traced the history of secret societies down through the ages and revealed that they had left clues to their existence in paintings, architecture, woodcuts, and books. "Many of the great minds of antiquity were initiated into these secret fraternities by strange and mysterious rites," Hall wrote. "After being admitted, the initiates were instructed in the secret wisdom which had been preserved for ages. Plato, an initiate of one of these sacred orders, was severely criticized because in his writings he revealed to the public many of the secret philosophic principles of the Mysteries."[15]

Like today's religions, these groups competed for control of the ancient secrets. Known as the mystery schools, these societies served as reservoirs of esoteric secrets, and their literature was carefully crafted to hide and reveal some of their knowledge. Some of the best-known successors of these early secret societies include the Gnostics, the Rosicrucian Order, and the order of the Knights Templar, a religious military order established during the Crusades that appeared "abruptly in an explosive outburst of popular hysteria, accusations of Satanism, mass arrests and fiery executions." It was during this time that the Knights Templar, a wealthy organization of Gnostics headquartered at the site of King Solomon's Temple in Jerusalem, are believed to have discovered treasure and scrolls containing esoteric secrets from the ancient world.

The Knights Templar, known for their association with the Holy Grail and the ark of the covenant, gained international fame in recent decades with films such as *The Da Vinci Code, Indiana Jones and the Last Crusade*, and *National Treasure*. Their Gnostic beliefs, which originated in Mesopotamia, held that "inner enlightenment" would bring wisdom.[16]

"Gnosis means knowledge or enlightenment, and the path of Gnosis can be found in various historical myths such as that of Semiramis, who looks like the [Statue of Liberty], including seven rays of light emanating from her head," wrote Dennis L. Cuddy, an author, historian, political analyst, and senior associate with the U.S. Department of Education during the Reagan administration.[17]

In the early eighteenth century, the remnants of the Knights Templar and mystical Rosicrucian movement, which laid the groundwork for modern science, began to associate under a central group whose founders hoped would one day "rule the world after all existing religions and governments had been destroyed." This fraternity, which sought the destruction of Christian civilization, referred to itself as the "Philosophes," according to historian and Bavarian Illuminati expert William H. McIlhany. "Inspired by the radical Philosophes and instructed by a mysterious occultist named Kolmer from what is now Denmark, Adam Weishaupt, a professor of Canon Law at the University of Ingolstadt... established a continuing organizational structure to direct the worldwide attack on religion and monarchy—a structure which would, he hoped, eventually rule the world," McIlhany wrote.[18]

This organization—founded by Weishaupt and four associates on May 1, 1776—was christened the Order of the Illuminati, a group of intellectuals who exalted the teachings of the ancient philosophers. One of Weishaupt's cofounders was reportedly William of Hesse, an employee of Mayer Amschel Rothschild—a "small merchant and money-changer" who founded the famed European banking dynasty. In 2005, *Forbes* magazine listed him as one of "The Twenty Most Influential

Businessmen of All Time." Another one of Weishaupt's associates was a merchant known only as Kolmer, who learned the esoteric knowledge of Egypt and Persia and "preached a secret doctrine based on an ancient form of Gnosticism...that had used the word 'Illuminated' prior to the third century." Additionally, Kolmer had gained esoteric knowledge from a French court magician named Cagliostro whom he met on the island of Malta, a Knights Templar stronghold. Kolmer passed these secrets on to Weishaupt.[19]

This "radical and secular occultist movement" was known for its secrecy and hierarchical structure, Librarian of Congress James H. Billington wrote in *Fire in the Minds of Men*, a phrase from Fyodor Dostoyevsky's book *The Possessed*. Upon founding the Illuminati, Weishaupt and his associates recruited about twenty-five hundred of Bavaria's leading intellectuals, including many dukes, princes, and writers. This included famed German author Johann Wolfgang von Goethe, a close friend of Schiller's who wrote *Faust*—a play about a scholar who sells his soul to the devil in exchange for knowledge, wealth, and power. These elite bankers, businessmen, and intellectuals found most of their recruits among the ranks of Germany's Masonic orders. Eerily, but living up to its satanic reputation, their Illuminist initiation rite involved getting naked and "drinking blood before seven black candles."[20]

At the time, the public had become fascinated with magic, astrology, "ghost-raising, exorcism, and alchemy," wrote Vernon Stauffer, dean and professor of New Testament and church history at Hiram College, in *The Bavarian Illuminati in America: The New England Conspiracy Scare, 1798*. The Rosicrucian Order was flourishing and rival systems had split Freemasonry—a secret fraternal order created in 1717 that evolved from the stonemason guilds of the Middle Ages (and, according to Freemason historian Dr. Albert C. Mackey, may trace its ancient origins to Nimrod)—into many hostile camps. This period during the Enlightenment was marked by an increase in religious skepticism. "To give effect to this campaign of seduction, the lodges of Freemasonry were invaded and their secret assemblies employed to spread free-thinking and cosmopolitan ideas," Stauffer wrote. "At such an hour, according to Robison, Weishaupt founded the Order of the Illuminati. Employing the opportunities afforded him by his connections with the Masons, he exerted himself to make disciples and to lay the foundations of an 'Association...which, in time, should govern the world,' the express aim of which 'was to abolish Christianity and overturn all civil government.'"[21]

These "men of rank and fortune" planned to overthrow the governments and religious establishments of Europe and "rule the world with uncontrollable power."[22]

To ensure secrecy, Weishaupt created a spy network whose members kept tabs on one another. The order's secret police—the "Insinuating Brethren," who adopted the all-seeing eye as their insignia—were charged with killing anyone who attempted to inform the authorities about the conspiracy. Two years after its creation, all but two of the chairs at the University of Ingolstadt were held by members of the Illuminati. Many were judges, lawyers, ministers, and doctors, along with princes and members of the literati. "The influence of the Order on German education and the German clergy was devastating," William McIlhany wrote. "By 1800, many German ministers no longer believed the most basic tenets of Christian doctrine. They had been converted to the worship of 'reason.'"[23]

The Illuminati, an "occult mystical-spiritualistic movement," had a distinct political agenda and infiltrated many segments of society through Freemasonry, according to Princeton University professor emeritus of German Theodore Ziolkowski. "Taking as their symbol of wisdom the owl of Minerva, they pursued essentially the same ideals as traditional Freemasonry—liberty, equality, fraternity—but, in distinction from the other movement, had a specifically political agenda: to educate people through ethics and enlightenment to a level at which government of any sort would no longer be necessary and, in the process, to infiltrate government with members of the order," Ziolkowski wrote in *Lure of the Arcane*.[24]

"A New World Order Through Revolution"

At the height of its growing influence in 1784, one of the Illuminati's messengers was reportedly struck by lightning on his way to Paris. The authorities discovered papers on his dead body titled "The Original Shift in Days of Illumination." "It described the Illuminati's ultimate goal for a 'New World Order through Revolution.' It also spoke of the French Revolution (which hadn't happened yet)," Devra Newberger Speregen and Debra Mostow Zakarin wrote in the special publication *Secret Societies: The Truth Revealed*. "Bavarian authorities discovered more revealing documents in Weishaupt's home about controlling all facets of Freemasonry, overthrowing European monarchies, and putting an end to the Catholic Church." One of the documents made this startling admission: "It is necessary to establish a universal regime and empire over the whole world."[25]

Not long afterward, the Bavarian monarch issued an order banning all secret societies. In 1786, police found a number of books and more than two hundred letters that had passed between Weishaupt and an associate. "Here was the complete range of evidence the authorities had long waited for," Vernon Stauffer wrote. "By the admissions of its leaders, the system of the Illuminati had the appearance of an organization devoted to the overthrow of religion and the state, a band of poisoners and forgers, an association of men of disgusting morals and depraved tastes. The publication of these documents amounted to nothing less than a sensation."[26]

Afterward, official inquiries were conducted and action was taken to eradicate the order. Weishaupt lost his professorship and was banished from the Bavarian States. Nonetheless, their philosophies continued to spread, and secret Illuminati chapters sprang up in France, Italy, England, and America. Soon, the Illuminati was resurrected as the German Union reading society and spread throughout Europe. The German Union came to control the bookselling business and helped ensure that only Illuminati-approved books were available to the public. Meanwhile, after purportedly helping to instigate the French Revolution, the Illuminati brought Jacobin-style revolution to the United States according to William McIlhany. "Shortly thereafter, agents of the Illuminati, such as French agitator Edward Genet [sic], began organizing insurrectionary and secessionist movements to destroy the American Republic," McIlhany wrote. "Their efforts were delayed by widespread public exposure, thanks in no small measure to George Washington who condemned 'the nefarious, and dangerous plan, and doctrines of the Illuminati.'"[27]

In a 1798 letter, Washington wrote, "It was not my intention to doubt that, the Doctrines of the Illuminati, and principles of Jacobinism had not spread in the United States. On the contrary, no one is more truly satisfied of this fact than I am." About that time, Washington and others warned of plans by the secret societies to create a central bank. "They didn't want a central bank to take over the nation," says Gerald Celente, a trend forecaster and publisher of the *Trends Journal*. "That's why Andrew Jackson got elected. He was a defender of the system against the central banks that have now taken over. Today, we've got a private bank running the show. Look at the decline of the dollar since the Federal Reserve came into power in 1913. There are six words that destroyed America: *Harvard, Princeton, Yale, bullets, bombs,* and *banks.* I mention this because going back to 1913 the president of Princeton, Woodrow Wilson, became president of the United States. He sold the country out with the Federal Reserve. It happened on Christmas Eve when no one was paying attention." In addition to Washington, Timothy Dwight, president of Yale University and the grandson of preacher Jonathan Edwards—father of the First Great Awakening—gave a 1798 sermon warning Americans about secret societies. Edwards described the Illuminati as a "higher order of Masons" that had spread to America and Europe, where it was having a "malignant" impact on government and religion. He said its doctrines struck at the "root of all human happiness and virtue" and had declared "murder, butchery and war" justifiable "if necessary for their purposes." Edwards went on, saying the Illuminati were "rapidly spreading through the world, to engage mankind in an open and professed war against God."[28]

At the time, Harvard University president Rev. Joseph Willard also issued a warning about the Illuminati infiltrating America: "There is sufficient evidence that a number of societies, of the Illuminati, have been established in this land of Gospel light and civil liberty, which were first organized from the grand society, in France. The enemies of all order are seeking our ruin. Should infidelity generally prevail, our independence would fall of course. Our republican government would be annihilated."[29]

By 1815, the Illuminati had extended its influence throughout Europe and America and had reportedly formed the League of the Just, which commissioned Karl Marx to write *The Communist Manifesto*. "Following publication of the *Manifesto*, the League of the Just changed its name to the Communist League," McIlhany wrote. "The Illuminists provided the unseen hand behind the staged communist revolts of 1848, which convulsed France, Austria-Hungry, and Russia. This inaugurated the era of communist subversion, infiltration, and control of governments across the globe—an era which has not ended, contrary to 'polite' opinion."[30]

Today, many experts in this field believe the Illuminati—a "clandestine, compartmentalized, hierarchical" organization often identified as the "original Marxist-Leninist group"—is far more powerful than it was in the late eighteenth century, and its "goals are nothing less than the abolition of all government, private property, inheritance, nationalism, the family unit, and organized religion."[31]

James Billington explored this question in *Fire in the Minds of Men*, challenging the conventional assumption that the Illuminati "lived on only in legend." He wrote that there is good reason to believe the Illuminati's influence was not so much a " 'legend' as an imperfectly perceived reality." "Illuminist ideas influenced revolutionaries not just through left-wing proponents, but also through right-wing opponents," Billington wrote. "As the fears of the Right became the fascination of the Left, Illuminism gained a paradoxical posthumous influence far greater than it had exercised as a living movement."[32]

Speregen and Zakarin delved into this question, too, claiming the Illuminati was "instrumental in the French Revolution, World Wars I and II, and to this day is still known as the Illuminati."[33]

However, a recent *Time* magazine publication titled *Secret Societies* expressed doubt as to whether the world's most ultrasecret society still exists:

Those free-thinking views, and the tropes in which he [Weishaupt] expressed them—including the all-seeing eye adapted from Egyptian mythology, the urge to wrest "order from chaos," and the search for an enlightened *Novus Ordo Seclorum*, or New World Order—continued to percolate through Europe and the U.S., some ultimately landing on the back of the U.S. dollar bill and, more recently, in the popular video game *Deus Ex* and in Hollywood movies. The Illuminati, like the Rosicrucians, lives on in popular culture, a handy magnet for suspicion and rumor, and for conspiracy theorists who view a Bavarian professor's failed attempt to institute a New World Order as an enterprise that still thrives in the form of a shadowy super elite.[34]

Are the "Shadowy Super Elite" Still Pursuing World Domination?

The late Dr. Stanley Monteith, a California doctor who once led a delegation of physicians in a decade-long battle to address the AIDS epidemic, traced the path of this "shadowy super elite" from the days of the Bavarian Illuminati to its modern-day counterparts, the Bilderberg Group, Yale's Skull and Bones, Bohemian Grove, and other secretive organizations: "We were told that the Illuminati were disbanded in the 1780s, but I don't believe so," Monteith, author of *Brotherhood of Darkness*, said in an interview before his death at age eighty-five in late 2014. "Weishaupt had made arrangements for it to continue, and there is evidence that it continues even up until this day."[35]

In *America's Secret Establishment*, Antony Sutton explored the question of whether Yale's Skull and Bones—a secret society whose membership rolls involve "some of the most powerful men of the 20th century"—can be traced to the Bavarian Illuminati. Interestingly, both of these secret societies were founded at prestigious universities. The Order of the Illuminati had its origins at the University of Ingolstadt—the setting, eerily enough, for the novel *Frankenstein* by Mary Shelley. The Order of Skull and Bones, or the "Brotherhood of Death," was founded at Yale in 1832 as a chapter of a German secret society started by Gen. William H. Russell and Alphonso Taft. Both groups are known internally as "The Order," and both are "intensively secret organizations." "The secret German society may have been none other than the mysterious and infamous Illuminati," Marrs wrote in *Rule by Secrecy*. In an *Esquire* article, journalist Ron Rosenbaum noted that the official skull and crossbones emblem of Skull and Bones is the same official crest of the Illuminati. "I do seem to have come across definite, if skeletal, links between the origins of Bones rituals and those of the notorious Bavarian Illuminists," Rosenbaum wrote. In his book *The Illuminati in America, 1776–2008*, former MI6 intelligence agent John Coleman described the secret society as the "Illuminati Order of Skull and Bones." "Today, secret instructions given to members of Skull and Bones are carried out in paneled boardrooms of the Committee of 300 banks, insurance companies and large corporations, instructions that originated in the Council on Foreign Relations (CFR) Harold Pratt House in New York," Coleman wrote. With membership rolls including presidents, high court justices, cabinet officers, intelligence agents, and titans of industry, Sutton argues that the influence of Skull and Bones today can be understood only through what is known as the Hegelian dialectic process, the notion that "conflict creates history." "The synthesis sought by the Establishment is called the New World Order," Sutton wrote. "Without controlled conflict this New World Order will not come about... This explains why the international bankers backed the Nazis, the Soviet Union, North Korea, North Vietnam, ad nauseam, against the United States. This 'conflict' built profits while pushing the world ever closer to one-world government. The process continues today."[36]

The phrase "New World Order" reappeared in modern times among scholars and policy gurus at the Pratt House, Christian Broadcasting Network founder Pat Robertson wrote in *The New World Order*. "It was only an idea, a catch phrase, but it offered an apt expression for Woodrow Wilson's premature vision of world unity which sparked the Fourteen-Point Plan and his ill-fated hopes for a League of Nations," Robertson stated. "To members of the Council on Foreign Relations (CFR)—the nongovernmental body that has advised presidents and politicians since Wilson's time—the concept of a new world order became a useful paradigm for expressing the image of a managed global economy where reason and order supplanted the shifty and uncertain machinations of public policy debates."[37]

The Brotherhood of Darkness and Bohemian Grove

Cecil John Rhodes, a South African diamond-mining magnate who established the Rhodes scholarships at Oxford University, played a key role in the effort to create a world government, Stanley Monteith wrote in *Brotherhood of Darkness*. Monteith argues that Rhodes, initially inspired by John Ruskin's lectures at Oxford to unite the world under British rule, has "done more to unite the world than any other man in history." When he realized he wouldn't live to see his vision fulfilled, he used his fortune to establish the Rhodes Trust, which has indoctrinated thousands of men, including President Bill Clinton, General Wesley Clark, Strobe Talbott, and many others, "in socialism and world government," Monteith wrote. Today, these former Rhodes scholars work at international banks and in government and media, have seats on the boards of multinational corporations, oversee tax-exempt foundations, and are members of the U.S. Supreme Court and the CFR, which wields enormous political influence. The major force behind the "global governance" movement today can be directly traced to a secret society Rhodes created in 1891 known as the Round Table Group. In his 1981 book, *The Anglo-American Establishment*, Carroll Quigley wrote that Rhodes and his fellow "imperial federalists" formed this group in conjunction with the Rothschild family. It became one of the "most important forces in the formulation and execution of British imperial and foreign policy," setting up the Rhodes Trust, creating the Royal Institute for International Affairs and the League of Nations, and exerting control over the *Times* in London, according to Quigley. Through the skillful use of propaganda, Quigley wrote, the Round Table Group was a key influence on British policy regarding Palestine from 1917 to 1945, was an important influence on the policy of appeasement toward Germany from 1920 to 1940, and "played a considerable role in the Second World War." "There were three other people with Cecil Rhodes when he created his secret society in 1891," Monteith says. "We know that at least two of them were Masons and the other was deeply involved in the occult and in theosophy. And out of that little group of four men came a series of secret societies that culminated in what we have today, the Council on Foreign Relations, the Bilderberg Group, the Trilateral Commission, Skull and Bones, and Bohemian Grove. A large number of these secret societies are all working together for a common goal—a one-world government, a one-world financial system, and certainly a one-world religion—and they are all intent upon destroying Christianity."[38]

Of these modern secret societies, one of the strangest is Bohemian Grove. When we first heard about it, Bohemian Grove sounded like a crazy conspiracy theory, but public records, news stories, documentaries, and photographs have revealed that very strange rituals occur at the secluded twenty-seven-hundred-acre campground in a redwood grove in Northern California. Since the late nineteenth century, U.S. presidents and "some of the richest and most powerful men in the world" have gathered for "two weeks of heavy drinking, super-secret talks, druid worship (the group insists they are simply 'revering the Redwoods') and other rituals," according to the *Washington Post*. This includes the Cremation of the Care ceremony, which filmmaker Alex Jones described as an "ancient Canaanite, Luciferian, Babylon mystery religion ceremony" in his documentary titled *Dark Secrets: Inside Bohemian Grove*. The planning for the Manhattan Project took place at Bohemian Grove in 1942, leading to the development of the atomic bomb, according to the *Washington Post*. "People ask me, why would our government be anti-Christian? It's because it's not our government," Monteith says. "Our government has been taken over by this Luciferian group of guys, a small group that hates Christianity and wants to destroy it. That's why they've taken God and prayer and the Ten Commandments and morality out of the schools. Immorality is a way of life in America along with support for abortions, support of homosexuality and certainly the support of sex outside of marriage. All these things are the direct result of the effort to destroy the moral fabric of our society and destroy America from within, and they are doing a very good job of it. They know exactly what they are doing. I call them the 'Brotherhood of Darkness.' It's a small group of perhaps five thousand people who control both political parties here in America and make a mockery of our electoral process."[39]

As disorienting and perplexing as this may be, the evidence we unearthed during our five-year investigation supports the conclusions of Monteith and many others and reveals that the world is not what it seems at all. While most of us have been taught that wars, depressions, revolutions, and other historical events happen largely by accident and are the "product of chaos," the reality, if the evidence is seriously considered, is exactly the opposite. Interestingly, powerful historical figures with inside knowledge of how the world really works share this view too. For instance, President Franklin D. Roosevelt, who led the United States through two of its greatest crises—the Great Depression and World War II—once opined: "In politics, nothing happens by accident. If it happens, you can bet it was planned that way." In 1909, Walter Rathenau, a German industrialist and statesman who served as the foreign minister of Germany during the Weimar Republic and was later assassinated, said, "Three hundred men, all of whom know one another, direct the economic destiny of Europe and choose their successors from among themselves." In America, Joseph P. Kennedy, a businessman and the father of President John F. Kennedy, once quipped, "Fifty men have run America and that's a high figure." Quigley, the Georgetown expert on secret societies whom President Clinton cited as an important influence, studied the small, wealthy ruling elite and wrote about it in *Tragedy & Hope*: "There does exist, and has existed for a generation, an international Anglophile network which operates, to some extent, in the way the radical Right believes the Communists act. In fact, this network, which we may identify as the Round Table Group, has no aversion to cooperating with the Communists, or any other groups, and frequently does so. I know of the operations of this network because I have studied it for twenty years and was permitted for two years, in the early 1960s, to examine its papers and secret records." As mind-boggling as this all is—especially for those of us who learned the official version of history through public schools and a mainstream media dominated by six major corporations—the reality is that an "unseen hand" of highly secretive forces is behind many of history's most significant events. It's a conspiracy theory that just happens to be true. And as a recent University of Chicago survey found, surprisingly large numbers of Americans are coming to the same conclusion.[40]

"Almost all the elite in this Luciferian movement have accumulated a great deal of wealth and fortune . . . and because of this they are utilizing that wealth to promote this idea of a one-world government," Stanley Monteith says. "With this accumulation of wealth, they have been able to buy up the major news outlets and control how the American people think. They own and control the six major banks and those banks control 67 percent of the financial assets of the United States. They use those banks to finance the major corporations. As a result, this small group that I call the 'Brotherhood of Darkness' controls most of the major corporations and through this are able to dominate the major financial aspects of our society."[41]

"Therefore Be Wise as Serpents and Harmless as Doves"

Since ancient Babylon, members of secret societies have acted as a kind of invisible elite wielding an inordinate degree of control over the affairs of mankind and the direction of civilization.

In our investigation of secret societies and other clandestine organizations, it was important for us to maintain both intellectual and historical integrity in our portrayal of the powerful individuals involved in these groups.

First of all, it is intellectually dishonest to say that all of these individuals and groups have malevolent motives. The reality is that these groups, like mankind itself, are composed of both good and bad people, and in many cases composed of individuals who possess good and bad qualities. To stigmatize secret societies and their members with a broad brush wouldn't be fair or accurate.

In investigating the prophetic mystery involving Babylon, we studied how biblical characters interacted with the occult hierarchies, secret societies, and power structures of their time, and we sought to follow the biblical model. For instance, if we examine the biblical account of powerful occult groups and secret societies, we read about how Joseph was promoted by the pharaoh to be second in command and to rule over all of Egypt. The pharaohs of Egypt were part of an occult god-king system with roots in ancient Babylon. When Joseph was supernaturally interpreting the pharaoh's dreams, he was competing with the pharaoh's most powerful occult advisers.

Joseph did not stand up in the middle of the pharaoh's occult government and denounce the pharaoh, wizards, soothsayers, prophets, magicians, and occult advisers. Instead, Joseph demonstrated the reality of God's power by supernaturally interpreting the pharaoh's dreams and helping the Egyptians prepare for a time of famine. God used Joseph to help both the Egyptians and the children of Israel. It was Joseph's character and supernatural God-given abilities that revealed to the pharaoh and the Egyptians the reality of the power of the biblical God.

A second example in Scripture involves the story of the prophet Daniel, who supernaturally interpreted dreams of the Babylonian king. Daniel was intensively trained in the occult and Babylonian system, but he remained true to God even in this training. He was placed in the very center of an occult-based empire. He was exposed to and lived in the midst of the most powerful occult, supernatural, and political forces on earth. Like Joseph, Daniel did not stand up and denounce the powerful wizards, prophets, soothsayers, and masters of the occult forces. Daniel supernaturally interpreted the dreams and visions of the king of Babylon. And although Daniel faced fierce opposition and persecution, his character, supernatural gifts, and faithfulness to God inspired the Babylonian king to accept the biblical God as the true God.

According to the Bible, we live in a world system under the temporary control of Lucifer. Every sphere of activity is affected by this reality. As such, when we examine the history of secret societies, it is not a black-and-white issue of good and evil any more than the pharaoh and the king of Babylon could be classified neatly into categories of all evil or all good. Certainly, there is justification of specific categorization on a case-by-case basis, but broad-brush classifications are most often inaccurate.

Let's take the historical facts surrounding both the creation and the founding of America. Sir Francis Bacon, the head of the Rosicrucian Order that later evolved into the Bavarian Illuminati, played an instrumental role in America's creation. Bacon planned for America to be the head of the New Atlantis, a future, scientific-utopian society. Regardless of Bacon's motives, America was ultimately structured in such a way that allowed Christianity and freedom of religion and speech to flourish.

When we examine the founding of America, we find a very strange hybrid of Illuminati, Masonic, and biblical beliefs. On the one hand, the Pilgrims and the Puritans came to America and entered into a covenant with God based on the one that God made with the children of Israel. Large numbers of Bible-believing Christians came from England and other parts of Europe to escape religious persecution. The original colonies were greatly impacted by the First Great Awakening and the biblical preaching of men like Jonathan Edwards. As a result, biblical truths were embedded in the U.S. Constitution, the Bill of Rights, and the Declaration of Independence.

Ironically, the Illuminati and America were founded in the same year—1776. Many of our Founding Fathers embraced a combination of Christian, Deist, Masonic, and Illuminist beliefs. This is not to imply that these conflicting ideas were blended into one belief. These beliefs were in conflict, as President Washington argued at the time, but they did provide a synergy that contributed to the Revolutionary War and the birth of America. Thomas Paine, author of *Common Sense* and other papers that influenced the American Revolution, had purported ties to secret societies and supported the French Revolution. Yet Paine's *Common Sense* was critical in motivating Christians, who seemed content to do nothing, to fight the British in the American Revolution.

From the very beginning, as evidenced by the Masonic architecture in Washington, DC, America was never a purely Christian nation. Some of the ideas contained in the U.S. Constitution and Bill of Rights were Illuminist in nature, but they did provide an original structure for Christianity to flourish too.

Throughout America's history, many of America's most powerful political and cultural figures were either influenced by or members of these secretive organizations. In studying the lives of these individuals, it's apparent that many had a very positive and beneficial impact on society. A list of them would read like a who's who of American presidents, U.S. Supreme Court justices, U.S. senators and representatives, governors, industrialists, businessmen, philanthropists, writers, scientists, educators, and others.

Those who could be called the "illumined ones"—the members of various secret societies—are not a monolithic group. Many of the central ideas of the elite are borrowed from the Greek philosopher Plato, who in *The Republic* described in detail the ideal city-state ruled by philosopher-kings. This idea of mass society ruled by the benevolent elite, or what U.S.

president Dwight Eisenhower described as the "scientific-technological elite," can be very noble and benevolent when the elite are acting on the French principle of noblesse oblige, in which they seek to help their fellow man.

The concept comes from Homer's *Iliad*, in which those with power and prestige help those who are less fortunate. But, on the dark side, the hidden and secretive elite can be and have been absolutely diabolical and evil—often enslaving and exterminating their fellow man throughout history.

In the past century, the majority of American presidents and high-level leaders were members of secret societies or worked closely with them. For example, President John F. Kennedy, who said in a 1961 speech to the American Newspaper Publishers Association that "we are as a people inherently and historically opposed to secret societies," was a member of the CFR along with many members of his cabinet. Clearly, President Kennedy did many good things for the nation and the world.[42]

Ronald Reagan, the president admired by most conservatives and Christians and who has been on Gallup's list of the world's most admired men more times than any other figure besides Billy Graham, did many things to advance religious and personal freedoms and strengthen America as a free nation. Reagan, who was given a copy of the *"Doc" Beshore Prophecy Study Bible* in the early 1980s, was an avid student of Bible prophecy and wanted to prepare America militarily for Armageddon-like conflicts. Yet Reagan's wife, Nancy, demanded that he consult astrological readings before making any decision. Further, Reagan's administration was "packed with both current and former members" of the Order of Skull and Bones, the Trilateral Commission, and the CFR.[43]

As we review the list of U.S. presidents and political leaders, we find that many who are considered the most Christian, biblical, and conservative are often Freemasons or connected to secret societies. The point is that there are many conservative and Christian politicians and leaders who have connections to or are members of secret societies. Some of the most powerful people in media, entertainment, finance, economics, and politics are members of secret societies or are connected to them. Many of these individuals have been responsible for good things. This is not an endorsement of everything these groups stand for, but the reality is that these are the people who to one degree or another largely control our world.

In *The Babylon Code*, we have not ignored evil or things that directly oppose Judeo-Christian beliefs wherever they are found. We are called to expose the hidden works of darkness and evil, but these hidden works can be found throughout society, and perhaps the greatest center of potential evil is and has always been in religious circles and even within the church. The reality is that not everyone who calls themselves a Christian is truly a Christian, and some of the most horrific acts of evil have originated not in secret societies but in the church.

We are not called to be ignorant of the devices of evil, nor are we to turn a blind eye. Just as Jesus instructed us in Matthew 10:16 to be "wise as serpents and harmless as doves" (NKJV), we need to be prepared to be called into the highest centers of occult-based activity, and our responsibility is to walk by and be controlled by the Spirit as Daniel was in the heart of Babylon.

Order Out of Chaos

The world is now experiencing a massive acceleration and convergence in biblical end-times signs, much of it orchestrated by hidden forces. Whether we call it the Illuminati, the Bilderberg Group, or the shadow government, the operating principle is the same: "order out of chaos." The primary strategy these groups use is to deliberately create chaos in order to break down the current order and create the new order. They employ what is known as "manufactured crises" to accomplish these goals. These secret societies and organizations frequently change their names, but they're hiding in plain sight and the end goal is the same: the creation of a global government and economic system under the guise of sustainability, world peace, and the fair redistribution of wealth.

At the most basic level, this is a spiritual conspiracy with roots in the great spiritual battle between good and evil. Ever since Lucifer failed in his first attempt to install his acolyte Nimrod as ruler of the known world, he's been seeking to do it again. In 1 John 2:18, the apostle John wrote that the world would experience many "antichrists" before the final one emerged on the world stage: "As you have heard that antichrist is coming, so now many antichrists have come" (NRSV). Many of these historical figures—Nimrod, Nebuchadnezzar, Alexander the Great, Julius Caesar, Genghis Khan, Napoleon Bonaparte, Adolf Hitler, Vladimir Lenin, Joseph Stalin, and Mao Tse-tung—attempted to unite the world under their iron grip. Now the grand finale of history is approaching, and these hidden forces are at work to install a "satanic superman" at the helm of a coming global government, economic system, and false religion.[44]

One of the keys to understanding the Babylon code is to recognize that the powerful, secret occult societies that began with Nimrod constantly change their names. For example, the Illuminati emerged from the Rosicrucian Order and other prior secret societies. The Illuminati may well be one of the secretive organizations that help to usher into power the charismatic world leader known as the Antichrist to oversee the end-times political and economic system, or it could be another organization operating under a different name that few know of. Remember, Satan is the master of deceit, subterfuge, and lies.

Tim LaHaye, coauthor of the Left Behind series and one of the world's foremost experts on Revelation, says the Bible indicates that Satan wants to rule the world and will indwell a man who possesses "incredible gifts" for this very purpose. "He will try to do everything against Christ,"

LaHaye says. "He will defame Christ. He will imitate Christ. He even dies, according to the book of Revelation, and rises again when he's indwelt by Satan himself."[45]

As outlined in *Rapture (Under Attack)*, LaHaye believes the Illuminati will help bring the Antichrist to power to establish the end-times global system described in the Bible. "The devil has his emissaries in every language and in every country in the world working toward [a one-world government]," LaHaye says. "I see it in our own country and in Europe and other places where you hear this obsessive idea that if we could just have one-world government we could have peace. If you analyze that from a Christian standpoint, you can't have world government with one man, a depraved fallen human being, running the world. As Lord Acton said, 'Power corrupts, and absolute power corrupts absolutely.' A Dutch representative [Paul-Henri Spaak] from the United Nations said the world is ready for a one-world government led by one person and 'be he god or devil, we will receive him.' "[46]

Chapter Three

"Ode to Joy" and a Shared Destiny

There is no such thing as chance; and what seems to us merest accident springs from the deepest source of destiny.

—FRIEDRICH VON SCHILLER, POET,
PLAYWRIGHT, AND PHILOSOPHER

Schiller—recently named Europe's greatest playwright after William Shakespeare—penned this enigmatic line about chance and destiny more than two centuries ago. Despite the passage of time, the quote has a strangely serendipitous and prophetic connection to *The Babylon Code*.

The story behind this book—a true tale of poetry, music, a mysterious death, and the Apocalypse—has its modern origins in late eighteenth-century Europe.

In 1784, a wealthy member of the Bavarian Illuminati befriended the famed writer. Despite his earlier success with *The Robbers*—a play that turned him into an overnight sensation and hero of revolutionaries on both sides of the Atlantic—Schiller was deeply in debt. This mysterious figure paid off Schiller's creditors and supported him for several years. It was during this time that Schiller wrote the world-famous poem "Ode to Joy," the fashionable society's vision of a utopian New World Order. Beethoven would later immortalize the poem celebrating the "brotherhood of man" in his masterpiece the Ninth Symphony—widely considered the greatest piece of music ever written and now the European Union anthem.

But after witnessing the horrors of the French Revolution, Schiller saw through the facade of the Bavarian Illuminati and began writing a play to expose their diabolical plans. Tragically, he never got to finish the play. He died at age forty-five in 1805. The authorities listed tuberculosis and other ailments as the official cause of death, but some believed the Illuminati had poisoned him with arsenic.[1]

More than two centuries later, I (Troy) learned that my ancestor may have died under suspicious circumstances. Through a twist of fate I encountered internationally recognized prophecy expert Paul McGuire. After hearing Paul say at a 2009 prophecy conference that the world is undergoing the most radical transformation in history—transitioning from sovereign nation-states to a global government as predicted in the Bible—I began investigating the nexus between current events, secret societies, and end-times biblical predictions, writing stories for the *Los Angeles Daily News*, *Christianity Today*, *Charisma*, WND.com, and CBN.com.

Later, Paul and I—a Pulitzer Prize–nominated journalist and a media commentator for Fox News, CNN, and the History Channel—decided to join forces and investigate whether there is credible evidence to suggest that end-times signs are not only accelerating but converging for the first time in history.

The result is the book *The Babylon Code*—where in this chapter I reveal how my discovery of the mysterious circumstances surrounding Schiller's death propelled me to pick up where my ancestor left off more than two hundred years ago, and how Paul's and my unique backgrounds brought us together to begin to solve the Bible's greatest end-times mystery of how, and when, powerful, behind-the-scenes forces are helping to bring about the fulfillment of biblical prophecy.

The Summer of Love and the Prophet of Liberty

Born September 18, 1967, during the "Summer of Love," I was raised in a small fishing and logging town along the southern Oregon coast called Port Orford.

My father, Stan Anderson—eulogized by Los Angeles County supervisor Michael D. Antonovich as "an important figure in the Pacific Northwest fishing industry"—owned Cape Blanco Fisheries and put me to work at age seven sweeping the cannery floors. From an early age I learned the value of hard work—picking shrimp, boat pulling, bucking hay, and working at a lumberyard—but I also found time to spend many hours reading books and writing hundreds of songs and poems.[2]

When I was nine, my grandmother Trella Hope Schiller took me for a walk near her home in Apache Junction, Arizona, in search of gemstones. The rock hound there told me about Schiller—the "prophet of liberty, the poet of beauty."[3]

Widely regarded as one of Europe's greatest writers, Schiller wrote *Don Carlos* (an inspiration for George Lucas's *Star Wars*); *Mary Stuart* (the story of the last days of Mary, Queen of Scots); *Wilhelm Tell* (the inspiration for the theme song to *The Lone Ranger*); and *The Maid of Orleans* (the tale of Joan of Arc). Schiller was revered for his ideas regarding political and spiritual freedom and the "beautiful soul." During the 250th anniversary of his birth, Schiller was voted the greatest playwright in Europe after Shakespeare.[4]

"A universal genius generally regarded as the greatest German dramatist, Friedrich Schiller dominates a period of German literary history as no one else before or since," according to the *Encyclopedia of World Biography*. "Schiller revealed more vividly than any of his predecessors the power of drama and poetry to convey a philosophy; his works contain the strongest assertions of human freedom and dignity and the worth of the individual in all German literature. After his death, he rapidly became part of the cultural environment: streets and schools were named after him, statues and monuments were raised to his memory, his birthday was declared a national holiday and his major works became part of the educational curriculum."[5]

Schiller, a strikingly handsome writer immortalized in dozens of statues and monuments in Europe and America, was widely known in the United States until the outbreak of World War I, when Germany's cultural contributions were largely suppressed and censored. Schiller's ideas and his drama *Wilhelm Tell*—a play about a Swiss herdsman who freed himself from the tyrannical yoke of an emperor—played an important role in the Civil War. Schiller admirers becoming connected with anti-slavery activists helped elect President Abraham Lincoln and "to a large degree helped to win the Civil War for the anti-slavery forces." More than 250,000 German Americans, including several generals, fought on Lincoln's side during the Civil War and many carried Schiller's works in their knapsacks. Frederick Douglass, a former slave and leading spokesman for the rights of African Americans, called Schiller the "Poet of Freedom."[6]

Revolution Against Tyranny

Enthralling me with these tales, Trella Schiller further piqued my interest by noting that there was some intrigue surrounding Schiller's death. She said Napoleon—as well as Adolf Hitler—had banned his work because it encouraged revolution against tyranny and the overthrow of tyrants.

"His plays angered those in power, including Napoleon, and they ordered his death. He was a very brave man. I know you like to write poems and stories too," she said. "I have a sense you are going to follow in his footsteps."

The conversation between my grandmother and me occurred just a

few years after the Council of Europe, the predecessor of the European
Union, voted to adopt "Ode to Joy" in 1972 as its national anthem, a
poem expressing "Schiller's idealistic vision of the human race becoming brothers—a vision Beethoven shared." In 1985, EU leaders adopted
it as the official anthem of the EU. Today, "Ode to Joy" embodies the
utopian dreams of globalists in Europe and throughout the world. Schiller, especially beloved in Europe and Asia where choirs of hundreds and
sometimes thousands sing "Ode to Joy," is the apotheosis of this dream.
Some believe "Ode to Joy" will be the anthem of the prophesied world
state.

The unusual ascendance of this poem began with Schiller's first play,
The Robbers—a "huge sensation" that catapulted Schiller to fame at a
young age, says Gail K. Hart, a professor of German at the University of
California, Irvine.[7]

The play solidified Schiller's reputation as an "outlaw," says Jeffrey L.
High, a professor of German studies at California State University, Long
Beach, and one of the editors of *Who Is This Schiller Now?* "His first play,
The Robbers, struck a chord in kind of the way that Woodstock struck
a chord in 1969," High says. "No one had ever seen a drama like this
where insane heroes obsessed with freedom stood up for good or worse
and fought to the death."[8]

The Robbers in 1782 and "Ode to Joy" in 1785 emerged during a
period of radical political upheaval. The American Revolution had just
ended and the French Revolution was about to ignite. It was one of the
most pivotal moments in history and marked the end of the reign of
kings and queens and the rise of secular republics and liberal democracies. It was also a time of great intrigue. Controversies were swirling in
Europe and the United States about what role secret societies like the
Bavarian Illuminati were playing in the revolutionary fervor sweeping
the world.

During the American Revolution, the first in a series of worldwide revolutions over the past two centuries, people were willing to endure great hardship—even sacrifice their lives—for freedom and liberty. The French Revolution, however, was based on the secular-humanist ideals of the Bavarian Illuminati and the Jacobins. Some consider it the predecessor of the Communist Revolution—an event inspired by Karl Marx's *The Communist Manifesto*, a document eerily similar to Weishaupt's *The Illuminati Manifesto*.

At the time, most of Schiller's friends were Freemasons or members of the Bavarian Illuminati, including Christian Gottfried Körner—who paid off Schiller's debts and let him stay in his garden house—and Goethe. Schiller's favorite professor in college, Jacob Friedrich von Abel, was the president of the Illuminati at the Karlsschule Stuttgart, the elite military academy where Schiller wrote *The Robbers*. Interestingly, Schiller wrote one of the first "lodge novels" about secret societies—*The Ghost Seer*—helping inspire the wider conspiracy fiction genre, including Dan Brown's blockbuster novels, Theodore Ziolkowski says. *The Ghost Seer* was Schiller's greatest popular success during his lifetime.

"One of the poems he wrote [while living in Körner's garden house] was 'To the Friends,' or to friendship, generically," High noted. "That evolved into 'Ode to Joy,' which has an endlessly complicated history. The word 'freedom' appears in the poem several times, including the line 'Freedom from the chains of tyrants.' It doesn't get much more revolutionary than that, except for the next line: 'Crowns belong to the deserving; downfall to the brood of liars.' Schiller is calling for the death of the princes in 1785–86. It was a spectacularly, radical poem."[9]

After Beethoven set "Ode to Joy" to music in the Ninth Symphony, Ziolkowski says it gained its greatest influence and broadest familiarity in the world at large. "Beethoven was a revolutionary musician and Schiller was a revolutionary poet," Ziolkowski says.[10]

Schiller's "dangerous dramas"—based on pivotal historical events but embedded with powerful critiques of the eighteenth-century oligarchical world—encouraged revolutions and the overthrow of tyrants. Schiller wrote his most popular play, *Wilhelm Tell*—the tale of the Swiss hero who slew the tyrant who forced him to shoot an arrow through an apple atop his son's head—to encourage Germany's 250 feudal states to liberate themselves from Napoleon's despotic reign and create a democratic republic. If that had occurred, High says, it's "extremely likely that all the misery of the twentieth century [World Wars I and II and the rise of Adolf Hitler] could have been avoided."[11]

The Late Great Planet Earth and the Jesus Movement

In 1979, when I was eleven, my mother, Janet, and I encountered an Assemblies of God youth pastor at a restaurant in Charleston, Oregon, a charming fishing village along the coast. The youth pastor, Richard Wheeler, had studied Bible prophecy at the J. C. Light and Power Company seminary at UCLA under Hal Lindsey, author of *The Late Great Planet Earth*.[12]

This serendipitous meeting came near the end of the Jesus movement, a spiritual awakening that first ignited among West Coast youth disillusioned with the hippie counterculture. About a dozen "Jesus people" from Southern California moved to Port Orford in their VW vans. Richard invited me to join the youth group, Royal Rangers, and the Frontiersmen Camping Fellowship. One evening in the attic of his home—outfitted to resemble a mountain-man cabin with bear skins, muzzle-loaders, and tomahawks—Richard told me how the Bible predicted the Antichrist would one day lead a global government before the return of Christ.

"The book of Revelation is my favorite book in the Bible," Richard told me, reading Revelation 3 from the *"Doc" Beshore Prophecy Study*

Bible. "To many people, it's mysterious—even scary. But to me it's the Bible's greatest book of hope. In the end, God wins. That's the great hope of our faith."

Fascinated, I became a believer and started going to Richard's house after school to learn more about Bible prophecy. I subscribed to *Charisma* and Keith Green's *Last Days Ministries* newsletter and held Bible studies at school where I told students about the Second Coming.

During this time, I made a curious note in my *Scofield Reference Bible.* Next to the headline "Judgment upon Babylon" in Isaiah 47, I wrote, "America?"

The Late Great Correction

Following high school, I attended the University of Oregon and studied journalism, political science, and theater—heeding my grandmother's suggestion to follow in Schiller's footsteps. Amid controversy surrounding Hal Lindsey's purported prediction that the Rapture would occur by 1988—and former NASA engineer Edgar C. Whisenant's controversial book *88 Reasons Why the Rapture Will Be in 1988*—I became disillusioned with Bible prophecy and fell away.

In the late 1980s, Lindsey's book had come under fire for a portion in which he quoted Christ in Matthew 24:34 saying the generation that witnessed the signs given in the Olivet Discourse would live to see their fulfillment. "What generation?" Lindsey wrote in *The Late Great Planet Earth.* "Obviously, in context, the generation that would see the signs—chief among them the rebirth of Israel. A generation in the Bible is something like forty years. If this is a correct deduction, then within forty years or so of 1948, all these things could take place. Many scholars who have studied Bible prophecy all their lives believe that this is so."[13]

In a 2009 interview I had with Hal Lindsey, he argued that critics had misconstrued what he wrote. Lindsey says he missed an important word in the verse that helped to explain the type of generation Jesus had in mind. It's the average life span of those in the generation to which Jesus had pointed. "I believe we are the generation that will live to see the fulfillment of the 'birth pangs' that Jesus predicted would all come together in one time frame shortly before the Tribulation's events that bring about his return," Lindsey says. "I have never believed that the precise day or hour could be known. Otherwise, what was the point of giving signs that would indicate his coming was near?" Lindsey says the signs he wrote about in his book are still valid: "In fact more so now than ever before."[14]

Tim LaHaye and F. "Doc" Kenton Beshore, president of the World Bible Society and author of the *"Doc" Beshore Prophecy Study Bible*, agree. They say a biblical generation is at least seventy to eighty years. LaHaye says it could be up to a century. This is based on Psalm 90:10: "The days of our life are seventy years, or perhaps eighty, if we are strong" (NRSV). Given this, LaHaye and Beshore—college roommates who studied under Biblical Research Society president David L. Cooper—believe the Second Coming may take place between 2018 and 2028, or seventy to eighty years after Israel became a nation in 1948. Taking into account the seven-year Tribulation period, Beshore believes the Rapture may occur sometime between now and 2021. "Jesus says in Matthew 24:34 that this 'born one,' or 'this generation will not pass away until all these things be fulfilled,'" Beshore says. "He pictures Israel as a Jewish boy, born May 14, 1948, who would grow up and become an old man until he comes in glory to establish his millennial kingdom. Now, how long is this generation—this 'born one'? The first meaning of 'born one' is in Psalm 90:10. If you extend that from 1948, the outside date for the millennium would be 2028. Take off seven years for the Tribulation and the outside date for the Rapture would be 2021." However, LaHaye says a biblical generation, according to Genesis 15:13–16, could be one hundred years. "[Beshore] and I studied under the same prophecy teacher…and we heard him talk about this and Cooper made the mistake, even as Hal Lindsey did, too, that a biblical generation is forty years, but really a generation could be up to one hundred years," LaHaye says.[15]

A Spiritual Odyssey and an Appointment with Destiny

Exposed to so many radical new ideas and philosophies at the U of O, I quit going to church. During this part of my spiritual odyssey, I explored a variety of different beliefs—Zen Buddhism, Native American spirituality, and mysticism—and read numerous books about different religions and prophecies, including ones by Nostradamus and Edgar Cayce. It was during this time that I chanced upon a large section of Schiller's books at the college library and began to learn more about my mysterious ancestor.

After graduating with a bachelor's degree in 1991, I spent the next decade working as a journalist at newspapers in Nevada, Oregon, and California—fortunately winning more than two dozen local, state, and national journalism awards, including ones for investigative reporting.

Several months after the September 11, 2001, terrorist attacks—discerning the prophetic significance of the incident—I began attending church again, though I remained skeptical about end-times date setting. Not long afterward, concluding my spiritual journey and realizing that the faith of my youth was the right path, I rededicated my life to Jesus.

The Friedrich Schiller Code and KGB Files

In early 2009, now an investigative journalist at the *Los Angeles Daily News*, I learned about the mystery surrounding Schiller's death. At the time, I was working on a story about a controversy surrounding German composer Richard Wagner's four-opera cycle Ring Festival in Los Angeles. In an interview, the source mentioned that Europeans were about to celebrate the 250th anniversary of Schiller's birth. Intrigued, I searched the Internet and found stories about a mysterious chain of events surrounding Schiller's death, along with a German television documentary called *The Friedrich Schiller Code*.[16]

The stories in the *New York Times*, the *Guardian*, *Time*, the Associated Press, and Spiegel Online revealed that a question mark had hung over the location of Schiller's remains for more than two centuries. After his death in 1805, Schiller was hastily buried in a mass grave in Weimar. More than two decades later, Weimar's mayor decided that a common burial place was not fitting for such a "literary lion." He ordered the esteemed poet's remains dug up. The laborers unearthed about two dozen skulls.

With the help of two doctors and Schiller's son Ernst, the mayor picked the biggest, saying: "That must be Schiller's." In the early twentieth century, amid concerns that the mayor may have picked the wrong skull, an anatomist reopened the mass grave and collected another sixty-three skulls. He selected another one and it was placed, along with the first skull and various bones, in a princely crypt next to Schiller's friend Goethe. Since then, the mystery has only deepened. In the 1950s, East German scientists examined Schiller's sarcophagus and concluded that the first skull was probably Schiller's and the second belonged to a woman. Shortly before celebrations of the two-hundredth anniversary of Schiller's death in 2005, the Foundation of Weimar Classics permitted scientists to analyze the DNA of the skulls and skeletons. The tests, costing $170,000, also included chemical analysis and facial reconstruction. The remains of five members of Schiller's family were exhumed to provide DNA samples for comparison. In a paper titled

"The Friedrich-Schiller-Code," officials at the Institute of Legal Medicine at Innsbruck Medical University in Austria concluded that neither of the skulls belonged to Schiller and the bones belonged to at least six different people.[17] Intrigued by these stories, I continued searching the Internet and discovered the website of a Swedish journalist who wrote in a book—partially based on recently released KGB files—that the Bavarian Illuminati had allegedly poisoned Schiller. In a section titled "The Murders of Schiller and Mozart," Jüri Lina wrote that an "important Illuminatus"—Körner—had sent Schiller a letter in 1784 suggesting that he join the Bavarian Illuminati. "Korner saw to it that all Schiller's debts were paid off and following this, he joined the Order," Lina wrote. "Naturally, Friedrich von Schiller could not suspect that Heinrich Voss, a young doctor who took care of him, was one of the 'Insinuating Brothers' who reported everything he heard and saw to Weishaupt." At the time, Schiller was working on a play called *Demetrius* that would "uncover some of the atrocities behind the scenes of those in power. Heinrich Voss reported this to Weishaupt who wished to stop this play at any cost."[18]

In his book *Schiller*, University of Aberdeen professor of German William Witte noted some people felt Schiller's obscure and hasty burial was "hardly in keeping with his status in the world of letters." In a footnote, Witte referenced the theory that Schiller had been "poisoned by the Freemasons, with the connivance of Goethe."[19]

"That was a rumor that was quite widespread at the time," Theodore Ziolkowski says.[20]

However, Schiller had been sick most of his adult life and an autopsy revealed he had tuberculosis and cancer, Jeffrey High says. The arsenic discovered via DNA tests of his hair in all probability came from the wallpaper in his writing den, High stated. Allegations that the Bavarian Illuminati, Napoleon, or Goethe was involved in his death were raised in the past, but there is no evidence to support the claim, High believes. However, Gail Hart says Schiller wrote "a lot of inflammatory stuff," and his plays were banned at different times. "Wherever there is political instability, good luck if you are going to put on a production of *The Robbers* or *Wilhelm Tell* because those are such rabble-rousing kind of plays," Hart says. "The Nazis wouldn't allow *The Robbers* and some of his other plays to be performed. A Swiss student made an attempt on Hitler's life and after that they wouldn't allow *Wilhelm Tell* to be performed because it's about an assassination of the governor of the Swiss cantons. They didn't want other people getting the idea that they should kill Hitler and people in the upper government."[21]

The Illuminati and Altered States of Consciousness

Shocked by what I learned, I began researching the Bavarian Illuminati and ran across Paul McGuire's website. McGuire, author of *The Day the Dollar Died* and other bestselling books, described the role of secret societies in the end-times global government and economic system predicted in Scripture. Curious but skeptical, I learned that McGuire was going to speak at a Bible prophecy conference in Southern California. I asked my editor at the *Los Angeles Daily News* if I could cover the event and write a story about renewed interest in the end times. At the conference, McGuire told the audience that he was a former atheist who at age fifteen had demonstrated with radical activist Abbie Hoffman and was made an honorary member of the Black Panther Party. The world, McGuire told the crowd, is undergoing the most radical transformation in history—transitioning from sovereign nation-states to a global government as predicted in the Bible thousands of years ago. "We're on the verge of the greatest change since Adam and Eve," McGuire told thousands of people in attendance. "A coming one-world government, a coming one-world religion, a coming cashless society—and all of it predicted in specific detail in the book I once hated, the Bible, which is the inspired and inerrant Word of God. The Bible predicted that we'd be in a time like this."[22]

Stunned, I interviewed McGuire for his story.

An Unlikely Prophet of the Second Coming

Growing up in New York City and raised in an intellectual and atheistic home, Paul McGuire was taught to hate Christianity because his family believed it was antilife, antisex, and an antijoy, bloodstained religion.[23]

However, ever since he was a boy, McGuire had felt compelled to discover the answers to life's most important questions: "Why am I alive?," "Who am I?," and "What is my purpose?"

At age eleven, McGuire read the biographies of the great scientists in the city library and devoured books on science, psychology, and other fields. Yet he could not find the answers he was looking for. During this time, he would go to the Fillmore East to see bands like the Grateful Dead, the Who, and Led Zeppelin. "Radical activists were organizing young people into a movement," McGuire wrote in *The Day the Dollar Died*. "They had new slogans. Instead of 'Peace and Love,' they started saying things like 'armed love' with pictures of an automatic assault rifle. Instead of the two-fingered peace symbol, they began to use the raised clenched fist and shout Marxist slogans like 'Power to the People.'"[24]

By fifteen, McGuire was caught up in the 1960s counterculture of radical politics and Eastern mysticism. Once, while he was hanging out with hippies in Central Park, members of the Weather Underground tried to recruit him, but McGuire told them that he didn't believe in violence, guns, or armed revolution. Instead, McGuire said, he believed in a revolution of consciousness based on love.

At the University of Missouri, where he had a dual major in filmmaking and the new field "Altered States of Consciousness," McGuire met people for the first time who were practicing Christians. But McGuire despised them and would rip them apart in debate classes. Then, mysteriously, one day he was invited to a Christian religious retreat located along the back roads and cornfields of Missouri.

When he arrived, his worst fears about Christianity as a "country club religion" were confirmed, and he told the person who invited him that he would hitchhike back to the campus. McGuire stuck out his thumb on a remote road in what looked like a scene from the film *Field of Dreams*. He got his first ride from a Pentecostal preacher and his wife. Then when he hitched another ride, a Bible salesman pulled up in a station wagon full of hefty King James Bibles. As they were driving, the Bible salesman told McGuire that he was a sinner on his way to hell and that he needed to be born again. "And that was basically it," McGuire said on an episode of *Sid Roth's It's Supernatural!* "I'm from New York. I didn't even believe in the word 'sin.' That was an archaic concept. And he says, 'You want to pull over and say the sinner's prayer?' And I said, 'Yeah,' but inside my mind, I'm going, 'Great. He's a religious, ax murderer pervert. He's going to chop my head off before he does whatever and bury me in the bushes and say a couple of prayers over me.' So I prayed with him. It was a real short prayer, 'Jesus Christ, I ask you to forgive me of my sins. I ask you to come into my life and make me born again.'" A few days later, back at the University of Missouri, McGuire was discussing his hitchhiking experience when a minister's daughter approached him. During their conversation, she asked him if he believed Jesus was the Son of God. "And I'd never said this before, but the words blurted out of me, 'I believe that Jesus Christ is the son of God,'" McGuire told Roth. "At that moment, the sky cracked open and I saw God, not in the physical sense, but in a spiritual sense. And I knew, instantaneously, that all the cosmic consciousness, astral projections, altered states of consciousness—all that stuff were illusions and false—and I knew that Jesus Christ was the Son of God—instantaneously."[25]

A few years later, McGuire found himself on Broadway in New York City producing Christian rock concerts with some of the biggest acts of the time—Keith Green, Barry McGuire, and Love Song—and television programs featuring movie stars such as Pat Boone and Pat Robertson. During this time, he also worked with Campus Crusade for Christ founder Bill Bright in developing the first marketing plans for *The Jesus Film*, the most-watched film in history. McGuire met with the legendary British producer of the film, John Heyman. At the meeting, McGuire presented Heyman with a global marketing plan for "The Jesus Film Project." Considered "one of the greatest evangelistic tools of all time," the film has been viewed six billion times, and more than two hundred million people have indicated decisions to follow Jesus after watching it. It was Bright, who worked with Heyman on the film, who first taught McGuire to "think supernaturally" and "act supernaturally."

Then, as though some unseen force was guiding his life, he married an actress and ended up in Hollywood producing science-fiction feature films. The couple lived on Laurel Canyon Boulevard atop Lookout Mountain in the Hollywood Hills. McGuire's home was just a block or so away from where English writer Aldous Huxley lived in the 1930s, along with Church of Scientology founder L. Ron Hubbard and American psychologist Dr. Timothy Leary. Lookout Mountain was a nexus for writers, musicians, and media people who shared the vision of ushering in a New World Order. Ironically, it was here that McGuire began to research the ancient Babylonian occult religions and where he started writing books about his spiritual journey from atheism and the New Age movement to Christianity. Not long afterward, he received invitations to begin speaking at conferences and other venues across the nation. Later, McGuire and his wife decided to move to a suburb of the San Fernando Valley where they would have children and raise a family.

Then, at 4:41 a.m. on January 17, 1994, McGuire and his wife awoke to what sounded like a Mack truck crashing into their house—shaking it with such violent force that they thought it would collapse and rip apart. With three children in diapers upstairs, they gathered them up and met their neighbors outside in the pitch black of a city without electricity. Knowing he had written books about Bible prophecy, McGuire's non-Christian neighbors asked him, "Paul, are these the signs of the times that Jesus Christ talked about?" McGuire's home was located at the epicenter of the 6.7-magnitude Northridge earthquake.

The event jolted and transformed his life. He began to look at Bible prophecy not as a far-off future event but as a reality that the world is literally living in the last days. All his research into economics, globalism, spirituality, geopolitics, and ancient religions like those connected to the Tower of Babel and the Egyptian pyramids began to come alive before his eyes. McGuire's research led to the discovery that the New World Order actually began in ancient Babylon. For the first time, he began to see a pattern, or a secret code, in the Bible involving Babylon. Later, he realized that this code predicts what is happening now—the emergence of a global government, economic system, and New Age–style religious belief system.

McGuire went on to write many prophecy books and became the host of a nationally syndicated radio show, *The Paul McGuire Show*, which aired for a decade out of Los Angeles during drive-time weekdays.

Again, doors mysteriously began to open and McGuire soon found limousines from Fox News and CNN at his house to drive him to their studios, where he would debate the world's leading experts on economics, politics, and geopolitics. Other times, he would be picked to debate the publishers of leading financial magazines on various economic topics. In addition, McGuire made appearances on *The O'Reilly Factor*, *Your World with Neil Cavuto*, and *America's Newsroom* with Fox cohost Megyn Kelly.

As a professor of eschatology at Dr. Jack Hayford's King's University, McGuire also appeared on two of the History Channel's highest-rated specials, "7 Signs of the Apocalypse" and "Countdown to Apocalypse: Four Horsemen."

Each year, McGuire speaks to tens of thousands of people at Bible prophecy conferences. It was at a conference in 2009 that we met. Paul says today that he was struck by my grasp of difficult concepts in Bible prophecy. I pray that's true. Paul said later that he listened to that "still small voice within me, and sensed the supernatural hand of God in the meeting." The two of us struck up a close friendship and Paul became one of my spiritual mentors.

Over the next few years, I continued to investigate the nexus between current events, secret societies, and end-times biblical predictions—hoping to learn not only if secret societies were involved in my ancestor's death but what role wealthy globalists may play in the fulfillment of biblical prophecies. Also during this time, Paul McGuire and I had been in conversations about collaborating on an end-times book and film. In late 2009, Paul suggested we write a book about a prophetic code in the Bible involving Babylon. We began actively writing *The Babylon Code* in early 2013.

As we've watched world events unfold since that time—the rise of radical Islam and ISIS, the growing aggression of Russia and its alliance with Iran, and the developing "two-state solution" for Israel and Palestine—it's become increasingly clear to us that we were brought together to write *The Babylon Code* to reveal that the world is now in the run-up to the end-times political and economic system predicted in

Scripture. Through a strange and mysterious shared destiny, I've walked in the footsteps of Schiller, who dreamed of becoming a minister in his youth, and Paul has spent decades following the trail of evidence in his quest to unearth the secrets hidden within the Bible's greatest enigma. As we'll reveal in the next chapter, all the biblical signs are coming together. And just as the prophet Daniel predicted thousands of years ago, prophecy is now being unsealed for this end-of-time generation.

Chapter Four

A Prophetic Superstorm

God keeps his promises, and this is why we can be sure that the return of Christ is near. Scripture tells us that there will be signs pointing toward the return of the Lord. I believe all of these signs are evident today…What a time to take the news of the day in one hand and the Bible in the other and watch the unfolding of the great drama of the ages come together.

—BILLY GRAHAM, ICONIC EVANGELIST, IN
THE REASON FOR MY HOPE

He's known as "God's prophet." Now, just as Noah did in ancient times, world-renowned evangelist Billy Graham is sounding the alarm that the Second Coming is "near."

In an exclusive interview for a seven-part WND.com series shortly before the *My Hope America with Billy Graham* broadcast during the week of his ninety-fifth birthday on November 7, 2013, Graham told Troy Anderson that signs of the end of the age are converging for the first time in history.

"The fourth and last watch is the coldest hour before the dawn," Graham observed. "It's the one that most people dread because it is so cold and you're still sleepy. I think that we're in the fourth watch in our world."[1]

Graham is not alone in his assessment. Other prominent figures and world leaders have reached the same conclusion, including Israeli prime minister Benjamin Netanyahu, who told the United Nations General Assembly that "biblical prophecies are being realized"; Franklin Graham, who says the world is in the "last hours" before Christ's return; and Pope Francis, who believes mankind is in the beginning stages of a "piecemeal" Third World War.[2]

The remarks by Pope Francis, the Grahams, and Netanyahu come at a time of plummeting morality, spiritual apathy, exploding national debts, severe economic turmoil, political uncertainty, a spate of historic natural disasters, worsening worldwide drought, record-breaking extreme weather, the growing risk of a nuclear conflagration, and many other daunting challenges. A dizzying series of events in recent years has prompted many to ask whether the biblical end-times have finally arrived. This includes the September 11, 2001, terrorist attacks, Hurricane Katrina, the 2008 financial meltdown, the Fukushima Daiichi nuclear disaster, and the increasingly unstable situation in the Middle East with the rise of ISIS and Iran's suspected development of nuclear weapons.

As Franklin Graham sees it, the "spirit of Antichrist is everywhere." "As you watch the news, do you feel as I do—that it seems the world is coming apart at the seams? There appears to be no end to the bad news," Graham, president of the Billy Graham Evangelistic Association, wrote in a recent article. "The killing of Christians by Muslims from Indonesia to Bangladesh to Pakistan. China tearing down church buildings. Christians tortured, beheaded, and crucified in Iraq, with villages burned and churches destroyed, and much the same in Syria...As I read the news, I can't help but wonder if we are in the last hours before our Lord Jesus Christ returns."[3]

Thomas Ice, executive director of the Pre-Trib Research Center, agrees with the Grahams. "I believe these are signs of the end times, and I think that these signs do indicate that we are near the beginning of the Tribulation," Ice says. "I had a debate at Oxford University over these issues and I provided three signs of the end times: Number one, Israel is back in its land and that's God's supersign of the end times. God talks in the Old Testament about a regathering of the Jews before Judgment Day. Secondly is globalism. Everywhere you look, globalism is an issue. Thirdly, the EU appears to be a forerunner of the revived Roman Empire."[4]

As a growing number of political and faith leaders reach similar conclusions, many people are turning to the Bible for prophetic intelligence about the future.

What are the signs of the end of the age? Are these signs really accelerating and converging for the first time in history? And do scientists and experts in geopolitics, economics, and military affairs agree with the prophecy experts and theologians? Is the world indeed experiencing what some are calling a "prophetic superstorm"?

The World's Greatest Codebook

The answers are embedded in the world's greatest codebook—the Bible. Written over a period of sixteen hundred years by more than forty writers, the Bible is the most studied, influential, and bestselling book in human history—containing some of mankind's most beloved stories, ones that can brighten the eyes of almost any child and yet mystify the world's wisest and most learned minds. *Guinness World Records* estimates that more than five billion copies of the Bible have been printed, far exceeding the numbers of the closest competitor—*A Tale of Two Cities* by Charles Dickens at two hundred million copies sold. Among its authors are kings, prophets, poets, philosophers, fishermen, farmers, a physician, and even a tax collector. And while most didn't know one another and were separated by vast epochs of time, they wrote letters, histories, proverbs, poems, prophecies, and parables that together form what many consider the handbook to life. In short, the Bible is the cornerstone of Western civilization, and much of the world's greatest art, literature, and music has been based on the "rhetorical and poetic power of its language."[5]

"Only God could have put the Bible together," wrote Rick Warren, pastor of Saddleback Church in Lake Forest, California, and the author of the *New York Times* bestselling book *The Purpose Driven Life*, in his *Daily Hope* newsletter. "It's 66 books written over 1,600 years by 40 authors—and it has one theme. Having a single unified theme is one of the reasons we know that the Bible is God's Word. From Genesis to Revelation, the Bible is all about God redeeming man, and Jesus is its star."[6]

Like Warren, Ross also believes that fulfilled prophecies are evidence for the reliability of the Bible. "Unique among all books ever written, the Bible accurately foretells specific events—in detail—many years, sometimes centuries, before they occur. Approximately 2500 prophecies appear in the pages of the Bible, about 2000 of which already have been fulfilled to the letter—no errors," Ross wrote in a Reasons to Believe article. "(The remaining 500 or so reach into the future and may be seen unfolding as days go by.) Since the probability for any one of these prophecies having been fulfilled by chance averages less than one in ten (figured very conservatively) and since the prophecies are for the most part independent of one another, the odds for all these prophecies having been fulfilled by chance without error is less than one in 10^{2000} (that is 1 with 2000 zeroes written after it!)."[7]

Many believe the biblical writers were divinely inspired. This is especially true for those who have studied Bible prophecy and discovered that Scripture is able to foretell, with precise accuracy, events that will occur hundreds and even thousands of years in the future. Based on several decades of eschatological research, it's clear to us that this monumental literary work has a supernatural author who embedded a complex, multidimensional code involving patterns, cycles, symbols, numbers, letters, and names into the historical accounts of the Old and the New Testaments. From Genesis to Revelation, God infused the Bible with prophecies, enigmas, codes, riddles, and mysteries that not only unlock the destinies of nations but reveal the secrets of astronomy, quantum physics, and the DNA code, along with the rebirth of Israel, the Tribulation, the Battle of Armageddon, and the Second Coming. Amazingly, the prophet Daniel predicted more than five hundred years before Christ's birth that these prophecies would be unsealed shortly before the end of days: "Go your way, Daniel, for the meaning of the words of prophecy is shut up and sealed until the time of the end. Many shall travel about and knowledge shall increase. None of the wicked shall understand these words, but those who are wise shall in the last days understand."[8]

The Book of Prophecy

Surprisingly, more than a quarter of the Bible (27 percent) is prophetic in nature and devoted to what is going to happen in the future. The sheer amount of space dedicated to the Second Coming, in both the Old and the New Testaments, argues that it's an important topic. "I don't believe you can understand, much less apply, the Bible accurately unless you understand end-times events," says Robert Jeffress, pastor of the eleven-thousand-member First Baptist Church in Dallas, Texas (where Billy Graham was a member for many years), and a frequent commentator on *The O'Reilly Factor* on Fox News. "You can't make sense out of the Old Testament prophets, the Gospels, the Epistles, or certainly the book of Revelation without understanding prophecy. So many Christians today avoid the book of Revelation—forgetting that the book of Revelation [Rev. 1:3] is the only book in the Bible that has a special blessing attached to those who read and understand end-times events."[9]

In addition to this special blessing, there are many other reasons for studying Revelation and Bible prophecy. Revealing the conclusion of the human story, prophecy helps us put life in perspective. It's also a powerful evangelistic tool. An intensely fascinating subject, Revelation is often the first book many unbelievers read. It is about Bible prophecy, and many are inspired to turn to the Lord. Also, the fact that Jesus said that no one, except God, would know the "day or hour" of his return is a strong motivator for righteous living. Finally, hundreds of prophecies have come to pass just as the Bible predicted, proving the truth of God's Word.

And although Rick Warren is criticized for minimizing Bible prophecy in his teachings, he recently made an astonishing statement about how Bible prophecy proves the truth of the Bible—perhaps signaling a change in his views. "One of the reasons I can know that the Bible is true and trustworthy is that it has thousands and thousands of prophecies that have come true and will come true in history," Warren wrote in his *Daily Hope* newsletter. The Bible contains more than three hundred prophecies about Jesus—all written hundreds of years before he was born. Scripture predicted when, where, and how Jesus would be born. "He couldn't have manipulated his birth to fulfill those prophecies," Warren wrote. "It also predicted how he would die. A thousand years before Jesus died, David described Jesus' death on the cross in one of the psalms... Only God could have known that... It takes more faith to believe that the Bible's prophecies were a coincidence than to believe that God planned them."[10]

Here are some surprising statistics: The Old Testament contains more than 1,500 references to Christ's return. There are more than 300 references to the Second Coming in the New Testament—1 out of every 30 verses. Jesus himself refers to the Second Coming nearly two dozen times. Of the Bible's 333 prophecies regarding Christ, only 109 were fulfilled with his first coming. The rest will be fulfilled with his return. And for every prophecy in Scripture about Christ's first coming, there are eight regarding his second coming. Bible prophecy warrants study based on the sheer amount of space the Bible devotes to the topic. The books of Isaiah, Ezekiel, Daniel, Zechariah, and Revelation are prophetic in nature, and many other books contain large amounts of prophecy, including Jeremiah, Joel, Malachi, Matthew, and 1 and 2 Thessalonians.[11]

In Isaiah 46:9–10, God told the prophet that "there is none like me, declaring the end from the beginning, and from ancient times the things that are not yet done" (KJV). Isaiah 46:9–11 makes it clear that only God can predict the future. "For those who really research this carefully, there are more than eleven hundred prophecies in the Bible—over five hundred of which have already been fulfilled," Tim LaHaye says. "What does that prove to us? It proves that the person who was writing it knew the future in advance. Well, who can do that? Only God. This is evidence that Bible prophecy can be relied upon because he fulfilled the first five hundred prophecies and he's going to fulfill the others too. I'd also like to highlight the fact that Jesus is the subject... of 109 of those prophecies [about his first coming] and Jesus fulfilled them all. Now what is the likelihood that one person out of the thirteen billion who have ever lived would fulfill all 109 of those prophecies?"[12]

Apocalypse: The Hollywood Zeitgeist

People are intensely curious about the future. Drive around almost any major city and you'll see signs for psychics, palm readers, and astrologers— ready to tell you your future for the right price. But it's not just those interested in astrology and the occult who are intrigued by what lies ahead. As a confluence of world events has ignited debate about the end times, fascination with ancient predictions has rekindled among not only Christians but also Jews, Muslims, Hindus, and those of other faiths.

Not surprisingly, Hollywood has taken notice—channeling the zeitgeist, or spirit of the age—through a series of end-of-the-world films and television shows. In recent times, Hollywood has been obsessed with all things apocalyptic (consider the recent reboot of the *Left Behind* film starring Nicolas Cage and films and television shows such as *Planet of the Apes, Noah, Exodus: Gods and Kings, The Hunger Games, Revolution, Sleepy Hollow, Elysium, Oblivion, I Am Legend, The Road, The Book of Eli, 2012, This Is the End, After Earth,* and *World War Z*—to name a few).

"I think this has kind of fueled the popular imagination," says Clint Jenkin, vice president of research at the Barna Group, a Ventura, California–based polling firm. "We had *The Hunger Games, I Am Legend* a few years ago, and it seems every time I look at a bookrack there is another book about how people are surviving a horrible future. There has been a flood of this kind of thinking into the popular consciousness. Culturally, it's becoming a bigger issue, and it will be very interesting to see how it plays out in the faith community."[13]

Why Aren't Pastors Telling Their Congregations the End Is Near?

While we've learned about a growing number of ministers giving sermons on Bible prophecy in recent years, the vast majority of churches today still avoid the topic. In large part, this can be traced to the speculation— fueled by Edgar Whisenant's *88 Reasons Why the Rapture Will Be in 1988* and the misunderstanding surrounding the length of a biblical generation in Hal Lindsey's *The Late Great Planet Earth*—that the Rapture would occur in 1988. When 1988 came and went, many ministers stopped teaching prophecy, concluding it was too controversial.

"The most neglected teaching in the church today is the second coming of Christ," Billy Graham once said.[14]

With so many interpretations of biblical prophecies, ministers may be reluctant to wade into the fray. Others may be put off by date-setters (such as radio preacher Harold Camping, who convinced thousands of his followers that the world would end on May 21, 2011) and other sensational claims. Critics are quick to point out that end-of-the-world prognosticators have all been wrong—for two millennia. This includes Christopher Columbus's prediction in his 1502 *Book of Prophecies* that Judgment Day would fall in 1657, and the man whom *Time* magazine described as "perhaps the most famous false prophet in history," William Miller. In the 1840s, Miller preached that the end would come sometime between March 21, 1843, and March 21, 1844. Convinced by his calculations, as many as one hundred thousand "Millerites" sold their possessions and waited. When the date passed, Miller recalculated the end as October 22, 1844. When October 23 came and went, he and his followers offered an explanation, giving birth to the Seventh-Day Adventist movement. Miller is just one of many misguided date-setters who have incorrectly predicted the end of days over the past two thousand years.[15]

"There has been a 100 percent failure rate," says Ben Witherington, the Jean R. Amos professor of New Testament for doctoral studies at Asbury Theological Seminary and the author of *Revelation (New Cambridge Bible Commentary)* and *Jesus, Paul and the End of the World.* "The fundamental problem is a misunderstanding of the nature of biblical prophecy. Biblical prophecy is not really interested in calculations and prognostications of a specific date-setting sort. What biblical prophecy is trying to do is give you in some sort of a larger picture some hope and reassurance about the big character of how God will resolve human history and bring his plans to fruition."[16]

One of the dangers in interpreting Bible prophecy is to "overread it" or "underread it." "You underread it by not paying enough attention to it and overread it by trying to figure it all out when the text is pretty clear…that it is not something you are going to entirely figure out," Darrell Bock says. "Jesus is coming at a time that no one knows. Even he doesn't know when the end is. The Father sends him. Not only that, but the disciples asked the question, 'Is this the time you are going to restore the kingdom of Israel?' and basically Jesus said in Acts 1, 'That's the Father's business. In the meantime, you are to be in the Spirit and you are to go to the ends of the earth [preaching the gospel].'"[17]

While we agree with Witherington and Bock that date-setting is unbiblical and Christians should certainly be committed first and foremost to fulfilling the Great Commission, a recent *Charisma* story—"Most Pastors Avoid Controversial Issues to Keep Tithes Up"—sheds some light on why many pastors are not giving sermons on the end times. The story, based on a Barna Group study, found that nine out of ten pastors avoid giving sermons on controversial issues such as politics, abortion, and same-sex marriage—even though the Bible speaks to every one of these issues—for fear of alienating people or impacting tithing. In a survey, 90 percent of the pastors conceded that the Bible addresses all those issues. "Then we ask them, 'Well, are you teaching your people what the Bible says about those issues?'—and the numbers drop...to less than 10 percent of pastors who will speak to it," George Barna said. Then, when asked how they judge the success of their church, the pastors cited five factors: attendance, giving, number of programs, number of staff, and square footage. "Now all of those things are good measures, except for one tiny fact: Jesus didn't die for any of them," Barna said. "What I'm suggesting is [those pastors] won't probably get involved in politics because it's very controversial. Controversy keeps people from being in the seats, controversy keeps people from giving money, from attending programs."[18]

Jan Markell, host of the nationally syndicated *Understanding the Times* radio program and founder of Maple Grove, Minnesota–based Olive Tree Ministries, says it's an "unmistakable tragedy" that so many pastors are caught up in preaching feel-good sermons as end-times events unfold all around them. Markell believes only a fraction of the nation's pastors are teaching their congregations about the end times. "Some pastors are preaching the truth, but by and large we've got a seeker-sensitive gospel being preached from about 90 percent of our pulpits," Markell says. "They are afraid they are going to lose people if they talk about the end times."[19]

Is This History's Final Countdown?

The Barna study and Markell's remarks help explain an unfortunate paradox in today's world: Major faith leaders and prophecy experts— and a significant proportion of the public—believe the stage is now being set for the grand finale of history. Yet the church and mainstream news media are largely silent about what is happening. In more than one hundred interviews over the past five years with prominent faith leaders and Bible prophecy experts, the overwhelming consensus of opinion is that the world is almost certainly in the run-up to the end-times events predicted in Scripture. Even more astonishing, though, a cross section of secular humanists and experts in geopolitics, economics, and science agree that the world is in the countdown to the end of civilization.

"The likely end of the era of civilization is foreshadowed in a new draft report by the Intergovernmental Panel on Climate Change," Chomsky wrote in his article "The End of History?" "The report concludes that increasing greenhouse gas emissions risk 'severe, pervasive and irreversible impacts for people and ecosystems' over the coming decades. The world is nearing the temperature when loss of the vast ice sheet over Greenland will be unstoppable. Along with melting Antarctic ice, that could raise sea levels to inundate major cities as well as coastal plains. One index of human impact is the extinction of species, now estimated to be at about the same rate as it was 65 million years ago when an asteroid hit the Earth. That is the presumed cause for the ending of the age of the dinosaurs, which opened the way for small mammals to proliferate, and ultimately modern humans. Today, it is humans who are the asteroid, condemning much of life to extinction."[20]

In a recent report from the University of Oxford's Future of Humanity Institute and the Global Challenges Foundation titled "Global Challenges: 12 Risks That Threaten Human Civilisation," the authors wrote that the idea that a number of risks threaten "the very basis of our civilisation at the beginning of the 21st century is well accepted in the scientific community, and is studied at a number of leading universities." The report is the "first science-based list of global risks... where in extreme cases all human life could end." "Over the last century the world has changed in ways that humanity has never experienced within our history," the authors wrote. "The changes are being caused by the extremely rapid development of science and technology, by the population explosion that has quadrupled the number of people on Earth, and by a greatly improved but a very resource-demanding standard of living in developed countries... This means that we are now forced to live with the risk of various kinds of extreme disaster with the potential of severely affecting billions of people." The twelve risks outlined in the report include extreme climate change, nuclear war, global pandemic, ecological catastrophe, global system collapse, major asteroid impact, supervolcano, synthetic biology, nanotechnology, artificial intelligence, "unknown consequences," and "future bad global governance." In regard to the final risk—a stunning admission in an academic report—the authors cited the possibility of a "world dictatorship" or a "global totalitarian state." "Technology, political and social change may enable the construction of new forms of governance, which may be either much better or much worse," the authors wrote.[21]

This rather shocking report comes as there is a sense around the world that something momentous and radically world-altering is under way. Many believe doomsday is on the horizon, and hope for a savior is growing. Christians are expecting the return of Christ, Muslims are anticipating the Twelfth Imam, Buddhists are awaiting the Fifth Buddha, Hindus are looking for Krishna, and members of the New Age movement have set their eyes on the coming of the enigmatic Lord Maitreya. Polls confirm that many believe history is wrapping up. A 2010 poll by the Pew Research Center for the People & the Press found that 41 percent of Americans believe Jesus will return to earth by 2050. Meanwhile, 58 percent think another world war is definite or probable over the next four decades, and 53 percent expect the United States to face a nuclear terrorist attack. In addition, 41 percent believe the world will move toward a single global currency, and 31 percent expect an asteroid to strike the earth. "We certainly seem to be heading toward something," says Jerry B. Jenkins, coauthor of the Left Behind series who was described by *Newsweek* as one of "the new prophets of Revelation." "Natural disasters seem to increase in intensity and frequency, and the Scripture's two-millennium-old prophecy of wars and rumors of wars and nation rising against nation has reached fever pitch."[22]

A recent poll by the Public Religion Research Institute found that 49 percent of Americans, up from 44 percent in 2011, believe the surge in natural disasters is "evidence of the apocalypse" and the "end times."[23]

The world is undergoing a major convergence of forces—worldwide drought and famine, the growing possibility of World War III, super-earthquakes, mega-tsunamis and other cataclysmic disasters, and an emerging cashless society and global government. This panorama of forces is now converging in the same way the biblical prophets and Christ predicted it would in the end times. "The overwhelming majority of [22] Bible prophecy experts [we interviewed] focused on one word—convergence," wrote David R. Reagan, founder of Lamb & Lion Ministries, in his newsletter. "In other words, they said the main reason why they believe we are living in the season of the Lord's return is not because of any one particular sign, but because we have so many signs converging that are coming together for the first time. All the signs of the end times are coming together at once."[24]

Stan Guthrie, former managing editor of *Christianity Today* and author of *A Concise Guide to Bible Prophecy*, says the world is facing unprecedented dangers. "Iran looks like it's on the verge of getting nuclear weapons, there are certainly financial stresses…and you've got superbugs spreading in the world, so I think it's very valid and logical to be concerned about the future and wonder what God is doing," Guthrie says. "Does he have a plan for our lives and is he going to bring us through these things? We are going to see what happens, but I certainly think we are heading toward some scary and dangerous days… I personally think the Lord could come at any time. He made it clear that once the gospel is preached to the entire world that he could come back at any time and we're basically there. I mean, obviously, there are a few outposts here and there that haven't heard, but as far as the gospel going to all nations…that has happened…I think it's very helpful and healthy to be looking to the heavens to see when Jesus might return because I think that's one of our besetting sins. We kind of go along like things are just going to continue on and on forever and that the Lord isn't going to come back. That's a conceit we cannot afford."[25]

Fearful Sights and Great Signs

While signs regarding the end of days are interspersed throughout the Bible, Jesus spoke of many of them in Matthew 24; Mark 13; and Luke 12 and 21. In Matthew 24, Jesus told his followers to "keep watch" for the signs of his return (v. 42 NIV). In describing these signs, Jesus spoke of "wars and rumors of wars" and "famines and earthquakes in various places" (Matt. 24:6–7 NIV). In Luke 21:11, Jesus also spoke of "pestilences" and "fearful sights and great signs" in the heavens (NKJV). In Mark 13:8, he described "the beginnings of sorrows" (NKJV). As a result, many prophecy experts believe the end times will be marked by earthquakes, tsunamis, volcanic eruptions, drought, famine, storms, floods, and economic failures.

Not long before the Babylonian invasion and destruction of Jerusalem in 586 BC, the prophet Jeremiah warned Israel—an apostate nation given to promiscuous sex and idolatry that he compared to a wife who had left her husband to become a harlot—that God had brought about a devastating drought to warn the Israelites that repentance was their last possible chance to escape destruction. A recent survey by the Public Religion Research Institute found that 36 percent of Americans—and 65 percent of white evangelical Protestants—believe the severity of the worsening drought and megadisasters such as Superstorm Sandy are evidence that the world is nearing its expiration date.[26]

The poll comes amid a tsunami of bad news about megadroughts, floods, extreme weather, earthquakes, wildfires, and plagues such as the recent ebola outbreak in Africa and other parts of the world. At the time, the World Health Organization called it the "most severe acute health emergency in modern times." For many years, end-times skeptics pointed to conflicting data as to whether the number of earthquakes was on the rise. Now a recent study has found that there were more than twice as many big earthquakes in the first quarter of 2014 as the average since 1979. "We have recently experienced a period that has had one of the highest rates of great earthquakes ever recorded," Tom Parsons, the lead study author and a research geophysicist at the U.S. Geological Survey in Menlo Park, California, told LiveScience.com. The study found that the average rate of large earthquakes—those exceeding magnitude 7—has been ten annually since 1979. That number increased to an average of 12.5 per year beginning in 1992, and jumped to 16.7 starting in 2010—a 65 percent increase compared to the 1979 rate.[27]

Meanwhile, recent World Economic Forum "Global Risks" reports paint a dire picture of the next decade, including the possibility of "major systemic financial failure," a "killer bacteria that could turn into a pandemic," and the possibility that the world has already "passed a point of no return and the Earth's atmosphere is tipping rapidly into an inhospitable state." Other risks include the continuing spread of weapons of mass destruction, severe income disparity, the threat of "destabilizing hyper-inflation," an increase in "extreme weather events" and other catastrophic natural disasters, and worsening global food and water crises. The authors noted that any future shocks on the already stressed global economic and environmental systems "could trigger the 'global perfect storm,' with potentially insurmountable consequences." "The narrative emerging from the survey is clear: like a superstorm, two major systems are on a collision course. The resulting interplay between stresses on the economic and environmental systems will present unprecedented challenges to global and national resilience," the authors wrote.[28]

Recent news headlines paint a similarly apocalyptic picture of the future:

- "America's Worst Drought Since '56 Threatens World Food Supply" (Reuters, July 17, 2012).
- "Franklin Graham: World Turmoil Could Signal 'End of the Age'" (*Newsmax*, September 5, 2014).
- "Europe Is in an Epic Depression—and It's Getting Worse" (*The Week*, August 15, 2014).
- "The Typical Household, Now Worth a Third Less" (*New York Times*, July 26, 2014).
- "Los Angeles Awaits Earthquake That Could Be the 'Big One'" (*Telegraph*, July 19, 2014).
- "Ebola Rages in West Africa, Reigniting Humanity's Oldest Fear: The Plague" (*Daily Beast*, August 4, 2014).
- "US West Faces 'Worst Drought in 500 Years'" (*Newsmax*, February 2, 2014).

- "Far More Asteroids Have Hit the Earth Than We Thought, Astronauts Say" (*Huffington Post*, April 19, 2014).

In terms of the often-underestimated danger of asteroids, former NASA scientist Ed Lu made the stunning admission recently that it's mere happenstance that an "atomic bomb scale asteroid" hasn't hit a densely populated area in recent times. Lu, a former space shuttle astronaut, said the nation's nuclear weapons test warning network detected twenty-six multi-kiloton explosions since 2001, all of which are due to asteroid impacts. "This shows that asteroid impacts are NOT rare—but actually 3–10 times more common than we previously thought," Lu said. "The fact that none of these asteroid impacts shown in the video was detected in advance shows that the only thing preventing a catastrophe from a 'city-killer' sized asteroid is blind luck."[29]

In terms of the signs of the end of the age, F. Kenton Beshore argues that seven major end-times signs have already been fulfilled, including the "dry bones" prophecy regarding the return of the Jews to the Holy Land following the Balfour Declaration in 1917 (Zeph. 2:1–2; Ezek. 37:1–14); the "birth pangs" of World Wars I and II (Matt. 24:6–8); the rebirth of the nation of Israel in 1948 (Matt. 24:32); and the Six-Day War in 1967, which resulted in the Israeli recapture of Old Jerusalem (Luke 21:24).[30]

Of these, the rebirth of Israel in 1948 is considered the major end-times event that started the prophetic countdown. "Israel is the supersign," Tim LaHaye says. "The Jews were scattered in almost every country and now they have been brought back to Israel in the last 150 years. For more than seventeen hundred years, they did not have a homeland and now they have that homeland and Jews are coming back into it—nearly seven million in the Holy Land now. That's a miracle in itself."[31]

Five end-times signs are in the process of fulfillment now, including the "falling away" or apostasy of the church (2 Thess. 2:1–3; 2 Tim.

4:3–4); the explosion of knowledge and travel (Dan. 12:4); growing anti-Semitism (Ps. 83:1–5); development of mark of the Beast technologies (Rev. 13:15–18); and Jews living securely in Israel (Ezek. 38:8, 11, 14).[32]

Jan Markell believes that the world is experiencing a coming together of last days signs, including new technologies that could make the "Antichrist system" possible for the first time in history. "From 'chip' technology to a cashless society, technology is racing and on fast-forward like never before," Markell wrote. "The 'increase in knowledge' foretold in Daniel 12 is most prominent in the world of technology. The Antichrist system will be waiting for him to tap into (Revelation 13, 17; Daniel 12)."[33]

A total of fifteen end-times prophecies are yet to be fulfilled, including the "War of Gog and Magog," in which Russia and a coalition of Middle Eastern nations are expected to attack Israel (Ezek. 38–39); the rise of the False Prophet and a global false religion (Rev. 17:1–5, 18; 13:11–17); a global economic system (Rev. 13:15–18); a world government consisting of ten regional unions (Dan. 7:23–24); the rebuilding of the Temple in Jerusalem (Rev. 11:1–2; 2 Thess. 2:4); the rise of the Antichrist (Isa. 28:15; Dan. 9:27; 7:20, 24; Rev. 6:1–2; 13:1–10); and distress and fear among the nations (Luke 21:25–27).[34]

In her list of converging signs, Markell noted how many people are talking favorably about a one-world religion. "Tony Blair has stated that he will spend the rest of his life pushing for this," Markell wrote. "The heads of many denominations and faiths see ecumenism as positive now." She also mentioned the growing popularity of the occult and witchcraft and similarities to the "days of Noah." In Matthew 24:37, Jesus compared the time of his return to the "days of Noah," a reference to the antediluvian world in which the "sons of God," or fallen angels, are believed by some to have interbred with women—creating an unholy, corrupted genetic line known as the Nephilim. "The 'days of

Noah' similarities have never been stronger," Markell wrote. "Corruption and violence characterized times then and now. There was genetic manipulation then and now. There was a preaching of the truth that was ignored. A decline in man's character was dramatic then and now. Earthly pleasures were all that mattered."[35]

Transhumanism and the "Days of Noah"

The changes now facing the human race are at an epochal level. In fact, the global transformations before us are now are so great that some scientists believe we are at a major turning point in mankind's evolution as a species. Whether or not you subscribe to all the tenets of evolutionary theory, powerful forces are converging and accelerating that could result in widespread genetic change.[36]

A revolution is occurring in what is called the science of transhumanism, a scientific pursuit that promises to alter our very DNA and potentially turn us into a new race of bionic supermen and superwomen. If you think this is science fiction, read Ray Kurzweil, whom many call the father of the transhumanism movement. Kurzweil, the director of engineering at Google, believes humanity can achieve a form of immortality through genetic engineering, science, and technology.

"The Singularity will allow us to transcend these limitations of our biological bodies and brains," Kurzweil wrote in his *New York Times* bestselling book *The Singularity Is Near*. "We will gain power over our fates. Our mortality will be in our own hands. We will be able to live as long as we want (a subtly different statement from saying we will live forever)...By the end of this century, the non-biological portion of our intelligence will be trillions of trillions of times more powerful than unaided human intelligence."[37]

In his book *Superintelligence: Paths, Dangers, Strategies*, Nick Bostrom, a philosophy professor and founding director of the Future of Humanity

Institute at Oxford University, wrote that the potential development of "superintelligence" is in all likelihood the most important and daunting challenge humanity has ever faced. "If some day we build machine brains that surpass human brains in general intelligence, then this new superintelligence could become very powerful," Bostrom wrote. "And, as the fate of the gorillas now depends more on us humans than on the gorillas themselves, so the fate of our species would depend on the actions of the machine superintelligence."[38]

In recent years, the U.S. Department of Defense has researched the potential creation of super-soldiers. The movie *Spider-Man* is not as far-fetched as some may think. A recent *Daily Mail* story noted that scientists had created more than 150 human-animal hybrid embryos in laboratories in the United Kingdom, despite warnings of a "nightmare *Planet of the Apes* scenario." "We're on the cusp of the greatest evolutionary change in the history of mankind," says Daniel Estulin, author of *TransEvolution: The Coming Age of Human Deconstruction*. "What's coming over the next five or ten years will forever revolutionize the very definition of humanity. I can tell you without a doubt that the generations of children who are being born right now are the last truly 100 percent human generation of human beings on the planet. Their children will be transhuman children—post-human man-machines, cyborgs, and beings who are not totally human as a result of synthetic biology. It's absolutely inevitable—the whole idea of merging man and machines."[39]

These genetic changes are not just intended for the military. Scientists in the United States, France, Great Britain, Russia, China, Japan, and other nations are reportedly experimenting with mingling human, animal, and insect DNA. In addition, there is a convergence of the sciences and technologies of genetics, computers, neuroscience, biochemistry, and quantum physics. These are not futuristic technologies. These are technologies that are already in their initial phases. The synergy of robotics, computer-brain interfaces, nanochips, synthetic telepathy, mind-reading technologies, and H. G. Wells's prediction of a "world brain" are converging into what can be described only as a mass acceleration of human consciousness and ability. Scientists have discovered that the brain is essentially holographic in nature and that every neuron contains the DNA necessary to replicate the entire brain. Thus, from the perspective of neurological science, the brain is a highly advanced holographic computer. At the same time, physicists are discovering that we live in what is in essence a holographic world composed of subatomic particles with vast spaces between them. Many scientists believe we live in a multidimensional universe where the discoveries of futurist Nikola Tesla and Scalar Technologies are opening up before us. String theory, according to Michio Kaku, an American theoretical physicist and the Henry Semat professor of theoretical physics at the City College of New York, has suggested that the universe is composed of eleven dimensions—a truly mind-bending discovery.[40]

Every field of science and discipline of human study from psychology, geopolitics, science, economics, physics, biology, and mathematics is in hyperdrive. As a result of computer technologies and the convergence of these disciplines, mankind is in the midst of the most massive transformation since the Garden of Eden.

God's Cosmic Riddle

This acceleration in human consciousness not only has allowed humanity to reinvent the future but has also enabled it to revisit the secrets and codes of the past, such as the biblical cryptograms embedded in what we've coined the "Babylon code." For example, when we reexamine the ancient biblical texts, we discover that the account of Noah and the Flood is not just some story about an old man with a white beard and a giant boat filled with animals. Rather, it seems it is a targeted move of the infinite personal living God of the universe to eradicate human and animal DNA corrupted by an interdimensional source. The Bible is not some archaic book of fairy tales as its critics would like to argue. The God of the universe created mankind according to a specific code—the DNA code. The double helix is God's cosmic code for all living creation. In the Garden of Eden, God created Adam and Eve with the DNA of God: "And God said, Let us make man in our image, after our likeness," according to Genesis 1:26 (KJV).

After God's judgment of the corrupted DNA, he commanded Adam to "be fruitful, and multiply" (Gen. 1:28 KJV), and males and females began to reproduce and fill the earth once again. But shortly after that period a man named Nimrod appeared who built Babylon and the Tower of Babel. When properly considered within its context, the Tower of Babel likely involved advanced technologies. The Tower of Babel and the word *Babel*, or *Bab-ili*, means "gate of the gods." Often the only way to truly understand the Bible is to study the root meaning of words in the original biblical language. Thus, the purpose of the Tower of Babel may have been to act as a kind of portal for interdimensional beings to enter the earthly realm. It was there in ancient Babylon that all the ancient mystery religions and secret occult societies were birthed. An ancient code is weaved into the interdimensional fabric of ancient Babylon that is connected to a dimension outside of time and space that we are only now beginning to understand.[41]

All these converging forces and advanced technologies, including what some are calling mankind's evolutionary transformation, are directly connected to Babylon and the ancient civilizations that many believe existed before the Flood.

As we will explain, a powerful key in unlocking the Babylon code is coming to understand that the Bible is not a collection of myths, fables, allegories, and legends. The Bible itself is the ultimate cosmic code that is downloaded by God, not from "the cloud" but from another dimension of reality. The God of the Bible has embedded in the text and the biblical stories an infinite and personal code that explains the future from before the beginning of time. As mortal human beings we may feel overwhelmed and dizzied by the acceleration of change all around us. But God gave us supernatural advanced knowledge to help prepare us for the period we live in. When Jesus Christ said, "As it was in the days of Noah, so it will be at the coming of the Son of Man" (Matt. 24:37 NIV), he was alerting us nearly two thousand years ago about the advent of such things as transhumanism, interdimensional beings, holographic reality, DNA, and digital coding.

As you read *The Babylon Code*, it is our desire that you would recognize the "apps" that the Creator has placed inside every human being who has downloaded his Spirit and that you would activate these "apps" by faith. We live in a world where the convergence and the acceleration of change are moving so fast that ordinary human modalities of processing information and experience are simply not enough. For your survival, the survival of your family, and the survival of the human race, it is essential that you grasp the full extent of the Babylon code.

Chapter Five

America at the End

The Bible doesn't say what happens to us. But by the absence of us being clearly defined in the text, it means something has happened. The question is what—what will happen to us that will neutralize our ability or desire to be an influential player in the last days of history before the return of Jesus Christ?

—JOEL C. ROSENBERG

Many intuitively sense that the world has entered one of the most dangerous times in all of human history. Society is caught in a maelstrom of converging forces—the growing threat of thermonuclear war, worsening drought and famine, and intensifying calls for a "new international order" and "global authority" to address the mounting array of international crises.[1]

Experts are alarmed by the continued spread of weapons of mass destruction and threats by Iran, North Korea, and ISIS to bring about "Armageddon" in the West. Meanwhile, fears of an economic collapse are growing as nations continue to amass unprecedented levels of debt. At the same time, the world is experiencing an increase in large earthquakes and other megadisasters, and concerns are rising about the possibility of a global outbreak of some horrific pathogen.

The sense of foreboding about the future is especially intense in

America. Yet most prophecy experts say the Bible seems strangely silent about the fate of the wealthiest, most powerful nation in history. For decades, Bible scholars have been puzzled by the Scripture's apparent omission of America in the prophetic scenario. Some believe the nation will experience a total economic collapse, a surprise nuclear attack, a wave of devastating earthquakes and other cataclysmic disasters, or that millions will miraculously disappear in the Rapture—triggering a complete societal breakdown.

"This is the number one question I get asked whenever I speak around the country," says Rosenberg, author of the *New York Times* bestselling book *Implosion: Can America Recover from Its Economic & Spiritual Challenges in Time?* "What happens to America in the end times? Where is America in Bible prophecy?"[2]

In the midst of soaring federal debt, economic turmoil, declining morality, growing spiritual apathy, a weakened church, and a myriad of other daunting challenges, many are curious to know how America fits into the end-times biblical scenario. Many believe the United States is not merely in decline but faces the real and growing risk of catastrophic collapse. A number of scenarios could explain why America isn't specifically mentioned in the Bible.

"It could be war," says Rosenberg, whom *U.S. News & World Report* once called a "modern-day Nostradamus" for writing a novel about terrorists who hijack a jet to use on a kamikaze mission into a U.S. city nine months before the September 11, 2001, terrorist attacks. "It could be terrorism, natural disasters, or political paralysis. Economic implosion seems increasingly a real threat and of course there is the issue of the Rapture, which would take out millions upon millions of born-again followers of Jesus Christ in the U.S. in the blink of an eye. That would have a devastating effect on the American economy and society when that happens."[3]

Nine Harbingers, Four Blood Moons, and the Shemitah

While no one knows what tidal wave of terror might engulf the United States in the future, Rosenberg's book, along with Jonathan Cahn's *The Harbinger* and Pastor John Hagee's *Four Blood Moons: Something Is About to Change*—all *New York Times* bestsellers—signals a new wave of interest in the role America plays in the end times. Now, with the revelations contained in *The Babylon Code*, the question turns to whether America will suffer some terrible fate or could be subsumed into or even become the headquarters of the global political, economic, and religious end-times system foretold by the prophets.

Of these books, *The Harbinger* has gained the most attention, selling more than two million copies. It has reached Capitol Hill and has been "read, hailed and endorsed" by members of Congress, senators, and presidential candidates. The book has inspired two documentaries—*The Isaiah 9:10 Judgment*, the number one faith video of 2012 and 2013; and *The Harbinger Decoded*, the number one faith video of 2014.[4]

The Harbinger, based on a prophetic mystery Cahn discovered in Isaiah 9, frames a biblical warning of judgment in a narrative as a journalist encounters a figure known as "the Prophet" who claims that the same nine harbingers of judgment that preceded the destruction of Israel twenty-seven hundred years ago are manifesting in America today.

"Before God brings a nation into judgment, he sends warning," says Cahn, the senior rabbi at the nation's largest messianic congregation, the Beth Israel Worship Center in Wayne, New Jersey. "Before he brought judgment and destruction to ancient Israel, he warned them. I believe the reason why the book has gone forth in such a massive way is because it's a prophetic warning given to the nation."[5]

Even the timing of the book's release—January 2012—is no accident, Cahn says. That's the same year that America reached a "tipping point"—when the president and the majority of Americans came out against the biblical definition of marriage—or against the Bible, Cahn says. "Since that time, the nation's apostasy from God and defiance of his ways has greatly accelerated," Cahn says. "According to the mystery of *The Harbinger*, and the example of ancient Israel, there is a grace period given in which the nation is given the chance to either turn back to God or descend into calamity and judgment. Though millions have now read or heard the message of *The Harbinger*, America's mainstream culture has continued its rapid descent. Thus, the mystery of *The Harbinger* portends this: If America does not turn back to God in repentance, there will come great shakings to the nation, and the American age as we know it will come to an end. This sense of American decline is not something felt only by students of biblical prophecy, or even just born-again believers, but, more and more, it's a feeling shared by the wider public."[6]

This growing awareness that God seems to be removing his hand of protection over America and the world comes amid the convergence of two events—a rare set of four blood moons and the biblical Shemitah in 2014 and 2015. Cahn believes these events fit in with a seven-year biblical pattern of escalating judgments that began with the September 11, 2001, terrorist attacks.

The greatest stock-market crashes in American history occurred exactly seven years apart on Elul 29, the day of the Shemitah, or the Sabbath year. Every seventh year, according to Leviticus 25:1–10, the land was to lie fallow. At the end of that year, Elul 29 on the Hebrew calendar, all debts and accounts were released. The ancient Israelites eventually ignored the Shemitah, choosing to sow and reap during the Sabbath year and not leave their fields, vineyards, and groves open for the poor to eat from. Consequently, they spent seventy years in Babylonian captivity—one for every Sabbath year they ignored God's instructions—following the destruction of Solomon's Temple and the fall of Jerusalem in 587 BC.

Mysteriously, it's on these exact days that the greatest collapses in Wall Street and American history occurred. The first occurred six days after the September 11, 2001, terrorist attacks. The next occurred exactly seven years later on the biblical calendar, on September 29, 2008, amid the global economic meltdown. Cahn believes this biblical pattern is connected to numerous events in modern history, including the rise of America—the only nation other than Israel to make a covenant with God—to superpower status, World Wars I and II, the return of the Jews to their ancient homeland, the Six-Day War in Jerusalem, and even the construction of the World Trade Center.

"It's an ancient mystery and an amazing phenomenon: The two greatest crashes in American history both took place on the same exact biblical day, exactly seven biblical years apart, and on the day appointed to strike a nation's financial realm," Cahn says. "I am continuously asked, when is the next Shemitah? The next one begins on September 25, 2014, and goes until 2015, when it culminates on Elul 29, which, on the Western calendar, falls on September 13." Could another economic collapse or a stock-market crash occur during this time? "Yes. Does it have to happen at the same exact time? No. The issue isn't ultimately about the dates, but of repentance and getting right with God," Cahn says. "Regardless of dates, we need to be ready."[7]

The fact that an unusual set of four blood moons, or a tetrad of total lunar eclipses, appeared in 2014–15 has intrigued people worldwide. The moon takes on a reddish-orange hue, or a blood color, during a total lunar eclipse. Many are now asking whether this could be the beginning of the prophetic countdown to Armageddon.

One of the eclipses, the solar eclipse of 2015, took place on Elul 29, the day of the Shemitah. "Those who have studied the blood moons believe that the phenomenon is linked to Israel, the people, and the land," Cahn says. "As for the Shemitah, it originates in Israel, and yet it has carried colossal ramifications for the United States."[8]

Further, the "Super Shemitah"—the Year of Jubilee that comes at the end of seven cycles of the Shemitah—begins on Yom Kippur, or September 23, 2015, and runs through September 2016. "What people don't realize is one of the missing keys of end-times prophecy is the Shemitah," Cahn told about one thousand people gathered at the recent Prophecy in the News conference in Orlando, Florida. "What's the end of end-times prophecy? The Tribulation. How long is the Tribulation period? Seven years. It's a cycle of Shemitahs that goes back to Daniel's seventy sevens, which is linked to the Shemitah and linked to the judgment of Israel and the seventy years of judgment. Every seventh year is a Shemitah, but every seventh Shemitah is a Super-Shemitah, which we call the Jubilee where it says everyone shall return to their father's possession. Everyone shall return to their father's land. If you lost your land, that year you returned home...Now, we know the Jewish people lost their land. For two thousand years, they had no land, so could the Jubilee actually be linked to the prophetic end-times scenario? We know that the Lord cannot return until his people come back to Israel, come back to Jerusalem and come back to him...Could [the Shemitah] usher in the prophetic end-times event of restoration?"[9]

These prophetic mysteries are just some of many that prophetic scholars are beginning to uncover in the Bible. Others say they have found a series of "biblical codes" and parallels between ancient Israel and America that point to the possible fulfillment of end-times events in the period of 2015–28.[10]

They note intriguing parallels between ancient Israel and America, including that America is the only nation in the world other than Israel that was "built on biblical principles" and has also played an instrumental role in spreading the gospel throughout the world. The Pilgrims made a covenant with God in the Mayflower Compact—"America's first constitution"—in 1620, just a few years after the Jamestown settlement nearly floundered because of a lack of strong government and leadership. The notion of a social contract, which dated to biblical times, would receive fuller expression in the works of Thomas Hobbes and John Locke, whose writings influenced American Revolutionaries and are reflected in the Declaration of Independence. William Bradford, the Pilgrim governor of the Plymouth Colony, used the Hebrew language at the beginnings of his books because it was the same language God used to speak to the angels and Old Testament patriarchs. Likewise, the Founding Fathers considered making the Hebrew language the official language of the colonies. The early Ivy League universities taught Hebrew, and the seal of Yale University contains the Hebrew words that mean "light and perfection." Further, America's founding documents—the Constitution, Bill of Rights, and Declaration of Independence—all contain elements based on the Torah, the Psalms, and the four Gospels.[11]

The Blood Moons Debate

Just as there is debate whether the end of the Shemitah in September 2015—or the "Super-Shemitah," running from September 2015 through September 2016—could be the beginning of fulfillment of end-times prophecies, the blood moons prophecy has also set off an apocalyptic controversy. In 2012, Pastor John Hagee announced that the appearance of four blood moons on Jewish holy days between April 2014 and October 2015 points to a "world-shaking event" that could signify the beginning of events culminating in the Tribulation. Hagee, along with Mark Biltz, founder of El Shaddai Ministries and the first to discover the blood moons prophecy, believe this tetrad of blood moons signals some major event in Israel, America, or the world.

"The Bible speaks of signs in the heavens that have been discovered and recorded by NASA that you yourself can find on Google on the Internet," Hagee, pastor of the twenty-two-thousand-member Cornerstone

Church in San Antonio, Texas, told his congregation in October 2012. "The coming four blood moons point to a world-shaking event that will happen between April 2014 and October 2015. What does it mean? What is the prophetic significance? Is this the end of the age?"[12]

Hagee argues that several Bible verses indicate that God uses the sun, moon, and stars for signs. For instance, Genesis 1:14 records that the "lights in the dome of the sky" are for "signs and for seasons" (NRSV). In his discourse on signs of his return, Jesus says in Luke 21:25 that "there will be signs in the sun, the moon, and the stars" (NRSV). Or consider Joel 2:30–31: "I will show portents in the heavens and on the earth, blood and fire and columns of smoke. The sun shall be turned to darkness, and the moon to blood, before the great and terrible day of the LORD comes" (NRSV). Revelation 6:12 says the "full moon became like blood" (NRSV) following the opening of the sixth seal—the first of three sets of progressive judgments during the Tribulation.

"I believe that the heavens are God's billboard—and that he has been sending signals to planet Earth and we just haven't been picking them up," Hagee told his church. "Today, with the help of God's Word and some very astute scientists, I'm going to walk you through five hundred years [of four blood moons on Jewish feast days] and show you how God is literally screaming at the world: 'I am coming soon.' "[13]

This rare combination of four blood moons on Passover and the Feast of Tabernacles in 2014–15 has occurred only three times in the past five centuries—and all during periods involving significant historical events regarding the Jewish people. The first tetrad on Jewish feast days occurred in 1493–94, a year after the Jews' expulsion from Spain and Christopher Columbus's discovery of America, a haven for the Jewish people. The second happened in 1949–50, a year after the founding of Israel in 1948. The third transpired in 1967–68, a period during which the Jews recaptured Jerusalem in the Six-Day War.

However, the prediction has generated significant debate. NASA issued a statement saying it doesn't consider tetrads especially rare—noting there will be eight before the year 2100.[14]

Mark Hitchcock, a noted Bible scholar and author of a book debunking the blood moons prophecy—*Blood Moons Rising*—says he's examined the evidence Hagee and Biltz compiled and has concluded that "it's not a biblical sign." First, Hitchcock says, the biblical passages Hagee and Biltz cite are related to the Second Coming, not to events preceding the Tribulation. Second, these blood moons can't be omens of the Second Coming because that event is preceded by the Tribulation, and that obviously hasn't happened yet. Third, the four blood moons of 1493–94 occurred after Spain expelled the Jews and can't be a sign of something that already happened. Likewise, the four blood moons of 1949–50 occurred after Israel became a nation in 1948. "I examined their view of the Bible and history, their view of these blood moons as being signs in the heavens, and I just find that these don't stand up to common sense or scriptural scrutiny, and so I don't put any stock in this," Hitchcock says.[15]

In a CNN article, Kenneth L. Waters, an associate dean and professor of New Testament at Azusa Pacific University, wrote that the Bible often speaks of astronomical signs of the end times, but these signs are ambiguous and nonspecific. "In times of widespread fear, insecurity and uncertainty, religious leaders and secular theorists, some well-meaning and some who are not, will exploit the need for hope and assurance by declaring exclusive discovery of some secret plan hidden in the disorder," Waters wrote. "We have seen this before: the fear of Y2K in 2000; Harold Camping's predictions of the apocalypse in 2011; the 'Mayan' Apocalypse on December 21, 2012; and now the blood moons."[16]

When it comes to conjecture and jumping to conclusions, Waters is right, but just because humans fail to do the math properly does not mean that biblical equations are ambiguous metaphors. As for whether the blood moons and biblical Shemitah, or even the "Super-Shemitah," are portents of the approaching end of days, only time will tell. All previous prognosticators have been wrong, but at some point someone will be right.

Newton's Riddle: 2015–16 or 2060?

Another prediction that has attracted attention, though certainly less well-known than the blood moon and Shemitah prophecies, is known as "Newton's Riddle"—a phrase derived from the title of forty-one-year veteran Annapolis High School teacher Neill G. Russell's book, *Newton's Riddle: The Mystery of Daniel's 70th Week Revealed.*

"He [Sir Isaac Newton] regarded the universe as a cryptogram set by the Almighty—just as he himself wrapped the discovery of the calculus in a cryptogram when he communicated with Leibnez," wrote British economist John Maynard Keynes, who in 1936 purchased Newton's vast collection of writings stored at the library at Cambridge University where Newton was a professor of mathematics for many years. "By pure thought, by concentration of mind, the riddle, he believed, would be revealed to the initiate. He did read the riddle of the heavens. And he believed that by the same powers of his introspective imagination he would read the riddle of the Godhead, the riddle of the past and future events divinely foreordained."[17]

Newton, an English physicist and mathematician who is considered one of the most influential scientists in history and a key figure in the scientific revolution, devoted much of his later years to the study and interpretation of the prophecies of Daniel and Saint John—penning a book titled *Observations upon the Prophecies of Daniel & the Apocalypse of St. John.* Keynes wrote that Newton viewed "the whole universe and all that is in it as a riddle, as a secret which could be read by applying pure thought to certain evidence, certain mystic clues, which God had laid about the world to allow a sort of philosopher's treasure hunt to the esoteric brotherhood." Newton believed that these clues were to be found "partly in the evidence of the heavens and in the constitution of elements" and "also partly in certain papers and traditions handed down by the brethren in an unbroken chain back to the original cryptic revelation in Babylonia."[18]

"The prophecy is called the Revelation, with respect to the Scripture of Truth, which Daniel was commanded to shut up and seal, till the time of the end," Newton wrote in his book. "But in the very end, the Prophecy should be so far interpreted so as to convince many. Then saith Daniel, many shall run to and fro, and knowledge shall be increased. For the Gospel must be preached in all nations before the great tribulation, and end of the world…An Angel must fly through the midst of heaven with the everlasting Gospel to preach to all nations, before Babylon falls, and the Son of man reaps his harvest…If the general preaching of the Gospel be approaching, it is for us and our posterity that these words mainly belong: In the time of the end the wise shall understand, but none of the wicked shall understand. Blessed is he that readeth, and they that hear the words of this Prophecy, and keep those things that are written therein (Daniel 12:4, 10)."[19]

In 2003, a story in the *Telegraph* claimed that Newton had calculated the world would end in 2060. In the article, Jonathan Petre wrote that Newton had spent fifty years and wrote forty-five hundred pages "trying to predict when the end of the world was coming." "His theories about Armageddon have been unearthed by academics from little-known handwritten manuscripts in a library in Jerusalem," Petre wrote. "The thousands of pages show Newton's attempts to decode the Bible, which he believed contained God's secret laws for the universe. Newton, who was also a theologian and alchemist, predicted that the Second Coming of Christ would follow plagues and war and would precede a 1,000-year reign by the saints on earth—of which he would be one. The most definitive date he set for the apocalypse, which he scribbled on a scrap of paper, was 2060."[20]

Then, in a 2008 interview on *Sid Roth's It's Supernatural!*, Russell said Newton—based off an unusual interpretation of the seventy weeks prophecy in Daniel—had predicted a major prophetic event would occur in 2016, forty-nine years after Israel recaptured Jerusalem in 1967. "He looked at the ninth chapter of Daniel," Russell told Roth. "He interpreted the years . . . as prophetic years—each year being seven years. But he took a different slant. Most people add up those years and come up with 483 years. They add that up and come up with the time of Christ's first return. But he took a look at the last forty-nine years and . . . said the Jews would return to their homeland. Now this is three hundred years before that fact, and that once they were in their homeland that they would have Jerusalem as their capital again. Now that occurred in 1967 and what he did is he took the forty-nine years in Daniel 9, added those to 1967, and he came up with the year—and he admonished people: 'We are not date-setters.' God's Word says that. He knew God's Word. But the year he came up with was 2016."[21]

Inexplicably, Newton's prediction lines up with the end of the biblical Shemitah in September 2015 and the beginning of the "Super-Shemitah" on September 23, 2015—Yom Kippur. If one takes the Newton's riddle calculation—beginning June 7, 1967, with the restoration of Jerusalem—and adds seven, seven-year Shemitah cycles in biblical or prophetic years of 360 days, the date comes out to September 23, 2015—the beginning of the "Super-Shemitah" of 2015–16.

"I just read about this prophecy that Isaac Newton made," Jonathan Cahn told those gathered at the Prophecy in the News conference. "Isaac Newton, the [scientist] who discovered gravity that they made us study in school, was an ardent student of prophecy and he wrote a prophecy based on a calculation of Daniel's 'seventy weeks.' I'm not saying this is correct or anything, but I'm just saying it's interesting and you should be aware. If you follow the calculation ... it takes you to this event to be taking place around the time of 2016, but when they did it by what they call the prophetic years—360 days—it took them from the exact date of June 7, 1967, the date of the Six-Day War in Jerusalem, adding forty-nine years of 360-day years, to the date of September 23. September 23 is the Yom Kippur of 2015, the beginning of the Jubilee. I'm not saying it has to be, but I'm saying, 'Hey, it's Isaac Newton.' "[22]

Is America in Bible Prophecy?

Like the debates over the blood moons, the Shemitah, the Super-Shemitah, and Newton's riddle, prophecy experts have a range of opinions about what role, if any, the United States plays in the end times. Many believe the Bible is mysteriously silent about the fate of America.

Yet this position begs the obvious question: Why would God, who exists outside of time and space and knows the end from the beginning, omit the most powerful and wealthy nation in history from end-times prophecies? After all, no nation in history has wielded greater influence—politically, economically, militarily, culturally, and religiously—than America or is more closely aligned with Israel.

In terms of end-times events, the Bible refers to at least fifteen nations and regional alliances, including Israel, Iran, China, Russia, and Europe. Dozens of Bible verses refer to God's dealing with "all the nations," including a passage in Haggai 2:7 that says God would "shake all nations" (KJV) in the last days. Is there significance to the Bible's silence about America? Perhaps it's just one of many nations that aren't named in the Bible. But if America is the world's greatest military and political power, it seems odd that it's not mentioned in the Bible. Perhaps something happens to eliminate its status as a great military and political power.

Some believe the United States, weakened by its soaring debts, an economic collapse, or another catastrophe, will align itself with a unified Europe—the "revived Roman Empire"—during the Tribulation. In his book *One Nation Under Attack*, Grant Jeffrey wrote that powerful forces are working to undermine the United States politically, economically, and militarily. Already, these forces have largely succeeded in weakening the U.S. economy and military. "They will not stop until they have crippled the national economy, transforming the once-great United States into an impoverished nation with a severely weakened military and no influence on the world stage," Jeffrey notes. "A powerless America serves their purposes because it will not be able to resist the movement (led from within the European Union) that seeks to achieve global government... The United States will fall into a state of near-oblivion, becoming little less than a helpless bystander as the most dramatic events of history unfold."[23]

We also share the view that America is not just in decline but on the "road to collapse." The nation has nearly $18 trillion in federal debt, $60 trillion in total debt, and $116 trillion in unfunded liabilities, according to the U.S. National Debt Clock. A portion of these unfunded liabilities are promises the government has made to Americans regarding Social Security, Medicare, and Medicaid, which are coming due as seventy-six million baby boomers retire. Furthermore, Americans have aborted more than fifty-five million babies since 1973. "That's horrific in its own right," Joel Rosenberg says. "But on top of that, as if that weren't bad enough, it's having an economic effect that liberals didn't intend, which is if you build a social welfare system in which young people pay the bills of older people through taxes and then you kill fifty-five million younger workers, you are going to have a crisis." Further compounding these problems, families are imploding amid widespread divorce, out-of-wedlock births, fatherless homes, rising drug use, violent crime, pornography, and other social ills.[24]

"We are experiencing an epic failure of leadership at almost every level of American society right now," Rosenberg says. "Something has gone terribly wrong with the American experiment. Our families are imploding; our national debt is exploding, and experts on the left and right are warning us that we need to change direction because we're on an unsustainable trajectory economically, socially, and culturally. Unfortunately, too many leaders in our country are stuck in a business-as-usual mode and Americans are getting anxious that the ice is cracking under our feet."[25]

Given the dire state of the nation, many prophecy experts believe something "catastrophic" will occur in America, paving the way for a global leader to arise as predicted in the Bible. They believe the United States may be destroyed or severely weakened by an electromagnetic pulse (EMP) or nuclear attack. In recent years, experts have warned that a nuclear attack on the United States is "more likely than not." The odds of a terrorist-initiated nuclear strike within the next decade are placed at fifty-fifty. Furthermore, studies by Stanford University and a think tank found that a child today has a 10 percent chance of dying in a nuclear war. "The fact that no nuclear war has ever happened does not prove that deterrence works, but rather that we have been lucky," Seth Baum, executive director of the Global Catastrophic Risk Institute, wrote in an article for the Bulletin of the Atomic Scientists. Meanwhile, a congressional report from the Commission to Assess the Threat to the United States from Electromagnetic Pulse (EMP) Attack found a nuclear weapon detonated at a high altitude over the United States could severely damage or destroy the nation's electrical power systems, electronics, and information systems—taking "months to years" to recover from. "Even the secular experts are looking at the world and wondering what the future holds with weapons of mass destruction at the fingertips of national leaders, along with chemical and biological weapons," Tim LaHaye says. "The experts I've read said they see no future for the world beyond twenty-five to thirty years. Of course, there are those who say we need a one-world dictator to solve all these problems. That's exactly what the Bible says will happen. After Christ raptures the church, the Antichrist will come and set up a worldwide kingdom."[26]

"For in One Hour Is Thy Judgment Come"

Other prophecy experts believe the Bible makes symbolic or veiled references to America. They argue that the United States, or New York City, is the enigmatic Babylon mentioned in Revelation 17–18—the "great whore...seated on many waters" that is destroyed by "fire" (Rev. 17:1, 16 NRSV) in an hour near the end of the Tribulation.

In these chapters, the apostle John wrote that the world's merchants had "grown rich from the power of her luxury" (Rev. 18:3 NRSV). He wrote that she "lived luxuriously"—saying in her heart, " 'I rule as a queen; I am no widow, and I will never see grief' " (18:7 NRSV). Yet the apostle wrote that she would be destroyed in one hour and the merchants of the earth, watching her burn from the vantage point of their ships, would weep over her destruction because "in one hour all this wealth has been laid waste!" (18:17 NRSV). "Standing afar off for the fear of her torment, saying, 'Alas, alas that great city Babylon, that mighty city! for in one hour is thy judgment come,' " the apostle John wrote in Revelation 18:10 (KJV).

These prophetic scholars believe the verses refer to a nuclear attack on New York City or multiple cities throughout the United States. In 2009, David Wilkerson, who first outlined his vision of this "great calamity" in his 1974 book *The Vision*, issued an urgent message about an "earth-shattering calamity" that is "going to be so frightening, we are all going to tremble—even the godliest among us."[27]

"For ten years I have been warning about a thousand fires coming to New York City," wrote Wilkerson, who died in a traffic accident in 2011 at age seventy-nine. (McGuire believes the manner of Wilkerson's

death—just as the manner of death of the biblical prophets was pregnant with meaning—is symbolic of how the church is largely asleep at
the wheel as end-times events unfold.) "It will engulf the whole mega-
plex, including areas of New Jersey and Connecticut. Major cities all
across America will experience riots and blazing fires—such as we saw
in Watts, Los Angeles, years ago. There will be riots and fires in cities worldwide. There will be looting—including Times Square, New
York City. What we are experiencing now is not a recession, not even a
depression. We are under God's wrath. In Psalm 11 it is written, 'If the
foundations are destroyed, what can the righteous do?' God is judging
the raging sins of America and the nations. He is destroying the secular
foundations."[28]

It's also interesting to note that America, especially New York City
and Hollywood, is often referred to as Babylon in pop culture. For
instance, one of the first hits by the early punk rock band the New York
Dolls was titled "Babylon." The moniker "Hollywood Babylon" gained
popularity in the 1950s with the release of avant-garde filmmaker Kenneth Anger's book of the same name—detailing the sordid scandals of
many of Hollywood's famous denizens. Babylon is also the name of a
town on Long Island, New York.

Today, a growing number of prophecy experts believe the Babylon of
Revelation 18 is America, a center of world commerce, economic control, and political hegemony. They believe America is also mentioned
in the Old Testament as the "Daughter of Babylon" in Jeremiah 50–51;
Isaiah 13 and 47; and Zechariah 2.[29]

Based off the writings of these Old Testament prophets, some eschatologists believe the United States could be destroyed in a nuclear attack
by Russia, North Korea, Iran, or even China. Few realize that North
Korea has more than fifty submarines, one of the largest fleets in the
world. It is third in size only to Russia and America with about seventy
and eighty submarines, respectively. In recent years North Korea has

assisted Iran in developing long-range-missile technologies. "There is no question that the language used in Jeremiah and Isaiah talks about this 'great nation,' this 'great empire' that will be 'Sodom and Gomorrah,' which of course was destroyed by literal fire and brimstone," S. Douglas Woodward says. "So there is a theory that the U.S. may see some type of considerable destruction, a number of its cities may be destroyed. But you have to remember that America has a very survivable military. Its carrier groups are still all over the world, its submarines are still all over the world, and so even if we had megalopolises on both coasts destroyed... it's very believable that an American president would survive and would be in a position to retaliate dramatically on whoever attacked America. So Wilkerson's vision absolutely could be fulfilled in line with what's prophesied in the Old Testament about the battle of Babylon."[30]

Likewise, in a sermon titled "Is America Mystery Babylon?" Steve Cioccolanti asked whether "America may be encoded in the word 'Babylon'" in Revelation 17–18, chapters that seem to refer to a great end-times superpower.[31]

"Alfred Thayer Mahan, author of *The Influence of Sea Power upon History*, said 'Whoever rules the waves, rules the world.' If you understand that, you'll know why America is a superpower," Cioccolanti said in his sermon. "It's what makes America unique and the only superpower in the world and I don't think that can change. She is the only nation that has the ability to control both oceans—the Atlantic and the Pacific. If you can control both oceans, well, then nobody can beat that."[32]

By any measure, America is the world's undisputed naval power. It built the Panama Canal and has military bases in Guantánamo Bay, Hawaii, Guam, the Philippines, Singapore, Japan, South Korea, and many other parts of the world.

"Basically its reach is complete," Cioccolanti said. "It's total domination of the sea. If you dominate the sea, you dominate the world. You dominate the economy and you dominate trade. You control the flow of all goods. Isn't that what Revelation 18 was talking about? Now, do you know what the single, greatest display of military power is? It's not just having long-range missiles or big bombs. The greatest display of military power is the aircraft carrier. It's a floating city of war. We can bring the war to you. That's what it says. It's a very powerful statement of how dominant you are. In fact, the U.S. has built sixty-eight aircraft carriers. Compare that to China. People say, 'Oh, China is rising up.' But China only has one aircraft carrier in service. America currently has ten in service. In other words, ten times the power. This is how you measure military power—dominate the sea. Also, whoever controls the money controls the world. And guess what? It's not the UN; it's not the Euro. It's the dollar that has been the world's reserve currency since 1944. That makes me think that Babylon is referring to America. Saudi Arabia is the center of Islam; I grant you that. But America is literally the center of the physical, material world…America did not exist at the time of the Bible so it's understandable that an alternative had to be used and maybe the code was Babylon."[33]

"America! America! God Shed His Grace on Thee"

The term "American exceptionalism" has been attacked by American intellectuals and world leaders, including Russian president Vladimir Putin. Is America exceptional? The answer is yes. America is exceptional. In fact, it is perhaps the most unique nation in the history of mankind.

However, like ancient Israel, which was called for a special purpose, God warned Israel that they were not called because of some inherent virtue they possessed. They were called because of their faith and obedience. Alexis de Tocqueville, the French political thinker and historian best known for writing *Democracy in America*, made a similar observation about America, noting that its freedom and liberty could not be "established without morality, nor morality without faith." "America is great because she is good," Tocqueville said. "If America ceases to be good, America will cease to be great."[34]

It must be understood that America is exceptional, but not because of any inherent virtue or superiority of its people. America's historical record of failure and moral atrocities proves beyond a doubt that the American people are not any better than other people. In fact, they may actually be worse, because as a nation originally founded on biblical principles they had the law and knowledge of God but often rejected it.

Despite the fact that America was founded by Pilgrims and Puritans who made a covenant with God based on the covenant God made with Israel, America has consistently violated the law of God in egregious ways. There are many ways America has violated God's moral laws, which Jesus summed up in John 13:34: "A new command I give you: Love one another. As I have loved you, so you must love one another" (NIV). Despite this simple instruction, America has done the following:

Five Ways America Has Violated God's Law of Love
1. The early American colonists, and later the American government, broke numerous treaties with the Native Americans, stealing their land, slaughtering them in cold blood, and driving them onto reservations.

2. America bought slaves in Africa, stacked their chained bodies on top of one another on ships bound for America, and then forced them to work for free, largely for Christian families and businesses. Their family units were destroyed, their women and children were raped, and they were forced to toil on plantations without pay. The Civil War, the civil rights movement, and racial tensions in America are rooted in this unresolved transgression against human beings of African descent.

3. While not necessarily a completely American phenomenon, nor done with the consent or knowledge of the American people,

powerful international banking families artificially created the Great Depression, along with World Wars I and II and other conflicts, as a means of expanding the wealth of a small elite.

4. Powerful American families and dynasties began the scientific eugenics programs of the 1920s in an attempt to scientifically breed a superior race. This led to a resurgence of anti-Semitism and the creation of abortion clinics in mostly minority neighborhoods. The result was widespread abortion of minority children. These policies were funded by the same powerful dynasties that secretly cooperated in financing the rise of Hitler and the Third Reich, which adopted the eugenics policies created in America. Countless American corporations and financial institutions invested in the Third Reich, contributing to the construction of the concentration camps where more than seven million Jews and Christians were killed. After World War II, these same families, corporations, and dynasties profited heavily from the war. "Both Nazi science and ideology were brought to America in the aftermath of World War II with the aid and assistance of the very self-styled globalists who created National Socialism in the first place," Jim Marrs wrote in *The Rise of the Fourth Reich: The Secret Societies That Threaten to Take Over America.* "Their agenda matches that of the old Bavarian Illuminati, who were long thought to have perished soon after the time of George Washington. But if the order died, its credo lives on—power and control through wealth by any means possible."[35]

5. One of God's primary laws in the Ten Commandments is "Thou shalt not kill" (Exod. 20:13 KJV). The American people have willfully participated in the abortion of more than fifty-five million unborn babies since the passage of *Roe v. Wade* in 1973. With notable exceptions, the Christian churches in America were largely silent in this collective act of mass murder.

The Most Unique Set of Rights in History

These are just a few of the evils that America has committed. And while not to justify these actions, countless other nations have engaged in greater or equal offenses. For example, Communist nations such as Russia, China, Cuba, North Korea, and others slaughtered 94 million people in the revolutions of the twentieth century. During that time, fascist regimes killed 28 million. Meanwhile, 101 million died of famine. All of the world's worst famines during the twentieth century occurred in Communist countries such as China, the Soviet Union, and North Korea. The number of abortions in Communist nations, as well as in Europe and other countries, goes into the hundreds of millions. Human trafficking, modern-day slavery, and the theft of land and property are commonplace around the world.[36]

Despite its atrocities, America is exceptional because it is ruled by an exceptional form of government and the rule of law codified in the U.S. Constitution, the Bill of Rights, and the Declaration of Independence. These laws and the American form of government are completely distinct in human history, as no other nation in recorded history has ever been ruled by such laws. First of all, the first four amendments of the Bill of Rights are the most unique rights ever given to any people in world history.[37] In the Declaration of Independence, we have a completely unique and distinct language, philosophy, and freedoms that no other nation on earth has ever had. The foundation of American exceptionalism is based on the "Laws of Nature and of Nature's God."[38]

In every other nation, laws are based on governments granting rights to the people. In America, the people are given their rights as inalienable rights directly from God, and as such government does not have the power to grant them or take them away. Men and women in America have been endowed by their Creator with the right to "Life, Liberty and the pursuit of Happiness." In addition, the Declaration of Independence states that "all men are created equal." Finally, people have the right and obligation to dismantle any form of government that opposes these rights and create a new one. This is the essence of American exceptionalism, and it is from this fountainhead of freedom that unparalleled opportunity and prosperity have come to America.

America: An Alchemic Christianity-Illuminati Mixture

The irony is that this blend of unique freedoms is the creation of an odd mixture of ideas from our revolutionary Founding Fathers, who were both Christians and Deists and in many cases members of secret societies such as the Freemasons and the Illuminati. This strange amalgamation of biblical truths, along with the ideas and philosophies of the Illuminati and Freemasonry, produced America as we know it. It's a misnomer to say definitively that America is a Christian nation. That is simply not true. Clearly, America is built on Christian beliefs, but weaved into the fabric of American exceptionalism are Illuminist and secret society ideas.

This is what is so difficult to comprehend about America because on the one hand the Illuminist and Freemasonry beliefs that fueled the French and Bolshevik revolutions produced entirely different outcomes than the American Revolution. The Russian Revolution in 1917, which led to the spread of Communism, was based on the 1848 publication of *The Communist Manifesto* by Karl Marx and Friedrich Engels. If you read Adam Weishaupt's *The Illuminati Manifesto*, published about six decades before the *The Communist Manifesto*, you'll discover that *The Communist Manifesto* is little more than a copy of *The Illuminati Manifesto*.

Both *The Communist Manifesto* and *The Illuminati Manifesto* are blueprints for a world socialist state ruled by the elite. This flows from Plato's *Republic*, a Socratic dialogue concerning the ideal city-state. This political system, Plato asserted, should be like Atlantis, the legendary ancient civilization overseen by ten philosopher-kings. Plato wrote about Atlantis in *Timaeus* and *Critias*, though most historians consider Atlantis to be a fictional island. "Atlantis, therefore, is the archetype or the pattern of right government, which existed in ancient days but was destroyed by the selfishness and ignorance of men," Manly P. Hall wrote in *The Secret Destiny of America*. "[The king of Atlantis was] descended of a divine race; that is, he belonged to the Order of the Illumined; for those who come to a state of wisdom then belong to the family of the heroes—perfected human beings."[39]

When we look at America today, it is important to recognize that what we've dubbed the Babylon code has been carefully embedded into its framework. And like the digital alarm on your smartphone, this encrypted biblical code is set to activate on a prophetically prescribed date that only God is privy to.

What America was and what America is quickly becoming are two different things. English Renaissance statesman and philosopher Sir Francis Bacon—a fascinating figure whom Mark Twain, Walt Whitman, Ralph Waldo Emerson, and others identified as the true author of Shakespeare's works—planned in the mid-1600s for America to become the head of a scientific-utopian world he described in *The New Atlantis*. Both Shakespeare's *Tempest* and Bacon's *New Atlantis* predict future societies overseen by the elite who become gods through occult knowledge. Historically, the scientific revolution grew out of the "Occult Renaissance," the vestiges of which can be seen today with the names of branches of science such as chemistry—a word derived from "alchemy." The reality of this scientific-elite power structure is hidden on the back of the U.S. dollar, where we see the "Eye of Horus" above the pyramid. At the bottom are the words "Novus Ordo Seclorum," or "A New Order of the Ages." During his term from 1989 to 1993, President George H. W. Bush, a member of Yale's Skull and Bones secret society and the former director of the CIA, connected "Novus Ordo Seclorum" to his policy of launching a New World Order. On the right-hand side of the dollar, there is an eagle, or, as some believe, a phoenix. Both the pyramid and the phoenix are part of the Babylon code.[40]

"Is the American eagle actually a Phoenix?" Hall asked rhetorically in *The Secret Destiny of America*. "Selection of the fabulous bird of the ancients seems to have been the intention of the designer of our nation's Great Seal." The phoenix is a mystical bird that rises from the ashes of destruction, experiencing a kind of rebirth. "That was the kind of symbolism that was interesting to those who designed the Great Seal: 'Hey look, if we die, that's just the beginning of the journey,'" says Robert Hieronimus, who is considered one of the world's foremost authorities on the Great Seal. "Because of what's been done to the land—the land is poisoned—it has to go under the water, like Atlantis, to be reborn, and that is the symbol of the phoenix." The phoenix also appeared on the coinage of the late Roman Empire as a symbol of the Eternal City. The word *phoenix* originates in ancient Egypt, and Phoenicia is where, according to the book of Enoch, the fallen angels first descended upon Mount Hermon and had sex with women. Although the apocryphal book of Enoch is not in the Bible, early church leaders such as Justin Martyr, Origen, Irenaeus, Jerome, Augustine, and others referred to it. "Perhaps knowing something about God's future plans to give territory to Abraham's descendants, these angels plotted their strategy to introduce 'the seed of the serpent' into the human race," wrote J. R. Church, founder of Prophecy in the News, in his article "Mount Hermon: Gate of the Fallen Angels." "Also, Mount Hermon lay in the territory where Ham and his family migrated after God's judgment at the Tower of Babel."[41]

Bacon, who served as attorney general and Lord Chancellor of England until his resignation amid charges of corruption, was very familiar with this story and its connection to the mythical Atlantis. The ten god-kings who ruled Atlantis were the "sons of God" described in Genesis 6 or the "B'nai Elohim," according to Bacon—best known as the "father of modern science."[42]

The Phoenix, the "Alinskyites," and "the Plan"

Some believe the phoenix, or officially the eagle, on the back of the dollar is a reference to the god-kings of mythical Atlantis. The phoenix is a mystical bird that rises from the ashes. In the same way, those behind the New World Order have a motto—"Order out of Chaos." A contemporary term for "chaos" is "crisis." This is why political leaders use the term—coined by community organizer Saul Alinsky—"manufactured crisis," or make remarks such as one by former White House chief of staff Rahm Emanuel about never letting "a serious crisis go to waste." Alinsky dedicated his book, *Rules for Radicals*, to Lucifer as the "first radical known to man who rebelled against the establishment and did it so effectively that he at least won his own kingdom."

Alinsky believed in "orderly revolution" that requires the "consent of organized groups and the power brokers of society," *New York Times* bestselling author Dinesh D'Souza wrote in *America: Imagine a World Without Her*. Former U.S. secretary of state Hillary Clinton wrote her senior thesis at Wellesley College on Alinsky's work, and President Obama, a fellow "Alinskyite," got his first job as a community organizer working for the Alinsky network in Chicago. "If Hillary Clinton is elected in 2016, the baton will have passed from one Alinskyite to another," wrote D'Souza, a senior policy analyst in the Reagan White House who was named by *New York Times Magazine* as one of America's most influential conservative thinkers. "In this case, Alinsky's influence will have taken on a massive, almost unimaginable, importance. Obama will have had eight years to remake America, and Hillary will have another four or perhaps eight to complete the job. Together, these two have the opportunity to largely undo the nation's founding ideals." In the book, D'Souza wrote that "America's suicide" is "the result of a plan." "Obama is simply part of a fifty-year scheme for the undoing and remaking of America, and when he is gone there are others who are ready to continue the job. What makes the plan especially chilling is that most Americans are simply unaware of what's going on. Their ignorance, as we shall see, is part of the plan."[43]

The Babylon Code, which exposes "the plan," reveals a form of clandestine societal programming where a New World Order is designed to rise from the chaos of crisis. Again, think of the mystical phoenix bird rising from the ashes after being burned. If you study our nation's capital, you'll see the architectural evidence of the Babylon code everywhere, including the statue in Judiciary Square of Freemasonry leader Albert Pike, who predicted the world would experience three world wars and the third one would be so horrible that it would cause people to become bitter, turn away from God, and turn to Lucifer.

Could it be with the escalating tensions among the United States, Russia, Ukraine, Great Britain, the EU, China, Iran, Iraq, Israel, and ISIS that the fuse is now being lit for a global war? Could this happen? Could mushroom clouds billow over major American cities? Our government and military have been preparing for this for decades and have built dozens of massive underground cities across the nation that are able to withstand a direct nuclear hit, including ones in Colorado and the Washington, DC, area. "The shadow government in each nation maintains subterranean military bases and virtual cities designed to allow the continuity of vital government functions," Grant Jeffrey wrote in *Shadow Government: How the Secret Global Elite Is Using Surveillance Against You*. "The names and identities of members of this government are top secret. To facilitate this shadow government, a complex network of duplicate computers, records, and other vital material has been established. This on-call government can take over the country at a moment's notice following a national disaster."[44]

If America is destined to be the head of the New World Order and the New Atlantis, then something catastrophic would have to happen to change America and its present form of government. That catastrophe would have to be a monumental crisis characterized by widespread chaos.

Although Bible scholars debate the exact identity of Babylon—and we are in no way definitively suggesting that America is the Babylon of Revelation 17–18—it could be, even if America is not Babylon, that it plays a key leadership role in the Babylonian system described as the "fourth beast" in Daniel 7.

The Babylon code, embedded in the historical fabric of our nation and its national monuments, reveals a great mystery. Babylon is the center of all the mystery religions of the world, and given its connections to this ancient empire, America will likely play a key role as the head, or at least a significant leader, in the emerging end-times Babylonian system.

Part II

THE BABYLON CODE

Chapter Six

The Hidden Hand of History

Years of research among the records of olden peoples available in
libraries, museums, and shrines of ancient culture has convinced me
that there exists in the world today, and has existed for thousands
of years, a body of enlightened humans united in what might be
termed, an Order of the Quest. It is composed of those whose intellectual and spiritual perceptions have revealed to them that civilization has a Secret Destiny—secret, I say, because this high purpose is
not realized by the many; the great masses of peoples still live along
without any knowledge whatsoever that they are part of a Universal
Motion in time and space.

—MANLY P. HALL, A LEADING ESOTERIC SCHOLAR, IN
THE SECRET DESTINY OF AMERICA

For we wrestle not against flesh and blood, but against principalities, against powers, against the rulers of the darkness of this world,
against spiritual wickedness in high places.

—APOSTLE PAUL (EPHESIANS 6:12 KJV)

The unparalleled danger the world now faces has its origins in the age-
old battle of good and evil—the true hidden hand of history. Long ago,
according to the biblical account, a war broke out in heaven and a very

powerful angelic being named Lucifer led one-third of the angels in a revolution to overthrow the kingdom of God. But the revolt failed and God cast the devil and his demons out of heaven. At some point later, Satan tempted Eve, promising that she would be like God if she ate from the tree of the knowledge of good and evil.

This is the cardinal Luciferian message and the one that all secret societies since the Garden of Eden have promised their adherents. The essential Luciferian mandate, "Ye shall be as God," is the devil's attempt to enlist mankind to join him in overthrowing the rule of God so he can install himself as God.

In essence, it was the world's first conspiracy. "It started when the serpent and Eve conspired to shut Adam out," Theodore Ziolkowski says. "I'm sure as long as there have been two, three or four people getting together there's been beliefs in secret societies and conspiracies."[1]

Enticed by the lure of Lucifer's deceptive promise, Adam and Eve disobeyed God and ate of the tree—introducing the destructive effects of sin into the world and setting up the supernatural struggle between God and Satan.

The biblical story may seem fantastical to some, but a recent Pew Forum on Religion & Public Life survey found that 68 percent of Americans believe angels and demons are involved in a cosmic, supernatural battle for the souls of humanity.[2]

To fully understand the Babylon code and what it portends for the future of the world, eschatologists say history must be viewed in terms of an unseen battle between the forces of good and the forces of evil. Through this lens, historical events make far greater sense.

This prophetic mystery begins in Genesis with Satan's attempt to rule the world through one man, Nimrod. Ever since his failure to unite the world in satanic worship at the Tower of Babel, the devil has been zealously at work to try it again. Indeed, much of history is the record of ruthless dictators—Nimrod, Nebuchadnezzar, Alexander the Great,

Julius Caesar, Genghis Khan, Napoleon Bonaparte, Hitler, and many others—and their attempts to rule the world.

"Satan, the master globalist, has been trying inexorably to bring the world back together again," Mark Hitchcock says. "So we've gone throughout world history from tribalism to nationalism and now to globalism and so the Bible pictures at the end everything coming full circle. We are back to globalism again and now instead of Nimrod ruling the whole world, we are going to have the Antichrist—the Beast of Revelation. He's going to dominate the world for the final three and a half years of this age—the final half of the Great Tribulation—and then Christ will return."[3]

Throughout time, many leaders have chosen to align themselves with dark spiritual forces. In their pride, they believed that they, like Lucifer, could become gods and rule over their own twisted earthly paradise. This is what Nimrod attempted at the Tower of Babel—a place of occult worship where the "Mystery, Babylon" religions were first established. Likewise, this is the same deceptive strategy the Antichrist will employ in enticing the world to participate in the final Babylonian system and his last desperate effort to overthrow God.

"It's kind of a full circle in that we go from Babylon to Babylon and then ultimately in Revelation 21 and 22 we have God's city, the New Jerusalem, come down out of heaven with God," Hitchcock says. "Babylon is the city of man whereas the New Jerusalem is the city of God. It's a fascinating picture to me of how God is going to bring everything full circle."[4]

The History Kept Secret from the Beginning

There are two kinds of history: There's the history you have read in textbooks at public schools, colleges, and universities; and then there is the real history of the world, which has been kept secret since the beginning.

That sounds somewhat conspiratorial, doesn't it? But, just for the sake of argument, what if it's true?

There is an old aphorism by British prime minister Winston Churchill: "History is written by the victors."[5]

Although it may come as a surprise to some, mankind has been at war since the dawn of time. And while some people believe that the story of Adam and Eve is an allegory or fairy tale, there are many of us who believe it's far more than a myth.

According to the biblical account, a great spiritual war between the forces of good and the forces of evil began in a real place called the Garden of Eden. A powerful fallen angel named Lucifer, the "shining one" (Isa. 14:12 NET), morphed into a reptilian-like being and seduced Adam and Eve into disobeying God's Word. This gave Lucifer, or "that serpent of old" (Rev. 12:9 NKJV), the legal right to control earth and become the "god of this world" (2 Cor. 4:4 KJV). It also allowed Lucifer to subjugate mankind as his slaves. Since then, this malevolent entity has led an ongoing revolution with one-third of the angels against the throne room of God. He is the leader of the first and greatest conspiracy in history to occupy heaven and earth and become king of the universe.

That may be a difficult chunk to swallow. If it is true, this great spiritual war has now played out for thousands of years, and it is the central conflict beyond the illusion we call reality. From the beginning of this battle, there have been two kinds of people on earth: those who have chosen to be on God's side in this conflict, and those who have chosen to follow Lucifer.

Those who have followed God in this colossal war have written history, created laws, and lived their lives in the light of the Word of God. The followers of Lucifer, whether knowingly or unknowingly, have created an entirely different history, made a different set of rules, and lived according to the precepts of a powerful fallen angel. The book of Exodus story embodies this split. When Moses came down from the mountain with the Ten Commandments, he discovered that his people were openly violating God's Word by engaging in a sexual orgy and worshipping a golden calf.

"There Are Two Paths You Can Go By"

It was there on Mount Sinai that we saw—as Led Zeppelin so eloquently philosophized in "Stairway to Heaven"—that, yes, "there are two paths you can go by,"[6] the stairway to heaven and the highway to hell. In today's culture—even more enmeshed in the occult than when First Church of Satan founder Anton LaVey announced the beginning of the "Satanic Age" in 1966—we see many people who claim to be Luciferians openly wearing clothing with the motto of the great satanist Aleister Crowley: "Do what thou wilt shall be the whole of the Law." In other words, the followers of Lucifer have only one law: Do whatever you want to do and with no restraints. It is like obeying the 1960s and '70s maxim "If it feels good, do it," on steroids.[7]

In contrast, followers of Jesus are not supposed to "do what thou wilt." The Word of God requires believers to follow a higher law based on the law of love, the love of God, and a love for their fellow man, and that means self-denial.

In its simplest sense, the followers of these two different entities live two kinds of lives. Each side has its own account of history. For most of human history, the people who have served God have outwardly controlled many of the laws of society and written much of history from their perspective.

Up until relatively recently, Judeo-Christian civilization was largely controlled by those who believed in a biblical God and his laws. But it appears that mankind has now entered a new season—what many are calling a post-Christian or postmodern society. According to the biblical flow of history, we were warned by the ancient prophets Isaiah, Jeremiah, Ezekiel, and Daniel, along with New Testament apostles such as Paul and John, that a time would arise—what the Bible calls the "last days" (2 Pet. 3:3 KJV)—when those who chose to join Lucifer in rebellion against God would start to write our laws, codes, and history. That day has now arrived.

Crowley, dubbed by the popular press as the "Wickedest Man in the World," calls this the "New Eon," or the new age of the Egyptian sun god Horus—an era of unparalleled freedom, chaos, death, and destruction. "Satanic cults are expanding in every major city in the United States," Lindsey wrote in his 1972 book, *Satan Is Alive and Well on Planet Earth.* "In fact, the United States probably harbors the fastest-growing and most highly organized body of Satanists in the world." This Luciferian rebellion is not new. It goes all the way back to ancient Babylon and the Tower of Babel where men thought they could create the world's first New World Order and become gods. "Behind this movement are strong Luciferian forces," Stanley Monteith says. "This is a spiritual battle. Basically, what people don't understand is that there really are supernatural forces. There really is a spiritual dimension where there is a battle between God and Satan. But that battle is also being fought at our level of consciousness."[8]

In *The Late Great Planet Earth,* Hal Lindsey wrote that before the seven-year Tribulation began, a powerful, false religious system would emerge that would help the Antichrist subjugate the world under his absolute authority. The Bible offers several names for this universal religion, including the "great harlot," representing a false religious system that "prostitutes the true meaning of being wedded to Christ, and sells out all to the false religions of man." The apostle John calls this occult-based religious system "Mystery, Babylon." "The Scripture says that a great dictator is coming and he will be boosted to power, and strengthened in his grasp upon the world with the assistance of the ancient religion called Mystery, Babylon," Lindsey wrote. "This is the very religion which started in the Genesis account and made possible the first world dictator."[9]

The Greatest of Puzzles

Considered "one of the greatest of puzzles among many riddles" in the Bible, the secret code of "Mystery, Babylon" reveals how an "unseen hand" has helped orchestrate human events for thousands of years and will bring about the final manifestation of the Babylonian system under the Antichrist. Tom Horn, an internationally recognized lecturer, radio host, and bestselling author, says this "great, superhuman superman" is the prosopopoeia of an "invisible network of thousands of years of collective knowledge." "This person will represent the embodiment of a very old, superintelligent spirit," Horn says. "In other words, just as Jesus Christ was the seed of a woman, this person is going to be the seed of the serpent, according to Genesis 3:15. And even though his arrival was foretold by numerous Scriptures, the broad masses of the world are not going to recognize him for what he actually is, and that's the ultimate incarnation of the Beast of Revelation 13:1. All the prophecies we've been looking at indicate that this individual is here."[10]

Douglas Hamp, author of *Corrupting the Image*, made a similar observation. "Something ominous is coming upon the world: it is Satan's final effort in the battle to destroy the image that man was created in, which has been raging since the beginning of time," Hamp wrote. "If Satan can destroy the image, then he can avert his own destruction. God created man in his own image and likeness; when man sinned

164 • THE BABYLON CODE

that image was marred, but not lost. However, as a result man cannot be with God in his presence since man's genetic code (and spiritual composition) has been compromised (or corrupted). God sent his son to give his life to correct the genetic (and moral) problem through the cross."[11]

In his book *The Unseen Hand*, historian, author, and lecturer A. Ralph Epperson wrote that the satanic conspiracy behind the rise of the iniquitous figure of the Antichrist is "extremely large, deeply entrenched, and therefore extremely powerful. It is working to achieve absolute and brutal rule over the entire human race by using wars, depressions, inflations and revolutions to further its aims. The conspiracy's one unchanging purpose has been to destroy all religion, all existing governments, and all traditional human institutions, and to build a New World Order... upon the wreckage they have created."[12]

Robert Hieronimus, a critic of Epperson and others who claim the Bavarian Illuminati infiltrated Freemasonry in the late eighteenth century in order to one day bring about the New World Order, concedes that there is no question that groups of wealthy and influential people gather regularly to plot the course of the world. "Many of my esteemed colleagues have written books about this shadowy conspiracy that has probably run parallel with official history all along," Hieronimus wrote in *The United Symbolism of America*. "Libertarians and liberal intelligentsia...name the names of the power brokers doing the manipulating. The missions of the Council on Foreign Relations (CFR), the Trilateral Commission (TLC), the Bohemian Grove, the Bilderberg Group, the Brookings Institution, and the Skull and Bones are to control what we see in the mass media, and even trigger certain events to persuade passage of certain policies they support. They have members in high positions of power and authority in the fields of politics, entertainment, media, and business. This is all true, and many people more qualified than I am have tracked and documented the revolving doors between the power elite, politics, and the media."[13]

Breaking the Ancient Secret Code

As you read *The Babylon Code*, you will be given powerful tools to break an ancient secret code that reveals not only the identity of these modern power brokers but also their mysterious links to an esoteric and ancient world. Most reading this book may have never been taught about the existence of secret societies. Did your school textbooks, or the mainstream media, just happen to accidentally omit this part of history? Why do you think this is? Is it because it's not important? Certainly not.

If it were not important, you would not see the symbols of these secret societies throughout Washington, DC—the occult symbolism in the city's layout; the U.S. Capitol Building, a mirror of Rome's Pantheon; and the Washington Monument, a reflection of Egypt's Heliopolis. Is it mere chance that the Washington Monument's height is 6,660 inches and its width is 666 inches? Likewise, is the sexual symbolism intrinsic in the city's architecture—the womb-like shape of the U.S. Capitol and phallic-like shape of the Washington Monument—just happenstance? These symbols have their origins in ancient Babylon and are prevalent in Egypt, Europe, Vatican City, and all across the world. During a recent seven-day trip to Rio, Pope Francis even expressed concerns about a Masonic lobby purportedly at work inside the Vatican. "There is another problem, another one: the problem is to form a lobby of those who have this tendency, a lobby of the greedy people, a lobby of politicians, a lobby of Masons, so many lobbies. This is the most serious problem for me," Pope Francis said. This secret is hidden in plain sight right before our very eyes. As *New York Times* bestselling author Dan

Brown wrote in his novel *The Lost Symbol*, "All of the best kept secrets are hidden in plain view." "What would you say if I told you the city of Washington, D.C., has more astrological signs in its architecture than any other city in the world—zodiacs, star charts, cornerstones laid at precise astrological dates and times?" Brown's character Harvard symbologist Robert Langdon told a class of students in *The Lost Symbol*, "More than half the framers of the Constitution were Masons, men who strongly believed that the stars and fate were intertwined, men who paid close attention to the layout of the heavens as they structured their new world."[14]

Plato's *Republic* and Atlantis

Some of America's founders and many of the world's most influential people have read Plato's *Republic*. What is it about this book that would prompt some of the world's most powerful people to read it so religiously? The ancient Greek philosopher Plato wrote about the legendary supercivilization of Atlantis, a story purportedly passed down to him by poets, priests, and others. According to Plato, ten philosopher-kings—half god and half human—ruled Atlantis and the world before Atlantis was destroyed about nine thousand years before his time (ca. 428 BC–ca. 348 BC) in a great cataclysm and sank into a "western sea." In recent years, a host of sea explorers have claimed to have found the ruins of Atlantis, though most serious historians and archaeologists are highly skeptical of these reports. They consider Atlantis a legend, something Plato meant as an allegory and a cautionary tale about the fate of civilizations that become greedy and morally bankrupt.[15]

Yet some believe Atlantis actually existed, or at least some form of ancient advanced civilization, and theories have proliferated in recent years about how such a civilization could have just gotten "lost somewhere." Surprisingly, a 2006 survey by the Baylor Institute for Studies of

Religion found that 41 percent of Americans believe an ancient advanced civilization such as Atlantis once existed. Graham Hancock, a British journalist who worked at the *Economist*, the *Times*, the *Sunday Times*, and the *Guardian* and a bestselling author who specializes in investigations of historical mysteries, wrote in *Fingerprints of the Gods: The Evidence of Earth's Lost Civilization* that oceanographers have mapped the floors of the world's oceans and haven't found any lost continents. "Yet, as my research continued, the evidence kept mounting that precisely such a civilization had once existed," Hancock wrote. "In support of this hypothesis, among other anomalies, were the remarkable ancient maps of the world, the 'Pyramid Boats' of Egypt, the traces of advanced astronomical knowledge in the astonishing calendar system of the Maya, and the legends of seafaring gods like Quetzalcoatl and Viracocha. A nation of navigators, then. And a nation of builders, too: Tiahuanaco builders, Teotihuacan builders, pyramid builders, Sphinx builders, builders who could lift and position 200-ton blocks of limestone with apparent ease, builders who could align vast monuments to the cardinal points with uncanny accuracy."

Despite the remnants of what some researchers believe to be an advanced ancient civilization, the question is how and when it might have disappeared. "Commonsense suggested that an answer had to lie in a cataclysm of some kind, a planetary disaster capable of wiping out almost all physical traces of a large civilization," Hancock wrote. "As my research progressed I studied many of the great myths of flood, fire, earthquake and ice handed down from generation to generation around the world…During the short history of mankind's presence on this planet, I found that there was only one known and documented catastrophe that fitted the bill: the dramatic and deadly meltdown of the last Ice Age between 15000 and 8000 B.C. Moreover, as was more obviously the case with architectural relics like Teotihuacan and the Egyptian pyramids, many of the relevant myths appeared to have been designed to serve as vehicles for encrypted scientific information, again an indication of what I was coming to think of as 'the fingerprints of the gods.' What I had become sensitized to, although I did not properly realize its implications at the time, was the possibility that a strong connection might exist between the collapsing chaos of the Ice Age and the disappearance of an archaic civilization which had been the stuff of legend for millennia."[16]

Hieronimus also believes in the existence of Atlantis—the fabled civilization whose knowledge was purportedly preserved by a series of secret societies stretching over thousands of years. "Do I believe Atlantis existed? Yes, I believe it existed," Hieronimus says. "Of course, there are a number of theories as to where it might be. There are theories that put it in the Mediterranean. There are some that put it off the Yucatan. There are some that put it all the way down in Antarctica. But there was a civilization, regardless of what you want to call it—Atlantis or something else. There was a civilization that gave birth to our civilization, but it was destroyed."[17]

Today, many of the elite share Hieronimus's views and agree with Plato that an ideal society is one ruled by the scientific elite.

From Atlantis to Babylon

The system of rule by the elite, at least in recorded history, began in Babylon. Later, in ancient Egypt, the pharaoh and the royal family were considered god-kings with the divine right to rule the masses as slaves. It was a pharaoh-based, god-king system in which the children of Israel were indoctrinated to believe that they were destined to be slaves under pharaoh. The secrets of the Babylonian mystery religions were passed down for thousands of years among the ruling elite.

This is the key to unlocking the Babylon code. When you learn how to decode the global matrix appearing before our eyes today, you will understand the mysteries behind what many are now calling the emerging "shadow government."

Some say this is all a bunch of unproven conspiracy theories. However, most of the people who throw out the term "conspiracy theory" have spent little or no time investigating that assertion. In fact, some believe the term "conspiracy theory" is part of the conspiracy—a sophisticated way of brainwashing the masses to discount anything labeled a "conspiracy theory" by the media, government, or academia.

Once again, there are two kinds of history: the history you study in school, and the real history that is concealed from the masses. Remember Churchill's statement that "history is written by the victors." Most history books and the curriculum taught about history are carefully constructed to perpetuate the viewpoints of the winners and not the losers.

For decades, the elite have worked toward their goals through control of the economy and media and through science-based mind control and brainwashing. The primary evidence of their success is the fact that the belief systems, morality, and religious beliefs of average Americans have changed dramatically in recent decades. The elites have so perfected social engineering that they have now indoctrinated several generations into being anti-American, anti-Christian, and Marxist in their belief systems. These changes have become especially pronounced after the U.S. Supreme Court ruled in June 2015 that same-sex couples have a right to marry, upending the Judeo-Christian foundations of the nation.

"This year has been one of the most dramatic years in the moral transformation that is overtaking America and much of the world," Jonathan Cahn told those gathered at the International Alliance of Messianic Congregations and Synagogues conference in Orlando, Florida, in early 2015. "America's rejection of biblical values has accelerated. Since we were last together, eighteen states had ended the biblical definition of marriage. One year later, the number of states that have done that is thirty-six. Only fourteen states are left standing, and they are all under attack. This is the fastest moral transformation in world history since the Garden of Eden. It's a symptom of something deeper—of a civilization's rejection of its spiritual foundation, and this phenomenon is manifesting in other forms, the growing acceptance of cohabitation without marriage. The latest statistics are that the percentage of children being born out of wedlock to the new generation—millennials—is now 57 percent. Six out of every ten children don't know what marriage is. The other form in which this is manifesting is the ascent of atheism and of atheists' challenges of the faith and the continual removing of God and the name of Messiah from the public square and from mainstream culture. We're also seeing the rise of satanic challenges to the faith. This year we saw satanic displays on grounds which once held Nativity scenes."[18]

Not coincidentally, this moral transformation has occurred as the world has witnessed the transfer of vast amounts of wealth and power into the hands of less than 1 percent of the population. In his book *Superclass: The Global Power Elite and the World They Are Making*, *Foreign Policy* magazine editor David Rothkopf argues that six thousand to seven thousand people, a global superclass who have amassed unprecedented levels of wealth and power, run the world's governments, largest corporations, powerhouses of international finance, media, and religions. "They are the Davos-attending, Gulfstream/private jet–flying, money-incrusted, megacorporation-interlocked, policy-building elites of the world, people at the absolute peak of the global power pyramid," wrote Peter Phillips and Brady Osbourne of Project Censored in their book, *Project Censored 2014*.[19]

Today, six major corporations control nearly all our media and fewer than that control our educational systems. Every regime and government, benevolent or otherwise, has understood that in order to maintain power you must control the media, or means of communication, and education.

Do the elite want the general public to know what is really going on? Of course not, or they would lose their power—a power that mysteriously originates in one of the earliest centers of civilization, one steeped in astrology, sorcery, and the "magic of money manipulation."[20]

Chapter Seven

The Tower of Babel, Nimrod, and Magic Money

The magic of money manipulation may have been perfected in more modern times, but its roots go back far into history, and there appears to be a correlation between control by money, gold, and the ancient gods. In ancient times, the coinage of money was conducted and controlled by the priesthoods in obedience to their gods. In Babylon, descendant of the Sumerian culture, checks were in use as draws on deposits of valuables.

—JIM MARRS, A *NEW YORK TIMES* BESTSELLING AUTHOR,
IN *OUR OCCULTED HISTORY*

To solve the Bible's greatest riddle, we need to go far back into the distant past—to a time not long after Noah's flood in ancient Babylon. Here, in the cradle of civilization along the Euphrates River, are the clues we need to piece together a cosmic jigsaw puzzle that predicts what is happening in our world today.

This prophetic mind-twister originates in Genesis 11 at the Tower of Babel and culminates in Revelation 17–18 with "Mystery, Babylon" and "Babylon the Great." It's a code that foreshadows today's headlines and the coming geopolitical, economic, and religious Babylon of the last days.

The biblical enigma has its origins in Babylon—the idolatrous empire that epitomized pride, rebellion, greed, materialism, and idolatry. In the biblical story, the human race—speaking one language—gathered in the land of Shinar a few generations after the Great Flood.

At the time, Nimrod ruled Babylon—the first world government and occult-based religious system. He had built eight cities throughout southern, central, and northern Mesopotamia. Nimrod married an alluring prostitute named Semiramis and built a huge city, along with the Tower of Babel—or the "gate of the gods"—to worship astral deities, according to extrabiblical accounts and popular legends. In addition to its use as an astrological observatory, some prophecy scholars say the tower also served as an interdimensional portal for the Babylonian gods, or fallen angels, to enter the earthly realm. After observing their endeavor, God confused their languages to stop the project, saying in Genesis 11:6, "Look! If they are able to accomplish all this when they have just begun to exploit their linguistic and political unity, just think of what they will do later! Nothing will be unattainable for them!" (TLB).[1]

"Nimrod wanted to unite the world, but God had a different plan," Stanley Monteith says. "God did not want a one-world government so God intervened and caused people to speak different languages. Then, if you follow the history of the Assyrians, the Persians, the Medes, and the Babylonians, they all wanted to unite the world. And then the Greeks and Romans wanted to unite the world. There has always been this tendency to want to unite the world and always behind it there have been secret societies."[2]

Over the centuries, the symbols and the secret knowledge of ancient Babylon, along with a belief in the return of Nimrod—an archetype of the Antichrist—were passed down through various cultures and secret societies. The biblical narrative predicts a struggle that pits the seed of the woman (Jesus, a descendant of Eve) against the seed of the serpent—Lucifer. Satan intends to mimic the divine plan by offering his son to sit upon the throne of a world government. As Jesus was born of a virgin, the Antichrist will be born of a harlot. Nimrod's wife, Semiramis, was a prostitute, and it is thought that all the ancient occult religions originate with the religious system she created—"Mystery, Babylon," according to extrabiblical sources.

Noah's Flood and the Nephilim

The historical account of Babylon and the Tower of Babel in Genesis came at a pivotal time in human history. Nimrod had established Babylon and built the Tower of Babel as an occult and astrological tower to worship the hosts of heaven.

Nimrod was the first man to openly rebel against God after the Flood. He created a world government and a false religion. "This displeased Jehovah who stopped the building of the tower," F. Kenton Beshore wrote in *Daniel Decoded*. "He confused their language causing them to speak numerous languages. This act put an end to Nimrod's dream of a world empire. Later...Semiramis continued the work of her husband. She kept the false religion Nimrod had founded alive, and through it controlled all of the great empires of history—Egyptian, Assyrian, Babylonian, Medo-Persian, Greek and Roman. When the final world government is established, Babylon the Great, the Mother of Harlots, will be ruling over the nations of the world and the Antichrist. The Great Harlot is not just a religious organization. It is a coalition of numerous organizations both religious and secular."[3]

Located fifty miles south of Baghdad, ancient Babylon was a center of idolatry and false religion—the "city of Satan."[4]

In order to understand the Babylon code and its connection to Lucifer, we have to first understand the purpose of the Flood, Noah, and the ark.[5]

When God judged the world with water during the time of Noah, the Flood was a targeted judgment against the corrupted DNA of mankind. It's true that part of the reason why God judged the world was due to its wickedness and the widespread violence at the time. But the specific nature of the Flood judgment is revealed by the following facts: First, God directed Noah and his family, whose genetic code had not been corrupted, to enter the ark until the Flood was over. Second, God directed Noah to build the ark in such a way that it would accommodate the animal kingdom, "two of every kind" (Gen. 6:20 NKJV), both male and female. It is clear from these directives and God's command to Noah and his family to "be fruitful and multiply" (Gen. 8:17 NKJV) that the purpose of the Flood and the ark was largely centered upon repopulating the world with the genetically uncorrupted line of Noah.

The Flood was specifically sent to wipe out the vast majority of mankind and living creatures because their DNA had been tainted. In Genesis 6 we read about how the "sons of God"—translated in Hebrew as fallen angels—mated with women and produced an offspring called the Nephilim. While this idea is controversial, a growing number of Bible scholars believe the Nephilim were the product of interspecies breeding between fallen angels and women. "The Nephilim were on the earth in those days—and also afterward—when the sons of God went in to the daughters of humans, who bore children to them. These were the heroes that were of old, warriors of renown," according to Genesis 6:4 (NRSV).

The biblical descriptions of these beings highlight their "enormous, arguably superhuman, size and strength," Hugh Ross wrote in *Navigating Genesis*. "The Goliath whom David fought and killed...stood six-and-a-half cubits tall (at least nine feet, nine inches) and demonstrated remarkable agility while carrying at least 250 pounds of armor and weapons. Og, the king of Bashan, another of these giants, is said to have slept in an iron bed measuring nine by four cubits (at least 13.5 feet by 6 feet)...Ancient extra-biblical literature makes plentiful reference to giants. The Greeks, Romans, Phoenicians, Mesopotamians, and

Egyptians, for example, all told stories of great and terrible heroes, men of supernatural size and strength . . . In all these non-biblical accounts, the 'supermen' sprang from the sexual union between immortal 'gods' and mortal humans. These giants certainly resemble the biblical Nephilim in their penchant for fighting and in their tendency to manifest birth defects, such as extra fingers and toes."[6]

Ross argues that there is significant evidence in Scripture to suggest the Nephilim really existed and were the offspring of women and fallen angels. "Some support for that is the fact that the Nephilim were all masculine," Ross says. "We see no mention of female Nephilim. We also know that they had birth defects. They are constantly described as having six toes and six fingers, which is something you'd expect if there was some form of bestiality going on. And, finally, in Jude 6 [the Bible] accuses certain fallen angels of leaving their estate, which is a Greek phrase which would be consistent of them being accused of bestiality. So, that lends support to the fact that there is something supernatural about the Nephilim. They are all evil." While the Flood destroyed the Nephilim of Noah's time, the Bible indicates they returned later. "That's tied in with what you see in the book of Jude—how God made this place called the Abyss as a place of torment for those demons that disobeyed God's command to leave women alone," Ross says.[7]

Gate of the Fallen Angels

These fallen angels are believed to have originally descended to earth at Mount Hermon. This is referenced in Jude, which cites the extrabiblical book of Enoch. In the book of Enoch, we read how the fallen angels descended at Mount Hermon—"a port of entry for a group of wicked angels"[8]—and they not only mated with human women but imparted to man secret knowledge and technologies.

In his article "Mount Hermon: Gate of the Fallen Angels," Prophecy in the News founder J. R. Church wrote that these demonic spirits could "transform themselves into all kinds of shapes," had sex with women, and begat children called Anakim (giants) and Nephilim. The literature of early church theologians Justin Martyr, Origen, Irenaeus, Eusebius, Augustine, and others made reference to these book of Enoch stories. "Of all the places where angels could have descended, it was on the northern border of the Promised Land," Church wrote. "Perhaps knowing something about God's future plans to give territory to Abraham's descendants, these angels plotted their strategy to introduce 'the seed of the serpent' into the human race."[9]

Mount Hermon is located in the area where Noah's son Ham and his family migrated after God's judgment at the Tower of Babel. "It seems to me that the Tower of Babel (meaning 'Gate to God') may have been built in an effort to contact these dark forces and forge a defense against the threat of another judgment," Church wrote. "As noted in the Zohar, Rabbi Hiya said, '...to this day they exist and teach men the arts of magic.'"[10]

The "Seed of the Serpent"

The biblical figures Jacob and Moses believed the Antichrist would come from the "seed of the serpent," according to Church. "We discussed the fact that the Greek king, Alexander the Great, claimed to be born of the 'seed of the serpent,'" Church wrote. "Those fallen angels who descended to Mount Hermon introduced the 'seed of the serpent' into the human race."[11]

God would not allow his creation to be corrupted with the DNA of fallen angels, so he wiped out the entire corrupted DNA with Noah's flood.

That's why the DNA code is an integral component of the Babylon code. Nimrod understood this genetic concept when he established the mystery religions of ancient Babylon. At the core of the mystery religions is the mystery of occult reproduction. This is why beginning in Babylon we see throughout history the use of phallic symbols, or towers, and womb-like structures, or domes. The original Tower of Babel was a phallic symbol, representing the male organ of Nimrod. The first womb-like structures, or domes, represented the womb of Semiramis, who was declared a goddess and later associated with figures such as Isis, Ishtar, Venus, Aphrodite, and Diana, according to extrabiblical traditions. Since ancient Babylon, Semiramis has been the "mother goddess." Today, adherents of the "Mysteries—the secret teachings of the ancients," still hold the "Queen of Heaven" in the highest regard.[12]

"And the Gates of Hell Shall Not Prevail Against It"

In order to understand the Babylon code, we also need to understand that the Tower of Babel served as a type of interdimensional, occult-based technology that opened up a spiritual gate for demonic beings to enter the earthly dimension.

This concept actually has a surprisingly strong biblical basis. Tom Horn argues that Scripture supports the idea that spiritual entities exist behind barriers, or gates, located in the sky, sea, and earth. For example, the book of Ephesians speaks of principalities and powers in "high places" and "power of the air" (6:12; 2:2 KJV). In Nehemiah 9:6, the prophet speaks of more than one heaven, including the "heaven of heavens" (KJV). In 2 Corinthians 12:2, the apostle Paul speaks of a man "caught up to the third heaven'" (KJV). Between the first heaven, the skies, and the third heaven, the dwelling place of God, there is believed to be a spiritual war zone known as the second heaven. "This is a place of brass gates...the kosmos or Hebrew equivalent of the Persian *Ahriman-abad*— the place where Satan or Beelzebub (the 'lord of the height') abides as the prince of the power of the 'air' ... It was believed that from here powerful demons known as kosmokrators could overshadow cities, intrude upon, and attempt to influence the affairs and governments of men," according to Horn. In Matthew 16:18, Jesus tells Peter that he will build his church "upon this rock...and the gates of hell shall not prevail against it" (KJV). Deuteronomy 18:10–11 warns that demonic spirits would try to move beyond their confines through human invitation, and the Hebrews were warned not to communicate with fallen angels (1 Sam. 28). First Samuel 28 also references beings that ascended from "out of the earth" (v. 13 NKJV). "Based on such texts, it is reasonable to believe that beings of superintelligence sometimes referred to as 'gods' are equivalent to those whom the Bible depicts as moving through openings of sky, earth, and sea during interaction with this planet's creatures," Horn wrote. In 1918, Crowley attempted to create a "dimensional vortex" to summon spirits from the unseen realm. More recently, Jet Propulsion Laboratory cofounder Jack Parsons and Church of Scientology founder L. Ron Hubbard conducted a secret ritual known as "Babalon Working" to reopen Crowley's gateway. "Instead, they wanted the spirit of Babylon, the archetypal divine feminine, to pass through the portal and to incarnate itself within a human being," Horn wrote. "Many adepts of Enochian magic and Ordo Templi Orientis believe they succeeded and that she—the Whore of Babylon—walks the earth today. It would come as no surprise, Babylonian and earlier 'gods' have been depicted as coming through 'gates' for some time."[13]

The Transhumanism Nexus

In the New Testament, Jesus said that "as it was in the days of Noah, so it will be at the coming of the Son of Man" (Matt. 24:37 NIV). A growing number of prophecy scholars argue that Jesus was telling us that in the last days the Nephilim would return. Today, it's interesting to note that the science of transhumanism is exploding all around us. Global experimentation with the interspecies breeding of human and animal DNA is also on the rise.[14]

The international transhumanism movement has existed for decades but has grown in popularity in recent years, as evidenced by blockbuster Hollywood films such as *Lucy*; *Her*; and *Transcendence*, starring Johnny Depp. "Despite its growing popularity, many people around the world still don't know what 'transhuman' means," Zoltan Istvan, a futurist and journalist, wrote in a recent article for the *Huffington Post* titled "A New Generation of Transhumanists Is Emerging." "Transhuman literally means beyond human. Transhumanists consist of life extensionists, techno-optimists, Singularitarians, biohackers, roboticists, AI proponents, and futurists who embrace radical science and technology to improve the human condition. The most important aim for many Transhumanists is to overcome human mortality, a goal some believe is achievable by 2045."[15]

In a recent *Daily Mail* article, Damien Gayle claimed that future soldiers might be able to run at Olympic speeds, go for days without food or sleep, and even regrow limbs blown apart by bombs if new research into gene manipulation is successful. The plans were revealed by a writer who was given behind-the-scenes access to the Pentagon's high-tech Defense Advanced Research Projects Agency. "With a budget of almost $2 billion a year, DARPA, established in 1958 after the USSR's first successful space mission shocked America, has a goal of maintaining U.S. technological dominance on the battlefield," Gayle wrote. "But its most controversial work involves genetic modification."[16]

Science has made significant leaps in this area in recent years. One of the biggest breakthroughs is the creation of a synthetic genome that can self-replicate. Scientists have modified the genes of a cell by inserting DNA from another organism, enabling the bacteria to replicate itself and create a second generation of the synthetic DNA. "It's a living thing, but under the control of man," says Daniel Estulin, author of

TransEvolution: The Coming Age of Human Destruction. "What's amazing about this is that as the cell is assembled and sparked into life in the laboratory it has literally taken us across the threshold of science. In the coming years, we will be able to manufacture and design a human being in the laboratory. But it's not just human beings. We can literally take the DNA of anything here on earth and create organisms that never before existed from nonliving materials. So we are creating new life-forms. You can go from human to transhuman, which is half human and half machine, to posthuman, which is something entirely different and involves beings which have nothing to do with humanity."[17]

"A Powerful Delusion"

Daniel 2:43 makes an especially provocative allusion regarding the Antichrist's final empire, noting "they shall mingle themselves with the seed of men," according to Chuck Missler, a former business executive, founder of the Koinonia House ministry, and a prophecy expert who counts actor Robert Downey Jr. among his fans. "Just what (or who) are 'mingling with the seed of men?'" Missler wrote in his "The Return of the Nephilim?" article. "'They' would seem to refer to some beings that are not the seed of men themselves. Could this be a hint of a return of the mischief of Genesis 6? It staggers the mind to consider the potential significance of Daniel's passage and its implications for the future of global governance." In his "As the Days of Noah Were" article, Missler points out that many people believe widespread reports of UFO sightings and alien abductions are "demonic and are just another precursor to the end-time. Some also believe that the coming world leader...may boast of an 'alien connection.' It would be consistent from what else we can infer from Scripture."[18]

This theory, pertaining to what 2 Thessalonians 2:11 (NIV) describes as a "powerful delusion" in the end times, comes amid growing interest in UFOs, extraterrestrials, and the ancient astronaut theory popularized on programs such as the History Channel's "Ancient Aliens." The hypothesis of the program, first introduced by Erich von Däniken in his 1968 book *Chariots of the Gods*, is that extraterrestrials have been visiting Earth for eons and are responsible for essentially creating modern humans through genetic manipulation. The program is just one of many that have popularized the E.T. phenomenon in recent decades, including numerous films such as *Close Encounters of the Third Kind*, *Star Wars*, *Contact*, *Independence Day*, and *Avatar*. Not surprisingly, a recent poll by the *Huffington Post* found that half of Americans now think there is some form of life on other planets, and a quarter believe alien visitors have already come to visit Earth. Even more surprising, though, is another poll by the *Huffington Post* that found more United Kingdom residents—33 million—believe in extraterrestrial life than believe in God—27 million.[19]

The "Ancient Aliens" program has struck a chord with many people who believe extraterrestrials colonized Earth and created a highly advanced civilization that was destroyed in some cataclysm. "This has come down to us as the story of Atlantis and the story of Noah and the Flood, and because of these cataclysms mankind was thrown into a primitive state," Jim Marrs says. "Finally, we are just now regaining the scientific knowledge to be able to understand the meaning of artifacts, stories, and mythological tales that have come down to us through the years." For example, archaeologists in the 1800s unearthed cities in what is now Iraq, discovering the ancient civilization of Sumer. This was when archaeologists first became aware of the civilization of Sumer, which predates the Egyptian civilization by thousands of years. "When I was in school, we were taught that the first human civilization was the Egyptians," Marrs says. "Well, now we know that's not true." Curiously, today's elite trace their bloodlines back through the royalty of Europe, the Roman Empire, Greece, Egypt, Babylon, and an even earlier civilization, perhaps Atlantis. "And they were all pretty clear in establishing that they at least believed themselves to be from the blood-lines of the ancient god-kings that came from the sky, from the stars, and taught them civilization," Marrs notes.[20]

"Science, Magic and Money"

Throughout history, the elite have passed down their secret knowledge, and an "international money power" has helped them maintain their wealth and power through "the magic of money manipulation." This early system of banking began in Babylon where the "gods demanded gold and silver, as noted in the Laws of Hammurabi." Under the tight control of the rulers, Babylonian money consisted of clay-tablet letters of credit drawn on the surpluses of state goods. This Babylonian mon-etary system was widespread, and attacks on Babylon by the Assyrians and others served to disperse the merchant banking class to other coun-tries. The Babylonian monetary systems established branches on the coast of Greece and in the Mycenaean centers. It was the beginning of an "international class of bullion brokers" who were closely connected with religious leaders whose temples were dependent on the financial institutions.[21]

The modern credit-debit system originated in about 5000 BC in ancient Babylon, wrote Craig R. Smith, chairman of the Swiss Amer-ica Trading Corporation, an investment firm specializing in U.S. gold and silver coins, in his article "What Does the Bible Say About Mak-ing Money?" "Babylonian bankers loaned out credit (which they 'cre-ated' from thin air) and then charged interest or usury on top of it! Notice that credit and debit are intangibles, and can be easily manipu-lated by the powerful to enrich themselves at everyone else's expense," Smith wrote. "Our whole modern banking system is patterned after the Babylonians and is based on the premise that God's laws are not true.

184 • THE BABYLON CODE

Therefore, bankers have the divine right to create credit as a money substitute. Sadly, most of us have given our consent to the Babylonian banking system—without understanding the consequences."[22]

In *Babylon's Banksters: The Alchemy of Deep Physics, High Finance and Ancient Religion*, Joseph P. Farrell argues that from ancient Babylon to today's "Babylon-on-the-Hudson," bankers have sought to usurp the money and credit-creating power of the state and "substitute a facsimile of money-as-debt." Farrell, an author and theologian who as a doctoral student at Pembroke College had access to Oxford University's library, wrote that since ancient times an "international money power" has sought by a variety of means to "usurp the money- and credit-creating power of the various states it has sought to dominate, and to obfuscate and occult the profound connection between that money-creating power and the deep 'alchemical physics' that such power implies." This knowledge of the relationship between "science, magic and money" was preserved by secret societies, Mystery Schools, and various civilizations, including Sumer, Babylonia, Assyria, and Egypt. "The fact that so many ancient temples show evidence both of a profound association with the stars through their astrological alignments, and also of international banking through the prominent association of moneychangers with those temples, is an indicator that at a deep and profound level—perhaps as a legacy of the Very High Civilization from which they sprang—these classical civilizations through their marriage of banking and astrology preserved the dim memory of a lost science that unified physics, economics and finance," Farrell wrote.[23]

In terms of the future of this "vast and ancient conspiracy," Farrell argues that it seems the guardians of this ancient knowledge are now attempting to "reconstruct a lost mythical past: a global 'golden age' with a supremely sophisticated science with which they can dominate and subjugate the earth. But to reconstruct it, on the scale required and implied by their enterprise itself, will require that virtually the entire planet and its resources must be at their disposal. What they intend to do after that is beyond the scope and purpose of this essay, but an answer does suggest itself, for if, as was seen, at least one of these banking dynasties—the Rothschilds—are alleged to trace their lineage back to Nimrod, half-human half-divine offspring of the 'gods' who once descended to earth and sired children of human mothers, then perhaps they seek, ultimately, to return to the stars."[24]

Chapter Eight

Illuminati Pyramid or Ancient Wonder?

The Great Pyramid was not a lighthouse, an observatory, or a tomb, but the first temple of the Mysteries, the first structure erected as a repository for those secret truths which are the certain foundation of all arts and sciences. It was the perfect emblem of the microcosm and the macrocosm and, according to the secret teachings, the tomb of Osiris, the black god of the Nile.

—MANLY P. HALL, A THIRTY-THIRD-DEGREE MASON, IN
THE SECRET TEACHINGS OF ALL AGES

Most people remember the epic film starring Charlton Heston known as *The Ten Commandments*—mainly because it airs regularly on television decades after it was produced. Who could forget some of Heston's famous lines: "Thus sayeth the Lord God of Israel: 'Let my people go!' " or "It would take more than a man to lead the slaves from bondage. It would take a God."[1]

The film—nominated for seven Academy Awards and considered one of the best films of all time—features powerful images of the pharaoh, the Great Pyramid of Giza, and the Hebrew slaves.[2]

In the biblical story, God sent Moses to deliver his people from the rule of the pharaoh. Biblically, the pharaoh is considered a type of Lucifer, and the land of Egypt under the pharaoh is a type of the world system of this present age that is temporarily ruled by "the god of this age" (2 Cor. 4:4 NIV)—Satan. From this biblical viewpoint, all those who have not accepted God's deliverer Jesus as their Messiah are slaves living under the Luciferian world system.

As we'll learn in this chapter, the Bible is not a one-dimensional or simplistic book. It was supernaturally written through the hands of men and contains a multidimensional message that must be decoded through careful study and guidance by the Spirit of God. Consider the first five verses in the book of John, but replace "Word" with "code," and this idea will make more sense:

> In the beginning was the Word, and the Word was with God, and the Word was God. He was with God in the beginning. Through him all things were made; without him nothing was made that has been made. In him was life, and that life was the light of all mankind. The light shines in the darkness, and the darkness has not overcome it. (NIV)

The Pharaoh and the God-Kings

The central tenet of the mystery religions of Egypt and Babylon is the idea that man can become God—the same lie Lucifer used to deceive Adam and Eve in the Garden of Eden. This theology was passed down from culture to culture, beginning in ancient Babylon and then reemerging in Egypt, Greece, Rome, and ultimately Europe and America via a string of secret societies.

This belief in the god-king was especially prevalent in Egypt where the pyramid was the predominant symbol. The pharaohs possessed secret knowledge and partook of various occult rituals. In this hierarchal system of belief, the base of the pyramid represents the mass of humanity, and the tip is the scientific-occult elite who rule the masses. The pharaoh was considered the son of the sun god Ra, the incarnation of the god Horus during life, and after death Osiris.[3]

The pharaoh is believed to be a god-king in a long line stretching back to ancient Babylon and Atlantis, which, according to Plato, was ruled by ten philosopher-kings. Throughout the world, myths abound about an ancient civilization of supermen who inhabited Atlantis and the world prior to the Flood. It was these beings, according to these legends, who built the pyramids, Stonehenge, the Incan and Mayan temples, and other mysterious structures from the past. Atlantis, according to these legends, had a great university in the "form of an immense pyramid" with an observatory on top, and this pyramid and the rest of this ancient civilization perished in the Deluge. "From a careful consideration of Plato's description of Atlantis it is evident that the story should not be regarded as wholly historical but rather as both allegorical and historical," Manly P. Hall wrote in *The Secret Teachings of All Ages*. "The Deluge legend may be traced also to the Atlantean inundation, during which a 'world' was destroyed by water."[4]

Fascinatingly, accounts of the Nephilim are recorded in countless cultures across the world—though often under different names. Around the globe, as Graham Hancock discovered in his research adventures, archaeological ruins exist that are suggestive of the existence of an advanced ancient civilization. It seems the Nephilim are simply what different cultures over the centuries have called gods, beings, and aliens.

"Whether 'they' are labeled as angels and demons, good or bad aliens, gods of mythology, or multidimensional unknowns, history is replete with records of super-intelligent beings interacting with the process of human development," Tom Horn wrote. As examples, he cited thousands of prehistoric and colossal pictographs around the world that could not have been created from the earth's surface, the construction of pyramids "out of stones so large and with such astronomical precision that the same engineering feats could not be repeated until very recently, and with large machines," ancient Sumerian cylinder seals containing detailed knowledge of the solar system, including the recently discovered planet Pluto, and the discovery of the Antikythera mechanism, the world's oldest analog computer used for tracking lunar and solar eclipses. Some believe intelligent extraterrestrial beings traveled from distant planets or other dimensions, imparted "galactic wisdom" to people around the world, and then left through a wormhole—promising to return one day. "Students of theology have picked up on this concept in recent years, blending it with traditional demonology and suggesting that demons were (and are) mimicking visitors from another world in order to deceive the human race," Horn wrote.[5]

"We Are Not Alone in the Universe"

Remarkably, many people today, including a growing list of notable scientists, physicists, and astrobiologists, believe in the existence of extraterrestrials. During a special panel discussion at NASA headquarters, astronomer Kevin Hand said he anticipates that during the "next twenty years we will find out we are not alone in the universe." Some of these scientists have pondered the possibility that extraterrestrials "seeded" the earth with their DNA, using advanced genetic engineering techniques to essentially create modern humans. "If you really press me to think of how intelligence would ever have designed life on this planet, the only possibility would be alien seeding," Richard Dawkins, an Oxford University professor emeritus, the internationally bestselling author of *The God Delusion*, and "one of the most respected scientists in the world," said at the recent Starmus Festival in the Canary Islands. The event was attended by experts in space, science, and astronomy, including University of Cambridge theoretical physicist and cosmologist Stephen Hawking. At the festival, Dawkins told the audience that he wants biologists to start to consider what other life might be like in the event that humans discover "we are not alone, which is increasingly unlikely." These theories offer an alternative account to creationism, intelligent design, and the theory of evolution.[6]

Recently, even Pope Francis chimed in on this debate, saying he would baptize an alien if intelligent life in the universe were discovered. "The Vatican has already covered the angles, it seems," wrote Steve Rose in an article for the *Guardian* titled "The Pope Has Said That He Would Baptise a Martian—but Would They Want Our Religions?" "In 2008, [the Vatican's] chief astronomer, José Gabriel Funes, publicly accepted that there could be life on other planets. 'Why can't we speak of a 'brother extraterrestrial'? he said. 'It would still be part of creation.' Aliens might even be closer to God than us, Funes suggested, and humans could be the 'lost sheep' of the universe. In other words, alien visitors might well have a more advanced religion than ours. Rather than baptizing them, we might want to convert to their faith."[7]

The "Great Deception" and "Lying Wonders"

These strange and stunning pronouncements from the world's most prominent scientists and religious leaders may fit into what the Bible predicts regarding a "powerful delusion" or "great deception" preceding the arrival of both Jesus and the Antichrist, a spellbinding orator who will mesmerize the world with his lies. The Bible indicates that the Second Coming will be preceded by the "falling away" and the revealing of the "man of sin . . . whose coming is after the working of Satan with all power and signs and lying wonders," according to 2 Thessalonians 2:3, 9 (KJV). "He will use every kind of evil deception to fool those who are on their way to destruction, because they refuse to love and accept the truth that would save them. So God will cause them to be greatly deceived, and they will believe all these lies," the apostle Paul wrote (2 Thess. 2:10–11 NLT).

For nearly two thousand years, Bible scholars have admonished Jesus' followers that a final great deception would precede the end of days. "Informed students of Bible prophecy know this deception as 'The Lie,'" S. Douglas Woodward wrote in his book *Lying Wonders of the Red Planet: Exposing the Lie of Ancient Aliens*. "It will be so illusive, so distorted, but nonetheless so compelling the whole world will be led astray...If we who espouse this hypothesis are correct, that Ancient Alien Theory comprises 'The Lie of the Last Days' (and we're quite sure it does), it constitutes nothing less than a doctrine of demons straight from 'The Pit.'"[8]

Some prophecy experts have speculated that the Bible's descriptions of "signs in the heavens" during the last days may include UFO phenomena. A large amount of occult and psychic phenomena often accompanies reported UFO incidents. These phenomena have given rise to what the Bible describes as "doctrines of demons" (1 Tim. 4:1 NKJV), which 1 Timothy 4:1–2 and 2 Timothy 4:3–4 say will characterize the end times. Countless sightings of UFOs are reported throughout the world, and many say "space brothers" are contacting them through psychics and mediums, Ron Rhodes wrote in *The End Times in Chronological Order: A Complete Overview to Understanding Bible Prophecy*. "I find it highly revealing that this 'alien' contact is not through physical means, such as radios, but rather through the occult," Rhodes wrote. "Many of the 'revelations' coming from the 'space brothers' through psychics deny essential doctrines of Christianity, including humanity's sin problem, the reality of hell, and the need to trust in Jesus Christ for salvation. Moreover, one must wonder why these 'aliens' have come millions (billions?) of miles only to tell us the same kind of things that New Agers have been telling us for decades."[9]

The flood of mainstream media news stories, television shows, movies, and books about UFOs and extraterrestrials seems to be aimed at preparing humanity for the "visitation of the gods" and ultimately upending the world's religious beliefs. Once considered a fringe topic, the potential existence of UFOs has gained greater credibility in recent years, as demonstrated by a news conference in 2010 at the National Press Club when seven former U.S. Air Force personnel recounted UFO sightings over nuclear weapons facilities in prior decades—"accounts that a UFO researcher says show extraterrestrial beings are interested in the world's nuclear arms race and may be sending humans a message," according to a CNN story. Three of the former officers said the UFOs appeared to have "temporarily deactivated some of the nuclear missiles."

"The 'benevolent ETs' profess to watch over us and promise to appear at the appropriate time to assist us in our next evolutionary, spiritual, and technological step forward," Horn wrote. "To prepare us for their coming, popular movies, bestselling books, cultural trends, and religious ideas focus the earth's masses on 'help from above,' while supporters smile and explain: 'It's okay, they've been here before' and 'Don't worry, ancient men simply described flying saucers in terms of demons, angels, and gods, because they didn't understand what they were seeing.'" The reality, prophecy experts say, is that this colossal deception may very well help facilitate the rise of the Antichrist and the False Prophet. "This fact could be contemporary given that Jesus said the end times would be as the days of Noah, and the prophet Isaiah (chapters 13 and 14) also tied the return of the Nephilim to the destruction of the city of Babylon in the end of days," Horn wrote. "Throughout the Bible, spiritual Babylon is equivalent to the world system that is at enmity with God. Babylon began at the Tower of Babel, where at the macro level Satan's strategy to incarnate a one-world system was first attempted. It now appears that it will end there, as the world [hurtles] toward a final climatic encounter."[10]

The Antediluvian World and the Nimrod-Pharaoh Link

After the Flood, Nimrod rose to power and appeared to have many of the same supernatural abilities as the god-kings of the antediluvian world. Some argue that one of the wives of Noah's sons may have had illicit relations with a fallen angel. As a god-king, Nimrod built Babylon, Nineveh, and many other great cities, along with the legendary Tower of Babel.

Recent scientific discoveries suggest that the Tower of Babel incident occurred anywhere from eleven thousand to forty thousand years ago. Using "DNA fingerprinting" techniques that compare the genes of wild and cultivated wheat, researchers have learned that the launch of organized, large-scale agriculture began around 9000 BC in Turkey. This location is consistent with what has long been thought of as the cradle of civilization, the center of Mesopotamia's Fertile Crescent, and the "probable landing site of Noah's ark," Hugh Ross wrote. Anthropologists, by dating goat skeletons in this area, have discovered that the domestication of goats began about ten thousand years ago. Together, these findings are consistent with the biblical account in terms of the spread of human civilization after the Flood. "The Genesis 11:10–32 genealogy provides a bridge from the primeval past to a past that feels—and indeed is—much nearer to us," Ross stated. "Noah and his immediate descendants likely lived 30,000–50,000 years ago. The scattering of peoples following the Tower of Babel incident most likely took place between 40,000 years and 11,000 years ago. Abraham, on the other hand, was born only about 4,000 years ago. Scientific research has provided a burgeoning body of evidence that corresponds with and affirms the accuracy of the Bible's first eleven chapters."[11]

In light of this new research, and especially the possible older dates for the Flood and the Tower of Babel incident, the prophetic significance and credibility of the biblical and extrabiblical accounts of Nimrod and Semiramis, along with similarities to the Egyptian, Canaanite, Greek, and Roman gods, is bolstered. Starting in Babylon with Nimrod and Semiramis, many subsequent cultures—and ones separated by vast periods of time—apparently adopted the ancient tales of Nimrod and Semiramis into their own cultures by simply changing the names.[12]

Following this logic, the mighty empire of Egypt and the pharaohs was simply an extension of ancient Babylon using different names and symbols. Nimrod and Semiramis were viewed as a god and a goddess, but known as Ra and Osiris and Isis and Ishtar. Later, Nimrod became known under even more names in different cultures, including Orion, Apollo, and Zeus, according to the *Jewish Encyclopedia*. Likewise, Semiramis was worshipped as a goddess under names such as Diana, Venus, Virgo, and the queen of Babylon.[13]

"In my research, I found that Nimrod and Semiramis became deified and later showed up as the deities we read about in the Bible," Carroll M. Helm says.[14]

This religious meme—whether in ancient Babylon, Egypt, Greece, or Rome—is an imitation of the story of Mary and Jesus. For example, the myth of Osiris is analogous to the gospel story, as is Isis with the role of Mary. "It's sinister in the sense that typically there is a god and then there is the mother of the god," Ross says. "You can kind of see the analogy with Jesus and Mary and so this is, I would argue, Satan's strategy of trying to dissuade people from following Jesus Christ to following an Antichrist."[15]

In Egypt, Nimrod metamorphosed into Osiris, the "Egyptian god of the underworld, death and rebirth"; Semiramis reputedly became Isis; and Tammuz transfigured into Horus, the "god of the sky." Under the Egyptian system, the pharaoh was worshipped as a god like Nimrod. In Egyptian society, the pharaoh was the center of society and had a "superhuman role, being a manifestation of a god or of various deities on earth." In late antiquity, Egyptian religious beliefs played an influential role in the development of Gnosticism, an in-vogue belief system popularized in Brown's *The Da Vinci Code*. Some of these belief systems reemerged during the Renaissance. "Often the sources of these esoteric religions run deep—the Cabala, Gnosticism and the ancient wisdom of the Greek sage Hermes Trismegistos and the Egyptian god Thoth are all part of the esoteric soup from which secret societies draw their ideas," wrote Amy D. Bernstein in her *U.S. News & World Report* article "A Short History of Secret Societies."[16]

In fact, the concept of a "one world order" among secret societies didn't originate in modern times with pronouncements by various world leaders, Daniel Estulin says. "The concept was discussed way back when by the Romans, Egyptians, and others. We can talk about the Roman Empire, we can talk about the Byzantine Empire, we can talk about the Phoenician black nobility, the synergistic movement of empires, and we can talk about the Bilderbergers. The point isn't a one world order; the point today, the way we understand it, is a One World Company Limited Corporation that holds all the power and basically runs the world. What we are seeing now is important because it kind of puts the whole thing into perspective over the last six thousand years. If you go back to ancient Egypt or before, who wielded the power? It was controlled by the high priests and over the centuries and the millennia what we've had is secret societies, and very, very secret and private organizations—most of which we didn't even know…existed—that kind of passed on this secret information from one generation to the next among the privileged people, or the elite."[17]

"The House of Hidden Places"

A land of mystery and intrigue, Egypt is home to the Great Sphinx and what was until the early part of the twentieth century the largest structure on earth—the Great Pyramid of Giza, the oldest (and only surviving) of the Seven Wonders of the Ancient World.

Egyptologists believe the massive pyramid—"perhaps the most colossal single building ever erected on the planet"—was built as a tomb for the pharaoh Khufu in about 2530 BC, about six centuries after societies began to emerge in Egypt. While *Encyclopaedia Britannica* says the question of just how the pyramid was built has not received a "wholly satisfactory answer," the predominant theory is that tens of thousands of workers moved 5.75 million tons of stone blocks, some weighing up to nine tons, up an embankment encircling the pyramid using rollers, sledges, and levers.[18]

Despite this hypothesis, serious questions remain not only about how the pyramids were built but when. Some geologists say that water erosion near the Great Pyramid and the Sphinx indicate that both structures came under heavy rains, which have not occurred on the Giza Plateau for more than ten thousand years. This has led to speculation that the Egyptian civilization, which is dated to about 3100 BC, could not have built the Great Pyramid, and it must have been built much earlier.[19]

In order for it to be "true to its astronomical symbolism," Manly P. Hall estimated the Great Pyramid was constructed long ago, perhaps tens of thousands of years in the past. The pyramid, built by the gods, was the tomb of Osiris, Hall wrote in *The Secret Teachings of All Ages*.[20]

For thousands of years, Egypt's more than one hundred pyramids, including seventeen great pyramids, have drawn endless admiration and awe. Over the millennia, the pyramids have been places of religious worship and the target of grave robbers in search of Egypt's fabled treasures. In modern times, speculation has arisen that the pyramid could be a "giant power generator based on harmonic resonance," a weapon in a "great cosmic war that encompassed our entire solar system," and even an extraterrestrial "star map." Researchers claim the Giza pyramids reflect the position of the constellation Orion—"home of the reborn Pharaohs"—as it would have appeared in 10450 BC, along with star systems such as Sirius. They claim that fifty "star maps" found around the world revealed that the "'gods' of early humans originated from other solar systems." Even more bizarre, though, is the link between the discovery of a nine-foot-long sarcophagus in Egypt in 1999—the purported tomb of Osiris—and its alignment with one of these constellations. Oddly, none of the released photos of the sarcophagus have disclosed its contents, leading to speculation that the "mummy of Osiris was inside."[21]

Hall wrote about the predicted return of Osiris in *The Secret Teachings of All Ages*. In the book, he described the Great Pyramid of Giza as "the House of the Hidden Places"—a place where the "illumined of antiquity" passed, entering its "portals as men; they came forth as gods." In the depths of its mysterious recesses resided an unknown being called the "Illustrious One" and "Master of the Hidden House." "Though the modern world may know a million secrets, the ancient world knew one—and that one was greater than the million; for the million secrets breed death, disaster, sorrow, selfishness, lust, and avarice, but the one secret confers life, light, and truth," Hall wrote. "The time will come when the secret wisdom shall again be the dominating religious and philosophical urge of the world."[22]

The Mummy and the Osiris Myth

The practitioners of the ancient mystery religions of Egypt believed Osiris would one day return, rising from the dead, and thus they wrapped the pharaohs tightly with special herbal chemicals to create mummies.

In the *Book of the Dead*, magical steps were created centered around the Osiris myth to help Egyptians in their journey to the afterlife. The Egyptians believed that everyone has a *ka*—a spiritual and invisible duplicate—and that the ka accompanies them throughout eternity. "Since the *ka* provided each person with a resurrected body in the kingdom of the dead, yet could not exist without the maintenance of the earthly body, every effort was made to preserve the human corpse," Tom Horn wrote. The body was mummified in accordance with magic rituals passed down from Isis, who perfected this ritual through her work on Osiris, according to legend.[23]

Today, strangely enough, scientists are perfecting the ability to take a small piece of preserved body and extract the DNA from it. The day may come, and it may have already arrived, when DNA will allow scientists to clone a new body—perhaps even the body of a pharaoh.

In *Apollyon Rising 2012*, Horn claimed that the prediction of Osiris, or Nimrod, rising from the dead and ruling the world is "cleverly hidden in the Great Seal of the United States" and may actually be possible in the future through recombinant DNA, genetic modification, and similar technologies. "Could the same technology described above or some variation lead to the resurrection of the pagan deity Apollo/Osiris/Nimrod, who returns to rule the *Novus Ordo Seclorum*? Is material from the deity's 'body' concealed in a tomb at Giza...or in Washington, D.C.? If so, is it conceivable that plans to revive the Apollonian tissue using biotechnology have already been made—or worse, have already been accomplished and the pagan god waits the moment of its unveiling?" Horn wrote. "People not familiar with biblical eschatology may find this idea fantastic, that the being who becomes the Antichrist was once alive, then was dead, and returns from the grave to rule the *Novus Ordo Seclorum*. But this is exactly what Revelation 17:8 appears to say will happen: 'The beast that thou sawest was, and is not; and shall ascend out of the bottomless pit, and go into perdition [*Apoleia*, Apollo]; and they that dwell on the earth shall wonder...when they behold the beast that was, and is not, and yet is.'"[24]

At first, this figure will have profound answers to the world's most difficult Gordian knots, but ultimately he will make the atrocities of Hitler, Stalin, and Genghis Khan, all of whom were types of the Antichrist, seem minor in comparison. "He will champion worship of the 'old gods' and 'cause that as many as would not worship the image of the beast should be killed' (Revelation 13:15), and he will revive an ancient mystery religion that is 'the habitation of devils, and the hold of every foul spirit, and a cage of every unclean and hateful bird' (Revelation 18:2)," Horn wrote. "Nevertheless, the world is readied—indeed, hungry for—a political savior to arise now with a plan to deliver mankind from upheaval."[25]

An Illuminati Pyramid?

In *The Secret Destiny of America*, Manly P. Hall argued that the dream of a "world democracy" began among the ancients who were aware of the existence of the American continent and selected it as the place where this "philosophic empire" would one day emerge. The pharaoh of Egypt, Akhnaton, shared this vision of the "secret destiny" of America as the place that would help fulfill his "dream of the Brotherhood of Man"—the same vision Schiller wrote of in "Ode to Joy" and Lennon in "Imagine."[26]

"Some people believe that The Order of the Quest is the force behind unfolding world events," Stanley Monteith wrote in *Brotherhood of Darkness*. "Manly P. Hall wrote about it in his book, *The Secret Destiny of America*. He noted that members of that secret group placed an unfinished pyramid on the back of the Great Seal of the United States back in 1782." The Great Seal is "stamped with the signature of the Order of the Quest," and the reverse side of the design "is even more related to the old Mysteries." "Here is represented the great Pyramid of Gizah, composed of thirteen rows of masonry, showing seventy-two stones," Hall wrote. "The Pyramid is without a cap stone, and above its upper platform floats

a triangle containing the All-Seeing Eye surrounded by rays of light...
The combination of the Phoenix, the pyramid, and the all-seeing eye is
more than chance or coincidence...There is only one possible origin for
these symbols, and that is the secret societies which came to this country
150 years before the Revolutionary War."[27]

Today, researchers say the pyramid and the all-seeing eye are symbols
of secret societies such as the Illuminati and signify its control of the
New World Order. Some historians agree with Hall, saying secret societies such as the Rosicrucian Order, the Illuminati, and the Freemasons
were involved in the design of America's seal and the dollar bill. A significant number of the nation's founders and signers of the Declaration
of Independence were members of these groups.[28]

"World democracy was the secret dream of the great classical philosophers," Hall wrote. "Toward the accomplishment of this greatest of all
human ends they outlined programs of education, religion, and social
conduct directed to the ultimate achievement of a practical and universal brotherhood...Thousands of years ago, in Egypt, these mystical
orders were aware of the existence of the Western Hemisphere and the
great continent which we call America...So brilliant was the plan and
so well was it administered that it has survived to our time, and it will
continue to function until the great work is accomplished."[29]

Today, those behind this secret globalist plan are using the same symbolism as was used in ancient Babylon and Egypt.[30] These symbols often
have a connection to the occult. "In the 1960s, the seal's reverse became
an emblem of the counterculture, appearing on posters for dance concerts and in underground newspapers, periodicals, and comic books,"
Robert Hieronimus wrote in *Founding Fathers, Secret Societies*. "In the
1980s Peter Sellers employed the distinctive pyramid-and-eye-motif as
a tomb in one of his final films, *Being There*. Shirley MacLaine referred
to it in her 1984 book, *Out on a Limb*, when she described our Founding Fathers as transcendentalists. The character played by Madonna in

the film *Desperately Seeking Susan* had it embroidered on the back of her jacket, and this became an important recurring image...With the mainstream popularity of books and films like *National Treasure* (2004) and *The Da Vinci Code* (book, 2003; film, 2006), interest in these symbols selected by our Founding Fathers to represent the new nation seems to be at an all-time high."[31]

Like Hall, Hieronimus—who corresponded for many years with the famous Masonic mystic—believes the choice of symbols on the Great Seal, and hence the dollar bill, "strongly implicates an influence of the secret societies on its design. Perhaps Franklin and Washington and Jefferson approved our two-sided seal because they were capable of interpreting its symbols as detailing America's secret destiny."[32]

Chapter Nine

The Battle for America

Behold our secret: If in order to destroy Christianity...remember
that the end justifies the means...This can be done in no other
way but by secret associations, which will by degrees, and in silence,
possess themselves of the government of the States...The express
aim of this order was to abolish Christianity, and overthrow all civil
governments.

—ADAM WEISHAUPT, FOUNDER OF THE
BAVARIAN ILLUMINATI

The brotherhood of the Illuminati is also factual.

—DAN BROWN, *NEW YORK TIMES* BESTSELLING
AUTHOR OF *ANGELS & DEMONS*, IN HIS AUTHOR'S NOTE

The philosophical battle for America began in the seventeenth and
eighteenth centuries between the forces of the Bavarian Illuminati and
Christianity. This battle between secular-humanist ideals and Judeo-
Christian values has been raging for hundreds of years and is now intensifying exponentially.

Mysteriously, both America and the Illuminati were founded in 1776.
At the nation's founding, there was a clash of worldviews. Many of the
Founding Fathers had, to varying degrees, a biblical worldview. Others

were Deists and some were Freemasons or part of the Illuminati and the Rosicrucian Order.

While the Pilgrims and Puritans had come to America in the early 1600s to lay a biblical foundation for a new society based upon religious freedom, members of occult societies also came to the New World and founded the Jamestown Colony at about the same time. The colony, a business venture of the Virginia Company of London, was named after King James I, who oversaw the creation of the King James Version of the Bible.[1]

The Virginia Company was formed in 1606 by secret society members, including Bacon, a member of Britain's Parliament, the "founder of [English] Freemasonry" and the "guiding light of the Rosicrucian Order." Even more intriguing, some believe Bacon was the "real" Shakespeare, the English poet, dramatist, and actor who is widely considered the greatest dramatist of all time. It has been alleged that Shakespeare was actually an illiterate actor whose name was used to hide the controversial political prose of a clandestine Elizabethan society that included Bacon, Sir Walter Raleigh, and Edmund Spenser. Considering the scant amount of records documenting Shakespeare's life and the uncertainty regarding his education, some scholars have raised questions about the authorship of his works. Shakespeare is a literary figure whose personal history is widely considered something of a mystery, and no biography of him was written until a century after his death in 1616. None of his original scripts have been found and he made no mention of his literary works in his will, leaving his wife only his "second-best bed." He signed the document "William Shackspeare," misspelling his own name. A purported Latin anagram in *Love's Labour's Lost* has been translated as "These plays, the offspring of F. Bacon, are preserved for the world." The 2011 Roland Emmerich film—*Anonymous: Was Shakespeare a Fraud?*—explored this claim.[2]

As the author of *The New Atlantis*, a book describing the utopian vision of many secret societies, Bacon and others played an influential role in the growing power of a number of esoteric and occult societies in the following century.

"This was the start of what was to become the Eastern Liberal Establishments," John Coleman wrote in *The Conspirators' Hierarchy: The Committee of 300*. "It was also the beginning of the spiritual conflict that has bedeviled the United States ever since a number of the Brethren established themselves in the American colonies in New England. They were members of the Rite of Swedenborg, Gnostic, Rosicrucian, Unitarians and Humanists. Almost three hundred years later the most important of these families was the Rockefellers who owned and controlled the Rockefeller-Standard Oil dynasty. It was this network that was used by the '300' to usher in the Fabian Socialist 'New Deal' via Roosevelt."[3]

By the late 1700s, these secretive groups had gained significant power, and many were appalled by some of the Founding Fathers' plans to draft documents creating a nation based upon biblical precepts. In response, they and their European counterparts created the Bavarian Illuminati "to bring us back under their control," Dennis L. Cuddy says.[4]

"The Illuminati infiltrated the Masonic lodges in France and helped start the French Revolution who came up with the motto, Liberté, Égalité, Fraternité (freedom, equality, brotherhood)," Cuddy continued. "So out of that basically flowed a plot against America and biblical Christianity around the world. They came up with an indirect attack and fomented revolutions like the French Revolution—the beginning of communism and socialism."[5]

At the time, many of the Founding Fathers were fervent biblical Christians, as evidenced by the unique writings of the U.S. Constitution, the Bill of Rights, and the Declaration of Independence. These documents echoed Christian concepts: all men are created equal, checks and balances, and the balance of power. At the same time, however, members of the Illuminati, Freemasonry, and other secret societies also exerted a strong influence on the nation. Some of the Founding Fathers, including Washington, warned that the European Illuminati had infiltrated America's Masonic lodges and were intent on creating a central bank to consolidate their financial and political power over the new nation.

"The Society of the Illuminati, springing up at a time and professing itself to be a higher order of Freemasonry, availed itself of the secrecy, solemnity, and mysticism of Masonry, of its system of correspondence, to teach and propagate doctrines calculated to undermine and destroy all human happiness and virtue," Vernon Stauffer wrote in *The Bavarian Illuminati in America*. "Thus God's being was derided, while government was pronounced a curse, civil society an apostasy of the race, the possession of private property a robbery, chastity and natural affection groundless prejudices, and adultery, assassination, poisoning and other infernal crimes not only lawful but even virtuous. To crown it all, the principle that the end justifies the means was made to define the sphere of action for the members of the order."[6]

At America's beginning, two diametrically opposed plans were conceived—the plan of God carried to America by the Pilgrims and Puritans, and the secret occult plan created by Bacon and others to make America the head of the New Atlantis, or what is known today as the New World Order. This plan was put into action by the Illuminati and its interlocking political and financial networks hundreds of years ago.

"Utilizing organizational models taken from both the Jesuits and the Masons, Weishaupt created a secular organization whose aim was to free the world 'from all established religious and political authority,'" wrote Michael Barkun in his *U.S. News & World Report* article "The Bizarre Legacy of the Bavarian Illuminati." "An elaborate apparatus of secrecy and ritual was designed not only to protect the organization from state penetration but also to mold its members into an elite capable of achieving Weishaupt's grandiose objective."[7]

By the late 1780s, the Illuminati had been dissolved, but its sweeping goals, secrecy, and insistence on "unswerving personal dedication made it a model for a sizable number of early 19th-century revolutionary organizations," Barkun wrote. "In short, the Illuminati influenced subsequent revolutionaries, albeit indirectly, even though the organization seems on the most reliable evidence to have lasted no more than 11 or 12 years. Yet the irony is that if its sympathizers were eager to preserve its legacy and achieve the total liberation that had eluded Weishaupt, its enemies were even more eager to keep it alive. They insisted that it had never died, that its dissolution was only apparent and that in the ultimate act of clandestinity, it had survived its own death."[8]

The Ultimate Act of Subterfuge

Regardless of whether the Illuminati still exists or it morphed into or inspired the creation of other secret societies and front organizations, the evidence uncovered in our five-year investigation strongly suggests that some form of "secret cabal" is covertly orchestrating world events.

While some say the original Illuminati no longer exists, most researchers agree it helped inspire or contributed to the creation of other secretive organizations such as Skull and Bones, Bohemian Grove, and the Bilderberg Group.

In *America's Secret Establishment*, Antony C. Sutton traced the families, bloodlines, and business entanglements of the "Establishment" in America, detailing numerous connections between the Bavarian Illuminati, Skull and Bones, the Group, and Round Table. He also documented purported links between these organizations and the CFR, the Trilateral Commission, and the Bilderberg Group. "Finally, in conclusion, we can trace the foundation of three secret societies, in fact the most influential three secret societies that we know about, to universities," Sutton wrote. "The Illuminati was founded at University of Ingolstadt. The Group was founded at All Souls College, Oxford University in England, and The Order [of Skull and Bones] was founded at Yale University in the United States. The paradox is that institutions supposedly devoted to the search for truth and freedom has given birth to institutions devoted to world enslavement."[9]

Sutton wrote the book after receiving a thick batch of documents containing the membership roster of Skull and Bones members. Over the past two centuries, Skull and Bones initiates have become senators, cabinet secretaries, judges, spies, titans of finance and industry, and even presidents.

"Skull and Bones is the springboard for a young man to be brought in, trained, conditioned, and imbued with these doctrines and then placed into positions of power to carry out the agenda of the covert secret societies," Jim Marrs said on the History Channel special "Secret Societies." The ratio of Skull and Bones members who go on to significant positions of power is enormous, he observed. "The Skull and Bones society does not operate in isolation," David Icke said. "It is a strand within the greater web and an important one in America. Presidents are not elected by ballot; they are selected by blood."[10]

In an article for the *Politic*, the Yale undergraduate journal of politics, Tom Hayden, a former antiwar activist, author, and politician, and the ex-husband of actress Jane Fonda, discussed the fact that President George W. Bush and Secretary of State John Kerry were "Bonesmen" and how the political system in America really works. Hayden was a member of a University of Michigan secret society—the Druids.

"The political system is a moneyed oligarchy underneath its democratic trappings," Hayden wrote. "The vast majority of voters are like fans in the bleachers: We participate from the cheap seats, supposed to enjoy our place, and vote for whichever Bonesmen we prefer."[11]

The Black Nobility

If that admission isn't stunning enough, Marrs learned during research for *Our Occulted History* that nearly all U.S. presidents and most of the important political figures in America over the past century are related to one another. "It really kind of blew me away when I found that out," Marrs says. "According to Dick Cheney's wife, in researching their family history, they found out that they are cousins to the Bush family and to Barack Hussein Obama. Holy cow! And they can all be traced back to the royals of Europe and to what is known as the Black Nobility. These prominent, wealthy people go back through their bloodlines and their families—the Pierces, the Windsors, and others—all the way back to Charlemagne...the Roman caesars and...back even further." Other researchers found thirteen to fifteen intermarried families that are connected to the black nobility—the descendants of the "early priests and money changers" who rose to power in Venice and intermarried with existing European royalty.[12]

As members of these families, those who belong to Skull and Bones and other secret societies manipulate the levers of power through a framework known as the Hegelian dialectic process—the notion that "conflict creates history."[13]

In the Hegelian system, the individual has limited freedom. "There was no freedom in Hitler's Germany, there is no freedom for the individual under Marxism, neither will there be in the New World Order," Sutton wrote. "And if it sounds like George Orwell's *1984*—it is." In the New World Order, the state is supreme and conflict is used to bring about the utopian world. "So who or what is the State? Obviously it's a self-appointed elite," according to Sutton. "It is interesting that [German philosopher Johann] Fichte, who developed these ideas before [German philosopher Georg Wilhelm Friedrich] Hegel, was a Freemason, almost certainly Illuminati, and certainly was promoted by the Illuminati."

Goethe, one of Schiller's close friends and a member of the Illuminati, pushed to get Fichte an appointment at the University of Jena, the college where Schiller served as a history professor. The college, now named the Friedrich Schiller University, attracted some of the most influential minds of the late eighteenth and early nineteenth centuries.[14]

Since then, the Illuminati and other secret societies have grown enormously more influential—maintaining their power through the "occult, magic rituals, and ceremonies," according to an article titled "The Illuminati" in the special publication *Secret Societies: The Truth Revealed*. "They use this power to control banks, governments, industry and trade," Speregen and Zakarin wrote. "They also control Hollywood and the music industry. They use entertainment to control the minds of young people." In 1996, a young woman named Svali reportedly escaped from the Illuminati cult and revealed its secrets. "She reports that 'each region of the U.S. has nerve centers, or power bases for regional activity," according to the article. "The U.S. has been divided into seven major geographical regions, which contain military compounds. They are hidden. These bases are used to train Illuminati in military techniques, in preparation for the ultimate collapse of government."[15]

Today, there is widespread public interest in whether the Illuminati still exists and what plans this group of "puppet-masters" may have in store for the world.

Charlie Daniels, the country music legend and host of the documentary *Behold a Pale Horse: America's Last Chance*, about a looming world state, argues that powerful forces are now aligning against the nation for an "organized and intentional takeover of America."[16]

The film, featuring interviews with Marrs, Monteith, retired U.S. Army lieutenant general William G. "Jerry" Boykin, trends forecaster Gerald Celente, and others, details how over the past few decades there has been a "systematic eradication" of the U.S. Constitution as part of a process to merge the nation into a global socialist government. This has followed a classic Marxist pattern, including the nationalization of major sectors of the economy—the 2008 bailouts of the automobile and banking industries, redistribution of wealth through Obamacare and other government programs, discrediting of the opposition (faith leaders, the Tea Party, etc.), intimidation and censorship of pastors by threatening to revoke their nonprofit status, and attempts at passing hate-crime laws similar to those in Europe. "They have a lot more control over what goes on in this country and all over the world than most people realize," Daniels says. "These people are very powerful. They control a lot of money. They control a lot of politicians. Their tentacles are everywhere."[17]

For Tim LaHaye, it's a "commonsense conclusion" that powerful people are working to bring about a global political, economic, and religious system as predicted in the Bible. "Something is driving the world into... a way of acting and functioning that exalts all the things God condemns," LaHaye says. "For example, God created man and woman to marry and to propagate and have children and replenish the earth, and, as you know, we have different standards today. Well, where do they come from? It's a satanically inspired plan that is coming from many different avenues where man without God makes his own decisions about what's right and wrong and how to live."[18]

A Secret Occult Destiny Hidden in Plain Sight

America has a secret occult destiny whose roots go back to the pyramids of ancient Egypt and the ziggurat of the Tower of Babel. Over the millennia, a succession of secret societies served as the guardians of this hidden plan, including the Knights Templar, the Rosicrucian Order, the Freemasons, Illuminati, Skull and Bones, and today such organizations as the Bilderberg Group and Bohemian Grove.

The irony is that much of this secret occult destiny is right out in the open and in front of our eyes. For example, consider the unfinished pyramid with the all-seeing eye on the back of the dollar bill. The Great Seal's designer was Charles Thompson, a Freemason who served as the secretary for the Continental Congress. Likewise, many believe that the design of our nation's capital involves an architectural code of a Rosicrucian and Freemason vision that America will become the New Atlantis and head of the New World Order. This is expected to bring about a new golden age called the "Golden Age of Osiris."[19]

"As Dr. Horn points out, *Novus Ordo Seclorum* is derived from the prophecies of the Cumaean Sibyl, a prophetess of Apollo [Apollo is the Greek version of the Egyptian god Osiris] who predicted the return of this deity at a future date, when men would be rejoined by the gods," wrote Donna Anderson, a writer at Horn's ministry. "Horn further notes how this 'god' is specifically identified in the Bible as the spirit that will inhabit the Antichrist. In other words, unknown to most Americans, the Great Seal of their country heralds an ancient prophecy of the coming Man of Sin."[20]

The most prominent architecture in Washington, DC, is a cypher that depicts this ancient supernatural power from the time of the pharaohs. The U.S. Capitol is a dome, representing the womb of the goddess Isis. The Washington Monument, an obelisk, represents the phallic symbol of Osiris.

In Egyptian mythology, the sun represented Osiris and the star Sirius symbolized Isis, and thirteen was the number of pieces of Osiris that Isis was able to find after Osiris's evil brother Seth murdered him and threw fourteen pieces of his body into the Nile River. Isis searched the river, recovering every piece except his genitals. "Isis replaced the missing organ with an obelisk and magically impregnated herself with Horus," Horn wrote. "Therefore, in Masonic as well as in ancient Egyptian mythology, the number thirteen—used a total of thirteen times on the Great Seal, counting front and back—is the number that represents the return or resurrection of Osiris." By dedicating the United States through its astrological alignment with the Virgo constellation of Isis, the Founders had dedicated the destiny of America to fulfilling the predicted return of "Osiris/Apollo/Nimrod" as the Antichrist, Horn stated. "Interestingly, the same dedication to Osiris/Isis/Apollo exists in New York where the events of September 11, 2001, initiated the push toward the *Novus Ordo Seclorum*. The Statue of Liberty in New York's Harbor, which holds the Masonic 'Torch of Enlightenment,' was presented in 1884 as a gift to American Masons by the French Grand Orient Temple Masons. Designed by French Freemason and sculptor Frédéric Auguste Bartholdi...the statue was originally identified as 'the goddess Isis' with the statue's head formed to represent 'the Greek Sun-god Apollo.'"[21]

According to several key verses in the Bible, the Antichrist could be the progeny of the ancient spirit Apollo, says Horn. Second Thessalonians 2:3 (KJV) warns: "Let no man deceive you by any means: for that day shall not come, except there come a falling away first, and that man of sin be revealed, the son of perdition [Apoleia; Apollyon, Apollo]."

While no one can be certain whether the Antichrist will emerge from America, Europe, or elsewhere, the theory presented by Horn and others is intriguing. Rather than be caught off guard as the fulfillment of biblical predictions continues to unfold in the years ahead, it would be prudent to watch political, economic, and other developments in America closely.

The Great Falling Away

The biblical term "falling away" comes from the Greek word *apostasia*, which describes the time in the last days when many believers will fall away. This "falling away" will involve a powerful but very subtle supernatural deception.

We believe that the "falling away" from the true faith as revealed in the Bible is already under way. Even in America, large numbers of those who say they are Christians believe things that are the exact opposite of what the Bible teaches. Ultimately, this "falling away" will usher in the coming global religion headed by a figure the Bible calls the False Prophet. Through signs and wonders, the False Prophet will convince the deceived to worship the Antichrist as God. The Bible very clearly teaches in Revelation that all who worship the Antichrist as God will be sentenced to the Lake of Fire, a place of eternal torment.

As you read *The Babylon Code*, we encourage you to do what the apostle Paul commanded, "Examine yourselves to see whether you are in the faith" (2 Cor. 13:5 NIV). In the last days, the Bible says, many will depart from the faith. The only way you can make sure that you are still in the true faith of the Word of God is to compare your beliefs and actions with what the Bible actually teaches.

Part III

UNLOCKING THE BABYLON CODE

Chapter Ten

Geopolitical-Military Babylon

The Global Union will require the formation of appropriate global bodies (such as a World Commission, World Court of Justice and World Parliament), and there will be initial resistance to joining on the part of bigger states (the equivalent of Britain's reluctance to share sovereignty in the E.U.).

—MARK CORNER, A PROFESSOR AT VESALIUS COLLEGE IN
BRUSSELS, IN AN ESSAY FOR THE FEDERAL TRUST

The next fifteen years will be "some of the most transformative in human history." That's the prediction contained in a recent UN report about a sweeping new set of "sustainable development goals" costing trillions of dollars. The nations of the world are slated to approve this plan at an upcoming UN summit, including unspecified "reforms of the mechanisms of global governance."[1]

Unbeknownst to many, the push for global governance—described by proponents as the "global management of the planet"—has advanced significantly in recent years.

"Obama's election, coupled with the global economic crisis, has encouraged breathless expectations in some quarters that we may be in a rare 'moment of creation,' where the world order is suddenly in flux, and major institutional renovation is possible," wrote Stewart Patrick, a senior fellow and director of the International Institutions and Global

Governance program at the CFR, in a report titled "Global Governance Reform: An American View of US Leadership."[2]

The champions of global governance—wealthy globalists, the UN, the CFR, the Bilderberg Group, the Trilateral Commission, and many other powerful organizations—say it will be a boon for the global economy, helping avert financial crises and promoting peace and security. But many are skeptical.

John Fonte, a senior fellow at the Hudson Institute and the author of *Sovereignty or Submission: Will Americans Rule Themselves or Be Ruled by Others?*, has sounded the alarm about the "vastly underappreciated threat to American democracy posed by the global governance movement." "Today we are at the beginning of an epic world-wide political and ideological conflict between the forces of global governance and the liberal democratic nation-state, especially the United States and Israel," Fonte wrote.

In a *National Review* article about the book, Stanley Kurtz wrote that the global governance movement is an attempt to extend the "pooling of sovereignty" in the European Union to the rest of the world, especially the United States. "In his foreword to the book, former *National Review* editor-in-chief John O'Sullivan compares Fonte to Edmund Burke, whose early warnings about the French Revolution were poorly appreciated until the outbreak of the Terror," Kurtz wrote. "Fonte's book names, outlines, and dissects a movement of international elites that seeks to place the heretofore sovereign decisions of democratic nation-states under the authority of international standards and bodies answerable to nobody—no one but international elites, that is. Particularly in America, the global governance movement offers a way for liberals to invoke the help of European progressives to impose policy solutions on the United States that could never be achieved by democratic means."[3]

For the first time in history since the Tower of Babel, the potential for a global government is within humanity's grasp. Today, all the elements are in place for establishing a world authority—electronic banking, the surveillance state, the Internet, an increasingly global society, and international political bodies. And while globalism has lofty goals— eradicating poverty, ending hunger, a more equitable distribution of the planet's resources, reversing climate change, and world peace—the Bible predicts that the Antichrist will exploit these hopes and one day seize the reins of a world-state. This would place unprecedented political, economic, and military power in the hands of one individual—a person who would ultimately gain control of the planet's nuclear and conventional arsenals.

"The capacity for missile warfare also makes world rule possible," Mark Hitchcock wrote. "Missiles can be fired and guided by GPS to almost any spot in the world in less than thirty minutes. A ruler with nuclear submarines and missiles at his disposal could threaten any portion of the world—blackmailing it into submission with the threat of extinction. No ruler in history has had such fearful weapons to enforce his rule. In terms of economics, the Bible predicts that the world ruler will have absolute control of the economy, and no one will buy or sell without his permission (Revelation 13:17). Today, electronic fund transfers, electronic banking, and debit and credit cards make this literally possible for the first time in world history... The increasing availability of nuclear weapons, the propaganda power of the world media, and the blackmail power of international economic agreements and embargoes will make it possible for a world dictator to seize control that would have been impossible in any previous generation."[4]

This supremely intelligent and cunning figure will ultimately declare himself ruler of the world, in the same fashion as the Babylonian and Roman emperors. He will set up an image of himself in the rebuilt Temple in Jerusalem and demand that the world worship him as if he were God. "Revelation 13 tells us the Antichrist is going to rule the world," Hitchcock says. "It says all peoples, nations, and tongues are going to worship him. He's going to be this great end-times leader so the whole move toward a global economy and global governance is in keeping with that. I think it's going to be easier to get the world together economically than politically. The economic part will probably come first, just out of necessity, and then the global governance will follow."[5]

Revelation predicts that the Antichrist's end-times world government will consist of three facets—geopolitical, commercial, and religious. Revelation 16–19 is focused on the great political, economic, and spiritual system known as "Mystery, Babylon" and "Babylon the Great."

For more than two millennia, theories have abounded about this prophetic enigma. This final Babylon has been identified with many institutions, empires, nations, and cities, including the EU, the Roman Catholic Church, the United States, apostate Christendom, New York City, Rome, London, Strasbourg, Jerusalem, and even the partially rebuilt city of Babylon in Iraq, a project former Iraqi dictator Saddam Hussein commissioned before his death. Intriguingly, it is located in Iraq's Babil province. "The government of Iraq is moving forward with plans to protect the archaeological remains of the ancient City of Babylon, in preparation for building a modern city of Babylon," Joel Rosenberg wrote. "The project, originally started by the late Saddam Hussein, is aimed eventually at attracting scores of 'cultural tourists' from all over the world to see the glories of Mesopotamia's most famous city. What's more, the Obama Administration is contributing $700,000 towards 'The Future of Babylon Project,' through the State Department's budget."[6]

God's Last Days Plan for Babylon

God's end-times plan for Babylon has its roots in the historical account of the Tower of Babel, the first post-Flood rebellion against God. God had commanded humanity to spread out around the world following the Flood. But under the leadership of Nimrod, mankind gathered in the land of Shinar and built a city and a tower in rebellion against God's command.

God stopped this apostasy by confusing the builders' languages, preventing them from communicating with one another. God knew the devil could lead mankind away from the truth far more easily if only one government existed and it fell into the hands of those opposed to God. "However, with the existence of multiple nations, those nations that reject anti-God agendas can work together to restrain evil to some extent," Tim LaHaye and Ed Hindson wrote. "Consequently, since the Tower of Babel incident, God has decreed that humanity be ordered according to national boundaries rather than global government (Deuteronomy 32:8; Acts 17:26)."[7]

Does the Bible Really Predict a World Government?

These themes also appear in Isaiah 13–14 and Jeremiah 50–51, chapters that speak of Babylon's ultimate destruction. While the destruction of Babylon at the hands of the Medo-Persian Empire occurred in 539 BC, Babylon's fall at that time doesn't correlate with the descriptions Isaiah and Jeremiah give of its cataclysmic destruction.[8]

Often, the Old Testament prophets who peered into the future were able to see only what eschatologists describe as the "mountain peaks" of Christ's two comings. This current age, known as the church age, was a mystery to them. As a result, the prophets often blended Christ's two comings. The gaps between these events are known as "prophetic skips."[9]

This is what we observe in Isaiah 13–14 and Jeremiah 50–51. For instance, Isaiah 13:19–20 describes the day of the Lord's judgment upon Babylon when it "will be overthrown by God like Sodom and Gomorrah. She will never be inhabited or lived in through all generations"

222 • UNLOCKING THE BABYLON CODE

(NIV). In order for these prophecies to fulfilled, Babylon must be revived so it can be destroyed again.[10]

Describing the coming Babylonian world government, Revelation 13 introduces two beasts through which the devil establishes control over the earth—the Antichrist and the False Prophet.

A few chapters later in Revelation 17–18, this system is described as "Mystery, Babylon" and "Babylon the Great." "Mystery, Babylon," likened to a lamb beast and a great prostitute, refers to the false religious system under the control of the False Prophet. "Babylon the Great," compared to a leopard beast or a great city, refers to a global government overseen by a political ruler, the Antichrist. Nimrod, according to tradition and mythology, was considered the greatest hunter of the ancient world, and he trained a leopard to hunt with him and wore leopard skins. "The purpose of this alliance between the woman and the beast is that both are seeking world domination," John F. Walvoord wrote. "When this is finally achieved, as the end of this chapter indicates, the political power will no longer need the religious power to support it."[11]

Revelation 18 offers more details about geopolitical-military Babylon. In the Old Testament, Babylon had taken God's people captive. In Revelation, the apostle John uses the metaphor to describe the world power that enslaves the world's inhabitants in the end times. "Chapter 18 describes the destruction of the city of Babylon, which is the seat of the Antichrist's political and economic power," according to *Halley's Bible Handbook*. "Three groups mourn as they see the city of Babylon burn and be utterly destroyed, and with it the heart of the political and commercial system; the kings, the merchants, and the seaman (perhaps a figurative term referring to someone who makes or collects money from the 'sea' of mankind). Here John seems to describe a corrupt form of capitalism that eventually brings destruction to the world."[12]

Regardless of what role America may play in this Babylonian system, Jan Markell says the nation will likely become part of the end-times global government. "I think America as we speak is rapidly diminishing in every respect—culturally, morally, spiritually, and diplomatically," Markell says. "I think it's going to continue this way and I think America is going to slip into near irrelevancy and then blend into the end-times form of global government, which I believe is literally over the horizon. It's racing toward us like a freight train. Is it a month, ten years, twenty years, who knows? But I think it's very soon."[13]

"Babylon the Great"

While Revelation 17 refers to "Mystery, Babylon," Revelation 18 is focused on "Babylon the Great." In this chapter, the apostle John wrote that Babylon's destruction is mainly due to its "spiritual and economic adultery." In fact, God's people are commanded to "come out of her" (Rev. 18:4 NIV) so they will not experience God's wrath for her sins. The Bible indicates that God destroys Babylon for its excessive materialism and for killing the saints.[14]

As opposed to theories that contend the end-times Babylon is headquartered in one central location—the EU, America, the rebuilt city of Babylon, or elsewhere—we believe the apostle John is referring to a global geopolitical and military system that will dominate the world during the Tribulation. A key feature of this colossal power is its international scope.

For decades, and increasingly in recent years, globalists in Europe, America, and throughout the world have been slowly changing laws, enacting treaties, and taking other steps to guide an unsuspecting world into this worldwide matrix.

"Today's globalism is a sign of the end times," Thomas Ice says. "It's the fact that no matter what happens—globalism is the answer for the world community. You have the revived Roman Empire rising in the EU. These are preparations for what will happen after the Rapture. Even though they are not fulfillments of Bible prophecy, it's stage-setting. You see all this coming together for the first time in history. People say, 'Christians have always thought that Christ was going to come back in their day.' I have a couple of degrees in church history and I have studied this extensively. Usually, the indicators are things like moral decline and very flexible things rather than actual historical events like Israel coming back into the land...and the rise and development of globalism. In the last fifty years, there has been a global consciousness that has never happened before. Intellectuals around the world believe the only answers to man's problems are some type of global rule or community."[15]

Ice and other prophecy experts believe that today's globalism movement will ultimately help usher in the arrival of a political figure that will oversee this world state.

Daniel 7 and Revelation 13 and 16 indicate that this world dictator will usurp people's freedom of worship, speech, and commerce. Daniel 7:25 notes that he also will make alterations in God's most basic laws, yet will face little opposition to his reign of power at the beginning. "My thesis...is the reason he will be able to gain such power with little opposition is because people will already have been conditioned to surrendering their rights to government before the Antichrist ever comes on the scene," Robert Jeffress says. "I believe that's what we are seeing right now."[16]

For example, the federal government recently told a nuns' society, the Little Sisters of the Poor Home for the Aged, that they needed to surrender their personal objections to abortion and contraceptives for the greater good of providing contraception free of charge to all American women. In Colorado, the government ordered a baker, against his religious convictions, to create a cake for a gay wedding or face punitive fines. In this regard, Jeffress has concerns about President Obama's support for same-sex marriage. "Never in U.S. history had a president proposed such a sweeping change in God's moral law as President Obama has in his embrace of gay marriage," Jeffress says. "There is a fundamental law of God that says marriage is between a man and a woman, and yet President Obama was able to champion and lead an effort to support homosexual marriage, and after doing so…he was able to win reelection by a comfortable margin…I'm simply using some of his policies to illustrate how a future world dictator may be able to make such sweeping changes in society without opposition."[17]

Jeffress's remarks follow similar ones made by Hal Lindsey in 2008. In a WND.com column, the author of *The Late Great Planet Earth* noted how Obama in his famous Berlin speech described the crowd as "fellow citizens of the world." "People of Berlin—people of the world—this is our moment. This is our time…With an eye toward the future, with resolve in our hearts, let us remember this history, and answer our destiny, and remake the world once again," Obama told the crowd. Obama is correct in saying that the world is ready for someone like him—"a messiah-like figure, charismatic and glib and seemingly holding all the answers to all the world's questions," Lindsey observed. "And the Bible says that such a leader will soon make his appearance on the scene. It won't be Barack Obama, but Obama's world tour provided a foretaste of the reception he can expect to receive. He will probably also stand in some European capital, addressing the people of the world and telling them that he is the one that they have been waiting for…The Bible calls that leader the Antichrist," Lindsey wrote. "And it seems apparent that the world is now ready to make his acquaintance."[18]

Is America's Decline Paving the Way for a Global Leader?

In early 2014, Jan Markell followed up on Lindsey's prediction, examining whether America's decline is paving the way for the Antichrist. She noted that Pulitzer Prize–winning syndicated columnist Charles Krauthammer wrote several commentaries about the "lawlessness" now playing out in America. In his columns, Krauthammer opined that when national and world leaders act lawlessly the people feel empowered to do the same. "It was open season on Jews and Christians around the world," Markell wrote. "And while Christians paid with their lives in many places, Christians in America were monitored, censored, shamed, scolded, and called hate groups (such as the American Family Association). In the military, they were reprimanded and told they could not share their faith. Christian media called the war on Christians, particularly in the Middle East, 'the unreported catastrophe of our times.' And it doesn't seem to be a concern to people in the pews or behind the pulpit. It is just not talked about. The details are tragic, vulgar, painful, and make everyone uncomfortable. Perhaps that explains the silence. Since spying was and continues to be such big business, we can only assume that the Antichrist system is being installed... The worldwide system of control is progressing rapidly! Even the healthcare law is about control, not health."[19]

In recent years, many politicians and political commentators have expressed concerns about the similarities between new laws and policies in America and those in Nazi Germany in the run-up to World War II. For instance, Dr. Ben Carson, a retired neurosurgeon and Republican candidate for president in 2016, described the United States as being in a "pre-fascist" era. In the wake of revelations about National Security Agency spying, the government health care takeover, and Internal Revenue Service intimidation of conservatives, Carson says the elite are using the Alinsky method to "achieve their one-world vision and their utopian society." This method calls for the destruction of America's Judeo-Christian values by stirring up divisions at every level of American society—"women against men, old against young, race against race, rich against poor," Carson told WND.com. "This is pre-fascist thinking. A lot of the liberals don't realize that," Carson said. "They don't know that they're being used. As Lenin said, you know, useful idiots.

We can use these people to actually change America and they won't even know that they are our puppets and we are using them."[20]

Carson's concerns are echoed by many others, including Tom DeLay, the former House Majority Leader and Texas congressman who says President Obama has ignored constitutional principles and Americans are "now living under a government of tyranny." "What we have now is a president who has accelerated the progressive movement that started back with Teddy Roosevelt and Woodrow Wilson... to such an extent that I now can tell you that we're living under a government of tyranny," DeLay told *Newsmax*. "When you have a president that is cruel and unfair to the people using his powers to undermine the Constitution of the United States [in order] to create a... monarchy within the presidency, and ignores the Congress and the Judicial Branch, you have tyranny. Redistribution of wealth is tyranny. Taking private property is tyranny."[21]

In her newsletter article "Hope and Change: Haunting Comparisons," Markell wrote that Germans were seduced in the 1930s by promises of "hope and change," along with handouts and government checks. Today, about half of Americans are receiving some form of government funds. "They simply had no idea that Hitler's 'hope and change' would cause the swastika to be burned across the very fabric of Europe," Markell stated. "There are haunting comparisons in America to Nazi Germany." Markell listed a few of the comparisons between 1938 Germany and today's America, including the fact that few people resisted the demise of capitalism and the rise of socialism, the 1935 elimination of school prayer, widespread abortion, socialized medicine, proliferation of child daycare, soaring government spending and taxation, gun registration followed by gun confiscation, elimination of free speech, a "green agenda... steeped in paganism," a church that "did not want to make waves" or "tackle controversy," and pulpits that "would never address serious issues or politics" amid Hitler's rise to power.[22]

During a recent speech at the University of California, Berkeley, U.S. senator Rand Paul, R-Ky., expressed alarm over the nation's direction, saying he is concerned about "who is truly in charge of our government." "Most of you have read the dystopian nightmares and maybe, like me, you doubted that it could ever happen in America," Paul told the audience. "If the CIA is spying on Congress, who exactly can or will stop them? I look into the eyes of senators and I think I see real fear. Maybe it's just my imagination, but I think I perceive fear of an intelligence community drunk with power, unrepentant, and uninclined to relinquish power." In a *Newsmax* article, Paul said President Obama is turning the United States into a "socialist nightmare." During an appearance on Glenn Beck's radio show, Paul said that America's problems run far deeper than politics, and the nation is in need of a spiritual awakening and revival. "I think that our country needs a spiritual cleansing," Paul told Beck. "I really think we need a revival in this country...I think our country's problems are deeper than political—that we need spiritual leaders to come forward. We need something beyond just the politics of the day and, you know, I see it everywhere—something really depraved is rising in the country."[23]

"The Game Plan" to Create a Global Government

Amid these concerns, a growing number of prominent figures say there is a "plan" to create a global government. In rather stunning articles in *Newsmax* and the *Nation,* U.S. representative Dana Rohrabacher, R-Calif., said global warming is a "fraud" being used as a tool to create a "global government." "And at the federal government, they want to create global government to control all of our lives," Rohrabacher told those gathered at a Newport Mesa Tea Party group. "That's what the game plan is. It's step by step by step, more and bigger control over our lives by higher levels of government. And global warming is that strategy in spades."[24]

Going beyond simply calls for a New World Order or what Pope Benedict described as a "world political authority," the global governance movement is seeking to extend the EU model to the rest of the world, especially America. "Global governancers see America, along with countries like Israel and India, as stubborn hold-outs for supposedly dated notions of national independence," Stanley Kurtz wrote in his *National Review* article. "If the party of global governance can ensnare America, Gulliver-style, in a tangle of transnational principles, precedents, and institutions, American military independence can effectively be nullified, and even our domestic policies can be brought into conformity with European norms in time. If this seems unlikely, consider that the E.U.'s ruling bureaucratic elite has already captured a significant portion of the sovereign powers of its member states, although that elite is largely unanswerable to any voting public... How did it come about that Europe's sovereign democracies ceded their sovereignty to an independent elite whose policy views were substantially to the left of the European public? How was even Margaret Thatcher defeated in her attempt to prevent Britain from surrendering many of its sovereign powers to the E.U.? Fonte shows exactly how it happened, and why the United States is next in line—if the global governancers get their way... America's sovereignty could someday be substantially subordinated to a transnational progressive-elite-E.U.-style. That is the global governance movement's long-term plan."[25]

Already, the UN has divided the world into ten regions—raising concerns among prophecy scholars whether these regions could be the ten "horns," or kingdoms, of Revelation 17:12 (NLT) who "reign" with the Antichrist during the Tribulation: "The ten horns of the beast are ten kings who have not yet risen to power. They will be appointed to their kingdoms for one brief moment to reign with the beast," the apostle John wrote.[26]

In the early 1970s, the Club of Rome—a global think tank consisting of about one hundred wealthy and powerful individuals and thirty-five national associations—released a study that revealed the club's plan to divide the world into ten political-economic regions. The report found this would boost the world's economy. The authors also made the point that replacing currency with some type of cashless system would boost the world economy by as much as 20 percent. "All of that kind of fits into passages you see in the Bible where you can't buy or sell unless you submit to a governmental system and how everybody is going to get a number—666," Hugh Ross says. "The Club of Rome pointed out that this would have a huge boost to the economic well-being of the world. That may be the way we end up with a [world government] where you basically have these Technocrats saying, 'Hey, if you're willing to submit to a confederacy of ten nations that you are going to be a lot wealthier and you are going to have greater well-being.'"[27]

The elite recognize that it won't be possible to create a world government in one fell swoop because many people around the world, especially Christians, are opposed to it and know about the Bible's predictions regarding an end-times world system. For decades now, millions of Americans have read books or articles and seen films about how the Bible predicts the rise of a global government, economy, and religion in the end times. Nevertheless, billions of people outside of America are largely unaware of these biblical predictions or consider them ramblings of overzealous believers. "The people [in Europe] really don't want it, but of course the people of great wealth have put their own people into positions of power as rulers in most of the countries in Europe," Stanley Monteith says. "The plan here in the United States is to unite Mexico, the U.S., and Canada into the United States of North America. They want to do the same thing with Central America, South America,

Africa, and Asia. There are ten regions in the world, and the whole idea is to unite them all into a one-world government. The people of America don't want this, but of course they don't understand what's really going on because these elements dominate both political parties and are using the financial power of the U.S. to unite all these unions into a one-world government."[28]

This plan, experts say, has been carefully orchestrated for decades and involves a methodically laid-out series of steps. In a recent *Wall Street Journal* article about his book *World Order*, Henry Kissinger seemed to confirm this strategy, saying a "world order of states" should be "our inspiration." "But progress toward it will need to be sustained through a series of intermediary stages," Kissinger wrote.[29]

An Accelerated Plan for a World Federation

In 1958, the World Constitution and Parliament Association was founded to create an Earth Constitution and to promote its ratification. Since 1983, the organization has been holding sessions of the provisional World Parliament, says Glen T. Martin, president of the association and a professor of philosophy and chair of the Peace Studies Program at Radford University in Radford, Virginia.[30]

Martin's organization is just one of many federalist groups around the world that are working toward the creation of a global government. Some of the planet's "world government visionaries," according to the association, have included British prime minister Winston Churchill; broadcast journalist Walter Cronkite; theoretical physicist Albert Einstein; author and biochemistry professor Isaac Asimov; U.S. Supreme Court justice William O. Douglas; Soviet statesman Mikhail Gorbachev; poet, playwright, and novelist Victor Hugo; UN secretary-general Robert Muller; philosopher, mathematician, and historian Bertrand Russell; philosopher Jean-Jacques Rousseau; U.S. president Harry S. Truman; author

H. G. Wells; classical Greek Athenian philosopher Alfred Tennyson; and Greek philosopher Socrates. Today, the world federalist movement is especially strong in Europe.[31]

In his classic 1940 nonfiction book, *The New World Order,* Wells advocated the creation of a "new world order" to unite the nations to bring peace and end war. "Step by step and here and there it will arrive, and even as it comes into being it will develop fresh perspectives, discover unsuspected problems and go on to new adventures," predicted Wells, who is best known for his science-fiction novels *The War of the Worlds, The Time Machine,* and *The Island of Doctor Moreau.* "No man, no group of men, will ever be singled out as its father or founder. For its maker will be not this man nor that man nor any man but Man, that being who is in some measure in every one of us. World order will be, like science, like most inventions, a social product, an innumerable number of personalities will have lived fine lives, pouring their best into the collective achievement."[32]

In another one of his books, *The Open Conspiracy*—described as a "guidebook on world control and management"—Wells openly lays out the plan that globalists seem to be following today: "To avoid the positive evils of war and to attain the new levels of prosperity and power that now come into view, an effective world control, not merely of armed force, but of the production and main movements of staple commodities and the drift and expansion of population, is required," Wells wrote. "On the political side it is plain that our lives must be given to the advancement of that union."[33]

Today, Wells's vision is coming to fruition as the world undergoes a "paradigm shift." "People's thinking is transforming quickly because we are facing global climate collapse and we're facing repeatedly the possibility of a nuclear holocaust," Martin says. "People contact us all the time, and some of them are prominent people, who say, '...I found out what you are doing and I want to be a part of it.' So we think there is going to be a very large transformation of people's attitudes that is going to bring the Earth Constitution to prominence on earth."[34]

The calls for a world government and constitution come amid growing disenchantment with the current form of "global governance," the way in which global affairs are currently managed. "When discussing global governance, it is failures that come to mind rather than achievements," wrote the authors of a Brookings Institution report, "Pillars of Global Governance." "Never-ending wars in the Middle East, humanitarian interventions turning into humanitarian catastrophes, the remaining enormous North-South gap, a sequel to the 2008 financial crisis at the gates—these all bear witness to the fact that the current system of global governance does not quite work as well as it should."[35]

For years, federalists thought the dream of a world state would take many decades, possibly a century or more. "On the surface of it—in the early 21st century—our planet seems to be descending into global war and planetary chaos," Martin wrote in his article "Planetary Maturity and Our Global Social Contract." "The so-called 'war on terror,' the fragmentation of some 193 supposedly 'sovereign' nation-states, the egoism and greed of the tiny ruling class that controls 50 percent of the world's wealth and most of its power, the spread of weapons, wars, and violence around the globe—all these phenomena give the impression of a divided world that cannot conceive of a viable, coherent, and peaceful future."[36]

However, as a result of climate change and the growing threat of nuclear war, Martin says, momentum is building to accelerate plans to create a planetary federation. "We don't have to evolve over decades and decades and have the earth eventually write its own constitution and develop a system within the next hundred years or so," Martin says. "The climate collapse is happening now and the danger of nuclear holocaust continues now. We need to ratify this constitution as soon as possible."[37]

Currently, Democratic World Federalists, a San Francisco–based civil society that advocates world government, envisions several paths toward the creation of what they call a "World Federation." One of the most popular methods would involve fundamental changes in the UN to form a "World Federation." One of the leading organizations promoting this strategy is the Campaign for a United Nations Parliamentary Assembly. Others have proposed that a "World Federation" can be achieved by first uniting democratic nations around the globe. Over time, as nations see the benefits, countries would join the federation.

The most feasible plan, expert says, involves uniting regional federations—such as the EU, African Union, Association of Southeast Asian Nations, the Arab League, Organization of American States, and the Union of South American Nations—into a "World Federation." "Some have proposed that a democratic world federation can best be achieved in two steps," wrote the authors of the Democratic World Federalists article "Paths to a World Federation." "First, the regions of the world would integrate into separate federations. The United States did this in 1787 when it went from 13 colonies under the Articles of Confederation into the United States of America under a federal constitution. The nations of Europe are currently bringing that region together and creating a European Union. Many other regions of the world are in earlier stages of forming regional unions. In the second step these separate regional unions and federations would join together to form a World Federation with a world constitution."[38]

Currently, a number of organizations are researching the development of regional unions as a means to create a "World Federation," including the UN University Institute on Comparative Regional Integration and the Union of European Federalists.

"As a psychologist, if you look at the global system, the geopolitical system, it's pretty obvious that we're not going to get rid of nuclear weapons unless we have a world union," says Roger Kotila, a psychologist and peace activist, editor of *Earth Federation News & Views*, past president of Democratic World Federalists, and the vice president of the World Constitution and Parliament Association.[39]

But most experts say it will likely take some major crisis before the governments of the world agree to create a global union. Many believe world leaders won't agree to a world government until the planet suffers an apocalyptic catastrophe, such as economic collapse, uncontrolled climate change, nuclear war, or the growing chaos and violence resulting from increased competition for dwindling resources.

"I think as long as things are going along decently people will be okay," Mark Hitchcock says. "But another catastrophe or another near unraveling of the world economy is going to cause people to have to establish some new kind of framework—a New World Order or whatever they are going to call it—and that is definitely coming according to the Bible."[40]

Will Babylon Rise Again?

While most prophecy experts believe the New World Order will emerge out of the European Union or America, some believe it will be headquartered in the rebuilt city of Babylon in Iraq. We believe the end-times Babylonian system will have multiple geographic centers, and modern Babylon could very well be one of them.

Under Nimrod's rule, ancient Babylon was the world's first world government, economic system, and religion. According to Bible prophecy, this Babylonian system will arise again in the last days.

Today, some Bible scholars believe ancient Babylon will be rebuilt to its former glory as end-times events unfold. Former Iraqi dictator Saddam Hussein began the process of rebuilding ancient Babylon. Hussein believed he was the ancient king of Babylon—King Nebuchadnezzar—reborn in modern times. The prophet Daniel interpreted the dreams and visions of King Nebuchadnezzar during the seventy-year captivity of the Jews in Babylon in the sixth century BC. "It was at this time that God gave Daniel many of his prophetic visions," Thomas Ice wrote in his article "Babylon in Bible Prophecy." "Babylon is the first of four great kingdoms to arise during the 'time of the Gentiles' (Dan. 2 and 7). History reveals that Babylon declined until it was abandoned about two centuries after Christ. Although the city of Babylon sank beneath the sands of time during the past seventeen hundred years, it has begun to rise in [the twentieth century]. Watch for Babylon to become a dominant force in the world religiously, commercially and governmentally for Revelation 17–18 predicts the destruction of that city and, in order to be the city those prophecies require, it must be rebuilt on a grand scale like in the days of Nebuchadnezzar."[41]

Ironically, ancient Babylon was known as Bab-Ili or "Gate of Ili," which means "illumined ones." Today, it's no accident that the center of geopolitical and military conflict and control is in Iraq and the Middle East. Some believe Iraq is the location of the Garden of Eden, along with the Tower of Babel.

In Revelation, we read about the rise of a geopolitical and military Babylon in the last days. Is it mere coincidence that both President George H. W. Bush and his son, President George W. Bush, invaded Iraq? Is it merely circumstantial that the international terrorist organization ISIS is heavily concentrated in Iraq?

By comparing current events with biblical predictions, it seems clear that the world is moving toward a global government, economy, and religion that will be ruled by a charismatic ruler known as the Antichrist. As head of both the global economic system and the global religion, the False Prophet will require the entire world to worship the Antichrist as God. According to Revelation, those who refuse will be beheaded—a form of execution many thought was abandoned following the French Revolution but has been revived recently by ISIS and other terrorist groups in the Middle East. Meanwhile, the False Prophet will also manage a global cashless society where no one will be able to buy or sell without the mark of the Beast.

"The biblical prophecies portend a one-world government, currency, and religion," says Jerry B. Jenkins, coauthor of the Left Behind series. "The speed with which we're approaching those is astounding and alarming even to me."[42]

Since the mid-1600s, when Bacon planned for America to become the New Atlantis, America has played a significant role in the emergence of this global Babylonian order.

Currently, America is the world's predominant geopolitical and military superpower, but that could change. Curiously, the global battle against ISIS—a terrorist group gaining infamy worldwide for beheading Americans and crucifying Christians—may result in America once again occupying Iraq, one of the possible centers for the end-times Babylonian system. Even now there are American troops occupying Babylon once again.

Mystery, Babylon: "A Multiethnic, Multicultural Superpower"

While some prophecy experts believe the "Babylon" of Revelation 17–18 refers to the rebuilt city of Babylon in Iraq, Steve Cioccolanti says the apostle John chose to distinguish the "Babylon he saw prophetically from the Babylon his audience would have surely known about from history." The Bible offers clues to the identity of "Mystery, Babylon" and "Babylon the Great," describing it as a great economic power, a maritime power, located on "many waters" (Rev. 17:1 NKJV) and whose destruction brings mourning to the whole world. The apostle John wrote that the kings of the earth would "weep and lament" for her when "they see the smoke of her burning, standing at a distance for fear of her torment, saying, 'Alas, alas, that great city Babylon, that mighty city!' " (Rev. 18:-9–10 NKJV). The sea merchants will also "stand at a distance for fear of her torment, weeping and wailing, and saying, 'Alas, alas, that great city…such great riches came to nothing'" (Rev. 18:15–17 NKJV).

"'Alas, alas' is repeated three times by two different groups of ruling elites: the politicians and the businessmen," Cioccolanti says. "Three times it was reiterated that they 'stood at a distance' as if being in close proximity would endanger their lives. This is congruent with fear of nuclear radiation contamination or a natural catastrophe beyond our comprehension, such as would result from the meteorite impacts described in both trumpet and bowl judgments…The potential destruction of Saudi Arabia by earthquake, meteor strike, or nuclear bomb would certainly bring a lot of crying and wailing among the Muslims. I am not sure they would stand at a distance in this case rather than rush to the rescue of Mecca, Medina, or Riyadh. The only nation whose collapse would make a difference to the entire world, and keep the world at a literal distance, is America. The main reason behind this is not obvious to most Christians. It was Alfred Mahan in *The Influence of Sea Power upon History* who stated, 'Whoever rules the waves rules the world.' What makes America the only current superpower is her unsurpassed protection from both oceans and her ability to control both oceans: Atlantic and Pacific. Due to blessings of geography, America is uniquely positioned to control the world. This 'good fortune' is even more important than the fact that its dollar is the world's reserve currency. World currency could theoretically be changed, but what can never be changed is that America is the only superpower with an Atlantic and Pacific coastline…America also metaphorically 'sits on many waters.' God made a point of sending an angel to explain the metaphor to John, 'The waters which you saw, where the harlot sits, are peoples, multitudes, nations and tongues.' In other words, we have another clue about Mystery Babylon. It is a multi-ethnic, multicultural superpower."[43]

More than any other nation, Cioccolanti says, the apostle John's description in Revelation of "Mystery, Babylon" seems to describe

America. "By several measures, America fits the end-time description of a super-economic power which controls sea commerce and whose destruction by earthquake, meteor strike, or nuclear explosion will send shock waves across the world," Cioccolanti says. "Moreover, America controls the media. Literally, the eyes of the world are on America. It makes sense that God would mention America in his end-time scenario. America did not exist at the time of the writing of the Bible, so it's understandable that an alternative name had to be used. The apostle John may have referred to this mysterious country by a code name 'Mystery, Babylon' because the 'New World'...had not yet been named 'America' in honor of Italian cartographer Amerigo Vespucci [1454–1512]. It also makes sense that God does not name 'America' by its future name, for then God would have to be credited with naming two continents and a country before they were discovered. God does not privilege America with such distinction. The only nation on earth God personally named is Israel."[44]

Where Will the Antichrist Emerge?

Let's turn our attention now to the Antichrist and his role in the end-times Babylonian system.

The Bible notes that the Antichrist will be a false Christ, a counterfeit who takes the place of Christ. We believe the deception will be so strong that people of various faiths will accept the Antichrist as the world's savior.[45]

In his book *Who Is the Antichrist?: Answering the Question Everyone Is Asking*, Mark Hitchcock notes that the Antichrist will be an intellectual, oratorical, political, economic, military, and religious genius who will be "all things to all men" and together with the False Prophet will pull off the greatest deception in world history. Hitchcock believes the Antichrist will arise from a "confederation of nations that in some way corresponds to the Old Roman Empire"—a conclusion supported by numerous passages in Daniel and Revelation. In a particularly interesting section of the book, Hitchcock outlines the "Top 10 Keys to Antichrist's Identity." Hitchcock points out that the people will not recognize the Antichrist initially, he will rise to "world prominence as the pied piper of international peace," will be a Gentile world ruler from the geographic region of the Roman Empire, will rule over the reunited Roman Empire, will make a seven-year peace treaty with Israel, will be assassinated and "come back to life," will break his treaty with Israel at the midpoint of the Tribulation and invade the nation, will go into the rebuilt Temple and declare that he is God, will desecrate the Temple by placing an image of himself in it, and will rule the entire world.[46]

"While I want to emphasize that no one can say for sure whether the Antichrist is alive today, I wouldn't be surprised if he is," Hitchcock wrote. "Many of the key pieces of the prophetic puzzle for the last days seem to be coming together. We have the United States of Europe coming together before our eyes in the form of the European Union. Globalism is here, and the advanced technology necessary for starting up a one-world government and economy already exists. Crises of epic proportions are erupting with sobering frequency and regularity, paving the way for more and more change. The world is ripe for a peacemaker, especially one who can bring peace to the Middle East...Again, all the indicators that the end times are on the horizon seem to be coming together. The emergence of the Antichrist could take place very soon. Which would mean the coming of the Lord is even closer. Are you ready to meet Him at His coming?"[47]

Chapter Eleven

Economic Babylon

The devil, taking Him up on a high mountain, showed Him all the kingdoms of the world in a moment of time. And the devil said to Him, "All this authority I will give You, and their glory; for this has been delivered to me, and I give it to whomever I wish. Therefore, if You will worship before me, all will be Yours." And Jesus answered and said to him, "Get behind Me, Satan! For it is written, 'You shall worship the LORD your God, and Him only you shall serve.'"

—LUKE THE EVANGELIST (LUKE 4:5–8 NKJV)

As the world digs itself into unparalleled levels of debt, many are beginning to ask how it will all end. A recent International Monetary Fund report by two Harvard University professors found that debt levels in the Western world have reached a two-hundred-year high. Some financial experts estimate the world's debts, including public and private, unfunded liabilities, and outstanding derivatives, now exceed $1.5 quadrillion. Noting that policy makers and others worldwide are in "denial" about the magnitude of the problem, the Harvard professors wrote that the "endgame of the global financial crisis" is likely to require "financial repression" and a "restructuring" of the world's economic system.[1]

"The magnitude of the overall debt problem facing advanced economies today is difficult to overstate," Harvard economists Carmen

Reinhart and Kenneth Rogoff wrote in the report for the International Monetary Fund. "The current central government debt in advanced economies is approaching a two-century high-water mark."[2]

World leaders and economic experts are warning that the global economy is near collapse. "We are excluding an entire generation to sustain a system that is not good," Pope Francis was quoted as saying in the *Huffington Post* article titled "Pope Francis Warns the Global Economy Is Near Collapse." "Our global economic system can't take any more. The rate of unemployment is very worrisome to me, which in some countries is over 50 percent... That is an atrocity. We discard a whole generation to maintain an economic system that no longer endures, a system that to survive has to make war, as the big empires have always done. But since we cannot wage the Third World War, we make regional wars. And what does that mean? That we make and sell arms. And with that the balance sheets of the idolatrous economies—the big world economies that sacrifice man at the feet of the idol of money."[3]

James Rickards, the senior managing director of Tangent Capital Partners and the *New York Times* bestselling author of *The Death of Money: The Coming Collapse of the International Monetary System*, is warning that the prognosis for the global financial system is indeed dire. "I'm just trying to prepare the reader for first of all, the fact that it's coming, and secondly as an investor what you can do now to protect yourself," Rickards told *Newsmax*.[4]

Many prophecy scholars and others believe the worldwide recession and international debt crisis was just the initial stage in a series of events that will lead to a global economic system foretold by the prophets. "What if the global financial chaos is not just a massive economic meltdown but the genesis of a dramatic, tectonic shift toward a global economic system? A system that will ultimately be controlled by one man? A system that will ultimately require all people to be registered and submit to him," Mark Hitchcock wrote in *The End of Money*.[5]

Since the Great Recession plunged the world into chaos in 2008, governments have taken a series of steps to increase cooperation and oversight of the world economy. Many world leaders believe the creation of a new global financial system will help prevent future economic crises. Britain's former prime minister Gordon Brown has called for a "global New Deal" and said the global recession was an opportunity "to create a truly global society." Former secretary of state Kissinger, a member of the CFR, predicted that within the next several years the world would witness the emergence of a "New International Order."[6]

Incredibly, the Bible predicted nearly two thousand years ago that a global dictator would one day take control of the world economy and a cashless society. This prediction is contained in Revelation 13:16–18: "He calls all, both great and small, rich and poor, free and slave, to receive a mark on their right hand or on their foreheads, so that no one may buy or sell except one who has the mark or the name of the beast, or the number of his name. Here is wisdom. Let him who has understanding calculate the number of the beast, for it is the number of a man: His number is 666" (NKJV).

The Ultimate, Cosmic Businessman

The historical account of Babylon and the Tower of Babel is the record of the world's first world government, economic system, and religion. God judged this empire because it was an attempt by humanity to build a kingdom on earth that both rejected God and fulfilled the plan of Lucifer. The story of Babylon is also a prophetic warning of what is to come in the future.

The world's first economy existed in the Garden of Eden. It was a perfect world in every way and its inhabitants lacked nothing until they rejected the Word of God and obeyed Lucifer, who became the temporary god of this world. In Ezekiel 28—a chapter that Bible scholars describe as Satan's biography—we read how Lucifer is the ultimate, cosmic businessman with a supernatural understanding of economics. Ezekiel 28 provides a wealth of information about Satan and his activities involving the financial affairs of mankind:

> *Because your heart is lifted up,*
> *And you say, "I am a god,*
> *I sit in the seat of gods,*
> *In the midst of the seas"…*
> *With your wisdom and your understanding*
> *You have gained riches for yourself,*
> *And gathered gold and silver into your treasuries;*
> *By your great wisdom in trade you have increased your riches,*
> *And your heart is lifted up because of your riches…*
> *You were the seal of perfection,*
> *Full of wisdom and perfect in beauty.*
> *You were in Eden, the garden of God;*
> *Every precious stone was your covering:*
> *The sardius, topaz, and diamond,*
> *Beryl, onyx, and jasper,*
> *Sapphire, turquoise, and emerald with gold.*
> *The workmanship of your timbrels and pipes*
> *Was prepared for you on the day you were created.*
> *You were the anointed cherub who covers;*
> *I established you;*
> *You were on the holy mountain of God;*
> *You walked back and forth in the midst of fiery stones.*
> *You were perfect in your ways from the day you were created,*
> *Till iniquity was found in you.*
> *By the abundance of your trading*
> *You became filled with violence within,*

And you sinned;
Therefore I cast you as a profane thing
Out of the mountain of God;
And I destroyed you, O covering cherub,
From the midst of the fiery stones.
Your heart was lifted up because of your beauty;
You corrupted your wisdom for the sake of your splendor;
I cast you to the ground,
I laid you before kings,
That they might gaze at you.
You defiled your sanctuaries
By the multitude of your iniquities,
By the iniquity of your trading;
Therefore I brought fire from your midst;
It devoured you,
And I turned you to ashes upon the earth
In the sight of all who saw you.
All who knew you among the peoples are astonished at you;
You have become a horror,
And shall be no more forever. (vv. 2–5, 12–19 NKJV)

"The God of This World"

The Bible is the only book with supernatural authorship, and its detailed emphasis on the global economic activities of Lucifer is not an accident. When Lucifer, "the serpent of old," instigated the fall of man, he became the temporary "god of this world." As such, Lucifer created systems of economics, government, and religion based upon satanic ideas. Ultimately, this is called the Babylonian or world system. The Bible contains a firm prophetic warning that Satan's global economic system will be destroyed by God shortly before the Second Coming. The eighteenth chapter of Revelation describes what Bible scholars call economic or commercial Babylon.

Revelation 18 offers a detailed description of a great commercial nation. This chapter details how the entire world produces the products that Babylon consumes, how the world's nations trade with Babylon—surrounded by "many waters"—via ships, and how Babylon is destroyed in one hour, prompting the merchants to panic.[7] Revelation 18:17–20 offers this account:

> "For in one hour such great riches came to nothing." Every ship-master, all who travel by ship, sailors, and as many as trade on the sea, stood at a distance and cried out when they saw the smoke of her burning, saying, "What is like this great city?" They threw dust on their heads and cried out, weeping and wailing, and saying, "Alas, alas, that great city, in which all who had ships on the sea became rich by her wealth! For in one hour she is made desolate." Rejoice over her, O heaven, and you holy apostles and prophets, for God has avenged you on her! (NKJV)

Verse 21 goes on to say: "Then a mighty angel took up a stone like a great millstone and threw it into the sea, saying, 'Thus with violence the great city Babylon shall be thrown down, and shall not be found anymore'" (NKJV).

One of the most powerful truths in the Bible is that money, economics, business, and commerce are at their foundation spiritual systems. This was commonly known in ancient Babylon and has been passed down through various empires such as Egypt, Greece, and Rome and institutions such as the international banking system set up by the Bavarian Illuminati in the late eighteenth century. The very wealthiest people in the world are fully aware of this, and that is why the select few who actually control the world's wealth belong to organizations such as Skull and Bones, Bohemian Grove, and the Bilderberg Group. The elite understand that ultimately the economy is connected to a Luciferian spiritual-economic system.

Lucifer is the temporary god of this world and controls its economics. When the devil tempted Jesus with all the kingdoms of this world it was because he, at least in a temporal sense, owns and is ruler of the world's assets. The biographical accounts of Satan in the Old Testament depict him as a master economist, industrialist, and international financier— trading with the kings and businessmen of the world. The devil thrives on two principles: first, an absolute lust for power and a desire to become God; and second, the use of highly sophisticated economic strategies to accomplish that goal. Revelation describes Lucifer as the head of the Babylonian geopolitical, commercial, and religious system with control of the total world gross domestic product. There is a reason why the apostle Paul warned of the dangers of the "love of money" in 1 Timothy 6:10 and why Jesus said in Matthew 6:24 that people can't serve God and riches: "No one can serve two masters; for either he will hate the one and love the other, or else he will be loyal to the one and despise the other. You cannot serve God and mammon" (NKJV).

Embedded within the secret teachings of ancient Babylon is a code— one based upon satanic power—to control money, government, and humanity. This secret has been passed down from generation to generation through occult societies with an untold number of different names. Remember, it's all about subterfuge and secrecy.

The Satanic System of Economics

Many believe and there is strong evidence to suggest that actual Illuminati bloodline families do exist and comprise the ruling class of our world. Within the secrets of "Mystery, Babylon" is a satanic system of economics that has enabled Lucifer's followers to accumulate the world's wealth at a level no ordinary person could ever achieve.

In his book *The Illuminati in America, 1776–2008*, former MI6 intelligence agent John Coleman wrote that John Robison "uncovered considerable evidence in the British Museum" that Illuminati founder Adam Weishaupt was a "mere servant of the Rothschilds." In addition to this famous family, Coleman wrote that the Illuminati is composed of twelve other families that are part of a "political society" and "secret government" that use the organization's "great secrecy" to methodically advance its agenda to create a global government, economic system, and religion. "Skull and Bones is controlled by thirteen families, all members of the Order of Illuminati," Coleman wrote. "These families have, since 1785, held the destiny of the United States in their hands." Since its creation in the late eighteenth century, the Illuminati have operated behind the scenes, instigating many revolutions and wars as part of a long-term plan to consolidate the world's wealth and power, according to Coleman. "The third great revolution the Illuminati organized is going on in America today," he wrote. "It is a revolution of spiritual anarchy, evolving into political and social anarchy, which, unless checked, will lead to religious anarchy and the collapse of the Republic of the United States and the ideals it stands for, as written into the Constitution by the Founding Fathers. In this, we are paralleling the collapse of Greece and Rome."[8]

Madame Helena Blavatsky, one of the world's most influential occultists, wrote books such as *Isis Unveiled* that taught, in part, about the occult elite who control the world system of finances. Blavatsky's disciple Alice Bailey, along with her husband, Foster, created an organization and publishing house in New York City called the Lucifer Publishing Company. Due to protests, the nonprofit organization moved several blocks to Wall Street and changed its name to the Lucis Trust. Today, the Lucis Trust is on the roster of the UN Economic and Social Council.

"The Baileys' reasons for choosing the original name are not known to us, but we can only surmise that they, like the great teacher H. P. Blavatsky, for whom they had enormous respect, sought to elicit a deeper understanding of the sacrifice made by Lucifer," according to the Lucis Trust website. "Alice and Foster Bailey were serious students and teachers of Theosophy, a spiritual tradition which views Lucifer as one of the solar angels, those advanced beings who Theosophy says descended (thus 'the fall') from Venus to our planet eons ago to bring the principle of mind to what was then animal-man. In the theosophical perspective, the descent of these solar angels was not a fall into sin or disgrace but rather an act of great sacrifice, as is suggested in the name 'Lucifer' which means light-bearer."[9]

At the highest levels of government, finance, culture, science, and politics, the elite are busy constructing a global economic order that will culminate with what is described in Revelation as the mark of the Beast system. The purpose of this system is "commerce and worship." During the Tribulation, people will be required to receive the mark or name of the Beast before they can conduct any type of business transactions. Those who refuse will face beheading or suffer enormous hardship and persecution. With the development of biometrics, radio frequency identification (RFID) chips, electronic tattoos, electronic payments, and similar technologies, prophecy scholars say the mark of the Beast system is now possible for the first time in history. In the not-too-distant future, futuristic thinkers say that "when people go to the market they will pick up the items they need and leave—without the benefit of paying a cashier," according to the *Catholic Online* article "Is the 'Mark of the Beast' the Future of Money?" "Sensors will identify a consumer by a mark, their way of walking or facial recognition. Will cash money—paper and coins, become extinct, for a system that calls forth the 'Mark of the Beast' as spoken in the book of Revelation?" Experts say the "global establishment" is increasingly promoting a "cashless society"—a world in which all payments and transactions would be conducted electronically, creating a permanent record for governments to monitor at will. The UN, along with governments in Africa, Asia, Europe, and the Americas, are working toward this goal.[10]

The Prelude to Economic Babylon

Behind the crisis involving Russia and the Ukraine is an attempt by the BRICS countries—Brazil, Russia, India, China, and South Africa—to replace the dollar with a "new world currency and full-fledged global governance." Russia is interested in the Ukraine in order to control the importing and exporting of oil. Currently, the dollar remains the de facto world currency because of U.S. military dominance of strategic oil-producing regions. Meanwhile, the crisis in Syria, Iran, Iraq, and other Middle Eastern nations has to do with control of massive oil supplies by Russia and Iran, who are exporting oil from Syria to Europe and China. The United States wants to control those oil supplies and if necessary will do so by military force. This trifecta of converging forces could ultimately result in an all-out military conflict between Russia, the Ukraine, the European Union, the United States, Great Britain, China, Syria, Iraq, Iran, and Israel over oil and the push by the BRICS to topple the dollar as the world's reserve currency.[11]

James G. Rickards, an attorney, a regular television commentator on finance, and the author of *Currency Wars: The Making of the Next Global Crisis*, says the next financial crisis will likely result in a new global reserve currency. "The next financial crisis is going to be bigger than the Fed," Rickards said on a recent episode of the *Peter Schiff Show*. "If the Fed already had to print out $4 trillion to bail out the system and there is another panic or crisis tomorrow, or next year, they can't just print another $4 trillion. I mean legally they can, but it's going to be way past the confidence limit. They will destroy confidence in the dollar. So the next crisis is going to be bigger than the Fed. That's going to go to the IMF [International Monetary Fund]. The IMF has a printing press. Not too many people know about it, but they have a printing press. They can print what they call Special Drawing Rights or SDRs. It sounds geeky, but it's pretty simple. SDRs are a world currency issued by the IMF. It's another kind of fiat currency. It's not backed by anything, but basically it will replace the dollar. People talk about the Chinese yuan. The Chinese yuan is not a reserve currency. It's not even close to being a reserve currency. The SDR, backed by the IMF, can function as a reserve currency."[12] This is what the "elites" are planning, Rickards told Schiff.

"I'm just telling you what the elites are going to try," Rickards said. "Again, whether I think it will work is irrelevant. The elites are going to try this. And when I say elites, again, it's not a deep, dark conspiracy. These are finance ministers, academics, central bankers; you know, the usual suspects running the international monetary system. They are going to try it, but it may fail for the reasons you suggest, which is, 'Hey, if I've lost confidence in the dollar, why should I have confidence in SDRs?'"[13]

At the root of this conflict over the world's currency is an effort to establish a global economic system. This is simply the prelude to the world financial system that eschatologists describe as economic Babylon. Many Bible scholars believe the rise of this global economic system will precede the creation of an international geopolitical system.

As the world becomes more chaotic, people will increasingly rely on the government for economic security. Many will be willing to give up even more of their freedoms in exchange for financial stability. Likewise, many sovereign states will be willing to join a global political body to be spared economic devastation.

"The one thing people want in the world more than anything goes back to what President Clinton said: 'It's the economy, stupid.' People want stability," Hitchcock says. "They don't care about a lot of other things, but if people have money and stability . . . a lot of people are going to be happy. They will surrender more and more control of these things until one day they wake up and the government has total control."[14]

The "Global Financial Coup d'État"

Six years before the global financial crisis erupted in 2007, investment banker and former U.S. assistant secretary of housing Catherine Austin Fitts attended a private investment conference in London where she gave a presentation on a Wall Street partnership that had engineered a "housing and debt bubble," "shifted vast amounts of capital out of the U.S.," and engaged in other questionable practices. As she listened to other presenters, Fitts came to a "horrifying epiphany: the banks, corporations, and investors acting in each global region were the exact same players. They were a relatively small group that reappeared again and again in Russia, Eastern Europe, and Asia accompanied by the same well-known accounting firms and law firms. Clearly, there was a global financial coup d'état underway."[15]

Later, Fitts learned that the world was experiencing a "global 'heist': capital was being sucked out of country after country." In her newsletter, Fitts wrote that the presentation she gave in London revealed a piece of the puzzle that was difficult for the audience to fathom. This phenomenon was not simply occurring in the emerging markets. It was happening in America too. As Fitts continued to investigate, she learned that "significant amounts of money started leaving the U.S., including illegally." "Over $4 trillion went missing from the U.S. government," Fitts wrote. "No one seemed to notice. Misled into thinking we were in a boom economy by a fraudulent debt bubble engineered with force and intention from the highest levels of the financial system, Americans were engaging in an orgy of consumption that was liquidating the real financial equity we needed urgently to reposition ourselves for the times ahead... The question hung in the air, unspoken, once the bubble was over, was the time coming, when we, too, could be 'de-modernized?' "[16]

Fitts's claim that a "global financial coup d'état" is under way comes amid growing concerns regarding the world's precarious financial condition and what observers call the "Age of Oligarchy." In a recent *Daily Beast* article—"Dawn of the Age of Oligarchy: The Alliance Between Government and the 1%"—Joel Kotkin, the Roger Hobbs fellow in urban futures at Chapman University in Orange, California, wrote about a "new class of super-wealthy oligarchs" who continue to gain wealth and power as the "country's middle class shrinks."[17]

In *The New Class Conflict*, Kotkin explores this phenomenon in even greater detail, making ominous predictions about America's future. "In this emergent society, wealth and power are concentrated in ever fewer hands and threaten to erode much of the traditional appeal of America, its institutions, and sense of promise," Kotkin wrote. "Together they threaten to create a new social order that in some ways more closely resembles feudal structures—with its often unassailable barriers to mobility—than the chaotic emergence of industrial capitalism... In this sense, the new class order represents the apotheosis of economic centralization, as well as a growing alliance between the ultra-wealthy and the instruments of state power. This is reflected, and glaringly so, in finance. In 1995, the assets of the six largest bank holding companies accounted for 15 percent of gross domestic product; by 2011, aided by the massive bailout of 'too big to fail' banks, this percentage had soared to 64 percent."[18]

In *Superclass*, *Foreign Policy* magazine editor David Rothkopf goes on to reveal how six thousand to seven thousand people, the world's "superclass—the most powerful of the world's most powerful people"—are able to exert enormous influence over the world of politics and government. "A global elite has emerged over the past several decades that has vastly more power than any other group on the planet," Rothkopf wrote. "Each of the members of this superclass has the ability to regularly influence the lives of millions of people in multiple countries worldwide. Each actively exercises this power, and they often amplify it through the development of relationships with others in this class...That such a group exists is indisputable. Heads of state, CEOs of the world's largest companies, media barons, billionaires who are actively involved in their investments, technology entrepreneurs, oil potentates, hedge fund managers, private equity investors, top military commanders, a select few religious leaders, a handful of renowned writers, scientists, and artists, even terrorist leaders and master criminals, meet the above criteria for membership." As the former managing director of Kissinger Associates, Rothkopf wrote that Kissinger's firm was "like a revolving door for the superclass." "Every U.S. national security adviser since Henry Kissinger has either worked with or for Kissinger—or he or she has worked with or for someone who worked with or for Kissinger: two degrees of separation. Many went to the same schools," Rothkopf stated. "Many had fathers and brothers in the same line of work. Mostly old white guys. Not too many women. A classic elite."[19]

Kissinger, a CFR member who predicted the creation of a "New International Order" in the near future, and his associates often attend Bilderberg Group meetings, according to Daniel Estulin. "Bilderberg is a medium, a means, of bringing together [representatives] of financial institutions which are the world's most powerful and predatory financial interests of the times," Estulin says. "It is that combination that represents the worst of humanity...The concept is a One-World Company, Ltd., made up of corporations that have a lot more power than any government on the planet. We've seen in recent years that elected presidents...have very little to do with the actual course of history. You can talk about foreign policy or national policy, but these policies have very little to do with how the world is run. It's global policy that matters and that global policy is not run by presidents and prime ministers. It's run by people far above the government level and the Bilderberg Group is just one of the nodes of these above-government level organizations whose objective is through consensus to reach an understanding of how the world is going to be run on behalf of the aristocracy."[20]

The Rise of the Spirit of Babel

Jonathan Cahn introduces readers to the Shemitah and its link to the September 11, 2001, terrorist attacks and the economic calamities that befell America in 2001 and 2008 in *The Mystery of the Shemitah*. Cahn also explores the connection between the Great Depression and similar economic events and the Shemitah, how the World Trade Center was birthed, completed, and destroyed during Shemitah years, and how the rise—and possibly the demise—of America is connected to the Shemitah.

Cahn claimed that a biblical pattern of sevens involving the Shemitah predicted the 9/11 terrorist attacks to the "exact hour" and how the mystery would converge with a second dynamic, the mystery of the towers, a phenomenon that began with the construction of the Tower of Babel and culminated with the 9/11 attacks on the World Trade Center towers.[21]

Since the beginning of history, towers have stood as symbols of pride. In the last millennium, European cathedrals were the highest man-made structures on the planet. At the same time, the church in Europe was one of the greatest centers of power in the world. But in the late 1800s, the cathedrals of Europe were replaced by secular skyscrapers as the tallest buildings on earth—heralding a "massive shift from ecclesiastical power to secular power." *The Mystery of the Shemitah* reveals the link between the rising of towers and the rising of nations. A year after America built the highest secular tower on earth in 1870, it became the world's strongest economic power, surpassing the British Empire.[22]

Over the next century, as America continued to construct even taller skyscrapers, the nation reached previously unattained heights of power. In 1930, construction began on the Empire State Building. The project was completed the following year—a Shemitah year. At a height of 1,454 feet, it was the tallest building in the world. Then, just before the end of World War II, officials from forty-four nations gathered in Bretton Woods, New Hampshire, to lay the groundwork for a new international economic system. In 1945, also a Shemitah year, former Florida governor David Scholz first proposed what would later become the World Trade Center in Lower Manhattan. "The Shemitah brings about the transformation of the economic and financial realms," Cahn wrote in a section of the book titled "The New World Order." "What took place at Bretton Woods would bring about the transformation of the global economic and financial order. It would establish such institutions as the World Bank and the International Monetary Fund. But most dramatically it would set up a new world economic and financial order in which world currencies would be tied to the U.S. dollar." In 1958, David Rockefeller created the master plan for the office complex dedicated to world trade. In 1961, New York governor Nelson Rockefeller signed the World Trade Center bill. Construction started four years later on a Shemitah year. The project was completed in 1972, and the World Trade Center became the highest building on earth.[23]

"One of the most unexpected revelations in *The Mystery of the Shemitah* begins at Babel," Cahn wrote in an article for *Charisma*. "It involves the connection between the building of high towers and the rise of world powers. This particular mystery is especially revealing concerning the rise (and fall) of America."[24]

Strangely, the Shemitah is connected to one of the most shocking events in modern American history—the September 11, 2001, terrorist attacks. "As the [21st century began], the tower that represented our eminence or economic dominance falls and crashes on 9/11, which if the rising of towers speaks of the rising of nations, what does the fall speak of? The other thing is the World Trade Center is linked to the Shemitah," Cahn says. "It was conceived in the year of the Shemitah, it was built in another year of the Shemitah. It was built for seven years, the time of the Shemitah. It was completed in 1972, the year of the Shemitah. It was destroyed in 2001, the year of the Shemitah. And as the towers speak of rising, rising—'we will ascend'—it's just like 'we will rebuild' in Isaiah 9:10. The Shemitah in Hebrew means the fall and so in the year of the fall it happens." In the aftermath of what some viewed as "divine judgment" and a "terrible catalyst to begin the end times," American leaders responded with defiance. Shortly after the terrorist attacks, American officials, quoting Isaiah 9:10, repeated the same vow uttered by Israel's leaders in its final days: "The bricks have fallen down, but we will rebuild with hewn stones." The verse in Isaiah was first repeated by Senate Majority Leader Tom Daschle a day after the terrorist attacks. On the third anniversary of the attacks, U.S. senator John Edwards quoted the verse again. The third time occurred when President Obama, in his first major address as president, uttered a paraphrase of the ancient vow. Then, in June 2012, Obama traveled to ground zero to dedicate what was known at the time as the Freedom Tower. On a steel beam set to be the highest beam on the structure, President Obama wrote eight words: "We remember. We rebuild. We come back stronger." That vow is now inscribed at the top of America's tallest building. "It's the highest words on the highest structure in North America," Cahn says. "It's a paraphrase of the vow that was spoken in ancient Israel that was an ominous vow because it said in the wake of a shaking—this attack on the nation—that instead of seeking God and turning from their course they vowed a vow of defiance, which the Bible reveals led to their judgment and ultimately their destruction."[25]

Ironically, the Freedom Tower, now called One World Trade Center, is located at the same place where President George Washington dedicated America to God more than two centuries ago. At the time, the nation's capital wasn't Washington, DC. It was New York City.

"Two hundred and twenty-four years ago, our first president placed his hands on the Bible and the American nation as we know it came into existence," Cahn said during a May 8, 2013, speech to members of Congress in the Capitol Building's Statuary Hall. "And in that first-ever presidential address, a prophetic warning was given forever embedded in our national foundation. Washington's warning was this: 'The propitious smiles of heaven can never be expected on a nation that disregards the eternal rules of order and right which heaven itself has ordained.' In other words, if America should ever turn away from God, if it should ever disregard the eternal rules of order and right ordained by God, then the blessings of heaven—its peace, its prosperity, its power, and its protection—would be removed from the land. If that should ever happen, if America should ever turn away from God, how would that turning come? It would come on the day that America abandoned the ways of God as ordained in his Word—the day it redefined what is right and wrong, when it called sin righteousness and righteousness sin, when it turned against its own foundation and that foundation cracked asunder. Members of Congress and those who love America here, that day has come."[26]

Statue of Liberty or Queen of Babylon?

In describing the destruction of the end-times Babylonian system, the apostle John noted that "she glorified herself and lived luxuriously"—believing she was safe because "'I sit as queen, and am no widow, and will not see sorrow.' Therefore her plagues will come in one day—death and mourning and famine. And she will be utterly burned with fire, for strong is the Lord God who judges her" (Rev. 18:7–8 NKJV).

Ominously, not far from One World Trade Center across New York

Harbor is Liberty Island, the location of the colossal copper sculpture known as the Statue of Liberty or "Liberty Enlightening the World"—an 1886 gift to America from France.

From Charlton Heston's famous scene in *The Planet of the Apes* depicting the Statue of Liberty as one of the world's remaining relics following a nuclear holocaust to a myriad of pop culture images today that employ it as an image of America's apocalyptic future, the 151-foot "pagan statue" is often depicted as a symbol of doomsday. Why is that?[27]

The Statue of Liberty was designed by French Freemason and sculptor Frédéric-Auguste Bartholdi, and a plaque at the pedestal's entrance is inscribed with the sonnet "The New Colossus"—a reference to the Colossus of Rhodes statue of the sun god Helios in the ancient Greek city of Rhodes, one of the Seven Wonders of the Ancient World.[28]

Recognized as a "universal symbol of freedom and democracy," the statue is generally believed to be based on the Roman goddess of freedom, Libertas. However, some prophecy scholars say the Statue of Liberty is a symbol of the end-times Babylonian system and its creation was ultimately inspired by the legendary Semiramis, the "Queen of Babylon." "Semiramis and Nimrod lie behind the pantheons of gods beginning with Sumeria, then Egypt, then Phoenicia, then Babylon, then Nineveh, and then Neo-Babylon," S. Douglas Woodward says. "Finally, Greco-Roman gods emerge which match the Egyptian gods. Lady Liberty is Libertas, the goddess of liberty, paraded around Paris during the French Revolution. Her head reflects spires of the sun and suggests Apollo too. America's mythology strives to reflect the glory of ancient Greece and Rome...But it is obvious even to children that the gods applauded in Washington, DC, are pagan deities. That a Masonic Frenchmen designed Lady Liberty mandates the case be closed." The "Queen of Babylon" refers to many women who some researchers say all have their root in the mother-wife of Nimrod—Semiramis. "Cybele is the Roman version," Woodward says. "Minerva is on top of the U.S.

Capitol Building. The Phoenicians worshipped Europa, whom Zeus carried on his back [The Woman Rides the Beast; the statue outside the EU headquarters building]. Europa was a Canaanite at least one thousand years before she was 'European.' "[29]

Other researchers say the statue is symbolic of the Egyptian mother goddess Isis. "Graham Hancock and Robert Bauval have connected the dots to show that Bartholdi may have been thinking about Isis when he designed his Suez Canal lighthouse and therefore, by extension, the Statue of Liberty," Robert Hieronimus wrote in *The United Symbolism of America*. "Bartholdi himself had compared his earlier proposed statue to the great Alexandrian Pharos Lighthouse, which, though not in the shape of a woman, had been dedicated to the goddess Isis."[30]

If this is true, it stands to reason that the original inspiration for the Statue of Liberty is actually Semiramis. If correct, America could very well be the "daughter of Babylon" spoken of in Isaiah 47:1; Jeremiah 50:42; and Psalm 137:8, and the Statue of Liberty would be her symbol.

"[We believe] the final Babylon of the Bible's prophets is New York City while the land of Babylon [Chaldea] is the United States of America," Douglas W. Krieger, Dene McGriff, and S. Douglas Woodward wrote in *The Final Babylon*. "New York with her Statue of Liberty standing like a sentinel in its harbor fulfills the stark and ominous symbol of Babylon (and as Old Testament prophets refer to it—the daughter of Babylon)."[31]

In his article "Statue of Liberty," Dennis L. Cuddy raises this possibility, too, noting that an engraved marker was attached to the St. John the Divine Cathedral in New York City in 1997 that depicted the final destruction of the world-class megalopolis. "This, no doubt, refers to the Rev. 14:8 saying that a 'great city' will be attacked, as it reads: 'Babylon is fallen, is fallen, that great city.' We know that this modern Babylon will fall in large part due to sexual license (fornication) for which Semiramis (which looks like the [Statue of Liberty]) was known. We know that 'the great whore...sitteth on many waters,' and [New York City] is at the juncture of the Hudson River, East River, New York Bay, and the Atlantic Ocean. We know the destroyed city is on the coast because Rev. 18:17–18 states that 'every shipmaster, and all the company in ships, and sailors...cried when they saw the smoke of her burning.' We know that her burning occurs in modern times because Rev. 18:9 states 'the kings of the earth...shall see the smoke of her burning.' And that would only be possible with instantaneous televised pictures. We also know the destruction will probably be caused by some type of nuclear device because Rev. 18:19 indicates that 'in one hour is she made desolate.' "[32]

Chapter Twelve

Spiritual-Technological Babylon

We believe that we are seeing, with all of the other signs, the revival of Mystery, Babylon—not just in astrology, but also in spiritism, a return to the supernatural.

—HAL LINDSEY, AUTHOR OF *THE LATE GREAT PLANET EARTH*

Some call it the "Illuminati Capital." CNN describes it as the "world's weirdest capital city." Shooting up nearly overnight in a remote and deserted area of the Asian Steppes, Astana, Kazakhstan, is described by critics as a "futuristic occult capital embracing the New World Order."[1]

Others say its architecture reflects ancient Babylonian sun worship. One of its most prominent features is the Pyramid of Peace—a sixty-meter-tall glass pyramid dedicated to the unification of the world's religions. The pyramid routinely attracts hundreds of the world's most prominent religious leaders to the Congress of World and Traditional Religions to hear Kazakhstan president Nursultan Nazarbayev, a top Communist leader in the former U.S.S.R.

Bathed in the golden and pale blue glow of the glass (colors from the Kazakhstan flag), they meet in a circular chamber based on the UN Security Council meeting room in New York City. In 2012, hundreds of world leaders, prime ministers, and top managers at international organizations, transnational corporations and businesses, along with twelve

Nobel laureates and renowned scientists, gathered for the V Astana Economic Forum, where Nazarbayev proposed the creation of a single world currency as a solution to the global economic crisis.[2]

During another meeting of the Congress of World and Traditional Religions, representatives of Islam, Christianity, Judaism, Hinduism, Buddhism, Daosism, Shintoism, and the Anglican Church discussed ways for peaceful coexistence between the world's religions. The congress also received letters from influential political leaders, including Kofi Annan, George W. Bush, Vladimir Putin, Hosni Mubarak, Jacques Chirac, and Mikhail Gorbachev. "The congress should serve as an example for cooperation and dialogue between religions—a bridge of its kind over the abyss," Nazarbayev told the participants. "Where methods of political regulation do not work, the role of religion is the only means for reconciliation and hope."[3]

While no one knows what role, if any, Astana and Nazarbayev may play in end-times events, we believe that "Mystery, Babylon," or the spiritual-technological Babylonian system described in Revelation 17, will involve a similar embrace of the world's religions and mark of the Beast technologies.

During the Tribulation, two world leaders will arise—the Antichrist and the False Prophet. Employing "great signs and wonders" (Matt. 24:24 NIV), the False Prophet will convince the world that the Antichrist has the solution to all its problems. Eventually, the False Prophet will oversee a new global religion. Many Bible scholars believe this new religious system will be a pagan, New Age religion that embraces all faiths but will ultimately require everyone to take the mark of the Beast and worship the Antichrist.

In recent decades, the belief that there are many ways to God, or that all paths lead to heaven and "all religions lead to the same truth," has gained in popularity, especially among young people. This phenomenon comes, not surprisingly, at a time when biblical literacy has reached an "all-time low." Research by David Campbell at the University of Notre Dame and Robert Putnam at Harvard University indicates that nearly two-thirds of evangelicals under age thirty-five believe non-Christians can go to heaven, compared to 39 percent of those over age sixty-five.[4]

A recent Pew Forum on Religion & Public Life survey found that 70 percent of Americans agree with the statement "Many religions can lead to eternal life." "Even more remarkable was the fact that 57 percent of evangelical Christians were willing to accept that theirs might not be the only path to salvation, since most Christians historically have embraced the words of Jesus, in the Gospel of John, that 'no one comes to the Father except through me.' Even as mainline churches had become more tolerant, the exclusivity of Christianity's path to heaven has long been one of the evangelicals' fundamental tenets. The new poll suggests a major shift, at least in the pews," wrote David Van Biema in his *Time* magazine article "Christians: No One Path to Salvation."[5]

This increasingly prevalent belief system is conveniently summed up in the yuppie "Coexist" bumper sticker. In the design, which uses symbols from various religions and pagan belief systems, the "C" represents the crescent moon of Islam, the "o" contains a peace symbol, the "e" is a male/female symbol, the "x" is the Star of David representing Judaism, the "i" is a pagan/Wiccan symbol, the "s" is the Chinese yin-yang symbol, and the "t" is a cross representing Christianity. Many prophecy experts believe some form of this universal belief system will be the one embraced by the world during the Tribulation.

The Rise of a Luciferian One-World Religion

One of the central teachings of Bible prophecy is that in the last days there will be the return of a spiritual-technological Babylonian system and the creation of a Luciferian world religion. An essential aspect of this world religion is that it will be based on the religious system set up in Babylon—the "fountainhead of all false religions."[6]

"Like other pagan peoples of the Ancient East, the Babylonians believed in many false gods and goddesses," Ron Rhodes, president of Reasoning from the Scriptures Ministries, wrote in *The 8 Great Debates of Bible Prophecy*. "Each city in Babylon had a patron god with an accompanying temple. A number of small shrines were also scattered about each city, and people often met in these to worship various other deities. The chief of the Babylonian gods was Anu, considered the king of heaven. The patron god of Babylon was Marduk. The Babylonians were well known for their practice of divination. Astrology can trace its roots back to Babylon... The priests of Babylon tried to understand and predict movements of these planets so that perhaps they could use this knowledge to benefit their nation. To study and worship these deities, the Babylonians built towers called ziggurats. The Tower of Babel was apparently such a ziggurat."[7]

The religious system set up by Nimrod at the Tower of Babel is called "Mystery, Babylon," and it is the source of all the occult and satanic religions throughout history. The Tower of Babel was the center of the ancient Babylonian occult religious system. Some researchers believe the Tower of Babel was a type of portal that allowed for the entrance of demonic entities into the earthly plane.

Nimrod was a descendant of Noah, who had saved his family from the Flood that some experts believe God used to wipe out the corrupted DNA resulting from the interbreeding of fallen angels with women. It is important to remember Jesus' warning in Luke 17:26, "And as it was in the days of Noah, so it will be also in the days of the Son of Man" (NKJV). Many prophecy experts believe Jesus was referring to the interspecies breeding of fallen angels and women that produced what the Bible describes as Nephilim. Some prophecy scholars argue that Nimrod was a Nephilim or Rephaim. They believe the Tower of Babel facilitated the return of the Nephilim to the earth after the Flood. They argue this concept is essential to understanding "Mystery, Babylon" and the one-world religion that will emerge in the last days.

The Antichrist/False Prophet Conspiracy

During the Tribulation, according to Revelation 13, the world's economic system will come under the control of the False Prophet. He will also control the global religious system on behalf of the Antichrist.

In Matthew 24, Jesus warned his disciples about the coming of the False Prophet, who would perform "great signs and wonders" that could "deceive the very elect" (v. 24 KJV). In a following verse, Jesus may have made a reference to the role secret societies would play in the rise of the False Prophet—describing these groups as meeting in "secret chambers." "Wherefore, if they shall say unto you, Behold, he is in the desert; go not forth: behold, he is in the secret chambers; believe it not," the apostle Matthew wrote (v. 26 KJV). Some also believe the apostle John's mention of the "synagogue of Satan" in Revelation 2:9 (KJV) is a reference to secret societies and their role in end-times events.

The centerpiece of the return of the spiritual-technological and commercial Babylon will be the mandatory distribution of some kind of microchip, biochip, nanochip implant, or similar technology placed underneath the skin of the forehead or the right hand.

No one on earth will be able to buy or sell, or participate in the global economic system, unless they have received this chip implant—also known as the mark of the Beast—"666."

"The Greek word is *charagma* (which means 'a mark or stamp engraved, etched, branded, cut, imprinted')," Mark Hitchcock says. "So people will actually be taking his name upon them—a pledge of allegiance. If you are going to be a great world leader and you are going to dominate the world economy, [this person]...is going to make every use of whatever technology is available to control people's lives. Today, with RFID and other technologies, we already know where every piece of merchandise is in the world, and through global positioning systems they can know where every person in the world is at any given time. Certainly, whoever this world leader is, he will avail himself of and exploit every kind of technology to exert his worldwide control."[8]

In order to receive the mark of the Beast, a person must specifically renounce Jesus as Lord and choose to worship the Antichrist as God. If they refuse to do this, they will be beheaded, according to the Bible. All of this is a central component of the one-world religion known as "Mystery, Babylon."

Curiously, money and currency have always been based on a spiritual system. The False Prophet, who will be head of the one-world religion, is the person who will administrate the mark of the Beast system because the mark of the Beast is both economic and spiritual in nature.

The Latest Craze: Microchip Implants and "Wearable Tech"

The world has now arrived at a time in human history when all kinds of microchips, biochips, and nanochip implants are being used for various purposes. The technology now exists for a mark of the Beast system to be put in place. This has never happened before in human history.

Currently, people are receiving medical chips that are designed to fire electrical impulses and facilitate healing. These medical chips can monitor vital signs and help improve the health of people with dementia, Alzheimer's disease, diabetes, and other ailments.

Movie stars, celebrities, politicians, and the superwealthy are getting chip implants as protection against kidnapping and terrorist groups. Parents are buying chip implants for their young children and infants to protect them from child abduction and from being sold into sexual slavery. An increasing number of schools are using special tracking chips embedded in student identification cards, which also store personal academic, medical, and psychological information about the students. A growing number of parents are unhappy about this, especially Christian parents who are aware of what the Bible says about mark of the Beast technologies.

Yet a recent survey by Cisco Systems found that a fourth of professionals ages eighteen to fifty would be willing to get a surgical brain implant to allow them to "instantly link their thoughts to the Internet." "I really think it's the cool factor. When they see something that's cutting-edge, they really don't stop to think about the implications," Liz McIntyre, a privacy expert and coauthor of the book *Spychips: How Major Corporations and Government Plan to Track Your Every Purchase and Watch Your Every Move*, told WND.com. "It's part of this whole wave now where the [tech] industry feels like they have an in, and they're going to push it right through on the cool factor."[9]

The technology of the mark of the Beast is not only commercial, but it's about total control of every human on earth.

"Again, because of technology, the world shrinks daily," says Jerry B. Jenkins, coauthor of the Left Behind series. "We really are becoming one village. I'm not a theologian, and neither am I a geopolitical animal. All I know is what everyone else recognizes from the news we all see every day. Everything seems to point to a cashless society, fewer borders, one-world government, et cetera."[10]

The term "wearable tech" applies to a wide spectrum of technology manufacturers who want technology implanted under the skin. One product is literally called "Project Underskin," a health-tracking tattoo that would run on the body's electrochemical energy and could be used to exchange data in a handshake or unlock your home when you touch the doorknob.[11]

In the decades Paul McGuire has been researching, writing, and speaking on Bible prophecy, people have periodically come up to him at conferences and shared that they were in the military, had some kind of operation, and believe a microchip implant was placed inside them. Often they are afraid to tell anyone. In a spirit of brotherly love and acceptance, McGuire listens and assures them they're not crazy.

Some have claimed that their health has been affected by these chips. They hear voices, see a variety of images, and experience what some have described as electronically induced mood and psychological changes. The reality is that it is now fairly well-known that technologies exist that can cause people to hear voices, see images, and experience mood changes ranging from depression to ecstasy, anxiety to serenity, and paranoia to a deep sense of well-being.

Amy Zalman, the chief executive officer at the Washington, DC–based World Future Society, says the world's largest and oldest membership organization for futurists is watching this trend in which "chips move ever close to us: from our clothing into our phones and, ultimately, into our bodies" with great interest. "The World Future Society prides itself on its neutrality, so we would not take a position on whether this is good or bad," Zalman says. "We will ask what this trend and these technologies mean for human society. There will be questions about technology, ethics, surveillance, privacy, and our public selves. These technologies are going to raise deep questions about who we are and what it means to be human."[12]

Operation Paperclip, MKULTRA, and Nazi Mind Control

The development of these technologies began in the 1950s when the U.S. government brought in thousands of high-level Nazi rocket and mind control scientists through what was known as Operation Paperclip to pioneer aggressive programs to combat the scientific brainwashing techniques used by Communist nations such as the former Soviet Union, East Germany, North Korea, North Vietnam, and China.

Following World War II, many Nazi rocket scientists relocated to America, where they obtained jobs in what President Eisenhower called "the military-industrial complex." Some believe they came to America with the "loot of Europe" as well as advanced technologies that remain classified even today.[13]

At the same time, Russia was caught beaming electromotive waves into a U.S. embassy, causing severe mental confusion. As a result, the U.S. military responded with very aggressive mind control programs such as Project MKULTRA, Project BLUEBIRD, and Monarch Mind Control. Powerful nations like Russia and China were developing mind control programs, so the CIA, the U.S. Office of Naval Intelligence, the Defense Advanced Research Projects Agency (DARPA), and many branches of the military began their own programs. This included ones dedicated to psychic spying, remote viewing, telepathy, and one called Operation Star Gate, the purported inspiration for the film *The Men Who Stare at Goats* starring George Clooney. In fact, the 1962 film *The Manchurian Candidate* starring Frank Sinatra depicted a programmed assassin who was ordered to kill a prominent political figure. The movie came out at the time the CIA was involved in a similar program, "thanks in great part to the groundwork laid down years earlier by Nazi mind-control experts."[14]

Captain America and Real Super-Soldiers

Today, a vast array of new technologies in neuroscience, quantum physics, and computer-brain interfaces are being developed to create what were once considered superhuman abilities limited to fictional characters such as the one played by actor Lee Majors in the 1970s television show

The Six Million Dollar Man. One of these technologies involves bio-chips and nanochips surgically implanted into the body and brain with computer-brain interfaces.

In the 1960s, the Department of Defense began to develop what are known as super-soldiers using genetic enhancements, implants, drugs, neuroscience, computer technologies, and chips. In a *PC Magazine* article titled "5 Ways Scientists Are Building Real World Super Soldiers," Chandra Steele wrote that "scientists are working hard to create the modern-day super soldier." "It sounds as preposterous as anything you might see this weekend in *Captain America: The Winter Soldier,* but the Defense Advanced Research Projects Agency (DARPA) and others are working on some very sci-fi projects that wouldn't be out of place in the Marvel world."[15]

Today, the Department of Defense and other institutions are developing chips to cure post-traumatic stress disorder, mental illness, and a variety of medical and psychological problems.

Ultimately, some claim genetic experiments involving the breeding of animal and human DNA could lead to the creation of genetically modified super-soldiers and humans. "A mouse that can speak? A monkey with Down's Syndrome? Dogs with human hands or feet? British scientists want to know if such experiments are acceptable, or if they go too far in the name of medical research," wrote Kate Kelland in her Reuters article "Scientists Want Debate on Animals with Human Genes." "To find out, Britain's Academy of Medical Sciences launched a study... to look at the use of animals containing human material in scientific research."[16]

Perhaps the global religion of "Mystery, Babylon" will involve a hidden code—a corruption of human DNA—that God anticipated ahead of time. After all, God created man "in our image, after our likeness" (Gen. 1:26 KJV), and any alteration in that code would be an abomination.

272 • UNLOCKING THE BABYLON CODE

The Babylon-DNA Code

In order to grasp the multidimensional nature of the DNA code, we need to understand how the Babylon code interfaces with the "image" of God. When we look back at the origins of mankind with the first male and female in the Garden of Eden, we see that the Creator made the first man and woman in the image of God. In scientific terms, this means that Adam and Eve were created with the DNA of God. Since Adam and Eve were created with the DNA of God, they had supernatural power to rule over the earth under the direction of God. However, when Lucifer appeared, he tempted Adam and Eve to reject the Word of God—tripping a "cosmic switch" that allowed the "death force," or the law of sin and death, to be activated, and the fall of man ensued.

God gave Adam and Eve specific commands to be fruitful and multiply. However, Lucifer was in the process of leading a revolution with one-third of the angels to install himself as the new ruler of heaven. Part of this plan was to corrupt the DNA of God that existed in mankind. This is thought to have begun on Mount Hermon, where Lucifer directed fallen angels to bestow mankind with advanced technologies and mate with women, producing a hybrid race with demon and human DNA. This race of beings is what Genesis 6:1–4 calls the Nephilim—the "sons of God," which is derived from the Hebrew words *b'nai Elohim*, meaning "fallen angels."

As we read about the Flood in the Bible, it seems that its primary purpose was to eradicate corrupted DNA. Thus, we must understand that one of the primary battlefields between God and Lucifer is the battle involving DNA—the code of life. After all, Christ was born through the line of King David, and everyone whose DNA has not been corrupted can receive salvation.

In order to unravel the Babylon code, we must consider that Nimrod was in all likelihood a Nephilim with corrupted DNA. Those who believe in the existence of Atlantis argue that the ten philosopher-kings of the fabled city-state were also Nephilim. In deciphering the Babylon code, it's important to understand that it is embedded with a corrupted genetic code, and the highly advanced mathematics contained in that code are in conflict with the divine mathematics of God. Today, scientists believe that the universe and life itself are essentially mathematics. "There's something very mathematical about our Universe, and...the more carefully we look, the more math we seem to find," says MIT professor Max Tegmark, author of *Our Mathematical Universe: My Quest for the Ultimate Nature of Reality*.[17]

In fact, it's no accident that the Bible contains an array of precise mathematical sequences beginning with the seven-day Creation in Genesis and ending with a seven-year judgment consisting of seven seals, seven trumpets, and seven bowls. In Genesis, Joseph supernaturally prepared Egypt for seven years of famine. Joshua marched around Jericho for seven days before its destruction. In Leviticus, the Year of Jubilee occurs at the end of seven cycles of sabbatical years, or Shemitahs, when all the children of Israel were to be released from debt. In Daniel 9, we learn about the master prophetic clock that outlines what are known as the "seventy weeks of Daniel," or the "seventy 'sevens' of years" culminating in one final seven-year period known as the "time of Jacob's trouble"—the Tribulation period. Many of the numbers throughout the Bible involve mathematically precise timetables outlining future prophetic events.

Interestingly, Babylon was built using a precise mathematical system known as Babylonian mathematics. The Babylonian Empire developed what later become known as the Pythagorean theorem. At the end of the age, the biblical mathematical system will collide with the Babylonian mathematical system. At its most basic level, the battle of good versus evil is a war of codes—mind-boggling mathematical cryptograms that will determine the fate of the universe, the world, and mankind. And as scientists and mathematicians are now discovering, the entire universe, life, and our genetic code are part of the most mind-bending mathematical equation ever conceived. As Microsoft founder Bill Gates relates it, DNA is "like a software program, only much more complex than anything we've ever devised."[18]

Nietzsche's Übermensch—the "Superman"

The most aggressive area of science today is what is known as transhumanism—the science of evolving man through genetic and technological manipulation. Chip implants have already become an important aspect of transhumanism. With chip implants, the military can potentially enhance human performance to a point where super-soldiers—what German philosopher Friedrich Nietzsche called the "Übermensch," or "Superman"—become a reality.

Occult scholars claim that the superiority of Hitler's fighting force was due to a combination of the application of the science of eugenics, the breeding of a master race, and occult training that taught the Nazis how to enhance their energy, health, concentration, focus, and strength.

According to Nazi beliefs, based in part on Nordic legends and Greek mythology, a superior Aryan master race came from the stars and mated with human women to produce a race of god-men—a story that seems to parallel the account in Genesis 6 of fallen angels mating with human women. This superrace, according to Nazi beliefs, gave mankind advanced technologies, but a cataclysmic flood occurred and this super-race retreated into a vast underground world in the far north known as Thule/Hyperborea. Today, the U.S. Air Force's Thule Air Base is located 750 miles north of the Arctic Circle and is home to the Twenty-First Space Wing's "global network of sensors providing missile warning, space surveillance and space control to North American Aerospace Defense Command and Air Force Space Command."

Were these Nordic and Greek myths based on the existence of the Nephilim before the Flood? Many ancient civilizations have similar legends. If there is any truth to these myths, it would help explain what the *Daily Mail* describes as Hitler's "mad schemes of eugenics" to create a "new 'breed' of supposedly genetically-superior German beings" that would safeguard the future of the Thousand-Year Reich. After all, Hitler was a member of the Thule Society, a group of wealthy conservatives, nationalists, and anti-Semites who "delved into radical politics, race mysticism, and the occult under its emblem—a swastika superimposed over a sword." "The society also served as a front for the even more secretive Germanenorden, or German Order, a reincarnation of the old Teutonic Knights, which had branches throughout Germany patterned after Masonic Lodges," Jim Marrs wrote. "It is believed that these lodges carried on the agenda of the outlawed Bavarian Illuminati." The Thule Society, along with occult literature publisher Dietrich Eckart—whom Hitler described as the "spiritual founder of National Socialism"—helped fund the Germany Workers Party, which later changed its name to the National Socialist German Workers Party, or Nazi Party. In sum, the Thule Society and its bizarre beliefs helped facilitate Hitler's rise to power and resulted in two of the greatest tragedies the planet has ever known—World War II and the Holocaust.[19]

Resurrecting the Pharaoh

Hidden in the Babylon code, going all the way back to ancient Babylon and Egypt, are the secret teachings and practices of a purportedly genetically superior race. This could be the purpose of preserving the pharaohs, who were thought to be gods in ancient Egypt, as mummies and storing their mummified bodies deep inside giant pyramids.

What if supernatural "principalities and powers" knew that the mechanism for bringing them back to life one day would be transhumanism and genetic modification? Were the ancient pharaohs Nephilim? Is it conceivable that preserved DNA of the pharaohs could be used one day to impregnate a woman who would then give birth to a Nephilim? While speculative at this point, there are reports that Nephilim DNA has been recovered from bodies frozen in the ice in Antarctica, Iraq, and other locations around the globe. Some researchers even believe there are secret projects involving the use of Nephilim DNA for the purpose of interspecies breeding. Once again, it's important to not disregard the words of Jesus when he said, "As it was in the days of Noah, so it will be also in the days of the Son of Man" (Luke 17:26 NKJV).

"In recent years, astonishing technological developments have pushed the frontiers of humanity toward far-reaching morphological transformation that promises in the very near future to redefine what it means to be human," Tom Horn wrote in an article titled "The Hybrid Age" in Chuck Missler's "Personal Update." In the article, Horn argued that the genetic modification of plants and animals will soon apply to people. "An international, intellectual, and fast-growing cultural movement known as Transhumanism supports this vision, as does a flourishing list of U.S. military advisors, bioethicists, law professors, and academics, which intend the use of genetics, robotics, artificial intelligence, nanotechnology and synthetic biology (GRINS technologies) as tools that will radically redesign our minds, our memories, our physiology, our offspring, and even perhaps—as Joel Garreau, in his bestselling book *Radical Evolution*, claims—our very souls," Horn wrote. "Though the transformation of man to his post-human condition is in its fledgling state, complete integration of the technology necessary to replace existing Homo sapiens as the dominant life-form on earth is approaching an exponential curve with many experts predicting the first substantive steps in GRINS human-enhancement starting any time after the year 2012. *National Geographic* magazine concurred in 2007, speculating that within ten years, the first 'human non-humans' would walk the earth, and retired San Diego State University professor and computer scientist Vernor Vinge (who delivered the now-famous lecture, 'The Coming Technological Singularity,' at the Vision-21 Symposium sponsored by NASA Lewis Research Center and the Ohio Aerospace Institute in 1993), agreed recently that we are entering that period of history when questions like, 'What is the meaning of life?' will be nothing more than an engineering question."[20]

The Rockefeller Plan

In recent years, researchers have uncovered links between secret occult groups such as the Rosicrucian Order and the Hermetic Order of the Golden Dawn. Aleister Crowley was believed to be the head of the Golden Dawn, which was connected to both English and German occult societies. Essential to their belief system was that mankind is on the brink of a giant evolutionary leap.[21]

Today, members of these secret societies believe in enhancing the performance of human beings through genetics and technology. Dating back to ancient Babylon and Egypt, and passed down through various occult societies, is the core belief that men will one day become like gods.

It all started with the original Luciferian deception when Satan promised Adam and Eve, "Ye shall be as gods" (Gen. 3:5 KJV). History is replete with human efforts to achieve immortality and reach godhood. In modern times, the goal to enhance humanity began with the Rockefeller-financed experiments in eugenics in the early twentieth century. By 1900, thirty states had laws that called for the sterilization of mental patients and imbeciles. In Germany, the Nazis adopted similar laws targeting those they considered unworthy of life, ultimately leading to the Holocaust.[22]

Transhumanism and the "Great Rebellion"

The science that is the driving force at the center of all this is transhumanism. Ultimately, transhumanism is about upgrading the human species and scientifically improving human genetics. It is simply the same science of eugenics financed by the Rockefellers, and by its very nature it asserts a belief in superior races. While all this is carefully hidden from the public, the goal is the same as in Nazi Germany: to create a genetic superrace who will rule the world and eradicate what they perceive to be the inferior races.[23]

The term "transhumanism," popularized by futurist Ray Kurzweil, was first used by English biologist Julian Huxley, the brother of novelist Aldous Huxley. "Many of this movement's adherents point to the 'Singularity' (an exponential increase in technological advancement so rapid the unaided human mind is unable to grasp its implications) as the climax of human civilization," wrote Britt Gillette in his RaptureReady.com article, "Transhumanism and the Great Rebellion." "Believing this event will usher in a new era for the human race in which limited mortals transcend their biological bodies and set out to conquer the universe; Transhumanist anticipation of the Singularity is comparable to Christian anticipation of the Second Coming of Jesus Christ."[24]

Strange Days

Today, there is a growing acceptance by many scientists of the possibility of the existence of alien life-forms and even that our planet may have been "seeded" by an extraterrestrial civilization. Movies like *Prometheus* and others have popularized this notion. In 2010, Cardiff University professor Chandra Wickramasinghe claimed that new evidence from astrobiology "overwhelmingly" supports the view that "life was seeded from outside Earth," according to a *BBC News* story. "The astrobiologist has helped develop the panspermia theory which suggests an extra-terrestrial origin for life," the author wrote. "He accepts this model still does not explain how life actually began in the first place, but says there is no hard evidence to support the theory that life only began in a 'primordial soup' on Earth." The idea of the earth being seeded by an alien civilization has become a central feature in the movement toward a one-world religion. Even the Vatican is preparing for some kind of disclosure of extraterrestrial life. In a recent article titled "Aliens Are My Brother" in the official Vatican newspaper, Vatican observatory director Father José Gabriel Funes wrote that intelligent beings created by God could exist in outer space, and this would not contradict belief in God.[25]

"The new president of the Vatican Observatory Foundation has said that it is only a matter of time before alien life forms are discovered, which will pave the way to questions about God's relationship to intelligent beings outside our planet," Stoyan Zaimov wrote in a story for the *Christian Post*, "Vatican Astronomer Says Alien Life Will Be Discovered, but Will Not Prove or Disprove God." "Jesuit Brother Guy Consolmagno speculated that the general public will not be too surprised when life on other planets is eventually discovered, and will react in much the same way it did when news broke in the '90s that there are other planets orbiting far off stars. Consolmagno, a planetary scientist who has studied meteorites and asteroids as an astronomer with the Vatican Observatory since 1993, told *Catholic News Service* that the discovery of alien life will not prove or disprove the existence of God, but will pave the way to questions on salvation and how it relates to intelligent species."[26]

It now appears that the world is on the verge of a revolution in science in which the traditional theory of evolution could be replaced by new theories that claim life came from outer space. "I think there is a racial memory that, yes, there is some truth to all this and basically what it is I think is that these ancients were telling us the truth when they said that these beings came from the skies, landed on earth, and began to colonize and to create cities and empires that [exhibited] technology, which I think because of the ancient cataclysms have come down to us as the story of Atlantis and the story of Noah and the Flood," Marrs says.[27]

A growing number of prophecy experts believe that some kind of public pronouncement regarding the existence of extraterrestrial life could be made in the not-too-distant future. They believe such an announcement by world leaders could radically impact religious beliefs and potentially lead to the creation of a new global religion. Some are calling this the "Alien Disclosure Event." The phrase is inspired by the Disclosure Project, the organization that sponsored the National Press Club Disclosure Event in 2001 when more than twenty military, government, intelligence, and corporate officials gave "compelling testimony regarding the existence of extraterrestrial life forms visiting the planet, and the reverse engineering of the energy and propulsion systems of their spacecraft." The officials claimed that extraterrestrials have been visiting earth for a long period of time, but would not make contact until the human race evolves to a certain point. At the press conference seen and heard by more than one billion people via worldwide media, project founder Dr. Steven Greer and other officials claimed a "shadow government of military leaders and others" have kept information about aliens a secret, including purported energy-generation and antigravity-propulsion systems that have the potential to solve environmental problems and help avert a future energy crisis. Greer, who alleged that people "have been killed to keep this quiet," also expressed concerns about space-based weapon systems. "If we begin to put these weapons in space, we will upset not just a geopolitical order, but possibly a cosmic order," said Greer, former chairman of the Department of Emergency Medicine at Caldwell Memorial Hospital in Lenoir, North Carolina, and founder of the Center for the Study of Extraterrestrial Intelligence (CSETI).[28]

While many Bible scholars are highly skeptical of the existence of extraterrestrial life, they note that the Bible predicts a "strong delusion" will precede the end-times events described in Scripture. In 2 Thessalonians 2, the apostle Paul admonishes believers not to be deceived because the Lord's return will not occur until the "falling away" occurs and the "son of perdition" (v. 3 NKJV) is revealed:

> The coming of the lawless one is according to the working of Satan, with all power, signs, and lying wonders, and with all unrighteous deception among those who perish, because they did not receive the love of the truth, that they might be saved. And for this reason God will send them strong delusion, that they should believe the lie, that they all may be condemned who did not believe the truth but had pleasure in unrighteousness. (vv. 9–12 NKJV)

Some prophecy experts believe this "strong delusion" may involve fallen angels, appearing as extraterrestrials and entering our dimension in what appears to be advanced spacecraft to help the world avert nuclear war or some other potentially cataclysmic threat. As far-fetched as this may seem, Hebrews 13:2 (KJV) does speak of entertaining "angels unawares"—indicating that angels can assume a human likeness. Another scenario, perhaps a more plausible one, may involve a "manufactured crisis" designed to convince the earth's inhabitants to accept a world government. The elite know that the middle class, especially in America, are not going to willingly give up their freedoms and hard-earned wealth to join a world state. Therefore, some major crisis—an economic collapse, a nuclear terrorist attack, or even something more powerful—will be necessary before people are willing to live under such a system.

Some claim that this crisis might involve a highly sophisticated *War of the Worlds*-like mind control operation featuring technologically simulated extraterrestrial contact. For decades, the public has been indoctrinated with the idea of benevolent alien contact with films like *Contact*, *E.T. the Extra-Terrestrial*, *Close Encounters of the Third Kind*, and *2001: A Space Odyssey*. The subtext, at least in these and other films, is that extraterrestrials will one day appear with solutions to humanity's intractable problems, helping us "evolve" to the next stage in our planetary evolution. Amid a steady increase in reported UFO sightings in recent years and the recent press conference in which military personnel claimed UFOs flew over nuclear missile silos and shut down the weapon systems, the public may now be primed for such an announcement. As bizarre as it may seem, government and religious authorities are openly talking today about the possibility of extraterrestrial life and what this would mean for the world. Not long ago, the UN even announced the creation of a "space ambassador to greet alien visitors," the *Telegraph* reported. Some even believe the UN plans to use Schiller's "Ode to Joy" "as the anthem for the introduction for the New Age one-world religion" following contact with extraterrestrial intelligence.[29]

"Despite the skeptic's enduring challenge to question God's existence, humanity cannot quench its innate thirst for its maker: humankind will not accept the finality of an atheistic materialistic (i.e. naturalist) answer," S. Douglas Woodward wrote in *Lying Wonders of the Red Planet*. "There has to be a reason why we are here—there has to be someone out there who cares what happens to us . . . Even if humanity ardently argues it has outgrown the need for God, it never stops looking for someone bigger than itself to explain why it exists . . . We may alter our DNA, but the lesson learned from the Frankenstein monster still holds true: we will strive for our maker's affirmation. Indeed we persevere in our belief that God exists, although it does now appear humanity has been conditioned to dramatically alter its creed regarding the identity of this deity and how we relate to him . . . This affirmation—that our Creator and Nurturer *comes* from the stars rather than being the *One who made them*—is the Great Deception of the time in which we live, a time this author believes constitutes 'the last days' before Jesus Christ returns to this earth. It is the final world religion."[30]

The Final World Religion

Regardless of whether the final world religion is the result of a "great deception" (2 Thess. 2:11 NLT) involving extraterrestrials, a New Age False Prophet uniting the apostate church and the globe's other faiths by promising peace and safety during a time of global turbulence, or some other diabolically sophisticated scheme, the outcome will be the same.

As the Bible predicts, humanity will fall for the age-old lie that we can create our own utopian world—on our own terms, of course—and become gods. In believing the lie that all paths lead to heaven, humanity will succumb to the master of deception's greatest scheme—submitting to the "Mystery, Babylon" religious system that forces people to take the mark of the Beast and pledge allegiance to Lucifer or face beheading.

Tragically, the Bible indicates that this false religious system will be embraced by the apostate church and the world's other faiths. The Bible speaks of a time of apostasy in the last days. "I think, unfortunately, what we see even in our churches today is a watering-down of the gospel," Greg Laurie says. "I think you have people who are professing to be Christians that really aren't Christians at all because there is no fruit, no spiritual fruit or results that would give evidence of that. So one of the things I think we need to be aware of is that there are going to be false teachers that will arise among the good teachers giving an aberrant, deluded, or false gospel, and it is only the biblically literate Christians that will know the difference between what is true and what is false."[31]

In an interview shortly before the *My Hope* evangelistic outreach on Graham's ninety-fifth birthday in 2013, his son Franklin Graham expressed grave concerns about the state of the church, especially the American church. "We have turned our back morally and spiritually on God," he says. "We are so concerned with being relevant to the culture. God never called us to be relevant to the culture. Our Father in heaven has called us to be obedient to him. We are to be faithful and to be true.

We are losing our country. We have all these religions coming into our country. We have opened up the door to Islam, Hinduism, and many other things that have come in. They are making great strides, but the church is asleep. My father has almost a century that he can look back over, and he sees how far our nation has fallen from where we were fifty, sixty, or seventy years ago and to where we are today. He loves our country, but he sees how wicked we have become as a nation—the abortions that take place, the pornography that is on television and on the Internet. He sees the moral decay and corruption that has taken place in Washington, DC, and the laws that are now being passed. It just breaks his heart and my father sees this and he just has a burden. He's approaching the age of ninety-five, but he can still do something to try to help wake the church of America up."[32]

Laurie says that many people in the church say they want to "see a healing of the land"—a spiritual awakening in America. "We need to get back to the Judeo-Christian roots that we founded our country upon, but it seems to me it would need to start in the church," Laurie says. "You know when God sees the spiritual and moral breakdown of a nation it's interesting that he looks to his people first. I would say our primary problem is not in the White House; it's in God's house and among God's people. The individual followers of Jesus need to ask themselves this question: Am I walking as closely with the Lord as I could? Am I living a compromised life? Are there sins that I need to turn from? I think if this were to happen in a widespread way, that to me would be a clear indication that we're having a revival. A mere increase in [church] attendance is not the indicator of that. What I want to see, or what I think we need to see in America, is Christians living up to their names as true followers of Christ."[33]

Chapter Thirteen

The Babylon-Jerusalem Matrix
(The Great Tribulation and the Fall of Babylon)

Babylon is Satan's attempt to deceive man about God. It's a parallel to Jerusalem and the Holy City of God, the place of peace. And it's a capital. It's always been the capital of Satan and in the end times even more so. The destruction of Babylon is predicted at a time when it will be the geopolitical center of the world, the economic center of the world, and the religious center of the world, and all dominated by the Antichrist, who is trying to supplant the faith of humanity in the death, burial, and resurrection of Jesus. He's going to try to use every means at his disposal, but thanks be to God, he'll only have seven years to do it.

—TIM LaHAYE, BESTSELLING COAUTHOR OF THE LEFT
BEHIND SERIES, IN AN EXCLUSIVE INTERVIEW

No human author, playwright, or screenwriter could ever have conceived of a story as infinitely complex, yet profoundly simple, as the one the Bible tells. As prophecy scholars are discovering, the Old and the New Testaments contain the encrypted past and future of humanity—a code so sophisticated that only a highly advanced supercomputer will be able to break it, and when this cosmic cryptogram is deciphered, it will constitute definitive proof of the existence of a superintelligence knowing the end from the beginning.

This prophetic enigma is embedded in the Bible's primary conflict—one that centers upon the fall of man from paradise, where Lucifer appeared to Adam and Eve in the form of a serpent and tempted them, saying "Ye shall be as gods" (Gen. 3:5 KJV).

In the first account of Babylon in Genesis, God offers clues as to where all of human history is heading. At the end of the story in Revelation, mankind's final rebellion is expressed in their worship of the Antichrist as Babylon returns. Babylon is the world system headed by Lucifer, and it is man's attempt to create a counterfeit of paradise and the kingdom of heaven. But just as God judged the first Babylon, God will judge "Babylon the Great" and "Mystery, Babylon" too.

The word *mystery* in "Mystery, Babylon" is a secret code of rebellion from God that was activated by Adam and Eve when they joined Lucifer and his angelic minions in their revolt against God. When Adam and Eve disobeyed God's Word, they activated the law of sin and death—the death force. This death force will result in what the Bible calls in 2 Thessalonians 2:7 "the mystery of iniquity" (KJV) or the "mystery of lawlessness" (ESV). One Bible translation describes it as the "secret power of lawlessness" (NIV).

In contrast to Babylon is Jerusalem, the "city of God" (Ps. 46:4 NIV). When God judges and destroys Babylon at the end of Revelation, he is destroying the world system. Babylon is described as a harlot because as a spiritual system it is unfaithful to the Word of God. God and his Word are the same and Jesus is the Word who assumed human form.

Babylon and the world system are built entirely on Lucifer's rebellion against God. In contrast, both the Jewish people in the Old Testament and the Christians in the New Testament, who are faithful to the Word of God, are referred to as God's bride. Any person who chooses to receive Jesus as their Savior supernaturally becomes part of the bride of Christ (see Rev. 21:2)—one of the Bible's most fascinating mysteries involving the God of love.[1]

The Bride of Christ and the Whore of Babylon

In a prophetic sense, the Bible—and the history of mankind—is the story of the conflict between Babylon and Jerusalem. Babylon is symbolic of mankind's rebellion against God. It is the queen of harlots. Jerusalem represents the faithful bride of Christ. It is the "holy city" (Rev. 21:2 KJV) in the heavenly age to come.

In Genesis, Babylon was both a city-state and a false religious system under the rule of Nimrod. Later, King Nebuchadnezzar oversaw the Neo-Babylonian Empire and invaded Judah three times.[2]

Throughout the Old Testament, the prophets repeatedly warned the Israelites to repent of their sins or God would use the Babylonians to punish them. After the Babylonians destroyed the Temple in Jerusalem in 586 BC, this prophetic message changed. The prophets then predicted that God would one day repay Babylon for her iniquity.[3]

Babylon doesn't appear again until Revelation—a book that combines nearly six hundred Old Testament references into a "comprehensive sequence of events"—as the geopolitical, financial, and false religious system under the authority of the Antichrist.[4]

Jerusalem Takes Center Stage in the End Times

In the final days of planet Earth, the prophets predicted Jerusalem would take center stage in the end-times epic. Thousands of years ago, long before the predicted rebirth of Israel in 1948, the biblical writers foresaw that the ancient Hebrew nation would play a leading role in the closing act of the human drama.

At a time when people are bombarded with images of ISIS beheading

Christians, heavily armed Russian troops surrounding the Ukraine, and Islamic extremists overrunning the ancient Babylonian region, many are asking whether the Middle East is about to explode into all-out war.[5]

It certainly seems that the nuclear showdown between Iran and Israel is about to enter the "critical 'end game' phase"—a sign that the prophetic time clock is about to go into hyperdrive. In recent years, Iranian leaders have repeatedly threatened to annihilate Israel. "[Netanyahu] called the Iranian a 'messianic, apocalyptic' regime bent on genocide, a reference to the Shia eschatology Khamenei holds that Iran must annihilate Israel and the U.S. to usher in the reign of the Twelfth Imam," Joel Rosenberg wrote. "Netanyahu also called the incoming Iranian president, Hassan Rouhani, 'a wolf in sheep's clothing' who has bragged in the past about negotiating with the West while secretly advancing nuclear enrichment. What's more, Netanyahu vowed not to 'wait too long' to stop Iran."[6]

A growing number of Middle East experts believe Iran already has several nuclear weapons and has been working with North Korea to develop the missile technologies necessary to attack Israel, Europe, and the United States. North Korean ships have been intercepted with materials and parts on board to assist the Iranians with their nuclear ambitions. Interestingly, Persia, or Iran, is specifically mentioned in Ezekiel 38 as an instigator of the "War of Gog and Magog."[7]

Many prophecy scholars believe the Israel-Iran nuclear showdown will result in the fulfillment of prophecies in Ezekiel 38 and 39—chapters pertaining to the "War of Gog and Magog." They say these chapters describe an end-times attack on Israel by Russia, Iran, and a coalition of other Middle Eastern nations.

They point to the fact that Russia and Iran have formed their first alliance in history, as predicted in the Bible. As a result, many believe the prophetic scenario the prophet Ezekiel foresaw twenty-six hundred years ago could soon come to pass. Under Vladimir Putin, the first Russian leader to form close ties with the Iranian regime, Russia is supplying nuclear expertise and armaments to the Islamic nation.

In Ezekiel 38, the prophet wrote that "Gog"—a word many believe refers to a Russian dictator—would lead a confederation of nations in a last days attack on Israel, triggering God's supernatural intervention and destruction of the invading forces. The Bible speaks of a "great earthquake," along with "torrents of rain, hailstones and burning sulfur," that rain down and incinerate the attacking armies (Ezek. 38:19, 22 NIV). "This will be a day of great judgment when God turns his supernatural fury against the enemies of Israel," Rosenberg said at a conference at Biola University in La Mirada, California.[8]

Prophecy experts believe several factors could motivate this confederation of nations to attack Israel, not the least of which is their hostility toward Israel and a desire to control the Middle East and plunder Israel's wealth and energy reserves.[9]

The most widely discussed scenario involves Israel engaging in a preemptive airstrike against Iran's nuclear facilities—sparking a massive counterattack. For years, the world has watched and wondered when Israel might carry out this assault. Recently, following failure of negotiations to reach an agreement on Iran's nuclear program, speculation has grown that this attack could happen in the near future.[10]

"As we observe the instability in the world today—as we see a superpower like Russia moving aggressively—it helps us see how the scenario we read about in Ezekiel 37 and 38 could unfold," Greg Laurie says. "This chain of events could be likened to dominoes stacked closely together. Once the first domino falls, all of them will fall rapidly."[11]

Some prophecy experts believe the Gog-Magog war will happen after the Rapture but several years before the Tribulation starts. This view is based on Ezekiel 39:9, which notes it will take the Israelites seven years to burn the weapons of war remaining on the battlefield. "The Bible says it takes seven years to burn the instruments of war, and since they are going to be out of the land in the last half of the seven-year Tribulation, then this would allow for seven years to burn the weapons and that would mean the interval between the Rapture and Tribulation is at least three and a half years," Thomas Ice says. "So that would give them seven years to burn the instruments up to the midpoint of the Tribulation. I think the Rapture will occur and then the Gog-Magog war will occur and then you'll have the revived Roman Empire."[12]

The Fullness of Iniquity and the Prophetic Time Crunch

Before the Tribulation begins, prophecy scholars believe several events must first take place, including the Gog-Magog war and what the prophet Daniel described as the "fullness of iniquity." When the world's cup of iniquity is full, the Antichrist will appear and prophetic events will quickly unfold. "At the 'time of the end' . . . the hundreds of remaining prophecies concerning Israel, the Antichrist, the Tribulation, and the return of Christ will begin to merge into a set time frame," Perry Stone, founder of Perry Stone Ministries, wrote in *Deciphering End-Time Prophetic Codes*. "Because we are in the time of the end, what would normally take centuries to fulfill will before our eyes occur within months, weeks, or hours—as we have entered the prophetic crunch time."[13]

While many eschatologists agree that prophetic events are accelerating, they differ on the sequence of these events. Prophecies are interspersed throughout the Bible, and opinions vary widely as to the order. For example, some believe the Gog-Magog war will occur prior to the Tribulation, while others think it will occur during this seven-year period.

The predominant end-times scenario is fairly easy to understand, though. Traditionally, the sequence begins with the Rapture followed by the seven-year Tribulation, Battle of Armageddon, Second Coming,

Millennium, the Great White Throne judgment, and the creation of the new heaven and the new earth.

Mark Hitchcock offers a fairly traditional chronology of events in the appendix of his book *The End*. However, even he concedes it's not easy assembling the pieces of the end-times puzzle in sequential order.[14]

Likewise, in his book *When?*, F. Kenton Beshore outlines fifteen prophetic events he expects to occur in the run-up to the Tribulation. Further, John F. Walvoord offers a chronology in *The Prophecy Knowledge Handbook*. Based on these sources and our own research, we've compiled a chronological timeline of how prophetic events might unfold. Given the wide range of opinions about when the Rapture will occur—before, at the midpoint, or at the end of the Tribulation—we left it off the timeline. While no one can be certain of the exact sequence of events, the following chronology offers a general overview. It should be noted that some of the events expected to happen during the Tribulation, including the formation of a global government and economic system and the rebuilding of Babylon, are already under way.[15]

Pretribulation Period
- War of Gog and Magog (Ezekiel 37–38; Daniel 11:40–45).
- Antichrist signs a peace treaty with Israel starting the seven-year Tribulation (Daniel 9:27; Ezekiel 38:8, 11).

First Half of the Seven-Year Tribulation
- Construction begins on third Jewish Temple in Jerusalem (Daniel 9:27; Revelation 11:1).
- Global government begins to form out of ten regional unions (Daniel 2:40–44; 7:7, 23; Revelation 17:12).
- World church arises (Revelation 17:1–5, 18; 13:11–17).
- Global economic system emerges (Revelation 13:15–18).
- Rebuilding of ancient Babylon in Iraq (Zechariah 5:5–11).

- Christ breaks open the seven-sealed scroll (Revelation 6; 8:1).
- 144,000 "Jewish Billy Grahams" preach the gospel (Revelation 7).
- Two witnesses preach (Revelation 11:2–3).
- Two witnesses killed, but God resurrects them (Revelation 11:7–12).
- Seven trumpet judgments sounded (Revelation 8–9).

Second Half of the Seven-Year Tribulation

- Antichrist breaks peace agreement and invades Israel (Daniel 9:27; 11:40–41).
- Antichrist erects abomination of desolation in the rebuilt temple (Daniel 9:27; 11:45; Matthew 24:15; 2 Thessalonians 2:4; Revelation 13:5, 15–18).
- False Prophet mandates mark of the Beast (Revelation 13:16–18).
- Antichrist slain (Daniel 11:45; Revelation 13:3, 12, 14; 17:8).
- Antichrist raised from the dead (Revelation 13:3).
- Seven bowl judgments poured out, including greatest earthquake in history (Revelation 16).

Battle of Armageddon

- Battle of Armageddon starts (Revelation 16:16).
- Babylon destroyed (Revelation 18).
- Jesus returns and eliminates enemies at Battle of Armageddon (Revelation 19:11–16; Isaiah 34:1–6; 63:1–5).

The Interval

- Antichrist and False Prophet thrown into the Lake of Fire (Revelation 19:20–21).
- Lucifer bound in the Abyss (Revelation 20:1–3).
- Millennial Temple constructed (Ezekiel 40–48).

Millennium
- One-thousand-year reign of Christ (Revelation 20).
- Satan's last revolt and defeat (Revelation 20:7–10).
- Great White Throne judgment (Revelation 20:11–15).

New Heaven and New Earth
- New heaven and new earth created (Isaiah 65:17; 66:22; 2 Peter 3:13; Revelation 21:1).
- God's people live in eternity (Revelation 21:9–22:5).

The Prophetic Countdown to Armageddon

While prophecy teachers may disagree on the order of events, most agree that the Tribulation will begin sometime after the Antichrist negotiates a peace treaty between Israel and its neighbors—dividing Jerusalem.

During the Gog-Magog war, God will supernaturally deliver Israel by wiping out the invading armies, leaving a power vacuum in the Middle East. If this occurs before the Tribulation, as many believe, the Antichrist will likely use the opportunity to seize control, consolidate his power, and negotiate a peace agreement between Israel and its neighbors. After God's supernatural destruction of the invaders, the Islamic nations will likely be willing to compromise—leading to the long-awaited two-state solution.[16]

For decades, many world leaders have sought to negotiate this treaty, but the agreement has eluded them—mostly because Israel is surrounded by about two dozen Islamic countries that are largely hostile to the Jews. "They hate the Jews and they are trying to destroy the Jews," Tim LaHaye says. "I watch Fox News a lot, and they're [Islamic leaders] on the news almost every night, talking about the Holocaust and how they want to exterminate the Jews, which is a fulfillment of prophecy.

They just have an obsessive hatred, and it can only be explained by a satanic inspiration."[17]

Soon, though, a diabolical genius will appear on the world stage, a figure so cunning that even the globe's most avowed enemies will accept his offer to lay down their arms and sign a peace agreement.

"In this geopolitical atmosphere, the belief is if we could just have one person lead the world, then we'd have peace—we'd have a one-world government," LaHaye says. "That's exactly what the book of Revelation teaches—that there will be an Antichrist coming on the scene. He will [bring peace to the Middle East] and diplomatically take control of the whole world. We're seeing the initial stages toward that now. I like to say that 'we're living in the end times of the end times.'"[18]

A Techno-Utopian Planet of Peace?

After brokering this pact between Israel and its neighbors, the Antichrist will propose an even more ingenious plan to bring the world together, fulfilling the dreams of globalists in a techno-utopian world of peace, prosperity, and coexistence. At long last, Lucifer will have accomplished what he set out to do in ancient Babylon, uniting the world under his puppet protégé via great "intrigue" (Dan. 11:21 NIV).

"The Antichrist will likely emerge from a major crisis," S. Douglas Woodward says. "It's certainly been the point of view of scholars that some major crisis, some major war in the Middle East, will in effect stimulate and cause this final seven-year period called the Tribulation period—sometimes equated to Daniel's seventieth week—that will kick off the Antichrist's rise to power."[19]

Whether the Antichrist arises out of Europe, America, or another region of the world, the Bible indicates that the "man of lawlessness" will feign being Israel's savior. Daniel and Luke indicate that he will initially lead a coalition of Western nations and eventually gain control of the whole world. "In Daniel's prophecies, the Antichrist is always associated with the final phase of the Roman Empire (the fourth kingdom)," Ed Hindson wrote. "Daniel 9:25–27 states that he will come from among the people who will destroy the Second Temple—that is, the Romans."[20]

His empire, the "fourth beast" in Daniel's vision, will be the Roman Empire "revived in a more powerful form" prior to the Second Coming, according to the late prophecy scholar Dave Hunt. "Since the Roman Empire was never ruled by ten kings at one time as foreseen in the image's ten toes and the fourth beast's ten horns ('ten kings that shall arise'— Dan. 7:24), it must be revived worldwide divided into ten regions under separate sub-rulers accountable to Antichrist," Hunt wrote in his "Mystery Babylon Identified" article. "Ten nations in Western Europe could hardly represent the revival of an empire which included far more in its day. Moreover, we are clearly told that 'power was given unto him over all kindreds, and tongues, and nations. And all that dwell upon the earth shall worship him...' (Rev. 13:7-8). Interestingly, today's world has already been divided into ten regions by the Club of Rome."[21]

During this time, the Antichrist and the False Prophet will establish a global economic system and false religious system.[22]

Then the Antichrist will commission the rebuilding of the Third Temple in Jerusalem, once a magnificent center of worship that housed the ark of the covenant. The ark, made famous in the film *Indiana Jones and the Raiders of the Lost Ark*, disappeared after the Babylonians destroyed Solomon's Temple in 586 BC. Roman soldiers destroyed the Second Temple in AD 70.[23]

The Seven-Sealed Scroll

In his prophetic vision of the end as described in Revelation, the apostle John watched as the resurrected Christ—whose hair was as "white as snow," eyes "like a flame of fire," and voice like the "sound of many waters" (1:14–15 NKJV)—broke a seven-sealed scroll, unleashing the Four Horsemen of the Apocalypse and fearsome judgments upon the earth. The rider on the white horse, the Antichrist, will inaugurate the greatest time of suffering and death in all of history, while simultaneously representing himself as a savior and man of peace. This will begin after Jesus breaks the second seal and riders on the red, black, and pale horses burst forth, bringing war, famine, and death to the world. Prophecy scholars estimate that anywhere from one-half to two-thirds or more of the world's population will die during the Tribulation—a holocaust unparalleled in magnitude and horror.

Then, when Christ breaks the sixth seal, a great earthquake will violently shake the world. At the same time, asteroids and comets will pummel the planet, immolating and upending mountains and unleashing a global storm of debris that blackens the light of the sun and turns the moon bloodred—making it unmistakable that God's wrath is being poured out on a rebellious world.

"It starts with the first seal judgment in the book of Revelation and then you have nineteen seal, trumpet, and bowl judgments," Ice says. "I believe the seal judgments will happen in the first half of the Tribulation. I believe many Jews will be saved by that point so when the abomination of desolation takes place they will flee to the wilderness. I also believe the two witnesses and 144,000 Jewish witnesses will help evangelize the world during the first half of the Tribulation."[24]

Two Witnesses and "144,000 Jewish Billy Grahams"

In an interlude prior to the breaking of the seventh seal, the apostle John in Revelation 7 describes 144,000 people from the twelve tribes of Israel who receive a "seal" on their foreheads that protects them from harm during the Tribulation. F. Kenton Beshore calls them the "144,000

Jewish Billy Grahams"—a special group of Jews who evangelize the world during the Tribulation.

Beshore, whose World Bible Society ministry has mailed millions of *Jewish Scriptures* booklets containing prophecies about Jesus' first and second comings to Jews worldwide, believes many Jews will read these and similar publications during the Tribulation, realize Jesus is the Messiah, and lead hundreds of millions to Christ.

"As I see it, 144,000 Jewish Billy Grahams are going to take the gospel to the world during the Tribulation," says Beshore, a prominent prophecy scholar who is the father of Kenton Beshore, pastor of Mariners Church in Irvine, California—one of the nation's twenty-five largest churches. "I know that I'll be gone when they turn to the Lord so they won't be able to hear my radio program. The only way they can be reached that I can see is to give them, by the literary method, specially prepared *Jewish Scriptures* now. They may not read it now, but Isaiah says they will hear a voice behind them, saying, 'This is the way, walk ye in it.' They will take the *Jewish Scriptures,* read them, and 144,000 will be called out. Then they will go out, Spirit-empowered, to take the gospel to every tongue, tribe, and nation. I see billions coming to the Lord during the Tribulation."[25]

During this time, angels will also fly throughout the world, preaching the "everlasting gospel...and communicating to every living person at that time." "Who but a loving God would plan that this would be the only time in history where angels would be entrusted with spreading the gospel? At the same time, he commissions 144,000 Jews go out and reach multitudes that no one can number," LaHaye says. "An innumerable host of people will come to faith in Christ during the Tribulation period. That's why I'm thrilled about the fact that we can lay a foundation in this generation for those people to carry and communicate the power of the Spirit...Can you imagine 144,000 Apostle Pauls going out to reach multitudes that no one can number? One day I decided to see how many expressions of love from God I could find in the book of Revelation, and I have actually come up with thirty-two of them. Now when you think about the love of God expressed in his mercy and forgiveness thirty-two times in the book of Revelation, you find it's not a book of wrath; it's a book of blessings—spiritual blessings."[26]

It's also during this time that God will raise two witnesses to preach the gospel to the world. Many believe these figures will be Moses and Elijah, two of the most influential figures in Jewish history. Both appeared on the Mount of Transfiguration with Jesus. The story in Matthew 17:2 notes that Elijah and Moses appeared in the presence of a few disciples and Jesus was "transfigured before them. His face shone like the sun, and his clothes became as white as the light" (NIV). The ministry of the two witnesses is described in Revelation 11:3–6:

"And I will appoint my two witnesses, and they will prophesy for 1,260 days, clothed in sackcloth." They are "the two olive trees" and the two lampstands, and "they stand before the Lord of the earth." If anyone tries to harm them, fire comes from their mouths and devours their enemies. This is how anyone who wants to harm them must die. They have power to shut up the heavens so that it will not rain during the time they are prophesying; and they have power to turn the waters into blood and to strike the earth with every kind of plague as often as they want. (NIV)

In the Old and the New Testaments, God often used "miracles to authenticate His messengers." "In the Tribulation period, when the world is overrun by supernatural demonic activity, false religion, murder, sexual perversion, and unrestrained wickedness, the supernatural signs performed by these two witnesses will mark them as true prophets of God," Ron Rhodes wrote.[27]

The apostle John wrote that the "beast" will arise from the "bottomless pit" and kill the two witnesses, their bodies will lie unburied on the streets of Jerusalem for three and a half days, people worldwide will be able to "gaze" at them (Rev. 11:7–9 ESV), and then God will resurrect them. "That would not have been possible a hundred years ago," Greg Laurie says. "But we have satellite technology today and a majority of the population has cell phones—even more to the point, smartphones, which is like a computer in your pocket. You realize that a prophecy like that could happen today when everybody could access the event as it's happening in real time—watching it."[28]

One of the primary purposes of the Tribulation is to give the billions of people alive at that time a chance to decide whether to receive or reject Christ. Daniel 9:27 describes this as "the consummation" (NKJV). If they accept Christ, Revelation 7:3 says they will receive the mark of the Father on their foreheads. "But they will then be 'open season' for martyrdom at the hands of the religious system of Babylon, the government leaders headed by Antichrist, the False Prophet, and the people whose lust for sin is surpassed only by their hatred of Christians," LaHaye and Ice wrote. "It is doubtful that many Tribulation saints will survive to the Millennium...In grace and love, He will give more supernatural signs and leadings of His Spirit than at any time in the history of the world, proving that He is 'not willing that any should perish, but that all should come to repentance' (2 Peter 3:9)."[29]

The Abomination of Desolation and the Mark of the Beast

At the midpoint of the Tribulation, the Bible predicts, the Antichrist will break his peace agreement with Israel, enter the Holy of Holies of the rebuilt Temple, and declare himself as God. Matthew 24:15 describes this as the "abomination of desolation" (KJV). Matthew admonished the Jewish people to "flee into the mountains" when this happens (v. 16 KJV).

"The Jewish people will flee to Petra where they will be protected for three-and-a-half years," Ice says. "I believe this will be supernatural protection. Some people call it the Second Exodus where the language in Revelation 12 is remindful of the language in Exodus where it says he will nourish them and hide them away. I take it to mean he will provide manna and other sustenance for the Jewish remnant in Petra."[30]

At this time, Revelation 13:1–3 indicates, the Antichrist will suffer a "mortal wound" (v. 3 ESV)—perhaps from an assassination attempt—but Satan will miraculously heal him. "It is within the power of Satan to heal, and it is possible that he would heal this ruler and restore him to life," John F. Walvoord wrote. "In any event and regardless of what the interpretation is, the supernatural origin and special powers of this world ruler are revealed."[31]

During the second half of the Tribulation, the Antichrist and the False Prophet will mandate that people receive the mark of the Beast. Throughout history, interpretations regarding the mark and the number 666 have differed. As the number 777 reflects the "perfect Trinity, perhaps 666 points to a being who aspires to perfect deity." Others have suggested that the number 666 refers to the Roman emperor Nero because the numerical value of the letters in Nero's name in Hebrew totals 666. "One thing is certain," Ron Rhodes wrote. "In some way that is presently unknown to us, this number will be a crucial part of his identification. It is sobering to realize that receiving this mark of the beast is apparently an unpardonable sin (Revelation 14:9–10)... Once made, there is no turning back... The choice will cause a radical polarization... One chooses either for or against the Antichrist... One must choose to either receive the mark and live (being able to buy and sell) or reject the mark and face suffering and death. One must choose to follow Antichrist and eat well or reject the Antichrist and starve."[32]

The Seven Trumpets

Following the breaking of the seventh seal, the apostle John recorded a brief silence in heaven followed by the sounding of the trumpet judgments—ones even more terrifying than the seal judgments. The seventh seal contains all the trumpet judgments.

The first three will involve a combination of asteroids, meteors, comets, and volcanic eruptions. The first burns a third of the earth's vegetation, the second destroys a third of sea life, and the third poisons a third of the world's fresh water. The fourth judgment brings partial darkness upon the earth. Then the fifth trumpet brings a demonic locust plague, and the sixth results in the deaths of a third of the earth's inhabitants through "another demonic visitation." Some Bible scholars believe Revelation 9 refers to an actual demonic army that is released from the "bottomless pit" upon the earth during the Tribulation.[33]

"It's known as the overflowing scourge," Beshore says. "It's also pictured in Joel 2:1–14 where Joel sees…a terrible host of demons…He likens them to a plague of locusts."[34]

The Bowls of God's Wrath

Then, following the seal and trumpet judgments, the worst punishments of all befall the world and its inhabitants—the infamous bowls of God's wrath. These horrific judgments are designed to break the power of Babylon—the coalition of forces under control of the Antichrist and the False Prophet.

These judgments, including painful sores on those who took the mark, water turning to blood, scorching heat, engulfing darkness, and the greatest earthquake in history, are directed against the Babylonian world system and are reminiscent of the plagues God visited upon ancient Egypt. Revelation 16:18–21 offers a terrifying picture of the severity of this series of final punishments that level cities and mountains and smash humankind with hundred-pound hailstones from the heavens:

> Then there came flashes of lightning, rumblings, peals of thunder and a severe earthquake. No earthquake like it has ever occurred since mankind has been on earth, so tremendous was the quake. The great city split into three parts, and the cities of the nations collapsed. God remembered Babylon the Great and gave her the cup filled with the wine of the fury of his wrath. Every island fled away and the mountains could not be found. From the sky huge hailstones, each weighing about a hundred pounds, fell on people. And they cursed God on account of the plague of hail, because the plague was so terrible. (NIV)

The Battle of Armageddon

Amid this final series of bowl judgments, the Battle of Armageddon will ignite in the Middle East. In this apocalyptic showdown, the "kings of the earth" will gather in the Valley of Esdraelon, near the ancient city of Megiddo in northern Israel, for what the Bible calls the "battle on that great day of God Almighty" (Rev. 16:14 NKJV).

The Antichrist and his allied armies will gather to attack Israel in a last-ditch attempt to prevent the return of Christ by eradicating the Jewish people—hoping to thwart Jesus' promise in Matthew 23:39 to only return once the Jews and their leaders asked him to return.[35] At the end of this ferocious battle—actually a culmination of a series of military conflicts—God will confound their foolish scheme.

"Armageddon will be the last great world war of history, and it will take place in Israel in conjunction with the Second Coming of Christ," Thomas Ice wrote. "According to the Bible, great armies from the East and the West will gather and assemble to strike a final blow against Israel...Its human purpose will be to gather the armies of the world to execute the Antichrist's 'final solution' to the Jewish problem. This is why Jesus Christ chooses this moment in history for his return to earth—to thwart the Antichrist's attempted annihilation of the Jews and to destroy the armies of the world. It seems only fitting, in light of mankind's bloody legacy, that a worldwide military conflict against Israel should precipitate the return of Christ."[36]

"Fallen! Fallen Is Babylon the Great!"

As the Battle of Armageddon continues, Revelation 17–18 and Jeremiah 50 describe how a great northern military force will attack and destroy the "daughter of Babylon" in one hour.

"While the Antichrist is with his armies at Armageddon, his capital will be attacked and destroyed," Ice wrote. "The irony is that while [the] Antichrist is gathering his armies in northern Israel for the purpose of attacking Jerusalem (God's city), God attacks the Antichrist's city—Babylon...According to Isaiah 13:19 and Jeremiah 50:40, the destruction will be as devastating and complete as was that of Sodom and Gomorrah. Once the attack and destruction are finished, Babylon will be uninhabitable and will never again be rebuilt."[37]

Afterward, as described in Revelation 18:2–3, the apostle John hears an angel announce:

> *"Fallen! Fallen is Babylon the Great!"*
> *She has become a dwelling for demons*
> *and a haunt for every impure spirit,*
> *a haunt for every unclean bird,*
> *a haunt for every unclean and detestable animal.*
> *For all the nations have drunk*

the maddening wine of her adulteries.
The kings of the earth committed adultery with her,
and the merchants of the earth grew rich from her excessive
luxuries. (NIV)

Babylon—the great political, economic, and religious capital of the Antichrist's empire—will be finally destroyed.[38]

In heaven, the news of Babylon's destruction is met with great rejoicing as the heavenly host acknowledge that the Lord has judged "the great prostitute who corrupted the earth by her adulteries" and has "avenged on her the blood of his servants" (Rev. 19:2 NIV).

The Second Coming

Meanwhile, undeterred by the destruction of his capital, the Antichrist and his armies attack Jerusalem with overwhelming force—winning an initial victory. Afterward, the Antichrist targets the remnants of the Jews in Petra and Bozrah.

Realizing the Antichrist's forces are about to destroy them, the Jews call out to their Messiah as God removes their spiritual blindness and they experience spiritual regeneration. "This is in keeping with Joel 2:28–29, which informs us that there will be a spiritual awakening of the Jewish remnant," Ron Rhodes wrote. "In terms of chronology, the Israelites will confess their national sin (Leviticus 26:40–42; Jeremiah 3:11–18; Hosea 5:15) and then be saved, thereby fulfilling Paul's prophecy in Romans 11:25–27. In dire threat of Armageddon, Israel will plead for their newly found Messiah to return and deliver them (Zechariah 12:20; Matthew 23:37–39; see also Isaiah 53:1–9), and their deliverance will surely come (see Romans 10:13–14)...It is sad to recognize that according to Zechariah 13:7–9, some two-thirds of the Jewish people will lose their lives during the Tribulation period. However, one-third—the remnant—will survive, turn to the Lord, and be saved (see Isaiah 64:1–12)."[39]

Suddenly, in the most climactic moment in all of history, the spiritual heavens will literally open—revealing the true nature of all reality in all its celestial glory—and Jesus Christ will return to earth. Known as the "blessed hope," this is the account the apostle John gave of "the appearing of the glory of our great God and Savior, Jesus Christ" (Titus 2:13 NIV):

> I saw heaven standing open and there before me was a white horse, whose rider is called Faithful and True. With justice he judges and wages war. His eyes are like blazing fire, and on his head are many crowns. He has a name written on him that no one knows but he himself. He is dressed in a robe dipped in blood, and his name is the Word of God. The armies of heaven were following him, riding on white horses and dressed in fine linen, white and clean. Coming out of his mouth is a sharp sword with which to strike down the nations. "He will rule them with an iron scepter." He treads the winepress of the fury of the wrath of God Almighty. On his robe and on his thigh he has this name written: KING OF KINGS AND LORD OF LORDS. (Rev. 19:11–16 NIV)

Jesus Wins

The glorious appearing of Christ not only will bring to consummation victory over Satan, the Antichrist, and the False Prophet but will also usher in the millennial kingdom—the thousand-year reign of Christ on earth.

Following the Second Coming and during an interval of seventy-five days, preparations will begin for the millennial kingdom. During this time, the Antichrist and the False Prophet will be thrown into the Lake of Fire, Lucifer will be bound in the Abyss, and construction will begin on the millennial Temple. After this interval, the thousand-year reign of Christ on earth will commence.

"Christ will sit on the throne of David and rule the world, bringing peace and righteousness," LaHaye and Ice wrote. "The Bible describes the Millennium as a time of righteousness, obedience, holiness, truth, and fullness of the Holy Spirit as never before."[40]

At the end of the Millennium, Satan will be released from the Abyss and will gather people throughout the world in a final rebellion to destroy Christ, Jerusalem, and his people. But God will destroy them. Afterward, Satan will be cast into the Lake of Fire forever.

This will be followed by the Great White Throne judgment, in which God will judge all unbelievers. Those who have not accepted Jesus as their Savior and whose names are not found in the Book of Life will be cast into the Lake of Fire. Afterward, God will create the new heaven and the new earth where his people will live for eternity.

During a recent sermon at Saddleback Church, Jud Wilhite, pastor of the twenty-one-thousand-member Christian Central Church in Las Vegas and a *New York Times* bestselling author, told the audience how the book of Revelation is ultimately a book of hope.

"The first thing I want to point out here is that the book of Revelation is at its very core a revelation about Jesus... It's an unveiling of who he is. And this is like the big idea for the book of Revelation... Are you ready? Jesus wins. There it is. Jesus wins. And through faith we can share in that victory, even in the middle of the mess. We can share in that victory in our lives today."[41]

The book of Revelation is a reminder to the world that God is "working a bigger plan that we don't understand," Wilhite told the congregation. "He is large and in charge. He's not finished. He's not done. He's not checked out. He's not kind of off in la-la land. He's working and he's moving and all of history is marching toward the culmination of what God ultimately has prepared. Revelation 1:7 says, 'Look, he comes with the clouds of heaven and everyone will see him, even those who pierced him and all the nations of the world will mourn for him.'...The overall thrust of the entire book of Revelation and really the Bible is hope. It's looking forward. It's looking forward with anticipation that Christ will return and that when he returns evil will be dealt the final blow and God's justice will ultimately prevail."[42]

The Babylon Code Is Broken

The final chapters of Revelation reveal the end of the enigmatic Babylon code and the final defeat of Lucifer. Ultimately, the Babylonian system, the Tower of Babel occult knowledge, and the entire New World Order are revealed as a counterfeit of the kingdom of heaven.

When Adam and Eve rejected God's Word, the rule of Lucifer or the Babylonian system began. The Babylonian or world system was a multidimensional and spiritual system built on a precise mathematical coding system that created a virtual reality energized by the law of sin and death.

This is why the Tower of Babel was constructed as not only an inter-dimensional portal but as a mathematical time system that used the stars and planets as algorithms. It was as if Satan broke into God's eternal system and temporarily hacked into the coding systems of God in an attempt to corrupt the system and overthrow the master programmer.

The world or Babylonian system functioned as a kind of holographic reality projected from the minds of Lucifer, his fallen angels, and fallen men. It's a vast satanic illusion superimposed over the creation of God. This illusion was referred to by the illumined ones as magic or science. When Jesus died upon the cross, he destroyed the power of sin and death, and thus the energy force driving this planetary matrix that has enslaved billions of people.

The breaking of the Babylon code will initiate the great cosmic reboot in which the Babylonian system is destroyed and all creation will be rebooted according to the original "God code," or source code, granting eternal life to all who have accepted Jesus as their Savior.

The Most Incredible and Joyous Cosmic Celebration

When Jesus returns, the saints of God will be taken to heaven to participate in the most incredible and joyous cosmic celebration known as the "Marriage Supper of the Lamb."

Those who have chosen to accept God's free offer of salvation in Jesus Christ, who have been cleansed by the blood of the Lamb, will experience perfect love and union with God and the restoration of all that was lost in the Garden of Eden. As such, not on the basis of trying to be good, but on the basis of receiving God's free gift of salvation, they will supernaturally be made pure and holy and will be taken to heaven to join in on the greatest party in the universe, the "Marriage Supper of the Lamb."

As these prophetic events unfold, Babylon—the entire worldly system and the old heavens and earth—will be completely burned up as Jesus brings into being a new heaven, a new earth, and the New Jerusalem. In Revelation 21:2–4, the heavenly Jerusalem is described as God's bride descending in all its glory and magnificence as a supernatural city that literally will hover above the new earth:

I saw the Holy City, the new Jerusalem, coming down out of heaven from God, prepared as a bride beautifully dressed for her husband. And I heard a loud voice from the throne saying, "Look! God's dwelling place is now among the people, and he will dwell with them. They will be his people, and God himself will be with them and be their God. He will wipe every tear from their eyes.

There will be no more death or mourning or crying or pain, for the old order of things has passed away." (NIV)

There are no human words to describe the beauty, love, joy, and peace that will radiate from this New Jerusalem. There will be no more need for the sun because the very glory of God will light up this brand-new world and the streets of the heavenly city will glow magnificently as translucent gold.

This was the city that Abraham was looking for as he obeyed God during his earthly pilgrimage. Unlike "Mystery, Babylon—the Mother of Harlots," God is faithful to his Word. That is why Revelation 19:11 says this about when Jesus Christ returns to the earth at his Second Coming to destroy Babylon: "I saw heaven opened, and behold a white horse; and he that sat upon him was called Faithful and True" (KJV). Jesus Christ, in distinct contrast to the "Mystery, Babylon" world system built on lies, is the Truth.

This means for everyone reading these words that if you choose to accept Jesus as your Savior, he will be faithful and true to save you and give you eternal life in the new heaven, the new earth, and the New Jerusalem.

If you have not yet made that choice, as the authors of *The Babylon Code*, we strongly encourage you to do that before you finish reading this book. Your eternal destiny rests upon this decision.

Chapter Fourteen

"God's Prophet" and Hope for the World

The New Testament is full of hope and expectancy. The Bible says, "For our hope is in heaven; from whence also we look for the Savior, the Lord Jesus Christ" (Philippians 3:20). "And there were great voices in heaven, saying, The kingdoms of this world are become the kingdoms of our Lord, and of his Christ; and he shall reign forever and ever" (Revelation 11:15). That promise will someday become literal history, and with God's help we're going to be a part of that history that is yet to come. Only Jesus Christ when He comes back again is going to bring it. He will defeat every enemy. Sin will be eliminated. Death will be eliminated. War will be eliminated. Crime will be eliminated. The hope of the second coming of Christ generates energy and sacrifice and faithfulness and diligence and zeal.

—BILLY GRAHAM, "AMERICA'S PASTOR," IN AN
EXCLUSIVE INTERVIEW

In the summer of 2012, Billy Graham wrote an open letter to America, calling the nation to turn back to God. In the letter, the world-renowned evangelist asked what his late wife, Ruth, would think of the United States today.

"Some years ago, my wife, Ruth, was reading the draft of a book

I was writing," Graham wrote. "When she finished a section describing the terrible downward spiral of our nation's moral standards and the idolatry of worshipping false gods such as technology and sex, she startled me by exclaiming, 'If God doesn't punish America, He'll have to apologize to Sodom and Gomorrah.' She was probably thinking of a passage in Ezekiel where God tells why He brought those cities to ruin: 'Now this was the sin of...Sodom: She and her daughters were arrogant, overfed and unconcerned; they did not help the poor and needy. They were haughty and did detestable things before me. Therefore I did away with them as you have seen' (Ezekiel 16:49–50). I wonder what Ruth would think of America if she were alive today. In the years since she made that remark, millions of babies have been aborted and our nation seems largely unconcerned. Self-centered indulgence, pride, and a lack of shame over sin are now emblems of the American lifestyle."[1]

In the letter, Graham went on to describe how a chaplain in a police department in the South was ordered not to mention the name of Jesus in prayer. He noted how similar incidents are now commonplace across America as "society strives to avoid any possibility of offending anyone—except God."

"My heart aches for America and its deceived people," Graham wrote. "The wonderful news is that our Lord is a God of mercy, and He responds to repentance. In Jonah's day, Nineveh was the lone world superpower—wealthy, unconcerned, and self-centered. When the Prophet Jonah finally traveled to Nineveh and proclaimed God's warning, people heard and repented. I believe the same thing can happen once again, this time in our nation."[2]

Believing America could experience another "great spiritual awakening," the Billy Graham Evangelistic Association held its largest outreach in American history on November 7, 2013—Graham's ninety-fifth birthday. The *My Hope America with Billy Graham* event involved more than twenty-six thousand churches—one in every twelve nationwide—and hundreds of thousands of people. More than four million people tuned in to watch Graham's message on the Fox News Channel, Christian cable networks, and more than one hundred local television stations. Millions of others connected online through the website, YouTube, Facebook, and other avenues. In addition, the video was shown in churches, living rooms, bookstores, coffee shops, prisons, rescue missions, and even drive-in theaters and aboard cruise ships. More than 110,000 people indicated making a commitment to Jesus during the *My Hope America* campaign. A second broadcast took place on Graham's ninety-sixth birthday in 2014.

"Our plan is to do *My Hope* each year for the next five years—we want the week of my father's birthday (November 7) to be Evangelism Week across America," says Franklin Graham, president of the Billy Graham Evangelistic Association. "We want to continue to produce powerful evangelistic programs and material that churches and individuals can use to reach the lost around them for Christ."[3]

The broadcast of Graham's messages came as a number of major evangelists—Greg Laurie, Reinhard Bonnke, Luis Palau, Banning Liebscher, and others—had turned their attention toward America in the hope of helping inspire a resurgence of faith. Since then, a growing number of religious leaders have joined Graham in encouraging believers to share their faith with family, friends, neighbors, and coworkers.

Many believe *My Hope* has helped to inspire a new evangelistic movement and energized believers to share their faith with others.

"We are thrilled by what we are hearing of the impact of *My Hope America with Billy Graham* across the nation," says Preston Parrish, the BGEA vice president for *My Hope America*. "We are daily receiving reports of people who made decisions for Jesus Christ as a result of the effort, but at the same time we are also getting a very clear picture that this movement has not run its course. This is indeed ongoing and may even be developing steam and additional momentum."[4]

Is Graham right? Is it possible to halt the countdown to the end of history as it was in Nineveh? And if so, is there enough momentum behind the *My Hope* movement and similar evangelistic efforts to turn America and the world back to God before it's too late?

We believe there is. We believe there is still hope.

In this final chapter of *The Babylon Code*, we'll detail a vision Paul McGuire had of just this—a potential "golden fire" of spiritual awakening sweeping across America and the world. It's a vision shared by many faith leaders and ministers with prophetic gifting worldwide.

In this vision, God indicated that he wants to pour out his mercy, but the key is repentance—first among God's people. God wants to bring a final Great Awakening in the last days, specifically to America first, and from there it will spread around the world.

But it's contingent on genuine repentance, especially among God's people.

A Vision and Prophetic Word from Paul McGuire

On July 4, 2012, I was praying with my wife for our nation. I began repenting and confessing my sins before God, and then, as an intercessor, I began repenting for and confessing the sins of the church, specifically in America. What happened next I want to describe to you in the most rational, calm, and detailed manner I can. I am not one who is given easily into what people may describe as "mystical" religious experiences. I have a very strong, logical, and rational mind, and what I am about to share with you will be presented in that manner.

Immediately, as I was repenting for my sins and then the sins of the church, my body and hands were set on fire with the most intense heat I have ever experienced. I held up my hands before my face, and not wanting to be swayed by emotion, I related to my wife in a very calm, methodical, and almost clinical manner what was happening to me.

I said, "My fingers are burning with the most intense heat I have ever experienced in my life; they are on fire. In fact, my entire body is burning with fire, and I am surprised I am not in physical pain because I am literally burning." Then what felt like a wave of power went through my body, heating up certain regions of my body, and I simply sighed this deep breath as I was released of something. I said to my wife, "I have just been healed of something very profound, but I do not specifically know what I was healed from." It was just a deep inner knowing that I was healed.

About two years later, I had to go to the doctor for somewhat serious medical tests, but when I completed the tests, the doctor was surprised to discover that everything was fine and that I was in perfect health.

Before I continue with what happened, I want to carefully define my experience. In many years of walking with the Lord I had experienced many things of a miraculous nature. For example, I had experienced what some people call the "Baptism of Fire" or being "set on fire" in revival. I am also very aware of the difference between when the Lord speaks to us through our inner spirit or simply inspires our imagination to see pictures or what some people, I believe mistakenly, call visions. Although these experiences may be legitimate, as long as they don't conflict with the Scripture, they are what I refer to as God-inspired pictures and imaginations. However, they are not visions in the strict, biblical definition of the word.

The incredible heat I experienced and knowing that I was being set on fire and burning was far beyond any previous experience I'd had. It was at a completely different level. As I was "burning," the next thing I knew was that I was looking down on the North American continent as if I was watching from a satellite. First, I saw the same fire that I was burning with ignite God's people specifically in Southern California and up and down the state of California. I had the distinct sense that I was watching a biblical, last days revival break out in California. Then I saw the fires of this revival begin to spread slowly from California to neighboring states. At this point the fire began to look like the intense glory of God coming upon millions of God's people who were in darkness. The glory illuminating the earth in certain states was so intense that I understood that this revival had become another Great Awakening.

The Biblical, Last Days Revival

The color of the glory of God illuminating the people was of a distinct brilliant and golden hue. It was similar to the color of light that the film industry calls the "magic hour." This is not to be confused with anything mystical. In my work as a former feature-film producer in Hollywood, we shot a number of films during sunrise and sunset when the light has this beautiful golden hue that bathes the actors and the scenes in a very remarkable color.

So from the point of view of a satellite over the North American continent I began to see the glory of God move slowly from the West Coast to the East Coast, and at the same time it was spreading to states in the North and the South. As I watched, this intense supernatural glory began to illuminate millions of God's people with light and they began to rise out of the darkness and into prayer. I heard the Lord say, "They are starting to rise; they are starting to rise in prayer." I was overwhelmed with the holiness and majesty of God as I saw God's people begin to rise in a Great Awakening that moved across the entire United States and then began to spread across the world.

The next thing I knew I was taken out of this vision and found myself contemplating what I had just seen. I want to emphasize that I don't use the word *vision* casually. Again, I believe it's important to carefully define the nature of what I saw. First, although I've had numerous pictures or movie-like images play through my head, these were almost always where my own human imagination was creating the pictures and I was participating in what was being generated.

During my life, I've experienced a number of powerful, supernatural miracles, but as far as I can recall this was the first time I'd had a true vision—under the biblical definition—where I supernaturally saw something and it was not generated by my human imagination.

Upon reflection, I believe the Lord allowed me to experience this to show me his will and desire for America and how it would affect the world. I saw a vision of what God desires to do in America because of his great love for his people.

However, because God must operate within his own laws in balance with his holiness, righteousness, and love, he cannot do this until his people come to him in personal repentance, gather together in small groups and at churches, and specifically repent of their sins and then ask God for his mercy, revival, and another Great Awakening.

I believe I have been directed by the Lord to share this experience with God's people, teach about its biblical basis, and lead God's people in this kind of prayer, which I have been doing at meetings and live on Christian television and radio. By God's grace, I have been able to share this with millions of people around the world.

I want to emphasize that what I saw was conditional and based on God's people responding in true repentance. In addition, what I saw should not be misconstrued as something that in any way can change what God has carefully written in his prophetic Word. Finally, I understand that what I saw was God supernaturally responding to the prayers of his people. It does not mean that God is going to wave a "magic wand" over America and that all our problems will go away. Nor does it mean that some kind of Reconstructionist event will take place in America and transform the country into a Christian nation.

Could God Suspend the Prophetic Time Clock?

What the vision means is that God is willing to whatever degree he chooses to give people real hope for the future. It means that God may grant us temporary relief, delay the timing of certain judgments, grant us an extension of time, and supernaturally bless, guide, and protect his people in the middle of adversity.

The problems in America and the world are deeply entrenched, and there are many prophetic signs that would indicate that we live in a time of an acceleration and convergence of prophetic events.

But if God's people are truly willing to repent and seek his face, God will offer his supernatural mercy and send us a biblical, last days revival and Great Awakening that would, to a significant degree, drive back the powers of darkness and supernaturally protect God's people.

The biblical basis for this is found in 2 Chronicles 7:14: "If my people, who are called by my name, will humble themselves and pray and seek my face and turn from their wicked ways, then I will hear from heaven, and I will forgive their sin and will heal their land" (NIV).

Although this verse was specifically given to the children of Israel, it may be applied to varying degrees to the church, although the church has not replaced Israel in God's prophetic program. The Pilgrims and Puritans who founded America made a covenant with God based on the same covenant God made with ancient Israel, and to whatever degree, God has honored that covenant.

There are many people who look at what is going on in America and the world and say that there is nothing anyone can do because America is under the judgment of God for its sins. Many of these people are Christians. Others say the growing evil in the hearts of men and women is evidence of the fact that we are in the last days and all we can do is look for Jesus to return.

However, the Bible does not teach fatalism or escapism.

The biblical message is that as long as we are here on earth, we are to obey the words of Jesus Christ to communicate the gospel to all people and to love our neighbors as ourselves. All those who call themselves believers are to pray for an end to the violence in the world, and the church is to visibly demonstrate before the world the love we have for people.

While hosting my nationally syndicated radio show, the *Paul McGuire Show*, a man called and said, "Paul, it's like I am sitting in a movie theater, eating popcorn and watching the end times unfold." This man's attitude reflects the feelings of millions of people who are Christians. But does the Bible say we are to just sit passively by and watch things get worse and worse until Jesus returns?

Let's consider what the apostle Paul wrote in 2 Timothy 3:1–5:

But mark this: There will be terrible times in the last days. People will be lovers of themselves, lovers of money, boastful, proud, abusive, disobedient to their parents, ungrateful, unholy, without love, unforgiving, slanderous, without self-control, brutal, not lovers of the good, treacherous, rash, conceited, lovers of pleasure rather than lovers of God—having a form of godliness but denying its power. (NIV)

Then in the final part of the chapter the Bible says, "Evildoers and impostors will go from bad to worse, deceiving and being deceived. But as for you, continue in what you have learned" (3:13–14 NIV). The apostle Paul is teaching all followers of God not to be passive in the face of evil, but to actively continue in the fight against evil and to do what is right.

The Bible Doesn't Teach End-Times Fatalism

The prevalent belief among Christians is that in the last days the world will continue to get worse and worse because men and women will become more evil. However, well-meaning, misinformed people jump to the conclusion that all we can do is hold on until the end. But nowhere does the Bible teach this kind of fatalism.

Another man called my radio show and asked, "Are we not in danger of undoing God's prophetic program in asking God to intervene?" I said to him as kindly as I could, "No, because not even one tiny item in God's prophetic timeline as he has revealed in his prophetic Word can be changed! God is the sovereign King of the universe, and if our prayers were to conflict with his will, he would simply overrule them by saying no. Don't give yourself too much credit; you cannot overrule the will of God with your prayers."

Finally, after giving an overview of all the evil in the last days, Paul says in 2 Timothy 3:16–17, "All Scripture is God-breathed and is useful for teaching, rebuking, correcting and training in righteousness, so that the servant of God may be thoroughly equipped for every good work" (NIV).

The apostle Paul is telling all believers that the Bible has a supernatural author and that the Bible is not to be viewed as myths or concocted stories. God has given us the entire Bible to equip us for every good work that he wants us to be doing in the last days.

The apostle Paul is not giving any of us any "wiggle room" in order to rationalize being apathetic, fatalistic, or disengaged from our divine assignment to do the "good work" God has called all of us to do. We are not trying to earn our salvation through this work, but it is part of our job description. This means that all true believers in Jesus, even in the last days, should be actively involved in sharing our faith in Jesus, feeding the poor, clothing the naked, ministering to orphans and widows, and finding ways to love people through practical actions so that they might come to Jesus. This also means being good citizens and getting involved in the community and the political process. If you truly "love your neighbor as yourself," as God originally commanded in Leviticus

19:18 (NIV), then you will become informed and vote because your vote is a tangible way to make sure laws are passed to protect and help people.

Finally, we are commanded to pray for "kings and all those in authority, that we may live peaceful and quiet lives in all godliness and holiness" (1 Tim. 2:2 NIV). That means praying for those in both political parties whether or not we agree with them or happen to like them. How can God move in their lives if we do not pray for them?

The way people will know that God exists is when they see that we as Christians love one another and reach out and love them in practical ways. In John 13:35, the apostle John wrote, "By this all will know that you are My disciples, if you have love for one another" (NKJV).

God's Judgment and the Next Great Awakening

As people have watched all the wars, freak weather, tsunamis, and mega-earthquakes in recent years, many have asked, "Is this the end of the world?" It's one of the most common questions people ask me.

> For nation will rise against nation, and kingdom against kingdom.
> And there will be famines, pestilences, and earthquakes in various
> places. (Matt. 24:7 NKJV)

On January 17, 1994, at 4:41 a.m., my wife and our three young children were awakened to an earsplitting noise that sounded as if a locomotive had crashed through our house. Our home began to rock so violently that we thought it would collapse at any second.

We made it safely to our driveway at the end of a cul-de-sac. We were wrapped in blankets and all the lights of the city were off. Slowly, our neighbors also came outside wrapped in their blankets. It was pitch-black, with the stars above us burning more brightly than usual.

Several of our neighbors, including agnostics and those of different faiths, asked me this question repeatedly: "Are these the signs of the times that Jesus Christ talked about, and does this mean this is the end of the world?" They had heard that I write books about Bible prophecy and so in this moment of vulnerability they began to ask these questions. We found out later that the block we lived on was at the epicenter of the 6.7-magnitude Northridge earthquake.

Questions such as "Is this the end of the world?" or "Is America under the judgment of God?" have become increasingly common as many people have come to realize that there is something very strange going on in our nation and world.

However, there is a certain degree of danger in asking these kinds of questions because many people presume to know with certainty what God is doing, and in many cases they are wrong. For example, purely on a technical, theological level, mankind has been in the "last days" since the birth of the early church on Pentecost (see Heb. 1:2).

Second, no one knows precisely where we are on God's prophetic timetable, although many claim to know. Since Israel is God's prophetic supersign, and the Jews returned to their land in 1948 after about two thousand years, many prophecy scholars believe that 1948 marks the beginning of a prophetic countdown period. But that does not tell us precisely where we are.

In addition, there are various perspectives on events like the Rapture of the church. Many popular Bible teachers believe that the church will be removed from the earth prior to the revealing of the Antichrist before the Tribulation period begins. This view is known as the pretribulation Rapture. Other Bible scholars believe that the church will be raptured sometime at the midpoint of the seven-year Tribulation period, which is known as the midtribulation or prewrath Rapture theory. Still other Christians hold to the more historic position that the Second Coming, the end of the Tribulation, and the Rapture are one event in what is called the posttribulation Rapture. In addition to those three primary viewpoints, there are numerous other perspectives on Bible prophecy.

I am not dismissing the importance of the timing of the Rapture, but I would like to address a greater truth, which is that whenever the Rapture occurs, we are to be faithfully doing what God has called us to do no matter when he comes.

"Occupy till I Come"

There is an often overlooked Scripture verse in which Jesus says, "Occupy till I come" (Luke 19:13 KJV). This is not a militaristic commandment; it is a commandment to spiritually occupy the land or territory God has given you until he returns.

In this verse, Jesus is directly confronting the spiritual error of fatalism. So how do we occupy until Christ returns, especially in places like America and other parts of the world?

First, we understand that America was founded by Pilgrims and Puritans who settled here for the religious freedom America offered. They entered into a covenant with God based on the same covenant that ancient Israel had with God. They recognized that God was the source of everything, and whenever they had a problem they would humble themselves and pray until they saw God move.

Now, it's true that America was also founded by Deists, Illuminists, and Freemasons. The fact that the symbolism of secret societies is all over our nation's capital proves without a doubt that the ideas of Francis Bacon and others were very much alive at the founding of America.

It's a myth to believe that America was purely a Christian nation. Throughout American history, there have been many incidents that were antithetical to Christianity even though those involved claimed to be Christians. One of the primary examples involves bringing slaves from

Africa who were stacked on top of one another in slave ships and then sold to "Christian" slave owners who brutally exploited them in every way. Another example is the betrayal and theft of the lands of Native Americans whose population was decimated by disease, the military, and enslavement.[5] Finally, up until Martin Luther King Jr. and the civil rights movement, racial segregation was openly practiced in America.

These are just a few of the inconsistencies in a nation that has claimed to be Christian, and they cannot be swept under the carpet. Despite these atrocities, there has always been a large remnant of true believers in America. This remnant still exists today and will play a decisive role in whether God decides to suspend the prophetic countdown and send another Great Awakening to America.

How Does America Fit into the Babylon Code?

What we have shared with you in *The Babylon Code*—a book based on decades of careful research, more than one hundred interviews, and the review of hundreds of books and tens of thousands of pages of government and academic documents and news articles—is that long before the founding of America there were two competing visions for the nation.

The first vision flows directly from ancient Babylon and was passed on through secret societies and orders throughout the ages. Then, in the mid-1600s, Bacon planned for America to become the head of the New Atlantis—what globalists today call the New World Order. Many of the secret societies our Founding Fathers belonged to held to this belief.[6]

At the same time, Bible-believing Christians like the Pilgrims and the Puritans made a covenant with God regarding America. In addition, the First Great Awakening radically transformed the thirteen colonies, and its biblical beliefs were embedded in the U.S. Constitution, the Bill of Rights, and the Declaration of Independence.

The reality is that America, from the beginning, has been a strange synthesis of biblical and Christian beliefs, along with those of the Freemasons, Illuminati, and other secret societies. There is the official version of American history that people learned in school and then there is the historical reality. Both of these parallel paths have taken America into the present hour as Bible prophecy is now unfolding all around us.

I'm often asked the question, "Where is America in Bible prophecy?"

In order to answer that, you must first understand the Babylon code and how America fits into this prophetic mystery. Perhaps sooner than we think, a world government, economic system, and religion outlined in Revelation will emerge. When it is time for this to happen, it will happen according to God's prophetic timetable, and nothing will be able to stop it.

How Are We to Live?

In light of this, the questions that should be asked are, "What are we to do?" and "How are we to live?"

Clearly, as long as the church is on the earth, God has a destiny for us to fulfill. That destiny can be fulfilled in one word: *faithfulness*. Our responsibility is to be faithful to God's Word and directives. The church is the body of Christ, or the Bride of Christ, which is supernaturally composed of all true believers in Jesus who have received salvation by faith in Christ and have the Holy Spirit living inside them.

The reality is that every believer is in the world, but not spiritually of the world, because heaven is our true home. But in the world, or the world system, we must be faithful to God.

In the Old Testament, we see how God placed the prophet Daniel among the most powerful occult forces on earth in the courts of the king of Babylon. Daniel's relationship with the elite occult power center was not confrontational. Daniel did not call them names or denounce them. Daniel walked with God and allowed God to supernaturally move through him.

In the Old Testament, Joseph was called to be the second in command under the pharaoh of Egypt. The courts of the pharaoh were also the highest centers of occult power on earth. Joseph did not get into a confrontation with the pharaoh but walked with God, and God supernaturally used him to help God's people and demonstrate the reality of God's existence.

Many Christians falsely believe they are called to denounce and engage in all-out confrontation with the occult elite. But that is not what Daniel, Joseph, or even Jesus did, except on very specific occasions. The battle we are in is a spiritual one, and we are to use spiritual weapons. This is what Moses had to learn as a deliverer of God's people. God was not calling him to lead a military-style revolution, but to rely on the power of God.

The call that every person who believes in God has at this time is to obey the Word of God, rely on the power of the Holy Spirit, and use the spiritual weapons God has given us such as prayer, repentance, worship, and evangelism.

"There's Still Time to Change the Road You're On"

We are now living in the last days of history, and the world is quickly moving toward the end-times Babylonian system predicted in Scripture. As this happens, mankind is dividing into two camps—Lucifer's and God's.

The Luciferian plan to usher in the Illuminati's New World Order is coming to fruition in our time. And while this satanic plan is coming to pass before our very eyes, God knew all about it long ago and laid out the story from beginning to end in the Bible.

This brings us to America.

How does America fit into *The Babylon Code*—this book that decodes an ancient mystery that began at the Tower of Babel, ends with the Battle of Armageddon, and explains everything that is happening in our world today?

The reality is that at some point America will likely become part of, or perhaps the head of, the predicted world-state, economic system, and religion.

America is in the greatest crisis it's ever been in since the inception of the nation. If America falls, the great light of truth based on God's Word will stop being communicated to the world, and the rest of the planet will quickly be subsumed into the end-times Babylonian world system.

America, specifically, and the world are now on the brink of the fulfillment of the fearsome judgments described in Revelation—an apocalyptic vision of unimaginable terror the world has never experienced in all of history.

Lucifer's game plan for a world government, economy, and religion under the control of the Antichrist and the False Prophet is almost here. Nearly all of the more than one hundred faith leaders and prophecy scholars we interviewed for *The Babylon Code* agreed with this assessment. It's just a question at this point of how much time is left on God's prophetic time clock and if people will repent and turn back to God, stopping the prophetic countdown.

At this time, mankind has a choice to either listen to the voice of God or reject the voice of God and yield to the temptation that "ye shall be as gods" and follow Lucifer as God. Everything that is happening now is a massive repeat of what happened at the beginning of human history. Everyone must make the choice to either listen to Lucifer or listen to God. There is no middle ground.

This is the most important decision you'll ever make. There are two kingdoms—the kingdom of God and the kingdom of Lucifer, which is

Babylon. All of us have to choose whether to follow God's plan, which leads to paradise and the real Utopia, or to follow Lucifer's secret occult society plan, which leads to a nightmare world, hell, and ultimately the Lake of Fire (see Luke 20:15).

The essential prophetic message in *The Babylon Code* is that time is running out, but God's hand of mercy is still being extended. "There's still time to change the road you're on," as Led Zeppelin sang in "Stairway to Heaven."[7]

If enough people collectively choose God and his plan, he will extend mercy and deliverance just as he did through Moses and the ancient Hebrews, Lot and his family at Sodom and Gomorrah, and Noah and his family during the Great Flood. God will faithfully rescue you if you turn from the lie of Lucifer and embrace the Word of God and God's all-consuming love.

The Alpha and Omega and Getting Back to the Garden

One of the primary questions believers ask is whether they will experience the Tribulation. In essence, their question is whether the Rapture will occur before the Tribulation begins—sparing them from the wholesale suffering and death that will occur during that time.

Today, prophecy scholars debate the timing of the event called the Rapture, or if there will even be a Rapture. But the purpose of *The Babylon Code* is not to deal with God's supernatural deliverance of his people in terms of a specific timetable but to look at prophetic events in terms of the big picture.

The Rapture is an interpretation of Scripture that essentially teaches that there are two comings of the Lord. According to those who believe and teach the Rapture, Jesus comes before the Tribulation begins to supernaturally remove his church as well as all those who died believing in Jesus. As such, the church of Jesus Christ will not be here when the

Antichrist is revealed and during the Tribulation judgments. But there are various positions as to the timing of the Rapture.

No matter what your position is regarding the prophetic timetable, the time is quickly coming when a majority of people on earth will opt to worship the coming Antichrist as God and receive a microchip implant distributed by the False Prophet. During this time, and specifically when the Antichrist breaks his peace treaty with Israel and sets himself up in the Temple to be worshipped, the wrath of God will be poured out on the earth.

At the end of the Tribulation, God will judge geopolitical, commercial, and spiritual Babylon—the satanic world system of this present age.

During the Battle of Armageddon, all the nations of the earth will invade Israel, but Jesus as the King of kings and Lord of lords will return with his heavenly forces and defeat the world's armies and rule and reign over planet Earth for the thousand-year millennial period when Jerusalem will become the capital of the world.

At the end of the Millennium, God will destroy the present earth and heavens with an intense fire and will supernaturally create the new heaven, the new earth, and the New Jerusalem. All those who put their faith in Jesus, along with all the Old Testament saints, will receive brand-new glorified bodies and eternal life.

Revelation describes the New Jerusalem as a bride coming down from heaven. At the Great White Throne judgment, God will judge all those who rejected his free offer of salvation in Christ. God will sentence to the Abyss and the Lake of Fire all those who received the mark of the Beast, including Satan, the Antichrist, and the False Prophet.

The bride coming down from heaven will be the pure and eternal heavenly city. In contrast, "Mystery, Babylon" and "Babylon the Great" will be destroyed with fire.

The curse of the Babylon code—triggered in the Garden of Eden when "the serpent of old" tempted Adam and Eve with the false promise of godhood—will be undone. Paradise will be restored and humanity will finally get back to the Garden.

That's the world's hope, and the answer to the greatest question of our time.

"It is the hope of the Second Coming of Christ that thrills me every day of my life," Graham says. "I know that He's coming again, and I know that He's going to set up a kingdom of which there will be no end. In Titus 2, it says, 'Looking for that blessed hope, and the glorious appearing of the great God and our Savior Jesus Christ.'"[8]

Acknowledgments

The only logical explanation for *The Babylon Code* is the supernatural intervention and guidance of God.

While space won't permit a complete recounting of all the divine coincidences and miraculous events that came together to bring you this book, we'd like to acknowledge some of the key people that God inspired to help us.

I (Paul) dedicate this book to my wife, Kristina, whose love and courage are a constant encouragement to me, and to all those who love the truth, because the truth shall set you free!

I (Troy) dedicate this book to my sweet, angelic, and godly-hearted wife, Irene. Truly, without her enthusiasm for Bible prophecy and immense encouragement, *The Babylon Code* never would have been written. I'd also like to thank my childhood youth pastor Richard Wheeler, who studied Bible prophecy at the JC Light and Power Company seminary at UCLA under Hal Lindsey, author of *The Late Great Planet Earth*. He led me to the Lord at age eleven and inspired in me a great love for the Bible and its prophecies.

Further, I'd like to thank my grandmother Trella Schiller; my father and mother, Stan and Janet Anderson; and my brother Dempsey Anderson, who played instrumental roles in my faith odyssey. They encouraged me to follow in the footsteps of my great-grandfather-plus—famed poet and playwright Friedrich von Schiller—and become a writer. I'd also like to thank Paul, whom I met at a Bible prophecy conference at

Calvary Chapel Chino Hills in early 2009. Shortly afterward, he proposed the idea of writing a book about a "code" in the Bible that reveals how powerful forces are now working to create a global government, economic system, and religion.

At the time, I was a government and investigative reporter at the *Los Angeles Daily News* and was skeptical about some of his claims. But over time, as our friendship developed and I read many books and did numerous interviews and extensive research, I came to the conclusion that he had uncovered what is in all probability the biggest story and political scandal in modern history.

Since that time, numerous people have played important roles in the development of *The Babylon Code*. First, I'd like to thank the founding editor of *Charisma* magazine, Steve Strang, who published one of my first end-times articles—the "Last Days Fever" cover story in October 2009. That marked the beginning of what would become a five-year journalistic investigation into the nexus between current events, secret societies, and end-times biblical predictions. In December 2012, *Charisma* published my follow-up story, "America at the End." Afterward, I was contacted by successful Hollywood producers who were interested in turning it into a docudrama and feature film. In early 2013, Paul and I began actively writing *The Babylon Code*—conducting the first of what would total more than one hundred interviews.

We'd like to thank everyone who so graciously took the time to do interviews, including Billy Graham, Dr. Tim LaHaye, Jerry B. Jenkins, Rabbi Jonathan Cahn, Joel Rosenberg, Hal Lindsey, Noam Chomsky, Pastor Greg Laurie, Mark Hitchcock, Dr. F. "Doc" Kenton Beshore, Jim Marrs, Daniel Estulin, Dr. Tom Horn, Pastor Ray Bentley, Dr. Robert Jeffress, Pastor Jud Wilhite, Ed Stetzer, Gerald Celente, Dr. Philip Ryken, Dr. Darrell Bock, Stan Guthrie, Dr. Ben Witherington, Dr. Robert Hieronimus, Jan Markell, Dr. Hugh Ross, Jesse Walker, John W. Whitehead, Dr. Jeffrey L. High, Dr. Gail K. Hart, Dr. Stanley Monteith, Trevor

W. McKeown, S. Douglas Woodward, Steve Cioccolanti, Dr. Thomas Ice, Neill G. Russell, Carroll M. Helm, Dr. Martin Gilens, Dennis L. Cuddy, Dr. Theodore Ziolkowski, and Charlie Daniels. I'd especially like to thank Rabbi Cahn, whom I first interviewed in early 2012 before the release of his *New York Times* bestselling book *The Harbinger*. Since that time, Cahn has prayed with me on several occasions, believing God would use my journalistic efforts to spread the end-times messages of many faith leaders and prophecy experts to the world.

During the research, interviewing, and writing process, three Bible study groups in Irvine, California, including one led by David and Esther, played key roles—encouraging us in our work and praying for God's guidance and spiritual protection. A member of one of these groups was kind enough to transcribe dozens of the interviews. Another group, led by Sam and Ming, invited an excellent Bible prophecy expert to take us through Revelation.

We'd also like to give special thanks to Dr. F. "Doc" Kenton Beshore, president of the World Bible Society, and his executive assistant Mary Dolkas. We attended Dr. Beshore's Bible Study Plus class at Mariners Church—one of the nation's largest churches—for a couple of years, gaining a deep understanding of Revelation and Bible prophecy. Serendipitously, I later learned that Richard Wheeler had led me to the Lord when I was a boy, using the *"Doc" Beshore Prophecy Study Bible*. I'd also like to thank John DeSimone, an author and ghostwriter we met at Dr. Beshore's class. He invited me to attend the Orange County Christian Writers Conference, planting the seed for what would become *The Babylon Code*. And I'd like to thank Glen Moss and other members of the intercessory prayer group at Mariners for covering this project in prayer.

In addition, we'd like to thank the Alive Literary Agency—"the largest, most influential literary agency for inspirational content," whose authors have written more than a dozen number one *New York Times* bestsellers. Alive represented Dr. Tim LaHaye and Jerry B. Jenkins, coauthors of the Left Behind series of end-times thrillers that sold more than eighty million copies and inspired several films, including the recent *Left Behind* movie with Nicolas Cage. We'd especially like to thank our outstanding agent, Bryan Norman, for his excellent work.

Finally, we'd like to thank all those who took the time to write an endorsement for *The Babylon Code*, including Dr. Tim LaHaye, Sid Roth, Dr. Robert Jeffress, Rabbi Jonathan Bernis, Dr. Hugh Ross, Dr. F. "Doc" Kenton Beshore, Pastor Michael Youssef, Dr. Thomas R. Horn, Jan Markell, and Michael Snyder. Lastly, we'd like to give a special thanks to our editing and publicity team at FaithWords, including editor Joey Paul, editorial assistant Becky Hughes, publicist Sarah Falter, director of marketing Andrea Glickson, vice president of marketing/publicity Patsy S. Jones, and senior vice president and publisher Rolf Zettersten.

Appendix A

Prayer of Salvation

To everyone reading this book, if you have not already done so, this is your opportunity to make your way back to Eden and walk one day in the unimaginable paradise of all your dreams with the Alpha and the Omega—"the beginning and the end, the first and the last" (Rev. 22:13 KJV). All you have to do is accept the free offer of salvation in Jesus Christ.

To do so, here is a simple prayer of salvation. Feel free to use this as a model for your own personal prayer to Jesus:

Dear Jesus,
Father, forgive me of all my sins.
I know that I am a sinner who
has broken your laws and commandments.
I am guilty;
however, today I turn away
from sin and my past sinful life.
Please forgive me, and help me
to walk in purity and righteousness.

I believe that your only begotten Son, Jesus Christ,
willingly died for me on the cross of Calvary,
and that he was buried and resurrected
from the dead on the third day,
and ascended up into glory.
I believe he will come again

to judge the living and the dead.
I surrender my life to you
and make you my Lord and Savior.
I give you permission to rule and reign
in my heart from this day forward.
Come into my life and fill me
with your Spirit in Jesus' holy name.
Amen.

Appendix B

Secret Society Quotes by World Leaders and Other Credible Sources

It was not my intention to doubt that, the Doctrines of the Illuminati, and principles of Jacobinism had not spread in the United States. On the contrary, no one is more truly satisfied of this fact than I am.

—GEORGE WASHINGTON, FIRST PRESIDENT OF THE UNITED STATES

The revolutionary movement which began in 1789 in the Cercle Social, which in the middle of its course had as its chief representatives Leclerc and Roux, and which finally with Babeuf's conspiracy was temporarily defeated, gave rise to the communist idea which Babeuf's friend Buonarroti re-introduced in France after the Revolution of 1830. This idea, consistently developed, is the idea of the new world order.

—KARL MARX, GERMAN PHILOSOPHER, ECONOMIST, SOCIOLOGIST,
HISTORIAN, JOURNALIST, AND REVOLUTIONARY SOCIALIST WHO
WROTE *THE COMMUNIST MANIFESTO* AND *DAS KAPITAL*

Behind the ostensible government sits enthroned an invisible government owing no allegiance and acknowledging no responsibility to the people.

—THEODORE ROOSEVELT, TWENTY-SIXTH PRESIDENT
OF THE UNITED STATES

I am a most unhappy man. I have unwittingly ruined my country. A great industrial nation is controlled by its system of credit. Our system of credit is concentrated. The growth of the nation, therefore, and all our activities are in the hands of a few men. We have come to be one of the worst ruled, one of the most completely controlled and dominated governments in the civilized world. No longer a government by free opinion, no longer a government by conviction and the vote of the majority, but a government by the opinion and duress of a small group of dominant men.

—WOODROW WILSON, TWENTY-EIGHTH PRESIDENT
OF THE UNITED STATES

From the days of Spartacus-Weishaupt to those of Karl Marx, and down to Trotsky (Russia), Bela Kun (Hungary), Rosa Luxembourg (Germany), and Emma Goldman (United States), this world-wide conspiracy for the overthrow of civilisation and for the reconstitution of society on the basis of arrested development, of envious malevolence, and impossible equality, has been steadily growing. It played, as a modern writer, Mrs. Webster, has so ably shown, a definitely recognisable part in the tragedy of the French Revolution. It has been the mainspring of every subversive movement during the Nineteenth Century; and now at last this band of extraordinary personalities from the underworld of the great cities of Europe and America have gripped the Russian people by the hair of their heads and have become practically the undisputed masters of that enormous empire.

—WINSTON CHURCHILL, PRIME MINISTER OF THE
UNITED KINGDOM FROM 1940 TO 1945 AND 1951 TO 1955

It is the system of nationalist individualism that has to go...We are living in the end of the sovereign states...In the great struggle

to evoke a Westernized World Socialism, contemporary governments may vanish...Countless people...will hate the New World
Order...and will die protesting against it.

—H. G. WELLS, AN ENGLISH WRITER, IN HIS 1940 BOOK,
THE NEW WORLD ORDER

We shall have world government, whether or not we like it. The
question is only whether world government will be achieved by consent or by conquest.

—JAMES WARBURG, A GERMAN-BORN AMERICAN BANKER
WHOSE FATHER, PAUL WARBURG, WAS THE "FATHER" OF
THE FEDERAL RESERVE, IN TESTIMONY ON
FEBRUARY 17, 1950, BEFORE THE U.S. SENATE
COMMITTEE ON FOREIGN RELATIONS

The drive of the Rockefellers and their allies is to create a one-world
government combining supercapitalism and Communism under the
same tent, all under their control...Do I mean conspiracy? Yes, I
do. I am convinced there is such a plot, international in scope, generations old in planning, and incredibly evil in intent.

—LARRY MacDONALD, DEMOCRATIC FORMER
MEMBER OF THE U.S. HOUSE OF REPRESENTATIVES
FROM GEORGIA

The very word *secrecy* is repugnant in a free and open society; and we
are as a people inherently and historically opposed to secret societies,
to secret oaths and to secret proceedings.

—JOHN F. KENNEDY, THIRTY-FIFTH PRESIDENT
OF THE UNITED STATES, WHO WAS ASSASSINATED IN 1963

Out of these troubled times, our objective—a new world order—can emerge. Today, that new world order is struggling to be born, a world quite different from the one we have known.

—GEORGE H. W. BUSH, FORTY-FIRST PRESIDENT
OF THE UNITED STATES AND FORMER
DIRECTOR OF THE CIA

For more than a century, ideological extremists, at either end of the political spectrum, have seized upon well-publicized incidents, such as my encounter with Castro, to attack the Rockefeller family for the inordinate influence they claim we wield over American political and economic institutions. Some even believe we are part of a secret cabal, working against the best interests of the United States, characterizing my family and me as "internationalists," and of conspiring with others around the world to build a more integrated global political and economic structure—one world, if you will. If that's the charge, I stand guilty, and I am proud of it.

—DAVID ROCKEFELLER, AN AMERICAN BUSINESSMAN AND
PHILANTHROPIST WHO SERVED AS CHAIRMAN AND
CHIEF EXECUTIVE OF CHASE MANHATTAN BANK,
IN HIS 2002 BOOK, *MEMOIRS*

Notes

Introduction: The Great Biblical Mystery

Epigraph: Sherlock Holmes, *The Boscombe Valley Mystery*, Sherlock Holmes Quotes, www.sherlockholmesquotes.com.

1. Billy Graham, e-mail interview by Troy Anderson for a seven-part WND.com series and www.tothesource.org story about the *My Hope America with Billy Graham* evangelistic outreach, August 20, 2013; "94-Year-Old Billy Graham's Warning for America," WND.com, August 4, 2013, http://www.wnd.com/2013/08/94-year-old-billy-grahams-warning-for-america; "Famed Evangelist: God Told Me 'America Will Be Saved,'" WND.com, August 18, 2013, www.wnd.com/2013/08/famed-evangelist-god-told-me-america-will-be-saved; "Billy Graham: Now Is Time for 'Fresh Awakening,'" WND.com, September 22, 2013, http://www.wnd.com/2013/09/billy-graham-now-is-time-for-fresh-awakening; "Billy Graham Sounds Alarm for 2nd Coming," WND.com, October 20, 2013, http://www.wnd.com/2013/10/billy-graham-sounds-alarm-for-2nd-coming; "Prophecy Scholar: America at Crossroads," WND.com, November 2, 2013, http://www.wnd.com/2013/11/prophecy-scholar-america-at-crossroads; "Man Who Walked Across U.S. Saw Revival Signs," WND.com, November 3, 2013, http://www.wnd.com/2013/11/man-who-walked-across-u-s-saw-revival-signs; "Billy Graham to Give 'Final, Most Important' Message," WND.com, November 5, 2013, http://www.wnd.com/2013/11/billy-graham-to-give-final-most-important-message; Troy Anderson, "Billy Graham's Hope for America," tothesource.org, September 26, 2013, http://www.tothesource.org/9_25_2013/9_25_2013.htm.

2. Catherine Austin Fitts, "Financial Coup d'Etat," Solari Report, August 8, 2011, https://solari.com/blog/financial-coup-detat.

3. Jim Marrs, *Our Occulted History: Do the Global Elite Conceal Ancient Aliens?* (New York: William Morrow, 2013), 213.

4. Barna Group, "Shock Poll: Startling Numbers of Americans Believe World Now in the 'End Times,'" Christian Newswire, September 10, 2013, http://www.christiannewswire.com/news/511072762.html; Joel Rosenberg, telephone interview by Troy Anderson for *The Babylon Code*, January 13, 2015.

5. Joel C. Rosenberg, "Here's My List of the Top Five Most Important Events in the Mideast in 2013," *Joel C. Rosenberg's Blog*, December 31, 2013, http://flashtrafficblog.wordpress.com/2013/12/31/heres-my-list-of-the-top-five-most-important-events-in-the-mideast-in-2013; "Full Text of Netanyahu's 2013 Speech to the

UN General Assembly," *Times of Israel*, October 1, 2013, http://timesofisrael.com/full-text-netanyahus-2013-speech-to-the-un-general-assembly; Stefano Rellandini, "Pope Says World's Many Conflicts Amount to Piecemeal World War Three," Reuters, September 13, 2014, http://news.yahoo.com/pope-says-worlds-many-conflicts-amount-piecemeal-world-104917232.html; Russell Shaw, "Devil Is Working Hard on Securing End Times," *OSV Newsweekly*, February 26, 2014, https://www.osv.com/osvnews weekly/article/tabid/535/artmid/13567/articleid/14188/devil-is-working-hard-on-securing-end-times.aspx.

6. Joel C. Rosenberg, "Exclusive New Poll Finds 80% of Americans Fear a 'Second Holocaust," *Joel C. Rosenberg's Blog*, March 20, 2014, http://flashtrafficblog.wordpress.com/2014/03/20/exclusive-poll-80-of-americans-fear-second-holocausti-discussed-this-today-on-cbn-see-poll-details-and-video-of-interview; Rosenberg, "68% of Americans Fear a 'Nuclear Holocaust' Here in U.S. If Iran Is Permitted to Build Nuclear Weapons, Exclusive Poll Finds," *Joel C. Rosenberg's Blog*, March 24, 2014, https://flashtrafficblog.wordpress.com/2014/03/24/68-of-americans-fear-a-nuclear-holocaust-here-in-u-s-if-Iran-is-permitted-to-build-nuclear-weapons-exclusive-poll-finds; Rosenberg, "With Iran & ISIS Threats Rising, Why Is President Obama Turning Against Israel? Analysis. (Also: in New Video, ISIS Threatens to 'Reach America' & Behead President Obama)," *Joel C. Rosenberg's Blog*, January 29, 2015, https://flashtrafficblog.wordpress.com/2015/01/29/with-iran-isis-threats-rising-why-is-president-obama-turning-against-israel-analysis-also-in-new-video-isis-threatens-to-reach-america-behead-president-obama.

7. Public Policy Polling, "Conspiracy Theory Poll Results," April 2, 2013, http://www.publicpolicypolling.com/main/2013/04/conspiracy-theory-poll-results-.html; Public Policy Polling, "Conspiracy Theories Round Two: Republicans More Likely to Subscribe to Government Conspiracy Theories," October 2, 2013, http://www.publicpolicypolling.com/main/2013/10/conspiracy-theories-round-two-republicans-more-likely-to-subscribe-to-government-conspiracy-theories.html.

8. World Economic Forum, "Global Risks 2014 Report," www.weforum.org/reports/global-risks-2014-report; Carmen M. Reinhart and Kenneth S. Rogoff, "Financial and Sovereign Debt Crises: Some Lessons Learned and Those Forgotten," IMF Working Paper, December 2013, http://www.imf.org/external/pubs/ft/wp/2013/wp13266.pdf; Drew MacKenzie, "ISIS, in Magazine, Warns of 'Armageddon' Against US, West," *Newsmax*, September 16, 2014, http://www.newsmax.com/Newsfront/ISIS-recruitment-terrorism-jihadists/2014/09/16/id/594870.

9. Justin Gillis, "Panel's Warning on Climate Risk: Worst Is Yet to Come," *New York Times*, March 31, 2014, http://www.nytimes.com/2014/04/01/science/earth/climate.html; Larry Elliott, "Climate Change Will 'Lead to Battles for Food,' Says Head of World Bank," *Guardian*, April 3, 2014, http://www.theguardian.com/environment/2014/apr/03/climate-change-battle-food-head-world-bank.

10. Hakan Altinay, "Global Governance Audit," Brookings Institution Global Working Papers No. 45, February 6, 2012, http://brookings.edu/research/papers/2012/02/global-governance-altinay.

11. Noam Chomsky, "The End of History?: The Short, Strange Era of Human Civilization Would Appear to Be Drawing to a Close," *In These Times*, September 4, 2014, http://inthesetimes.com/article/17137/the_end_of_history.

12. Chomsky, e-mail interview by Troy Anderson for *The Babylon Code*, January 18, 2015.

13. Safa Motesharrei (University of Maryland); Jorge Rivas (University of Minnesota); and Eugenia Kalnay (University of Maryland), "A Minimal Model for Human and Nature Interaction," November 13, 2012, http://www.ara.cat/societat/handy-paper-for-submission-2_ARAFIL20140317_0003.pdf; Nafeez Ahmed, "Nasa-Funded Study: Industrial Civilisation Headed for 'Irreversible Collapse'?" *Guardian*, March 14, 2014, http://www.theguardian.com/environment/earth-insight/2014/mar/14/nasa-civilisation-irreversible-collapse-study-scientists.

14. Ricardo Fuentes-Nieva and Nicholas Galasso, "Working for the Few: Political Capture and Economic Inequality," Oxfam International, January 20, 2014, http://www.oxfam.org/en/policy/working-for-the-few-economic-inequality; Reuters, "Richest 1 Percent Hold 46 Percent of the World's Wealth," *Huffington Post*, October 9, 2013, http://www.huffingtonpost.com/2013/10/09/richest-1-percent-wealth_n_4072658.html.

15. Sophie McBain, "Apocalypse Soon: The Scientists Preparing for the End Times," *New Statesman*, September 25, 2014, http://www.newstatesman.com/sci-tech/2014/09/apocalypse-soon-scientists-preparing-end-times; University of Oxford Future of Humanity Institute and the Global Challenges Foundation, "Global Challenges: 12 Risks That Threaten Human Civilisation," February 2015, http://globalchallenges.org/wp-content/uploads/12-Risks-with-infinite-impact-full-report-1.pdf.

16. Shanta Premawardhana, "Greed: How Can Religions Address the Deepening Spiritual Crisis of Our Time?" Council for a Parliament of the World's Religions, February 13, 2014, http://www.parliamentofreligions.org/news/index.php/2014/02/greed-how-can-religions-address-the-deepening-spiritual-crisis-of-our-time.

17. Graham, interview by Anderson, August 20, 2013; Jeffrey M. Jones, "Barack Obama, Hillary Clinton Extend Run as Most Admired," Gallup, December 29, 2014, http://www.gallup.com/poll/180365/barack-obama-hillary-clinton-extend-run-admired.aspx.

18. Billy Graham, "Billy Graham: 'My Heart Aches for America,'" Billy Graham Evangelistic Association, July 19, 2012, http://billygraham.org/story/billy-graham-my-heart-aches-for-america.

19. Billy Graham, *The Reason for My Hope: Salvation* (Nashville: Thomas Nelson, 2013), 172–73.

20. Greg Laurie, telephone interview by Troy Anderson for a WND.com story about *My Hope America*, July 10, 2013.

21. Jonathan Cahn, e-mail interview by Troy Anderson for an end-times magazine series, February 10, 2014.

22. Ibid.

23. Philip Ryken, telephone interview by Troy Anderson for *The Babylon Code*, March 4, 2014.

24. Joel C. Rosenberg, telephone interview by Troy Anderson for a *Charisma* magazine story and *The Babylon Code*, January 3, 2014.
25. Darrell Bock, telephone interview by Troy Anderson for *The Babylon Code*, February 5, 2014.
26. Rosenberg, interview by Anderson, January 3, 2014.
27. Neil King Jr. and Patrick O'Connor, "Poll Finds Americans Anxious Over Future, Obama's Performance," *Wall Street Journal*, January 28, 2014; Mariam Karouny, "Apocalyptic Prophecies Drive Both Sides to Syrian Battle for End of Time," Reuters, April 1, 2014, http://www.reuters.com/article/2014/04/01/us-syria-crisis -prophecy-insight-idUSBREA3013420140401.
28. Robert Hieronimus, *Founding Fathers, Secret Societies: Freemasons, Illuminati, Rosicrucians, and the Decoding of the Great Seal* (Rochester, VT: Destiny Books, 2006), 152; Paul Rodgers, "Elon Musk Warns of Terminator Tech," *Forbes*, August 5, 2014, http://www.forbes.com/sites/paulrodgers/2014/08/05/elon-musk-warns-ais -could-exterminate-humanity; Nick Bostrom, *Superintelligence: Paths, Dangers, Strategies* (Oxford: Oxford University Press, 2014), 2.
29. Barna Group, "The State of the Bible: 6 Trends for 2014," report commissioned by the American Bible Society, April 8, 2014, https://www.barna.org/barna-update/ culture/664-the-state-of-the-bible-6-trends-for-2014.
30. Greg Laurie, "Money and Motives," Crosswalk.com, September 4, 2008, http:// www.crosswalk.com/faith/spiritual-life/money-and-motives-11581312.html.
31. George Russell, "UN Brewing Up New—and Expensive—Global 'Sustainability Development Goals,'" FoxNews.com, October 3, 2013, http://www.foxnews .com/world/2013/10/03/un-brewing-up-new-and-expensive-global-sustainability -development-goals; United Nations, "A New Global Partnership: Eradicate Poverty and Transform Economies Through Sustainable Development," May 2013, http://www.post2015hlp.org/wp-content/uploads/2013/05/UN-Report.pdf; John Brandon, "Is There a Microchip Implant in Your Future?," FoxNews.com, August 30, 2014, http://foxnews.com/tech/2014/08/30/is-there-microchip-implant -in-your-future; "Joe Biden Says There Is an Agenda to Get Everyone Microchipped and Brain Scanned," YouTube video, 1:12, posted by 91177 info, April 25, 2011, https://www.youtube.com/watch?v=FQw68jl7KXc.
32. Scott A. Shay, "Cashless Society: A Huge Threat to Our Freedom," CNBC.com, December 12, 2013, http://www.cnbc.com/id/101266173.
33. John Fonte, "Sovereignty or Submission: Liberal Democracy or Global Governance?," Foreign Policy Research Institute, October 2011, http://www.fpri.org/ enotes/2011/201110.fonte.sovereignty.html.
34. Ibid.
35. Gideon Rachman, "And Now for a World Government," *Financial Times*, December 8, 2008, http://www.ft.com/cms/s/0/7a03e5b6-c541-11dd-b516-000077b07658.html.
36. John W. Whitehead, telephone interview by Troy Anderson for *The Babylon Code*, April 9, 2014.
37. Ibid.
38. Drew Zahn, "Kissinger: Obama Primed to Create 'New World Order': Policy Guru Says Global Upheaval Presents 'Great Opportunity,'" WND.com, January 6, 2009, http:// www.wnd.com/2009/01/85442; Political Transcript Wire, "Vice President Joseph

R. Biden Jr. Delivers Remarks at the Export-Import Bank Annual Conference," High Beam Research, April 5, 2013, http://www.highbeam.com/doc/1P3-2936974091 .html; *Wikipedia*, s.v. "New World Order (Politics)," http://en.wikipedia.org/wiki/ New_world_order_(politics); Mark Hitchcock, *The End of Money: Bible Prophecy and the Coming Economic Collapse* (Eugene, OR: Harvest House, 2013), 13–19; Pontifical Council for Justice and Peace, "Towards Reforming the International Financial and Monetary Systems in the Context of Global Public Authority," Vatican, October 24, 2011, http://www.vatican.va/roman_curia/pontifical_councils/just peace/documents/rc_pc_justpeace_doc_20111024_nota_en.html; Thomas Horn, "The Man of Sin and the New World Order," Rapture Ready, http://raptureready. com/soap/horn4.html; Terry L. Cook and Thomas R. Horn, *Beast Tech: Is the Mark of the New World Order Secretly Under Development?* (Crane, MO: Defender, 2013), 32–37; Matthew C. Quinn, "Critics Troubled by Bush's Call for a 'New World Order,'" *Times Union* (Albany, NY), February 17, 1991; Walter Friedenberg, "Bush Tries to Explain 'New World Order' in Speech, Action," Scripps Howard News Service, April 20, 1991; John T. Harding, "Kissinger Calls the U.S. Unready for New Order," *Star-Ledger* (Newark, NJ), September 26, 1991; Pat Robertson, *The New World Order* (Dallas: Word, 1991), 5; Aaron Klein, "Biden, Hagel Obsessed with Creating 'New World Order,'" WND.com, May 29, 2014, http://www.wnd .com/2014/05/biden-hagel-obsessed-with-creating-new-world-order.

39. Jim Marrs, telephone interview by Troy Anderson for *The Babylon Code*, February 28, 2014; Donald J. Sterling, "Another New World Order? Bra-ack!" *Oregonian*, February 22, 1991; Robertson, *New World Order*, 36.

40. Jon Meacham, "We Are All Socialists Now: The Perils and Promise of the New Era of Big Government," *Newsweek*, February 6, 2009, http://www.newsweek.com/ we-are-all-socialists-now-82577; "H. G. Wells Biography," Biography.com, http:// www.biography.com/people/hg-wells-39224; Jerry Bowyer, "Barack Obama, Fabian Socialist," Forbes.com, November 3, 2008, http://www.forbes.com/2008/11/03/ obama-fabian-socialist-oped-cx_jb_1103bowyer.html; John Coleman, *The Conspirators' Hierarchy: The Committee of 300* (Carson City, NV: World International Review, 2010), 45.

41. Greg Laurie, telephone interview by Troy Anderson for a follow-up story to the seven-part WND.com series about *My Hope America*, an end-times magazine series, and *The Babylon Code*, March 5, 2014.

42. Mark Hitchcock, telephone interview by Troy Anderson for an end-times magazine series and *The Babylon Code*, January 23, 2014.

43. Cadie Thompson, "Wearable Tech Is Getting a Lot More Intimate," Entrepreneur .com, December 26, 2013, http://www.entrepreneur.com/article/230555.

44. Hitchcock, interview by Anderson, January 23, 2014.

45. Daniel 7:23; "ABC's of Prophecy: Revived Roman Empire," Rapture Ready, http:// www.raptureready.com/abc/Roman_Empire.html.

46. Paul McGuire, telephone interview by Troy Anderson for *The Babylon Code*, September 9, 2013.

47. Coleman, *Conspirators' Hierarchy*, iii–2.

48. Carroll Quigley, *Tragedy & Hope: A History of the World in Our Time* (New York: Macmillan, 1966), 130–38.

49. Stefania Vitali, James B. Glattfelder, and Stefano Battiston, "The Network of Global Corporate Control," *PLOS ONE*, October 26, 2011, http://www.plosone.org/article/info%3Adoi%2F10.1371%2Fjournal.pone.0025995.

50. Antony C. Sutton, *America's Secret Establishment: An Introduction to the Order of Skull & Bones* (Walterville, OR: TrineDay, 2004), http://www.antonysutton.com.

51. McGuire, interview by Anderson, September 9, 2013; Marrs, interview by Anderson, February 28, 2014; Stanley Monteith, *Brotherhood of Darkness* (Crane, MO: Highway, 2000), 56–58; F. Kenton Beshore, *When?: When Will the Rapture Take Place?* (Costa Mesa, CA: World Bible Society, 2009), 197–208; Hieronimus, *Founding Fathers*, 38–39; Manly P. Hall, *The Secret Destiny of America* (Los Angeles: Philosophical Research Society, 1944), 53; William H. McIlhany, "A Primer on the Illuminati," *New American*, June 12, 2009, http://www.thenewamerican.com/culture/history/item/4660-a-primer-on-the-illuminati.

52. Tim LaHaye, *Rapture (Under Attack): Will You Escape the Tribulation?* (Sisters, OR: Multnomah, 1998), 138; Rob Boston, "Left Behind: If Best-Selling End-Times Author Tim LaHaye Has His Way, Church-State Separation Will Be…Left Behind," Americans United for Separation of Church and State, February 2002, https://www.au.org/church-state/february-2002-church-state/featured/left-behind.

53. John Robison, *Proofs of a Conspiracy: Against All the Religions and Governments of Europe, Carried on in the Secret Meetings of Free Masons, Illuminati, and Reading Societies* (London: Forgotten Books, 2008), 10–12; Devra Newberger Speregen and Debra Mostow Zakarin, *Secret Societies: The Truth Revealed* (Plain City, OH: Media Source, 2013), 10; Hieronimus, *Founding Fathers*, 26.

54. Trevor W. McKeown, telephone interview by Troy Anderson for *The Babylon Code*, April 7, 2014.

55. Robert Hieronimus, *The United Symbolism of America: Deciphering Hidden Meanings in America's Most Familiar Art, Architecture, and Logos* (Pompton Plains, NJ: New Page Books, 2008), 24.

56. "Secret Societies—David Icke and Jim Marrs" YouTube video, 29:46, posted by Brain Stream Media, February 12, 2001, https://www.youtube.com/watch?v=T6sICgrFQVo&feature=youtu.be.

57. Marc Lamont Hill, "Why Are People Obsessed with the Illuminati?," *HuffPost Live*, March 19, 2014, http://live.huffingtonpost.com/r/segment/why-are-people-obsessed-with-the-illuminati/5327354e2b8c2a49cc0003f6.

58. Ibid.

59. Theodore Roosevelt, "Behind the ostensible government sits enthroned an invisible government owing no allegiance and acknowledging no responsibility to the people," http://brainyquote.com/quotes/quotes/t/theodorero169571.html; McGuire, interview by Anderson, September 9, 2013; Marrs, interview by Anderson, February 28, 2014; Monteith, *Brotherhood of Darkness*, 56–58; Beshore, *When?*, 197–208; Arthur Unger, "Secrecy vs. Democracy: Moyers Probes America's Clandestine 'Shadow Government,'" *Christian Science Monitor*, November 3, 1987.

60. George Washington, "It was not my intention to doubt that, the Doctrines of the Illuminati, and principles of Jacobinism had not spread in the United States. On the contrary, no one is more truly satisfied of this fact than I am," http://en.wikiquote.org/wiki/freemasonry; Abraham Lincoln, "I see in the near future a

crisis approaching that unnerves me and causes me to tremble for the safety of my country. As a result of the war corporations have been enthroned and an era of corruption in high places will follow, and the money power of the country will endeavor to prolong its reign by working upon the prejudice of the people until all wealth is aggregated in a few hands and the republic is destroyed," http://en.wikiquote.org/wiki/Talk:Abraham_Lincoln; Woodrow Wilson, "I am a most unhappy man. I have unwittingly ruined my country. A great industrial nation is controlled by its system of credit. Our system of credit is concentrated. The growth of the nation, therefore, and all our activities are in the hands of a few men. We have come to be one of the worst ruled, one of the most completely controlled and dominated Governments in the civilized world no longer a Government by free opinion, no longer a Government by conviction and the vote of the majority, but a Government by the opinion and duress of a small group of dominant men," http://wikiquote .org/wiki/talk:Woodrow_Wilson; Winston Churchill, "From the days of Spartacus-Weishaupt to those of Karl Marx, and down to Trotsky (Russia), Bela Kun (Hungary), Rosa Luxembourg (Germany), and Emma Goldman (United States), this world-wide conspiracy for the overthrow of civilisation and for the reconstitution of society on the basis of arrested development, of envious malevolence, and impossible equality, has been steadily growing. It played, as a modern writer, Mrs. Webster, has so ably shown, a definitely recognisable part in the tragedy of the French Revolution. It has been the mainspring of every subversive movement during the Nineteenth Century; and now at last this band of extraordinary personalities from the underworld of the great cities of Europe and America have gripped the Russian people by the hair of their heads and have become practically the undisputed masters of that enormous empire," http://en.wikiquote.org/wiki/conspiracy; John F. Kennedy, "The very word 'secrecy' is repugnant in a free and open society; and we are as a people inherently and historically opposed to secret societies, to secret oaths and to secret proceedings," http://www.jfklibrary.org/Research/Research -Aids/JFK-Speeches/American-Newspaper-Publishers-Association_19610427 .aspx; Timothy Dwight, "Is it that we may change our holy worship into a dance of Jacobin phrenzy, and that we may behold a trumpet impersonating a Goddess on the altars of Jehovah? It is that we may see the Bible cast into a bonfire...and our children...uniting in the mob, chanting mockeries against God...Shall our sons become the disciples of Voltaire, and the dragoons of Marat, or our daughters the concubines of the Illuminati?" *The Duty of Americans, at the Present Crisis, Illustrated in a Discourse, Preached on the Fourth of July, 1798* (New Haven, CT: Thomas and Samuel Green, 1798), 20–21; Joseph Willard, "There is sufficient evidence that a number of societies, of the Illuminati, have been established, in this land of Gospel light and Civil liberty, which were first organized from the grand Society, in France. They are doubtless, secretly striving to undermine all our ancient institutions, civil and sacred. These societies are closely leagued with those of the same Order, in Europe; they have all the same object in view. The enemies of all order are seeking our ruin. Should infidelity generally prevail, our independence would fall of course. Our republican government would be annihilated," quoted in Richard N. Rhoades, *Lady Liberty: The Ancient Goddess of America* (Bloomington, IN: iUniverse, 2013), 123–24.

61. Matt Taibbi, "Everything Is Rigged: The Biggest Price-Fixing Scandal Ever," *Rolling Stone*, April 25, 2013, http://www.rollingstone.com/politics/news/everything-is-rigged-the-biggest-financial-scandal-yet-20130425.

62. Jim Marrs, *The Trillion-Dollar Conspiracy: How the New World Order, Man-Made Diseases, and Zombie Banks Are Destroying America* (New York: Harper, 2010), 3–4; Marrs, interview by Anderson, February 28, 2014.

63. Marrs, interview by Anderson, February 28, 2014.

Chapter One: "Mystery, Babylon"—the World's Greatest Prophetic Riddle

1. Drew Zahn, "Kissinger: Obama Primed to Create 'New World Order': Policy Guru Says Global Upheaval Presents 'Great Opportunity,'" WND.com, January 6, 2009, www.worldnetdaily.com/index.php?pageId=85442; Mark Corner, "Towards a Global Sharing of Sovereignty," Federal Trust for Education & Research, August 2008, http://www.fedtrust.co.uk/wp-content/uploads/2014/12/Essay44_Corner.pdf.

2. Mark Hitchcock, *The End: A Complete Overview of Bible Prophecy and the End of Days* (Carol Stream, IL: Tyndale, 2012), 361–69.

3. Darrell Bock, telephone interview by Troy Anderson for *The Babylon Code*, February 5, 2014.

4. Philip Ryken, telephone interview by Troy Anderson for *The Babylon Code*, March 4, 2014.

5. Jeff Kinley, telephone interview by Troy Anderson for *The Babylon Code*, April 10, 2014.

6. Hitchcock, *The End*, 361–69; *Encyclopaedia Britannica*, s.v. "Babylon," http://www.britannica.com/EBchecked/topic/47575/Babylon.

7. Douglas W. Krieger, Dene McGriff, and S. Douglas Woodward, *The Final Babylon: America and the Coming of Antichrist* (Oklahoma City: Faith Happens, 2013), 247; Isaiah 13:19; 14:4 (KJV); Henry H. Halley, *Halley's Bible Handbook* (Grand Rapids, MI: Zondervan, 2007), 397.

8. Greg Laurie, *Revelation: The Next Dimension* (Austin, TX: Allen David Books, 2014), 343–44.

9. C. I. Scofield, *The New Scofield Reference Bible: Authorized King James Version* (Oxford: Oxford University Press, 1967), 1014; Steve Cioccolanti, e-mail interview by Troy Anderson for *The Babylon Code*, January 14, 2015.

10. 2 Thessalonians 2:7 (KJV); Mark 4:11 (KJV); Daniel 2:28 (NRSV); 1 Peter 5:13 (KJV); "Babylon in the New Testament," BibleStudyTools.com, http://www.biblestudytools.com/encyclopedias/isbe/babylon-in-the-new-testament.html; Reference.com, http://www.reference.com/browse/Mysterion; Dave Hunt, "Mystery Babylon Identified," Pre-Trib Research Center, Liberty University, http://www.pre-trib.org/articles/view/mystery-babylon-identified; Thomas Ice, "Babylon in Bible Prophecy," Pre-Trib Research Center, Liberty University, http://www.pre-trib.org/articles/view/babylon-in-bible-prophecy.

11. S. Douglas Woodward, telephone interview by Troy Anderson for *The Babylon Code*, August 14, 2013.

12. *Encyclopaedia Britannica*, s.v. "Babylon"; Hugh Ross, *Navigating Genesis: A Scientist's Journey Through Genesis 1–11* (Covina, CA: Reasons to Believe, 2014), 193–95.

13. Hugh Ross, telephone interview by Troy Anderson for *The Babylon Code*, April 10, 2014; *Encyclopaedia Britannica*, s.v. "Noah," http://Britannica.com/EBchecked/topic/416799/Noah; *Wikipedia*, s.v. "Ussher Chronology," http://en.wikipedia.org/wiki/Ussher_chronology; *Wikipedia*, s.v. "Noah's Ark," http://en.wikipedia.org/wiki/Noah's_Ark; "Ancient Flood Narratives," in *Archaeological Study Bible* (Grand Rapids, MI: Zondervan, 2005), 13.

14. Mark Hitchcock, telephone interview by Troy Anderson for *The Babylon Code*, January 23, 2014.

15. Krieger, McGriff, and Woodward, *Final Babylon*, 39; Bodie Hodge, "Who Were the Nephilim?," Answers in Genesis, July 9, 2008, http://www.answersingenesis.org/articles/aid/v2/n1/who-were-the-nephilim; *Wikipedia*, s.v. "Nimrod," http://en.wikipedia.org/wiki/Nimrod; Dr. Henry Morris, *The Henry Morris Study Bible*, footnotes to Genesis 6:4.

16. Kevin Farrington, telephone interview by Troy Anderson for *The Babylon Code*, April 3, 2013.

17. "ABC's of Prophecy: Revived Roman Empire," Rapture Ready, http://www.raptureready.com/abc/Roman_Empire.html; "Imagine," Beatles Bible, http://www.beatlesbible.com/people/john-lennon/songs/imagine; Rich Lowry, "The Anthem of Joy," *National Review*, December 24, 2013, http://www.nationalreview.com/article/367011/anthem-joy-rich-lowry; Fraser McAlpine, "The London Games Opening Ceremony: Recap," BBC America, July 27, 2012, http://www.bbcamerica.com/anglophenia/2012/07/the-london-games-opening-ceremony-recap.

18. Mark Hitchcock, *The End of Money: Bible Prophecy and the Coming Economic Collapse* (Eugene, OR: Harvest House, 2013), 140–41; Tricia McCannon, *Jesus: The Explosive Story of the 30 Lost Years and the Ancient Mystery Religions* (Charlottesville, VA: Hampton Roads, 2010), ix.

19. Ross, interview by Anderson, April 10, 2014.

20. *Encyclopaedia Britannica*, s.v. "Mystery Religion," http://www.britannica.com/EBchecked/topic/400805/mystery-religion.

21. Ray Bentley, telephone interview by Troy Anderson for *The Babylon Code*, December 20, 2013.

22. Ray Bentley, *The Holy Land Key: Unlocking End-Times Prophecy Through the Lives of God's People in Israel* (Colorado Springs: WaterBrook Press, 2014), 122.

23. Bentley, interview by Anderson, December 20, 2013; Krieger, McGriff, and Woodward, *Final Babylon*, 33–43.

24. Alexander Hislop, *The Two Babylons*, http://www.biblebelievers.com/babylon; *Wikipedia*, s.v. "Semiramis," http://en.wikipedia.org/wiki/Semiramis; Paul McGuire, telephone interview by Troy Anderson for *The Babylon Code*, January 23, 2014.

25. *Encyclopaedia Britannica*, s.v. "Sammu-ramat," http://www.britannica.com/EBchecked/topic/520556/Sammu-ramat.

26. Ralph Woodrow, *The Babylon Connection?* (Palm Springs, FL: Ralph Woodrow Evangelistic Association, 1997), 19.

27. "The Last Days of Tim LaHaye (1 of 4)," YouTube video, 13:16, posted by Truth, Faith, and Grace, March 8, 2012, https://www.youtube.com/watch?v=QGLtw1r35xI&list=PLEG3-DIe-0-2xr6vsNtlbeRMsvxeyHz4-.

28. John F. Walvoord, *The Prophecy Knowledge Handbook: All the Prophecies of Scripture Explained in One Volume* (Wheaton, IL: Victory Books, 1990), 605.

29. *Encyclopaedia Britannica*, s.v. "Re," http://www.britannica.com/EBchecked/topic/492674/Re; Robert Hieronimus, *The United Symbolism of America: Deciphering Hidden Meanings in America's Most Familiar Art, Architecture, and Logos* (Pompton Plains, NJ: New Page Books, 2008), 39; Thomas Horn, *Apollyon Rising 2012: The Lost Symbol Found and the Final Mystery of the Great Seal Revealed* (Crane, MO: Defender, 2009), 110; Paul McGuire, "Stargates of God Kings and Breaking Through the Neurological Firewall," NewsWithViews.com, February 10, 2014, www.newswithviews.com/McGuire/paul203.htm.

30. Paul McGuire, in-person interview by Troy Anderson at a Newport Beach, California, restaurant for *The Babylon Code*, June 5, 2013; Walvoord, *Prophecy Knowledge Handbook,* 605.

31. Carroll M. Helm, telephone interview by Troy Anderson for *The Babylon Code*, March 19, 2014.

32. Ibid.

33. McGuire, interview by Anderson, June 5, 2013; Manly P. Hall, *The Secret Destiny of America* (Los Angeles: Philosophical Research Society, 1944), 42; Halley, *Halley's Bible Handbook*, 876; Corner, "Towards a Global Sharing of Sovereignty."

34. *Encyclopaedia Britannica*, s.v. "Babylon"; "Ancient Babylonia-History of Babylonia," Bible History Online, http://www.bible-history.com/babylonia/BabyloniaHistory_of_Babylonia.htm.

35. J. Daniel Hays and J. Scott Duvall, eds., *The Baker Illustrated Bible Handbook* (Grand Rapids, MI: Baker Books, 2011), 321; *Encyclopaedia Britannica*, s.v. "Jeremiah," http://www.britannica.com/biography/Jeremiah-Hebrew-prophet.

36. Ross, interview by Anderson, April 10, 2014.

37. Halley, *Halley's Bible Handbook*, 404–5; Hays and Duvall, *Baker Illustrated Bible Handbook*, 379; Hitchcock, *The End*, 66–70.

38. Halley, *Halley's Bible Handbook*, 874.

39. Hitchcock, *The End*, 361. Mark Hitchcock, telephone interview by Troy Anderson for *The Babylon Code*, January 23, 2014; Tim LaHaye and Ed Hindson, eds., *The Popular Encyclopedia of Bible Prophecy* (Eugene, OR: Harvest House, 2004), 332.

40. Hitchcock, interview by Anderson, January 23, 2014.

41. Joel C. Rosenberg, "Iraq Rebuilding Its Military, Even As They Rebuild Babylon: Prophetic Significance?" *Joel C. Rosenberg's Blog*, April 13, 2012, http://flashtrafficblog.wordpress.com/2012/04/13/iraq-rebuilding-its-military-even-as-they-rebuild-babylon-prophetic-significance; Steven Lee Myers, "A Triage to Save the Ruins of Babylon," *New York Times*, January 2, 2011, http://www.nytimes.com/2011/01/03/arts/03babylon.html.

42. Hitchcock, interview by Anderson, January 23, 2014.

43. Cioccolanti, interview by Anderson, January 14, 2015.

44. Joel C. Rosenberg, "The Biggest Threat Now Is Not Radical Islam. It Is 'Apocalyptic Islam.' Let Me Explain. (Excerpts from my address to the National Religious Broadcasters Convention)," *Joel C. Rosenberg's Blog*, February 27, 2015, https://flashtrafficblog.wordpress.com/2015/02/27/the-biggest-threat-now-is-not-radical

-islam-it-is-apocalyptic-islam-let-me-explain-excerpts-from-my-address-to-the
-national-religious-broadcasters-convention.

45. Grant R. Jeffrey, *One Nation, Under Attack: How Big-Government Liberals Are Destroying the America You Love* (Colorado Springs: WaterBrook Press, 2012), 2–7.

46. Ibid.

47. Jonathan Cahn, telephone interview by Troy Anderson for the "America at the End" story in the December 2012 issue of *Charisma* magazine, January 25, 2012; "Quotes from David Wilkerson," *Charisma*, http://www.charismamag.com/spirit/devotionals/loving-god?view=article&id=13370:quotes-from-david-wilkerson&catid=1532.

48. Woodward, interview by Anderson, August 14, 2013.

49. Ibid.

50. Jim Marrs, *Our Occulted History: Do the Global Elite Conceal Ancient Aliens?* (New York: William Morrow, 2013), 213–14.

51. Joseph P. Farrell, *Babylon's Banksters: The Alchemy of Deep Physics, High Finance and Ancient Religion* (Port Townsend, WA: Feral House, 2010).

52. Jim Marrs, telephone interview by Troy Anderson for *The Babylon Code*, February 28, 2014.

53. Ibid.

Chapter Two: The World's Most Infamous Secret Society

Epigraph: Sherlock Holmes, *The Hound of the Baskervilles*, Sherlock Holmes Quotes, http://sherlockholmesquotes.com/Sherlock-Holmes-on-Deduction-and-Deductive-Reasoning.html.

1. Grant R. Jeffrey, *Shadow Government: How the Secret Global Elite Is Using Surveillance Against You* (Colorado Springs: WaterBrook Press, 2009); Theodore Roosevelt, "Behind the ostensible government sits enthroned an invisible government owing no allegiance and acknowledging no responsibility to the people," http://brainyquote.com/quotes/quotes/t/theodorero169571.html; Manley P. Hall, *The Secret Destiny of America* (Los Angeles: Philosophical Research Society, 1944), 44.

2. *Time, Secret Societies: Decoding the Myths and Facts of History's Most Mysterious Organizations* (New York: Time Books, 2010), 4, 8.

3. "Secret Societies—David Icke and Jim Marrs," YouTube video, 29:46, posted by Brain Stream Media, February 12, 2001, https://www.youtube.com/watch?v=T6sICgrFQVo&feature=youtu.be.

4. Larry Bartels, "Rich People Rule!" *Washington Post*, April 8, 2014, http://www.washingtonpost.com/blogs/monkey-cage/wp/2014/04/08/rich-people-rule.

5. Martin Gilens, telephone interview by Troy Anderson for *The Babylon Code*, April 28, 2014; Bartels, "Rich People Rule!"; Martin Gilens and Benjamin I. Page, "Testing Theories of American Politics: Elites, Interest Groups, and Average Citizens," *Perspectives on Politics* 12, no. 3 (September 2014): 564–81, http://scholar.princeton.edu/sites/default/files/mgilens/files/gilens_and_page_2014_-testing_theories_of_american_politics.doc.pdf.

6. "Secret Societies—David Icke and Jim Marrs," History Channel.

7. Jim Marrs, telephone interview by Troy Anderson for *The Babylon Code*, February 28, 2014.

8. Daniel Estulin, *The True Story of the Bilderberg Group* (Walterville, OR: TrineDay, 2005), xxv, 4; *Encyclopaedia Britannica*, s.v. "Bilderberg Conference," http://www.britannica.com/EBchecked/topic/65237/Bilderberg-Conference.

9. Daniel Estulin, telephone interview by Troy Anderson for *The Babylon Code*, May 27, 2014.

10. "Secret Societies—David Icke and Jim Marrs," History Channel.

11. J. Eric Oliver and Thomas J. Wood, "Conspiracy Theories, Magical Thinking, and the Paranoid Style(s) of Mass Opinion," University of Chicago Department of Political Science, June 2012, 20–21.

12. Ibid.

13. Jesse Walker, telephone interview by Troy Anderson for *The Babylon Code*, March 24, 2014.

14. "Secret Societies—David Icke and Jim Marrs," History Channel; *Encyclopaedia Britannica*, s.v. "Mystery Religion," http://www.britannica.com/EBchecked/topic/400805/mystery-religion/15850/Secular-mystery-communities#ref363182; Jim Marrs, *Rule by Secrecy: The Hidden History That Connects the Trilateral Commission, the Freemasons, and the Great Pyramids* (New York: Perennial, 2000), 366.

15. Manly P. Hall, *The Secret Teachings of All Ages: An Encyclopedic Outline of Masonic, Hermetic, Qabbalistic, and Rosicrucian Symbolical Philosophy* (Seattle, WA: Pacific Publishing Studio, 2011), 1; Stanley Monteith, *Brotherhood of Darkness* (Crane, MO: Highway, 2000), 8–9; Mitch Horowitz, *Occult America: White House Séances, Ouija Circles, Masons, and the Secret Mystic History of Our Nation* (New York: Bantam, 2009), 154–55.

16. Marrs, *Rule by Secrecy*, 346, 348–49; William H. McIlhany, "A Primer on the Illuminati," *New American*, June 12, 2009; *Encyclopaedia Britannica*, s.v. "Templar," http://www.britannica.com/EBchecked/topic/586765/Templar; *Time*, *Secret Societies*, 4.

17. Dennis L. Cuddy, "Statue of Liberty," NewsWithViews.com, May 17, 2010, http://www.newswithviews.com/Cuddy/dennis181.htm.

18. McIlhany, "Primer on the Illuminati"; *Time*, *Secret Societies*, 24; Amy D. Bernstein, "A Short History of Secret Societies," *U.S. News & World Report* special publication, "Mysteries of History: Secret Societies," May 19, 2009.

19. Vernon Stauffer, *The Bavarian Illuminati in America: The New England Conspiracy Scare, 1798* (Mineola, NY: Dover Publications, 2006; orig. pub. 1918), 142–228; Marrs, *Rule by Secrecy*, 235–36; Paul McGuire, e-mail interview by Troy Anderson for *The Babylon Code*, April 2, 2014; JewishEncyclopedia.com, s.v. "Rothschild," http://www.jewishencyclopedia.com/articles/12909-rothschild; Michael Noer, "The Twenty Most Influential Businessmen of All Time," *Forbes*, July 29, 2005, http://www.forbes.com/2005/07/29/most-influential-businessmen-cx_mn_0729bizmenintro.html.

20. James H. Billington, *Fire in the Minds of Men: Origins of the Revolutionary Faith* (New York: Basic Books, 1980), 93–99; Theodore Ziolkowski, *Lure of the Arcane: The Literature of Cult and Conspiracy* (Baltimore, MD: Johns Hopkins University Press, 2013), 65.

21. Stauffer, *Bavarian Illuminati in America*, 207–8; Albert C. Mackey, "Nimrod," *Encyclopedia of Freemasonry and Its Kindred Sciences*, http://www.phoenixmasonry.org/mackeys_encyclopedia/n.htm.

22. John Robison, *Proofs of a Conspiracy: Against All the Religions and Governments of Europe, Carried on in the Secret Meetings of Free Masons, Illuminati, and Reading Societies* (London: Forgotten Books, 2008), 7–11.

23. Stauffer, *Bavarian Illuminati in America*, 209; Robison, *Proofs of a Conspiracy*, vii, 69, 71; McIlhany, "Primer on the Illuminati."

24. Ziolkowski, *Lure of the Arcane*, 67.

25. Devra Newberger Speregen and Debra Mostow Zakarin, *Secret Societies: The Truth Revealed* (Plain City, OH: Media Source, 2013), 10; Stauffer, *Bavarian Illuminati in America*, 173; Pat Robertson, *The New World Order* (Dallas: Word, 1991), 6.

26. Stauffer, *Bavarian Illuminati in America*, 175–83.

27. Ibid., 178–79, 210–11; Robison, *Proofs of a Conspiracy*, 12, 58, 77; Robert Hieronimus, *Founding Fathers, Secret Societies: Freemason, Illuminati, Rosicrucians, and the Decoding of the Great Seal* (Rochester, VT: Destiny Books, 1989), 39; Marrs, *Rule by Secrecy*, 239; McIlhany, "Primer on the Illuminati."

28. George Washington, "It was not my intention to doubt that, the Doctrines of the Illuminati, and principles of Jacobinism had not spread in the United States. On the contrary, no one is more truly satisfied of this fact than I am," http://en.wikiquote .org/wiki/freemasonry; Timothy Dwight, "The Duty of Americans at the Present Crisis," 1798, http://books.google.com/books?id=NVAuAAAAYAAJ&printsec= frontcover&source=gbs_ge_summary_r&cad=0#v=onepage&q&f=false; Gerald Celente, telephone interview by Troy Anderson for *The Babylon Code*, September 26, 2014.

29. Joseph Willard, Harvard University, "A Sermon Preached in Lancaster, New Hampshire on the Anniversary of Our National Independence," http://quotes.liberty -tree.ca/quote/joseph_willard_quote_5025.

30. McIlhany, "Primer on the Illuminati."

31. Marrs, *Rule by Secrecy*, 242; Robison, *Proofs of a Conspiracy*, vii.

32. Billington, *Fire in the Minds of Men*, 99.

33. Speregen and Zakarin, *Secret Societies*, 33–38.

34. *Time, Secret Societies*, 27.

35. Stanley Monteith, telephone interview by Troy Anderson for *The Babylon Code*, August 5, 2014.

36. *Wikipedia*, s.v. "Ingolstadt," http://en.wikipedia.org/wiki/Ingolstadt; Antony C. Sutton, *America's Secret Establishment: An Introduction to the Order of Skull & Bones* (Walterville, OR: TrineDay, 2004), 115, 212; Marrs, *Rule by Secrecy*, 91; Bernstein, "A Short History of Secret Societies"; John Coleman, *The Illuminati in America, 1776–2008* (Carson City, NV: World International Review, 2008), 27.

37. Robertson, *New World Order*, 44.

38. Monteith, interview by Anderson, August 5, 2014; Monteith, *Brotherhood of Darkness*, 21–23, 66; Carroll Quigley, *The Anglo-American Establishment* (San Pedro, CA: GSG, 1981), ix, 4–6, 38, 134–35, 303.

39. Monteith, interview by Anderson, August 5, 2014; Elizabeth Flock, "Bohemian Grove: Where the Rich and Powerful Go to Misbehave," *Washington Post*, June 15, 2011; Philip Weiss, "Masters of the Universe Go to Camp: Inside the Bohemian Grove," *Spy Magazine*, November 1989; Alex Jones, *Dark Secrets: Inside Bohemian Grove*, InfoWars.com, 2000, https://archive.org/details/DSIBG.

40. A. Ralph Epperson, *The Unseen Hand: An Introduction to the Conspiratorial View of History* (Tucson: Publius Press, 1985), 6–9; Franklin D. Roosevelt, "In politics, nothing happens by accident. If it happens, you can bet it was planned that way," BrainyQuote.com, http://www.brainyquote.com/quotes/quotes/f/franklind164126.html; Marrs, *Rule by Secrecy*, 12; Carroll Quigley, *Tragedy & Hope: A History of the World in Our Time* (New York: Macmillian, 1966), 950; Jim Naureckas, telephone interview by Troy Anderson for *The Babylon Code*, September 5, 2014.

41. Monteith, interview by Anderson, August 5, 2014.

42. John F. Kennedy, "The President and the Press: Address Before the American Newspaper Publishers Association," April 27, 1961, http://www.jfklibrary.org/Research/Research-Aids/JFK-Speeches/American-Newspaper-Publishers-Association_19610427.aspx; Jim Marrs, *The Rise of the Fourth Reich: The Secret Societies That Threaten to Take Over America* (New York: William Morrow, 2008), 220.

43. Mitch Horowitz, "Ronald Reagan and the Occultist: The Amazing Story of the Thinker Behind His Sunny Optimism," Salon.com, January 5, 2014.

44. Greg Laurie, *Revelation: The Next Dimension* (Austin, TX: Allen David Books, 2014), 325.

45. Tim LaHaye, telephone interview by Troy Anderson for *The Babylon Code*, August 29, 2014; Lord Acton, "Power tends to corrupt and absolute power corrupts absolutely," http://www.brainyquote.com/quotes/quotes/l/lordacton109401.html.

46. LaHaye, interview by Anderson, August 29, 2014; Henri Spaak, "What we want is a man of sufficient stature to hold the alliances of all people and to lift us out of the economic morass into which we are sinking. Send us such a man, and be he god or devil, we will receive him," RaptureReady.com, http://www.raptureready.com/soap/garcia13.html.

Chapter Three: "Ode to Joy" and a Shared Destiny

1. William Witte, *Schiller* (Oxford: Blackwell, 1949), 39; Juri Lina, *Under the Sign of the Scorpion: The Rise and Fall of the Soviet Empire* (Stockholm: Referent Publishing, 2002), 32–36.

2. Los Angeles County Board of Supervisors Transcript, Adjournment in Memory of Stanley Richard Anderson, May 17, 2005, http://file.lacounty.gov/bos/transcripts/05-17-05%20Board%20Meeting%20Transcript%20(C).pdf.

3. "Friedrich von Schiller," *Grand Rapids Press*, May 9, 1905, http://www.genealogybank.com/gbnk/newspapers/doc/v2%3A1231FD919F0.

4. "Schiller, Friedrich (1759–1805)," research article from *Encyclopedia of Philosophy*, http://www.bookrags.com/research/schiller-friedrich-17591805-eoph; "Schiller's 250th Birthday," YouTube video, 4:27, posted by DW (English), November 10, 2009, http://www.youtube.com/watch?v=5XbGn53-tO8; Luke Harding, "Tale of Two Skulls Divides Germany," *Guardian*, May 8, 2005, http://www.theguardian.com/world/2005/may/08/artsandhumanities.germany; Walter Hinderer, ed., *Friedrich Schiller Plays: Intrigue and Love and Don Carlos* (New York: Continuum, 1994), x.

5. "Johann Christoph Friedrich von Schiller Biography," *Encyclopedia of World Biography*, http://www.bookrags.com/biography/friedrich-von-schiller-dtx.

6. "Friedrich Schiller the Freedom Fighter," Spiegel Online International, May 10, 2005, http://www.spiegel.de/international/spiegel-surfs-the-web-friedrich-schiller -the-freedom-fighter-a-355415.html; Harding, "Tale of Two Skulls Divides Germany"; Hinderer, *Friedrich Schiller Plays*, xi; Gabriele Chaitkin, "'For He Was One of Us': Friedrich Schiller, the Poet of America," *American Almanac*, October 1996, http://members.tripod.com/american_almanac/schill96.htm.

7. "The European Anthem," European Union, http://europa.eu/about-eu/basic -information/symbols/anthem/index_en.htm; Gail K. Hart, in-person interview by Troy Anderson at the University of California, Irvine, for *The Babylon Code*, September 23, 2014; Esteban Buch, *Beethoven's Ninth: A Political History*, trans. Richard Miller (Chicago: University of Chicago Press, 2003), 1, 49.

8. Jeffrey High, telephone interview by Troy Anderson for *The Babylon Code*, July 10, 2013.

9. Ibid.

10. Hinderer, *Friedrich Schiller Plays*, xiv.

11. High, interview by Anderson, July 10, 2013.

12. "The Who's Who of Prophecy: Hal Lindsey," RaptureReady.com, https://rapture ready.com/who/Hal_Lindsey.html.

13. Hal Lindsey and C. C. Carlson, *The Late Great Planet Earth* (Grand Rapids, MI: Zondervan, 1970), 54.

14. Hal Lindsey, e-mail interview by Troy Anderson for the "Last Days Fever" cover story in *Charisma* magazine, July 2009; Troy Anderson, "Last Days Fever," *Charisma*, July 13, 2012; http://www.charismamag.com/spirit/prophecy/6745-last-days-fever.

15. F. Kenton Beshore, *When?: When Will the Rapture Take Place?* (Costa Mesa, CA: World Bible Society, 2009), 177; Tim LaHaye, telephone interview by Troy Anderson for the "America at the End" story in *Charisma*, August 29, 2012; Troy Anderson, "The Late Great Correction," *Charisma*, December 2012, http://www .charismamag.com/spirit/prophecy/15875-the-late-great-correction.

16. "Bones of Contention: DNA Tests Reveal 'Schiller's' Skull Not His," Spiegel Online International, May 5, 2008, http://www.spiegel.de/international/zeitgeist/bones -of-contention-dna-tests-reveal-schiller-s-skull-not-his-a-551557.html; Troy Anderson, "Wagner Series Splits Community," *Los Angeles Daily News*, May 3, 2009.

17. Harding, "Tale of Two Skulls Divides Germany"; Nicholas Kulish, "2 More Skulls, but Still No Schiller," *New York Times*, May 8, 2008, http://www .nytimes.com/2008/05/08/world/europe/08iht-journal.4.12715118.html; *Wikipedia*, s.v. "Friedrich Schiller's Skull," http://en.wikipedia.org/wiki/Friedrich _Schiller%27s_skull; Kate Connolly, "Schiller's Family Exhumed as Scientists Work to Crack Mystery of the Two Skulls," *Guardian*, July 24, 2007, http://www .theguardian.com/world/2007/jul/24/germany.kateconnolly.

18. Lina, *Under the Sign of the Scorpion*, 32–33; Claudia Pilling, Diana Schilling, and Mirjam Springer, *Friedrich Schiller* (Hamburg: Rowohlt Taschenbuch, 2002), 54–55.

19. Witte, *Schiller*, 38–39.

20. Theodore Ziolkowski, telephone interview by Troy Anderson for *The Babylon Code*, September 26, 2014.

21. Hart, interview by Anderson, September 23, 2014.

22. Paul McGuire, speech given at Southern California Prophecy Conference, Calvary Chapel Chino Hills, February 20, 2009.

23. Paul McGuire, e-mail interview by Troy Anderson for *The Babylon Code*, September 9–10, 2014.

24. Paul McGuire, *The Day the Dollar Died* (Los Angeles: M House Publishers, 2009), 77–78.

25. "Paul McGuire," *Sid Roth's It's Supernatural!*, June 10, 2013, http://sidroth.org/television/tv-archives/paul-mcguire.

Chapter Four: A Prophetic Superstorm

Epigraph: Billy Graham, *The Reason for My Hope: Salvation* (Nashville: Thomas Nelson, 2013), 172–73.

1. Billy Graham, e-mail interview by Troy Anderson for a seven-part WND.com series and www.tothesource.org story about the *My Hope America with Billy Graham* evangelistic outreach, August 20, 2013; "94-Year-Old Billy Graham's Warning for America," WND.com, August 4, 2013, http://www.wnd.com/2013/08/94-year-old-billy-grahams-warning-for-america; "Famed Evangelist: God Told Me 'America Will Be Saved,'" WND.com, August 18, 2013, www.wnd.com/2013/08/famed-evangelist-god-told-me-america-will-be-saved; "Billy Graham: Now Is Time for 'Fresh Awakening,'" WND.com, September 22, 2013, http://www.wnd.com/2013/09/billy-graham-now-is-time-for-fresh-awakening; "Billy Graham Sounds Alarm for 2nd Coming," WND.com, October 20, 2013, http://www.wnd.com/2013/10/billy-graham-sounds-alarm-for-2nd-coming; "Prophecy Scholar: America at the Crossroads," WND.com, November 2, 2013, http://www.wnd.com/2013/11/prophecy-scholar-america-at-crossroads; "Man Who Walked Across U.S. Saw Revival Signs," WND.com, November 3, 2013, http://www.wnd.com/2013/11/man-who-walked-across-u-s-saw-revival-signs; "Billy Graham to Give 'Final, Most Important' Message," WND.com, November 5, 2013, http://www.wnd.com/2013/11/billy-graham-to-give-final-most-important-message; Troy Anderson, "Billy Graham's Hope for America," tothesource.org, September 26, 2013, http://www.tothesource.org/9_25_2013/9_25_2013.htm.

2. Joel C. Rosenberg, "Here's My List of the Top Five Most Important Events in the Mideast in 2013," *Joel C. Rosenberg's Blog*, December 31, 2013, http://flashtraffic blog.wordpress.com/2013/12/31/heres-my-list-of-the-top-five-most-important-events-in-the-mideast-in-2013; "Full Text of Netanyahu's 2013 Speech to the UN General Assembly," *Times of Israel*, October 1, 2013, http://timesofisrael.com/full-text-netanyahus-2013-speech-to-the-un-general-assembly/#ixzz2z0sX0vtG; Stefano Rellandini, "Pope Says World's Many Conflicts Amount to Piecemeal World War Three," Reuters, September 13, 2014, http://news.yahoo.com/pope-says-worlds-many-conflicts-amount-piecemeal-world-104917; Russell Shaw, "Devil Is Working Hard on Securing End Times," *OSV Newsweekly*, February 26, 2014, https://www.osv.com/osvnewsweekly/article/tabid/535/artmid/13567/articleid/14188/devil-is-working-hard-on-securing-end-times.aspx; "Michele Bachmann: Obama 'Funding' Terrorists Is Proof That We're Living in the End Times," *Huffington Post*, October 7, 2013, http://www.huffingtonpost.com/2013/10/07/michele-bachmann-end

-times_n_4060063.html; Franklin Graham, "Franklin Graham: Are We in the Last Hours Before Christ's Return?," Charisma News, September 3, 2014, http://www.charismanews.com/opinion/45248-franklin-graham-are-we-in-the-last-hours-before-christ-s-return.

3. Franklin Graham, "Franklin Graham: Is the World Coming Apart at the Seams?," Billy Graham Evangelistic Association, September 10, 2014, http://billygraham.org/story/franklin-graham-is-the-world-coming-apart-at-the-seams; David A. Patten, "Franklin Graham: Spirit of Anti-Christ Is Everywhere," Newsmax, January 20, 2011, http://www.newsmax.com/InsideCover/Franklin-Graham-Jesus-Christ/2011/01/20/id/383454.

4. Thomas Ice, telephone interview by Troy Anderson for The Babylon Code, December 18, 2014.

5. Henry H. Halley, Halley's Bible Handbook (Grand Rapids, MI: Zondevan, 2007), 27; Troy Anderson, "King James Bible Turns 400," tothesource.org, September 16, 2010, http://www.tothesource.org/9_15_2010/9_15_2010.htm; "Best-Selling Book of Non-Fiction," Guinness World Records, http://www.guinnessworldrecords.com/world-records/best-selling-book-of-non-fiction; Wikipedia, s.v. "List of Best-Selling Books," http://en.wikipedia.org/wiki/List_of_best-selling_books.

6. Rick Warren, "The Bible Has One Theme, and That's a Miracle," Daily Hope, September 20, 2014, http://rickwarren.org/devotional/english/the-bible-has-one-theme-and-that-s-a-miracle.

7. Hugh Ross, "Fulfilled Prophecy: Evidence for the Reliability of the Bible," Reasons to Believe, August 22, 2003, http://www.reasons.org/articles/articles/fulfilled-prophecy-evidence-for-the-reliability-of-the-bible.

8. Hal Lindsey and C. C. Carlson, The Late Great Planet Earth (Grand Rapids, MI: Zondervan, 1970), 180.

9. Robert Jeffress, telephone interview by Troy Anderson for The Babylon Code, January 9, 2014; Mark Hitchcock, The End: A Complete Overview of Bible Prophecy and the End of Days (Carol Stream, IL: Tyndale, 2012), 23.

10. Hitchcock, The End, 4–16; Rick Warren, "What the Bible Predicts, Comes True," Daily Hope, May 21, 2014, http://rickwarren.org/devotional/english/what-the-bible-predicts-comes-true; Mark Hitchcock, 101 Answers to Questions About the Book of Revelation (Eugene, OR: Harvest House, 2012), 25.

11. Hitchcock, The End, 4–5; Hitchcock, telephone interview by Troy Anderson for The Babylon Code, January 23, 2014.

12. Tim LaHaye, telephone interview by Troy Anderson for The Babylon Code, August 29, 2014.

13. Clint Jenkin, telephone interview by Troy Anderson for The Babylon Code, January 2, 2014.

14. Billy Graham, speech at the Southern Baptist Convention, St. Louis, June 1987.

15. Claire Suddath, "It's the End of the World as We Know It," Time, October 21, 2011, http://content.time.com/time/specials/packages/article/0,28804,2097462_2097456_2097489,00.html; David A. Patten, "Will He Ever Return?," Newsmax, April 2009; "Newton's End Times Calculation Corrected!," WND.com, September 16, 2008, http://www.wnd.com/2008/09/75434.

16. Ben Witherington, telephone interview by Troy Anderson for *The Babylon Code*, February 21, 2014.

17. Darrell Bock, telephone interview by Troy Anderson for *The Babylon Code*, February 5, 2014.

18. Jennifer LeClaire, "Most Pastors Avoid Controversial Issues to Keep Tithes Up," Charisma News, August 13, 2014, http://www.charismanews.com/us/45009-most -pastors-avoid-controversial-issues-to-keep-tithes-up.

19. Jan Markell, telephone interview by Troy Anderson for *The Babylon Code*, February 11, 2014.

20. Noam Chomsky, "The End of History?" *In These Times*, September 4, 2014, http:// inthesetimes.com/article/17137/the_end_of_history.

21. University of Oxford Future of Humanity Institute and the Global Challenges Foundation, "Global Challenges: 12 Risks That Threaten Human Civilisation," February 2015, http://globalchallenges.org/wp-content/uploads/12-Risks-with-infinite -impact-full-report-1.pdf.

22. Public Religion Research Institute, "Six-in-Ten Americans Believe Climate Change Responsible for Recent Natural Disasters," December 13, 2012, http://publicreligion .org/newsroom/2012/12/news-release-six-in-ten-americans-believe-climate -change-responsible-for-recent-natural-disasters; Pew Research Center for the People & the Press, "Section 3: War, Terrorism and Global Trends," June 22, 2010, http://www.people-press.org/2010/06/22/section-3-war-terrorism-and-global -trends; Jerry B. Jenkins, e-mail interview by Troy Anderson for *The Babylon Code*, March 31, 2014.

23. Robert P. Jones, Daniel Cox, and Juhem Navarro-Rivera, "Believers, Sympathizers, & Skeptics: Why Americans Are Conflicted About Climate Change, Environmental Policy, and Science," Public Religion Research Institute, November 22, 2014, http://publicreligion.org/site/wp-content/uploads/2014/11/2014-Climate-Change -FINAL.pdf.

24. David R. Reagan, "An End Times Sign More Important Than Israel?," Lamb & Lion Ministries, April 23, 2014, http://www.lamblion.com/enewsletter1/new _enewsletter_template_140423.html; Constance Cumbey, *The Hidden Dangers of the Rainbow: The New Age Movement and Our Coming Age of Barbarism* (Lafayette, LA: Huntington House, 1983), 14; Joel C. Rosenberg, "Understanding Egypt: The Twelfth Imam, and the End of Days," TheBlaze.com, February 9, 2011, http://www.theblaze.com/blog/2011/02/09/understanding-egypt-the-twelfth-iman -and-the-end-of-days.

25. Stan Guthrie, telephone interview by Troy Anderson for *The Babylon Code*, January 27, 2014.

26. Dan Merica, "Survey: One in Three Americans See Extreme Weather as a Sign of Biblical End Times," CNN, December 13, 2012, http://religion.blogs.cnn .com/2012/12/13/survey-one-in-three-americans-see-extreme-weather-as-a-sign-of -biblical-end-times; Public Religion Research Institute, "Six-in-Ten Americans Believe Climate Change Responsible for Recent Natural Disasters"; Henry H. Halley, *Halley's Bible Handbook* (Grand Rapids, MI: Zondervan, 2007), 364–65.

27. Becky Oskin, "Big Earthquakes Double in 2014, but They're Not Linked," LiveScience .com, June 27, 2014, http://www.livescience.com/46576-more-earthquakes-still

-random-process.html; "WHO Chief: Ebola Outbreak 'Most Severe Health Emergency in Modern Times,'" *Newsmax*, October 13, 2014, http://www.newsmax.com/Newsfront/Health-Ebola-WAfrica-WHO/2014/10/13/id/600332/?ns_mail_uid=26940664&ns_mail_job=1590219_10132014&s=al&dkt_nbr=2mwwjpnp.

28. World Economic Forum, "Global Risks 2013" and "Global Risks 2014," http://www.weforum.org/reports/global-risks-2013-eighth-edition; http://www.weforum.org/reports/global-risks-2014-report.

29. B612 Foundation, "Protecting Our Planet from Dangerous Asteroids," press release, April 22, 2014, http://sentinelmission.org/newsroom/press-releases.

30. Matthew 24:42, in *NIV Archaeological Study Bible* (Grand Rapids, MI: Zondervan, 2005); F. Kenton Beshore, *When?: When Will the Rapture Take Place?* (Costa Mesa, CA: World Bible Society, 2009), 11, 31–34; *Encyclopaedia Britannica*, s.v. "Six-Day War," http://www.britannica.com/EBchecked/topic/850855/Six-Day-War.

31. LaHaye, interview by Anderson, August 29, 2012.

32. Beshore, *When?*, 35–40.

33. Jan Markell, "The Convergence," April 7, 2014, http://olivetreeviews.org/images/Newsletter-March-April-May-2014.pdf.

34. Beshore, *When*, 41–56.

35. "Nephilim," BibleStudyTools.com, http://www.biblestudytools.com/encyclopedias/isbe/nephilim.html; Markell, "The Convergence."

36. Paul McGuire, e-mail interview by Troy Anderson for *The Babylon Code*, September 17, 2014.

37. Ray Kurzweil, *The Singularity Is Near: When Humans Transcend Biology* (New York: Penguin, 2005), 9.

38. Nick Bostrom, *Superintelligence: Paths, Dangers, Strategies* (Oxford: Oxford University Press, 2014), vii.

39. Daniel Estulin, telephone interview by Troy Anderson for *The Babylon Code*, May 27, 2014; Daniel Martin, "150 Human Animal Hybrids Grown in UK Labs: Embryos Have Been Produced Secretively for the Past Three Years," *Daily Mail*, July 22, 2011, http://www.dailymail.co.uk/sciencetech/article-2017818/Embryos-involving-genes-animals-mixed-humans-produced-secretively-past-years.html.

40. *Dr. Michio Kaku on Why the Universe Has 11 Dimensions*, AOL.com, http://on.aol.com/video/dr--michio-kaku-on-why-the-universe-has-11-dimensions-517068278.

41. "Babel, Tower of," BibleStudyTools.com, http://www.biblestudytools.com/encyclopedias/isbe/babel-tower-of.html.

Chapter Five: America at the End

Epigraph: Joel C. Rosenberg, interviewed by Troy Anderson for his "America at the End" story in *Charisma*, December 2012, http://www.charismamag.com/spirit/prophecy/15873-america-at-the-end.

1. Stephen G. Brooks and William C. Wohlforth, "Reshaping the World Order," *Foreign Affairs*, March/April 2009, http://www.foreignaffairs.com/articles/2009-03-01-reshaping-the-world-order; Philip Pullella, "Vatican Urges Economic Reforms, Condemns Collective Greed," Reuters, October 24, 2011, http://uk.reuters.com/assets/print?aid=UKL5E7L01LS20111024.

2. Joel C. Rosenberg, telephone interview by Troy Anderson for *Charisma* story "America at the End," June 13, 2012.

3. Ibid.

4. Jonathan Cahn, e-mail interview by Troy Anderson for *The Babylon Code*, February 10, 2014.

5. Ibid.

6. Ibid.

7. Ibid.

8. Ibid.

9. Troy Anderson and Jessilyn Justice, "The Shemitah Unraveled: What 2015–2016 Could Bring," CharismaNews.com, March 10, 2015, http://www.charismanews .com/world/48667-the-shemitah-unraveled-what-2015-2016-could-bring.

10. Perry Stone, *Deciphering End-Time Prophetic Codes* (Lake Mary, FL: Charisma House, 2015), 5–6, 51, 63–69.

11. Ibid., 5–6, 63–69; "The Mayflower Compact (1620)," http://usa.usembassy.de/ etexts/democrac/2.htm.

12. John C. Hagee, sermon on four blood moons given in October 2012 at Cornerstone Church, http://www.youtube.com/watch?v=4lqk3XdMkDY.

13. Ibid.

14. Sarah Pulliam Bailey, " 'Blood Moon' Sets Off Apocalyptic Debate Among Some Christians," *Washington Post*, April 15, 2014, http://www.washingtonpost .com/national/religion/blood-moon-sets-off-apocalyptic-debate-among-some -christians/2014/04/15/00b76502-c4be-11e3-9ee7-02c1e10a03f0_story.html.

15. Mark Hitchcock, telephone interview by Troy Anderson for *The Babylon Code*, January 23, 2014.

16. Kenneth L. Waters, "Does the Bible Predict the 'Blood Moon'?" CNN, April 14, 2014, http://religion.blogs.cnn.com/2014/04/14/whats-up-with-the-blood-moons -prophecies.

17. David Flynn, *Temple at the Center of Time: Newton's Bible Codex Deciphered and the Year 2012* (Crane, OR: Official Disclosure, 2008), 21.

18. Ibid.

19. "Isaac Newton, Bible Code Pioneer?," BibleCodeDigest.com, http://www.bible codedigest.com/page.php?PageID=74.

20. Jonathan Petre, "Newton Set 2060 for End of World," *Telegraph*, February 22, 2003, http://www.telegraph.co.uk/news/uknews/1422794/Newton-set-2060-for-end -of-world.html.

21. "Neil and Cindy Russell," *Sid Roth's It's Supernatural!* April 7, 2008, http://sidroth .org/television/tv-archives/neill-and-cindy-russell.

22. Anderson and Justice, "The Shemitah Unraveled."

23. Grant R. Jeffrey, *One Nation, Under Attack: How Big-Government Liberals Are Destroying the America You Love* (Colorado Springs: WaterBrookPress, 2012), 6–7; Ron Rhodes, *The 8 Great Debates of Bible Prophecy* (Eugene, OR: Harvest House, 2014), 58.

24. U.S. National Debt Clock, http://www.usdebtclock.org; Rosenberg, interview by Anderson, June 13, 2012.

25. Rosenberg, interview by Anderson, June 13, 2012.

26. Tim LaHaye, telephone interview by Troy Anderson for the "America at the End" story in *Charisma*, August 29, 2012; Stephen Mulvey, "Could Terrorists Get Hold of a Nuclear Bomb?," *BBC News*, April 12, 2010, http://news.bbc.co.uk/2/hi/americas/8615484.stm; Rhodes, *8 Great Debates of Bible Prophecy*, 61–63; John S. Foster Jr., Earl Gjelde, William R. Graham, Robert J. Hermann, Henry M. Kluepfel, Richard L. Lawson, Gordon K. Soper, Lowell L. Wood Jr., and Joan B. Woodard, "Report of the Commission to Assess the Threat to the United States from Electromagnetic Pulse (EMP) Attack," 2004, http://www.empcommission.org/docs/empc_exec_rpt.pdf; Michael Bryne, "Dying in a Nuclear Apocalypse Is Still a Pretty Likely Outcome," Motherboard, November 30, 2014, http://motherboard.vice.com/read/dying-in-a-nuclear-apocalypse-is-still-a-pretty-likely-outcome; Seth Baum, "Nuclear War, the Black Swan We Can Never See," *Bulletin of the Atomic Scientists*, November 21, 2014, http://thebulletin.org/nuclear-war-black-swan-we-can-never-see7821.

27. David Wilkerson, "An Urgent Message," David Wilkerson Devotions, March 7, 2009, http://davidwilkersontoday.blogspot.com/2009/03/urgent-message.html.

28. Ibid.

29. Douglas W. Krieger, Dene McGriff, and S. Douglas Woodward, *The Final Babylon: America and the Coming of the Antichrist* (Oklahoma City: Faith Happens, 2013), 59–60.

30. S. Douglas Woodward, telephone interview by Troy Anderson for *The Babylon Code*, August 14, 2013.

31. "Is America Mystery Babylon?" YouTube video, 19:11, posted by Discover Ministries TV, January 16, 2014, https://www.youtube.com/watch?v=nOL_Ozm4P90&feature=youtu.be.

32. Ibid.

33. Ibid.

34. Alexis de Tocqueville, "America is great because she is good. If America ceases to be good, America will cease to be great," http://www.goodreads.com/author/quotes/465.Alexis_de_Tocqueville.

35. Jim Marrs, *The Rise of the Fourth Reich: The Secret Societies That Threaten to Take Over America* (New York: William Morrow, 2008), 5.

36. John J. Walters, "Communism Killed 94M in 20th Century, Feels Need to Kill Again," Reason, May 13, 2013, http://reason.com/blog/2013/03/13/communism-killed-94m-in-20th-century.

37. Bill of Rights, Bill of Rights Institute, http://billofrightsinstitute.org/founding-documents/bill-of-rights.

38. Declaration of Independence, Bill of Rights Institute, http://billofrightsinstitute.org/founding-documents/declaration-of-independence.

39. *Encyclopaedia Britannica*, s.v. "Atlantis," http://www.britannica.com/EBchecked/topic/41264/Atlantis; Manley P. Hall, *The Secret Destiny of America* (Los Angeles: Philosophical Research Society, 1944), 44.

40. *Encyclopaedia Britannica*, s.v. "George H. W. Bush," http://www.britannica.com/EBchecked/topic/86083/George-HW-Bush; Robert Hieronimus, *Founding Fathers, Secret Societies: Freemasons, Illuminati, Rosicrucians, and the Decoding of the Great Seal* (Rochester, VT: Destiny Books, 2006), 105; Jim Marrs, *Rule by Secrecy: The Hidden History That Connects the Trilateral Commission, the Freemasons, and the Great Pyramids* (New York: Perennial, 2000), 229; Flynn, *Temple at the Center of Time*, 2.

41. *Encyclopaedia Britannica*, s.v. "Phoenix," http://www.britannica.com/EBchecked/topic/457189/phoenix; J. R. Church, "Mount Hermon: Gate of the Fallen Angels," Prophecy in the News, May 1, 2011, http://www.prophecyinthenews.com/mount-hermon-gate-of-the-fallen-angels; Hall, *The Secret Destiny of America*, 125; Robert Hieronimus, telephone interview by Troy Anderson for *The Babylon Code*, April 3, 2014.
42. "Rephaim," Jewish Virtual Library, http://www.jewishvirtuallibrary.org/jsource/judaica/ejud_0002_0017_0_16648.html; "Rephaim," BibleStudyTools.com, http://www.biblestudytools.com/dictionary/rephaim; Paul McGuire, "America in Prophecy, Babylon and the New World Order," NewsWithViews.com, March 4, 2013, http://newswithviews.com/McGuire/paul163.htm; "Francis Bacon," Famous Scientists, http://www.famousscientists.org/francis-bacon.
43. *Encyclopaedia Britannica*, s.v. "Saul Alinsky," http://www.britannica.com/EBchecked/topic/15483/Saul-Alinsky; Kevin Jackson, "Obama, Alinsky and the Devil," *American Thinker*, July 29, 2013, http://www.americanthinker.com/blog/2013/07/obama_alinksy_and_the_devil.html; Dinesh D'Souza, *America: Imagine a World Without Her* (Washington, DC: Regnery, 2014), 4, 76–87; Rahm Emanuel, "You never let a serious crisis go to waste. And what I mean by that it's an opportunity to do things you think you could not do before," BrainyQuotes.com, http://www.brainyquote.com/quotes/quotes/r/rahmemanue409199.html; Hall, *The Secret Destiny of America*, 125.
44. William M. Arkin, "Back to the Bunker," *Washington Post*, June 4, 2006, http://www.washingtonpost.com/wp-dyn/content/article/2006/06/02/AR2006060201410.html; Tom Vanderbilt, "Is This Bush's Secret Bunker?," *Guardian*, August 28, 2006, http://www.theguardian.com/world/2006/aug/28/usa.features11; Stephen I. Schwartz, "Near Washington, Preparing for the Worst," *Washington Post*, August 9, 2006, http://www.washingtonpost.com/wp-dyn/content/article/2006/08/08/AR2006080801220.html; "Underground Bases and Tunnels," Project Camelot, http://projectcamelot.org/underground_bases.html; Grant R. Jeffrey, *Shadow Government: How the Secret Global Elite Is Using Surveillance Against You* (Colorado Springs: WaterBrook Press, 2009), 104.

Chapter Six: The Hidden Hand of History

Epigraph: Manley P. Hall, *The Secret Destiny of America* (Los Angeles: Philosophical Research Society, 1944), 19.
1. Theodore Ziolkowski, interview by Troy Anderson, September 26, 2014.
2. Pew Forum on Religion & Public Life / U.S. Religious Landscape Survey, June 1, 2008, http://www.pewforum.org.
3. Mark Hitchcock, telephone interview by Troy Anderson for *The Babylon Code*, January 23, 2014.
4. Ibid.
5. Winston Churchill, "History is written by the victors," ThinkExist.con, http://thinkexist.com/quotation/history_is_written_by_the_victors/150112.html.
6. Led Zeppelin, "Stairway to Heaven," AZLyrics.com, http://www.azlyrics.com/lyrics/ledzeppelin/stairwaytoheaven.html.
7. Hal Lindsey, *Satan Is Alive and Well on Planet Earth* (Grand Rapids, MI: Zondervan, 1972), 20; Aleister Crowley, "Do what thou wilt shall be the whole of the Law,"

http://en.wikiquote.org/wiki/Aleister_Crowley; David D. Nowell, "If It Feels Good Do It?," *Psychology Today*, February 6, 2011, http://www.psychologytoday.com/blog/intrinsic-motivation-and-magical-unicorns/201102/if-it-feels-good-do-it-0.

8. Mike Dash, "The Mysterious Mr. Zedzed: The Wickedest Man in the World," Smithsonian.com, February 16, 2012, http://www.smithsonianmag.com/history/the-mysterious-mr-zedzed-the-wickedest-man-in-the-world-97435790; Stanley Monteith, telephone interview by Troy Anderson for *The Babylon Code*, August 5, 2014; Lindsey, *Satan Is Alive and Well on Planet Earth*, 20–21.

9. Hal Lindsey and C. C. Carlson, *The Late Great Planet Earth* (Grand Rapids, MI: Zondervan, 1970), 114–18.

10. Tom Horn, telephone interview by Troy Anderson for a story about *Petrus Romanus: The Final Pope Is Here*, May 2, 2012; Douglas W. Krieger, Dene McGriff, and S. Douglas Woodward, *The Final Babylon: America and the Coming of the Antichrist* (Oklahoma City: Faith Happens, 2013), 25.

11. Douglas Hamp, *Corrupting the Image: Angels, Aliens, and the Antichrist Revealed* (Crane, MO: Defender, 2011), 17.

12. A. Ralph Epperson, *The Unseen Hand: An Introduction to the Conspiratorial View of History* (Tucson: Publius Press, 1985), 8.

13. Robert Hieronimus, *The United Symbolism of America: Deciphering Hidden Meanings in America's Most Familiar Art, Architecture, and Logos* (Pompton Plains, NJ: New Page Books, 2008), 61.

14. Krieger, McGriff, and Woodward, *Final Babylon*, 124–25; Dan Brown, *The Lost Symbol* (New York: Doubleday, 2009), 28–29; Alexander Lucie-Smith, "Most of Us Would Laugh at the Idea of a Masonic Mafia at Work in the Vatican. I'm Not Sure We Should," *Catholic Herald*, July 30, 2013, http://www.catholicherald.co.uk/commentandblogs/2013/07/30/most-of-us-would-laugh-at-the-idea-of-a-masonic-mafia-at-work-in-the-vatican-im-not-sure-that-we-should.

15. Willie Drye, "Atlantis—True Story or Cautionary Tale?," *National Geographic*, http://science.nationalgeographic.com/science/archaeology/atlantis; Jim Marrs, *Rule by Secrecy: The Hidden History That Connects the Trilateral Commission, the Freemasons, and the Great Pyramids* (New York: Perennial, 2000), 377.

16. Graham Hancock, *Fingerprints of the Gods: The Evidence of Earth's Lost Civilization* (New York: Three Rivers Press, 1995), 462–64; Baylor Institute for Studies of Religion, "American Piety in the 21st Century," September 2006, http://www.baylor.edu/content/services/document.php/33304.pdf.

17. Robert Hieronimus, telephone interview by Troy Anderson for *The Babylon Code*, April 3, 2014.

18. Jonathan Cahn, in a speech before the International Alliance of Messianic Congregations and Synagogues (IAMCS) in Orlando, Florida, January 7, 2015.

19. Peter Phillips and Brady Osborne, *Project Censored 2014: Fearless Speech in Fateful Times*, http://www.projectcensored.org/financial-core-of-the-transnational-corporate-class.

20. John 8:32, Common English Bible, BibleGateway.com; Jim Marrs, *Our Occulted History: Do the Global Elite Conceal Ancient Aliens?* (New York: William Morrow, 2013), 213.

Chapter Seven: The Tower of Babel, Nimrod, and Magic Money

Epigraph: Jim Marrs, *Our Occulted History: Do the Global Elite Conceal Ancient Aliens?* (New York: William Morrow, 2013), 213.

1. Thomas R. Horn, *Nephilim Stargates: The Year 2012 and the Return of the Watchers* (Crane, MO: Anomalos, 2007), 17–28; Hugh Ross, *Navigating Genesis: A Scientist's Journey Through Genesis 1–11* (Covina, CA: Reasons to Believe, 2014), 186.

2. Stanley Monteith, telephone interview by Troy Anderson for *The Babylon Code*, August 5, 2014.

3. F. Kenton Beshore, *Daniel Decoded: An Examination of Bible Prophecy* (Costa Mesa, CA: World Bible Society, 2013), 93.

4. Tim LaHaye and Ed Hinson, eds., *The Popular Encyclopedia of Bible Prophecy* (Eugene, OR: Harvest House, 2004), 42.

5. David Livingston, "Search for the Tower of Babel," Answers in Genesis, October 17, 2010, https://answersingenesis.org/tower-of-babel/search-for-the-tower-of-babel.

6. Ross, *Navigating Genesis*, 132–33.

7. Hugh Ross, telephone interview by Troy Anderson for *The Babylon Code*, April 10, 2014.

8. J. R. Church, "Mount Hermon: Gate of the Fallen Angels," Prophecy in the News, May 1, 2011, http://www.prophecyinthenews.com/mount-hermon-gate-of-the-fallen-angels.

9. Ibid.

10. Ibid.

11. Ibid.

12. Tricia McCannon, *Jesus: The Explosive Story of the 30 Lost Years and the Ancient Mystery Religions* (Charlottesville, VA: Hampton Roads, 2010), 26.

13. Horn, *Nephilim Stargates*, 17–28; S. Douglas Woodward, *Lying Wonders of the Red Planet: Exposing the Lie of Ancient Aliens* (Oklahoma City: Faith Happens, 2014), 42–45.

14. Paul McGuire, "America's Three Futures—Part 3: The Nephilim Alien Disclosure Event," http://www.paulmcguire.org/?p=531.

15. Zoltan Istvan, "Transhumanism Has a Conspiracy Theory Problem," Motherboard, October 2, 2014; http://motherboard.vice.com/read/transhumanist-a-conspiracy-theory-problem; Istvan, "A New Generation of Transhumanists Is Emerging," *Huffington Post*, March 10, 2014, http://www.huffingtonpost.com/zoltan-istvan/a-new-generation-of-trans_b_4921319.html.

16. Damien Gayle, "Army of the Future: Soldiers Will Be Able to Run at Olympic Speed and Won't Need Food or Sleep with Gene Technology," August 12, 2012, http://archive.today/bH76w.

17. Daniel Estulin, telephone interview by Troy Anderson for *The Babylon Code*, May 27, 2014.

18. Chuck Missler, "As the Days of Noah Were," Koinonia House, January 1996, http://www.khouse.org/articles/1996/43; Missler, "The Return of the Nephilim?," Koinonia House, September 1997, http://www.khouse.org/articles/1997/22; Alex Murashko, "Is Robert Downey Jr. Tracking End Times Prophecy by Chuck Missler?," *Christian Post*, May 22, 2013, http://www.christianpost.com/news/is-robert-downey-jr-tracking-end-times-prophecy-by-chuck-missler-96395.

19. Emily Swanson, "Alien Poll Finds Half of Americans Think Extraterrestrial Life Exists," *Huffington Post*, June 21, 2013, http://www.huffingtonpost .com/2013/06/21/alien-poll_n3473852.html; Lee Speigel, "More Believe in Space Aliens Than in God, According to U.K. Survey," *Huffington Post*, October 18, 2012, http://www.huffingtonpost.com/2012/10/15/alient-believers-outnumber-god _n_1968259.html.

20. Jim Marrs, telephone interview by Troy Anderson for *The Babylon Code*, February 28, 2014.

21. Marrs, *Our Occulted History*, 213–14.

22. Craig R. Smith, "What Does the Bible Say About Making Money?" *Whistleblower*, November 2008.

23. Joseph P. Farrell, *Babylon's Banksters: The Alchemy of Deep Physics, High Finance and Ancient Religion* (Port Townsend, WA: Feral House, 2010), 20, 47, 159, 173.

24. Ibid.

Chapter Eight: Illuminati Pyramid or Ancient Wonder?

Epigraph: Manly P. Hall, *The Secret Teachings of All Ages: An Encyclopedic Outline of Masonic, Hermetic, Qabbalistic, and Rosicrucian Symbolical Philosophy* (Seattle, WA: Pacific Publishing Studio, 2011), 32.

1. Wikiquotes, "The Ten Commandments," http://en.wikiquote.org/wiki/The_Ten _Commandments_(1956_film).

2. J. Daniel Hays and J. Scott Duvall, eds., *The Baker Illustrated Bible Handbook* (Grand Rapids, MI: Baker Books, 2011), 57.

3. Thomas Horn, *Apollyon Rising 2012: The Lost Symbol Found and the Final Mystery of the Great Seal Revealed* (Crane, MO: Defender, 2009), 161–62.

4. Manley P. Hall, *The Secret Destiny of America* (Los Angeles: Philosophical Research Society, 1944), 128; Hall, *The Secret Teachings of All Ages*, 17–18; Paul McGuire, "Armageddon: A Space War Coming to You Soon," NewsWithViews.com, July 2, 2012, http://www.newswithviews.com/McGuire/paul132.htm.

5. Thomas R. Horn, *Nephilim Stargates: The Year 2012 and the Return of the Watchers* (Crane, MO: Anomalos, 2007), 93–99.

6. Jonathan O'Callaghan, "Do Aliens Hold the Key to Why We Have Sex? Richard Dawkins Says ET Could Reveal Why Animals Use It to Reproduce—and Even the Origins of Life," *Daily Mail*, September 23, 2014, http://www.dailymail.co .uk/sciencetech/article-2766475/Do-ALIENS-hold-key-sex-Richard-Dawkins -says-ET-reveal-animals-use-reproduce-origins-life.html; "Aliens and the Creation of Man: Did Humans Evolve from More Primitive Life Forms, or Did Our Intelligence and Creativity Develop from Contact with an Otherworldly Source?" "Ancient Aliens," History Channel, http://www.history.com/shows/ancient-aliens/ videos/ancient-aliens-aliens-and-the-creation-of-man?m=5189717d404fa&s=All &f=1&free=false; Eric Pfeiffer, "NASA Says Discovering Alien Life in Next 20 Years Is 'Within Reach,'" Yahoo.com, July 16, 2014, http://news.yahoo.com/blogs/ sideshow/nasa-says-alien-life-will-be-discovered-within-20-years-220544489 .html.

7. Steve Rose, "The Pope Has Said That He Would Baptise a Martian—but Would They Want Our Religions?" *Guardian*, May 14, 2014, http://www.theguardian

.com/science/shortcuts/2014/may/14/pope-francis-baptise-martian-would-they
-want-our-religions.

8. S. Douglas Woodward, *Lying Wonders of the Red Planet: Exposing the Lie of Ancient Aliens* (Oklahoma City: Faith Happens, 2014), xvii–xix.

9. Ron Rhodes, *The End Times in Chronological Order: A Complete Overview to Understanding Bible Prophecy* (Eugene, OR: Harvest House, 2012), 101–2.

10. Horn, *Nephilim Stargates*, 148–49, 186–87, 196; Jason Hanna, "UFOs Eyed Nukes, Ex–Air Force Personnel Say," CNN, September 27, 2010, http://news.blogs .cnn.com/2010/09/27/ufos-showed-interest-in-nukes-ex-air-force-personnel-say.

11. Hugh Ross, *Navigating Genesis: A Scientist's Journey Through Genesis 1–11* (Covina, CA: Reasons to Believe, 2014), 194–95.

12. Jim Marrs, *Rule by Secrecy: The Hidden History That Connects the Trilateral Commission, the Fremasons, and the Great Pyramids* (New York: Perennial, 2000), 372.

13. McGuire, "Armageddon"; "Bible Verses About Osiris," Bible Tools, http://www .bibletools.org/index.cfm/fuseaction/Topical.show/RTD/cgg/ID/773/Osiris.htm; Hall, *The Secret Teachings of All Ages*, 34.

14. Carroll M. Helm, telephone interview by Troy Anderson for *The Babylon Code*, March 19, 2014.

15. Hugh Ross, telephone interview by Troy Anderson for *The Babylon Code*, April 10, 2014.

16. *Encyclopaedia Britannica*, s.v. "Osiris," http://www.britannica.com/topic/Osiris-Egyptian-god; *Encyclopaedia Britannica*, s.v. "Egyptian Religion," http://www .britannica.com/topic/Egyptian-religion; Jim Marrs, *Our Occulted History: Do the Global Elite Conceal Ancient Aliens?* (New York: William Morrow, 2013), 85; Amy D. Bernstein, "A Short History of Secret Societies," *U.S. News & World Report* special publication "Mysteries of History: Secret Societies," May 19, 2009.

17. Daniel Estulin, telephone interview by Troy Anderson for *The Babylon Code*, May 27, 2014.

18. Jonathan Shaw, "Who Built the Pyramids?," *Harvard Magazine*, July–August 2003, http://harvardmagazine.com/2003/07/who-built-the-pyramids.html; David Down, "The Pyramids of Ancient Egypt," Answers in Genesis, September 1, 2004, https:// answersingenesis.org/archaeology/ancient-egypt/the-pyramids-of-ancient-egypt; *Encyclopaedia Britannica*, s.v. "Pyramids of Giza," http://www.britannica.com/topic/ pyramids-of-Giza.

19. Marrs, *Our Occulted History*, 99.

20. Hall, *The Secret Teachings of All Ages*, 56.

21. Marrs, *Our Occulted History*, 99–105.

22. Hall, *The Secret Teachings of All Ages*, 32–33.

23. Horn, *Apollyon Rising 2012*, 159–60.

24. Ibid., 209–10.

25. Ibid., 88.

26. Hall, *The Secret Destiny of America*, 15, 23.

27. Ibid., 127–29.

28. Paul McGuire, "Murder of President Kennedy, New World Order Prophecy," McGuire Prophecy Report, September 19, 2013; Dennis L. Cuddy, "The Election

of 2012," NewsWithViews.com, November 26, 2012, http://www.newswithviews
.com/Cuddy/dennis247.htm; Hall, *The Secret Destiny of America*, 127–29.

29. Hall, *The Secret Destiny of America*, 20–21; Hall, *The Secret Teachings of All Ages*, 18, 169.
30. Paul McGuire, "Deception in the Last Days Prophecy Conference," GOD TV, http://www.god.tv/deception-in-the-last-days-prophecy-conference/deception-in -the-government.
31. Robert Hieronimus, *Founding Fathers, Secret Societies: Freemasons, Illuminati, Rosi-crucians, and the Decoding of the Great Seal* (Rochester, VT: Destiny Books, 2006), 107–8.
32. Ibid., 80.

Chapter Nine: The Battle for America

Epigraphs: John Coleman, *The Conspirators' Hierarchy: The Committee of 300* (Carson City, NV: World International Review, 2010), 30; Jim Marrs, *Rule by Secrecy: The Hidden History That Connects the Trilateral Commission, the Free-masons, and the Great Pyramids* (New York: Perennial, 2000), 237; Dan Brown, *Angels & Demons* (New York: Atria Books, 2000), "Author's Note."

1. Marrs, *Rule by Secrecy*, 227–28.
2. Ibid., 228–30; *Encyclopaedia Britannica*, s.v. "Jamestown Colony," http://www
.britannica.com/EBchecked/topic/300134/Jamestown-Colony; "William Shake-speare," Biography.com, http://www.biography.com/people/william-shakespeare -9480323#synopsis.
3. Coleman, *Conspirators' Hierarchy*, 21–22.
4. Dennis L. Cuddy, telephone interview by Troy Anderson for *The Babylon Code*, July 29, 2014.
5. Ibid.
6. Vernon Stauffer, *The Bavarian Illuminati in America: The New England Conspiracy Scare, 1798* (Mineola, NY: Dover Publications, 2006; orig. pub. 1918), 249–50.
7. Michael Barkun, "The Bizarre Legacy of the Bavarian Illuminati: Two Centuries After Their Demise, Conspiracy Theorists Still Fear Them," *U.S. News & World Report* special publication "Mysteries of History: Secret Societies," May 19, 2009.
8. Ibid.
9. Antony C. Sutton, *America's Secret Establishment: An Introduction to the Order of Skull & Bones* (Walterville, OR: TrineDay, 2004), 80.
10. "Secret Societies—David Icke and Jim Marrs," YouTube video, 29:46, posted by Brain Stream Media, February 12, 2001, https://www.youtube.com/watch?v=T6s ICgrFQVo&feature=youtu.be.
11. Tom Hayden, "When Bonesmen Fight," *Politic*, May 17, 2004, http://www.alternet
.org/story/18726/when-bonesmen_fight.
12. Jim Marrs, telephone interview by Troy Anderson for *The Babylon Code*, February 28, 2014; Marrs, *Our Occulted History: Do the Global Elite Conceal Ancient Aliens?* (New York: William Morrow, 2013), 241, 247.
13. Sutton, *America's Secret Establishment*, 115.
14. Ibid., 34, 79.

15. "The Illuminati," in Devra Newberger Speregen and Debra Mostow Zakarin, *Secret Societies: The Truth Revealed* (Plain City, OH: Media Source, 2013).
16. *Behold a Pale Horse: America's Last Chance*, press materials.
17. Charlie Daniels, telephone interview by Troy Anderson for *The Babylon Code*, October 4, 2013.
18. Tim LaHaye, telephone interview by Troy Anderson for *The Babylon Code*, August 29, 2014.
19. Donna Anderson, "Why Are There Domes, Obelisks, and Magic Squares in Washington, D.C.?: How the Most Powerful Nation on Earth Beckons the Evil One," Raiders News Network, February 27, 2011, http://www.raidersnewsupdate.com/leadstory70.htm.
20. Ibid.
21. Thomas Horn, *Apollyon Rising 2012: The Lost Symbol Found and the Final Mystery of the Great Seal Revealed* (Crane, MO: Defender, 2009), 250–53.

Chapter Ten: Geopolitical-Military Babylon

Epigraph: Mark Corner, "Towards a Global Sharing of Sovereignty," Federal Trust for Education & Research, August 2008, http://fedtrust.co.uk/up-content/uploads/2014/12/Essay44_Corner.pdf.
1. George Russell, "UN Brewing Up New—and Expensive—Global 'Sustainability Development Goals,'" FoxNews.com, October 3, 2013, http://www.foxnews.com/world/2013/10/03/un-brewing-up-new-and-expensive-global-sustainability-development-goals; United Nations, "A New Global Partnership: Eradicate Poverty and Transform Economies Through Sustainable Development," May 2013, http://www.un.org/sg/management/pdf/HLP_P2015_Report.pdf.
2. Stewart Patrick, "Global Governance Reform: An American View of US Leadership," Stanley Foundation, February 2010, http://www.stanleyfoundation.org/publications/pab/PatrickPAB210.pdf.
3. John Fonte, "Sovereignty or Submission: Liberal Democracy or Global Governance?," Foreign Policy Research Institute, October 2011, http://www.fpri.org/enotes/2011/2011/10-sovereignty-or-submission-liberal-democracy-or-global-governance; Stanley Kurtz, "John Fonte's 'Sovereignty or Submission,'" *National Review*, September 13, 2011, http://nationalreview.com/node/277019/print.
4. Mark Hitchcock, *The End: A Complete Overview of Bible Prophecy and the End of Days* (Carol Stream, IL: Tyndale, 2012), 117.
5. Mark Hitchcock, telephone interview by Troy Anderson for *The Babylon Code*, January 23, 2014; Hitchcock, *The End of Money: Bible Prophecy and the Coming Economic Collapse* (Eugene, OR: Harvest House, 2013), 35–36.
6. William Dunlop, "Restoring the Glory of Long-Abused Ancient Babylon," FoxNews.com, June 24, 2013, http://www.foxnews.com/world/2013/06/24/restoring-glory-long-abused-ancient-babylon; Joel C. Rosenberg, "U.S. to Help Rebuild City of Babylon in Iraq," *Joel C. Rosenberg's Blog*, February 14, 2009, https://flashtrafficblog.wordpress.com/2009/02/14/us-to-help-rebuild-city-of-babylon-in-iraq.
7. Tim LaHaye and Ed Hindson, eds., *The Popular Encyclopedia of Bible Prophecy* (Eugene, OR: Harvest House, 2004), 43.
8. Ibid.

9. Hitchcock, *The End*, 58.

10. LaHaye and Hindson, *Popular Encyclopedia of Bible Prophecy*, 43.

11. John F. Walvoord, *The Prophecy Knowledge Handbook: All the Prophecies of Scripture Explained in One Volume* (Wheaton, IL: Victor Books, 1990), 607; Henry H. Halley, *Halley's Bible Handbook* (Grand Rapids, MI: Zondervan, 2007), 878; Douglas W. Krieger, Dene McGriff, and S. Douglas Woodward, *The Final Babylon: America and the Coming of the Antichrist* (Oklahoma City: Faith Happens, 2013), 35.

12. Halley, *Halley's Bible Handbook*, 877–78.

13. Jan Markell, telephone interview by Troy Anderson for *The Babylon Code*, February 11, 2014.

14. J. Daniel Hays and J. Scott Duvall, eds., *The Baker Illustrated Bible Handbook* (Grand Rapids, MI: Baker Books, 2011), 986.

15. Thomas Ice, telephone interview by Troy Anderson for *The Babylon Code*, December 18, 2014.

16. Robert Jeffress, telephone interview by Troy Anderson for *The Babylon Code*, January 9, 2014; Morgan Canclini, "Robert Jeffress Claims Obama's Policies Are Paving the Way for a Future World Dictator in His New Book, *Perfect Ending*," Worthy Publishing statement, January 3, 2014.

17. Jeffress, interview by Anderson, January 9, 2014; *NBC News*, "Supreme Court Halts Contraception Mandate for Nuns' Group," December 31, 2013, http://usnews.nbcnews.com/_news/2013/12/31/22128010-supreme-court-halts-contraception-mandate-for-nuns-group.

18. Hal Lindsey, "How Obama Prepped World for the Antichrist," WND.com, August 1, 2008, http://www.wnd.com/2008/08/71144/print.

19. Jan Markell, "America's Decline Paves the Way for a Global Leader," *Understanding the Times*, January/February 2014.

20. Leo Hohmann, "Ben Carson: America Now in 'Pre-Fascist' Era," WND.com, July 6, 2014, http://www.wnd.com/2014/07/ben-carson-uncorks-on-whats-wrong-with-america.

21. "Tom DeLay: Americans Now Live 'Under a Government of Tyranny,'" *Newsmax*, February 14, 2014, http://www.newsmax.com/Newsfront/tom-delay-constitution-obama/2014/02/14/id/552917.

22. Jan Markell, "Hope and Change: Haunting Comparisons," May 13, 2014, www.olivetreeviews.org.

23. Rand Paul, speech at the University of California, Berkeley, March 20, 2014, http://www.randpaul2016.com/2014/03/video-senator-rand-paul-speech-at-university-of-california-berkeley; Billy Hallowell, "Rand Paul Declares America Needs a 'Spiritual Cleansing' and' Revival': 'Something Really Depraved Is Rising in the Country,'" *Blaze*, February 13, 2013; "Rand Paul: Obama Turning US into 'Socialist Nightmare,'" *Newsmax*, February 5, 2014.

24. Lee Fang, "Member of Congressional Science Committee: Global Warming a 'Fraud' to Create 'Global Government,'" *Nation*, August 10, 2013, http://www.thenation.com/blog/175697/science-committee-congressman-global-warming-fraud-create-global-governent; Courtney Coren, "Rohrabacher: Global Warming Is a 'Fraud' to Create 'Global Government,'" *Newsmax*, August 13, 2013, http://www.newsmax.com/US/rohrabacher-global-warming/2013/08/13/id/520131.

25. Vatican, "Vatican International Financial Global Public Authority Paper Full Text," Public Intelligence.net, http://publicintelligence.net/Vatican-global-financial-authority; Kurtz, "John Fonte's 'Sovereignty or Submission.'"

26. United Nations, "The Millennium Development Goals Report, 2012," p. 67.

27. Hugh Ross, telephone interview by Troy Anderson for *The Babylon Code*, April 10, 2014; ConspiracyWiki.com, "Club of Rome," http://conspiracywiki.com/articles/new-world-order/club-of-rome.

28. Stanley Monteith, telephone interview by Troy Anderson for *The Babylon Code*, August 5, 2014.

29. Henry Kissinger, "Henry Kissinger on the Assembly of a New World Order," *Wall Street Journal*, August 29, 2014, http://online.wsj.com/articles/henry-kissinger-on-the-assembly-of-a-new-world-order-1409328075.

30. Glen T. Martin, telephone interview by Troy Anderson for *The Babylon Code*, April 18, 2014.

31. Democratic World Federalists, "Gallery of World Government Visionaries," http://www.dwfed.org/gallery-of-world-visionaries.php.

32. H. G. Wells, *The New World Order* (Minneapolis: Filiquarian Publishing, 2007), 121.

33. H. G. Wells, *The Open Conspiracy: What Are We to Do with Our Lives?* (Great Britain: C. A. Watt, 1935), iii, 11, 37.

34. Martin, interview by Anderson, April 18, 2014.

35. Hakan Altinay, "Global Governance Audit," Brookings Institution Global Working Papers No. 49, February 2012, http://www.brookings.edu/research/papers/2012/2/global-governance-altinay.

36. Glen T. Martin, "Planetary Maturity and Our Global Social Contract: Part One—Planetary Maturity," OpEdNews.com, March 8, 2014, http://www.opednews.com/populum/printer_friendly.php?content=a&id=177672.

37. Martin, interview by Anderson, April 18, 2014.

38. Democratic World Federalists, "Paths to a World Federation," http://www.dwfed.org/paths-to-a-world-federation.php.

39. Roger Kotila, telephone interview by Troy Anderson for *The Babylon Code*, August 12, 2014.

40. Hitchcock, interview by Anderson, January 23, 2014.

41. Thomas Ice, "Babylon in Bible Prophecy," Pre-Trib Research Center, Liberty University, http://www.pre-trib.org/articles/view/babylon-in-bible-prophecy.

42. Jerry B. Jenkins, e-mail interview by Troy Anderson for *The Babylon Code*, March 31, 2014.

43. Steve Cioccolanti, e-mail interview by Troy Anderson for *The Babylon Code*, January 14, 2015.

44. Ibid.

45. "Antichrist (Beast)," RaptureReady.com, https://www.raptureready.com/abc/antichrist.html.

46. Mark Hitchcock, *Who Is the Antichrist?: Answering the Question Everyone Is Asking* (Eugene, OR: Harvest House, 2011), 56, 72, 175, 181–82.

47. Ibid.

Chapter Eleven: Spiritual-Technological Babylon

1. John Morgan, "Harvard Economists to IMF: Global Government Debt Is the Worst in 200 Years," *Newsmax*, January 3, 2014, http://www.moneynews.com/Economy/IMF-debt-Rogoff-Reinhart/2014/01/03/id/545071.

2. Ibid.

3. Alexander C. Kaufman, "Pope Francis Warns the Global Economy Is Near Collapse," *Huffington Post*, June 13, 2014, http://www.huffingtonpost.com/2014/06/13/pope-francis-economy_n_5491831.html.

4. Dan Weil, "James Rickards: International Monetary System Headed for Collapse," *Newsmax*, March 23, 2014, http://www.moneynews.com/StreetTalk/Rickards-international-monetary-collapse/2014/03/23.

5. Mark Hitchcock, *The End of Money: Bible Prophecy and the Coming Economic Collapse* (Eugene, OR: Harvest House, 2013), 9.

6. Ibid., 14–17.

7. Douglas W. Krieger, Dene McGriff, and S. Douglas Woodward, *The Final Babylon: America and the Coming of the Antichrist* (Oklahoma City: Faith Happens, 2013), 150–51.

8. John Coleman, *The Illuminati in America, 1776–2008* (Carson City, NV: World International Review, 2008), 9, 31.

9. Lucis Trust, "The Esoteric Meaning of Lucifer," http://www.lucistrust.org/en/arcane_school/talks_and_articles/the_esoteric_meaning_of_lucifer.

10. Tim LaHaye and Ed Hindson, eds., *The Popular Encyclopedia of Bible Prophecy* (Eugene, OR: Harvest House, 2004), 203–5; Alex Newman, "Establishment Pushing 'Cashless Society' to Control Humanity," *New American*, July 2, 2014, http://www.thenewamerican.com/tech/item/18619-establishment-pushing-cashless-society-to-control-humanity; "Is the 'Mark of the Beast' the Future of Money?," Catholic Online, April 2, 2014, http://www.catholic.org/news/business/story.php?id=54795.

11. Alex Newman, "BRICS Regimes Forge New World Bank, Call for Global Currency," *New American*, April 3, 2013, http://www.thenewamerican.com/world-news/africa/item/14983-brics-regimes-forge-new-world-bank-call-for-global-currency.

12. James G. Rickards, interview on the *Peter Schiff Show*, March 25, 2014, https://www.youtube.com/watch?v=D-QiJ0XuG0g&feature=youtu.be.

13. Ibid.

14. Mark Hitchcock, telephone interview by Troy Anderson for *The Babylon Code*, January 23, 2014.

15. Catherine Austin Fitts, "Financial Coup d'Etat," Solari Report, August 8, 2011, https://solari.com/blog/financial-coup-detat.

16. Ibid.

17. Joel Kotkin, "Dawn of the Age of Oligarchy: The Alliance Between Government and the 1%," *Daily Beast*, June 28, 2014, http://www.thedailybeast.com/articles/2014/06/28/dawn-of-the-age-of-oligarchy-the-alliance-between-government-and-the-1.html.

18. Joel Kotkin, *The New Class Conflict* (Candor, NY: Telos Press, 2014), 1–3.

19. David Rothkopf, *Superclass: The Global Power Elite and the World They Are Making* (New York: Farrar, Straus and Giroux, 2008), xvii–xxvii.

20. Daniel Estulin, *The True Story of the Bilderberg Group* (Walterville, OR: TrineDay, 2005), 5; Estulin, telephone interview by Troy Anderson for *The Babylon Code*, May 27, 2014.

21. Jonathan Cahn, *The Mystery of the Shemitah* (Lake Mary, FL: FrontLine, 2014), 3.

22. Ibid., 159–60.

23. Ibid., 160–62, 170–73, 200.

24. Jonathan Cahn, "America in the Balance: Revival or Judgment?," *Charisma*, October 1, 2012, http://www.charismamag.com/spirit/prophecy/15570-america-in-the-baiance-revivai-or-judgment.

25. James F. Fitzgerald, *The 9/11 Prophecy: Startling Evidence the Endtimes Have Begun* (Washington, DC: WND Books, 2013), i and back cover; Jonathan Cahn, telephone interview by Troy Anderson, September 6, 2012; Cahn, "America in the Balance."

26. "Jonathan Cahn Speaks to Capitol Hall," YouTube video, 10:29, posted by Hope of the World, June 20, 2013, https://www.youtube.com/watch?v=wlp_6L07rvU.

27. Robert Hieronimus, *The United Symbolism of America: Deciphering Hidden Meanings in America's Most Familiar Art, Architecture, and Logos* (Pompton Plains, NJ: New Page Books, 2008), 101.

28. *Encyclopaedia Britannica*, s.v. "Statue of Liberty, http://www.britannica.com/EBchecked/topic/339344/Statue-of-Liberty; *Encyclopaedia Britannica*, s.v. "Colossus of Rhodes," http://www.britannica.com/EBchecked/topic/501620/Colossus-of-Rhodes.

29. S. Douglas Woodward, telephone interview by Troy Anderson for *The Babylon Code*, August 14, 2013.

30. Hieronimus, *United Symbolism of America*, 101, 121; National Park Service, "Statue of Liberty," http://www.nps.gov/stli/index.htm.

31. Krieger, McGriff, and Woodward, *Final Babylon*, 130–31.

32. Dennis L. Cuddy, "The Statue of Liberty," NewsWithViews.com, May 3, 2010, http://www.newswithviews.com/Cuddy/dennis180.htm.

Chapter Twelve: Spiritual-Technological Babylon

Epigraph: Hal Lindsey and C. C. Carlson, *The Late Great Planet Earth* (Grand Rapids, MI: Zondervan, 1970), 124.

1. Daisy Carrington, "Astana: The World's Weirdest Capital City," CNN, July 13, 2012, http://www.cnn.com/2012/07/13/world/asia/eye-on-kazakhstan-astana/index.html; "The Illuminati Capital ASTANA Kazakhstan," Before It's News, August 7, 2013, http://beforeitsnews.com/alternative/2013/08/the-illuminati-capital-astana-kazakhstan-2731548.html.

2. Astana Economic Forum 2012, "Establishment of a Single World Currency and Overcoming the Economic Crisis," PR Newswire, May 21, 2012.

3. Khabar Television, "Kazakhstan Is Link Between Asia and Europe," BBC Monitoring International Reports, September 23, 2003.

4. Albert Mohler, "All Roads Lead to Heaven?—Kathleen Parker Does Theology," AlbertMohler.com, May 12, 2010, http://www.albertmohler.com/2010/05/12/all-roads-lead-to-heaven-kathleen-parker-does-theology; Lillian Kwon, "Biblical

Illiteracy in US at Crisis Point, Says Bible Expert," *Christian Post*, June 16, 2014, http://www.christianpost.com/news/biblical-illiteracy-in-us-at-crisis-point-says-bible-expert-121626.

5. David Van Biema, "Christians: No One Path to Salvation," *Time*, June 23, 2008, http://content.time.com/time/nation/article/0,8599,1817217,00.html.

6. Mark Hitchcock, *101 Answers to Questions About the Book of Revelation* (Eugene, OR: Harvest House, 2012), 194.

7. Ron Rhodes, *The 8 Great Debates of Bible Prophecy* (Eugene, OR: Harvest House, 2014), 147–48.

8. Mark Hitchcock, telephone interview by Troy Anderson for *The Babylon Code*, January 23, 2014.

9. Leo Hohmann, "Generation WiFi Wants Brains Hooked to Internet," WND.com, November 13, 2014, http://www.wnd.com/2014/11/generation-wifi-wants-brains-hooked-to-internet.

10. Jerry B. Jenkins, e-mail interview by Troy Anderson for *The Babylon Code*, March 31, 2014.

11. Véronique Hyland, "Can Opening Ceremony Make Wearable Tech Cool?," *New York*, November 17, 2014, http://nymag.com/thecut/2014/11/can-opening-ceremony-make-wearable-tech-cool.html; "In Five Years, Wearables Could Be Under Your Skin," Yahoo.com, October 10, 2014, http://news.yahoo.com/five-years-wearables-could-under-skin-133133473.html.

12. Amy Zalman, telephone interview by Troy Anderson for an *NBIZ Magazine* story, "Science Fiction Becomes Reality," September 6, 2014.

13. Jim Marrs, *The Rise of the Fourth Reich: The Secret Societies That Threaten to Take Over America* (New York: William Morrow, 2008), 4.

14. Ibid., 194, 202.

15. Chandra Steele, "5 Ways Scientists Are Building Real-World Super Soldiers," *PC Magazine*, April 4, 2014, http://www.pcmag.com/slideshow/story/322349/5-ways-scientists-are-building-real-world-super-soldiers.

16. Paul McGuire, "A Transhuman Replicant Future," http://paulmcguire.com/america_in_prophecy_a_transhuman.htm; Kate Kelland, "Scientists Want Debate on Animals with Human Genes," Reuters, November 9, 2009, http://www.reuters.com/article/2009/11/10/us-science-animal-human-idUSTRE5A900R20091110.

17. Max Tegmark, "Is the Universe Made of Math?," *Scientific American*, January 10, 2014, http://www.scientificamerican.com/article/is-the-universe-made-of-math-excerpt.

18. Mario Seiglie, "DNA: The Tiny Code That's Toppling Evolution," Good News, http://www.ucg.org/science/dna-tiny-code-thats-toppling-evolution.

19. Andrew Malone, "Stolen by the Nazis: The Tragic Tale of 12,000 Blue-Eyed Blond Children Taken by the SS to Create an Aryan Super-Race," *Daily Mail*, January 9, 2009, http://www.dailymail.co.uk/news/article-1111170/Stolen-Nazis-The-tragic-tale-12-000-blue-eyed-blond-children-taken-SS-create-Aryan-super-race.html; Paul McGuire, "Armageddon: A Space War Coming to You Soon," NewsWithViews.com, July 2, 2012, http://www.newswithviews.com/McGuire/paul132.htm; Marrs, *Rise of the Fourth Reich*, 19–20; U.S. Air Force, "Peterson Air Force Base," http://www.peterson.af.mil/units/821stairbase/index.asp.

20. Tom Horn, "The Hybrid Age," Personal Update, February 2012.

21. *Time*, "The Rosicrucians: The Mystical Underpinnings of Modern Science," in *Secret Societies: Decoding the Myths and Facts of History's Most Mysterious Organizations* (New York: Time Books, 2010), 24; Devra Newberger Speregen and Debra Mostow Zakarin, "The Hermetic Order of the Golden Dawn," in *Secret Societies: The Truth Revealed* (Plain City, OH: Media Source, 2013), 68–69.

22. Jim Marrs, *Our Occulted History: Do the Global Elite Conceal Ancient Aliens?* (New York: William Morrow, 2013), 302.

23. David Turner, "Foundations of Holocaust: Eugenics and America's Master Race," *Jerusalem Post*, December 23, 2012, http://www.jpost.com/Blogs/The-Jewish-Problem ---From-anti-Judaism-to-anti-Semitism/Foundations-of-Holocaust-Eugenics-and -Americas-Master-Race-365015.

24. Britt Gillette, "Transhumanism and the Great Rebellion," RaptureReady.com, http://www.raptureready.com/featured/gillette/transhuman.html.

25. David Willey, "Vatican Says Aliens Could Exist," *BBC News*, May 13, 2008, http://news.bbc.co.uk/2/hi/7399661.stm; "Professor's Alien Life 'Seed' Theory Claimed," *BBC News*, February 1, 2010, http://news.bbc.co.uk/2/hi/uk_news/ wales/south_east/8491398.stm.

26. Stoyan Zaimov, "Vatican Astronomer Says Alien Life Will Be Discovered, but Will Not Prove or Disprove God," *Christian Post*, September 22, 2014, http://www .christianpost.com/news/vatican-astronomer-says-alien-life-will-be-discovered -but-will-not-prove-or-disprove-god-126813.

27. Jim Marrs, telephone interview by Troy Anderson for *The Babylon Code*, February 28, 2014.

28. Lila Arzua, "Forum Seeks Space Aliens," *Miami Herald*, August 20, 2001; David Clarke, "Group: Tell Public UFOs, Aliens Are Out There" (Durham, NC) *Herald-Sun*, May 10, 2001; "Steven M. Greer, MD," Disclosure Project, http://www.dis closureproject.org/presskit/sgbio.shtml.

29. Heidi Blake, "UN 'to Appoint Space Ambassador to Greet Alien Visitors,'" *Telegraph*, September 26, 2010, http://www.telegraph.co.uk/science/space/8025832/ UN-to-appoint-space-ambassador-to-greet-alien-visitors.html; Serge Monast, *Project Blue Beam*, 1994, p. 4, http://educate-yourself.org/cn/projectbluebeam25jul05 .shtml.

30. S. Douglas Woodward, *Lying Wonders of the Red Planet: Exposing the Lie of Ancient Aliens* (Oklahoma City: Faith Happens, 2014), 7.

31. Greg Laurie, telephone interview by Troy Anderson for *The Babylon Code*, March 5, 2014.

32. Franklin Graham, telephone interview by Troy Anderson for the seven-part WND .com series on the *My Hope America with Billy Graham* evangelistic outreach, July 2, 2013.

33. Laurie, interview by Anderson, March 5, 2014.

Chapter Thirteen: The Babylon-Jerusalem Matrix

Epigraph: Tim LaHaye, telephone interview by Troy Anderson for *The Babylon Code*, August 29, 2014.

1. Mike Bickle, "Studies in the Bride of Christ," http://mikebickle.org/resources/ series/the-bride-of-christ-2010.

2. Mark Hitchcock, *101 Answers to Questions About the Book of Revelation* (Eugene, OR: Harvest House, 2012), 188.

3. Ibid., 188–89.

4. Ibid., 27, 195.

5. Daniel 8:17, New International Version, BibleGateway.com.

6. Joel C. Rosenberg, "Has the End Game Begun? Privately, Senior Israeli Officials Now Warning Iran War Could Come in 2013. Netanyahu Preparing Public," *Joel C. Rosenberg's Blog*, July 15, 2013, https://flashtrafficblog.wordpress.com/2013/07/15/has-the-end-game-begun-privately-senior-israeli-officials-now-warning-iran-war-could-come-in-2013-netanyahu-preparing-public.

7. Perry Stone, *Deciphering End-Time Prophetic Codes* (Lake Mary, FL: Charisma House, 2015), 77.

8. Troy Anderson, "Israel-Iran Nuclear Showdown: Is This the War of Gog and Magog?" CharismaNews.com, April 4, 2012, http://www.charismanews.com/world/33150-israel-iran-nuclear-showdown-is-this-the-war-of-gog-and-magog.

9. Stone, *Deciphering End-Time Prophetic Codes*, 79.

10. "Speculation Concerning Israeli Pre-Emptive Strike on Iranian Nuclear Facilities Emerges as U.S. Privately Accuses Tehran of 'Cheating,'" Prophecy News Watch, December 11, 2014, http://www.prophecynewswatch.com/2014/December11/112.html.

11. Greg Laurie, telephone interview by Troy Anderson for *The Babylon Code*, March 5, 2014.

12. Thomas Ice, telephone interview by Troy Anderson for *The Babylon Code*, December 18, 2014.

13. Stone, *Deciphering End-Time Prophetic Codes*, 46–52.

14. Mark Hitchcock, *The End: A Complete Overview of Bible Prophecy and the End of Days* (Carol Stream, IL: Tyndale, 2012), 463.

15. Ibid., 463–67; F. Kenton Beshore, *When?: When Will the Rapture Take Place?* (Costa Mesa, CA: World Bible Society, 2009), 41–55; John F. Walvoord, *The Prophecy Knowledge Handbook: All the Prophecies of Scripture Explained in One Volume* (Wheaton, IL: Victor Books, 1990), 382–85.

16. Stone, *Deciphering End-Time Prophetic Codes*, 80.

17. LaHaye, interview by Anderson, August 29, 2014.

18. Ibid.

19. S. Douglas Woodward, telephone interview by Troy Anderson for *The Babylon Code*, August 14, 2013.

20. Tim LaHaye and Ed Hindson, eds., *The Popular Encyclopedia of Bible Prophecy* (Eugene, OR: Harvest House, 2004), 24–25.

21. Dave Hunt, "Mystery Babylon Identified," Pre-Trib Research Center, Liberty University, http://www.pre-trib.org/articles/view/mystery-babylon-identified.

22. Ron Rhodes, *The End Times in Chronological Order: A Complete Overview to Understanding Bible Prophecy* (Eugene, OR: Harvest House, 2012), 124.

23. Ibid., 95–96.

24. Ice, interview by Anderson, December 18, 2014.

25. F. Kenton Beshore, in-person interview by Troy Anderson at the World Bible Society office in Costa Mesa, California, for end-times magazine stories, March 4, 2012.

26. LaHaye, interview by Anderson, August 29, 2014.
27. Ron Rhodes, *The 8 Great Debates of Bible Prophecy* (Eugene, OR: Harvest House, 2014), 169.
28. Laurie, interview by Anderson, March 5, 2014.
29. Tim LaHaye and Thomas Ice, *Charting the End Times: A Visual Guide to Understanding Bible Prophecy* (Eugene, OR: Harvest House, 2001), 58.
30. Ice, interview by Anderson, December 18, 2014.
31. Walvoord, *Prophecy Knowledge Handbook*, 583.
32. Rhodes, *End Times in Chronological Order*, 154–55.
33. LaHaye and Hindson, *Popular Encyclopedia of Bible Prophecy*, 334–35.
34. Beshore, in-person interview by Anderson, March 4, 2012.
35. Thomas Ice, "An Interpretation of Matthew 24–25," RaptureReady.com, https://www.raptureready.com/featured/ice/AnInterpretationofMatthew24_25_1.html.
36. LaHaye and Hindson, *Popular Encyclopedia of Bible Prophecy*, 37, 42.
37. Ibid., 39.
38. Hitchcock, *The End*, 363.
39. Rhodes, *End Times in Chronological Order*, 169–71.
40. LaHaye and Ice, *Charting the End Times*, 70.
41. Jud Wilhite, in a sermon given at Saddleback Church, Lake Forest, CA, May 18, 2013.
42. Ibid.

Chapter Fourteen: "God's Prophet" and Hope for the World

Epigraph: Billy Graham, e-mail interview by Troy Anderson for a seven-part WND.com series and www.tothesource.org story about the *My Hope America with Billy Graham* evangelistic outreach, August 20, 2013.

1. Billy Graham, "Billy Graham: 'My Heart Aches for America,'" Billy Graham Evangelistic Association, July 19, 2012, http://billygraham.org/story/billy-graham-my-heart-aches-for-america.
2. Ibid.
3. Franklin Graham, "Plans Underway to Continue My Hope into 2014; Churches Encouraged to Show 'The Cross' This Easter," Billy Graham Evangelistic Association, February 3, 2014, http://billygraham.org/press-release/more-than-110000-have-made-commitments-to-christ-through-billy-grahams-my-hope-america.
4. Preston Parrish, telephone interview by Troy Anderson for a *My Hope America* follow-up story, November 26, 2013.
5. *Encyclopaedia Britannica*, s.v. "Native American," http://www.britannica.com/EBchecked/topic/1357826/Native-American.
6. *Encyclopaedia Britannica*, s.v. "Rosicrucian," http://www.britannica.com/EBchecked/topic/510019/Rosicrucian; James H. Billington, *Fire in the Minds of Men: Origins of the Revolutionary Faith* (New York: Basic Books, 1980), 102; Robert Hieronimus, *The United Symbolism of America: Deciphering Hidden Meanings in America's Most Familiar Art, Architecture, and Logos* (Pompton Plains, NJ: New Page Books, 2008), 50.
7. Led Zeppelin, "Stairway to Heaven," GoodReads.com, http://www.goodreads.com/quotes/149110-yes-there-are-two-paths-you-can-go-by-but-in.

8. Graham, interview by Anderson, August 20, 2013; "94-Year-Old Billy Graham's Warning for America," WND.com, August 4, 2013, http://www.wnd.com/2013/08/94-year-old-billy-grahams-warning-for-america; "Famed Evangelist: God Told Me 'America Will Be Saved,'" WND.com, August 18, 2013, www.wnd.com/2013/08/famed-evangelist-god-told-me-america-will-be-saved; "Billy Graham: Now Is Time for 'Fresh Awakening,'" WND.com, September 22, 2013, http://www.wnd.com/2013/09/billy-graham-now-is-time-for-fresh-awakening; "Billy Graham Sounds Alarm for 2nd Coming," WND.com, October 20, 2013, http://www.wnd.com/2013/10/billy-graham-sounds-alarm-for-2nd-coming; "Prophecy Scholar: America at the Crossroads," WND.com, November 2, 2013, http://www.wnd.com/2013/11/prophecy-scholar-america-at-crossroads; "Man Who Walked Across U.S. Saw Revival Signs," WND.com, November 3, 2013, http://www.wnd.com/2013/11/man-who-walked-across-u-s-saw-revival-signs; "Billy Graham to Give 'Final, Most Important' Message," WND.com, November 5, 2013, http://www.wnd.com/2013/11/billy-graham-to-give-final-most-important-message; Troy Anderson, "Billy Graham's Hope for America," tothesource.org, September 26, 2013, http://www.tothesource.org/9_25_2013/9_25_2013.htm.

Scripture Permissions

About the Authors

Paul McGuire is an internationally recognized Bible prophecy expert and regular commentator on Fox News, CNN, and the History Channel. He is the host of a GOD TV prophecy television show. McGuire's work has earned him the praise of Director Oliver Stone, the *Huffington Post*, and many world leaders. He is the bestselling author of *Mass Awakening, A Prophecy of the Future of America*, and *The Day the Dollar Died* and has written extensively about Bible prophecy. He is a professor of eschatology at Dr. Jack Hayford's King's University. He appeared on two of the History Channel's highest-rated specials, "7 Signs of the Apocalypse" and "Countdown to Apocalypse: Four Horsemen."

For a decade, McGuire was the nationally syndicated radio talk show host of the *Paul McGuire Show*, which aired out of Los Angeles for three hours during drive time Monday through Friday. On the program, he interviewed numerous world leaders, presidents, and prime ministers, including former president Jimmy Carter, U.S. senator John McCain, former White House press secretary Tony Snow, Israeli prime minister Ehud Olmert, Oliver North, Pastor Rick Warren, Joel Rosenberg, Dr. Tim LaHaye, Dr. James Dobson, and Ann Coulter. He also interviewed secretaries of state, generals, and high-ranking members of the Pentagon and the Palestine Liberation Organization, along with Israeli Defense Forces generals. He's debated many of the nation's leading economists on Fox News. The late Israeli general Shimon Erem said, "Paul McGuire is a Watchman on the walls of Jerusalem, one of the best."

Each year, McGuire speaks to tens of thousands of people at Bible prophecy conferences. He has made featured appearances on numerous award-winning documentaries such as *American Empire: An Act of Collective Madness*, which Director Oliver Stone called a "revolution in film" and the *Huffington Post* described as a "provocative production that makes you think."

McGuire grew up in New York City. A former atheist and countercultural radical, McGuire demonstrated with activist Abbie Hoffman, was made an honorary member of the Black Panther Party, and was recruited by the Weather Underground. He studied film and "Altered States of Consciousness" at the University of Missouri. He lives in the Los Angeles area.

www.paulmcguire.us

https://www.facebook.com/pages/Paul-McGuire/143707940365

https://www.facebook.com/paul.mcguire.7798

https://twitter.com/radiomcguire

Troy Anderson is a Pulitzer Prize–nominated investigative journalist, author, and speaker and the executive editor of *Charisma* magazine and Charisma Media, one of the nation's largest Christian media outlets with five million readers. Anderson spent two decades as a reporter, bureau chief, editorial writer, and editor at the *Los Angeles Daily News*, the *Press Enterprise*, and other newspapers. He's also written for Reuters, *Newsmax*, *National Wildlife*, *Christianity Today*, *Charisma*, *Human Events*, Watchdog.org, *Outreach*, and many other media outlets. He has interviewed many prominent national figures, including Billy Graham, Franklin Graham, Rick Warren, Dr. Tim LaHaye, Hal Lindsey, Greg Laurie, Joel Rosenberg, Jonathan Cahn, Mark Hitchcock, Nick Vujicic, Lee Strobel, Pat Boone, and Kirk Cameron.

During his career, Anderson has received numerous journalistic accolades: more than two dozen local, state, and national writing awards;

2011 and 2012 Eddie Awards (*Folio:* magazine's prestigious journalism awards); and a Pulitzer Prize nomination. He's a member of the American Society of Journalists and Authors, the nation's premier association of writers of nonfiction who have met ASJA's exacting standards of professional achievement.

He's made many media appearances and given numerous speeches over the years, including a recent one at the Twenty-Third Annual Movieguide Awards in Universal City, California. During his eleven-year stint at the *Los Angeles Daily News*, radio show hosts often interviewed him. He's also appeared on various TV news programs and in an award-winning documentary produced by actress Ally Walker (*Profiler, Law & Order*, and *Sons of Anarchy*). The documentary *For Norman... Wherever You Are* was inspired by a foster care series Anderson wrote for the *Los Angeles Daily News*. The series was nominated for a Pulitzer Prize. The film won Best Documentary Feature at the San Fernando Valley International Film Festival, as well as the Champion of Conscience Award at the Wine Country Film Festival.

At age eleven, Anderson met a Jesus movement youth pastor from Southern California who studied Bible prophecy at the UCLA Light and Power House seminary under Hal Lindsey, author of the bestselling nonfiction book of the 1970s—*The Late Great Planet Earth*. The youth pastor told Anderson how the Bible predicts the Antichrist would lead a global government and economic system before the Second Coming.

Fascinated, Anderson became a Christian. Later, Anderson attended the University of Oregon and studied journalism, politics, and theater. After graduating with a bachelor's degree in 1991, Anderson spent the next two decades working as a journalist at newspapers in Nevada, Oregon, and California.

In 2009, he wrote the "Last Days Fever" cover story for *Charisma*, followed by the "America at the End" article in 2012. Afterward, successful Hollywood producers contacted him. During the summer of

2014, he sold his first book—*The Babylon Code: Solving the Bible's Greatest End-Times Mystery*—to FaithWords, an imprint of the Hachette Book Group. A docudrama and feature film based on the book is in development. In early 2015, he was named the executive editor of *Charisma* magazine and Charisma Media. Anderson lives in Lake Mary, Florida.

www.troyanderson.us
www.charismamag.com
www.mediabistro.com/Troy-Anderson-profile.html
https://www.facebook.com/troyandersonwriter
https://twitter.com/TroyMAnderson
https://www.linkedin.com/profile/view?id=18209645